MULTIDIRECTIONAL SPEED IN SPORT

During field- and court-based sports, players are continually required to perceive their environment within a match and select and perform the most appropriate action to achieve their immediate goal within that match instance. This ability is commonly known as agility, considered a vital quality in such sports and may incorporate a variety of locomotion and instantaneous actions.

Multidirectional speed is a global term to describe the competency and capacity to perform such actions: accelerate, decelerate, change direction, and ultimately maintain speed in multiple directions and movements within the context of sports-specific scenarios, encompassing agility, speed, and many other related qualities. Multidirectional speed in sport depends on a multitude of factors, including perceptual-cognitive abilities, physical qualities, and the technical ability to perform the previously mentioned actions.

Multidirectional Speed in Sport: Research to Application reviews the science of multidirectional speed and translates this information into real-world application in order to provide a resource for practitioners to develop multidirectional speed with athletes, bringing together knowledge from a wealth of world-leading researchers and applied practitioners in the area of speed and agility to provide a complete resource to assist practitioners in designing effective multidirectional speed development programmes.

This text is critical reading for undergraduate and graduate sports science students, all individuals involved in training athletes (e.g. coaches, physiotherapists, athletic trainers), and researchers in the field of sports science and sports medicine.

Paul A. Jones is a lecturer in sports biomechanics/strength and conditioning (S&C) at the University of Salford, UK. He has over 20 years of experience in biomechanics and S&C support to athletes and teams, primarily in athletics, football, and rugby, and was a former sports science coordinator for UK disability athletics. He is a BASES Fellow, has been BASES-accredited for over 17 years, is a Chartered Scientist, and currently serves on the BASES accreditation committee. Paul has also been a certified strength and conditioning specialist (CSCS) with the National Strength and Conditioning Association (NSCA) for over 18 years, recertifying with distinction on the last two occasions.

Thomas Dos'Santos is a lecturer in S&C and sports biomechanics at Manchester Metropolitan University (MMU), UK. Thomas is an NSCA-certified S&C specialist (with distinction). He is currently a physical performance coach for England Para-Football, and he consults on strength and movement profiling with sport technology companies and sports teams, such as Sale Sharks Rugby and Manchester United FC.

MULTIDIRECTIONAL SPEED IN SPORT

Research to Application

Edited by
Paul A. Jones and Thomas Dos'Santos

Routledge
Taylor & Francis Group
NEW YORK AND LONDON

Designed cover image: Getty

First published 2023
by Routledge
605 Third Avenue, New York, NY 10158

and by Routledge
4 Park Square, Milton Park, Abingdon, Oxon, OX14 4RN

Routledge is an imprint of the Taylor & Francis Group, an informa business

ISBN: 978-1-032-21333-0 (hbk)
ISBN: 978-1-032-21332-3 (pbk)
ISBN: 978-1-003-26788-1 (ebk)

DOI: 10.4324/9781003267881

Typeset in Bembo
by Apex CoVantage, LLC

CONTENTS

FIGURES

TABLES

BOXES

CONTRIBUTORS

Liam Anderson, PhD, is an applied exercise physiologist who works at the University of Birmingham, UK. He has held both applied practitioner and research roles in professional football both in the UK and abroad. He is particularly interested in the applied physiology of intermittent sports. He has worked at the Liverpool Football Club, Everton Football Club, and Crewe Alexandra Football Club in the UK and worked abroad at the Mol Fehervar Football Club in Hungary. Alongside his current academic work, he consults for football clubs in the English Premier League and English Football League. Liam utilises his extensive applied experience to undertake research aimed at identifying methods to improve performance and preparation processes in intermittent sports.

Steve Atkins, PhD, FBASES, is an accredited sports scientist with BASES who has a long-standing interest in how best to optimise performance. He currently works as Director of Psychology and Sport at the University of Salford, UK. He has written articles published in peer-reviewed journals, and his primary research areas relate to the determinants of performance, including the use of advanced technologies to optimise performance profiling. Steve has worked with many elite and amateur athletes and supports clients within the University of Salford's physiology testing service. He has lectured for over 25 years and is a senior fellow of the Higher Education Academy, seeking to create optimal learning environments for students via the use of creative heutagogical approaches.

Anne Benjaminse, PhD, obtained her bachelor's degree in physical therapy in 2004 at the Hanze University Groningen, Netherlands. After this, Anne started to specialise in sports medicine. In 2005–2006 she worked as a student researcher at the American Sports Medicine Institute in Birmingham, Alabama, USA. Anne earned her master's degree in 2008 at the School of Health and Rehabilitation Sciences of the Department of Sports Medicine and Nutrition at the University of Pittsburgh, Pennsylvania, USA. With a graduate assistantship, she worked as a student researcher in the Neuromuscular Research Laboratory from 2006 to 2008. In 2015, Anne finished her PhD and currently works as an assistant professor at the Center for Human Movement Sciences,

University of Groningen, and at the School of Sport Studies, Hanze University Groningen. Anne was awarded an NWO-ZonMw Veni grant in 2017 and a European Erasmus+ grant in 2018. In both projects, motor learning to reduce the knee and ankle injury incidence is the central theme. Her goal is to deliver a useful contribution to the field of sports medicine in the community through innovative research, interventions, publications, presentations, workshops, and teaching.

Molly Binetti is Director of Women's Basketball Performance for the 2022 NCAA Division I National Champions, University of South Carolina Gamecocks, USA. She is a proud graduate of Marquette University, where she earned a bachelor of science degree in exercise physiology, and the University of Minnesota, where she earned a master of education degree in applied kinesiology. The Eau Claire, Wisconsin, native is a member of the National Strength and Conditioning Association and Collegiate Strength and Conditioning Coaches Association, where she holds the CSCS and RSCC certifications and the SCCC certification, respectively. She has contributed to two publications, both in the *Journal of Strength and Conditioning Research*, focused on the mechanical and physical determinants of elite women's basketball players.

Micheál Cahill, PhD, is currently Vice President of Strategy and Registrar at Setanta College. He is also Head of Athletic Performance for the Clare Senior Footballers. Prior to this role, Micheál served as Chief Performance Officer and interim Chief Executive Officer at Athlete Training and Health in Texas. Micheál completed his bachelor's degree in health, fitness, and leisure and master's degree in sports performance. He earned a PhD at Auckland University of Technology, New Zealand, in sports science and performance.

Paul Caldbeck, DSport ExSci, ASCC, CSCS, is an experienced sports performance expert, with extensive experience as a practitioner within Premier League soccer and a wide variety of other sports and levels. With a doctoral thesis investigating the contextual nature of sprinting in Premier League soccer, Paul has studied in-depth and applied multidirectional speed theories with a range of athletes. He now works as Account Director at Sportlight Technology, where he is utilising a novel technology solution to provide physical performance practitioners with the tools to make better decisions.

Sarah M. Churchill, PhD, graduated from the University of Worcester with a BSc in sport and exercise science with associated biological science. She worked at the Motion Analysis Research and Rehabilitation Centre (MARRC) at the University of Worcester as a technical engineer conducting applied biomechanics (in particular, gait analysis) before joining the University of Bath to study for a PhD. Her thesis, 'Biomechanical Investigations of Bend Running Technique in Athletic Sprint Events', involved the data collection, analysis, and interpretation of three-dimensional sprint videography and force data of elite athletes. Sarah has also provided biomechanics support to elite athletes and Paralympic athletes. She joined Sheffield Hallam University in 2013 to teach on a range of sport and exercise science and sport and exercise technology undergraduate and postgraduate modules. She was the course leader for the BSc (hons) sport and exercise technology degree from 2018 to 2021, when she joined the Directorate of Student Engagement, Teaching, and Learning.

Paul Comfort, PhD, is Professor in Strength and Conditioning at the University of Salford United Kingdom, where he is also Programme Leader for MSc in strength and conditioning. Paul is also an adjunct professor at Edith Cowan University (Western Australia), a founding member and accredited member of the United Kingdom Strength and Conditioning Association, and a current National Strength and Conditioning Association board member. Professor Comfort regularly consults with numerous sports teams in the UK and has co-authored more than 150 peer-reviewed journal articles. Paul is also a co-editor of the textbooks *Advanced Strength and Conditioning: An Evidence-Based Approach* and *Performance Assessment for Strength and Conditioning*.

Thomas Dos'Santos, PhD, MSc, PGCLTHE, BSc (Hons), CSCS*D, FHEA, is a lecturer in strength and conditioning and sports biomechanics at Manchester Metropolitan University (MMU), having earned a PhD in sports biomechanics at the University of Salford (2020), where he investigated the biomechanical determinants of performance and injury risk during change of direction. Thomas has published over 80 peer-reviewed journal articles, with research interests including change-of-direction biomechanics, anterior cruciate ligament injury screening and intervention, inter-limb asymmetry, and assessment and development of strength and power characteristics, and he is also a research member of the Musculoskeletal Science and Sports Medicine Research Centre (MMU), Football Science Institute (Granada, Spain), Human Braking Performance Research Group (UCLAN), and the England Para-Football Research Centre. Thomas is an NSCA-certified strength and conditioning specialist (with distinction), having previously worked as a strength and conditioning coach for Manchester United FC, Salford City FC, England North-West Netball, England Lacrosse Academy, and Manchester BMX Club. Thomas is currently a physical performance coach for England Para-Football, and he consults on strength and movement profiling with sport technology companies and sports teams such as Sale Sharks Rugby and Manchester United FC, and he has previously consulted with the England Football Association on change-of-direction biomechanics. Thomas is also a visiting lecturer on postgraduate programmes at Middlesex University, the University of Girona, the Chinese University of Hong Kong, and the Football Science Institute, and he is an editor for the *International Journal of Strength and Conditioning* and *International Journal of Environmental Research and Public Health*.

Barry Drust is an applied exercise physiologist who works at the University of Birmingham, UK as Director of Graduate School of Sport and Professional Practice, Industrial Professional Fellow, and Business Engagement Champion. He is a world-leading expert with over 25 years of experience leading applied practice and research projects in the UK and internationally. Alongside his academic work, he has worked for several elite football clubs, including the Liverpool Football Club, Glasgow Rangers Football Club, West Bromwich Albion Football Club, Middlesborough Football Club, and England Senior Men's Football Team. Barry's extensive experience has allowed him to become an internationally recognised researcher and practitioner and is continuing to develop the future applied researchers in the UK and abroad.

Laura J. Elstub, PhD, graduated from Leeds Beckett University, UK, with a BSc in sport and exercise therapy. She worked with the Adidas Innovations Team (Portland, Oregon) using biomechanics to inform sports bra design before joining Sheffield Hallam university to study for a PhD. Her thesis, 'Investigation of the Biomechanical Adaptations in the Acceleration Phase of Bend Sprinting', involved the modelling the multi-segment foot and using statistical parametric mapping to understand force production and injury mechanisms during bend sprinting. Her postdoctoral work at Vanderbilt University (Nashville, Tennessee) has focused on the development of wearable technology to reduce the risk of injury in the general population.

Jon Goodwin is Director of Performance Services for the SOTC. He has worked previously in athletics coaching and S&C delivery in a number of sports. Prior full-time roles include Head of Academy Sport Science with Fulham Football Club, Head of Strength and Conditioning for the Saudi Olympic Committee, and Programme Director for the BSc and MSc in strength and conditioning programmes at St Mary's University in Twickenham.

Damian Harper, PhD, CSci, ASCC, FHEA, is an accredited sport and exercise scientist and strength and conditioning coach and currently lecturer in coaching and human performance at the University of Central Lancashire (UCLan). Damian completed his PhD at UCLan in 2021 where he investigated the neuromuscular determinants of horizontal deceleration in team sport athletes. Following his PhD in 2022 Damian founded Human Braking Performance with a vision to further develop and disseminate information on the importance of deceleration and braking for sports performance and injury-risk reduction. He has published extensively on the topic of deceleration, presented at international conferences, and consulted with many professional sporting organisations from around the world, including the English Football Association (TheFA), English Premier League (EPL), National Basketball Association (NBA) and National Football League (NFL), amongst many other leading sports organisations and technology companies. Damian is internationally recognised for the impact his research has had on applied sports performance practices.

Lee Herrington, PhD, MSc, MCSP, is a physiotherapist and Senior Lecturer in Sports Injury Rehabilitation at the University of Salford, UK, where he is Programme Leader for MSc in sports injury rehabilitation. Lee is an athlete health consultant for the English Institute of Sport, leading on issues related to lower limb injury rehabilitation, and a consultant physiotherapist to various premiership and championship football and rugby union clubs. He has worked as part of the Team GB medical team at the London 2012 and Rio 2016 Olympic Games. Lee has previously worked with British Swimming, Great Britain women's basketball team, Wigan Warriors, Great Britain rugby league teams, and England table tennis and netball teams. His research interests are the treatment and rehabilitation of sports injuries, specifically anterior knee pain and hamstring strain injuries, and rehabilitation from knee surgery (principally ACL reconstruction). Lee has published more than 150 peer-reviewed articles, along with numerous book chapters. Lee is also Editor in Chief of *Physical Therapy in Sport*.

Paul A. Jones, PhD, MSc, BSc (Hons), FBASES, BASES Accredited, CSCS*D, CSci, is a lecturer in sports biomechanics/strength and conditioning (S&C) at the University of Salford. Paul earned a BSc (Hons) and MSc in sports science at Liverpool John Moores University and a PhD in sports biomechanics at the University of Salford. He has over 20 years of experience in biomechanics and S&C support to athletes and teams, primarily in athletics, football, and rugby, and was a former sports science coordinator for UK disability athletics. He is a BASES Fellow, has been BASES-accredited for over 17 years, is a Chartered Scientist, and currently serves on the BASES accreditation committee. Paul has also been a certified strength and conditioning specialist (CSCS) with the NSCA for over 18 years, recertifying with distinction on the last two occasions. Paul has authored/co-authored over 100 peer-reviewed journal articles and six book chapters, mainly in change-of-direction biomechanics, assessment and development of change-of-direction speed, and strength diagnostics, and previously co-edited a book by Routledge, *Performance Assessment in Strength and Conditioning.*

Cameron Josse is an athletic performance coach for American football at Indiana University in Bloomington, Indiana. Prior to Indiana University, he spent eight years working for DeFranco's Training Systems, preparing and managing multiple levels of athletes, including professional athletes from the NFL, NHL, UFC, and WWE. He is currently pursuing a PhD at the University of Saint-Etienne in France, under the supervision of Dr J.B. Morin, and holds a master's degree in exercise science from William Paterson University in New Jersey, as well as a bachelor's degree in kinesiology from the University of Rhode Island.

Chris McLeod has been working in elite sport for over 15 years and holds a postgraduate certificate in creativity, leadership, and innovation from Cass Business School. During his time in elite sport, he has worked alongside coaches to prepare athletes and practitioners for multiple world championships and Olympic Games (Beijing 2008, London 2012, and Rio 2016) across a range of sports and most recently within British Tennis. He is currently SNR Innovation Consultant for the English Institute of Sport, which involves working in partnership with sports coaches to innovate and create positive changes in training design and performance planning. Chris has previously worked for British Tennis and the English Institute of Sport as Head of Strength and Conditioning and has also supported Team GB at the 2016 Olympics as a performance scientist.

Robert W. Meyers, PhD, is Principal Lecturer and also Principal Lead for Undergraduate Programmes in Sport at Cardiff Metropolitan University. He earned a PhD in youth physical development, focused on the development of speed with age, growth, and maturation. He is also a UKSCA-accredited strength and conditioning coach (ASCC) and a member of the Youth Physical Development Research Group at Cardiff Metropolitan University.

Mark Quinn, PhD, is an academic and practitioner working within the subject areas of sports science and performance analysis. He currently works as a lecturer at the University of Salford and leads the degree programmes for BSc (hons) in sports science and MSc in performance analysis in sport. Mark has worked within elite and amateur sport, supporting athletes with coaching, strength and conditioning, sports science, and performance analytics. He was an integral part of the Wigan Warriors Rugby League team, which had success in winning the Challenge Cup (2011, 2013), League Leaders Shield (2012), Super League Grand Final (2013, 2016), and World Club Challenge (2017). He has previously held an assistant coaching role with England Wheelchair Rugby League, and his research interests span performance analysis, monitoring athletes, and training load.

John M. Radnor, PhD, is a senior lecturer at Cardiff Metropolitan University, where he is the programme director of the MSc in youth athletic development course. He earned a PhD in paediatric strength and conditioning and is an S&C coach for the Cardiff Met Football Club and also in the Youth Physical Development Centre at Cardiff Metropolitan University.

Tania Spiteri, PhD, earned her master's and doctor's degree in biomechanics at Edith Cowan University. She is an internationally recognised practitioner and researcher for her work in applied exercise science, having published and presented her work as a keynote speaker at several national and international conferences. These efforts lead to Tania being awarded the Young Investigator of the Year Award (2017) by the National Strength and Conditioning Association, USA. Tania has held sport science roles with the National Football League, Purdue University, and Basketball Australia in preparation for the Rio Olympics, overseeing and implementing the health, well-being, and sport science initiatives with athletes to improve performance outcomes and reduce injury incidence. Tania currently holds a position as a health and well-being manager and is an adjunct lecturer in the Sport, Exercise and Rehabilitation at the University of Technology Sydney.

Christopher Thomas, PhD, MSc, BSc (Hons), CSCS*D, ASCC, is a strength and conditioning coach and performance support lead at Aspire Academy, Qatar. His main role is overseeing athlete support and research projects from creation to execution while also collaborating on innovation initiatives with key stakeholders across the Academy. Chris earned a PhD in sports biomechanics at the University of Salford, where his passion for sciences and innovation has seen him feature in over 60 peer-reviewed journal articles, primarily in the areas of change-of-direction biomechanics, asymmetry, and strength and power diagnostics.

James Wild, PhD, is a research and innovation and speed consultant with Harlequins Rugby Club and a lecturer in sport and exercise science at the University of Surrey. Using a blend of physical preparation and biomechanics techniques with skill acquisition and motor learning principles, James has worked with coaches and athletes across a full spectrum of abilities, including medal-winning teams and athletes at major international competitions. James is also a book author and has a PhD in the biomechanics and motor control of initial sprint acceleration.

PART 1

Theoretical Basis for Developing Multidirectional Speed

1

INTRODUCTION TO MULTIDIRECTIONAL SPEED

Paul A. Jones and Thomas Dos'Santos

Introduction

During field- and court-based sports, players are continually required to perceive their environment within a match and select and perform the most appropriate action to achieve their immediate goal within that match instance. This ability is commonly known as *agility* and has been comprehensively defined as 'as a rapid and accurate whole-body movement with change of velocity, direction, or movement pattern in response to a stimulus' (Jones & Nimphius, 2018). Although physical capacities are important in sport, ultimately the ability to perform and execute multidirectional speed/agility movements is fundamental for successful attacking and defensive plays in sport, thus highlighting the importance of multidirectional speed. Whilst agility is often considered a vital quality in field- and court-based sports, it is important to consider what agility is by considering the potential underpinning factors. Figure 1.1 illustrates that agility is largely dependent on perceptual-cognitive factors that leads to the selection and execution (i.e. physical component) of an action (perception-action coupling). A plethora of different agility actions are available and may be performed by athletes within the contextual demands of sport (which we will cover in Part 1 of this book). These actions could be instantaneous (i.e. change of direction or vertical jump) or have a timed duration and involve travel (sprinting, side-shuffling, backpedalling, etc.). For example, in American football, a running back looking to penetrate the defensive line may, on receiving the ball, perform a lateral shuffle motion as a 'ready position' to scan for an opening (transitional phase); once an opening presents itself, the running back may perform a sharp side-step cutting manoeuvre (an initiation again) to evade an opponent and accelerate and sprint into the gap and gain yards in the play (actualisation phase) in a curvilinear path. Effectively, the final phase dictates the success of the play (yards gained), but the preceding phases are equally important to the player in preparation for that final phase. Locomotion and instantaneous actions (Figure 1.1) are dependent on technical and physical factors that are specific to each action. Collectively, in developing agility, whilst attention should be paid to the development of perceptual-cognitive abilities (e.g. improve the thinking element), the ability to perform instantaneous and locomotion actions efficiently, effectively (e.g. make the athlete a fast mover; physical

DOI: 10.4324/9781003267881-2

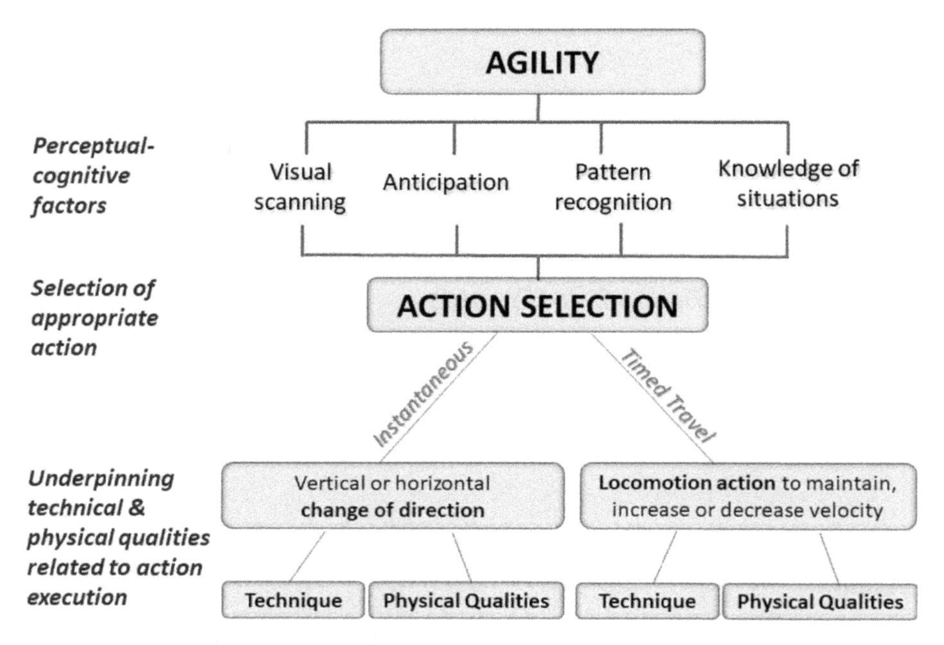

FIGURE 1.1 A deterministic model for agility taken from Dos'Santos and Jones (2022). Training for change of direction and agility, in *Advanced Strength and Conditioning* (second edition) (eds. A. Turner and P. Comfort), Routledge.

component), and safely (i.e. reducing tissue mechanical loading) is a major consideration and requires both technical and physical development to do so.

With these principles in mind, this book uses the term *multidirectional speed* (MDS). *Multidirectional speed* is a global term to describe 'the competency and capacity to accelerate, decelerate, change direction, and ultimately maintain speed in multiple directions and movements within the context of sports specific scenarios' (McBurnie & Dos'Santos, 2022). Akin to the term *strength*, which contains various components and utilities (concentric, isometric, eccentric, ballistic, reactive, dynamic, etc.), we propose MDS is similar, and is an umbrella term which encompasses the range of different agility and locomotive actions available to athletes, including linear sprinting (acceleration and maximum speed), change of direction, deceleration, and curvilinear speed. Sports are often chaotic and require a range of different actions to be performed in response to opponents/implements/balls to various locations on the pitch or court, often within a 360° radius. Having the competency and capacity to perform a variety of different manoeuvres, across a range of angles and velocities, from both limbs, would undoubtedly be advantageous for sports which involve open, random multidirectional movements, and this should be the overarching philosophy of most MDS programmes. Essentially, MDS in sport is about following a holistic approach to agility development, having an appreciation of the various locomotor actions which are required to be successful in the sport, whereby the physical capacity and technical competency in a range of movements are catered for whilst embracing the athletes target context (i.e. contextual speed). Consequentially, for the remainder of this chapter, it is important to define and understand the several components of MDS to allow us to more effectively evaluate and develop qualities that underpin each in the following chapters (Table 1.1).

TABLE 1.1 Definitions of Key Terms Related to Multidirectional Speed

Term	*Definition*
Multidirectional speed	'Competency and capacity to accelerate, decelerate, change direction, and ultimately maintain speed in multiple directions and movements, within the context of sports-specific scenarios.' (McBurnie & Dos'Santos, 2021)
Agility	'A rapid and accurate whole-body movement with change of velocity, direction or movement pattern in response to a stimulus.' (Jones & Nimphius, 2018)
Game speed	'The ability to exploit the qualities of speed and agility within the context of a sport.' (Jeffreys, 2010)
Change-of-direction ability	'The skills and abilities needed to change movement direction, velocity, or modes. Describes the physical event of changing direction.' (DeWeese & Nimphius, 2016)
Manoeuvrability	'The ability to maintain velocity during a COD, when performed without a clear "plant" step (i.e. a curvilinear path of movement); or the ability to perform or change mode of travel to and from "transitional" movements (i.e. side shuffle or back pedal).' (DeWeese & Nimphius, 2016)
COD speed	'The ability to decelerate, reverse or change movement direction and accelerate again.' (Jones et al., 2009) 'The ability to change initial direction to a predetermined location and space on a field or court' – applicable to specific situations in open skilled sports. (Nimphius, 2014)
Change of direction	'A reorientation and change in the path of travel of the whole-body centre of mass towards a new intended direction.' (McBurnie & Dos'Santos, 2021)
Curved sprinting	'The upright running portion of the sprint completed with the presence of some degree of curvature.' (Caldbeck, 2019)
Deceleration	The action of reducing horizontal momentum (negative acceleration) during a locomotor task across a series of foot contacts as an isolated agility action or prior to COD manoeuvre (Dos'Santos et al., 2022) or the ability to proficiently reduce whole body momentum, within the constraints, and in accordance with the specific objectives of the task (i.e. braking force control), whilst skilfully attenuating and distributing the forces associated with braking (i.e. braking force attenuation).
Attacking agility	In the context of invasion team sports (i.e. court-and field-based sports with the objective to score goals/points), defined as 'distinct, sharp, change of directions (COD) or decelerations performed for attacking purposes (i.e. team in possession) while being actively defended by an opponent(s)' (Fox et al., 2014)
Sprinting	Running at maximal or near-maximal speeds. (McMillan & Pfaff, 2018)

Components of Multidirectional Speed

Sprinting

Linear running speed is no doubt an essential quality regarding expressions of agility in sport and may even mask inabilities of the athlete in other elements identified in Figure 1.1. Indeed, data in male soccer highlights that sprint (or linear advancing motions) is the most common action by an attacker preceding a goal (Faude et al., 2012; Martinez et al., 2022), and sprint capacity is typically a discriminating factor in playing levels across numerous sports (Gabbett et al., 2008; Dobbin et al., 2019; Thomas et al., 2016). Figure 1.2 shows a typical velocity distance graph based on Usain Bolt's world 100 m record in 2009. A sprint such as this can be divided into acceleration, maximum velocity, and velocity maintenance phases. Each phase is characterised by differing locomotion mechanics; in short, acceleration phases involve greater forward lean with triple lower-limb extension behind the trunk, whereas maximum velocity running is characterised by a more upright trunk position. The acceleration phase can be further divided into early (0–5 steps), mid (5–15 steps), and late (15–25 steps) acceleration, whereby distinct kinematic differences (e.g. foot contacting ground ahead of centre of mass, support knee flexion, and a plateau in step frequency [early to mid]; postural changes, lower intensity of hip movements [mid to late]) distinguish these phases (Nagahara et al., 2014). However in team sports, such as soccer, the acceleration phase is likely to be over shorter distances leading to shorter distances for early (2.5 m), mid (6 m), and late acceleration (12 m) (Bellon et al., 2019) due to differing contextual demands and achievement of lower maximum velocity compared to elite sprinting.

Time-motion studies in field-based sports, such as soccer and rugby, suggest that most sprints during match play are <20 m or <5 seconds (Di Salvo et al., 2010; Andrzejewski, 2013; Gabbett, 2012). Whilst court dimensions for racket sports (e.g. tennis – average running distance of 3 m and 8–12 m per point [Parsons & Jones, 1998]) and team sports (e.g. basketball [Scanlan et al., 2011; Abdelkarim et al., 2007]; netball [Thomas et al., 2017]) dictate that sprint activity may typically be of shorter duration (<10 m; <2 seconds). Hence, maximum velocity sprinting maybe seldom achieved during field-based matches and less likely during court-based sports, placing the emphasis on developing acceleration (the rate of change in movement velocity increase) ability in the majority of field- and court-based sports. However, it is important to remember whilst infrequent, longer sprints (>20 m) whereby maximum velocity maybe achieved by the athlete/player do occur in certain field sports match instances (e.g. a counterattack in soccer or a lengthy throw

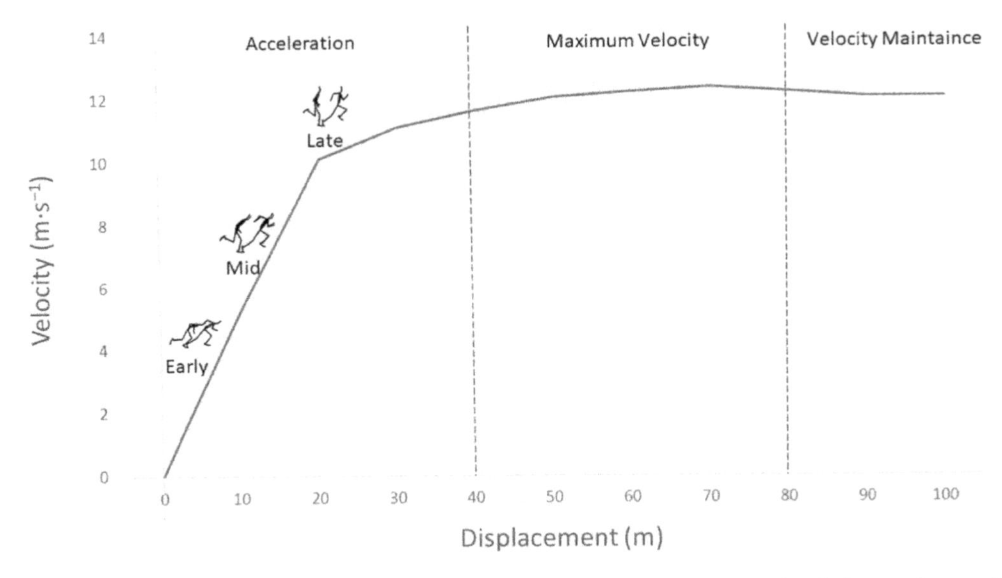

FIGURE 1.2 A velocity-displacement profile for an elite sprinter illustrating the different phases of a sprint.

and catch and subsequent yards gained after the catch in American football). Thus, development of maximum velocity sprint mechanics is still important, and the inclusion of longer sprints in training are essential for metabolic and physical conditioning requirements and injury mitigation.

Another important aspect to recognise is that particularly in the case of field-based sports, such as soccer and American football, many sprints are not directly linear. Caldbeck (2019) in analysis of maximum velocity sprinting in EPL soccer found that 85% of sprints are curvilinear. Furthermore, sprint activities in soccer have been shown to be rarely linear (Fitzpatrick et al., 2019), and such sprint actions in soccer may vary from 3.5 to 11 m in radii (Brice et al., 2004), suggesting that whilst the ability to sprint is no doubt important, the ability to modify technique and maintain speed whilst running along a curvilinear path (*curvilinear sprint ability*, otherwise known as *manoeuvrability*) is perhaps even more important. This is commonly observed post-attacking agility COD actions with the aim to reaccelerate and deviate their path of travel when penetrating the defensive line. Manoeuvrability is defined as the ability to maintain velocity during a change of direction that does not involve a clear 'plant' step (i.e. a curvilinear path of movement or 'arc' run) or the ability to perform or change mode of travel to and from 'transitional' movements (i.e. side-shuffle or backpedal) (DeWeese & Nimphius, 2016; Jones & Nimphius, 2018) and can be considered important in passages in play where a sequence of various agility actions are required and performed over short time intervals (for example, a defender who is pressing opponents while chasing after the ball in soccer).

As Figure 1.1 shows, locomotion actions such as linear and curvilinear sprints are dependent on technical and physical factors and form the cornerstone for the development of these qualities with athletes. In addition, sprint-running actions are commonly associated with hamstring strain injuries (Heiderschiet et al., 2005; Thelen et al., 2005; Schache et al., 2012) due to the propensity to generate large hamstring stretch loads during the terminal swing phase in preparation for ground contact. Whilst the aetiology of musculoskeletal injuries such as this are complex, risk factors for hamstring injuries point to intrinsic physical (e.g. eccentric hamstring strength [Jonhagen et al., 1994; Opar et al., 2015; Timmins et al., 2015]; muscle architecture [Timmins et al., 2015]) and technical (e.g. reducing anterior pelvic tilt and 'backside' mechanics, promoting more 'frontside' mechanics [Mendiguchia et al., 2021]) factors. This presents programming considerations for more holistic multidirectional speed development.

Change of Direction

Often central to expressions of agility is *changing direction* as this often is the action involved in creating separation (i.e. a forward attempting to lose their defensive marker) from – or responding to movements of an opponent (i.e. a centre back responding to the movements of a centre forward). *Change of direction* (COD) is defined as 'a reorientation and change in the horizontal path of travel of the whole-body centre of mass (COM) towards a new intended direction', and such manoeuvres are frequently performed in sports such as soccer (Bloomfield et al., 2007; Robinson et al., 2011; Martinez et al., 2022), netball (Fox et al., 2014; Sweeting et al., 2017), basketball (Svilar et al., 2018a, 2018b), rugby (Sayers & Washington-King, 2005; Wheeler et al., 2010; Zahidi & Ismail, 2018), and Gaelic football (Talty et al., 2022). For example, male soccer players in the English Premier League (EPL) have been shown to perform ~600 cuts of 0–90° and ~100 turns of 90–180° during games (Bloomfield et al., 2007), whilst in male (n = 24) EPL academy soccer (U18 and U23) (Morgan et al., 2021), an average of 305 ± 50 CODs has been reported, with 77% of these reported to be ≤90° and on average 19.2 ± 3.9 s recovery between

CODs (differences between studies likely due to different methods, definitions, and inclusion/exclusion criteria used to identify changes of direction). Gaelic football players (averaged across attacking middle third, defensive middle third, inside forward line, and inside defensive line positions) have been shown to perform 6.8 ≤ 90°-COD·min^{-1} and 2.4 90–180°-COD·min^{-1} during games (Talty et al., 2022), while directional changes of 45°, 90°, and 180° have been found to be frequent actions in netball (Sweeting et al., 2017). CODs have also been shown to be a common action involved in critical match deciding events such as goals scored in EPL soccer (Martinez et al., 2022) and penetrating defensive lines in rugby union (Zahidi et al., 2018). Hence, the literature highlights the importance and breadth of COD actions involved in field- and court-based sports.

COD ability, or *COD speed*, in a measurement context is considered 'the ability to decelerate, reverse or change movement direction and accelerate again' (Jones et al., 2009) or, in the context of specific situations in open skilled sports, 'the ability to change initial direction to a predetermined location and space on a field or court' (Nimphius, 2014) (Table 1.1). It is worth pointing out at this stage that previous definitions and models of agility has led to a coaching assumption that all COD actions are performed in 'open' situations and subject to perceptual-cognitive factors, highlighting the need to perform such drills in an unanticipated manner. However, even in field-based sports where there is a variety of sports-specific visual stimuli, it could be argued that in some 'offensive' or 'attacking' COD actions, a player acts as the 'instigator' and thus performs the action in a 'semi pre-planned' manner, whilst aware of external stimuli to initially look for the opening. For example, a defensive end 'spins' to evade an offensive tackle to pass rush the quarterback. Here, the defensive end is the instigator, and thus, their actions are planned to achieve the goal of evading the offensive tackle and then attacking the quarterback but regulated by external visual stimuli. In contrast, in 'defensive' plays, an athlete acts as the arbitrator and performs directional manoeuvres in response to an opponent or passage of play (e.g. a central defender performs a side-step cut to change direction to track and close-down a centre forward). Athletes may also perform pre-planned routes, set plays or attacking transitions in open, random sports (e.g. a corner kick routine in soccer, a wide receiver performing a slant route or a power forward in basketball performing a backdoor cut). Therefore, performing COD and related actions in a variety of contexts in training is vital to develop technical competency and adaptability (Dos'Santos et al., 2022). Furthermore, execution of pre-planned drills in training, from a skill acquisition and motor skill learning perspective, allows the development of technique and physical capacity in a controlled environment, initially, before executing such drills in unanticipated situations where task complexity, cognitive loading, and mechanical loading increases (Dos'Santos et al., 2019, 2022). Developing linear sprint ability and landing mechanics are often practised and rehearsed in a pre-planned manner regardless of the sport. Just like sprint running and landing, changing direction is a movement action all the same; thus, why wouldn't such an action be practised initially in a pre-planned manner? Therefore, changing directions needs to be practised in closed environments before initially increasing complexity and contextual interference when developing technique (Chapter 10). The objective of this method is to develop an athlete's mechanical and physical ability to execute the action which should help improve agility performance (i.e. fast mover), irrespective of perceptual-cognitive speed.

Directional changes, particularly side-step cutting manoeuvres, are also the most common actions involved in non-contact anterior cruciate ligament (ACL) injuries in handball (Olsen et al., 2004), soccer (Faude et al., 2005; Brophy et al., 2015; Walden et al., 2015; Lurcano et al., 2021), rugby union (Montgomery et al., 2018), and American football (Johnstone et al.,

2018) due to the propensity to generate high knee joint loads (e.g. knee abduction and rotation moments and anterior shear forces) (McLean et al., 2003; McLean et al., 2004) during the 'plant' step of the manoeuvre that increase ACL strain (Shin et al., 2009, 2011). Changing direction has also been identified as an action associated with lateral ankle sprains (Fong et al., 2009), adductor injuries (Serner et al., 2019), hamstring strain injuries (Kerin et al., 2022), and development of athletic groin pain (Franklyn-Miller et al., 2017), but the short- and long-term consequences of ACL injury has led to widespread research interest. Developing safer COD techniques and the physical capacity to perform COD manoeuvres is therefore an important prerequisite not only for performance but for injury mitigation to maximise player welfare and availability.

Deceleration

A largely overlooked high-intensity locomotion action is *deceleration* (i.e. the rate of decrease in movement velocity [negative acceleration]), which refers to 'the action performed during sporting scenarios that precedes a COD manoeuvre or an action immediately performed following a sprint to reduce momentum' (McBurnie et al., 2022). A systematic review and meta-analysis by Harper et al. (2019) revealed that in most field-based sports, except for American football (e.g. hockey, rugby league, rugby union, rugby sevens, and soccer), high-intensity (< -2.5 m·s^{-2}) decelerations determined through global positioning systems devices are performed more frequently than high-intensity accelerations during competitive match play. In soccer (professional reserve, U21 and U18 level) 43–62 high-intensity decelerations (≤ -3 m·s^{-2}) per game are performed (Russell et al., 2016; Tierney et al., 2016), whilst in the first and second halves of professional rugby union matches, 28.3 ± 10.6 and 25.9 ± 12.1 decelerations (≤ -3 m·s^{-2}), respectively, have been reported (Jones et al., 2015). Moreover, playing position in both soccer (Tierney et al., 2016) and rugby union (Cunningham et al., 2016) have been shown to influence the number of decelerations performed, suggesting that distinct playing boundaries in field-based sports influence the intensity and duration of decelerations during match play. As with CODs (Morgan et al., 2021), the frequency of high- and very-high-intensity accelerations and decelerations from the first- to the second-half periods of elite team sport match play tends to show a slight reduction (Harper et al. 2019), which highlights that these intense movement actions could be particularly vulnerable to neuromuscular fatigue and consequently to an increased risk of encountering injury (Harper et al., 2019; McBurnie et al., 2022).

Rapid deceleration manoeuvres are vital in both offensive and defensive situations to help avoid or pursue an opponent. For instance, in soccer, deceleration has also been found to be the second most common action by attackers (scorer and assistant) and defenders (defender of scorer and assistant) in goals scored in the men's EPL (Martinez et al., 2022). Furthermore, Rhodes et al. (2021) reported that, in a soccer team, they tended to win more matches when a greater frequency of decelerations were performed. However, the often-sudden imposed deceleration involving rapid reductions in velocity enforced in short time frames and constrained spaces give rise to large mechanical loading (e.g. magnitude of ground reaction forces and rate of loading during braking steps). These large mechanical loads experienced present a concern to coaching teams, as players are exposed to high eccentric braking, placing increased vulnerability of the muscle/tendon to tissue damage and neuromuscular fatigue (Harper & Kiely, 2018; McBurnie et al., 2022). Furthermore, effective deceleration mechanics involving preparatory steps (e.g. antepenultimate [Dos'Santos et al., 2021] and penultimate [Jones et al., 2016; Dos'Santos et al., 2017, 2019] steps), leading into a COD or a complete stop allows an athlete to dissipate braking forces, reduce momentum, and arrive in an optimal position for these instances and in turn reduce hazardous multi-planar knee joint loads and injury susceptibility. Thus, multidirectional speed athletes need to be able to skilfully dissipate braking loads, develop mechanically robust musculoskeletal structures, and ensure frequent high-intensity horizontal deceleration exposure to accustom individuals to the potentially damaging nature of intense decelerations (McBurnie et al., 2022).

Aims and Objectives of This Book

The multifactorial underpinning of multidirectional speed presents difficulties to practitioners in trying to develop *multidirectional speed* with athletes, in that practitioners require a good biomechanical understanding of the range of sports actions associated with expressions of agility (i.e. knowing what optimal technique is for these actions and how they could be developed and coached), a thorough knowledge of strength and conditioning practices to be able to prepare an athlete for the physical demands of these actions, and knowledge of how to improve an athlete's/player's ability to 'read the game' and select and execute the most appropriate movement action during match play. This book aims to review the science of multidirectional speed and translate this information into real-world application to provide a resource for practitioners to develop multidirectional speed with athletes. This book brings together knowledge from a wealth of world-leading researchers and applied practitioners in the area of multidirectional speed to provide a complete resource to assist practitioners in designing effective multidirectional speed development programmes. In order to achieve this aim, this book is divided into three parts, each with a particular objective:

1. Critically review the scientific literature to provide a theoretical basis of multidirectional speed. Here the contextual importance of multidirectional speed is examined before a review of the literature regarding the biomechanical and physical demands of the previously mentioned actions associated with multidirectional speed to provide a theoretical framework to work from in subsequent chapters (Part 1 – Chapters 1–5).
2. Critically examine the strategies for the assessment and development of core elements of multidirectional speed, including the development of muscle strength qualities, technique modification and coaching strategies for multidirectional speed, metabolic conditioning, and developing perceptual-cognitive abilities (Part 2 – Chapters 6–13).
3. Present programming solutions for multidirectional speed development and consider adaptations for the rehabilitating and youth athlete (Part 3 – Chapters 14–17).

References

Abdelkrim, B. N., El Fazaa, S., & El Ati, J. (2007). Time-motion analysis and physiological data of elite under-19- year-old basketball players during competition. *British Journal of Sports Medicine, 41*(2), 69–75.

Andrzejewski, M., Chmura, J., Pluta, B., Strzelczyk, R., & Kasprzak, A. (2013). Analysis of sprinting activities of professional soccer players. *Journal of Strength & Conditioning Research, 27*(8), 2134–2140.

Bellon, C. R., DeWeese, B. H., Sato, K., Clark, K. P., & Stone, M. H. (2019). Defining the early, mid, and late subsections of sprint acceleration in division 1 men's soccer players. *Journal of Strength & Conditioning Research, 33*, 1001–1006.

Bloomfield, J., Polman, R., & O'Donoghue, P. (2007). Physical demands of different positions in FA Premier League soccer. *Journal of Sports Science and Medicine, 6*(1), 63.

Brice, P., Smith, N., & Dyson, R. (2004). Frequency of curvilinear motion during competitive soccer play. *Journal of Sports Sciences, 22*, 485–593.

Brophy, R. H., Stepan, J. G., Silvers, H. J., & Mandelbaum, B. R. (2015). Defending puts the anterior cruciate ligament at risk during soccer: A gender-based analysis. *Sports Health, 7*, 244–249.

Caldbeck, P. (2019). *Contextual sprinting in football* [thesis]. Liverpool, UK: Liverpool John Moores University.

Cunningham, D., Shearer, D. A., Drawer, S., Eager, R., Taylor, N., Cook, C., & Kilduff, L. P. (2016). Movement demands of elite U20 international rugby union players. *PLoS ONE, 11*, 1–10.

DeWeese, B. H., & Nimphius, S. (2016). Program design and technique for speed and agility training. In *Essentials of strength training and conditioning* (4th edition) (Eds. G. G. Haff & N. T. Triplett). Champaign, IL: Human Kinetics, pp. 521–557.

Di-Salvo, V., Baron, R., Gonza´Lez-Haro, C., Gormasz, C., Pigozzi, F., & Bachl, N. (2010). Sprinting analysis of elite soccer players during European Champions League and UEFA Cup matches. *Journal of Sports Sciences, 28*, 1489–1494.

Dobbin, N., Highton, J., Moss, S. L., & Twist, C. (2019). The discriminant validity of a standardized testing battery and its ability to differentiate anthropometric and physical characteristics between youth, academy, and senior professional rugby league players. *International Journal of Sports Physiology and Performance, 14*(8), 1110–1116.

Dos'Santos, T., & Jones, P. A. (2022). Training for change of direction and agility. *In Advanced strength and conditioning* (2nd edition) (Eds. A. Turner & P. Comfort). Abingdon, UK: Routledge, pp. 328–362

Dos'Santos, T., McBurnie, A., Thomas, C., Comfort, P., & Jones, P. A. (2019). Biomechanical comparison of cutting techniques: A review and practical applications. *Strength & Conditioning Journal, 41*, 40–54.

Dos'Santos, T., Thomas, C., & Jones, P. A. (2021). How early should you brake during a 180° turn? A kinetic comparison of the antepenultimate, penultimate, and final foot contacts during a 505 change of direction speed test. *Journal of Sports Sciences, 39*(4), 395–405, doi:10.1080/02640414.2020.1823130

Dos'Santos, T., Thomas, C., Jones, P. A., & Comfort, P. (2017). Mechanical determinants of faster change of direction speed performance in male athletes. *Journal of Strength & Conditioning Research, 31*, 696–705.

Faude, O., Junge, A., Kindermann, W., & Dvorak, J. (2005). Injuries in female soccer players. A prospective study in the German national league. *American Journal of Sports Medicine, 33*, 1694–1700.

Faude, O., Koch, T., & Meyer, T. (2012). Straight sprinting is the most frequent action in goal situations in professional football. *Journal of Sports Sciences, 30*(7), 625–631.

Fitzpatrick, J. F., Linsley, A., & Musham, C. (2019). Running the curve: A preliminary investigation into curved sprinting during football match-play. *Sport Performance & Science Reports, 55*, 1–3.

Fong, D. T.-P., Hong, Y., Shima, Y., Krosshaug, T., Yung, P. S.-H., & Chan, K.-M. (2009). Biomechanics of supination ankle sprain: A case report of an accidental injury event in the laboratory. *American Journal of Sports Medicine, 37*(4), 822–827.

Fox, A., Spittle, M., Otago, L., & Saunders, N. (2014). Offensive agility techniques performed during international netball competition. *International Journal of Sports Science and Coaching, 9*, 543–552.

Franklyn-Miller, A., Richter, C., King, E., Gore, S., Moran, K., Strike, S., & Falvey, E. (2017). Athletic groin pain (part 2): A prospective cohort study on the biomechanical evaluation of change of direction identifies three clusters of movement patterns. *British Journal of Sports Medicine, 51*(5), 460–468.

Gabbet, T. J. (2012). Sprinting patterns of national rugby league competition. *Journal of Strength & Conditioning Research, 26*(1), 121–130.

Gabbett, T. J., Kelly, J. N., & Sheppard, J. M. (2008). Speed, change of direction speed, and reactive agility of rugby league players. *Journal of Strength & Conditioning Research, 22*(1), 174–181.

Harper, D. J., Carling, C., & Kiely, J. (2019). High-intensity acceleration and deceleration demands in elite team sports competitive match play: A systematic review and meta-analysis of observational studies. *Sports Medicine, 49*, 1923–1947.

Harper, D. J., & Kiely, J. (2018). Damaging nature of decelerations: Do we adequately prepare players? *BMJ Open Sport & Exercise Medicine, 4*, e000379. doi:10.1136/bmjsem-2018-000379

Heiderscheit, B. C., Hoerth, D. M., Chumanov, E. S., Swanson, S. C., Thelen, B. J., & Thelen, D. G. (2005). Identifying the time of occurrence of a hamstring strain injury during treadmill running: A case study. *Clinical Biomechanics, 20*, 1072–1078.

Jeffreys, I. (2010). *Gamespeed: Movement training for superior sports performance*. Monterey, CA: Coaches Choice.

Johnston, J. T., Mandelbaum, B. R., Schub, D., Rodeo, S. A., Matava, M. J., Silvers, H. J., Cole, B. J., Elattrache, N. S., Mcadams, T., & Brophy, R. H. (2018). Video analysis of anterior cruciate ligament tears in professional American football athletes. *American Journal of Sports Medicine, 46*(4), 862–868.

Jones, M. R., West, D. J., Crewther, B. T., Cook, C. J., & Kilduff, L. P. (2015). Quantifying positional and temporal movement patterns in professional rugby union using global positioning system. *European Journal of Sport Science, 15*, 488–496.

Jones, P. A., Bampouras, T., & Marrin, K. (2009). An investigation into the physical determinants of change of direction speed. *Journal of Sports Medicine and Physical Fitness, 49*(1), 97–104.

Jones, P. A., Herrington, L., & Graham-Smith, P. (2016). Braking characteristics during cutting and pivoting in female soccer players. *Journal of Electromyography & Kinesiology, 30*, 46–54.

Jones, P. A., & Nimphius, S. (2018). Change of direction and agility. In *Performance assessment in strength and conditioning* (Eds. P. Comfort, P. A. Jones, & J. J. McMahon). Abingdon, UK: Routledge, pp. 140–165.

Jonhagen, S., Nemeth, G., & Eriksson, E. (1994). Hamstring injuries in sprinters. The role of concentric and eccentric hamstring muscle strength and flexibility. *American Journal of Sports Medicine, 22*, 262–266.

Kerin, F., Farrell, G., Tierney, P., McCarthy Persson, U., De Vito, G., & Delahunt, E. (2022). It's not all about sprinting: Mechanisms of acute hamstring strain injuries in professional male rugby union – a systematic visual video analysis. *British Journal of Sports Medicine*. Published Online First: 19 January 2022. doi:10.1136/bjsports-2021-104171

Lucarno, S., Zago, M., Buckthorpe, M., Grassi, A., Tosarelli, F., Smith, R., & Della Villa, F. (2021). Systematic video analysis of anterior cruciate ligament injuries in professional female soccer players. *American Journal of Sports Medicine, 49*(7), 1794–1802, June. doi:10.1177/03635465211008169. Epub: 14 May 2021. PMID: 33989090.

Martínez Hernández, D., Quinn, M., & Jones, P. A. (2022). Linear advancing actions followed by deceleration and turn are the most common movements preceding goals in male professional soccer. *Science and Medicine in Football*. doi:10.1080/24733938.2022.2030064

McBurnie, A. J., & Dos'Santos, T. (2022). Multidirectional speed in youth soccer players: Theoretical underpinnings. *Strength and Conditioning Journal, 44*(1), 15–33. doi:10.1519/SSC.0000000000000658

McBurnie, A. J., Harper, D., Jones, P. A., & Dos'Santos, T. (2022). Deceleration training in team sports: Another potential 'vaccine' for sports-related injury? *Sports Medicine, 52*, 1–12

McLean, S. G., Lipfert, S. W., & Van Den Bogert, A. J. (2004). Effect of gender and defensive opponent on the biomechanics of sidestep cutting. *Medicine and Science in Sports and Exercise, 36*(6), 1008–1016.

McLean, S. G., Su, A., & Van Den Bogert, A. J. (2003). Development and validation of a 3-d model to predict knee joint loading during dynamic movement. *Journal of Biomechanical Engineering, 125*, 864–874.

Mcmillan, S., & Pfaff, D. (2018). *The ALTIS Kinogram method*. (ebook).

Mendiguchia, U., Castaño-Zambudio, A., Jimenez-Reyes, P., Morin, J. B., Edouard, P., Conceição, F., Dodoo, J., & Colyer, S. L. (2021). Can we modify maximal speed running posture? Implications for performance and hamstring injuries management. *International Journal of Sports Physiology and Performance*. doi:10.1123/ijspp.2021–0107.

Montgomery, C., Blackburn, J., Withers, D., Tierney, G., Moran, C., & Simms, C. (2018). Mechanisms of ACL injury in professional rugby union: A systematic video analysis of 36 cases. *British Journal of Sports Medicine, 52*(15), 944–1001.

Morgan, O. J., Drust, B., Ade, J. D., & Robinson, M. A. (2021). Change of direction frequency off the ball: New perspectives in elite youth soccer. *Science and Medicine in Football*. doi:10.1080/24733938.2021.1986635

Nagahara, R., Matsubayashi, T., Matsuo, A., & Zushi, K. (2014). Kinematics of transition during human accelerated sprinting. *Biology Open, 3*, 689–699. doi:10.1242/bio.20148284

Nimphius, S. (2014). Increasing agility. In *High-performance training for sports* (Eds. D Joyce & D. Lewindon). Champaign, IL: Human Kinetics, pp. 185–198.

Olsen, O. E., Myklebust, G., Engebretsen, L., & Bahr, R. (2004). Injury mechanisms for anterior cruciate ligament injuries in team handball. A systematic video analysis. *American Journal of Sports Medicine, 32*, 1002–1012.

Opar, D. A., Williams, M. D., Timmins, R. G., Hickey, J., Duhig, S. J., & Shield, A. J. (2015). Eccentric hamstring strength and hamstring injury risk in Australian footballers. *Medicine and Science in Sports and Exercise, 47*(4), 857–865.

Parsons, L. S., & Jones, M. T. (1998). Development of speed, agility and quickness for tennis athletes. *Strength & Conditioning, 20*, 14–19.

Rhodes, D., Valassakis, S., Bortnik, L., Eaves, R., Harper, D., & Alexander, J. (2021). The effect of high-intensity accelerations and decelerations on match outcome of an elite English league two football team. *International Journal of Environmental Research and Public Health, 18*(18), 9913.

Robinson, G., O'Donoghue, P., & Nielson, P. (2011). Path changes and injury risk in English FA Premier League Soccer. *International Journal of Performance Analysis in Sport, 11*, 40–56.

Russell, M., Sparkes, W., Northeast, J., Cook, C. J., Love, T. D., Bracken, R. M., & Kilduff, L. P. (2016). Changes in acceleration and deceleration capacity throughout professional soccer match-play. *Journal of Strength & Conditioning Research, 30*, 2839–2844.

Sayers, M., & Washington-King, J. (2005). Characteristics of effective ball carries in super 12 rugby. *International Journal of Performance Analysis in Sport, 5*, 92–106.

Scanlan, A., Dascombe, B., & Reaburn, P. (2011). A comparison of the activity demands of elite and sub-elite Australian men's basketball competition. *Journal of Sports Sciences, 29*(11), 1153–1160.

Schache, A. G., Dorn, T. W., Blanch, P. D., Brown, N. A. T., & Pandy, M. G. (2012). Mechanics of the human hamstring muscles during sprinting. *Medicine and Science in Sports and Exercise, 44*(4), 647–658.

Serner, A., Mosler, A. B., Tol, J. L., Bahr, R., & Weir, A. (2019). Mechanisms of acute adductor longus injuries in male football players: A systematic visual video analysis. *British Journal of Sports Medicine, 53*(3), 158–164.

Shin, C. S., Chaudhari, A. M., & Andriacchi, T. P. (2009). The effect of isolated valgus moments on ACL strain during single-leg landing: A simulation study. *Journal of Biomechanics, 42*(3), 280–285.

Shin, C. S., Chaudhari, A. M., & Andriacchi, T. P. (2011). Valgus plus internal rotation moments increase anterior cruciate ligament strain more than either alone. *Medicine and Science in Sports and Exercise, 43*(8), 1484–1491

Svilar, L., Castellano, J., Jukic, I., & Casamichana, D. (2018a). Positional differences in elite basketball: Selecting appropriate training-load measures. *International Journal of Sports Physiology and Performance, 13*(7), 947–952.

Svilar, L., Jukić, I., & Castellano, J. (2018b). Load monitoring system in top-level basketball team. *Kinesiology, 50*(1), 25–33.

Sweeting, A. J., Aughey, R. J., Cormack, S. J., & Morgan, S. (2017). Discovering frequently recurring movement sequences in team-sport athlete spatiotemporal data. *Journal of Sports Sciences, 35*, 2439–2445.

Talty, P. F., Mcguigan, K., Quinn, M., & Jones, P. A. (2022). Agility demands of Gaelic football match-play: A time-motion analysis. *International Journal of Performance Analysis in Sport*. doi:10.1080/24748668.2022.2033519

Thelen, D. G., Chumanov, E. S., Best, T. M., Swanson, S. C., & Heiderscheit, B. C. (2005). Simulation of biceps femoris musculo-tendon mechanics during the swing phase of sprinting. *Medicine and Science in Sports and Exercise, 37*, 1931–1938.

Thomas, C., Comfort, P., Jones, P. A., & Dos'Santos, T. (2017). Strength and conditioning for netball: A needs analysis and training recommendation. *Strength and Conditioning Journal, 39*(4), 10–21. doi:10.1519/SSC.0000000000000287

Thomas, C., Ismail, K. T., Comfort, P., Jones, P. A., & Dos'Santos, T. (2016). Physical profiles of regional academy netball players. *Journal of Trainology, 5*(2), 30–37.

Tierney, P. J., Young, A., Clarke, N. D., & Duncan, M. J. (2016). Match play demands of 11 versus 11 professional football using global positioning system tracking: Variations across common playing formations. *Human Movement Science, 49*, 1–8.

Timmins, R. G., Bourne, M. N., Shield, A. J., Williams, M. D., Lorenzen, C., & Opar, D. A. (2015). A short biceps femoris long head fascicle length and eccentric knee flexor weakness increase risk of hamstring injury: A prospective cohort study in 152 elite professional football players. *British Journal of Sports Medicine*. doi:10.1136/bjsports-2015-095362

Walden, M., Krosshaug, T., Bjorneboe, J., Andersen, T. E., Faul, O., & Hagglund, M. (2015). Three distinct mechanisms predominate in non-contact anterior cruciate ligament injuries in male professional football players: A systematic video analysis of 39 cases. *British Journal of Sports Medicine*, *49*(22), 1452–1460.
Wheeler, K. W., Askew, C. D., & Sayers, M. G. (2010). Effective attacking strategies in rugby union. *European Journal Sport Science*, *10*, 237–242.
Zahidi, N. N. M., & Ismail, S. I. (2018). Notational analysis of evasive agility skills executed by attacking ball carriers among elite rugby players of the 2015 Rugby World Cup. *Movement Health and Exercise*, *7*, 99–113.

2

CONTEXTUAL IMPORTANCE OF MULTIDIRECTIONAL SPEED IN FIELD- AND COURT-BASED SPORTS

Paul Caldbeck

Introduction

It is widely taught and understood that there are fundamental differences between agility and change of direction. While no universally accepted definitions truly exist, it is commonly accepted that agility involves 'a rapid whole-body movement with a change of velocity or direction in response to a stimulus' (Sheppard and Young, 2006), whereas change of direction refers to pre-planned tasks (Young et al., 2015). The essential difference is related to the presence of stimuli and an individual's response to these (i.e. perception-action coupling). In sport these stimuli are highly specific to the sport itself and the specific contexts that occur within it.

All multidirectional speed actions in field- and court-based sports occur in relation to the sport itself. These speed actions are believed to be initiated and attained through a constant exchange of information between organism, environment, and task. This dynamical systems theory approach defines the organism as the individual's characteristics, be they physical capacities or psychological; the environment as the physical and sociocultural variables in nature; and the task as the activity itself, such as the rules of the game (Immonen et al., 2017; Myszka, 2018). These constraints coalesce to create the 'perceptual-motor workspace' within which the athlete operates. This ultimate interaction and exchange between athlete, environment, and task leads to movement solutions through perception-action coupling, whereby actions are taken in response to the individual's perception of the relationship between oneself, the environment, and the task.

Often in strength and conditioning and sports science, a focus is overwhelmingly made to the physical capacities of an individual, with little to no appreciation for the complex relationship between the athlete and the environment and task. An example of this would be a programme focused on closed-skill change-of-direction ability. Whilst such physical development is important, appreciation must be made to the nature of how these actions present themselves within a competitive environment. Often such tasks are not completed solely at maximal intensities, with aspects such as timing being important. Similarly, the presence of an opposition will dictate the ultimate movement solutions selected. The athlete must first process the information presented to them (perception) before an action occurs. This is an ongoing process rarely present in closed-skill movements.

DOI: 10.4324/9781003267881-3

Such multidirectional speed skills have been previously termed *game speed*, whereby an athlete seeks to exploit the capacities of speed and agility in the context of a match (Jeffreys, 2011; Jeffreys et al., 2018). This definition would suggest that enhanced game speed abilities will lead to maximal efficiency of ones' physical capacity within their sport. And thus, an individual is limited by the ability in achieving this. Therefore, an athlete may see on field/court improvements through enhancement of either their physical capacity or their ability to maximally exploit this capacity in a game situation. It is often said in soccer of experienced professionals that the 'first yards are in their head'. As a simplistic example, an elite track sprinter may possess a larger capacity for maximal speed than an NFL wide receiver, but ultimately lacks in their ability to employ this in a football-related context of responding to the ball and teammates and avoiding the opposition defensive players, without even considering the additional physical qualities required such as deceleration. The sprinter could therefore be deemed a 'slow thinker' within this context of football game speed, lacking such highly tuned perceptual-cognitive abilities as visual scanning, anticipation and pattern recognition (Jackson et al., 2006; Murphy et al., 2018). Leading to longer and less accurate decision-making than the NFL Wide Receiver who possess an inferior maximum velocity.

There exists a natural tendency in education and learning to reduce complex systems down to easy-to-manage factors distinct from their complex interactions. As discussed, this often manifests in sports performance as improvements on easy-to-control closed-skill speed tests, assumed to be directly observed in on pitch/court improvements. However, this association is rarely the case, particularly as an athlete progresses from junior to elite levels. Small enhancements in maximal sprinting speed (0.2 m/s) are arguably unlikely alone to transfer to a noticeable increase in sporting performance in field- and court-based sports, whereas an enhancement of decision-making during a crucial moment, such as tracking an offensive player as a pass is made to them during a defensive phase of play, may be vital.

It is often assumed that the physical practitioner's role ends with closed speed skills, such as linear sprinting and change-of-direction ability. Any aspects beyond this are often deemed the remit of the sport coach. However, their focus is often primarily sporting techniques, tactical coaching, and more global strategy, without a direct appreciation for the movement patterns these consist of. Thus, this key area is regularly omitted from programming, when it is likely this highly specific zone could carry the greatest transfer to ultimate sports performance.

If game speed can be enhanced through both physical qualities and the means by which an individual applies these in their sport, then it is crucial to understand the context within which these multidirectional skills occur. This can then subsequently inform training provisions and provide an athlete with a more holistic development programme. Only through an appreciation of these contexts can a practitioner truly seek to achieve the desired transfer to performance.

In soccer it has been suggested that 'full integration' of physical actions accounts for tactical, technical, and physical actions (Ade et al., 2016; Bradley and Ade, 2018) (Figure 2.1), with each existing on a Venn diagram suggesting a particular actions predominance in a category – for example, a physical action with a tactical outcome being a recovery run where an athlete runs at high velocity to recover position within a wider tactical structure. Such an action requires the individual to respond to the evolving situation around them and choose the best movement solution to achieve the selected task outcome, recovering position. This may involve physical actions, such as a change in direction and a high-velocity run, that may include more nuanced physical actions, such as torso dissociation or a manipulation of velocity or direction (curve). Likewise, this run may not all be completed at maximal effort as the player times their action through a

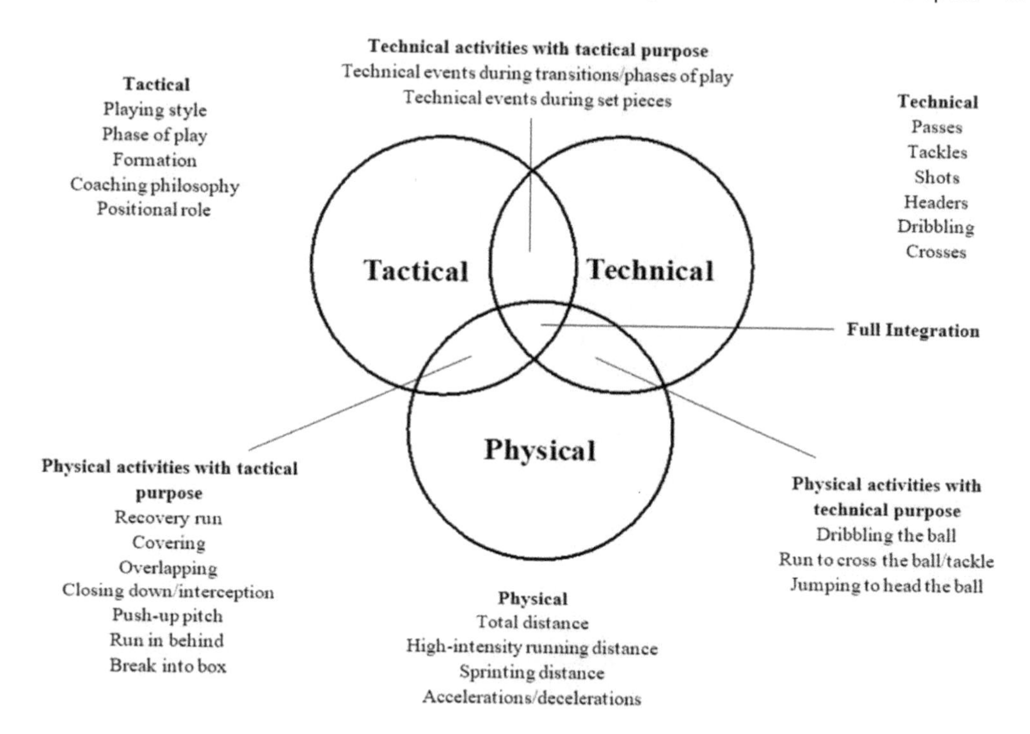

FIGURE 2.1 A Venn diagram displaying an integrated approach to understanding match actions in soccer (adapted from Bradley and Ade, 2018). Note the figure is not an exhaustive list of all possible actions, merely a representation.

consistent exchange of the information presented to them. The individual may self-regulate their velocity to a speed that affords them the greatest number of possible options for accurate and effective execution of sport-specific actions. The direction of the ball may also change course mid-action, demanding response, and solution, to a new, different task.

In the outlined example of a recovery run in soccer, inefficient decision-making or broader game speed skills, such as changing direction or torso dissociation to monitor play, can easily undo an outstanding maximal velocity ability by causing the athlete to be unsuccessful in recovering their position within the wider tactical formation too late. It would thus be remiss to ignore such abilities in the development of an athlete.

Of course, physical capacities are imperative to the ultimate presentation of effective game speed ability. But without a true understanding of the contextual application of these capacities in a game context, performance enhancement programmes can be seen as incomplete. Therefore, to attain truly holistic development, intricate knowledge of the context within which speed actions are performed must be gained. By understanding why and how these actions occur in competition, a practitioner can begin to reverse engineer these contexts and designing effective training as a result. Development of skills such as anticipation and an ability to 'read the game' is said to be a key differentiator between skilled and less skilled athletes (Williams, 2000; Jackson et al., 2006).

The process of reverse engineering in sports performance is well described (Turner et al., 2022), originally defined as a process where products are deconstructed to extract their design information so they may be recreated (Turner et al., 2022). The application of such thinking to multidirectional speed is fairly simple. Once a desired outcome is selected, a practitioner would then work backwards to establish the underlying determinants. In certain sports, such as track and field sprinting, this may be a desired competition winning race time. In more complex sports such as field- and court-based ones, where there is less of a direct link between physical performance and outcome, one may select aspects that support sporting success, such as key tactical outcomes.

To continue the example of a recovery run in soccer, what positions predominantly complete this action? How do these actions manifest in a match? Such factors as frequency, phase of play, and location on the pitch are all imperative to understand and appreciate. Full backs often complete recovery runs in soccer subsequent to an attacking phase of the play. These often occur following a loss of possession and thus a defensive transition where the previously offensive team attempts to recover their defensive structure. Full backs are a position that features laterally on the soccer pitch, therefore inducing constraints on space and likely demanding differing 'scanning of the field' demands than a centrally located player. All of these factors will affect the ultimate completion of the action of a recovery run and consequently its success.

What We Know

As noted, agility and game speed involve cognitive aspects absent in pure speed and agility actions and are thus often distinguished as open skill versus closed skill. Whilst it is crucial this coalescence of perception and action is always appreciated, it is often useful to observe these as constituent parts. An understanding of the actions employed allows for a biomechanical appreciation of key movement patterns that may have implications for skill development, physical development, and injury prevention. For example, the repetition of a particular movement pattern may create stress to physical structures that lead to injury. Knowledge of such movements allows for injury reduction programmes to be designed accordingly.

However, with that being said, an ecological dynamics approach to understanding movements in sport suggests it ineffective to attempt to seek to elicit an exact movement response from an athlete to a given scenario through stored memory. Rather, dexterity of movement should be the ultimate goal. Dexterity is defined by Bernstein as 'the ability to find a motor solution for any external situation, that is, to adequately solve any emerging motor problem' (Bernstein, 1967). The overarching premise suggests that each given task within a sport varies significantly between match plays and even within a match play, as do the environmental constraints. Therefore, rote memory of a situation is impossible to attain.

If perception and action are inherently linked, then enhancing perception likely attunes action (Seifert et al., 2016). Information that is perceived by an athlete is thus said to specify affordances. Affordances, or opportunities for action, are highly specific to the organism (i.e. athlete) and the task within a given environment (Fajen et al., 2009; Seifert et al., 2016). Therefore, by enhancing an athlete's appreciation and knowledge of a given task within an environment, it is suggested possible to increase potential affordances (Davids et al., 2013). These action opportunities, being specific to an individual, mean different individuals will display different behaviours within the same scenario. Consequently, while patterns may exist within a sport or position, focus should be made predominantly to the contexts faced rather than the actions observed.

Beyond performance, there is developing evidence in sports such as soccer that suggest that injuries such as ACL ruptures occur overwhelmingly in reactive situations with high cognitive loads. The vast majority of these devastating injuries are non-contact and, beyond that, typically seen in defensive actions, predominantly when 'pressing' (Waldén et al., 2015). Thus, recommendations have been made to train running and changing direction techniques in such 'out of balance' situations and reactive situations, reinforcing optimal mechanics (Olsen et al., 2004; Waldén et al., 2015; Taberner et al., 2020). Pressing actions in soccer typically involve a high-speed run towards an opposition player, which may involve a reactive change of direction or velocity directly in response to this opposition player. There is thus a critical perceptual element to such an action that may lead an athlete into biomechanically compromised positions (Chapter 4 discusses the neurocognitive element of the ACL injury in further detail). A targeted training programme seeking exposure to these contexts with effective coaching could be a potential route to reduction of risk, alongside typical physical protective provisions considering the performance-injury conflict (Dos'Santos et al., 2018, 2022b).

As noted, it is often useful to think of game speed movements within categories of transition, initiation, and actualisation (Jeffreys, 2008; Jeffreys et al., 2018). Transition movements are associated with actions that are employed as preparation for subsequent actions, the goal being to maintain opportunity for effective action through effective positioning. These may be static or in motion. The classic 'athletic position' is a good example of an effective transition movement where the individual is afforded movement in the most possible directions with the most efficiency. Other motion-based examples are linear controlled running, lateral shuffling or crossover running, and rearwards backpedalling, amongst others. Transition movements are a particularly good example of the paradigm shift in viewing game speed movements within context rather than merely as physical actions alone. Evaluation of a transition movement should be based more upon efficiency of movements and the options it affords rather than any measure of time to complete. A 30 m backpedalling distance is unlikely to be linked to performance in many sports.

Initiation movements are those that are used to start or change motion. These can be categorised as the starting direction of the action or whether any change of direction takes place. Typically, the starting direction can be linear, lateral, or rear. Commonly categorised movements are then applied by the athlete to attain these: acceleration pattern, hip turn, or drop steps. To instigate a change in direction, plant and cut steps are utilised, depending on the degree of angle change.

Finally, there are actualisation movements, which are the key movements that ultimately decide the degree of success of the movement, be these key sporting actions or a moving to a position as quickly as possible. These can be described as consisting of acceleration and/or maximum speed elements. And may be from static position or rolling and be linear or curved in nature. As noted, these are often the key maximal effort movements and are traditionally tested based upon time to completion.

Many varying means of classifying movement exist, and it is likely that a practitioner should refine their own specific system of classification specific to their population and sport (Bloomfield et al., 2007; Ade et al., 2016; Dos'Santos et al., 2022a). Similarly, though important to understand one's own specific context, within the literature exist detailed data regarding the types of movements observed in many sports across many levels (Bloomfield et al., 2007; Morgan et al., 2022; Dos'Santos et al., 2022a). While this knowledge can inform practice, it is fundamental to understand the contexts within which these movements present themselves. The common presence of a given movement does not necessarily indicate a most effective strategy for an individual or equate to importance to, or impact upon, match outcome. For example, walking is one of the most common actions seen in soccer, yet it is not associated directly with the key, decisive moments of a match (Bradley et al., 2009; Faude et al., 2012). And similarly, jumping in rugby is rare but can be key to certain moments related to catching the ball to complete or prevent a try and lineouts (Deutsch et al., 2007).

Once a classification of movement is established, key multidirectional speed actions can be observed within their context and key themes noted. This allows a blend of approaches that can target the typical movements observed and allow dextrous development within key context experienced. A defining work in the space of contextualising these high-speed actions in soccer employed a novel high-intensity movement programme (HIMP), observing actions where a velocity of >21 km·h^{-1} was achieved (Ade et al., 2016). The applied HIMP then defined the movement pattern, technical skill, tactical outcome, and pitch location of each action, displayed by playing position. Such an analysis of course does not weight importance of an action, merely frequency. But such data can be then used to establish a training programme specific to an individual or position category and also assist in testing battery selection and rehabilitation of previously injured players.

Without considering the physical movement patterns associated with the actions, it is clear to see differing contexts between positions in soccer. For example, centre backs' most common high-speed movements were achieved during actions, such as covering, push-up pitch, and track running, whereas a centre forward would most commonly close down, drive through the middle, and challenge CB (Ade et al., 2016; Caldbeck, 2019). If we consider these high-speed actions in more depth, clear distinctions in the types of movements that would be employed to achieve success would be seen.

As a centre back, covering is clearly an important action for tactical integrity; the player moves to cover space or a player on the pitch whilst remaining goal side. This action occurs whilst the team is out of possession and thus in a defensive phase of play (transition or organisation). Although a conjecture, it would be reasonable to assume such an action can be crucial to match outcome if unsuccessful. Ineffective covering may lead to a pass to an attacking player in space that can threaten the goal of the defensive team or an attacking player in possession of the ball being unopposed if they are able to dribble past a single defensive player. The action is thus a 'safety net' for the defensive team. For a centre back specifically, this action would naturally have higher importance as they are typically the last line of defence before the goalkeeper.

The commonality of such an action displays the importance of centre back 'pairs' in the regularly utilised four defensive player formations (4–4–2, 4–4–3). One player will engage the opposition and the other provide cover. It is simple to then consider the perceptual and cognitive demands associated with such an action. The covering defender must first detect the development of play that demands a covering run, consider the timing of their run to maintain integrity of the offside line, decide the best placement of themselves between attacker and goal, and then respond constantly to any change in the circumstance of the play (regaining of possession, a switch of play). This information is then factorised by the consideration of one's own physical ability and the potential ability of all other players involved in the action. For example, if I am covering a player, with my back to goal to observe play, and my opposition are facing my goal, how confident in my physical ability am I that I can change my direction of facing and beat my opposite number to the ball to make an interception or tackle should a pass in behind me be made.

A useful analogy of this is the application of John Boyd's OODA loop developed for military strategy (Jeffreys, 2016). Accordingly, decision-making occurs in a constant loop of *o*bserving, *o*rienting, *d*eciding, and *a*cting. Suggesting effective decision-making can be achieved through effectively observing and reacting to events as they unfold. Higher-performing athletes tend to anticipate situations better through 'cue utilisation' and 'act' earlier than their opposition to achieve outcomes such as the creation or reduction of space more effectively. The key being the constant exchange of information. Rarely in a field- or court-based sport does an athlete merely compete a maximal effort linear sprint. These actions overwhelmingly would be made in response to stimuli and require constant readjustments in aspects such as velocity and direction as the environment and task develop.

As noted, though, perception and action are inexorably linked. The player should, hopefully, be moving whilst maintaining this constant exchange of information with the environment. These abilities are thus the organismic constraints to the task. Consider an example of a covering run that involves supporting my co-centre back who is tracking an attacking player with the ball, whilst I am covering space and another attacking player. This may involve any number of transition movements, such as in-place jockeying (should the in possession attacker hold up the player and maintain a defensive line but maintain visibility of the ball and attacking opposition), linear movement (whereby I am submaximally running in a straight line, in constant response to my opposition and my own defensive line – not too fast as to break the line, not too slow as to lose the line or my designated attacker), diagonal cross-step running (where I travel towards my own goal but also towards the lateral side of the field where the ball is), and rearwards backpedalling (if the ball is a comfortable distance back from myself and my goal).

Naturally, I may transition between the transition movements constantly as the play develops, I may begin backpedalling as the opposition gain possession away from my goal, then as the attacking team travel closer to my goal but forced wide by my teammates, I may move to diagonal cross-steps, then if the play builds in speed, I could begin travelling linearly as I ramp up my own speed travelling towards my goal and maintaining cover of the space between defence and goal. It is therefore imperative that a centre back be able to compete the movement patterns efficiently but transition between them seamlessly. All of these must also occur whilst I am maintaining visibility of not only the ball, but any other players in the vicinity of the action to provide me with the clearest understanding of the play for effective decision-making. This would therefore require constant dissociation of my torso and lower body as I observe play in differing directions to that of my travel.

Such a description, hopefully, displays the limitation of solely focusing on physical capacities without consideration of more intricate COD and game speed skills and the perceptual elements that are occurring constantly at the same time. Again, these transition actions are not focused on maximal outputs but provide a platform for effective application of key actualisation movements. Unsuccessful applications of any of these during a covering run could lead to a goal conceded. For example, during the transition from backpedalling to diagonal cross-stepping, if the attacker in possession makes a pass behind the defensive line, the covering player must have afforded themselves the ability to instigate a maximal acceleration in a different direction of travel as quickly as possible to meet the pass. A step wrong during this transition between state would give an advantage to the attacking player. The only effective means of avoiding this is an exemplary coalescence between perception and action, which allows the player to read, anticipate, or react to the play and select and execute the appropriate action.

Training

As discussed, there is no doubt to the merits of technical and physical development of an athlete when seeking improvements in multidirectional speed in field- and court-based sports. However, true game speed ability cannot separate action from perception, and practitioners should always consider the ultimate on-pitch performance in designing effective programmes (Dos'Santos et al., 2022a). These may be trained separately or as a whole as part of multi-component agility or game speed framework (McBurnie et al., 2022). Similarly, testing may exist across a spectrum following a reverse engineering model from the ultimate sporting action.

A popularly employed means of classifying exercises is based upon the work of Anatoly Bondarchuk (Bondarchuk, 2007). Described are four categories of exercise progressing from those that are most specific to more general. Working backwards from the event (or action within a sport) itself, the first class is competitive exercise, which refers to exercises that are identical, or almost identical, to the competition event (or action). Here there would be only a small number of potential exercise options as a result of the required specificity. The second class is known as specific development exercise. As with competitive exercise, this category trains the competitive movement pattern, alongside the physiological systems. The exercise still repeats the competition event, but in its separate parts, and may begin to include resistance. Following the two highly specific classes is specific preparatory exercise, where the focus is paid more to the underlying physiology and muscle groups involved rather than attempting to mimic the event or action. The number of options for selection here continues to rise as focus moves to more general adaptations. Finally, general preparatory exercises is all-purpose and seeks very general adaptations without aiming to replicate the event movements or physiology directly. Such a classification can be applied more widely to understand all athletic development provisions and testing. However, the described classes should be considered as a spectrum of exercises rather than truly separate types.

As an example, a 'run in behind' in soccer involves an offensive player seeking to exploit space in behind a defensive structure by performing a high-velocity run (Table 2.1). To truly assess the effectiveness of an individual in this key tactical context, a practitioner must observe game footage of the individual and attempt to qualitatively evaluate performance. Often this may also be through discussions with coaching staff on an athlete's perceived technical/tactical weaknesses in

TABLE 2.1 An Example Application of the Bondarchuk Exercise Classification Model (Bondarchuk, 2007) to a Specific Sprinting Action in Soccer

Event	*Competitive Exercise*	*Specific Development Exercise*	*Specific Preparatory Exercise*	*General Preparatory Exercise*
Run in Behind Player aims to beat the opposition offside trap to run through onto the opposition goal.	Identical, or almost identical, to the competition event.	Repeat the competition event, but in its separate parts, and may include overload.	Do not imitate the competition event but train the same muscles/ physiology.	Do not imitate the competition event and do not train the specific systems.
♣ Perception ♣ Linear/diagonal transition movements ♣ Lateral initiation ♣ Explosive acceleration ♣ Curved sprint ♣ Torso dissociation ♣ End with ball	♣ Full-sized match play ♣ Small-sided games to elicit exposure to the context ♣ Drills that replicate the exact context	♣ Unopposed replication of the context ♣ Multidirectional reactive sprinting ♣ Curved sprinting ♣ Sprinting to the ball in closed and open environments	♣ Linear sprinting ♣ Resisted sprinting ♣ Power training ♣ Lateral plyometrics ♣ Unilateral ♣ Torso dissociation	♣ Strength training ♣ Mobility

relation to physical actions. Alongside this, a battery of tests across the spectrum of specific to general may be employed that support the action. For the current example, this may consist of curve or linear sprinting ability, key facets of a run in behind. Testing of shallow cutting ability may also prove important, as the action may involve a sudden change of direction to initiate the run. Similarly, assessing key transition movements, such as travelling diagonally or laterally, may be useful. In support of these, general physical tests for lower limb power, strength, and mobility would support understanding why an athlete may be ineffective at such a task.

Following the application of such a testing battery, conclusions can be drawn to establish areas of focus. Often key common contexts will have overlap in the underpinning qualities, such as sprinting ability supporting both a 'run in behind' and 'break into the box' for attacking soccer situations. A spectrum of testing allows for establishing whether the weaknesses lay with specific factors, such as perception, decision-making, and technical (sprinting or change-of-direction skills) or physical qualities, such as concentric/eccentric strength or power. If an athlete's sprinting ability is deemed good, then it may be suggestive of poor application of this sprinting ability in specific game speed situations.

Within the umbrella of context-specific drills, there still exists a spectrum from those that directly replicate the context to less-specific drills that seek to replicate constituent parts (Taberner et al., 2019; Mota et al., 2022). In field sports it is unlikely, due to physical demand, an athlete will be able to replicate true game contexts during training repeatedly. Additionally, while certain scenarios may be deemed commonly occurring, they may still occur less than five times during a full match. Therefore, it is often necessary to design drills that elicit repetitive environments representative of the desired action. In the example of run in behind in soccer, this would involve the setting up of a drill with potentially two opposing full teams, but the play begins from a specific moment that will lead to the requirement for a run in behind to be performed. Play is then reset following this phase. These minimal constraints therefore lead to repetition without repetition, where the athlete is exposed to the context and action but from a wide variety of circumstances and must respond accordingly (Myszka, 2018; Yearby et al., 2022). This will support learning through adaptation in movement dexterity that leads to maximal affordances to the individual, which is achieved through a learning process of selecting the best physical action as a consequence of the perception of the task (Davids et al., 2013). Here coaching is key to achieving the desired outcome. Effective feedback during the drill can expedite the learning experience. Testing at this level is difficult and highly qualitative, as a successful execution of process may not always align with a successful outcome such as a goal scored due to additional factors.

Following this highly specific drill design, one can then begin to progress along the specific to general spectrum by removing a degree of specificity to allow for further overload and repetition of the desired context. In the example of a run in behind in soccer, beyond replicating an exact match context, a drill can be designed that involves fewer players within smaller spaces. This can then directly focus on repetitive run-in-behind efforts. An example would be setting up a high defensive line, with the ball beginning at the feet of an attacking player. The aim of the drill would then be for an attacking teammate to seek to make a run in behind this defensive line in a constrained time period. The drill then resets when a goal is scored or the defensive team gains possession. The drill can be repeated multiple times, within desired physical loading patterns, to develop physically and psychologically the action of running in behind. This will involve the learning of cues on when to make the run, creating an appreciation for one's physical abilities within the context and the most efficient and effective means of applying then to attain a successful outcome. Such small-sided games have been shown to enhance performance through increases in decision-making speed rather than movement speed (Young and Rogers, 2014; Mota et al., 2022). Of course, broader planning can lead to such a drill that creates contextual multidirectional speed development of the defensive players also involved in actions such as 'covering runs'.

A further step in the direction of more general movement skills could involve removing other players and working individually with the centre forward on their run-in-behind ability. Here drills could focus more on the physical actions involved and seek to be completed at high speed. For example, manikins can be placed to represent defensive players, and a coach could initiate the drill by playing a pass in behind this static defensive line. The attacking player would begin the drill by completing transition movements akin to those that have been identified as common to running in behind. Once the pass is made, the attacker would then react at speed and compete the action of running in behind to meet the pass, finishing with a shot on goal. Here, due to the removal of a large majority of the perceptual stimuli, focus is on effective and fast movement application. The goal is thus for the induvial to complete repetitive actions, such as cut steps, to initiate actualisation movements, such as sprinting on a curve whilst dissociating one's torso. Coaching should begin to consequently move towards a focus on the kinematics of the movements, to attain effective force application, and accordingly less on factors such as timing, anticipation, and decision-making. Progress can be monitored again through qualitative analysis of effective movement, and improvements here, it is hoped, would lead to more effective movements in a more specific drills and ultimately match performance.

Alongside successful application of such specific drills, more general qualities should be developed. Here, a practitioner may remove all context and perceptual stimuli completely and seek to complete the desired, representative movements in a controlled closed-skill manner. In a run-in-behind action, this could involve maximal effort sprinting along a curve or cutting steps to initiate a change of direction to begin a maximal acceleration. The goal here is to shift focus to capacity of relevant game-speed skills. A higher ceiling here should allow for greater performance levels under specific conditions. Naturally, again these drills and exercises exist on a spectrum of most to least specific. An example here would be curved sprinting versus linear maximal effort sprinting. It seems clear that most sprinting in soccer involves curvilinear efforts, but an enhancement of maximal velocity in linear sprinting allows for a greater ceiling in such an effort (Caldbeck, 2019). More quantitative measures can be used to monitor progression here.

Conclusion

In sports performance, there is often a focus made purely on the underpinning physical capacities of multidirectional speed. Whilst these are clearly fundamental to enhancing in-game performance, it would be remiss of a practitioner to ignore the more complex aspects that constitute these actions. Factors such as muscular strength are typically relatively simple to measure and enhance, particularly in untrained individuals. However, the true extent to which these transfer to ultimate performance, particularly in elite athletes, is likely more limited than many would like to admit.

A true holistic performance enhancement programme should therefore seek to reverse-engineer the key elements of competition in field- and court-based sports. By doing so, a practitioner can seek to enhance qualities at all levels along a spectrum from those most specific to least. A direct targeting of these multidirectional actions, rather than an assumption that sport training satisfies adequate development, would lead to an effective means of enhancing and monitoring sporting performance. To attain such an outcome, a practitioner must possess an intricate knowledge of the contextualised movements completed within the sport with consideration for *how* and *why* these actions occur, thus providing awareness of perception-action coupling, which would ensure adequate ecological validity to drills.

References

Ade, J., Fitzpatrick, J. and Bradley, P.S., (2016). High-intensity efforts in elite soccer matches and associated movement patterns, technical skills and tactical actions. Information for position-specific training drills. *Journal of Sports Sciences, 34*, 2205–2214.

Bernstein, N., (1967). *The Co-ordination and Regulations of Movements*. Oxford, NY: Pergamon Press.

Bloomfield, J., Polman, R. and O'Donoghue, P., (2007) Physical demands of different positions in FA Premier League soccer. *Journal of Sports Science and Medicine, 6*, 63–70.

Bondarchuk, A., (2007). *Transfer of Training in Sports*. Muskegon, MI: Ultimate Athlete Concepts.

Bradley, P.S. and Ade, J.D., (2018). Are current physical match performance metrics in elite soccer fit for purpose or is the adoption of an integrated approach needed? *International Journal of Sports Physiology and Performance, 13*, 656–664.

Bradley, P.S., Sheldon, W., Wooster, B., Olsen, P., Boanas, P. and Krustrup, P., (2009). High-intensity running in English FA Premier League soccer matches. *Journal of Sports Sciences, 27*, 159–168.

Caldbeck, P., (2019). *Contextual Sprinting in Football* [thesis]. Liverpool, UK: Liverpool John Moores University.

Davids, K., Araújo, D., Vilar, L., Renshaw, I. and Pinder, R., (2013). An ecological dynamics approach to skill acquisition: Implications for development of talent in sport. *Talent Development and Excellence, 5*, 21–34.

Deutsch, M.U., Kearney, G.A. and Rehrer, N.J., (2007). Time – motion analysis of professional rugby union players during match-play. *Journal of Sports Sciences, 25*, 461–472.

Dos'Santos, T., McBurnie, A., Thomas, C., Jones, P.A. and Harper, D., (2022a). Attacking agility actions: Match play contextual applications with coaching and technique guidelines. *Strength & Conditioning Journal, 44*, 102–118.

Dos'Santos, T., Thomas, C., Comfort, P. and Jones, P.A., (2018). The effect of angle and velocity on change of direction biomechanics: An angle-velocity trade-off. *Sports Medicine, 48*, 2235–2253. doi: 10.1007/s40279-018-0968-3.

Dos'Santos, T., Thomas, C., Comfort, P. and Jones, P.A., (2022b). Biomechanical effects of a 6-week change of direction speed and technique modification intervention: Implications for change of direction side step performance. *Journal of Strength & Conditioning Research, 36*, 2780–2791.

Fajen, B.R., Riley, M.A. and Turvey, M.T., (2009). Information, affordances, and the control of action in sport. *International Journal of Sport Psychology, 40*, 79–107.

Faude, O., Koch, T. and Meyer, T., (2012). Straight sprinting is the most frequent action in goal situations in professional football. *Journal of Sports Sciences, 30*, 625–631.

Immonen, T., Brymer, E., Orth, D., Davids, K., Feletti, F., Liukkonen, J. and Jaakkola, T., (2017). Understanding action and adventure sports participation – an ecological dynamics perspective. *Sports Medicine – Open, 3*, 18.

Jackson, R.C., Warren, S. and Abernethy, B., (2006). Anticipation skill and susceptibility to deceptive movement. *Acta Psychologica, 123*, 355–371.

Jeffreys, I., (2008). Movement training for field sports: Soccer: *Strength and Conditioning Journal, 30*, 19–27.

Jeffreys, I., (2011). A task-based approach to developing context-specific agility. *Strength and Conditioning Journal, 33*, 52–59.

Jeffreys, I., (2016). Agility training for team sports – running the OODA loop. *Professional Strength & Conditioning, 42*, 15–21.

Jeffreys, I., Huggins, S. and Davies, N., (2018). Delivering a gamespeed-focused speed and agility development program in an English Premier League soccer academy. *Strength and Conditioning Journal, 40*, 23–32.

McBurnie, A.J., Parr, J., Kelly, D.M. and Dos'Santos, T., (2022). Multidirectional speed in youth soccer players: Programming considerations and practical applications. *Strength & Conditioning Journal, 44*, 10–32.

Morgan, O.J., Drust, B., Ade, J. D. and Robinson, M. A., (2022). Change of direction frequency off the ball: New perspectives in elite youth soccer. *Science & Medicine in Football, 6*(4), 473–482. https://doi.org/10.1080/24733938.2021.1986635

Mota, T., Alfonso, J., Sá, M. and Clemente, F., (2022). An agility training continuum for team sports: From cones and ladders to small-sided games. *Strength and Conditioning Journal, 44*, 46–56.

Murphy, C.P., Jackson, R.C. and Williams, A.M., (2018). The role of contextual information during skilled anticipation. *Quarterly Journal of Experimental Psychology, 71*, 2070–2087.

Myszka, S., (2018). Movement skill acquisition for American football – Using 'repetition without repetition' to enhance movement skill. *NSCA Coach*, 54.

Olsen, O.-E., Myklebust, G., Engebretsen, L. and Bahr, R., (2004). Injury mechanisms for anterior cruciate ligament injuries in team handball: A systematic video analysis. *The American Journal of Sports Medicine, 32*, 1002–1012.

Seifert, L., Komar, J., Araújo, D. and Davids, K., (2016). Neurobiological degeneracy: A key property for functional adaptations of perception and action to constraints. *Neuroscience & Biobehavioral Reviews, 69*, 159–165.

Sheppard, J.M. and Young, W.B., (2006). Agility literature review: Classifications, training and testing. *Journal of Sports Sciences, 24*, 919–932.

Taberner, M., Allen, T. and Cohen, D.D., (2019). Progressing rehabilitation after injury: Consider the 'control-chaos continuum'. *British Journal of Sports Medicine, 53*, 1132–1136.

Taberner, M., van Dyk, N., Allen, T., Jain, N., Richter, C., Drust, B., Betancur, E. and Cohen, D. D. (2020). Physical preparation and return to performance of an elite female football player following ACL reconstruction: A journey to the FIFA Women's World Cup. *BMJ Open Sport & Exercise Medicine, 6*(1), e000843. https://doi.org/10.1136/bmjsem-2020-000843

Turner, A.N., Read, P., Maestroni, L., Chavda, S., Yao, X., Papadopoulos, K., Virgile, A., Spiegelhalter, A. and Bishop, C., (2022). Reverse engineering in strength and conditioning: Applications to agility training. *Strength & Conditioning Journal, 44*, 85–94.

Waldén, M., Krosshaug, T., Bjørneboe, J., Andersen, T.E., Faul, O. and Hägglund, M., (2015). Three distinct mechanisms predominate in non-contact anterior cruciate ligament injuries in male professional football players: A systematic video analysis of 39 cases. *British Journal of Sports Medicine, 49*, 1452–1460.

Williams, A.M., (2000). Perceptual skill in soccer: Implications for talent identification and development. *Journal of Sports Sciences, 18*, 737–750.

Yearby, T., Myszka, S., Roberts, W.M., Woods, C.T. and Davids, K., (2022). Applying an ecological approach to practice design in American football: Some case examples on best practice. *Sports Coaching Review*, 1–24.

Young, W. and Rogers, N., (2014). Effects of small-sided game and change-of-direction training on reactive agility and change-of-direction speed. *Journal of Sports Sciences, 32*, 307–314.

Young, W.B., Dawson, B. and Henry, G.J., (2015). Agility and change-of-direction speed are independent skills: Implications for training for agility in invasion sports. *International Journal of Sports Science & Coaching, 10*, 159–169.

3

BIOMECHANICAL BASIS OF LINEAR AND CURVILINEAR SPRINT PERFORMANCE

Laura J. Elstub and Sarah M. Churchill

The winner of the Olympic 100 m race is often touted as the fastest man or woman on earth and is known across the world. Our fascination with sprinting dates back to the original Olympic Games, which took place in the seventh century BC and featured a *stadion* race, where competitors raced from one end of the stadium to the other. Ancient Greek stadia featured rectangular running tracks, giving rise to 'there and back' or 'double *stadion*' sprint events. The 400 m was introduced at the modern Olympic Games (Athens, 1896) alongside the introduction of the oval running track at Panathinaiko Stadium, which consequently required athletes to run a bend. The 200 m event did not make its first appearance until the Paris 1900 Olympic Games. Whilst the 100 m takes place entirely on the straight (see Figure 3.1), approximately 58% of the 200 m and 400 m races take place on a curved portion of track (Figure 3.1; Meinel, 2008). The proportion of the distance run on the bend during the 200 m and 400 m races suggests that bend sprinting performance makes a substantial contribution to overall race performance. Therefore, bend sprinting should demand sufficient attention in training programmes that aim to improve sprint performance.

Whilst running is distinguished from walking by the presence of a flight phase (where neither foot is in contact with the ground; Novacheck, 1998), sprinting is the maximisation of speed 'with little regard to economy' (Bushnell and Hunter, 2007). In addition, running typically takes place over longer distances, whereas sprinting occurs at faster speeds over shorter distances and without any consideration for maintaining aerobic metabolism (Novacheck, 1998). For the purpose of this chapter, *straight-line* sprinting is considered as a linear translation on a straight portion of the track, such as during the 100 m, whereas *bend sprinting* is defined as curvilinear translation on a curved portion of the track – for example, in parts of the 200 or 400 m races.

Compared with straight-line sprinting, bend sprinting results in a 2% decrease in performance in the acceleration phase (Judson et al., 2020a) and 5% at maximal speed (Churchill et al., 2015) owing to fundamental differences in task execution. To put these differences into the context of race performance, the difference between first and second place in the women's 200 m final at the 2017 International Association of Athletic Federations (IAAF) World Championships was 0.03 s. Therefore, even small improvements in bend sprinting performance could be meaningful in terms of competitive race outcomes. To achieve these performance improvements, we must first

DOI: 10.4324/9781003267881-4

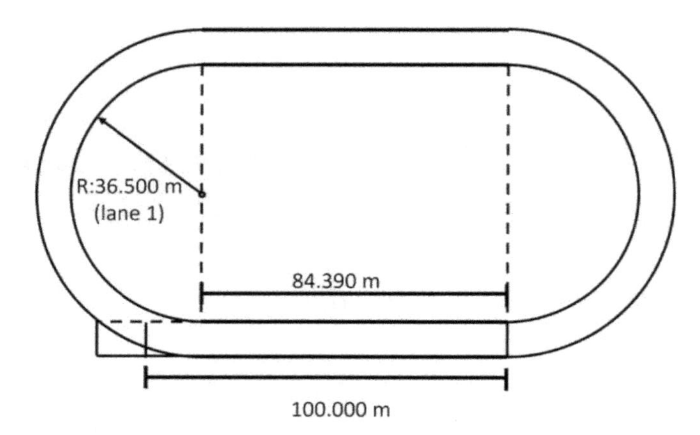

FIGURE 3.1 A schematic overview of a standard outdoor 400 m running track (adapted from Meinel, 2008).

understand the principles of technique and performance in both straight-line and bend sprinting. This chapter will outline the fundamental biomechanics of sprinting on the bend and straight during both the acceleration and maximal speed phases, with specific reference to the key kinematic and kinetic aspects of technique and performance. We also discuss the associated practical applications and provide recommendations for the physical development of athletes.

Acceleration Phase

The acceleration phase of sprinting typically refers to the first 30–50 m of a race (Mero et al., 1992). Due to step-by-step changes in technique, it is often broken down into two different phases, referred to as initial acceleration and the transition phase (Delecluse, 1995). The initial acceleration phase covers the first two steps of the race, including the portion where athletes are in the starting blocks, whereas the third step to the point where the athlete reaches 80% of their maximum velocity (usually around the sixth to thirteenth step; von Lieres Und Wilkau et al., 2020) is referred to as the transition phase (Delecluse, 1995). The acceleration phase makes an essential contribution to overall race performance (Delecluse, 1995; Mero et al., 1992) because the maximum speed an athlete is able to attain is ultimately dependent on their ability to accelerate. The ability to accelerate for longer periods has previously been linked to performance (Letzelter, 2006) since accelerating for longer means the athlete will reach a higher velocity and maintain this to finish the race first.

To understand the fundamental biomechanics of the acceleration phase of sprinting, we must refer to Newton's second law, which states that the acceleration of an object as produced by a net force is directly proportional to the magnitude of the net force, in the same direction as the net force, and inversely proportional to the mass of the object. This is often simplified to the following equation:

$$\mathbf{F} = \mathbf{ma}$$

where F = force, m = mass, and a = acceleration.

Therefore, if the net force were doubled, the acceleration of the object (in this case the athlete) would be twice as large. Similarly, if the mass of the object were doubled, its acceleration would be half as large. In sporting contexts, the mass under evaluation typically stays constant, particularly when we are referring to the acceleration of an athlete during competition. Therefore, to affect or influence the acceleration of the athlete, the net force being produced must increase or decrease. This concept has been demonstrated experimentally by Rabita et al. (2015), who found a strong relationship between straight-line acceleration performance and mean anterior force but not resultant or vertical ground reaction force. As such, ratio of force – a concept borrowed from cycling (Bini et al., 2013) – has been introduced in the evaluation of sprint acceleration performance (Morin et al., 2011, 2012; Rabita et al., 2015). The ratio of force expresses horizontal force as a percentage of resultant force and thus provides a measure of an athlete's ability to apply force effectively in the forward direction.

Whilst acceleration remains an important factor in sprint performance, the mechanical demands of the acceleration phase are fundamentally different when sprinting on the bend compared with the straight. The radius of the track (typically 36.8–45.34 m for an eight-lane track) and the need to stay in lane to avoid disqualification require athletes to change direction (deviate their path of travel) every time the foot is in contact with the ground. As such, unlike straight-line sprinting, the athlete must also generate centripetal force (i.e. the force that acts on a body moving in a circular path and is directed towards the centre around which the body is moving) to accelerate towards the centre of the bend. The need for this additional component of force has been shown to decrease ratio of force on the bend (Judson et al., 2019) due to a combination of reduced propulsive (horizontal) force and a required increase in mediolateral force. These results could be taken to suggest that athletes are applying propulsive force 'less effectively' on the bend than the straight. However, it should be noted that the demands of sprinting on the bend are different to sprinting on the straight and, therefore, so is what is considered 'effective'. For example, one way to improve ratio of force on the bend would be to reduce mediolateral force. However, doing so would be detrimental to race performance as without this the athlete would be unable to maintain a curved path of travel. Therefore, rather than achieving the highest ratio possible as with straight-line sprinting, there is most likely an optimum ratio that exists as a balance of propulsive and mediolateral forces.

The generation of centripetal force is accompanied by a lateral lean (towards the centre of curvature), which counteracts the torque that would otherwise cause an outward rotation of the athlete about the anteroposterior axis in the mediolateral direction (Figure 3.2). It is important to note that the magnitude of centripetal force produced is proportional to the square of velocity, so as the athlete reaches a faster velocity, they must also generate more centripetal force. Consequently, there are a number of adaptations that occur during bend sprinting to accommodate the lateral lean of the athlete and the need to produce centripetal force to change direction and stay in lane. Since the race is always completed in the same direction around the running track (anti-clockwise) and the athlete *leans into* the bend, this lateral lean involves the athlete leaning to their left. As such, the majority of adaptations occur whilst the left leg is in contact with the ground and these left-side adaptations will be the focus of the next few paragraphs.

During the acceleration phase of bend sprinting, there is a 2% decrease in absolute speed compared with the straight (Judson et al., 2020a). To identify the underlying cause of this reduction, we must first consider the spatiotemporal factors of performance. By referring to a deterministic model of overall sprint performance (bend and straight, Figure 3.3), we can see that sprint velocity is determined from step length and step frequency. To account for the reduction

FIGURE 3.2 Frontal plane ground reaction forces experienced by an athlete running on (A) the straight, where mediolateral forces are negligible, and (B) on the bend, where centripetal force is also present.

in performance observed during sprinting on the bend in the acceleration phase, one of these factors must be affected, and research from Judson et al. (2020a) confirms a reduction in left step frequency during the acceleration phase of bend sprinting. Moving to the next branch of the deterministic model, we can see that step frequency is determined from a combination of contact time (the amount of time the foot is in contact with the ground) and flight time (the amount of time both feet are in the air). Whilst left step contact time increases on the bend compared with the straight, flight time remains consistent and so the reduction in step frequency is likely a consequence of a longer contact time (Judson et al., 2020a).

There are numerous kinematic and kinetic adaptations that occur during bend sprinting alongside the spatiotemporal and ratio force differences already discussed. The hip joint is a region of particular interest, with rapid hip extension being linked to a greater propulsive impulse during the acceleration phase of straight-line sprinting (Hunter et al., 2005). In addition, increased muscular forces at the hip (and therefore increased joint moment) allow rapid accelerations of the hip, knee, and ankle joints and are also thought to be responsible for increasing step frequency (Dorn et al., 2012). However, there is a lower hip flexor moment (present towards the end of the stance phase) during sprinting on the bend than the straight (Judson et al., 2020b), which could explain the decrease in step frequency that was also observed.

A longer contact time in the left step appears to be a key adaptation that occurs during the acceleration phase of bend sprinting (Judson et al., 2020a), and an increase in energy absorption at the foot and ankle might be a contributing factor to this. *Energy* is defined as *the capacity to do work* and is calculated as the integral of the power-time curve where cumulative positive energy represents energy generation and cumulative negative energy represents energy absorption. Analysis of energy absorption and generation at the foot and ankle shows large amounts of energy are absorbed in the foot and ankle complex during bend sprinting, particularly in the left step (Judson et al., 2020b). It has previously been suggested that energy absorption within the foot could result in a slowing of the centre-of-mass (CoM) progression and subsequently a prolonged contact time to facilitate the production of the necessary propulsive impulse (Kelly et al., 2018).

The adaptations that have been discussed so far all occur in the sagittal plane. However, due to the three-dimensional (3D) nature of bend sprinting, we must also consider adaptations that occur in the non-sagittal planes, which likely hold additional insights into performance. One of the key adaptations that occur in the non-sagittal plane is a high peak left hip adduction and external rotation angle (8°, Judson et al., 2020a). These non-sagittal-plane kinematics likely influence the ability of lower-limb muscles to produce force in the sagittal plane, as seen in the lower-hip flexor moment discussed previously. For example, the complex arrangement of the left limb, which combines high hip adduction and external rotation with high midfoot eversion, may cause athletes to experience difficulties repositioning the left limb on the bend.

Moreover, the left metatarsophalangeal (MTP) joint has been shown to use a different push-off axis during bend sprinting (Judson et al., 2019). The MTP joint has two possible axes about which the foot can push off: transverse which runs through the heads of the first and second metatarsals and oblique runs through the second to fifth metatarsal heads (Bojsen-Møller, 1979) (Figure 3.3). When push-off occurs with the transverse axis, the calcaneocuboid joint is closely packed and consequently provides a more stable foot for push-off (Bojsen-Møller, 1979). As such, the transverse axis is considered more effective at generating propulsive force in the direction of progression and is thought to be used at higher speeds (Bojsen-Møller, 1979). This concept has been demonstrated empirically on the bend by Judson et al. (2019), who found the oblique axis was used by the left foot on the bend compared with the transverse axis on the straight. This difference in axis use at push-off coincided with a decrease in anterior force and propulsive impulse on the bend (Judson et al., 2019). As such, it appears that using the oblique axis is a necessary adaptation (dictated by the need to produce centripetal force) to support the change of direction that is required during bend sprinting.

The adaptions discussed thus far occur primarily in the left leg, owing to the anticlockwise direction used in competitive athletics and the lateral lean athletes use to lean into the bend and generate centripetal force (Figure 3.2). Consequently, the left and right legs perform different functions during bend sprinting. During bend sprinting, the left limb appears to have a controlling role with the aim of producing the necessary rotation and centripetal force to change direction and stay in the lane (Judson et al., 2019). However, the right limb is focused on producing force in the anterior direction (Judson et al., 2019) and therefore shares more characteristics with straight-line sprinting.

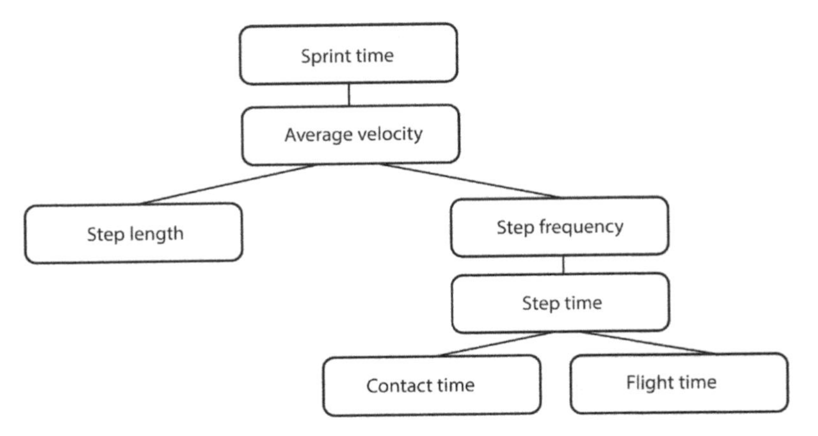

FIGURE 3.3 A deterministic model of factors affecting sprint performance, describing the relationships between step length, step frequency, and velocity.

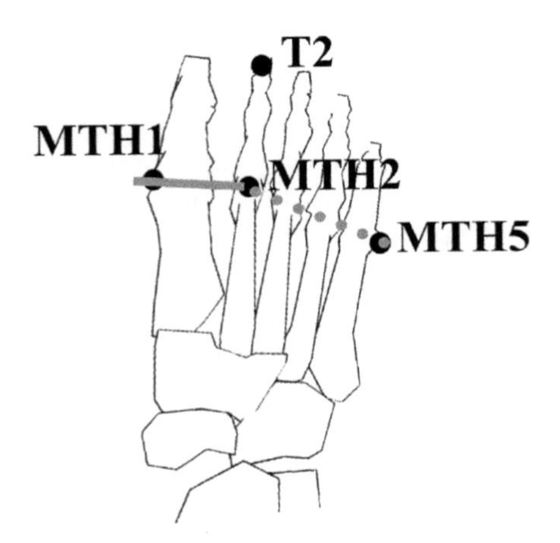

FIGURE 3.4 Right foot representation of the oblique (solid line) and transverse (dashed line) axes of the foot, where MTH 1, 2, and 5 represent the first, second, and fifth metatarsal heads, respectively.

Maximal Speed Phase

During straight-line sprinting, the maximal speed phase occurs once an athlete is no longer accelerating but instead has reached and is aiming to maintain maximal speed for as long as possible – typically until around the 50–60 m mark in the 100 m (Gajer et al., 1999). Once they can no longer maintain their speed, athletes typically experience a negative acceleration towards the end of the race. Thus, the ability to maintain maximal speed and delay deceleration is linked to performance in the 100 m.

From a biomechanical perspective, athletes improve maximal velocity during straight-line sprinting by applying force to the ground quickly – or minimising ground contact time and producing as much force as possible (Weyand et al., 2010). This is achieved by an 'active touchdown' whereby the anteroposterior distance between the point of foot contact at touchdown and the CoM, the touchdown distance, is as small as possible (Hunter et al., 2004b) and the positive velocity of the contact foot, relative to the CoM, is reduced as much as possible. Research investigated whether the 'constant limb force' hypothesis can be applied to bend sprinting on an athletics track and to understand how force production influences performance on the bend compared with the straight (Churchill et al., 2016). Force and video analyses performed on competitive athletes (n = 7) revealed that left-step mean peak vertical and resultant force decreased significantly on the bend (radius 37.72 m) compared with the straight (Churchill et al., 2016). However, force production in the right step was not compromised in the same way, with some athletes actually demonstrating substantial increases in force production with the right step on the bend compared with the straight (Churchill et al., 2016). In addition, there was more inward impulse in the left step compared with the right, which also coincided with 1.6° more turning during the left step on the bend. Combined, these results show that the constant limb force hypothesis is not entirely valid for maximal effort bend sprinting. Moreover, as previously alluded to within the chapter, the force requirements of sprinting on the bend are different to straight-line sprinting and are asymmetrical in nature. As such, sprint performance might be improved by bend-specific strength and technique training.

During the acceleration phase, a high ratio of the propulsive impulse to the braking impulse increases speed. In contrast, maximal-velocity sprinting is characterised by a net-zero anteroposterior impulse. That is, at maximal speed, braking and propulsive impulses are balanced. We can understand this by referring to Newton's first law of motion, which states that an object in motion will remain in motion at a constant speed until acted on by an external force. During this phase, better sprint performance is focused on generating high amounts of vertical and resultant force (Weyand et al., 2010). These high vertical forces are required for two reasons:

1. To arrest the downward movement caused by gravity attempting to accelerate the CoM towards the ground
2. To produce adequate upward movement to propel the athlete forwards into the next flight phase

Since velocity is determined from step length and step frequency (Figure 3.2), higher maximal speeds can be achieved by increasing step length or step frequency (or both), so long as the increase in one factor does not result in an overall detrimental decrease in the other. Generally, successful sprinters have a combination of a long step length and a high step frequency. Indeed, step length and step frequency have been found to increase as velocity increases (Luhtanen and Komi, 1978; Mero and Komi, 1986). At an individual athlete level, it is suggested that an improvement in step frequency has the largest effect on velocity at high speeds (Luhtanen and Komi, 1978; Mero and Komi, 1986; Weyand et al., 2000; Hunter et al., 2004a). For example, Mann (1985) suggested that an increase in step frequency, in addition to an acceptable or better-than-average step length characterises superior sprint performance. However, other research contradicts this, suggesting that faster athletes in fact exhibit longer step lengths (e.g. Gajer et al., 1999).

Salo et al. (2011) suggested that these inconsistent results over whether step length or step frequency was the most important factor for faster velocities may have been due to differences in groupings of athletes in previous studies. As such, it was hypothesised that individual athletes adopt different strategies and individualised optimal step length and step frequencies (Salo et al., 2011). To confirm this hypothesis, Salo et al. (2011) analysed TV footage of some of the world's best athletes and found considerable variation between athletes with some athletes demonstrating a clear reliance on high step frequencies for their best performances, some athletes demonstrating greater reliance on long step lengths, and others demonstrating no clear reliance on one or the other for their best performances. It is important to understand an individual's step length/step frequency reliance so that training programmes can be appropriately informed. For example, step-frequency-reliant athletes may need to consider neural activation to generate high leg 'turnover', whereas strength and hip flexibility may be important for athletes reliant on long step lengths (Salo et al., 2011).

As running velocity increases, the length of time the foot spends in contact with the ground (referred to as contact time) decreases both in absolute terms (Kivi et al., 2002; Weyand et al., 2000) and also as a percentage of the gait cycle – that is, the duty factor (Weyand et al., 2000). This is due to the fact that although, when running at top speed, faster runners have a shorter ground contact time than slower runners, swing time remains constant, resulting in a decreased duty factor for faster runners and a superior step frequency (Weyand et al., 2000). A smaller touchdown distance has also been shown to be related to shorter contact time (Hunter et al., 2004a, 2004b). Therefore, an active touchdown may have a positive effect on contact time and step frequency.

However, during bend sprinting, the athlete is continuously accelerating due to the need to change direction with each step to follow the curve of the track and stay in the lane. It is possible that achieving the necessary change in direction might be more difficult at the higher velocities observed during the maximal speed phase because higher velocities require the production of greater centripetal force (the magnitude of centripetal force is proportional to the square of velocity). Consequently, a greater degree of lateral lean is also required to counteract the rotational torque in the mediolateral direction and achieve the change in direction required to stay in the lane and follow the curve of the athletics track, and this is thought to affect force production on the bend.

At the time of writing, there is currently only one study that has examined force production in elite athletes running at maximal effort on the bend in conditions representative of a competitive track-and-field environment (Churchill et al., 2016). Lower peak resultant and vertical forces were observed in the left step on the bend compared with the straight at maximal velocity and were accompanied by a necessary increase in mediolateral force (Churchill et al., 2016). The combination of increased lateral lean and the need to produce greater amounts of centripetal force results in a reduction in speed reported as between 2.3% (Churchill et al., 2016) and 4.8% (Churchill et al., 2015) during maximal speed bend running, which is higher than that shown for the acceleration phase (2%, Judson et al., 2020a) compared with straight-line sprinting.

Referring back to the deterministic model of sprint performance, we can again identify spatiotemporal factors that are related to this decrease in performance during the maximal speed phase of bend sprinting (Churchill et al., 2015; Churchill et al., 2016). Differences in experimental protocols have resulted in inconsistent outcomes with regard to step frequency, step length, and flight time, which, whilst found to remain constant during submaximal bend sprinting (Alt et al., 2015) and at smaller radii (Chang and Kram, 2007), were shown to decrease at maximal effort (Churchill et al., 2015; Churchill et al., 2016). Therefore, it is possible that some adaptations are dependent on the velocity of the athlete and the radius of the curve.

There is, however, a strong consensus with regard to contact time, which appears to be a bend-specific adaptation since a longer left step contact time has been consistently reported despite the varying protocols used (Alt et al., 2015; Chang and Kram, 2007; Churchill et al., 2015).

Moreover, large effect sizes have been observed for left step contact time (d = 2.97, bend left: 0.116 s, straight left: 0.105 s, Churchill et al., 2015), which further strengthens the possibility that left step contact time is an important factor to consider during bend sprinting.

The horizontal distance between the CoM and the head of the second metatarsal of the stance foot is known as touchdown distance (Hunter et al., 2004a). To put this more simply, it is a measure of how far in front of the body the foot is when it comes in contact with the floor. A shorter touchdown distance (bringing the foot closer to the CoM in the anteroposterior direction) has been associated with a shorter contact time (Hunter et al., 2004b), which, as previously discussed, is related to the ability to achieve faster maximal speeds (Weyand et al., 2010). A longer touchdown distance (having the foot further in front of the CoM) has been observed in the left step during bend sprinting at maximal speed, suggesting this may also be a key adaptation to occur on the bend.

Similarly, to the acceleration phase, there are a number of kinematic adaptations to technique that occur during sprinting on the bend to accompany changes in spatiotemporal parameters. Unfortunately, there are few published studies in this area, and those that do exist have different protocols which make comparisons problematic. However, there is a consistent agreement to suggest that the left limb can be characterised by a greater hip adduction and ankle eversion (Alt et al., 2015; Churchill et al., 2016). In contrast, the right limb is thought to implement a rotational strategy which employs transverse-plane adaptions to control horizontal plane motion. This is highlighted by research at submaximal velocity using three-dimensional motion capture which found a greater right knee internal rotation in comparison to the left (mean difference 4.0°, Alt et al., 2015), which was combined with a high external rotation of the right ankle (mean difference 4.9°, Alt et al., 2015).

Until this point in the chapter, the adaptations reported to occur when sprinting on the bend have been with regard to lanes 1 and 2 of a standard athletics track, which typically have a radius of 36.5 and 37.7 m, respectively. However, competitive athletics typically takes place across eight lanes, each with varying radii. As the radius, and therefore the tightness, of the bend decreases in the outer lanes, the need to produce centripetal force decreases (for the same running velocity). Consequently, it has been empirically demonstrated that athletes in the inner lanes are at a competitive disadvantage due to the need to run on a tighter bend radius (Churchill et al., 2019), which supports conclusions from mathematical modelling (Greene, 1985; Jain, 1980; Usherwood and Wilson, 2006). Churchill et al. (2019) reported a decrease in velocity of 2.1% and 2.0% for the left and right step, respectively, in lane 5 compared with lane 8. A negligible further decrease in velocity (0.2%) was found for the left step only from lane 5 to lane 2. These results were reported to be due to decreased step frequency as the radius tightened. Further, step length decreased in lane 5 and 2 compared with lane 8, although the shortest step lengths were observed in lane 5. The experimental study of Churchill et al. (2019) provides useful empirical evidence of changes in spatiotemporal parameter and the authors suggested that the effect of the radius may be greater than previous models had suggested. Churchill et al. (2019) estimated that the difference in race times for an athlete running in lane 8 compared with lane 5 could be around 0.170 s and between lane 8 and lane 2 it could be 0.180 s. These estimates are greater than the 0.069 s (Jain, 1980) and 0.123 s (Greene, 1985) suggested previously in modelling. However, a more complete analysis across all lanes and measuring more variables is currently missing from the literature.

Despite the potential biomechanical advantages of competing in the outer lanes, anecdotal evidence suggests that many athletes prefer being in the inner lanes as this allows them to see and therefore 'chase down' other runners. This preference is reflected in the lane allocation process for outdoor competitions, where first-round lanes are randomly assigned. However, lane allocations for subsequent rounds are based on the finishing positions of each athlete within the first race, where the four highest ranked athletes are allocated lanes 3 to 6 at random, the fifth and sixth ranked athletes allocated lanes 7 and 8 at random, and the final two athletes allocated lanes 1 and 2 at random (World Athletics, 2022). The psychological interaction between lane allocation and performance notwithstanding, biomechanically, those athletes in the outer lanes are at an advantage, which is one reason why the indoor 200 m event (where the effect of the bend is even more pronounced) has been abandoned at the highest competition level.

While this chapter is primarily focused on track and field, the reported biomechanical differences across different radii also have implications for other sports, such as soccer. Studies of running on a curved path at much smaller radii than used in track and field tend to agree that performance is reduced when following a curved path (Chang and Kram, 2007; Smith et al., 2006). However, at very small radii, there are differences in force production compared with radii typical of an athletics track. For example, Chang and Kram (2007) studied running on very small radii curves (between 1 m and 6 m) and found speed to decrease but also found that the outer (right) leg generated greater peak inward forces than the inside leg. These findings were supported by previous research at similar radii (Smith et al., 2006), whereas Churchill et al. (2016) found inward force was greater for the inside leg on a radius of 37.72 m. During bend running, it has been suggested that the outside leg performs an action similar to an open, or side-step, cutting manoeuvre, whereas the inside leg performs a cross, or crossover, cutting manoeuvre (Rand and Ohtsuki, 2000). Indeed, larger vertical and mediolateral force production and greater muscle activation have been reported in open cutting manoeuvres than in cross cutting manoeuvres (Rand and Ohtsuki, 2000). While it does not appear that sprinters in athletic events are using cutting actions to turn, at very small radii this might be the case (Churchill et al., 2016). Therefore, in multidirectional field and court sports, it should be borne in mind that the tightness of the curvature and the fact that velocities will be considerably lower at very small radii may affect task execution, especially when making comparisons with the movements of track and field athletics.

Implications for Strength Training and Physical Development

As discussed throughout the chapter, there are distinct differences in the fundamental principles and task execution of bend sprinting compared with straight-line sprinting. In summary, sprinting on the bend is three-dimensional in nature and requires the production of centripetal force to produce a change in direction with each step. Consequently, athletes 'lean into' the bend. As such, the technique on the bend necessarily differs from the straight because the task itself is different. The biomechanics of bend sprinting can primarily be characterised by an increase in left hip adduction, left ankle eversion, and a longer contact time. These differences hold important implications for strength training and physical development for athletes who sprint on the bend, and potentially also for team sports where non-linear sprints take place. There are a number of factors to consider: asymmetry between limbs, specificity of training, and the transfer of skill from the bend to the straight. These concepts will be summarised here and discussed in further detail in subsequent chapters.

While high levels of asymmetry might indicate the presence of or be a precursor to injury, a certain level of asymmetry between limbs during straight-line sprinting is not necessarily dysfunctional or detrimental to performance (Exell et al., 2017) and could simply be a functional adaptation to the sport. In fact, asymmetry in the sprint cycle has been shown to be the norm rather than the exception and should therefore be expected (Haugen et al., 2018). This is of high importance in relation to bend sprinters, who sprint in the same anticlockwise direction around the bend and perform different functions with each leg, and so asymmetry in muscle strength might be expected. However, since the movement of bend sprinting is itself asymmetrical, there is a need for strength-training programmes that meet the differing demands of bend sprinting by ensuring the principle of specificity is being met.

The principle of training specificity is of paramount importance to ensure the effective and efficient transfer of strength training to sports performance (Young, 2006). Whilst there is a number of ways this principle can be met, it has been reported that coaches prefer specificity of training is achieved by adding resistance to sporting specific movements as opposed to trying to make gym-based exercises more sports-specific (Burnie et al., 2018). Therefore, supplementing training with the use of ropes or harnesses to provide resistance, as well as including a leaning position to account for technique on the bend, is recommended to improve performance (Churchill et al., 2016).

Moreover, strengthening lower-limb muscles in the non-sagittal (frontal and transverse) planes would be another way to increase the specificity of training, which could be beneficial in improving sprint performance on the bend. For example, research has shown that plyometric bounding exercises have similar contact times to those found in the acceleration phase of sprinting (Young, 1992). This similarity consequently aids the transfer of strength training to performance through comparable contraction velocity specificity (Young, 2006). Therefore, coaches and practitioners may wish to consider the inclusion of bounding exercises with a change of direction.

Finally, it is known anecdotally that some athletes do not like and therefore tend to avoid training on the bend. However, doing so is essential to promote further specificity of training. Therefore, training on the bend should not only include both the acceleration and maximal speed phases but also training across the different lanes of the running track (including the tightest lanes) or in the context of multidirectional sports training with different radii in different directions (clockwise and anticlockwise). In addition, during competitive sprinting, athletes are required to transition from sprinting on the bend to sprinting on the straight. However, as discussed throughout the chapter, there is a fundamental difference in task execution on the bend compared with the straight. Therefore, this transition requires a change in technique and should be included in training where possible so as to ensure that training completed on the bend does not have a negative impact on straight-line sprint performance. For the team sport athletes, drills should be developed that encompass both straight-line and curvilinear sprinting to ensure technique development/maintenance of each.

Increased understanding of the fundamental biomechanics of sprint performance on the bend can be used to inform strength and conditioning programmes with the aim of improving performance and reducing the risk of injury. While at the time of writing there is no direct evidence to suggest a relationship with sprint performance, several authors have recommended strengthening the intrinsic and extrinsic muscles of the foot (e.g. Judson et al., 2020b; Smith et al., 2014). This hypothesis is supported from an anatomical perspective since the plantar intrinsic muscles of the foot have been shown to contribute toward a stiffer forefoot during the late stance phase (Farris et al., 2019). Furthermore, Stefanyshyn and Nigg (1997) previously showed that the MTP joint absorbs large amounts of energy during contact with the ground, with the energy absorbed being dissipated into the shoe and foot complex. As such, it was proposed that performance improvements could be achieved through reducing energy loss at the MTP joint (Stefanyshyn and Nigg, 1997). This hypothesis is somewhat supported by research from Smith et al. (2014) which showed that sprint spikes are capable of enabling changes in MTP joint function, resulting in an increased sprint velocity and therefore sprint performance compared with a barefoot condition. Therefore, strength training aimed at the extrinsic muscles of the foot and ankle, such as tibialis anterior and posterior, in addition to the intrinsic foot muscles such as abductor hallucis and flexor digitorum brevis, might provide a further opportunity to influence sprint performance, particularly on the bend (Smith et al., 2014).

One possible alternative method to strength training that also has the additional benefit of being easy to implement is the use of minimalist shoes for walking. For example, an eight-week intervention where participants undertook a maximum of 7,000 steps in minimalist footwear at least five days a week resulted in increased muscular strength of both extrinsic and intrinsic foot muscles (Ridge et al., 2019). The observed increase in strength was comparable to the control group who performed a strength-training programme (Ridge et al., 2019). Moreover, a stiffer longitudinal arch has been associated with the habitual wearing of minimalist shoes (Holowka et al., 2018), which was identified earlier in the chapter as a factor affecting the production of propulsive force at push-off. In addition, it is possible that force produced by larger, more proximal muscles might offset energy loss at the foot (Kelly et al., 2018). Therefore, increasing energy generation at the hip might also be beneficial alongside reducing energy absorption at the foot.

In this chapter, we have summarised some key biomechanical effects of running on a curved path, mainly in relation to athletic sprint events. A growing body of literature is emerging in the field of bend sprinting, and this information can be useful to athletes and coaching teams to understand the mechanisms and consequences of sprinting on a curved path. While a greater evidence base of the effects of specific training interventions is required in the literature, some practical implications for strength training and physical development are suggested, and the recommendations provided later in this book for the development on curvilinear speed will be of use in this area.

References

Alt, T., Heinrich, K., Funken, J., & Potthast, W. (2015). Lower extremity kinematics of athletics curve sprinting. *Journal of Sports Sciences*, *33*, 552–560. https://doi.org/10.1080/02640414.2014.960881

Bini, R., Hume, P., Croft, J., & Kilding, A. (2013). Pedal force effectiveness in cycling: A review of constraints and training effects. *Research Outputs*, *2*(1), 11–24.

Bojsen-Møller, F. (1979). Calcaneocuboid joint and stability of the longitudinal arch of the foot at high and low gear push off. *Journal of Anatomy*, *129*, 165–176.

Burnie, L., Barratt, P., Davids, K., Stone, J., Worsfold, P., & Wheat, J. (2018). Coaches' philosophies on the transfer of strength training to elite sports performance. *International Journal of Sports Science & Coaching*, *13*, 729–736. https://doi.org/10.1177/1747954117747131

Bushnell, T., & Hunter, I. (2007). Differences in technique between sprinters and distance runners at equal and maximal speeds. *Sports Biomechanics*, *6*, 261–268. https://doi.org/10.1080/14763140701489728

Chang, Y.-H., & Kram, R. (2007). Limitations to maximum running speed on flat curves. *Journal of Experimental Biology*, *210*, 971–982. https://doi.org/10.1242/jeb.02728

Churchill, S.M., Salo, A.I.T., & Trewartha, G. (2015). The effect of the bend on technique and performance during maximal effort sprinting. *Sports Biomechanics*, *14*, 106–121. https://doi.org/10.1080/14763141.2015.1024717

Churchill, S.M., Trewartha, G., Bezodis, I.N., & Salo, A.I.T. (2016). Force production during maximal effort bend sprinting: Theory vs reality. *Scandinavian Journal of Medicine and Science in Sports, 26*, 1171–1179. https://doi.org/10.1111/sms.12559

Churchill, S.M., Trewartha, G., & Salo, A.I.T. (2019). Bend sprinting performance: New insights into the effect of running lane. *Sports Biomechanics, 18*, 437–447. https://doi.org/10.1080/14763141.2018.1427279

Delecluse, C.H. (1995). Analysis of 100 meter sprint performance as a multidimensional skill. *Journal of Human Movement Studies, 28*, S. 87–101.

Dorn, T.W., Schache, A.G., & Pandy, M.G. (2012). Muscular strategy shift in human running: Dependence of running speed on hip and ankle muscle performance. *Journal of Experimental Biology, 215*, 1944–1956. https://doi.org/10.1242/jeb.064527

Exell, T., Irwin, G., Gittoes, M., & Kerwin, D. (2017). Strength and performance asymmetry during maximal velocity sprint running. *Scandinavian Journal of Medicine and Science in Sports, 27*, 1273–1282. https://doi.org/10.1111/sms.12759

Farris, D.J., Kelly, L.A., Cresswell, A.G., & Lichtwark, G.A. (2019). The functional importance of human foot muscles for bipedal locomotion. *Proceedings of the National Academy of Sciences, 116*(5), 1645–1650. doi:10.1073/pnas.1812820116

Gajer, B., Thepaut-Mathieu, C., & Lehenaff, D. (1999). Evolution of stride and amplitude during course of the 100 m event in athletics. *New Studies in Athletics, 14*, 43–50.

Greene, P.R. (1985). Running on flat turns: Experiments, theory, and applications. *Journal of Biomechanical Engineering, 107*, 96–103. https://doi.org/10.1115/1.3138542

Haugen, T., Danielsen, J., McGhie, D., Sandbakk, Ø., & Ettema, G. (2018). Kinematic stride cycle asymmetry is not associated with sprint performance and injury prevalence in athletic sprinters. *Scandinavian Journal of Medicine and Science in Sports, 28*, 1001–1008. https://doi.org/10.1111/sms.12953

Holowka, N.B., Wallace, I.J., & Lieberman, D.E. (2018). Foot strength and stiffness are related to footwear use in a comparison of minimally- vs. conventionally-shod populations. *Scientific Reports, 8*, 3679. https://doi.org/10.1038/s41598-018-21916-7

Hunter, J.P., Marshall, R.N., & McNair, P.J. (2004a). Reliability of biomechanical variables of sprint running. *Medicine & Science in Sports & Exercise, 36*(5), 850–861. https://doi.org/10.1249/01.mss.0000126467.58091.38

Hunter, J.P., Marshall, R.N., & McNair, P.J. (2004b). Interaction of step length and step rate during sprint running. *Medicine & Science in Sports & Exercise, 36*(2), 261–271. https://doi.org/10.1249/01.MSS.0000113664.15777.53

Hunter, J.P., Marshall, R.N., & McNair, P.J. (2005). Relationships between ground reaction force impulse and kinematics of sprint-running acceleration. *Journal of Applied Biomechanics, 21*, 31–43.

Jain, P.C. (1980). On a discrepancy in track races. *Research Quarterly in Exercise & Sport, 51*, 432–436.

Judson, L.J., Churchill, S.M., Barnes, A., Stone, J.A., Brookes, I.G.A., & Wheat, J. (2019). Horizontal force production and multi-segment foot kinematics during the acceleration phase of bend sprinting. *Scandinavian Journal of Medicine and Science in Sports, 29*, 1563–1571. https://doi.org/10.1111/sms.13486

Judson, L.J., Churchill, S.M., Barnes, A., Stone, J.A., Brookes, I.G.A., & Wheat, J. (2020a). Kinematic modifications of the lower limb during the acceleration phase of bend sprinting. *Journal of Sports Sciences, 38*, 336–342. https://doi.org/10.1080/02640414.2019.1699006

Judson, L.J., Churchill, S.M., Barnes, A., Stone, J.A., & Wheat, J. (2020b). Joint moments and power in the acceleration phase of bend sprinting. *Journal of Biomechanics, 101*, 109632. https://doi.org/10.1016/j.jbiomech.2020.109632

Kelly, L.A., Cresswell, A.G., & Farris, D.J. (2018). The energetic behaviour of the human foot across a range of running speeds. *Scientific Reports, 8*, 10576. https://doi.org/10.1038/s41598-018-28946-1

Kivi, D.M.R., Maraj, B.K.V., & Gervais, P. (2002). A kinematic analysis of high-speed treadmill sprinting over a range of velocities. *Medicine & Science in Sports & Exercise, 34*, 662–666. https://doi.org/10.1097/00005768-200204000-00016

Letzelter, S. (2006). The development of velocity and acceleration in sprints. *New Studies in Athletics, 21*, 15–22.

Luhtanen, P., & Komi, P.V. (1978). Mechanical factors influencing running speed. In E. Asmussen & K. Jorgensen (Eds.), *Sixth international congress of biomechanics – international series on biomechanics, volume 2B*, 23–29. Copenhagen: University Park Press.

Mann, R. (1985). Biomechanical analysis of the elite sprinter and hurdler. In N. K. Butts, T. T. Gushiken & B. Zarins (Eds.), *The elite athlete*, 43–80. New York: Spectrum Publications, Inc.

Meinel, K. (2008). Competition area. In International Association of Athletics Federations (Ed.), *IAAF track and field facilities manual*, 31–54. Monaco: Multiprint.

Mero, A., & Komi, P.V. (1986). Force-, EMG-, and elastic-velocity relationships at submaximal, maximal and supramaximal running speeds in sprinters. *European Journal of Applied Physiology & Occupational Physiology, 55*, 553–561.

Mero, A., Komi, P.V., & Gregor, R.J. (1992). Biomechanics of sprint running. A review. *Sports Medicine, 13*, 376–392. https://doi.org/10.2165/00007256-199213060-00002

Morin, J.-B., Bourdin, M., Edouard, P., Peyrot, N., Samozino, P., & Lacour, J.-R. (2012). Mechanical determinants of 100-m sprint running performance. *European Journal of Applied Physiology, 112*, 3921–3930. https://doi.org/10.1007/s00421-012-2379-8

Morin, J.-B., Edouard, P., & Samozino, P. (2011). Technical ability of force application as a determinant factor of sprint performance. *Medicine & Science in Sports & Exercise, 43*, 1680–1688. https://doi.org/10.1249/MSS.0b013e318216ea37

Novacheck, T.F. (1998). The biomechanics of running. *Gait and Posture*, 7, 77–95. https://doi.org/10.1016/s0966-6362(97)00038-6

Rabita, G., Dorel, S., Slawinski, J., Sàez-de-Villarreal, E., Couturier, A., Samozino, P., & Morin, J.-B. (2015). Sprint mechanics in world-class athletes: A new insight into the limits of human locomotion. *Scandinavian Journal of Medicine and Science in Sports, 25*, 583–594. https://doi.org/10.1111/sms.12389

Rand, M.K., & Ohtsuki, T. (2000). EMG analysis of lower limb muscles in humans during quick change in running directions. *Gait and Posture, 12*, 169–183. https://doi.org/10.1016/s0966-6362(00)00073-4

Ridge, S.T., Olsen, M.T., Bruening, D.A., Jurgensmeier, K., Griffin, D., Davis, I.S., & Johnson, A.W. (2019). Walking in minimalist shoes is effective for strengthening foot muscles. *Medicine & Science in Sports & Exercise, 51*, 104–113. https://doi.org/10.1249/MSS.0000000000001751

Salo, A.I.T., Bezodis, I.N., Batterham, A.M., & Kerwin, D.G. (2011). Elite sprinting: Are athletes individually step-frequency or step-length reliant? *Medicine & Science in Sports & Exercise, 43*, 1055–1062. https://doi.org/10.1249/MSS.0b013e318201f6f8

Smith, G., Lake, M., & Lees, A. (2014). Metatarsophalangeal joint function during sprinting: A comparison of barefoot and sprint spike shod foot conditions. *Journal of Applied Biomechanics, 30*, 206–212. https://doi.org/10.1123/jab.2013-0072

Smith, N., Dyson, R., Hale, T., & Janaway, L. (2006). Contributions of the inside and outside leg to maintenance of curvilinear motion on a natural turf surface. *Gait and Posture, 24*, 453–458. https://doi.org/10.1016/j.gaitpost.2005.11.007

Stefanyshyn, D.J., & Nigg, B.M. (1997). Mechanical energy contribution of the metatarsophalangeal joint to running and sprinting. *Journal of Biomechanics, 30*, 1081–1085. https://doi.org/10.1016/s0021-9290(97)00081-x

Usherwood, J. R., & Wilson, A. M. (2006). Accounting for elite indoor 200 m sprint results. *Biology Letters, 2*(1), 47–50. https://doi.org/10.1098/rsbl.2005.0399

von Lieres Und Wilkau, H.C., Irwin, G., Bezodis, N.E., Simpson, S., & Bezodis, I.N. (2020). Phase analysis in maximal sprinting: An investigation of step-to-step technical changes between the initial acceleration, transition and maximal velocity phases. *Sports Biomechanics, 19*, 141–156. https://doi.org/10.1080/14763141.2018.1473479

Weyand, P.G., Sandell, R.F., Prime, D.N.L., & Bundle, M.W. (2010). The biological limits to running speed are imposed from the ground up. *Journal of Applied Physiology, 108*, 950–961. https://doi.org/10.1152/japplphysiol.00947.2009

Weyand, P.G., Sternlight, D.B., Bellizzi, M.J., & Wright, S. (2000). Faster top running speeds are achieved with greater ground forces not more rapid leg movements. *Journal of Applied Physiology, 89*, 1991–1999. https://doi.org/10.1152/jappl.2000.89.5.1991

World Athletics. (2022) *Book of rules, book C: Competition: Book C2.1 technical rules*. https://worldathletics.org/about-iaaf/documents/book-of-rules

Young, W.B. (1992). Sprint bounding and the sprint bound index. *National Strength and Conditioning Association Journal*, 14. https://doi.org/10.1519/0744-0049(1992)014<0018:SBATSB>2.3.CO;2

Young, W.B. (2006). Transfer of strength and power training to sports performance. *International Journal of Sports Physiology and Performance*, *1*, 74–83. https://doi.org/10.1123/ijspp.1.2.74

4

BIOMECHANICAL AND PHYSICAL BASIS OF CHANGE OF DIRECTION FOR PERFORMANCE AND INJURY RISK

Thomas Dos'Santos and Paul A. Jones

Introduction and Change-of Direction (COD) Action Classifications

A range of different CODs and agility actions (which contain CODs) are performed in multidirectional sports (Fox et al., 2014; Rayner, 2020; Wheeler et al., 2010), including side-step cuts, crossover cuts (XOC), split-step cuts, shuffle-step cuts, spin manoeuvres, turns, and decelerations. Definitions and descriptions of these actions are presented in Table 4.1 (Dos'Santos et al., 2022). A COD, simply, is defined as a 'reorientation and change in the path of travel of the whole-body centre of mass (COM) towards a new intended direction' (David et al., 2017; Wyatt et al., 2019) and can be performed for a plethora of reasons in multidirectional sports (Bourgeois et al., 2017; Young et al., 2015). For example, in invasion team sports (i.e. court- and field-based sports with the objective to score goals/points), from an attacking perspective, athletes may (1) perform a COD to evade and create separation from an opponent, (2) generate high exit velocities and momentums for penetrative or overlapping runs, or (3) facilitate a sharp redirection to draw out a defender (Dos'Santos et al., 2022). In defensive scenarios, defenders will usually perform CODs to restrict space for the defender to make a tackle, block, or covering run or to anticipate and/or react to the ball or implement to make an interception or restrict passing opportunities (Dos'Santos et al., 2022). In batting sports, CODs are a critical part of scoring points, such as running and turning between the wickets in cricket or around the bases of a diamond in softball/baseball (Bourgeois et al., 2017; Young et al., 2015). Moreover, in racket sports, such as badminton, tennis, and squash, generally after each stroke/shot from the shot-maker, the athlete would then perform a COD to return to the 'T' in preparation for the opponent's next shot. As such, given the importance of COD ability for numerous sports, understanding the COD techniques and biomechanical strategies that optimise performance while mediating and mitigating injury risk is of great interest.

As stated, there are a range of different COD actions available to athletes in order to achieve the objectives within the contextual scenario of that sport (Table 4.1) (Dos'Santos et al., 2022). These actions have subtle differences in kinetics and kinematics, which have their own unique advantages, disadvantages, and implications for performance and injury risk which are summarised in Box 4.1 and Figure 4.1 (Dos'Santos et al., 2022). For example, side-step cuts are an

DOI: 10.4324/9781003267881-5

TABLE 4.1 COD Actions and Descriptions

Action	*Description*
Side-step	Athlete plants their foot laterally opposite to the direction of travel to create a propulsive impulse into the new intended direction.
Shuffle-step	Athlete performs a series of lateral side-steps (often double/triple) with the final movement similar to the side-step action, sometimes known as double/triple step or stutter step.
Crossover cut (XOC)	Athlete positions the planted foot on the same side (ipsilateral) of the new direction (or sometimes medially across the pelvic midline) and then crossing the opposite leg (contralateral) in front of the body for the new step in the new direction, accelerating in the same direction of the push-off leg.
Split-step	Athlete performs a small jump (amplitude jump) prior to push-off, landing with both feet greater than or equal to shoulder width apart, and then, upon landing, the contralateral limb is used for push-off into the intended direction of travel.
Spin	Athlete plants the foot and pivots/rotates the foot and whole body using a 'blind turn'/spinning movement, generally rotating the whole body at ≥270°.
Turn	This is a unilateral or bilateral turning strategy where one foot rotates and remains in contact with the ground and redirects COM (typically for directional changes ≥110°).

Key: COD: change of direction; COM: centre of mass

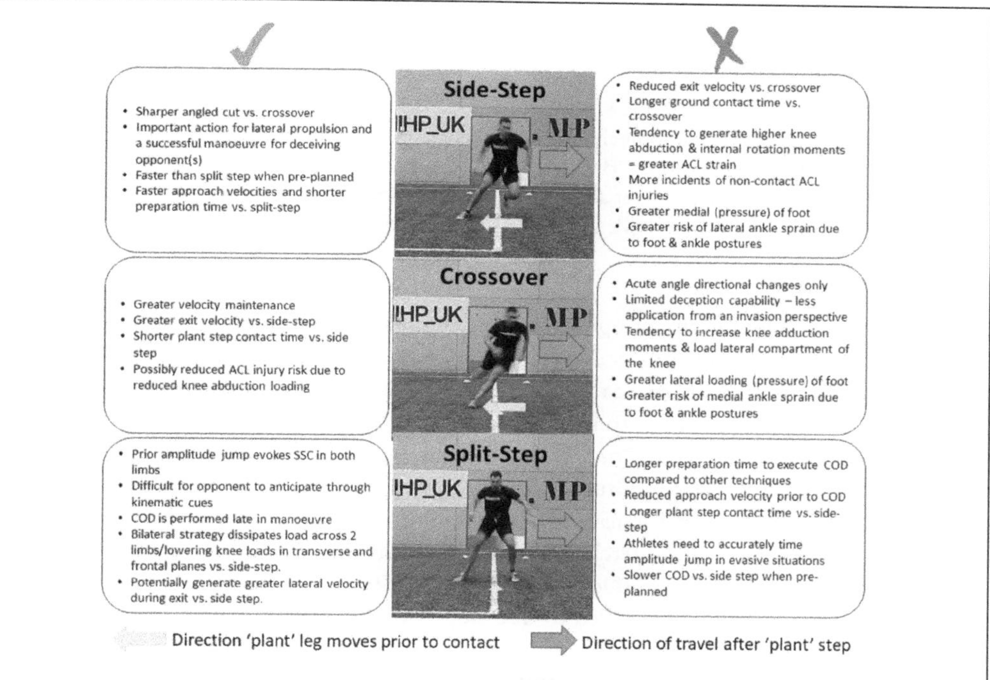

BOX 4.1 ADVANTAGES AND DISADVANTAGES OF THE DIFFERENT CUTTING MANOEUVRES

Based on Dos'Santos et al. reviews (Dos'Santos et al., 2022; Dos'Santos, McBurnie, et al., 2019) and adapted from Dos'Santos & Jones (2022). ACL: anterior cruciate ligament; COD: change of direction; SSC, stretch-shortening cycle.

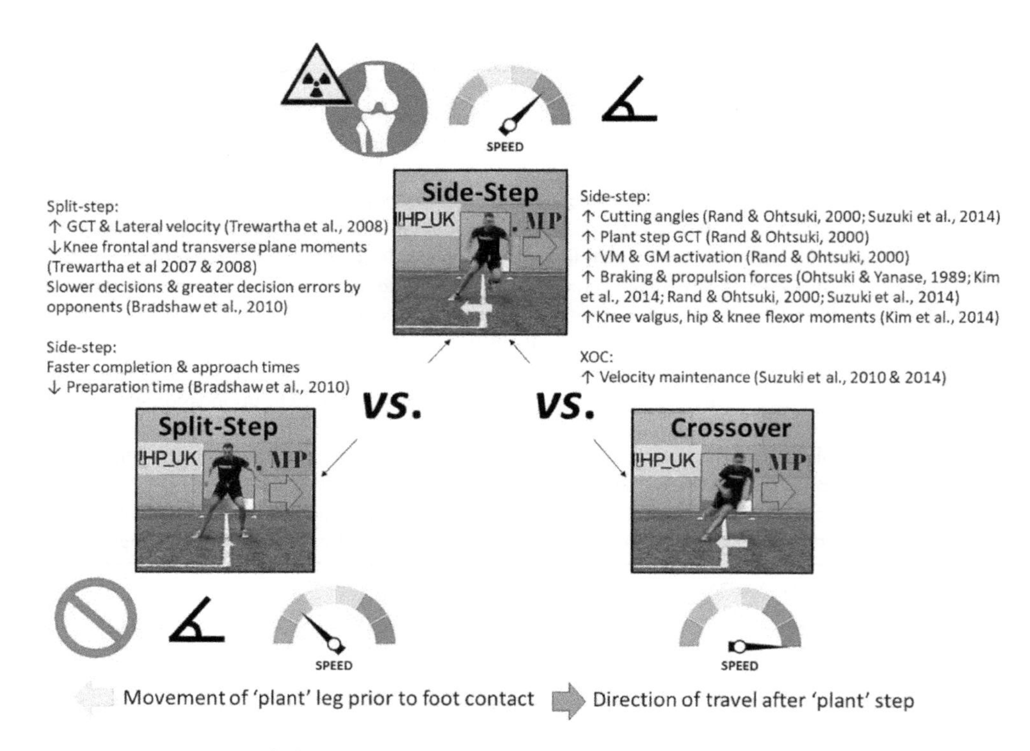

FIGURE 4.1 Summary of the biomechanical differences between side-step, crossover, and split-step cutting techniques. Based on Dos'Santos et al. reviews (Dos'Santos et al., 2022; Dos'Santos, McBurnie, et al., 2019) and adapted from Dos'Santos & Jones (2022). GCT: ground contact time; VM: vastus medius; GM: gluteus medius; XOC: crossover cut.

effective and applicable movement option in 1 vs 1 situations when acting as an instigator, and for evasion when a sharp cut or lateral propulsion is required (Dos'Santos et al., 2022), particularly from moderate- to high-approach velocities. Conversely, split- and shuffle-steps may be more suitable for scenarios at low- to moderate-approach velocities and isolated 1 vs 1 scenarios where longer preparation time is afforded and when greater deception and feint manoeuvres are needed (Dos'Santos et al., 2022). Crucially, the split-step may enable greater lateral propulsion and subsequent acceleration, particularly when initiating a COD from a stationary or low-entry velocity due to evoking a high stetch-load response from the stretch-shortening cycle (SSC) during the prior amplitude jump (Dos'Santos et al., 2022). Conversely, crossover cuts are not considered a deceptive action compared to side-steps, shuffle-steps, and split-steps but are critical when a subtle COD and redirection is needed, particularly when velocity maintenance is essential (Dos'Santos et al., 2022). For example, scenarios in sport may require a crossover cut, such as (1) channelling, overlapping, and driving runs to be deployed to get into space to receive a pass or destabilise defensive organisations; (2) creating high horizontal momentum to break through tackles or lines in collision sports; (3) forcing opposition defenders to change position during diversion and decoy runs; or (4) performing a slight deviation in path where a curvilinear/curved sprint enables attainment or maintenance of high velocities (Dos'Santos et al., 2022). Importantly, however, due to the multistep nature of COD that is needed to reorient and deflect the COM, a crossover cut is commonly performed following the main execution lateral step (e.g. side-step, shuffle-step, split-step) to help facilitate the redirection (David et al., 2018; Dos'Santos, McBurnie, et al., 2019; Dos'Santos et al., 2018).

Spin actions are underinvestigated but appear to be effective in manoeuvring successfully through crowded spaces, protecting an implement, particularly in ball-carrying sports (Dos'Santos et al., 2022). For example, ball carriers in rugby codes, American football, and basketball typically aim to protect the ball on the 'blind side' by turning away from the defender and successfully evade tackles and blocks by making themselves a smaller target (Dos'Santos et al., 2022). Finally, turns are necessary when large deflections of the COM are needed to be >110°, which can also be a potentially effective, deceptive, evasive action where sharp redirections and separations are required, such as V-cuts (Dos'Santos et al., 2022).

Biomechanics of Change of Direction

A COD's aim is simply to reorient and change in the path of travel of the whole-body COM towards a new intended direction (David et al., 2017; Wyatt et al., 2019), often involving a break in cyclical running (McBurnie & Dos'Santos, 2022) and some form of manipulation of the base of support (BOS) relative to the COM to generate perpendicular impulse to deflect and accelerate the COM towards the intended direction of travel for exit velocity, separation, or sharp redirections (Dos'Santos et al., 2022; Dos'Santos, McBurnie, et al., 2019; McBurnie & Dos'Santos, 2022). Despite subtle postural adjustments and manipulation of the BOS relative to the COM, the different COD actions outlined in Table 4.1 can be globally divided into four phases (Dos'Santos et al., 2022; Dos'Santos, McBurnie, et al., 2019; McBurnie & Dos'Santos, 2022):

1. Initiation: Linear/curvilinear/lateral motion
2. Preparation: Preliminary deceleration/preparatory postural adjustments
3. Execution: Main COD plant phase
4. Follow-through: Reacceleration

These four phases of COD will be influenced by the entry speed/velocity, athlete's physical capacity, COD angle, and the contextual and agility demands of the sport-specific scenario, with the biomechanical demands of directional changes angle- and velocity-dependent (Dos'Santos, McBurnie, et al., 2019; Dos'Santos et al., 2018; McBurnie & Dos'Santos, 2022) (which we expand on in the next section). COD actions are generally performed over multiple steps and are described as a multistep action (Dos'Santos, Thomas, et al., 2019b). For example, upon some form of linear/curvilinear/lateral initiation movement, the foot contacts preceding the main COD execution foot contact, such as the penultimate foot contact (PFC) (and potentially steps prior), play a critical role in braking or preparing the main execution foot contact (i.e. postural adjustments) for effective weight acceptance and push-off (Dos'Santos et al., 2019b; Dos'Santos et al., 2021a; Dos'Santos, Thomas, et al., 2019b). Additionally, because of the angle-velocity trade-off, full redirection and deflection of the COM is difficult to attain over the execution step (Daniels et al., 2021; Dos'Santos et al., 2018); thus, the following foot contact(s) are subsequently involved in redirection (i.e. crossover commonly performed) (David et al., 2018; Dos'Santos et al., 2018; Rovan et al., 2014). As such, multiple steps are necessary to facilitate rapid decelerations, redirections, deceptive/feinting manoeuvres, and reaccelerations, and thus, COD actions should be coached as a multistep strategy (Dos'Santos et al., 2022; Dos'Santos et al.,

2019b; McBurnie & Dos'Santos, 2022). The execution phase is primarily responsible for propulsion, thus the deflection of the COM and acceleration towards the intended direction of travel (Dos'Santos et al., 2022; Dos'Santos et al., 2019b; McBurnie & Dos'Santos, 2022). As stated earlier, a clear break in cyclical running is observed and a manipulation of the BOS relative to COM is demonstrated for perpendicular impulse generation. The action itself is characterised as an eccentric-concentric coupling movement (i.e. SSC) (Green et al., 2011; Plisk, 2000; Young et al., 2002), involving rapid lower-limb triple flexion (i.e. eccentric strength requirement) for braking before rapidly transitioning to a powerful lower-limb triple extension (i.e. concentric/reactive strength requirement) for propulsion. CODs are rapid movements, with typical ground contact times ranging between 0.15 and 0.40 seconds, subject to angle, entry velocity, and physical capacity of the athlete (Dos'Santos et al., 2018). Additionally, typical ground reaction force (GRF) profiles range from 2 to 5 × body weight, with high levels of lower-limb (knee-spanning and non-knee-spanning) and trunk muscle activation needed to support the large external lower-limb flexor moments and to facilitate effective braking and propulsion (Dos'Santos et al., 2022; Dos'Santos et al., 2019b; Dos'Santos et al., 2018).

The Angle–Velocity Trade-off During Directional Changes

CODs have been investigated in the literature across a spectrum of entry velocities (3–7 m/s) and angles (30–180°) (Donelon et al., 2020; Dos'Santos et al., 2018), while during multidirectional sports, athletes are often required to perform hundreds of CODs during training and match play across low-, medium-, and high-entry velocities and a diverse spectrum of angles (Kai et al., 2021; Morgan et al., 2021; Slaughter & Adamczyk, 2020). Because of the diversity in potential CODs that athletes may perform with respect to entry velocity and angle, it should be noted that the biomechanical demands of COD are angle- and velocity-dependent (Dos'Santos et al., 2021b; Dos'Santos et al., 2018), Critically, COD angle and entry velocity govern and regulate COD intensity (Dos'Santos et al., 2021b; Dos'Santos et al., 2018) and have unique implications for the kinetic, kinematics, muscle activity, screening, physical preparation, and technical requirements of COD (Dos'Santos et al., 2021b; Dos'Santos et al., 2018). For example, as intended, COD angle increases and ground contact times (GCTs) during the main foot contact of the execution phase progressively increase to facilitate greater net impulse (i.e. braking and propulsion) and COM deflection (Dos'Santos et al., 2021b; Dos'Santos et al., 2018), while horizontal momentum must reduce in order to facilitate the directional change (Dos'Santos et al., 2021b; Dos'Santos et al., 2018). In addition, the technical requirements of directional changes are also influenced by the COD angle, with differences in lower-limb and trunk kinematics, such as trunk lean, hip abduction, pelvic rotation, and knee flexion angles observed (Dos'Santos et al., 2021b; Dos'Santos et al., 2018; Havens & Sigward, 2015b). In addition, sharper-angled CODs are also potentially a more hazardous action, with researchers demonstrating greater knee joint loads during 90° versus 45° cutting tasks (Dos'Santos et al., 2021b; Havens & Sigward, 2015a; Schreurs et al., 2017) and similar knee joint loads between 180° and 90° CODs (Dos'Santos et al., 2021b; Jones et al., 2016a; Schreurs et al., 2017).

While approach velocity is a critical determinant of subsequent exit velocity during COD tasks (Dos'Santos et al., 2018; Dos'Santos, Thomas, McBurnie, Comfort, et al., 2021; Hader et al., 2015), practitioners and athletes should be conscious of the speed-accuracy trade-off, whereby greater approach speeds will make it more challenging to slow down and redirect the COM sharply (Dos'Santos et al., 2018). This is pertinent in specific scenarios in sport, whereby COD angle and subsequent COM deflection is a priority, such as evading a tackle and creating separation from an opponent (Dos'Santos et al., 2022). Notably, many biomechanical studies indicate that the actual angle achieved during a COD (i.e. execution) is often lower than the intended angle (Dos'Santos et al., 2018; Dos'Santos, Thomas, Comfort, et al., 2021b; Vanrenterghem et al., 2012). For example, Vanrenterghem et al. (2012) demonstrated intended COM travel was not achieved during a side-step cut, and this was exacerbated with increased entry velocities, suggesting the existence of an angle-velocity trade-off when executing CODs. This observation has subsequently been observed in several studies highlighted in the Dos'Santos et al. review (2018). Thus, practically, an angle-velocity (speed-accuracy) trade-off is present during COD, whereby the faster an athlete enters the COD, the more difficult it is to reorient and deflect their COM due to challenges in converting forward horizontal momentum into a lateral direction and the shorter GCTs associated with faster entry speeds for propulsive impulse (Dos'Santos et al., 2018; Dos'Santos, Thomas, Comfort, et al., 2021b; Vanrenterghem et al., 2012). In addition, as COD angle increases, deceleration distances and braking requirements have been reported to be greater (Dos'Santos et al., 2018; Dos'Santos et al., 2021b; Havens & Sigward, 2014), highlighting the importance of deceleration prior to sharper-angled COD. Collectively, to achieve the intended direction of travel, because of the speed-accuracy trade-off, the subsequent foot contacts after the main execution plant foot contact (which initiates the COD) is involved in redirecting the athlete (Andrews et al., 1977; Rovan et al., 2014), with the steps preceding playing a critical role in preparation and/or deceleration (Dos'Santos et al., 2018; Dos'Santos, Thomas, et al., 2019b).

In order to reduce momentum and perform a COD towards the intended direction of travel, braking over a series of steps is required (Andrews et al., 1977; Dos'Santos, McBurnie, et al., 2019b; Dos'Santos, Thomas, et al., 2019b). Specifically, the penultimate foot contact plays a key role in deceleration, creating posterior braking impulse to reduce momentum prior to changing direction (Dos'Santos, Thomas, et al., 2019b), with greater penultimate foot contact braking forces associated with faster sharper cutting (Dos'Santos, 2020; McBurnie, Dos'Santos, et al., 2021) and 180° turning performance (Dos'Santos et al., 2020; Dos'Santos et al., 2017; Dos'Santos, Thomas, et al., 2019b; Graham-Smith et al., 2009; Jones et al., 2017). Maximising braking forces during the penultimate foot contact is advantageous because this will enable greater impulse, thus decreasing momentum, but importantly allows the final foot contact to focus on propulsion, facilitating a shorter GCT (Dos'Santos, Thomas, et al., 2019b). Conversely, as highlighted earlier particularly for shallower CODs, the penultimate foot contact is considered a key 'positional' or 'preparatory' step for facilitating effective postures during the execution ('plant' step) phase to optimise braking and push-off (Dos'Santos et al., 2020; Dos'Santos, Thomas, et al., 2019b). It is not uncommon for athletes to start initiating the COD during the penultimate foot contact and redirecting their COM by making anticipatory postural adjustments, such as head, trunk, and pelvis rotation towards the intended direction of travel with subtle changes in foot placement (Lee et al., 2017; Mornieux et al., 2014; Wheeler & Sayers, 2010). This, in turns, helps reduce the redirection requirements during the final foot contact.

In summary, the traffic light in Figure 4.2 indicates that for shallow CODs, minimal braking is needed, with a greater emphasis on velocity maintenance (Dos'Santos et al., 2021b; Dos'Santos et al., 2018). CODs of this angle will require a greater reliance on concentric and dynamic strength characteristics in addition to fast SSC reactive strength qualities (Bourgeois et al., 2017; Dos'Santos et al., 2018). Conversely, as COD angle increases (the colours progress from amber to red in Figure 4.1), the braking requirements must increase to reduce horizontal momentum into the COD, and the GCTs typically increase in order to facilitate a greater propulsive impulse

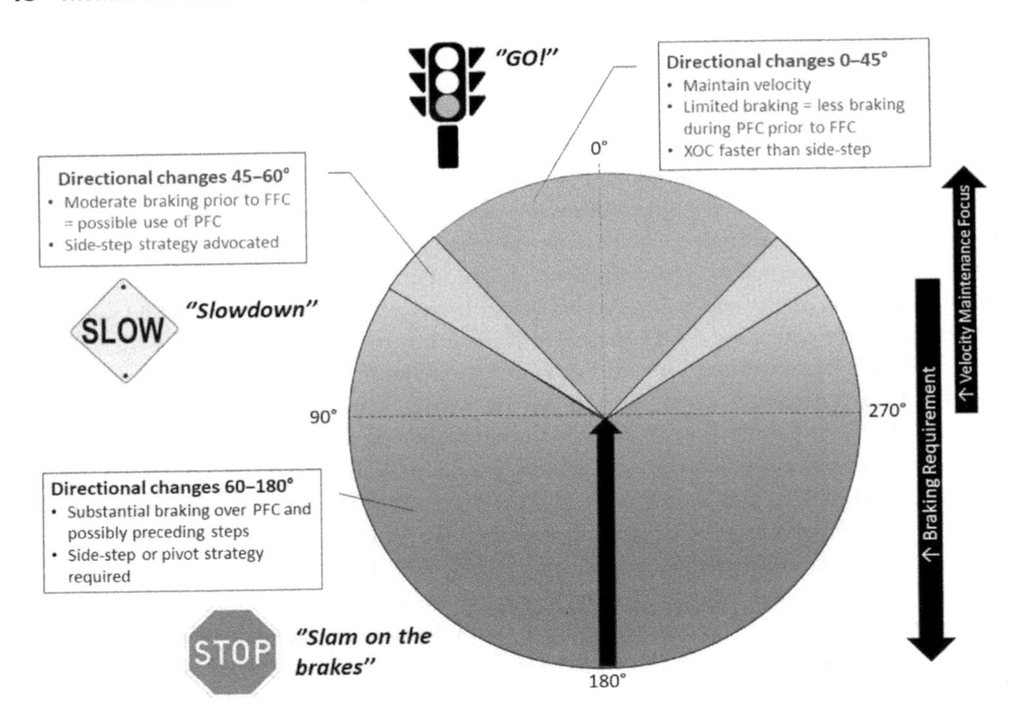

FIGURE 4.2 Braking strategy and technique requirements for different directional changes. FFC: final foot contact; PFC: penultimate foot contact; XOC: crossover cut.

to change momentum and deflect the COM (Dos'Santos et al., 2021b; Dos'Santos et al., 2018). CODs of greater angle have a greater reliance on eccentric strength characteristics due to greater braking emphasis and force production characteristics while the muscle tendon unit is lengthening and greater reliance on slow SSC characteristics due to the longer GCTs (Bourgeois et al., 2017; Dos'Santos et al., 2018; McBurnie, Harper, et al., 2021). Overall, velocity and COD angle regulate intensity, with greater mechanical loads with faster entry speed and sharper CODs (Dos'Santos et al., 2018; Dos'Santos et al., 2021b). Resultantly, angle and velocity are two crucial factors which regulate intensity during COD and should be progressed accordingly when coaching and designing MDS training programmes, particularly when working with novices or athletes rehabilitating from injury (Dos'Santos et al., 2018; Dos'Santos et al., 2021b).

Biomechanical and Technical Determinants of COD Performance

COD performance determinants are multifaceted and underpinned by an interaction of several factors, including an athlete's velocity (speed capacity), deceleration, mechanics, and physical capacity (Figure 4.3) (Jones et al., 2017; Jones et al., 2019; Spiteri et al., 2013). For example, greater braking and propulsive forces and impulse over short GCTs are associated with faster COD speed performance (Dos'Santos et al., 2020; Dos'Santos, Thomas, McBurnie, Comfort, et al., 2021; Spiteri et al., 2015). These findings can be attributed to the impulse-momentum relationship, whereby greater propulsive net forces oriented in the optimal direction, for a given contact time, increases propulsive impulse, thus changing the momentum, and subsequent exit

FIGURE 4.3 Change of direction (COD) underpinned by the interaction between velocity, deceleration, mechanics, and physical capacity. PFC: penultimate-foot contact.

velocity toward the new direction of travel (the impulse applied is a three-dimensional vector and so can be applied to change the initial momentum vector) (Dos'Santos, Thomas, McBurnie, Comfort, et al., 2021). Moreover, due to the dual role of the plant step (i.e. braking and propulsion), which consists of an eccentric-concentric coupling action (i.e. rapid transition from lower-limb triple flexion to extension) (Green et al., 2011; Plisk, 2000; Young et al., 2002), shorter GCTs are advantageous because less time is required to generate braking and propulsive impulse, which may facilitate greater SSC utilisation (i.e. energy release and stretch reflex) (Bosco et al., 1981; Welch et al., 2019), and overall less time performing the COD action (Dos'Santos, Thomas, McBurnie, Comfort, et al., 2021). Additionally, greater braking forces may increase storage and utilisation of elastic energy as the muscle lengthens under an eccentric load (Hunter et al., 2005; Spiteri et al., 2013; Spiteri et al., 2015), thus effectively reducing horizontal momentum and facilitating superior exit velocity. In addition to the importance of the braking and propulsive force and impulse magnitudes (Dos'Santos, Thomas, McBurnie, Comfort, et al., 2021; Spiteri et al., 2013; Spiteri et al., 2015), the orientation of force application (i.e. force-vector specificity) during the braking and propulsive phases are also important characteristics of cutting (Dos'Santos, 2020; Dos'Santos, Thomas, McBurnie, Comfort, et al., 2021; Welch et al., 2019) and turning performance (Dos'Santos et al., 2020; Dos'Santos et al., 2021a; Dos'Santos et al., 2017). Thus, for effective COD performance, athletes are required to (1) be able to produce high and rapid magnitudes of net braking and propulsive force and (2) be able to transmit force effectively in the optimal direction to facilitate effective net deceleration and acceleration.

For *side-step cutting performance* (30–90°), technical, kinetic, and kinematic determinants of faster cutting performance include greater ankle power, greater ankle plantar-flexor moments, greater torso lean and rotation, greater hip power and extensor moments, rapid knee and hip extension, wider lateral foot plants, reduced hip and knee flexion, and low COM (David et al., 2018; Dos'Santos, Thomas, McBurnie, Comfort, et al., 2021; Havens & Sigward, 2015a;

Marshall et al., 2014; Welch et al., 2021). For instance, an athlete that lowers their COM during the preparation into the execution phase increases stability, and this postural adjustment enables them to adopt a wide lateral foot plant, which is necessary to generate perpendicular impulse (Havens & Sigward, 2015a; Jones, Herrington, et al., 2015). Additionally, a rapid transition from weight acceptance (i.e. braking) to powerful simultaneous triple extension of ankle, knee, and hip (i.e. simultaneous joint movements) is integral for propulsion (Dos'Santos et al., 2019b). However, the ability to maximise propulsive force is reliant on a firm base of support (i.e. foot-to-ground contact and interaction) for effective braking and propulsion (Dos'Santos et al., 2022; Dos'Santos et al., 2019b; McBurnie & Dos'Santos, 2022). The combination of high braking and propulsive forces and reduced hip and knee flexion could indicate a 'stiffer' strategy to permit a rapid transition from braking to drive-off (i.e. propulsion), thus facilitating a shorter GCT and greater SSC utilisation for more effective force generation, particularly as COD angle reduces (Dos'Santos, Thomas, McBurnie, Comfort, et al., 2021). Moreover, dynamic trunk control is also imperative for cutting performance because reducing lateral trunk flexion and encouraging medial trunk lean will shift the COM more towards the intended direction of travel (i.e. they minimise COM displacement) (Dos'Santos, Thomas, McBurnie, Comfort, et al., 2021; King et al., 2018; Marshall et al., 2014), while greater whole-body, pelvic, and foot rotation permits a more effective alignment of the whole-body COM towards the intended direction of travel, subsequently reducing the redirection demands during the COD (David et al., 2018; Havens & Sigward, 2015a, 2015b). It is worth noting, however, from an attacking agility perspective, some athletes may 'drop the shoulder' (i.e. lateral trunk flexion) and rotate towards their plant foot contact during weight acceptance to deceive the opponent before a rapid trunk reversal towards the intended direction of travel (Dos'Santos et al., 2022).

Although more investigations have been conducted into side-step biomechanical determinants, there has been recent emphasis placed on examining *turning biomechanical determinants* (Dos'Santos et al., 2021a; Dos'Santos et al., 2020). Early research investigations, akin to side-step cutting investigations, initially confirmed greater braking and propulsive forces in shorter GCTs as strong associates with turning performance (Dos'Santos et al., 2017; Graham-Smith et al., 2009; Spiteri et al., 2015). Sasaki et al. (2011) reported smaller forward angular trunk displacements, and shorter GCTs were associated with faster 180° COD performance. Additionally, Dos'Santos et al. (2020) investigated the biomechanical determinants of the modified and traditional 505 and observed that faster performers demonstrated greater peak and mean horizontal propulsive forces in shorter GCTs, more horizontally oriented peak resultant braking and propulsive forces, greater horizontal-to-vertical mean and peak braking and propulsive ratios, greater approach velocities, and greater reductions in velocity over key instances of the COD. Additionally, greater triple flexion (e.g. hip, knee, and ankle) during the PFC, greater medial trunk lean, and greater internal pelvic and foot rotation were demonstrated by faster performers. Thus, as illustrated in previous work for 180° COD (Dos'Santos & Jones, 2022; Jones et al., 2021), a turning strategy which encompasses COM lowering via PFC triple flexion from preparation to execution phases is advocated to facilitate an effective braking position, increase braking impulse, and emphasise a horizontally oriented GRF. Moreover, during the preparation phase (i.e. PFC), early whole-body (i.e. trunk, pelvis, lower-limb) rotation towards the intended direction of travel to minimise COM displacement and effectively align the COM is advantageous, while a large anterior placement of the execution plant foot (i.e. to maximise BOS relative to COM) (Santoro et al., 2021) coupled with forceful triple extension for rapid propulsion to exit the turn are further recommended technical characteristics (Dos'Santos et al., 2020; Dos'Santos et al., 2021a). Recently, in the case for high entry velocity 180° turning performance, greater horizontally oriented braking forces in the antepenultimate foot contact were associated with faster performance and may play a critical role in facilitating effective deceleration for high entry velocity turning (Dos'Santos et al., 2021a). However, further research is needed that explores the joint kinematics and kinetics role of the antepenultimate foot contact during COD particularly as such an early braking strategy would be dependent on increasing preparation time through greater perceptual-cognitive abilities.

It is also worth highlighting that practitioners should be conscious of braking strategy variance adopted during sharp 180° turns (Dos'Santos, Thomas, et al., 2019b). For example, some athletes have been observed to adopt a bilateral (i.e. dual-support) 180° turning strategy whereby the braking is performed in a transverse rotated position to reduce the redirection demands of the execution foot contact, whereby the PFC remains in contact with the ground during final foot contact weight acceptance, thus distributing loading across two foot contacts (Dos'Santos, Thomas, et al., 2019b). In this scenario, the antepenultimate foot contact likely performs a greater proportion of braking and is generally performed to a greater extent in the sagittal plane (Dos'Santos et al., 2021a). Conversely, some athletes have been observed to adopt a clear flight phase between the PFC and FFC, thus resulting in primarily unilateral loading of the final plant foot and potentially slower performance as athletes will rotate their body during the flight phase to redirect towards the intended direction of travel (Dos'Santos, Thomas, et al., 2019b). Further research is needed, which empirically quantifies both turning actions; however, due to the chaotic demands of multidirectional sport, it would theoretically be important that athletes have the capacity to display both aforementioned turning strategies, so they possess adaptable movement strategies to mitigate injury risk through movement variability (i.e. redistribution loading through proximal and distal joints) and improve movement solutions in sport (Dos'Santos et al., 2022).

Although strong relationships between linear sprint times and COD completion time have been observed (Nimphius et al., 2013; Nimphius et al., 2017; Sayers, 2015), and linear speed may mask deficiencies in COD ability when evaluating COD ability solely on completion time and be biased toward faster athletes (Nimphius et al., 2017), novel methods have been adopted to better quantity COM velocity during CODs for a more holistic overview of COD ability (Dos'Santos, 2020; Hader et al., 2015; Jones et al., 2019). Hader et al. (2015), using laser speed guns to assess COM related kinematics, demonstrated that minimum speed reached during the COD was a large to very large determinant of 45° and 90° cutting performance, while peak acceleration and peak speed additionally contributed. Additionally, Dos'Santos et al. (2021), using 3D motion analysis, found COM horizontal velocity at key instances of a 90° cut such as PFC touchdown (approach velocity), final foot contact touchdown, and toe-off, were strong determinants of faster cutting performance. This finding is further corroborated by Jones et al. (2019) who, using hierarchal multiple regression, found minimum COM horizontal velocity and approach velocity during a 70–90° cut could explain 82% (79% adjusted) of variation in cutting time. The finding that faster approach velocities and velocities at key instances are major determinants of cutting performance is unsurprising because faster athletes will attain greater horizontal displacements in shorter times, and the ability to maintain speed during the cut will make it easier to transition from the preparation (approach) to reacceleration phase (exit). Thus, the ability to maintain velocity or minimise the decline in velocity prior to and during cuts of 45–90° (depending on the sport-specific scenarios) and shallow directional changes (≤ 45°) is noteworthy and appears advantageous for faster cutting performance.

The ability to maintain velocity or minimise the decline in velocity during COD will be influenced by the intended angle of COD, approach distance, athlete physical capacity, and subsequent entry velocity because larger braking forces; thus, net horizonal impulse and deceleration will be required during CODs of sharper angles (Havens & Sigward, 2014; Jones et al., 2016a; Sigward et al., 2015) and greater approach velocities and momentums (Dai et al., 2016; McBurnie, Harper, et al., 2021; Vanrenterghem et al., 2012). Nonetheless, akin to the previously mentioned cutting research, faster 180° turning performance is associated with greater approach velocities (Dos'Santos et al., 2020; Jones et al., 2017; Ken-ichi et al., 2019; Santoro et al., 2021). However, in contrast to cutting where COM velocity can be ~2–5 m/s during the execution phase (Dos'Santos, 2020), athletes will be required to reduce their horizontal COM velocity to zero upon turning 180° (Ken-ichi et al., 2019). Thus, to overcome inertia and deflect the COM effectively, athletes possessing greater momentum (mass × velocity) will require greater deceleration/braking impulse prior to turning to effectively decelerate prior to turning (Dos'Santos et al., 2020; Jones et al., 2017; Ken-ichi et al., 2019). Thus, the ability to approach fast and decelerate late (i.e. over shorter distances and duration) and brake hard (i.e. greater braking impulse) will be advantageous (Dos'Santos et al., 2020; Dos'Santos, Thomas, et al., 2019b; Jones et al., 2017; Ken-ichi et al., 2019; Santoro et al., 2021). The ability to decelerate effectively, however, will be influenced by the preparation times available for postural adjustments to facilitate braking and limited by the available visual and auditory cues to anticipate the directional change (McBurnie, Harper, et al., 2021). Moreover, a 'self-regulatory' concept has been observed with respect to COD (Dos'Santos et al., 2018; Jones et al., 2019; Jones et al., 2017), demonstrating that athletes sprint at a velocity and enter a COD based on a deceleration load that they can tolerate. For example, eccentrically (knee flexor and extensor) stronger female soccer players have been shown to approach faster and display greater reductions in velocity and braking forces during 180° CODs (Jones et al., 2017), while eccentrically stronger (knee flexor and extensor) soccer players were better able to maintain velocity and attain higher minimum speeds and tolerate greater joint loads during a 90° cutting task (Jones et al., 2019). Therefore, although improving athletes' speed does indeed appear intuitive, it is essential that athletes have the physical capacity (i.e. neuromuscular control, rapid force production, muscular strength and activation) (Dos'Santos et al., 2018; Jones et al., 2017; Maniar et al., 2019; Nimphius, 2017) to (1) tolerate the mechanical loads associated with greater entry velocities and sharper directional changes, (2) provide the physical affordances to adopt the favourable postures associated with faster COD performance, (3) provide the neuromuscular foundation to generate high magnitude and rapid braking and propulsive impulse, and (4) provide muscular activation and coordination to support and assist in ligament unloading and centre-of-mass control. A summary of underpinning physical qualities for COD ability is provided in previous work (Dos'Santos & Jones, 2022; Jones et al., 2021)

Determinants of Knee Joint Loads During COD Manoeuvres

COD actions, particularly those which involve lateral foot plants, are injury inciting events associated with non-contact lower-limb injuries, such as ACL (Cochrane et al., 2007; Johnston et al., 2018; Krosshaug et al., 2007; Montgomery et al., 2018), hamstring strain (Kerin et al., 2022), medial and lateral ankle sprains (Fong et al., 2009; Wade et al., 2018), and adductor injuries (Serner et al., 2019), particularly in cutting dominant sports. Simply, injuries to tissue occur because of a mechanical load which exceeds the tissues' tolerance capacity (Edwards, 2018; Kalkhoven et al., 2021; Meeuwisse et al., 2007) or because of a 'fatigue failure mechanism' due to repeated and chronic exposure to mechanical loads, without adequate rest and recovery, which reduces the structural integrity and tolerance threshold, resulting in failure from mechanical loads it could previously tolerate (Beaulieu et al., 2021). When performing COD actions, potentially hazardous and high mechanical loads (Donelon et al., 2020; Dos'Santos, Thomas, McBurnie, Donelon, et al., 2021; Fox, 2018; Kalkhoven et al., 2021), particularly knee joint loads, can be generated, which are amplified if there are aberrant movement quality and neuromuscular control (i.e. high-risk deficits) (Donelon et al., 2020; Fox, 2018), high approach velocities and sharper directional changes, and externally directed attention with high cognitive loading (Brown et al., 2014; Donelon et al., 2020; Dos'Santos, 2020; Dos'Santos et al., 2019a; Dos'Santos, Thomas, Comfort, et al., 2021b; Dos'Santos, Thomas, McBurnie, Donelon, et al., 2021; Fox, 2018).

Readers are encouraged to read the review articles for comprehensive overviews of the biomechanical and neuromuscular deficits associated with greater knee joint loading during COD and potential injury risk; thus, a brief overview is presented here (Donelon et al., 2020; Dos'Santos, Thomas, McBurnie, Donelon, et al., 2021; Fox, 2018). Figure 4.4 and Table 4.2 summarise several biomechanical factors associated with greater peak knee abduction moments (KAMs) during 30–90° CODs and thus potential ACL injury risk (Hewett et al., 2005; Markolf et al., 1990; Shin et al., 2009). Furthermore, recent research has shown a strong relationship between frontal and transverse loads (Dos'Santos, Thomas, McBurnie, Comfort, et al., 2021; McBurnie, Dos'Santos, et al., 2021), which is concerning because a combination of loading in several planes (i.e. combined anterior tibial shear, knee abduction, and internal rotation moments) increases ACL strain to a greater extent than uniplanar loading alone (Markolf et al., 1995; Shin et al., 2011).

External joint moments are a product of the GRF and the moment arm distance between the joint axis and GRF vector (i.e. line of action of force). Thus, whole-body postures and joint

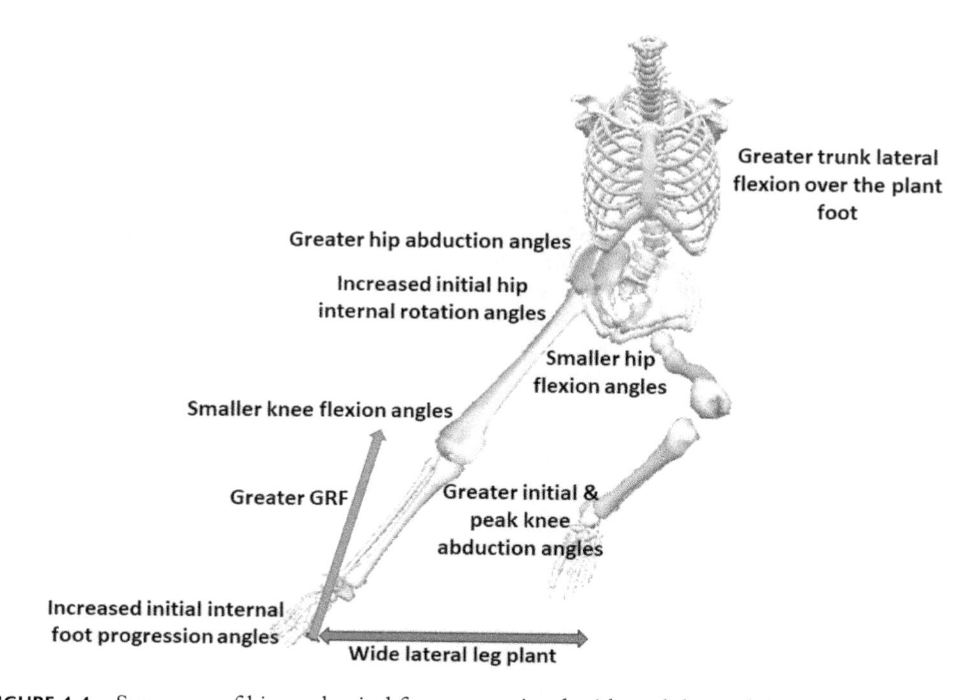

FIGURE 4.4 Summary of biomechanical factors associated with peak knee abduction moments based on literature (Donelon et al., 2020; Dos'Santos, Thomas, McBurnie, Donelon, et al., 2021; Fox, 2018).

TABLE 4.2 Side-Step Cutting Technique Checklist Regarding the Performance-Injury Risk Conflict

Determinant	*Should we intervene?*	*Rationale*	*Recommendation*
Approach velocity and COD angle	✗	Athletes are unlikely to sprint slower and avoid sharper CODs, and velocity is key determinant of performance.	Optimise technique and develop physical capacity to tolerate knee joint loads. Encourage PFC to brake during sharper COD and postural adjustment prior to COD to facilitate effective weight acceptance during execution of foot contact.
Lateral trunk flexion/ rotation	✓ (pre-planned) Deception?	Medial trunk lean is associated with faster performance and lower knee joint loads. However, during unplanned COD, athletes may laterally flex trunk (drop shoulder) to deceive (feint) opponents.	Coach upright/medial trunk lean during pre-planned COD. Coach upright trunk position for unplanned COD.
Wide lateral foot plant	✗	Although a wide lateral foot plant increases moment arm and KAM, it is necessary to generate ML GRF and perpendicular force to accelerate into the intended direction. Athletes are unlikely to adopt narrower foot plants at the expense of a slower performance.	If coaching a wide lateral foot plant, ensure that athletes avoid initial valgus postures with lateral trunk flexion. An amalgamation of several high-risk postures is worse than just lateral foot plant. Ensure high levels of muscular support before and during ground contact to support ligament unloading.
Knee valgus and hip rotation	✓	Knee valgus and internal hip rotation are linked to greater KAMs but offer no associated performance benefits.	Encourage strong frontal plane alignment of the hip, knee, and ankle.
Knee and hip flexion	?	Increasing knee flexion can reduce the impact of GRFs, KAMs, and anterior tibial shear, but increased flexion is also associated with longer GCTs and reduced exit velocity. Similar observations have been observed for hip flexion.	Encourage ankle, knee, and hip rapid co-flexion with rapid transition to forceful triple extension. Encourage active touchdown (initial flexed postures) with high muscular pre- and co-activation.
Foot position	✓	Excessive internally and externally rotated postures can increase KAMs and tibial rotation, respectively. Neutral foot position is the safest strategy without any detrimental impacts for performance.	Encourage neutral position during COD.

Determinant	*Should we intervene?*	*Rationale*	*Recommendation*
Impact GRF	?	High GRFs increase KAMs and are a by-product of running faster and reduced knee flexion. High-impact GRFs are needed to facilitate greater braking forces to reduce momentum.	Encourage braking during earlier foot contacts, such as PFC.
PFC braking	✓	PFC braking, particularly for sharper COD, is associated with faster performance and lower knee joint loads and is considered a safer strategy because braking generally occurs in the sagittal plane and through greater knee flexion. This, in turn, lowers knee joint loads during FFC and permits the FFC to focus on propulsion and redirection rather than braking.	Encourage PFC dominant braking strategies for sharper COD. Ensure optimal PFC placement for effective weight acceptance during shallower CODs.

Key: GRF: ground reaction force; COD: change of direction; PFC: penultimate foot contact; FFC: final foot contact; KAM: knee abduction moment; GCT: ground contact time

movements during initial contact and overweight acceptance during the COD manoeuvre have the potential to increase one or both of these (Kristianslund et al., 2014). Because ACL injuries are reported to occur within 50 milliseconds of ground contact during high-impact activities (Koga et al., 2010), this leaves limited time for postural readjustments through a feedforward mechanism. As such, improving biomechanical and neuromuscular deficits at initial contact could arguably be of greater importance in injury mitigation programmes and screening (Donelon et al., 2020). Nonetheless, increasing lateral foot plant distances produces a greater moment arm distance between the GRF vector and the knee in the frontal plane, resulting in a greater externally applied KAM (Dos'Santos, 2020; Jones, Herrington, et al., 2015; Sigward & Powers, 2007). Additionally, internally rotated postures at the foot and hip in combination with knee valgus position (i.e. abduction – distal tibia abducting from midline) can contribute to a medially positioned knee relative to the GRF vector, thus increasing frontal plane moment arm distance and subsequent external KAM (Havens & Sigward, 2015a; McLean et al., 2005; Sigward et al., 2015). Containing approximately half of the body's mass, dynamic trunk control is also a critical determinant of multiplanar knee joint loads (Donelon et al., 2020; Mendiguchia et al., 2011). For example, lateral trunk flexion and deviation from the midline creates a laterally directed GRF vector, which increases the moment arm distance between the GRF vector and knee joint centre (Dos'Santos, 2020; Havens & Sigward, 2015a; Jones, Herrington, et al., 2015).

Extended knee postures at initial contact and during weight acceptance can increase anterior tibial shear, increasing ACL strain (Markolf et al., 1990; Withrow et al., 2006), while reduced knee flexion can increase impact GRFs (Devita & Skelly, 1992; Zhang et al., 2000) – a key determinant of knee moments. Reduced knee flexion (Dos'Santos, Thomas, McBurnie, Comfort, et al., 2021; Kristianslund et al., 2014; Weir et al., 2019) and hip flexion (Dos'Santos, Thomas, McBurnie, Comfort, et al., 2021) are also associated with hazardous multiplanar knee joint loads. Greater GRFs, a key constituent part of a moment, are associated with greater KAMs (Dos'Santos, 2020; Jones et al., 2016a; Sigward et al., 2015), which can be partially attributed to final foot contact heel strike contacts (David et al., 2017; Donnelly et al., 2017; Kristianslund et al., 2014), and both can be offset through increased braking during the penultimate foot contact (Dos'Santos, 2020; Jones et al., 2016a, 2016b). Additionally, knee joint loading is amplified during faster and sharper CODs and is also amplified in unplanned situations (Almonroeder et al., 2015; Brown et al., 2014) and sport-specific cuts (Chan et al., 2009; Chaudhari et al., 2005; Fedie et al., 2010) and exacerbated under fatigue (Weinhandl et al., 2014; Whyte et al., 2018). As such, reducing and mitigating the aforementioned high-risk deficits are viable strategies to reduce knee joint loads and potential ACL injury risk during COD (Fox, 2018; Hewett, 2017; Padua et al., 2018).

Biomechanical Differences Between Pre-planned and Unplanned Manoeuvres

Three systematic reviews (Almonroeder et al., 2015; Brown et al., 2014; Giesche et al., 2021) have confirmed that compared to pre-planned (or anticipated) directional changes, unplanned (or unanticipated/reactive) directional changes evoke higher-risk knee mechanics and amplify multiplanar knee joint loads, which are disproportionately greater than the increased muscle activation (and support) (Weir, 2022). Specifically, greater sagittal (Besier et al., 2001; Dempsey et al., 2009; Kim et al., 2014), transverse (Besier et al., 2001; Dempsey et al., 2009), and frontal (Besier et al., 2001; Kim et al., 2014; Lee et al., 2013) plane knee joint loading have been observed during unplanned directional changes, while Weinhandl et al. (2013), via musculoskeletal modelling, reported significantly greater ACL loading during unanticipated side-steps through combined increased sagittal (62%), frontal (26%), and transverse (12%) plane loading. Visual observation studies of non-contact ACL-injury-inciting events generally confirm that the injured athlete has externally focused attention (i.e. divided attention) in response to one or more stimuli, with high visual and spatial-temporal constraints, such as evading or reacting to an opponent or reacting to a ball/implement (i.e. both attacking and defensive scenarios) (Brophy et al., 2015; Montgomery et al., 2018; Olsen et al., 2004). The potentially deleterious effects of unplanned or divided attention directional changes, through the introduction and response to stimuli or multiple stimuli, poses a greater challenge to the athlete, by increasing the task complexity and imposing temporal constraints on the central nervous system (Besier et al., 2001; Collins et al., 2016; Mornieux et al., 2014).

Known as perception-action coupling, is a mechanism by which an athlete must identify and process one or more stimuli (i.e. reaction), select and make a decision in response to the stimuli, then coordinate and execute a specific mechanical action (i.e. motor response). This introduction of stimuli, as well as the subsequent perceptual-cognitive requirements to process the stimuli and make a decision and execute an action, reduces the preparation time for athletes to appropriately adjust their whole-body posture (Lee et al., 2013; Lee et al., 2017; Mornieux et al., 2014) (i.e. coordinate and pre-activate multiple muscles, joints, and segments), in contrast to the anticipatory postural adjustments, which are afforded during pre-planned tasks (Weir, 2022). Moreover, any delay or deficits in attentional processing of stimuli (or information) may also contribute to greater injury risk, by reducing the ability and time affordances to potentially correct any sub-optimal coordination patterns (i.e. neuromuscular feed-forward) (Gokeler et al.,

2021), potentially resulting in positions of 'no return'. Collectively, this may explain the propensity to generate greater multiplanar knee joint loads during unplanned directional changes, which can potentially increase ACL strain and subsequent injury risk (Kiapour et al., 2016; Shin et al., 2009; Shin et al., 2011).

The ACL injury mechanism has been traditionally viewed as a biomechanical issue; however, it is important not to neglect the neurocognitive elements associated with the ACL injury mechanism (Giesche et al., 2021; Gokeler et al., 2021). Consequently, there has been a recent emphasis on the coaching and screening of COD biomechanics utilising generic stimuli or tasks with externally directed or divided attention (Hughes & Dai, 2021). Although the option of a generic stimuli (i.e. flashing light/arrow external stimulus) appears to be an attractive option for the coaching and screening of agility mechanics, with the majority of literature adopting a generic stimulus for biomechanical comparison (Giesche et al., 2021), it is worth noting the timing and type of stimuli can affect COD biomechanics and subsequent knee joint loading (Lee et al., 2013; Lee et al., 2017; Mornieux et al., 2014). Additionally, the use of flashing lights/arrows as an unanticipated stimulus has been criticised because they are not a sport-specific stimulus (Nimphius et al., 2017; Paul et al., 2016; Young & Farrow, 2013). In reality, athletes do not react to flashing lights and arrows in sport. Instead, they visually scan and process multiple visual, auditory, postural, and kinematic cues regarding the environment, sport (i.e. gameplay), and athletes (i.e. teammates and opposition) while processing proprioceptive stimuli when performing a COD (or other technical action) (Jeffreys, 2011; Weir, 2022; Young & Farrow, 2013), often in open, chaotic, unpredictable environments. Researchers have shown performance during reactive agility tasks using flashing lights/arrows does not differentiate skilful performers (Young et al., 2011; Young et al., 2015; Young & Farrow, 2013) – while these tasks do not allow athletes to make anticipatory decision-making and postural adjustments, which they normally would do in sports – and in fact is a more complex and hazardous task compared to reacting to 2D video footage (Lee et al., 2013). Additionally, athletes, when performing these unplanned tasks in response to a flashing light or arrow, still know that they are going to perform a time-constrained decision-making task in response to a stimuli in a laboratory environment (Giesche et al., 2021). Consequently, unplanned COD tasks containing generic stimuli, such as flashing lights and arrows, although argued to increase ecological validity and provide a more challenging scenario compared to pre-planned tasks, still does not provide the representative environments and the complex stimuli (i.e. cognitive loads) associated with dynamic sport (Giesche et al., 2021).

Unfortunately, it is difficult to provide a controlled (i.e. timing), 3D sport-specific stimulus in the laboratory when assessing unplanned COD biomechanics, which will truly reflect the complexities of open, chaotic, unpredictable environments in sport. In addition, due to the different types of agility actions (i.e. side-steps, crossovers, split-steps, pivots, shuffle-steps, turns) and contextual applications of these actions performed in sport (i.e. attacking, defending, 1 vs 1, multiple attackers and defenders, in position/out of possession, ball-carrying/non-carrier situations), and because COD biomechanics are task-dependent (Dos'Santos et al., 2018; Giesche et al., 2021; Hughes & Dai, 2021), a multitude of tests are likely needed to evaluate these qualities, which is impractical in most community to high-performance settings with time constraints for testing. Nevertheless, to increase sports specificity and the neurocognitive demands associated with match play, researchers have implemented sport-specific COD tasks with externally directed attention during a side-stepping task, such as attending to a ball (Chan et al., 2009; Fedie et al., 2010), side-stepping past a static opponent (Kristianslund et al., 2014; McLean et al., 2004), or carrying an object (e.g. ball or lacrosse stick) (Chaudhari et al., 2005), which can evoke higher-risk postures and increase knee joint loading compared to pre-planned tasks. These findings may partially explain why the ball carrier in rugby (Montgomery et al., 2018), American football (Johnston et al., 2018), and handball (Olsen et al., 2004) is commonly injured when side-stepping past an opponent, and the ACL injured limb is predominantly the racket-hand side during plant-and-cut actions in badminton (Kimura et al., 2010). Overall, unplanned directional changes appear to induce greater ACL injury risk compared to planned directional changes due to the neurocognitive challenges and reduced preparation time to better adopt coordinative movement and muscle activation strategies. Consequently, practitioners should be conscious of the biomechanical, perceptual-cognitive, and physical differences between pre-planned and unplanned actions and acknowledge these implications when coaching, screening, rehabilitating, and physically preparing athletes for the agility and COD demands of multidirectional sport.

Mediating the Performance-injury Risk Conflict During Change of Direction: A Multidimensional Approach

Concerningly for athletes and practitioners, a paradox may exist between maximising performance and injury risk mitigation during COD, with recent evidence revealing that technical and mechanical factors associated with superior exit velocities, deflections/redirections of the COM, and deceptive movements are at odds and may conflict with safer performance (i.e. reduced mechanical loads) (Dos'Santos, Thomas, McBurnie, Comfort, et al., 2021; Fox, 2018; Havens & Sigward, 2015a; McBurnie, Dos'Santos, et al., 2021; Sankey et al., 2020). This paradox has been referred to as the 'performance-injury risk conflict' (Dos'Santos, Thomas, McBurnie, Comfort, et al., 2021; McBurnie, Dos'Santos, et al., 2021). For instance, modulating postures and movement strategies, such as lateral foot plant distance, hip and knee flexion, foot and pelvis rotation approach velocity, high-impact GRFs, and lateral trunk flexion and rotation (from a deception perspective), can indeed reduce potentially hazardous knee joint loads but most likely to the detriment of faster and effective COD performance (Dos'Santos, Thomas, McBurnie, Comfort, et al., 2021; Fox, 2018; Havens & Sigward, 2015a; McBurnie, Dos'Santos, et al., 2021; Sankey et al., 2020). This conundrum is a problem for practitioners working in sports science and medicine whose primary objectives are to improve athletic performance and mitigate injury risk, while receiving athlete and coach adherence will also be challenging as they are unlikely to adopt safer movement strategies at the expense of faster and effective performance (Havens & Sigward, 2015a).

Despite several technical and mechanical variables being linked to both faster COD performance and greater multiplanar knee joint loads and potential knee injury risk, some characteristics are mutually beneficial to performance and injury risk mitigation, or some factors could be modified without negatively affecting performance while reducing injury risk (Table 4.2) (Dos'Santos, Thomas, Comfort, et al., 2021a; Dos'Santos, Thomas, McBurnie, Comfort, et al., 2021). For instance, knee valgus is a primary determinant of external KAMs (Dos'Santos, 2020; Jones, Herrington, et al., 2015; Kristianslund et al., 2014) but offers no associated performance benefits (Dos'Santos, Thomas, McBurnie, Comfort, et al., 2021; Marshall et al., 2014; McBurnie, Dos'Santos, et al., 2021). Moreover, medial trunk lean is associated with faster pre-planned COD performance (Dos'Santos, Thomas, McBurnie, Comfort, et al., 2021; Marshall et al., 2014) and lower knee joint loads (Dempsey et al., 2007; Jamison et al., 2012; Jones, Herrington, et al., 2015), though practitioners and athletes must be mindful of lateral trunk flexion as a deceptive action in agility contexts, and the rapid trunk reversal can be an effective evasive agility action (Dos'Santos et al., 2022). Finally, greater PFC braking forces, particularly for sharper COD, have been shown to be associated with faster performance (Dos'Santos et al., 2020; Dos'Santos, 2020; Dos'Santos, Thomas, et al., 2019b; Dos'Santos, Thomas, McBurnie, Comfort, et al., 2021) and potentially lower knee joint loads (Dos'Santos, Thomas, et al., 2019b; Dos'Santos, Thomas, McBurnie, Comfort, et al., 2021; Jones, Barber, et al., 2015; Jones et al., 2016a), and are considered a safer strategy because braking generally occurs in the sagittal plane and through greater knee flexion (Dos'Santos, Thomas, et al., 2019b; Graham-Smith et al., 2018). Consequently, Table 4.2 present a side-step cutting technical model which attempts to satisfy and mediate the performance-injury risk conflict.

Inevitably, there will be some inherent risk of injury when performing high-intensity actions, such as COD, often in chaotic, unpredictable environments (Dos'Santos et al., 2022), and due to the complexity of the injury mechanism and interaction of internal, external, modifiable, and non-modifiable factors (Bittencourt et al., 2016), it would potentially be erroneous to assume that all non-contact injuries during COD are preventable. That said, particularly in the context of knee injuries, practitioners have a duty of care to maximise athletic development and should drive for a multidimensional approach (Figure 4.5) to best mediate the performance-injury conflict and best prepare athletes for the competitive demands of training and competition (Dos'Santos et al., 2022; Weir, 2022).

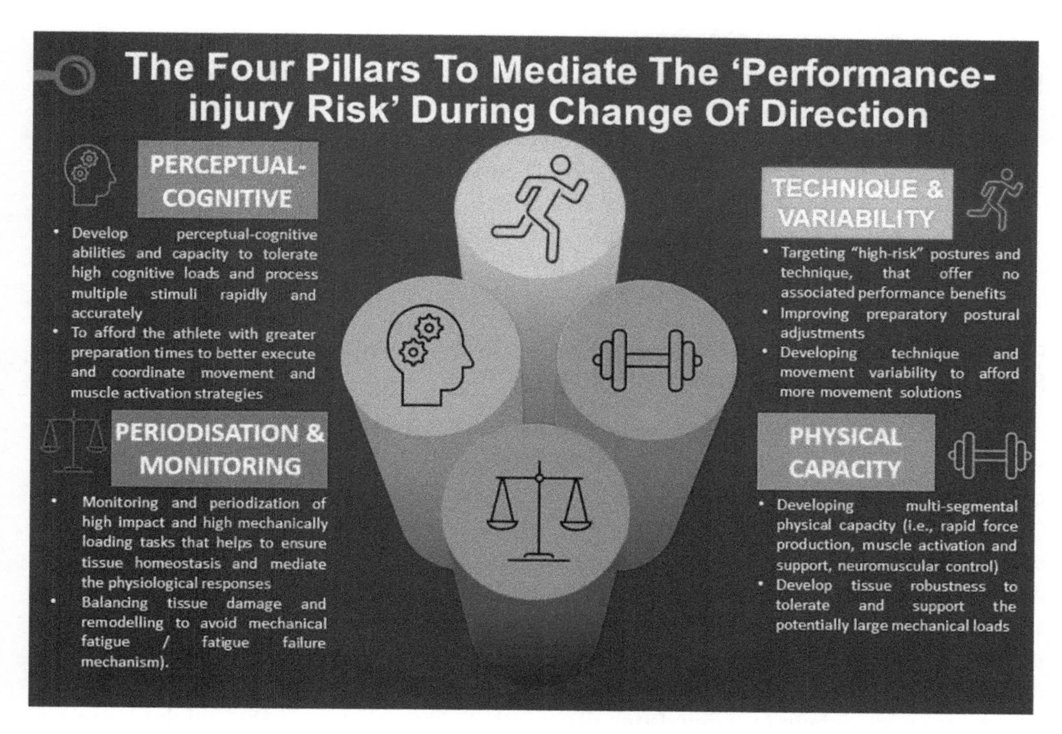

FIGURE 4.5 The four pillars to mediate the performance-injury risk during change of direction.

Four viable strategies as part of the multidimensional approach (Figure 4.5) include (Dos'Santos et al., 2022; Weir, 2022):

1. Targeting 'high-risk' postures and techniques that offer no associated performance benefits (e.g. reducing knee valgus through resistance, neuromuscular control, jump-landing training), improving preparatory postural adjustments (e.g. PFC braking and placement via technique modification training and eccentric strength training) (Dos'Santos, Thomas, Comfort, et al., 2021a; Dos'Santos, Thomas, McBurnie, Comfort, et al., 2021; Weir, 2022), and developing technique and movement variability to offer more affordances/movement solutions and potentially avoid repetitive loading of same tissues (Dos'Santos et al., 2022; Weir, 2022)
2. Developing multi-segmental (i.e. knee- and non-knee-spanning musculature) physical capacity (i.e. rapid force production, muscle activation and support, neuromuscular control) and tissue robustness to tolerate and support the potentially large mechanical loads via a multicomponent training program (i.e. which integrates resistance, plyometric, balance, and dynamic trunk stabilisation training) (Dos'Santos, Thomas, et al., 2019a; Lloyd & Buchanan, 2001; Maniar et al., 2018; Weir, 2022)
3. Developing athletes' perceptual-cognitive abilities and capacity to tolerate high cognitive loads and process multiple stimuli rapidly and accurately (i.e. developing players situational awareness, visual scanning, anticipatory skills, reaction times, and decision-making ability and speed via agility training and feedback and video training) (Dos'Santos et al., 2022; Hughes & Dai, 2021; Weir, 2022), in order to afford the athlete with greater preparation times to better execute and coordinate movement and muscle activation strategies (Gokeler et al., 2021; Hughes & Dai, 2021; Weir, 2022)
4. Monitoring and periodising high-impact and high mechanically loading tasks that help to ensure tissue homeostasis and mediate the physiological responses (i.e. balancing tissue damage and remodelling to avoid mechanical fatigue/fatigue failure mechanism) (Beaulieu et al., 2021; Edwards, 2018; Kalkhoven et al., 2021) associated with these sporting environmental challenges (e.g. use of player tracking and/or wearable devices to monitor frequency and intensity of metrics, such as decelerations, accelerations, and directional changes) (Edwards, 2018; Kalkhoven et al., 2021; Lipps et al., 2013)

Physical Determinants of COD Performance and Key Considerations for Physical Preparation (Capacity Building)

A range of different physical qualities are associated with faster COD performance and are needed when changing direction (Bourgeois et al., 2017). High levels of eccentric, isometric, and concentric strength are required for the braking, plant and transition, and propulsion phases of COD (Spiteri et al., 2013; Spiteri et al., 2014; Spiteri et al., 2015), respectively, and because of the rapid braking and propulsive (i.e. SSC requirements), reactive strength is also a key physical quality to develop in training programmes (Jarvis et al., 2021). Additionally, because of the time constraints associated with changing direction, the ability to produce rapid and high magnitudes of net force (i.e. rate of force development and impulse) to accelerate the mass and change direction is fundamental (Dos'Santos et al., 2018). It is worth noting, however, that power and the ability to produce force rapidly is built on a foundation of strength (Suchomel et al., 2018), and thus, maximal strength training should still form a cornerstone component of a periodised training programme.

Additionally, the biomechanical and physical demands are angle-dependent (Dos'Santos et al., 2018), and thus, the angle should be considered when designing physical training programmes.

With athletes who are required to be proficient at shallow CODs, typically <45°, the deceleration and braking requirements are limited, with short GCTs of ~0.20 seconds during plant foot contact observed (Dos'Santos et al., 2018). Thus, the ability to approach fast, attain high minimum speeds, and maintain velocity is imperative (Dos'Santos et al., 2018; Hader et al., 2015). Consequently, practitioners may consider targeting their programme design and exercise selection on the 'velocity' spectrum of the force-velocity curve, utilising ballistic and fast SSC exercises, while developing concentric, dynamic, and reactive strength (Bourgeois et al., 2017; Dos'Santos et al., 2018). Conversely, athletes who are required to be proficient at sharper CODs of ≥60°, and acknowledging approach velocity is still important, the ability to decelerate and brake hard, late, and quickly is fundamental for faster COD performance (Jones et al., 2017; Ken-ichi et al., 2019). Thus, sharper CODs from greater approach velocities require greater braking distances and longer GCTs of ~0.30–0.50 seconds during the COD foot plant to facilitate the directional change (Dos'Santos et al., 2018; Hader et al., 2015). Consequently, practitioners should target their programme design and exercise selection on the 'force' aspect of the force-velocity curve through high-load resistance training and slow SSC plyometric exercises (Bourgeois et al., 2017; Dos'Santos et al., 2018) while considering eccentric (Jones et al., 2019; Jones et al., 2017; McBurnie, Harper, et al., 2021) and isometric strength development (Lum & Barbosa, 2019; Oranchuk et al., 2019). However, as most sports will require athletes to COD across a spectrum of shallow, moderate, and sharp directional changes, a training programme which emphasises different muscle actions and force-velocity characteristics (Figure 4.6) across multiple segments of knee- and non-knee-spanning musculature is needed to best physically prepare athletes for the physical demands of chaotic multidirectional sport (Dos'Santos et al., 2022; Dos'Santos, Thomas, et al., 2019a; McBurnie, Harper, et al., 2021). An overview of the physical and anatomical requirements for COD are presented in Figure 4.5 (Dos'Santos and Jones, 2022; Jones et al., 2021) to better prepare for the 'performance-injury conflict' which is present during COD.

Changing direction will impose multiplanar knee joint loading, and this is inevitable when athletes become faster (i.e. the primary aim of strength and conditioning). Athletes will ultimately seek to adopt COD strategies that enhance performance, even at the expense of greater knee joint loading, and it is not feasible to instruct athletes to avoid sharp CODs and perform CODs slower with reduced approach velocities (Dos'Santos et al., 2018). It is worth noting, however, that an athlete's ability to execute particular agility and COD actions could be constrained by their physical capacity (Davies et al., 2022; Jones et al., 2017; Jones et al., 2019; Spiteri et al., 2013; Thomas et al., 2020), and the athlete's awareness of their own physical limitations (i.e. the so-called affordances for action) could influence the agility and COD actions they decide to perform in sport (Dos'Santos et al., 2022). Therefore, to best physically prepare athletes to tolerate and support the mechanical loading, provide the foundation for impulsive braking and propulsion, and permit the physical affordances to execute a range of different COD actions, it is recommended that practitioners develop their athletes' physical capacity (i.e. neuromuscular control, rapid force production, muscular strength, and activation) (Donnelly et al., 2012; Lloyd & Buchanan, 2001; Maniar et al., 2018). This, in turn, should allow the athlete to (1) improve their ability to produce and transmit braking and propulsive impulse, (2) permit athletes to adopt favourable postures associated with faster performance (i.e. physical affordances), (3) enable athletes to sprint and enter CODs at greater velocities as they will possess a greater load

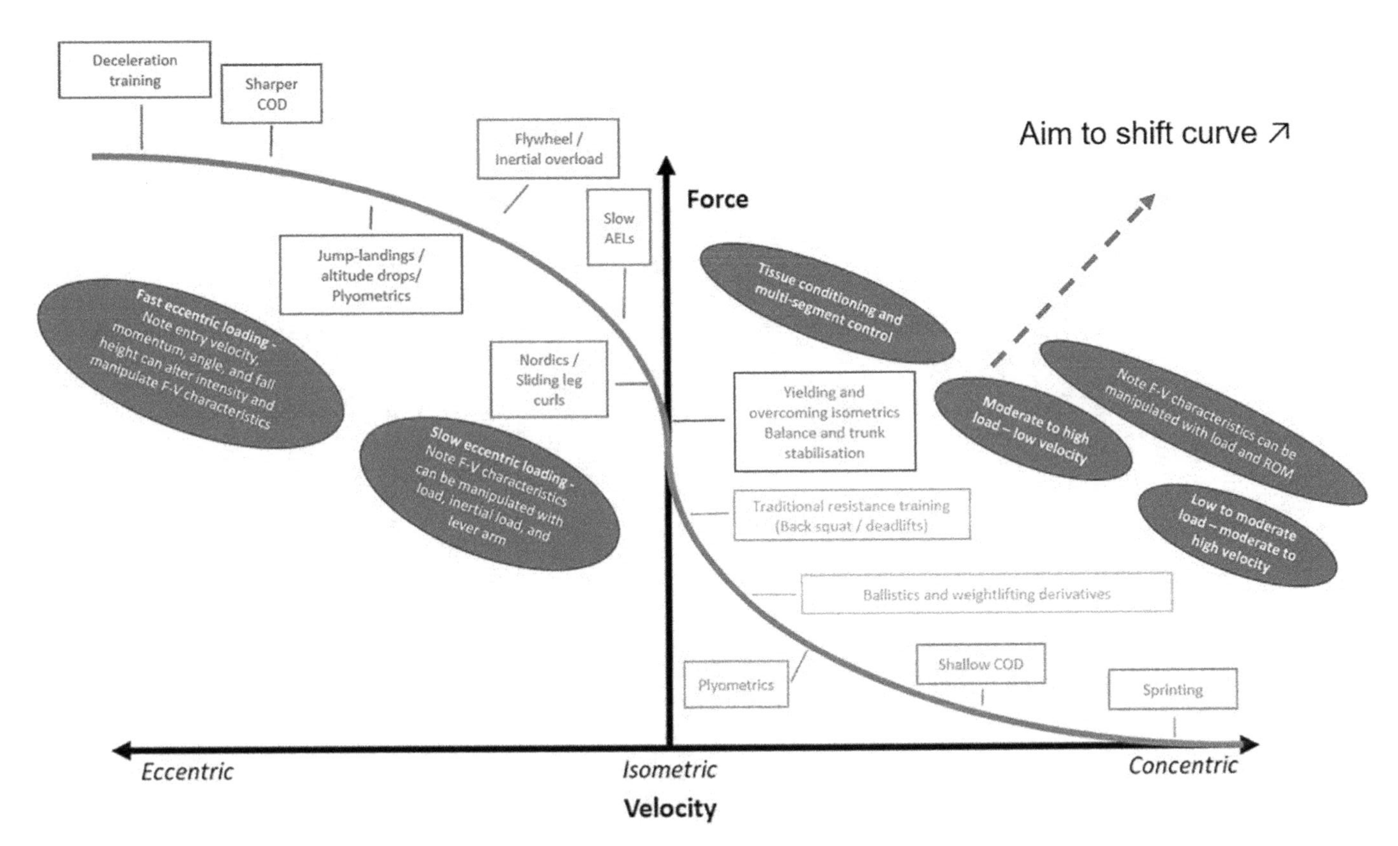

FIGURE 4.6 Physical qualities needed for a successful COD performance. COD: change of direction; GCT: ground contact time; SSC: stretch-shorten cycle; AEL: augmented eccentric loading; F-V: Force-velocity.

TABLE 4.3 Important Physical Preparation Considerations for Change-of-Direction Actions: Developing Physical Capacity for Load Tolerance

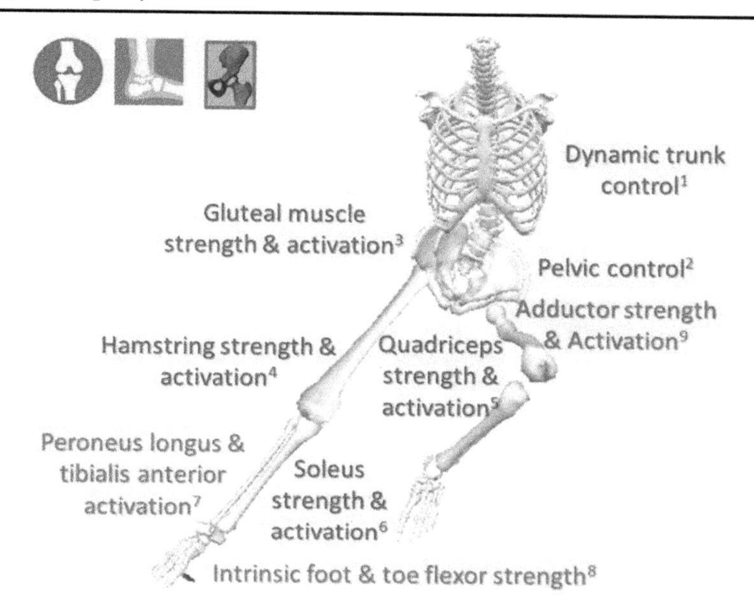

Dynamic trunk control[1]

- Trunk contains approximately half of the body's mass, which must be supported on one limb during COD.
- Lateral trunk flexion increases frontal-plane moment arm distance and GRF vector orientation; thus, greater knee joints load during COD (Donnelly et al., 2012; Hewett & Myer, 2011). Additionally, deficits in trunk control are associated with ACL injury (Zazulak et al., 2007;. Zazulak et al., 2007), and computed simulated modelling of side-stepping has shown a reduction in knee valgus loading through shifting whole-body COM more medially (Donnelly et al., 2012).
- Medial trunk lean is also associated with faster performance (Dos'Santos, 2020; Dos'Santos et al., 2020; Marshall et al., 2014).
- Anterior trunk flexion can increase hamstring stretch load (Kerin et al., 2022)

Pelvic control[2]

- Pelvic obliquity can directly influence lateral trunk flexion angle (Staynor et al., 2018), permitting the trunk to be more upright when aligned towards the direction of travel.

External hip rotator (gluteal) strength and activation[3]

- To reduce KAA thus, frontal-plane moment arm and KAM (Hewett et al., 2005; McLean et al., 2004). Greater knee valgus angles are associated with ACL injury (Hewett et al., 2005), and an increase in knee valgus angle of 2° can lead to a 40 Nm change in valgus moment (McLean et al., 2004).
- Gluteal strength is required to oppose knee valgus moments and rotator moments (Maniar et al., 2020; Maniar et al., 2018), and lower gluteus medius force (with greater vertical and lateral GRF) is associated with greater KAM (Ueno et al., 2020).
- Gluteal strength (hip extension) is required to support large hip flexion moments (Dos'Santos, Thomas, et al., 2019b) during deceleration, PFC, FFC, and trunk stabilisation to prevent excessive anterior flexion and to facilitate effective propulsion (Maniar et al., 2019).
- Isometric external rotation and abduction strength have been found to be associated with the incidence of non-contact ACL injuries (Khayambashi et al., 2016).

(Continued)

TABLE 4.3 (Continued)

Hamstring strength and activation[4]

- To reduce ACL loading (Weinhandl et al., 2014), enable greater knee flexion (Donnelly et al., 2012), and reduce anterior tibial shear and impact GRF (Lloyd & Buchanan, 2001; Maniar et al., 2020; Maniar et al., 2018).
- Deficits in medial hamstring activity (semitendinosus) and greater vastus lateralis activity associated with greater ACL injury (Smeets et al., 2019; Zebis et al., 2009). Hamstrings play a crucial assisting in braking and propulsion during hip extension (Besier et al., 2003; Maniar et al., 2019) (particularly medial hamstring strength and activation).

Quadriceps strength and activiation[5]

- Facilitate effective braking (eccentric) and propulsion (concentric) (Besier et al., 2003; Lloyd & Buchanan, 2001; Maniar et al., 2019) and support large knee flexor moments created during weight acceptance (Dos'Santos, Thomas, et al., 2019b; Hader et al., 2016).
- Weak eccentric quadriceps may result in a braking strategy with minimal knee flexion and increased hip and trunk flexion (i.e. hip dominant strategy), resulting in high eccentric loads placed on the hamstrings, elevating risk injury (Mateus et al., 2020; Warrener et al., 2021).

Soleus strength and activation[6]

- To oppose anterior tibial translation, create posterior shear force, and facilitate braking and propulsion (Maniar et al., 2019; Maniar et al., 2018; Sinclair et al., 2019).

Peroneus longus and tibialis anterior activation[7]

- For ankle joint stability to control inversion, supination, and internal rotation (Fong et al., 2009; Konradsen & Ravn, 1991; Neptune et al., 1999).

Intrinsic foot and toe flexor strength[8]

- Intrinsic foot muscles contribute to elastic energy storage and return (Kelly et al., 2019), support medial longitudinal arch (McKeon et al., 2015; Tourillon et al., 2019), facilitate energy absorption, and facilitate propulsion (Tourillon et al., 2019; Yuasa et al., 2018) and ankle stability (Fraser et al., 2016).

Adductor strength and activation[9]

- During push off (final 30%) where the hip and knee extends, the hip is abducted, and the pelvis rotated towards direction of travel, there is increased lengthening and activation of adductor longus (Dupré et al., 2021). Gracilis also shows greatest lengthening velocity during last quarter of push-off, and this extreme and potentially vulnerable position can increase eccentric loading (stretch-type loading).
- Reduced strength in the hip adductor muscles has been prospectively linked to increased groin muscle injury in soccer players (Markovic et al., 2020; Moreno-Pérez et al., 2019).

Key: COD: change of direction; GRF: ground reaction force; ACL: anterior cruciate ligament; KAA: knee abduction angle

tolerance, (4) reduce high-risk deficits and facilitate improvements in neuromuscular control, (5) elicit positive tissue adaptations and develop tissue robustness, and (6) improve muscular strength and co-activation to assist in ligament unloading and COM control.

To develop athletes' physical capacity, a mixed multicomponent programme incorporating multi-segmental strength capacity and tissue conditioning, balance, trunk control, plyometrics, and COD/agility training are necessary for ACL injury mitigation, and such modalities commonly feature in an athlete's holistic strength and conditioning programme and recommended features of ACL injury mitigation programmes (Dos'Santos, Thomas, et al., 2019a; Padua et al., 2018). Additionally, a meta-analysis confirmed that plyometric, strength, COD, and combined training methods positively enhance COD speed and manoeuvrability performance (Falch et al., 2019). As such, to enhance COD performance and mitigate ACL injury risk, practitioners are encouraged to implement a mixed multicomponent programme which integrates multi-segmental strength capacity and tissue conditioning (Table 4.3), plyometric/

jump-landing training, balance, dynamic trunk stabilisation, COD speed, agility, small-sided games, and COD technique modification. These components must be prioritised, periodised, and phased appropriately (Dos'Santos et al., 2022), and readers are directed to Chapter 8 for further information.

Summary

Overall, COD is a complex skill with a plethora of technical and movement solutions available for athletes to perform, which have their own distinct technical requirements and associated advantages and disadvantages. As the biomechanical demands of COD are angle- and velocity-dependent, these two factors regulate intensity and have important implications for coaching (see Chapter 10), screening (see Chapters 6 and 16), rehabilitation (see Chapter 16), and physical preparation (see Chapter 8). Moreover, we have introduced the concept of a performance-injury risk conflict during COD and agility, where some of the techniques and mechanics required for faster performance are at odds with safer execution. It is highly unlikely that practitioners can fully eliminate and mitigate all non-contact injuries due to the complex interaction of internal and external factors. However, to best mediate the performance-injury conflict and better prepare athletes for the physical and perceptual-cognitive demands of multidirectional sports, we recommended a four-pillar multidimensional approach that develops (1) technique and movement variability, (2) physical capacity, and (3) perceptual-cognitive ability while (4) periodising and monitoring high mechanically loading activity in athletes.

References

Almonroeder, T. G., Garcia, E., & Kurt, M. (2015). The effects of anticipation on the mechanics of the knee during single leg cutting tasks: A systematic review. *International Journal of Sports Physical Therapy, 10*(7), 918.

Andrews, J. R., McLeod, W. D., Ward, T., & Howard, K. (1977). The cutting mechanism. *The American Journal of Sports Medicine, 5*(3), 111–121.

Beaulieu, M. L., Ashton-Miller, J. A., & Wojtys, E. M. (2021). Loading mechanisms of the anterior cruciate ligament. *Sports Biomechanics*, 1–29.

Besier, T. F., Lloyd, D. G., & Ackland, T. R. (2003). Muscle activation strategies at the knee during running and cutting maneuvers. *Medicine and Science in Sports and Exercise, 35*(1), 119–127.

Besier, T. F., Lloyd, D. G., Ackland, T. R., & Cochrane, J. L. (2001). Anticipatory effects on knee joint loading during running and cutting maneuvers. *Medicine and Science in Sports and Exercise, 33*(7), 1176–1181.

Bittencourt, N. F. N., Meeuwisse, W. H., Mendonça, L. D., Nettel-Aguirre, A., Ocarino, J. M., & Fonseca, S. T. (2016). Complex systems approach for sports injuries: Moving from risk factor identification to injury pattern recognition-narrative review and new concept. *British Journal of Sports Medicine, 50*, 1309–1314.

Bosco, C., Komi, P. V., & Ito, A. (1981). Prestretch potentiation of human skeletal muscle during ballistic movement. *Acta Physiologica Scandinavica, 111*(2), 135–140.

Bourgeois, F., McGuigan, M. R., Gill, N. D., & Gamble, G. (2017). Physical characteristics and performance in change of direction tasks: A brief review and training considerations *Journal of Australian Strength and Conditioning, 25*(5), 104–117.

Brophy, R. H., Stepan, J. G., Silvers, H. J., & Mandelbaum, B. R. (2015). Defending puts the anterior cruciate ligament at risk during soccer: A gender-based analysis. *Sports Health*, 7(3), 244–249.

Brown, S. R., Brughelli, M., & Hume, P. A. (2014). Knee mechanics during planned and unplanned sidestepping: A systematic review and meta-analysis. *Sports Medicine, 44*(11), 1573–1588.

Chan, M. S., Huang, C. F., Chang, J. H., & Kernozek, T. W. (2009). Kinematics and kinetics of knee and hip position of female basketball players during side-step cutting with and without dribbling. *Journal of Medical and Biological Engineering, 29*(4), 178–183.

Chaudhari, A. M., Hearn, B. K., & Andriacchi, T. P. (2005). Sport-dependent variations in arm position during single-limb landing influence knee loading implications for anterior cruciate ligament injury. *The American Journal of Sports Medicine, 33*(6), 824–830.

Cochrane, J. L., Lloyd, D. G., Buttfield, A., Seward, H., & McGivern, J. (2007). Characteristics of anterior cruciate ligament injuries in Australian football. *Journal of Science and Medicine in Sport, 10*(2), 96–104.

Collins, J. D., Almonroeder, T. G., Ebersole, K. T., & O'connor, K. M. (2016). The effects of fatigue and anticipation on the mechanics of the knee during cutting in female athletes. *Clinical Biomechanics, 35*, 62–67.

Dai, B., Garrett, W. E., Gross, M. T., Padua, D. A., Queen, R. M., & Yu, B. (2016). The effect of performance demands on lower extremity biomechanics during landing and cutting tasks. *Journal of Sport and Health Science, 43*(9), 1680–1608.

Daniels, K. A., Drake, E., King, E., & Strike, S. (2021). Whole-body change-of-direction task execution asymmetries after anterior cruciate ligament reconstruction. *Journal of Applied Biomechanics, 1*(aop), 1–6.

David, S., Komnik, I., Peters, M., Funken, J., & Potthast, W. (2017). Identification and risk estimation of movement strategies during cutting maneuvers. *Journal of Science and Medicine in Sport, 20*(12), 1075–1080.

David, S., Mundt, M., Komnik, I., & Potthast, W. (2018). Understanding cutting maneuvers–The mechanical consequence of preparatory strategies and foot strike pattern. *Human Movement Science, 62*, 202–210.

Davies, W. T., Ryu, J. H., Graham-Smith, P., Goodwin, J. E., & Cleather, D. J. (2022). Stronger subjects select a movement pattern that may reduce anterior cruciate ligament loading during cutting. *The Journal of Strength & Conditioning Research, 36*, 1853–1859.

Dempsey, A. R., Lloyd, D. G., Elliott, B. C., Steele, J. R., & Munro, B. J. (2009). Changing sidestep cutting technique reduces knee valgus loading. *The American Journal of Sports Medicine, 37*(11), 2194–2200.

Dempsey, A. R., Lloyd, D. G., Elliott, B. C., Steele, J. R., Munro, B. J., & Russo, K. A. (2007). The effect of technique change on knee loads during sidestep cutting. *Medicine & Science in Sports & Exercise, 39*(10), 1765–1773.

Devita, P., & Skelly, W. A. (1992). Effect of landing stiffness on joint kinetics and energetics in the lower extremity. *Medicine & Science in Sports & Exercise, 24*(1), 108–115.

Donelon, T. A., Dos'Santos, T., Pitchers, G., Brown, M., & Jones, P. A. (2020). Biomechanical determinants of knee joint loads associated with increased anterior cruciate ligament loading during cutting: A systematic review and technical framework. *Sports Medicine-Open, 6*(1), 1–21.

Donnelly, C., Elliott, B. C., Ackland, T. R., Doyle, T. L., Beiser, T. F., Finch, C. F., Cochrane, J., Dempsey, A. R., & Lloyd, D. (2012). An anterior cruciate ligament injury prevention framework: Incorporating the recent evidence. *Research in Sports Medicine, 20*(3–4), 239–262.

Donnelly, C. J., Chinnasee, C., Weir, G., Sasimontonkul, S., & Alderson, J. (2017). Joint dynamics of rear- and fore-foot unplanned sidestepping. *Journal of Science and Medicine in Sport, 20*(1), 32–37.

Donnelly, C. J., Lloyd, D. G., Elliott, B. C., & Reinbolt, J. A. (2012). Optimizing whole-body kinematics to minimize valgus knee loading during sidestepping: Implications for ACL injury risk. *Journal of Biomechanics, 45*(8), 1491–1497.

Dos'Santos, T. (2020). *Biomechanical determinants of injury risk and performance during change of direction: Implications for screening and intervention*. University of Salford.

Dos'Santos, T., & Jones, P. (2022). 18 Training for change of direction and agility. *Advanced Strength and Conditioning: An Evidence-based Approach*, 328.

Dos'Santos, T., McBurnie, A., Donelon, T., Thomas, C., Comfort, P., & Jones, P. A. (2019a). A qualitative screening tool to identify athletes with "high-risk" movement mechanics during cutting: The cutting movement assessment score (CMAS). *Physical Therapy in Sport, 38*, 152–161.

Dos'Santos, T., McBurnie, A., Thomas, C., Comfort, P., & Jones, P. A. (2019b). Biomechanical comparison of cutting techniques: A review and practical applications. *Strength & Conditioning Journal, 41*(4), 40–54.

Dos'Santos, T., McBurnie, A., Thomas, C., Comfort, P., & Jones, P. A. (2020). Biomechanical determinants of the modified and traditional 505 change of direction speed test. *The Journal of Strength & Conditioning Research, 34*(5), 1285–1296.

Dos'Santos, T., Thomas, C., Comfort, P., & Jones, P. A. (2018). The effect of angle and velocity on change of direction biomechanics: An angle-velocity trade-off. *Sports Medicine, 48*(10), 2235–2253.

Dos'Santos, T., Thomas, C., Comfort, P., & Jones, P. A. (2019a). The effect of training interventions on change of direction biomechanics associated with increased anterior cruciate ligament loading: A scoping review. *Sports Medicine*, *49*(12), 1837–1859. https://doi.org/10.1007/s40279-019-01171-0

Dos'Santos, T., Thomas, C., Comfort, P., & Jones, P. A. (2019b). The role of the penultimate foot contact during change of direction: Implications on performance and risk of injury. *Strength & Conditioning Journal*, *41*(1), 87–104.

Dos'Santos, T., Thomas, C., Comfort, P., & Jones, P. A. (2021a). Biomechanical effects of a 6-week change-of-direction technique modification intervention on anterior cruciate ligament injury risk. *The Journal of Strength & Conditioning Research*, *35*(8), 2133–2144.

Dos'Santos, T., Thomas, C., Comfort, P., & Jones, P. A. (2021b). Biomechanical effects of a 6-week change of direction speed and technique modification intervention: Implications for change of direction side step performance. *Journal of Strength and Conditioning Research*, *36*, 2780–2791.

Dos'Santos, T., Thomas, C., & Jones, P. A. (2021a). How early should you brake during a 180° turn? A kinetic comparison of the antepenultimate, penultimate, and final foot contacts during a 505 change of direction speed test. *Journal of Sports Sciences*, *39*(4), 395–405.

Dos'Santos, T., Thomas, C., & Jones, P. A. (2021b). The effect of angle on change of direction biomechanics: Comparison and inter-task relationships. *Journal of Sports Sciences*, *39*(12), 2618–2631.

Dos'Santos, T., Thomas, C., Jones, P. A., & Comfort, P. (2017). Mechanical determinants of faster change of direction speed performance in male athletes. *The Journal of Strength & Conditioning Research*, *31*, 696–705.

Dos'Santos, T., Thomas, C., McBurnie, A., Comfort, P., & Jones, P. A. (2021). Biomechanical determinants of performance and injury risk during cutting: A performance-injury conflict? *Sports Medicine*, *51*, 1983–1998.

Dos'Santos, T., Thomas, C., McBurnie, A., Donelon, T., Herrington, L., & Jones, P. A. (2021). The Cutting Movement Assessment Score (CMAS) qualitative screening tool: Application to mitigate anterior cruciate ligament injury risk during cutting. *Biomechanics*, *1*(1), 83–101.

Dupré, T., Tryba, J., & Potthast, W. (2021). Muscle activity of cutting manoeuvres and soccer inside passing suggests an increased groin injury risk during these movements. *Scientific Reports*, *11*(1), 1–9.

Edwards, W. B. (2018). Modeling overuse injuries in sport as a mechanical fatigue phenomenon. *Exercise and Sport Sciences Reviews*, *46*(4), 224–231.

Falch, H. N., Rædergård, H. G., & van den Tillaar, R. (2019). Effect of different physical training forms on change of direction ability: A systematic review and meta-analysis. *Sports Medicine-Open*, *5*(1), 53.

Fedie, R., Carlstedt, K., Willson, J. D., & Kernozek, T. W. (2010). Effect of attending to a ball during a side-cut maneuver on lower extremity biomechanics in male and female athletes. *Sports Biomechanics*, *9*(3), 165–177.

Fong, D. T.-P., Hong, Y., Shima, Y., Krosshaug, T., Yung, P. S.-H., & Chan, K.-M. (2009). Biomechanics of supination ankle sprain: A case report of an accidental injury event in the laboratory. *The American Journal of Sports Medicine*, *37*(4), 822–827.

Fox, A. S. (2018). Change-of-direction biomechanics: Is what's best for anterior cruciate ligament injury prevention also best for performance? *Sports Medicine*, *48*(8), 1799–1807.

Fox, A. S., Spittle, M., Otago, L., & Saunders, N. (2014). Offensive agility techniques performed during international netball competition. *International Journal of Sports Science & Coaching*, *9*(3), 543–552.

Fraser, J. J., Feger, M. A., & Hertel, J. (2016). Clinical commentary on midfoot and forefoot involvement in lateral ankle sprains and chronic ankle instability. Part 2: Clinical considerations. *International Journal of Sports Physical Therapy*, *11*(7), 1191.

Giesche, F., Stief, F., Groneberg, D. A., & Wilke, J. (2021). Effect of unplanned athletic movement on knee mechanics: A systematic review with multilevel meta-analysis. *British Journal of Sports Medicine*, *55*(23), 1366–1378.

Gokeler, A., Benjaminse, A., Della Villa, F., Tosarelli, F., Verhagen, E., & Baumeister, J. (2021). Anterior cruciate ligament injury mechanisms through a neurocognition lens: Implications for injury screening. *BMJ Open Sport & Exercise Medicine*, 7(2), e001091.

Graham-Smith, P., Atkinson, L., Barlow, R., & Jones, P. (2009). Braking characteristics and load distribution in 180 degree turns. (Ed.),^(Eds.). *Proceedings of the 5th Annual UKSCA Conference*.

Graham-Smith, P., Rumpf, M., & Jones, P. A. (2018, September 10–14). Assessment of deceleration ability and relationship to approach speed and eccentric strength. (Ed.),^(Eds.). *ISBS Proceedings Archive*, Auckland, New Zealand.

Green, B. S., Blake, C., & Caulfield, B. M. (2011). A comparison of cutting technique performance in rugby union players. *The Journal of Strength & Conditioning Research, 25*(10), 2668–2680.

Hader, K., Mendez-Villanueva, A., Palazzi, D., Ahmaidi, S., & Buchheit, M. (2016). Metabolic power requirement of change of direction speed in young soccer players: Not All is what it seems. *PloS one, 11*(3), e0149839.

Hader, K., Palazzi, D., & Buchheit, M. (2015). Change of direction speed in soccer: How much braking is enough? *Kineziologija, 47*(1), 67–74.

Havens, K. L., & Sigward, S. M. (2014). Whole body mechanics differ among running and cutting maneuvers in skilled athletes. *Gait & Posture, 42*(3), 240–245.

Havens, K. L., & Sigward, S. M. (2015a). Cutting mechanics: Relation to performance and anterior cruciate ligament injury risk. *Medicine and Science in Sports and Exercise, 47*(4), 818–824.

Havens, K. L., & Sigward, S. M. (2015b). Joint and segmental mechanics differ between cutting maneuvers in skilled athletes. *Gait & Posture, 41*(1), 33–38.

Hewett, T. (2017). Preventive biomechanics: A paradigm shift with a translational approach to biomechanics. *American Journal of Sports Medicine, 45*(11), 2654–2664.

Hewett, T., & Myer, G. D. (2011). The mechanistic connection between the trunk, knee, and anterior cruciate ligament injury. *Exercise and Sport Sciences Reviews, 39*(4), 161.

Hewett, T., Myer, G. D., Ford, K. R., Heidt, R. S., Colosimo, A. J., McLean, S. G., Van den Bogert, A. J., Paterno, M. V., & Succop, P. (2005). Biomechanical measures of neuromuscular control and valgus loading of the knee predict anterior cruciate ligament injury risk in female athletes a prospective study. *The American Journal of Sports Medicine, 33*(4), 492–501.

Hughes, G., & Dai, B. (2021). The influence of decision making and divided attention on lower limb biomechanics associated with anterior cruciate ligament injury: A narrative review. *Sports Biomechanics*, 1–16.

Hunter, J. P., Marshall, R. N., & McNair, P. J. (2005). Relationships between ground reaction force impulse and kinematics of sprint-running acceleration. *Journal of Applied Biomechanics, 21*(1), 31–43.

Jamison, S. T., Pan, X., & Chaudhari, A. M. W. (2012). Knee moments during run-to-cut maneuvers are associated with lateral trunk positioning. *Journal of Biomechanics, 45*(11), 1881–1885.

Jarvis, P., Turner, A., Read, P., & Bishop, C. (2021). Reactive strength index and its associations with measures of physical and sports performance: A systematic review with meta-analysis. *Sports Medicine*, 1–30.

Jeffreys, I. (2011). A task-based approach to developing context-specific agility. *Strength & Conditioning Journal, 33*(4), 52–59.

Johnston, J. T., Mandelbaum, B. R., Schub, D., Rodeo, S. A., Matava, M. J., Silvers, H. J., Cole, B. J., ElAttrache, N. S., McAdams, T. R., & Brophy, R. H. (2018). Video analysis of anterior cruciate ligament tears in professional American football athletes. *The American Journal of Sports Medicine, 46*(4), 862–868.

Jones, P. A., Barber, O. R., & Smith, L. C. (2015). Changing pivoting technique reduces knee valgus moments. Free communication. *Journal of Sports Sciences (BASES Annual Conference), 33*(Supplement 1), S62.

Jones, P. A., Dos'Santos, T., McMahon, J. J., & Graham-Smith, P. (2019). Contribution of eccentric strength to cutting performance in female soccer players. *Journal of Strength and Conditioning Research*, Published ahead of print

Jones, P. A., Herrington, L., & Graham-Smith, P. (2015). Technique determinants of knee joint loads during cutting in female soccer players. *Human Movement Science, 42*, 203–211.

Jones, P. A., Herrington, L., & Graham-Smith, P. (2016a). Braking characteristics during cutting and pivoting in female soccer players. *Journal of Electromyography and Kinesiology, 30*, 46–54.

Jones, P. A., Herrington, L., & Graham-Smith, P. (2016b). Technique determinants of knee abduction moments during pivoting in female soccer players. *Clinical Biomechanics, 31*, 107–112.

Jones, P. A., McBurnie, A., & Dos'Santos, T. (2021). Using qualitative technique analysis to evaluate and develop technique of agility actions with your athletes. *Professional Strength and Conditioning*(63), 25–33.

Jones, P. A., Thomas, C., Dos'Santos, T., McMahon, J., & Graham-Smith, P. (2017). The role of eccentric strength in 180° turns in female soccer players. *Sports, 5*(2), 42. www.mdpi.com/2075-4663/5/2/42

Kai, T., Hirai, S., Anbe, Y., & Takai, Y. (2021). A new approach to quantify angles and time of changes-of-direction during soccer matches. *PloS One, 16*(5), e0251292.

Kalkhoven, J. T., Watsford, M. L., Coutts, A. J., Edwards, W. B., & Impellizzeri, F. M. (2021). Training load and injury: Causal pathways and future directions. *Sports Medicine, 51*(6), 1137–1150.

Kelly, L. A., Farris, D. J., Cresswell, A. G., & Lichtwark, G. A. (2019). Intrinsic foot muscles contribute to elastic energy storage and return in the human foot. *Journal of Applied Physiology, 126*(1), 231–238.

Ken-ichi, K., Tomoya, H., Michio, Y., Yu, K., Noriko, H., Takahito, T., & Kazuo, F. (2019). Factors affecting the 180-degree change-of-direction speed in youth male soccer players. *Human Performance Measurement, 16*, 1–10.

Kerin, F., Farrell, G., Tierney, P., Persson, U. M., De Vito, G., & Delahunt, E. (2022). Its not all about sprinting: Mechanisms of acute hamstring strain injuries in professional male rugby union – a systematic visual video analysis. *British Journal of Sports Medicine*, Published ahead of print.

Khayambashi, K., Ghoddosi, N., Straub, R. K., & Powers, C. M. (2016). Hip muscle strength predicts noncontact anterior cruciate ligament injury in male and female athletes: A prospective study. *The American Journal of Sports Medicine, 44*(2), 355–361.

Kiapour, A. M., Demetropoulos, C. K., Kiapour, A., Quatman, C. E., Wordeman, S. C., Goel, V. K., & Hewett, T. E. (2016). Strain response of the anterior cruciate ligament to uniplanar and multiplanar loads during simulated landings: Implications for injury mechanism. *The American Journal of Sports Medicine, 44*(8), 2087–2096.

Kim, J. H., Lee, K.-K., Kong, S. J., An, K. O., Jeong, J. H., & Lee, Y. S. (2014). Effect of anticipation on lower extremity biomechanics during side-and cross-cutting maneuvers in young soccer players. *The American Journal of Sports Medicine, 42*(8), 1985–1992.

Kimura, Y., Ishibashi, Y., Tsuda, E., Yamamoto, Y., Tsukada, H., & Toh, S. (2010). Mechanisms for anterior cruciate ligament injuries in badminton. *British Journal of Sports Medicine, 44*(15), 1124–1127.

King, E., Franklyn-Miller, A., Richter, C., O'Reilly, E., Doolan, M., Moran, K., Strike, S., & Falvey, É. (2018). Clinical and biomechanical outcomes of rehabilitation targeting intersegmental control in athletic groin pain: Prospective cohort of 205 patients. *British Journal of Sports Medicine, 52*(16), 1054–1062.

Koga, H., Nakamae, A., Shima, Y., Iwasa, J., Myklebust, G., Engebretsen, L., Bahr, R., & Krosshaug, T. (2010). Mechanisms for noncontact anterior cruciate ligament injuries knee joint kinematics in 10 injury situations from female team handball and basketball. *The American Journal of Sports Medicine, 38*(11), 2218–2225.

Konradsen, L., & Ravn, J. B. (1991). Prolonged peroneal reaction time in ankle instability. *International Journal of Sports Medicine, 12*(03), 290–292.

Kristianslund, E., Faul, O., Bahr, R., Myklebust, G., & Krosshaug, T. (2014). Sidestep cutting technique and knee abduction loading: Implications for ACL prevention exercises. *British Journal of Sports Medicine, 48*(9), 779–783.

Krosshaug, T., Nakamae, A., Boden, B. P., Engebretsen, L., Smith, G., Slauterbeck, J. R., Hewett, T. E., & Bahr, R. (2007). Mechanisms of anterior cruciate ligament injury in basketball video analysis of 39 cases. *The American Journal of Sports Medicine, 35*(3), 359–367.

Lee, M. J. C., Lloyd, D. G., Lay, B. S., Bourke, P. D., & Alderson, J. A. (2013). Effects of different visual stimuli on postures and knee moments during sidestepping. *Medicine & Science in Sports & Exercise, 45*(9), 1740–1748.

Lee, M. J. C., Lloyd, D. G., Lay, B. S., Bourke, P. D., & Alderson, J. A. (2017). Different visual stimuli affect body reorientation strategies during sidestepping. *Scandinavian Journal of Medicine & Science in Sports, 27*(5), 492–500.

Lipps, D. B., Wojtys, E. M., & Ashton-Miller, J. A. (2013). Anterior cruciate ligament fatigue failures in knees subjected to repeated simulated pivot landings. *The American Journal of Sports Medicine, 41*(5), 1058–1066.

Lloyd, D. G., & Buchanan, T. S. (2001). Strategies of muscular support of varus and valgus isometric loads at the human knee. *Journal of Biomechanics, 34*(10), 1257–1267.

Lum, D., & Barbosa, T. M. (2019). Brief review: Effects of isometric strength training on strength and dynamic performance. *International Journal of Sports Medicine*, *40*(06), 363–375.

Maniar, N., Schache, A. G., Cole, M. H., & Opar, D. A. (2019). Lower-limb muscle function during sidestep cutting. *Journal of Biomechanics*, *82*, 186–192.

Maniar, N., Schache, A. G., Pizzolato, C., & Opar, D. A. (2020). Muscle contributions to tibiofemoral shear forces and valgus and rotational joint moments during single leg drop landing. *Scandinavian Journal of Medicine & Science in Sports*, *30*, 1664–1674.

Maniar, N., Schache, A. G., Sritharan, P., & Opar, D. A. (2018). Non-knee-spanning muscles contribute to tibiofemoral shear as well as valgus and rotational joint reaction moments during unanticipated sidestep cutting. *Scientific Reports*, *8*(1), 2501.

Markolf, K. L., Burchfield, D. M., Shapiro, M. M., Shepard, M. F., Finerman, G. A. M., & Slauterbeck, J. L. (1995). Combined knee loading states that generate high anterior cruciate ligament forces. *Journal of Orthopaedic Research*, *13*(6), 930–935.

Markolf, K. L., Gorek, J. F., Kabo, J. M., & Shapiro, M. S. (1990). Direct measurement of resultant forces in the anterior cruciate ligament. An in vitro study performed with a new experimental technique. *Journal of Bone and Joint Surgery. American*, *72*(4), 557–567.

Markovic, G., Šarabon, N., Pausic, J., & Hadžić, V. (2020). Adductor muscles strength and strength asymmetry as risk factors for groin injuries among professional soccer players: A prospective study. *International Journal of Environmental Research and Public Health*, *17*(14), 4946.

Marshall, B. M., Franklyn-Miller, A. D., King, E. A., Moran, K. A., Strike, S., & Falvey, A. (2014). Biomechanical factors associated with time to complete a change of direction cutting maneuver. *The Journal of Strength & Conditioning Research*, *28*(10), 2845–2851.

Mateus, R. B., Ferrer-Roca, V., João, F., & Veloso, A. P. (2020). Muscle contributions to maximal single-leg forward braking and backward acceleration in elite athletes. *Journal of Biomechanics*, *112*, 110047.

McBurnie, A., & Dos'Santos, T. (2022). Multi-directional speed in youth soccer players: Theoretical underpinnings. *Strength & Conditioning Journal*, *44*(1), 15–33.

McBurnie, A., Dos'Santos, T., & Jones, P. A. (2021). Biomechanical associates of performance and knee joint loads during an 70–90° cutting maneuver in sub-elite soccer players. *Journal of Strength and Conditioning Research*, *35*(11), 3190–3198.

McBurnie, A., Harper, D. J., Jones, P. A., & Dos'Santos, T. (2021). Deceleration training in team sports: Another potential 'vaccine' for sports-related injury? *Sports Medicine*, 1–12.

McKeon, P. O., Hertel, J., Bramble, D., & Davis, I. (2015). The foot core system: A new paradigm for understanding intrinsic foot muscle function. *British Journal of Sports Medicine*, *49*(5), 290–290.

McLean, S. G., Huang, X., & van den Bogert, A. J. (2005). Association between lower extremity posture at contact and peak knee valgus moment during sidestepping: Implications for ACL injury. *Clinical Biomechanics*, *20*(8), 863–870.

McLean, S. G., Lipfert, S. W., & Van den Bogert, A. J. (2004). Effect of gender and defensive opponent on the biomechanics of sidestep cutting. *Medicine and Science in Sports and Exercise*, *36*(6), 1008–1016.

Meeuwisse, W. H., Tyreman, H., Hagel, B., & Emery, C. (2007). A dynamic model of etiology in sport injury: The recursive nature of risk and causation. *Clinical Journal of Sport Medicine*, *17*(3), 215–219.

Mendiguchia, J., Ford, K. R., Quatman, C. E., Alentorn-Geli, E., & Hewett, T. E. (2011). Sex differences in proximal control of the knee joint. *Sports Medicine*, *41*(7), 541–557. https://doi.org/10.2165/11589140-000000000-00000

Montgomery, C., Blackburn, J., Withers, D., Tierney, G., Moran, C., & Simms, C. (2018). Mechanisms of ACL injury in professional rugby union: A systematic video analysis of 36 cases. *British Journal of Sports Medicine*, *52*(15), 944–1001.

Moreno-Pérez, V., Travassos, B., Calado, A., Gonzalo-Skok, O., Del Coso, J., & Mendez-Villanueva, A. (2019). Adductor squeeze test and groin injuries in elite football players: A prospective study. *Physical Therapy in Sport*, *37*, 54–59.

Morgan, O. J., Drust, B., Ade, J. D., & Robinson, M. A. (2021). Change of direction frequency off the ball: New perspectives in elite youth soccer. *Science and Medicine in Football*, *6*(4), 473–482. https://doi.org/10.1080/24733938.2021.1986635

Mornieux, G., Gehring, D., Fürst, P., & Gollhofer, A. (2014). Anticipatory postural adjustments during cutting manoeuvres in football and their consequences for knee injury risk. *Journal of Sports Sciences*, *32*(13), 1255–1262.

Neptune, R. R., Wright, I. C., & Van Den Bogert, A. J. (1999). Muscle coordination and function during cutting movements. *Medicine and Science in Sports and Exercise*, *31*, 294–302.

Nimphius, S. (2017). Training change of direction and agility. In A. Turner & P. Comfort (Eds.), *Advanced Strength and Conditioning* (pp. 291–308). Routledge.

Nimphius, S., Callaghan, S. J., Bezodis, N. E., & Lockie, R. G. (2017). Change of direction and agility tests: Challenging our current measures of performance. *Strength & Conditioning Journal*, *40*(1), 26–38.

Nimphius, S., Geib, G., Spiteri, T., & Carlisle, D. (2013). "Change of direction deficit" measurement in Division I American football players. *The Journal of Australian Strength and Conditioning*, *21*(S2), 115–117.

Olsen, O.-E., Myklebust, G., Engebretsen, L., & Bahr, R. (2004). Injury mechanisms for anterior cruciate ligament injuries in team handball a systematic video analysis. *The American Journal of Sports Medicine*, *32*(4), 1002–1012.

Oranchuk, D. J., Storey, A. G., Nelson, A. R., & Cronin, J. B. (2019). Isometric training and long-term adaptations: Effects of muscle length, intensity, and intent: A systematic review. *Scandinavian Journal of Medicine & Science in Sports*, *29*(4), 484–503.

Padua, D. A., DiStefano, L. J., Hewett, T. E., Garrett, W. E., Marshall, S. W., Golden, G. M., Shultz, S. J., & Sigward, S. M. (2018). National athletic trainers' association position statement: Prevention of anterior cruciate ligament injury. *Journal of Athletic Training*, *53*, 5–19.

Paul, D. J., Gabbett, T. J., & Nassis, G. P. (2016). Agility in team sports: Testing, training and factors affecting performance. *Sports Medicine*, *46*(3), 421–442.

Plisk, S. S. (2000). Speed, agility, and speed-endurance development. *Essentials of Strength Training and Conditioning*, 471–491.

Rayner, R. (2020). *Training and Testing of 1v1 Agility in Australian Football*. Federaration University Australia.

Rovan, K., Kugovnik, O., Holmberg, L. J., & Supej, M. (2014). The steps needed to perform acceleration and turning at different approach speeds. *Kinesiologia Slovenica*, *20*(1), 38–50.

Sankey, S. P., Robinson, M. A., & Vanrenterghem, J. (2020). Whole-body dynamic stability in side cutting: Implications for markers of lower limb injury risk and change of direction performance. *Journal of Biomechanics*, 109711.

Santoro, E., Tessitore, A., Liu, C., Chen, C.-H., Khemtong, C., Mandorino, M., Lee, Y.-H., & Condello, G. (2021). The biomechanical characterization of the turning phase during a 180° change of direction. *International Journal of Environmental Research and Public Health*, *18*(11), 5519.

Sasaki, S., Nagano, Y., Kaneko, S., Sakurai, T., & Fukubayashi, T. (2011). The relationship between performance and trunk movement during change of direction. *Journal of Sports Science & Medicine*, *10*(1), 112–118.

Sayers, M. G. L. (2015). Influence of test distance on change of direction speed test results. *The Journal of Strength & Conditioning Research*, *29*(9), 2412–2416.

Schreurs, M. J., Benjaminse, A., & Lemmink, K. A. (2017). Sharper angle, higher risk? The effect of cutting angle on knee mechanics in invasion sport athletes. *Journal of Biomechanics*, *63*, 144–150.

Serner, A., Mosler, A. B., Tol, J. L., Bahr, R., & Weir, A. (2019). Mechanisms of acute adductor longus injuries in male football players: A systematic visual video analysis. *British Journal of Sports Medicine*, *53*(3), 158–164.

Shin, C. S., Chaudhari, A. M., & Andriacchi, T. P. (2009). The effect of isolated valgus moments on ACL strain during single-leg landing: A simulation study. *Journal of Biomechanics*, *42*(3), 280–285.

Shin, C. S., Chaudhari, A. M., & Andriacchi, T. P. (2011). Valgus plus internal rotation moments increase anterior cruciate ligament strain more than either alone. *Medicine and Science in Sports and Exercise*, *43*(8), 1484–1491.

Sigward, S. M., Cesar, G. M., & Havens, K. L. (2015). Predictors of frontal plane knee moments during side-step cutting to 45 and 110 degrees in men and women: Implications for anterior cruciate ligament injury. *Clinical Journal of Sport Medicine*, *25*(6), 529–534.

Sigward, S. M., & Powers, C. M. (2007). Loading characteristics of females exhibiting excessive valgus moments during cutting. *Clinical Biomechanics*, *22*(7), 827–833.

Sinclair, J., Brooks, D., & Stainton, P. (2019). Sex differences in ACL loading and strain during typical athletic movements: A musculoskeletal simulation analysis. *European Journal of Applied Physiology, 119*(3), 713–721.

Slaughter, P. R., & Adamczyk, P. G. (2020). Tracking quantitative characteristics of cutting maneuvers with wearable movement sensors during competitive women's ultimate frisbee games. *Sensors, 20*(22), 6508.

Smeets, A., Malfait, B., Dingenen, B., Robinson, M. A., Vanrenterghem, J., Peers, K., Nijs, S., Vereecken, S., Staes, F., & Verschueren, S. (2019). Is knee neuromuscular activity related to anterior cruciate ligament injury risk? A pilot study. *The Knee, 26*(1), 40–51.

Spiteri, T., Cochrane, J. L., Hart, N. H., Haff, G. G., & Nimphius, S. (2013). Effect of strength on plant foot kinetics and kinematics during a change of direction task. *European Journal of Sport Science, 13*(6), 646–652.

Spiteri, T., Newton, R. U., Binetti, M., Hart, N. H., Sheppard, J. M., & Nimphius, S. (2015). Mechanical determinants of faster change of direction and agility performance in female basketball athletes. *The Journal of Strength & Conditioning Research, 28*(3), 2205–2214. https://doi.org/10.1519/jsc.0000000000000876

Spiteri, T., Nimphius, S., Hart, N. H., Specos, C., Sheppard, J. M., & Newton, R. U. (2014). The contribution of strength characteristics to change of direction and agility performance in female basketball athletes. *The Journal of Strength & Conditioning Research, 28*(9), 2415–2423.

Staynor, J., Donnelly, C., & Alderson, J. (2018). Pelvis obliquity in sidestepping: Implications for dynamic trunk control. *Journal of Science and Medicine in Sport, 21*, S17.

Suchomel, T. J., Nimphius, S., Bellon, C. R., & Stone, M. H. (2018). The Importance of muscular strength: Training considerations. *Sports Medicine, 48*(4), 765–785.

Thomas, C., Dos'Santos, T., Comfort, P., & Jones, P. A. (2020). Effect of asymmetry on biomechanical characteristics during 180° change of direction. *The Journal of Strength & Conditioning Research, 34*(5), 1297–1306.

Tourillon, R., Gojanovic, B., & Fourchet, F. (2019). How to evaluate and improve foot strength in athletes: An update. *Frontiers in Sports and Active Living, 1*, 46.

Ueno, R., Navacchia, A., DiCesare, C. A., Ford, K. R., Myer, G. D., Ishida, T., Tohyama, H., & Hewett, T. E. (2020). Knee abduction moment is predicted by lower gluteus Medius force and larger vertical and lateral ground reaction forces during drop vertical jump in female athletes. *Journal of Biomechanics*, 109669.

Vanrenterghem, J., Venables, E., Pataky, T., & Robinson, M. A. (2012). The effect of running speed on knee mechanical loading in females during side cutting. *Journal of Biomechanics, 45*(14), 2444–2449.

Wade, F. E., Mok, K.-M., & Fong, D. T.-P. (2018). Kinematic analysis of a televised medial ankle sprain. *Asia-Pacific Journal of Sports Medicine, Arthroscopy, Rehabilitation and Technology, 12*, 12–16.

Warrener, A., Tamai, R., & Lieberman, D. E. (2021). The effect of trunk flexion angle on lower limb mechanics during running. *Human Movement Science, 78*, 102817.

Weinhandl, J. T., Earl-Boehm, J. E., Ebersole, K. T., Huddleston, W. E., Armstrong, B. S., & O'connor, K. M. (2013). Anticipatory effects on anterior cruciate ligament loading during sidestep cutting. *Clinical Biomechanics, 28*(6), 655–663.

Weinhandl, J. T., Earl-Boehm, J. E., Ebersole, K. T., Huddleston, W. E., Armstrong, B. S., & O'connor, K. M. (2014). Reduced hamstring strength increases anterior cruciate ligament loading during anticipated sidestep cutting. *Clinical Biomechanics, 29*(7), 752–759.

Weir, G. (2022). Anterior cruciate ligament injury prevention in sport: Biomechanically informed approaches. *Sports Biomechanics*, 1–21.

Weir, G., Alderson, J., Smailes, N., Elliott, B., & Donnelly, C. (2019). A reliable video-based acl injury screening tool for female team sport athletes. *International Journal of Sports Medicine, 40*(3), 191–199.

Welch, N., Richter, C., Franklyn-Miller, A., & Moran, K. (2019). Principal component analysis of the associations between kinetic variables in cutting and jumping, and cutting performance outcome. *Journal of Strength and Conditioning Research*, Published ahead of print.

Welch, N., Richter, C., Franklyn-Miller, A., & Moran, K. (2021). Principal component analysis of the biomechanical factors associated with performance during cutting. *Journal of Strength and Conditioning Research, 35*(6), 1715–1723.

Wheeler, K. W., Askew, C. D., & Sayers, M. G. (2010). Effective attacking strategies in rugby union. *European Journal of Sport Science, 10*(4), 237–242. https://doi.org/10.1080/17461391.2010.482595

Wheeler, K. W., & Sayers, M. G. L. (2010). Modification of agility running technique in reaction to a defender in rugby union. *Journal of Sports Science & Medicine, 9*(3), 445–451.

Whyte, E. F., Richter, C., O'connor, S., & Moran, K. A. (2018). The effect of high intensity exercise and anticipation on trunk and lower limb biomechanics during a crossover cutting manoeuvre. *Journal of Sports Sciences, 36*(8), 889–900.

Withrow, T. J., Huston, L. J., Wojtys, E. M., & Ashton-Miller, J. A. (2006). The relationship between quadriceps muscle force, knee flexion, and anterior cruciate ligament strain in an in vitro simulated jump landing. *The American Journal of Sports Medicine, 34*(2), 269–274.

Wyatt, H., Weir, G., van Emmerik, R., Jewell, C., & Hamill, J. (2019). Whole-body control of anticipated and unanticipated sidestep manoeuvres in female and male team sport athletes. *Journal of Sports Sciences, 37*(19), 2269–2269.

Young, W. B., Dawson, B., & Henry, G. J. (2015). Agility and change-of-direction speed are independent skills: Implications for training for agility in invasion sports. *International Journal of Sports Science and Coaching, 10*(1), 159–169.

Young, W. B., & Farrow, D. (2013). The importance of a sport-specific stimulus for training agility. *Strength & Conditioning Journal, 35*(2), 39–43.

Young, W. B., Farrow, D., Pyne, D., McGregor, W., & Handke, T. (2011). Validity and reliability of agility tests in junior Australian football players. *The Journal of Strength & Conditioning Research, 25*(12), 3399–3403.

Young, W. B., James, R., & Montgomery, I. (2002). Is muscle power related to running speed with changes of direction? *Journal of Sports Medicine and Physical Fitness, 42*(3), 282–288.

Yuasa, Y., Kurihara, T., & Isaka, T. (2018). Relationship between toe muscular strength and the ability to change direction in athletes. *Journal of Human Kinetics, 64*(1), 47–55.

Zazulak, B. T., Hewett, T. E., Reeves, N. P., Goldberg, B., & Cholewicki, J. (2007). Deficits in neuromuscular control of the trunk predict knee injury risk: Prospective biomechanical-epidemiologic study. *The American Journal of Sports Medicine, 35*(7), 1123–1130.

Zazulak, B. T., Hewett, T. E., Reeves, N. P., Goldberg, B., & Cholewicki, J. (2007). The effects of core proprioception on knee injury: A prospective biomechanical-epidemiological study. *The American Journal of Sports Medicine, 35*(3), 368–373. https://doi.org/10.1177/0363546506297909

Zebis, M. K., Andersen, L. L., Bencke, J., Kjaer, M., & Aagaard, P. (2009). Identification of athletes at future risk of anterior cruciate ligament ruptures by neuromuscular screening. *The American Journal of Sports Medicine, 37*(10), 1967–1973.

Zhang, S.-N., Bates, B. T., & Dufek, J. S. (2000). Contributions of lower extremity joints to energy dissipation during landings. *Medicine and Science in Sports and Exercise, 32*(4), 812–819.

5

DECELERATION IN SPORT

Incidence, Demands, and Implications for Training

Damian Harper

Introduction

Deceleration is mechanically defined as decreasing velocity with respect to time and is fundamental to decreasing whole-body momentum (Winter et al., 2016). Therefore, in sports with repeated multidirectional speed demands, deceleration can be considered a critical component to achieving effective performance (Winter et al., 2016). Despite this fact, training-specific research and training practice in general has historically focused on acceleration and high-speed running capacities, with much less research and time devoted to deceleration (Harper & Kiely, 2018). As further illustration, at the time of writing, this is the very first chapter in the myriad of sports performance books purely devoted to deceleration! With evident evolutions and potential future evolutions in multidirectional sports likely leading to increased frequency of accelerations and high-speed running actions (Harper, Sandford, et al., 2021; Nassis et al., 2020), understanding the demands of deceleration and how to best prepare for these demands has never been more important to the performance, health, and well-being of athletes involved in multidirectional sports (Harper, McBurnie, et al., 2022; McBurnie et al., 2022).

For the purposes of this chapter, the term *deceleration* is referring to actions involving whole-body horizontal deceleration. This distinguishment is important since deceleration is a vector quantity and, in accordance with Newton's laws of motion, is directly proportional to the direction of force applied (Winter et al., 2016). Therefore, to manipulate the rate of horizontal deceleration, an athlete must adjust either the magnitude or duration of force (i.e. impulse) applied in the horizontal direction (Winter et al., 2016; Winter & Fowler, 2009). It is important to recognise early within this chapter that the optimisation of braking impulse requires a high level of technical ability (Harper, McBurnie, et al., 2022). Therefore, deceleration should be regarded as a skill where athletes capable of generating a greater horizontal component of the ground reaction force (GRF) vector will have superior deceleration performance.

Whilst acceleration and deceleration are underpinned by the same mechanical definition, it is important to recognise that these actions have unique mechanical and physiological demands (Harper & Kiely, 2018; McBurnie et al., 2022). For example, some braking steps when decelerating can be characterised with a unique GRF profile comprising high-impact peak forces

DOI: 10.4324/9781003267881-6

(up to around six times the body mass [BM]) and loading rates (Nedergaard et al., 2014; Verheul et al., 2021). Furthermore, another notable and unique feature of decelerations is the necessity to be able to skilfully attenuate and distribute the high-impact forces through the muscle-tendon structures of the lower limb, which may enforce some lower-limb muscles to operate primarily through eccentric muscle action, and therefore be more vulnerable to tissue damage (Harper & Kiely, 2018; McBurnie et al., 2022). Accordingly, an athlete's deceleration ability should not only consider the ability to rapidly reduce momentum but also the ability to attenuate and distribute the high mechanical forces that are associated with decelerating. Based on these considerations, a definition of deceleration ability has been proposed by Harper et al. (2022, p. 22) and will be adopted for this chapter:

> a player's ability to proficiently reduce whole body momentum, within the constraints, and in accordance with the specific objectives of the task (i.e. braking force control), whilst skilfully attenuating and distributing the forces associated with braking (i.e. braking force attenuation).

This definition highlights two key components: (1) braking force control and (2) braking force attenuation, both of which are illustrated in Figure 5.1.

FIGURE 5.1 An illustration of deceleration ability, including the two key components: (1) braking force control and (2) braking force attenuation.

The following sections of this chapter will cover the incidence of decelerations in multidirectional sports, the physical demands of deceleration, and the underpinning physical and technical qualities of deceleration and will conclude with implications for training deceleration for athletes involved in multidirectional sports.

Incidence of Decelerations in Multidirectional Sports

To ensure optimal preparation of athletes, it is important to firstly conduct a needs analysis to gain a thorough understanding of the physical demands an athlete may be exposed to during competitive match play, to then be able to design training approaches that most optimally prepare athletes for these demands. This process has also been referred to as 'reverse engineering' (Turner et al., 2021). Probably the first reported data of deceleration demands during competition was by Bloomfield and colleagues (2007) in male English Premier League (EPL) soccer players using an observational video notational approach that became known as the Bloomfield Movement Classification. They observed that EPL soccer players performed on average nine decelerations following high-speed running and sprinting actions every 15 minutes, meaning they would total approximately 54 decelerations per match, with the majority (77%) being performed after a sprint. Furthermore, they also observed that 72% of these decelerations were less than 1 s in duration, with almost all (96%) less than 2 s.

With advancements in wearable technologies (e.g. global positioning system [GPS] tracking devices), together with approval from sport's governing bodies to allow usage within official competitive match play, there has been an exponential increase in studies that have reported data on match play acceleration and deceleration demands (Harper et al., 2019). A very interesting finding in the study by Harper and colleagues (2019) was that high-intensity decelerations (<-2.5 m·s^{-2}) occurred more frequently than equivalent intensity accelerations in all elite field-based team sports (Australian football, field hockey, rugby league, rugby sevens, rugby union, and soccer) competitive match play, apart from American football. These differences ranged from large in soccer and rugby sevens to moderate in Australian football, hockey, rugby league, rugby sevens, and rugby union. Whilst American football had a larger frequency of high-intensity accelerations than decelerations across all positional groups, when very-high-intensity accelerations (>3.5 m·s^{-2}) and decelerations (<-3.5 m·s^{-2}) were compared differences were *unclear* in the majority of positions (i.e. running back, quarter back, tight end, defensive tackle, defensive end) with offensive linesman having a very larger frequency of very high-intensity decelerations ($n = 7$) compared to accelerations ($n = 2$). This perhaps highlights the unique nature of American football match play and the players' anthropometric profiles, which, together, require players to have the ability to reduce very high whole-body momentums and thus be able to generate and tolerate very high braking impulses (i.e. high magnitudes of braking forces in short time frames).

Table 5.1 illustrates the frequency of high-intensity accelerations and decelerations performed during competitive match play in popular field- and court-based team sports. The table also illustrates how much percentage greater or lower high-intensity decelerations are in comparison to equivalent intensity accelerations. This information helps to provide some further insight into which sports and positional roles may have greater high-intensity deceleration relative to high-intensity acceleration demands during match play, or vice versa.

Whilst the high-intensity deceleration data reported in Table 5.1 provides important information on high-intensity deceleration match demands across various field- and court-based multidirectional sports, it does not provide contextual information on why high-intensity decelerations

TABLE 5.1 Occurrence of High-Intensity Accelerations and Decelerations Observed During Elite Competitive Match Play in Various Multidirectional Team Sports

Sport, Standard	*Aim of Study*	*Measurement Details*	*Acceleration Frequency*	*Deceleration Frequency*	*Decelerations % Greater (+)/Lower (−)*
Australian Football, Australian Football League (AFL) (Rennie et al., 2020)	Describe the distribution of accelerations and decelerations during different phases of play in male professional players	10 Hz GPS devices (Catapult Sports, Optimeye S5) HI = >2.78 $m \cdot s^{-2}$	**Frequency (n)** T: **33** OF: **6** DF: **7** CP: **15**	**Frequency (n)** T: **43** OF: **10** DF: **12** CP: **18**	**Frequency (n)** T: **+30** OF: **+67** DF: **+71** CP: **+20**
Australian Football, Australian Football League (AFL) (Johnston et al., 2015)	Identify if accelerations and decelerations where capable of identifying differences between playing positions in male professional players	5 and 10 Hz GPS devices (Catapult Sports S3 and S4) HI = >2.78 $m \cdot s^{-2}$	**Frequency (n)** T: **46** MD: **50** FF: **40** FD: **41** RK: **38**	**Frequency (n)** T: **59** MD: **60** FF: **53** FD: **61** RK: **51**	**Frequency (n)** T: **+28** MD: **+20** FF: **+33** FD: **+49** RK: **+34**
American Football, NCAA Division 1 (Wellman et al., 2015)	Examine the physiological competitive movement demands of male NCAA players during official matches and determine if differences exist between positional groups	10 Hz GPS device (GPSports) HI = 2.6–3.5 $m \cdot s^{-2}$ VHI = >3.5 $m \cdot s^{-2}$	**Frequency (n)** WR HI: **39** VHI: **22** RB HI: **19** VHI: **8** QB HI: **21** VHI: **9** TE HI: **22** VHI: **6** OL HI: **17** VHI: **2** DB HI: **32** VHI: **21** DT HI: **15** VHI: **3** DE HI: **20** VHI: **7** LB HI: **26** VHI: **13**	**Frequency (n)** WR HI: **19** VHI: **16** RB HI: **8** VHI: **6** QB HI: **10** VHI: **6** TE HI: **9** VHI: **5** OL HI: **8** VHI: **7** DB HI: **19** VHI: **14** DT HI: **8** VHI: **3** DE HI: **11** VHI: **5** LB HI: **14** VHI: **10**	**Frequency (n)** WR HI: **−51** VHI: **−27** RB HI: **−58** VHI: **−25** QB HI: **−52** VHI: **−33** TE HI: **−59** VHI: **−17** OL HI: **−53** VHI: **+250** DB HI: **−41** VHI: **−33** DT HI: **−47** VHI: **0** DE HI: **−45** VHI: **−29** LB HI: **−58** VHI: **−23**
Basketball, Elite Spanish Basketball League (Vázquez-Guerrero et al., 2018)	Compare the number and intensity of accelerations and decelerations between playing positions during elite male competitive matches	100 Hz triaxial accelerometer (analogue devices) HI = >3.0 $m \cdot s^{-2}$	**Frequency ($n \cdot min^{-1}$)** PG: **1.4** SG: **1.0** SF: **0.8** PF: **1.4** CE: **1.5**	**Frequency ($n \cdot min^{-1}$)** PG: **4.5** SG: **4.1** SF: **3.2** PF: **3.5** CE: **3.7**	**Frequency ($n \cdot min^{-1}$)** PG: +**221** SG: **+310** SF: **+300** PF: **+150** CE: **+147**

(*Continued*)

TABLE 5.1 (Continued)

Sport, Standard	*Aim of Study*	*Measurement Details*	*Acceleration Frequency*	*Deceleration Frequency*	*Decelerations % Greater (+)/Lower (−)*
Field Hockey, Malaysian National Team (James et al., 2021)	Use data collected from a top 15 ranked male teams in the world to report the volume and intensity of accelerations and decelerations and identify differences between positional groups	10 Hz GPS devices (Catapult Sports G5 and S5) VHI = >3.5 $m{\cdot}s^{-2}$	**Frequency (n)** T: **50** DEF: **48** MID: **51** ATT: **50** **Frequency ($n{\cdot}min^{-1}$)** T: **1.3** DEF: **1.1** MID: **1.4** ATT: **1.5**	**Frequency (n)** T: **60** DEF: **61** MID: **63** ATT: **55** **Frequency ($n{\cdot}min^{-1}$)** T: **1.6** DEF: **1.3** MID: **1.7** ATT: **1.7**	**Frequency (n)** T: **+20** DEF: **+27** MID: **+24** ATT: **+10** **Frequency ($n{\cdot}min^{-1}$)** T: **+23** DEF: **+18** MID: **+21** ATT: **+13**
Rugby League, International Four Nations (Dempsey et al., 2018)	Quantify and compare game acceleration and deceleration demands of male senior competitive games for the first time	10 Hz GPS devices (GPSports SPI-ProX) HI = >2.78 $m{\cdot}s^{-2}$	**Frequency (n)** FW: **21** BK: **29** **Frequency ($n{\cdot}min^{-1}$)** FW: **0.3** BK: **0.4**	**Frequency (n)** FW: **44** BK: **61** **Frequency ($n{\cdot}min^{-1}$)** FW: **0.7** BK: **0.8**	**Frequency (n)** FW: **+110** BK: **+128** **Frequency ($n{\cdot}min^{-1}$)** FW: **+133** BK: **+100**
Rugby Union, International Six Nations (Cunningham et al., 2016)	Report acceleration and deceleration movement demands of male senior international competitions	10 Hz GPS device (STATSports, ViperPod) HI = 3.0–4.0 $m{\cdot}s^{-2}$ VHI = >4.0 $m{\cdot}s^{-2}$	**Frequency (n)** FW HI: **2.2** VHI: **0.7** BK HI: **4.9** VHI: **1.0**	**Frequency (n)** FW HI: **6.4** VHI: **2.4** BK HI: **9.9** VHI: **4.4**	**Frequency (n)** FW HI: **+178** VHI: **+243** BK HI: **+102** VHI: **+340**
Soccer, English Category 2 Academy (Smalley et al., 2022)	Compare acceleration and deceleration outputs across English U16, U18, and U23 academy soccer matches and investigate possible relationships with neuromuscular and aerobic capacities	18 Hz GPS devices (Apex, STATSports) HI = >3 $m{\cdot}s^{-2}$	**Frequency (n)** T U16: 58 T U18: 83 T U23: 81 **Frequency ($n{\cdot}min^{-1}$)** T U16: 0.82 T U18: 1.00 T U23: 0.94	**Frequency (n)** T U16: 62 T U18: 88 T U23: 91 **Frequency ($n{\cdot}min^{-1}$)** T U16: 0.89 T U18: 1.07 T U23: 1.06	**Frequency (n)** T U16: **+7** T U18: **+6** T U23: **+12** **Frequency ($n{\cdot}min^{-1}$)** T U16: **+6** T U18: **+7** T U23: **+13**

Soccer, Spanish LaLiga 2 (Oliva-Lozano et al., 2022)	Report the volume and intensity of accelerations and decelerations during competitive male matches and the influence of the length of the microcycle	10 Hz WIMU Pro tracking system (Real Track Systems) HI = >3 m·s^{-2}	**Frequency (n)** T SMC: **51** T MMC: **60** T LMC: **62**	**Frequency (n)** T SMC: **72** T MMC: **83** T LMC: **92**	**Frequency (n)** T SMC: **+41** T MMC: **+38** T LMC: **+48**
Soccer, Spanish LaLiga 2 (Arjol-Serrano et al., 2021)	Examine differences in acceleration and deceleration demands across two playing formations (4–2–3–1 and 4–4–2)	18 Hz GPS devices (Apex, STATSports) VHI + >4 m·s^{-2}	**Frequency (n)** T: 4–2–3–1: **14** 4–4–2: **17** CD: 4–2–3–1: **13** 4–4–2: **14** WD: 4–2–3–1: **15** 4–4–2: **19** CM: 4–2–3–1: **8** 4–4–2: **14** WM: 4–2–3–1: **13** 4–4–2: **15** OM: 4–2–3–1: **22** 4–4–2: **17** FW: 4–2–3–1: **23** 4–4–2: **23**	**Frequency (n)** T: 4–2–3–1: **28** 4–4–2: **30** CD: 4–2–3–1: **19** 4–4–2: **23** WD: 4–2–3–1: **33** 4–4–2: **35** CM: 4–2–3–1: **22** 4–4–2: **25** WM: 4–2–3–1: **33** 4–4–2: **34** OM: 4–2–3–1: **45** 4–4–2: **39** FW: 4–2–3–1: **32** 4–4–2: **31**	**Frequency (n)** T: 4–2–3–1: **+100** 4–4–2: **+76** CD: 4–2–3–1: **+46** 4–4–2: **+64** WD: 4–2–3–1: **+120** 4–4–2: **+84** CM: 4–2–3–1: **+175** 4–4–2: **+79** WM: 4–2–3–1: **+154** 4–4–2: **+127** OM: 4–2–3–1: **+104** 4–4–2: **+129** FW: 4–2–3–1: **+39** 4–4–2: **+35**
Soccer, Spanish LaLiga (Lorenzo-Martínez et al., 2021)	Examine the effects of chronological age on acceleration and deceleration match performance in professional soccer players	25 Hz computerised optical tracking system (TRACAB, ChronoHego) HI = >3 m·s^{-2}	**Frequency (n)** T A: **48** B: **48** C: **46** D: **43** WD A: **50** B: **52** C: **53** D: **47** CD A: **44** B: **46** C: **43** D: **39** WM A: **50** B: **53** C: **53** D: **52** CM A: **46** B: **42** C: **39** D: **41** FW A: **50** B: **57** C: **48** D: **42**	**Frequency (n)** T A: **64** B: **62** C: **61** D: **60** WD A: **71** B: **74** C: **71** D: **65** CD A: **52** B: **55** C: **55** D: **48** WM A: **68** B: **71** C: **68** D: **67** CM A: **62** B: **57** C: **58** D: **57** FW A: **61** B: **64** C: **62** D: **54**	**Frequency (n)** T A: **+33** B: **+29** C: **+33** D: **+40** WD A: **+42** B: **+42** C: **+34** D: **+38** CD A: **+18** B: **+20** C: **+28** D: **+23** WM A: **+36** B: **+36** C: **+28** D: **+29** CM A: **+35** B: **+36** C: **+39** D: **+41** FW A: **+22** B: **+12** C: **+29** D: **+29**

(*Continued*)

TABLE 5.1 (Continued)

Sport, Standard	*Aim of Study*	*Measurement Details*	*Acceleration Frequency*	*Deceleration Frequency*	*Decelerations % Greater (+)/Lower (−)*
Soccer, Spanish LaLiga 2 (Oliva-Lozano et al., 2021)	Compare acceleration and deceleration demands during the first, second, and third most demanding passages of play in professional soccer matches	10 Hz WIMU Pro tracking system (Real Track Systems) HI = >3 m·s^{-2}	**Frequency (n·min^{-1})** T 1st: **3.7** 2nd: **3.2** 3rd: **2.8** WD 1st: **3.0** 2nd: **2.4** 3rd: **1.9** CD 1st: **3.4** 2nd: **3.1** 3rd: **2.8** WM 1st: **4.3** 2nd: **3.5** 3rd: **3.1** CM **1st**: **3.8** 2nd: **3.1** 3rd: **2.8** FW 1st: **3.3** 2nd: **2.9** 3rd: **2.7**	**Frequency (n·min^{-1})** T 1st: **4.5** 2nd: **3.8** 3rd: **3.5** WD 1st: **4.5** 2nd: **3.7** 3rd: **3.5** CD 1st: **4.2** 2nd: **3.5** 3rd: **3.2** WM 1st: **5.0** 2nd: **4.2** 3rd: **3.8** CM 1st: **4.4** 2nd: **3.5** 3rd: **3.4** FW 1st: **4.2** 2nd: **3.5** 3rd: **3.2**	**Frequency (n·min^{-1})** T 1st: **+22** 2nd: **+19** 3rd: **+25** WD 1st: **+50** 2nd: +**54** 3rd: **+84** CD 1st: **+24** 2nd: **+13** 3rd: **+14** WM 1st: **+16** 2nd: **+20** 3rd: **+23** CM 1st: **+16** 2nd: **+13** 3rd: **+21** FW 1st: **+27** 2nd: **+21** 3rd: **+19**
Soccer, Spanish LaLiga 2 (Oliva-Lozano et al., 2020)	Describe acceleration and deceleration profiles of players and compare to positional roles and analyse starting speed based on intensity of acceleration and deceleration by playing position	10 Hz WIMU Pro tracking system (Real Track Systems) HI = >3 m·s^{-2}	**Frequency (n)** WD: **31** CD: **28** WM: **36** CM: **28** FW: **30**	**Frequency (n)** WD: **54** CD: **51** WM: **65** CM: **55** FW: **55**	**Frequency (n)** WD: **+74** CD: **+86** WM: **+81** CM: **+96** FW: **+83**
Soccer, Danish Women's Soccer League (Panduro et al., 2021)	Investigate the position-specific acceleration and deceleration demands of elite female soccer players	10 Hz GPS and 200 Hz triaxial accelerometer (Polar Team Pro) HI = 3 to 4.99 m·s^{-2}	**Frequency (n)** WD: **8** CD: **7** WM: **7** CM: **10** FW: **12**	**Frequency (n)** WD: **17** CD: **13** WM: **23** CM: **16** FW: **19**	**Frequency (n)** WD: **+113** CD: **+86** WM: **+229** CM: **+60** FW: **+58**

Soccer, English Premier League Reserve (Russell et al., 2016)	Profile the influence of soccer match play on the number of acceleration and deceleration efforts in professional reserve team soccer players	10 Hz GPS device (STATSports, ViperPod) HI = >3 m·s^{-2}	**Frequency (n.5min)** WD: **2** CD: **2** WM: **2** CM: **2** FW: **3** T: **26**	**Frequency (n.5min)** WD: **3** CD: **3** WM: **4** CM: **3** FW: **4** T: **44**	**Frequency (n.5min)** WD: **+50** CD: **+50** WM: **+100** CM: **+50** FW: **+33** T: **+69**
Soccer, U21 and U18 English Football League (Tierney et al., 2016)	Examine acceleration and deceleration demands of each playing position in various playing formations in male professional soccer players	10 Hz GPS device (STATSports) HI = >3 m·s^{-2}	WD: **34** CD: **27** WM: **35** CM: **33** FW: **38**	WD: **56** CD: **45** WM: **62** CM: **53** FW: **55**	WD: **+65** CD: **+67** WM: **+20** CM: **+61** FW: **+45**

Acceleration/deceleration threshold: HI = high-intensity, VHI = very high-intensity

Passages of play: OF = offensive play, DF = defensive play, CP = contested play, 1st = first most demanding passage of play, 2nd = second most demanding passage of play, 3rd = third most demanding passage of play

Playing positions: WR = wide receiver, RB = running back, QB = quarter back, TE = tight end, OL = offensive linesman, DB = defensive back, DT = defensive tackle, DE = defensive end, LB = linebacker, PG = point guard, SG = shooting guard, SF = small forward, PF = power forward, CE = centre, T = team, MD = midfielder, FF = fixed forward, FD = fixed defender, RK = ruck, DEF = defender, ATT = attacker, FW = forward, BK = back, WD = wide defender, CD = central defender, WM = wide midfielder, CM = central midfielder, OM = offensive midfielder

Phase of training: SMC = small microcycle (days), MMC = medium microcycle (days), LMC = long mesocycle (days)

Ages: U16 = under 16 years, U18 = under 18 years, U23 = under 23 years, A = 17 to 23 years, B = 24 to 27 years, C = 28 to 30 years, D = 31 to 38 years

are occurring alongside technical and tactical actions nor provide information on other contextual factors that may influence the frequency of high-intensity decelerations during match play (e.g. standard of opposition, home or away fixture, tactical formations, style of play). Rago et al. (2018) reported that total number of decelerations above -2 m·s^{-2} in a male professional Italian Serie B team to be significantly higher when playing against professional compared to amateur-level opponents and that declines in total decelerations were also greater during match play when competing against a higher standard of opposition. These findings align with Rhodes et al. (2021) who reported total decelerations above -3 m·s^{-2} to be significantly higher when winning official matches across an entire season in a male professional English League Two soccer team. Similarly, Oliva-Lozano et al. (2021) reported higher maximum deceleration values when games were won compared to lost across an entire season in male professional Spanish LaLiga 2 soccer players, highlighting the importance of players possessing the ability to decelerate at higher magnitudes in addition to higher frequencies. This is further highlighted in male EPL soccer players, where decelerations have been reported to be the second most frequent action preceding goals during competitive match play across a whole season, with high-intensity decelerations particularly important for defensive players in order to rapidly react to an attackers movement to prevent a goal scoring opportunity (Martínez-Hernández et al., 2022). Furthermore, Oliva-Lozano et al. (2021) reported that across all positional roles the highest frequency per minute of high-intensity decelerations occurred within the first 15-minute period of play, demonstrating that high-intensity decelerations are highly vulnerable to neuromuscular fatigue and subsequent declines during match play.

In addition to contextual information, simple frequency counts also do not provide information on the various types of decelerations being performed that would give important information for deceleration training prescription (Ellens et al., 2022). For example, Mara et al. (2016) reported that the maximum deceleration distance was significantly different amongst positional roles in elite female soccer players, with centre forwards reporting higher distances (10.5 m) than central defenders (7.5 m) and midfielders (7.1 m). Across all positional roles, the mean deceleration distance was between 1 and 4 m. Additionally, the authors also reported the speed at which the deceleration started and ended. For example, central defenders performed significantly less decelerations ($n = 16$) from high (5.4 m·s^{-1}) to low (3.4 m·s^{-1}) speeds compared to central attackers ($n = 34$). Such information provides more detailed insights into position specific deceleration demands and highlights the need to train decelerations across various distances and when starting and ending at various speeds. Finally, future research should consider exploring decelerations relative to individual player maximal deceleration capacities rather than using fixed arbitrary thresholds (Ellens et al., 2022). Furthermore, new technologies, such as wearable sensors (e.g. inertial measurement units, foot force pressure sensing insoles) and marker-less motion tracking combined with evolving machine learning algorithms, may advance tracking precision and provide new insights into inter-limb braking demands.

Biomechanical and physiological demands of deceleration

The biomechanical and physiological demands of deceleration have been discussed in detail in previous reviews (Harper, McBurnie, et al., 2022; McBurnie et al., 2022). Table 5.2 provides a summary of the biomechanical and physiological demands of deceleration together with the implications for multidirectional speed athletes from a performance and injury-risk perspective.

TABLE 5.2 Biomechanical and Physiological Demands of Deceleration and Implications for Multidirectional Speed Athletes from a Performance and Injury-Risk Perspective (Adapted from McBurnie et al., 2022)

Biomechanical and physiological demands	*Performance and injury-risk implications*
Biomechanical	
Rapid changes in whole body velocity across very short time frames and spaces	***Performance*** Increased ability to create and close down spaces ***Injury*** Increased braking impulse required to generate higher changes in velocity (deceleration)
Increased magnitude of braking impulse in the preparatory deceleration steps (APFC and PFC) relative to FFC	***Performance*** Effective application of force during preparatory deceleration steps to enhance force application in FFC and reacceleration into a new direction ***Injury*** Decrease in knee joint loads during FFC and risk of injuries such as ACL
High-impact peak forces (around six times the BM) and loading rates (i.e. tall-thin impulse)	***Performance*** Faster decreases in momentum to evade or pursue opponents, reflecting an impulse-momentum relationship ***Injury*** Increased lower-limb musculoskeletal loading and risk of overuse injuries
High ankle (up to 484°/s) and knee (up to 493°/s) joint flexion angular velocities	***Performance*** Increased attenuation of forces and rapid limb positioning to facilitate better orientation of braking forces ***Injury*** Reflective of increased loading severity and fast eccentric muscle demands that could increase susceptibility to soft tissue damage/injury
High ankle, knee, and hip internal joint extensor moments (triple extensor)	***Performance*** Help to maintain COM behind COP to generate higher braking impulse and thus higher deceleration; high hip extensor moment to control hip flexion ***Injury*** Increased attenuation and distribution of forces throughout the lower limb to reduce tissue damage and chance of lower-limb injuries
Physiological	
Highest forces for a given angular velocity during eccentric muscle actions compared to concentric or isometric	***Performance*** High eccentric forces permitting greater braking force application and faster deceleration and COD performances; increased use of passive elastic tissues during eccentric muscle actions permitting high metabolic efficiency ***Injury*** Increased forces leading to increased chance of tissue damage and neuromuscular fatigue
High internal quadriceps muscle forces compared to MVIC	***Performance*** Increased internal knee joint extensor moment generated by quadriceps contributing to higher braking forces (impulse) ***Injury*** Increased chance of knee injuries with increased force demands placed on quadriceps
Increased hamstring activation levels relative to quadriceps (improving hamstring-to-quadriceps ratio)	***Performance*** Increased knee joint stability and application of braking forces ***Injury*** Decreased risk of anterior displacement of the tibia through hamstring co-contraction leading to potential decrease in ACL injury risk
High pre-impact muscle activation	***Performance*** Increased ability to generate and attenuate braking forces ***Injury*** Decrease chance/rate of active muscle fascicle lengthening (mechanical strain) and subsequent damage to muscle fascicles

(*Continued*)

TABLE 5.2 (Continued)

Biomechanical and physiological demands	*Performance and injury-risk implications*
High rate of eccentric force production	***Performance*** Increased contribution of passive elastic structures, thereby enabling higher braking impulses and deceleration ***Injury*** Increased chance of active muscle fascicle lengthening, tissue damage, neuromuscular fatigue, and injury
High-impact forces demand increased mechanical buffering capacity of tendons	***Performance*** Increased braking force capacity and tolerance of braking forces permitting higher deceleration and ability to repeat decelerations ***Injury*** Decreased peak muscle forces and chance/rate of active muscle fascicle lengthening resulting in less tissue damage, neuromuscular fatigue, and injury

When compared to other high-intensity activities (i.e. plant step of 90° and 180° COD and 30 cm drop jump), the initial braking steps of deceleration have been described as the 'most demanding in terms of impact force characteristics' (Lozano-Berges et al., 2021, p. 673). Furthermore, in comparison to the initial steps of a maximal horizontal acceleration and the steps of maximum velocity sprint running, peak impact forces have been reported to be up to 2.7 (5.9 vs 2.2 times BM) to 1.3 (5.9 vs 4.4 times BM) times greater in magnitude, respectively (Bezodis et al., 2008; Verheul et al., 2021). As illustrated in Figure 5.2, high-impact peak forces and loading rates (i.e. 'tall-thin' impulse) occur during the first 10 to 40% of stance and must be rapidly attenuated and distributed over very short time periods (<50 ms) (Verheul et al., 2021).

During COD tasks demanding significant deceleration prior to turning (135 to 180°), similar GRF and trunk acceleration profiles have also been reported during the preparatory deceleration steps (i.e. antepenultimate and penultimate foot contacts) prior to turning (Dos'Santos et al., 2021; Nedergaard et al., 2014). Accordingly, an ability to produce greater deceleration in the steps prior to severe COD manoeuvres could be a deceleration strategy that not only enhances COD performance (Dos'Santos et al., 2017; Dos'Santos et al., 2021) but also reduces knee joint loads and injury-risk during the final plant foot contact of a COD manoeuvre. For example, non-contact anterior cruciate ligament (ACL) injury risk factors are commonly associated with an attempt to rapidly decelerate in multidirectional sports like soccer (Della Villa et al., 2021; Lucarno et al., 2021; Waldén et al., 2015), American football (Johnston et al., 2018), Australian football (Cochrane et al., 2007), and basketball (Schultz et al., 2021). In soccer, performing a rapid deceleration during defensive pressing has been reported to be the situational pattern leading to ACL injuries in male (33 to 66%) and female (58%) players (Della Villa et al., 2021; Lucarno et al., 2021; Waldén et al., 2015), highlighting the importance of deceleration ability to the potential reduction of major injuries like ACL ruptures.

The unique biomechanical forces observed with rapid decelerations are likely associated with the necessity for an initial heel strike with anterior foot placement and very high peak segmental accelerations of the braking foot, shank, and thigh (Nedergaard et al., 2014; Verheul et al., 2019). Interestingly, Jordan et al. (2021) reported both increased plantar flexion (307–484°/s) and knee joint flexion (325–469°/s) velocities with progressively increasing deceleration demands, highlighting the necessity for muscles around these joints to be able to generate high internal extensor moments in order to resist and control joint flexion imposed by braking hard. Indeed, high cumulative internal peak ankle, knee, and hip extensor moments were observed during the initial

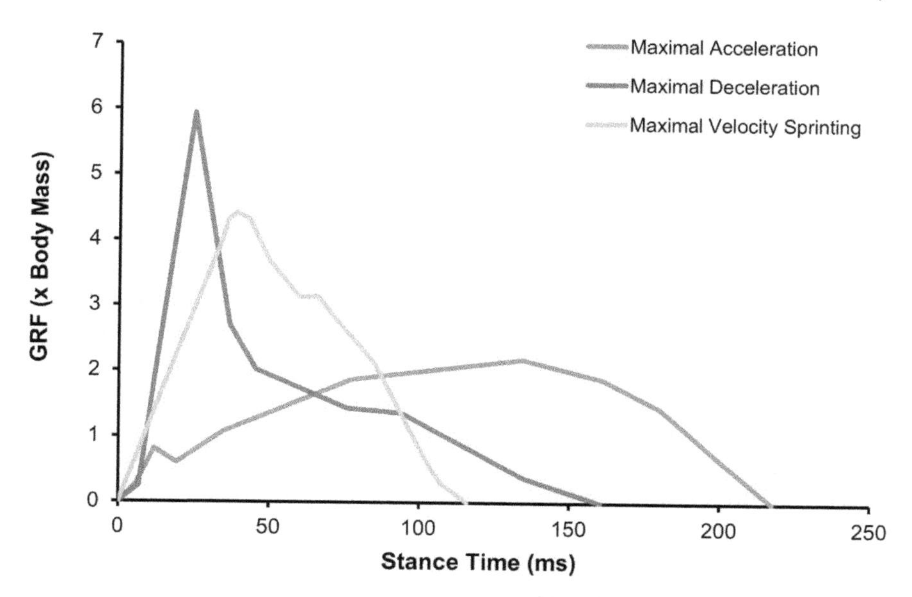

FIGURE 5.2 Comparison of ground reaction force (GRF) profiles for initial steps of maximal acceleration and deceleration and steps of maximal velocity sprint running. Data taken from Verheul et al. (2021) and Bezodis et al. (2008).

braking step of a rapid deceleration (Lozano-Berges et al., 2021). Notably, in the initial braking step, the highest internal peak extensor moment of any joint was reported at the hip extensor, highlighting the importance of the hip extensor muscles (i.e. hamstrings and gluteus maximus) for controlling hip flexion and the potential forward rotation (inertia) of the trunk imposed by sudden deceleration. This finding may also explain why braking hard during rapid decelerations have been observed to be a cause of hamstring injuries in multidirectional sports (Gronwald et al., 2022; Kerin et al., 2022), particularly when the knee is extending upon a forward rotating trunk imposing increased eccentric 'stretch-related' forces to the hamstrings (Gronwald et al., 2022). Therefore, in addition to maximal sprinting, deceleration field-based exercise training exercises may also be an important tool for helping to mitigate the high frequency of hamstring injuries in multidirectional sports with a particular emphasis on trunk control in the sagittal plane (Gronwald et al., 2022).

As illustrated in Figure 5.1, a critical component of deceleration ability is the necessity to skilfully attenuate and distribute the forces associated with deceleration. When decelerating from submaximal runs, the ankle and knee muscle tendon structures have been reported to attenuate between 68 and 77% of the impact forces emanating from ground contact (Gageler et al., 2013). In the same study when decelerations were more intense, the demands on the ankle and knee muscle-tendon structures to attenuate forces further increased, with the earlier braking steps (i.e. step 1 of 5), imposing greater peak segmental acceleration and shock attenuation demands. Conversely, when decelerations were less intense impact forces were of lower magnitude and distributed more evenly between limbs and across steps. These findings suggest that the ankle and knee muscle-tendon structures are the major shock absorbing structures when braking hard during deceleration. Indeed, the quadriceps (knee extensor) muscles have been reported to be the key contributors to centre-of-mass deceleration and for supporting the attenuation of braking forces (Mateus et al., 2020). As an indication of the extreme internal force demands placed on the quadriceps, a very high level of pre-activation has been observed prior to ground contact, and when required to attenuate the forces upon ground contact, electromyograph values can exceed 150% isometric maximal voluntary contraction (Colby et al., 2000). When the trunk assumes a more erect posture, increased demand to attenuate forces may be placed on the biarticular rectus femoris (Mateus et al., 2020; Mendiguchia et al., 2013), requiring specific consideration of eccentric focused exercises to target this muscle (Mendiguchia et al., 2013).

The soleus has also been identified as an important muscle contributing to the attenuation of impact forces during deceleration, in addition to resisting the vertical effect of gravity and preventing forward sway by 'locking the ankle' (Mateus et al., 2020). It is also important to note that in addition to the hamstrings, the soleus exerts posterior shear force that counteracts the anterior translation of the tibia that could decrease ACL strain and injury risk when decelerating rapidly (Mateus et al., 2020). Under conditions of fatigue resulting from repeated eccentric demands on the soleus, increased demands to attenuate forces may be placed on the knee and hip due to a local stiffening strategy of the ankle aiming to reduce stretch-amplitude and potentially damaging stimulus to the plantar-flexor muscles (Debenham et al., 2015). Given that decelerations are performed frequently during match play and that the soleus has important contributions to both performance and injury risk reduction when decelerating, careful consideration should be given to exercises that enhance the force and fatigue resilience capabilities of the soleus.

The mechanical stressors, implicit with deceleration activity discussed so far, likely increase the onset of neuromuscular fatigue and the risk of soft-tissue damage if the muscle-tendon structures are not adequately recovered or optimally prepared for these demands (Edwards, 2018; Harper & Kiely, 2018; McBurnie et al., 2022). These risks are likely further exacerbated when athletes perform a high frequency of intense decelerations or during periods of fixture congestion when full recovery may not be possible. As such, Harper and Kiely (2018) proposed deceleration load (frequency and intensity) to be the critical *mediator* driving neuromuscular fatigue and the risk of tissue damage in multidirectional sports, with the deceleration capacity of the athlete helping to reduce this risk (Figure 5.3).

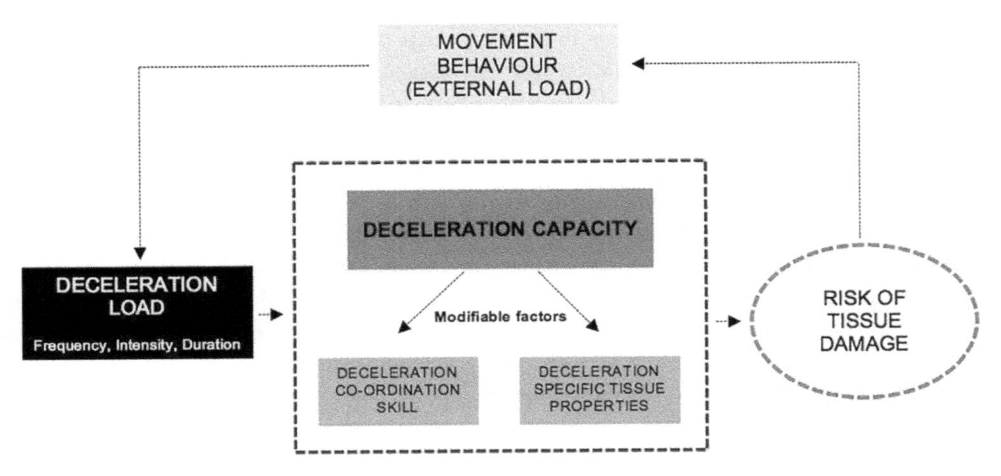

FIGURE 5.3 Deceleration capacity represented as a critical mediator moderating the performers risk of tissue damage. Taken from Harper and Kiely (2018).

As can be seen in Figure 5.3, deceleration capacity can be modified by two factors: (1) deceleration-specific tissue properties (i.e. load-bearing capacities) of the lower limb and (2) deceleration coordination skill. The physical and technical determinants that underpin each of these factors will be discussed in the following section.

Physical and Technical Determinants of Deceleration

Based on empirical evidence, the currently known physical and technical determinants of deceleration ability were summarised by Harper et al. (2022) and are illustrated in Figure 5.4. According to this diagram, deceleration ability is an interaction of various neuromuscular and biomechanical qualities that are required to optimise braking impulse and achieve the desired reductions in whole-body momentum (i.e. reflecting the impulse-momentum relationship) (Harper, McBurnie, et al., 2022).

From a physical perspective, eccentric, isometric, concentric, and reactive strength qualities have been reported to be important for enhanced deceleration ability (Figure 5.4). It has long been recognised that through increasing eccentric force capabilities of the muscles, higher braking forces can be achieved when decelerating, thereby permitting faster reductions in whole-body momentum (Hewit et al., 2011). The specific eccentric force capabilities highlighted to be important for deceleration in Figure 5.4 includes eccentric peak force (eccentric maximal

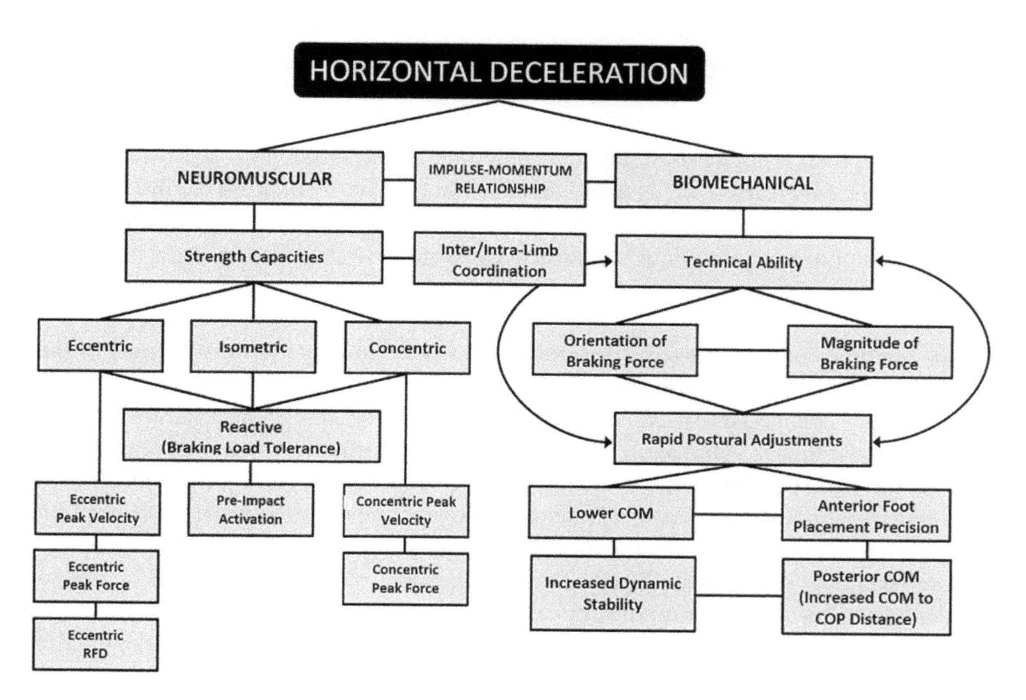

FIGURE 5.4 Horizontal deceleration ability represented by an interaction of the neuromuscular (strength) and biomechanical (technical) qualities required to optimise braking impulse. Taken from Harper et al. (2022).

strength), eccentric rate of force development (RFD), and eccentric peak velocity. Unilateral eccentric knee extensor (quadriceps) strength has been highlighted as particularly important for horizontal deceleration ability (Harper, Jordan, et al., 2021; Jones et al., 2017; Zhang et al., 2021). For example, when comparing players with high and low eccentric quadriceps strength, those with higher strength capacity had significantly greater ability to generate horizontal braking forces, enabling faster COD approach speeds, changes in velocity across key phases of the COD, and faster overall COD performance times (Jones et al., 2017). Rapid (0–100 ms) unilateral eccentric quadriceps torque may also be important for the generation of higher horizontal braking force, power, and impulse during a rapid deceleration (Zhang et al., 2021), permitting greater contribution of passive elastic tissue structures to the generation and attenuation of forces when braking hard. Therefore, training interventions that can increase maximal and 'explosive' unilateral eccentric quadriceps strength are important for enhanced deceleration ability.

Reactive strength has previously been proposed as an important neuromuscular quality underpinning better deceleration ability (Kovacs et al., 2015) and is often quantified using the reactive strength index (jump height/ground contact time) (Flanagan & Comyns, 2008). The reactive strength index is considered to be representative of the stretch-load capacity of the muscle-tendon unit during short (<0.25 s) high-force impacts with the ground and is a widely adopted assessment used to measure an athlete's capacity to counteract high eccentric-braking forces (Young, 1995). Harper et al. (2022) reported large significant associations between drop jump reactive strength index measured from both 20 and 40 cm drop heights and average deceleration ($m \cdot s^{-2}$) measured during a maximal deceleration from a 20 m sprint. Furthermore, the authors also identified a larger association with the early (peak velocity to 50% of peak velocity) compared to late (50% peak velocity to lowest velocity) deceleration sub-phase, suggesting those with greater reactive strength index were better able to generate greater horizontally oriented braking force within the initial braking steps when shorter ground contact times are available to generate force (i.e. braking impulse). Despite these findings, only one longitudinal study has investigated the potential link between reactive strength and deceleration (Lockie et al., 2014). In this study, only the group who performed enforced decelerations at the end of traditional speed and COD drills had significant improvements in drop jump reactive strength measured from a 40 cm drop height, further highlighting the potential importance of reactive strength for performing intense deceleration manoeuvres.

Whilst not previously considered a determinant of deceleration, concentric strength qualities have been identified as potentially important contributors to rapid deceleration ability (Harper, McBurnie, et al., 2022). Harper and colleagues (2021) suggested that concentric strength qualities (particularly at higher joint angular velocities) may help to facilitate the complex inter-limb movement patterns required to decelerate rapidly (i.e. facilitate rapid limb switching between ground contacts). Indeed, moderate associations have been reported between concentric knee extensor peak torque at faster (240°/s) joint angular velocities and maximal braking power during a rapid deceleration (Zhang et al., 2021). These authors also reported that a rapid rate of concentric hamstring-to-quadriceps torque ratio, indicative of dynamic agonist-antagonist knee joint control, had large associations with maximal braking power. It was hypothesised that optimal balance between rapid hamstring-to-quadriceps torque would contribute to lower limb stiffness to enhance force attenuation, knee joint stability, and force generation when braking hard during a maximal deceleration manoeuvre. A significant increase in concentric knee extensor peak torque of the left leg at 240°/s was also observed following six weeks of speed and agility training with enforced decelerations, although this was not observed in the right leg or in a group of players who followed the same speed and agility programme with no enforced decelerations (Lockie et al., 2014). Whilst further research is required to investigate the transference of fast velocity concentric strength gains to rapid deceleration abilities, training interventions that can enhance fast velocity concentric strength qualities may be important for enhanced deceleration ability.

Lower-body isometric strength (particularly unilateral) has also been highlighted as a foundational quality required to develop an athlete's deceleration ability (Griffin et al., 2021). This recommendation is based on studies that have identified male and female athletes who can generate greater lower-body isometric peak force can achieve faster COD performance times by adopting lower centre-of-mass positions to facilitate better orientation and higher magnitude of braking impulse (Spiteri et al., 2013; Spiteri, Nimphius, et al., 2014). Explosive isometric strength (i.e. the ability to increase force production rapidly) as measured using the isometric mid-thigh pull (at 100 and 300 ms) has also been associated with better performance in COD tasks with a large braking demand (Thomas et al., 2015). Similarly, both Behan et al. (2018) and Jakobsen et al. (2012) demonstrated the importance of isometric ankle plantar flexor RFD for enabling rapid adjustments and control of posture during highly dynamic sporting manoeuvres. This was suggested to be especially the case when a distal to proximal muscle activation sequence occurs, such as when braking during rapid horizontal decelerations. Accordingly, training interventions that enhance isometric peak force and RFD of the ankle and knee extensor muscles seem especially important for enhancing deceleration ability.

Isometric strength training is also a potent stimulus for facilitating architectural (e.g. tendon size) and functional (e.g. stiffness) tendon adaptations (Lazarczuk et al., 2022; Oranchuk et al., 2019a). With regard to the distribution and attenuation of braking forces when decelerating, elastic tendon structures have a critical role in helping to protect muscles from exercise induced eccentric muscle damage by providing a shock-absorbing mechanism that reduces peak muscle forces in addition to the amplitude and velocity of active muscle fascicle lengthening (Roberts & Konow, 2013; Werkhausen et al., 2017). Therefore, by focusing on interventions that may enhance elastic tendon properties, muscle fascicles may operate at safer lengths, be tolerant to higher forces, and be less prone to structural damage when braking during intense decelerations. Therefore, isometric strength training and the development of various isometric strength capacities should form an important element of a training programme focused on developing an athlete's deceleration ability.

Implications for Training Deceleration Ability

Using the neuromuscular and biomechanical qualities identified (Figure 5.4), training solutions can now be identified to target the required adaptations necessary to enhance deceleration ability. The braking performance framework (BPF) (Figure 5.5) acknowledges that optimal transfer can be achieved through a programme of structured, interconnected exercises that aim to combine the principles of *traditional* and *coordinative* overload — also referred to as a mixed-methods approach (Brearley & Bishop, 2019). Accordingly, the exercise categories and training solutions identified within the BPF move on a continuum from local (i.e. braking elementary exercises) to global (i.e. braking performance exercises) specificity, with a focus on either upgrading braking tissue properties or coordination skills. Developing 'damage resistance' of tissue structures commonly exposed to deceleration loads is an important health-related player feature of the braking

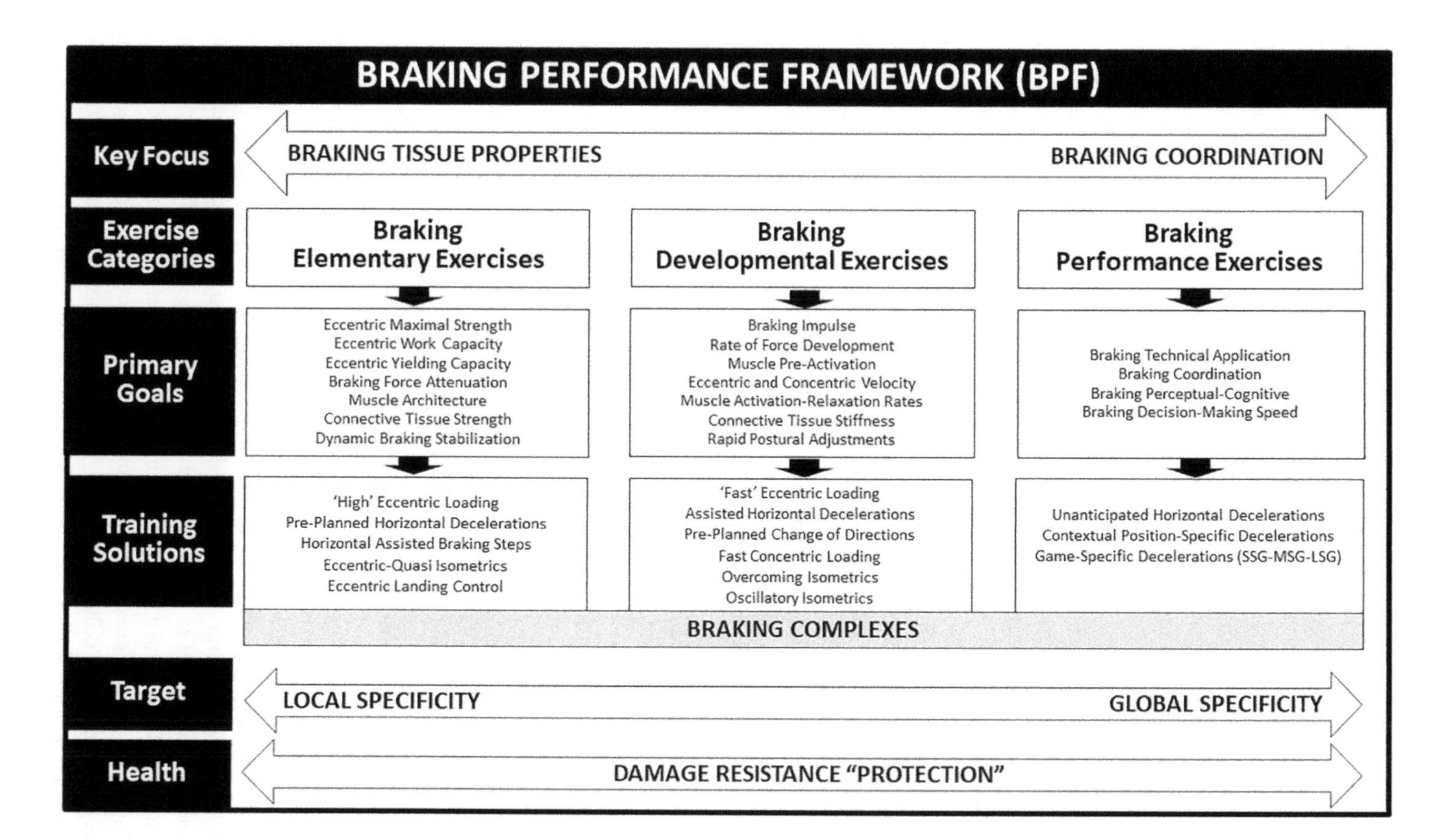

FIGURE 5.5 Braking performance framework (BPF) illustrating training solutions that can be used to target improvements in horizontal deceleration ability. Braking complexes represent combinations of exercises selected from different braking exercise categories. For example, an overcoming isometric exercise from the braking developmental exercise category could be paired with pre-planned decelerations from the braking elementary exercise category.

performance framework. Consequently, both acute and chronic training solutions that are known to enhance 'damage resistance' to high eccentric braking forces are important considerations within the BPF.

The BPF comprises three main exercise categories: (1) braking elementary exercises, (2) braking development exercises, and (3) braking performance exercises. Within each exercise category, there are a number of training solutions that can be chosen by practitioners to develop their athlete's deceleration ability. A brief overview of each exercise category together with the respective training solutions is discussed in the following sections.

Braking Elementary Exercises

Braking elementary exercises aim to target specific adaptations to neuromechanical muscle-tendon properties to enable players to produce and tolerate higher horizontal braking forces. To assist in effective force attenuation and to reduce the likelihood of injury when braking, a further goal is to enhance limb and trunk sensorimotor control (i.e. dynamic stabilisation). Training solutions within this category include: 'high' eccentric loading, pre-planned horizontal decelerations, assisted horizontal braking, eccentric quasi-isometrics, and eccentric landing control. Eccentric strength training is a potent stimulus for enhancing mechanical muscle-tendon function (e.g. strength, power, stiffness, stretch-shortening cycle) and for signalling positive structural adaptations (e.g. muscle and tendon cross-sectional area, type II fast-twitch muscle fibre size) (Douglas et al., 2017) and forms a pivotal part of the BPF. High eccentric loading exercises take advantage of the superior force capabilities that are possible with eccentric compared to concentric muscle actions by utilising training solutions that place an accentuated demand on the eccentric phase of an exercise. For more information on options for high eccentric load training, see Chapter 8.

Pre-planned horizontal decelerations involve high-force eccentric muscle actions that can increase the susceptibility of exercise induced eccentric muscle damage, particularly in less-accustomed players (Brown et al., 2016; Howatson & Milak, 2009). However, following short exposure to this activity, muscle damage response can be attenuated resulting in reduced soreness and enhanced ability to perform other high-speed movement actions (Brown et al., 2016), signifying a protective adaptive mechanism (i.e. repeated bout effect) (Hyldahl et al., 2017). An advantage of using this method is intensity can be systematically progressed or regressed by manipulating either or both the velocity and distance at which the deceleration is performed (Dos'Santos et al., 2018). For example, deceleration distance will increase with higher approach speeds or when the COD angle increases (i.e. >60°) (Graham-Smith et al., 2018; Hader et al., 2016). Accordingly, Dos'Santos et al. (2019) proposed that pre-planned horizontal decelerations with a progressive increase in approach velocity and COD angle were important components within the early phases of a six-week COD technique modification programme, aimed to enhance preparatory deceleration and COD performance.

Assisted horizontal braking can be performed across a predetermined series of braking steps and aim to increase eccentric-braking force capabilities by increasing the time available to apply a horizontal braking force (Mendiguchia et al., 2013). Assistance can be generated with additional force or velocity via low-cost equipment (i.e. elastics bands) or more precisely tuned using computer-controlled electro-motor devices (e.g. 1080 Sprint). Despite limited research, slow horizontal assisted braking steps have been used in eccentric-based training programmes to increase knee flexor and extensor peak force to longer muscle lengths, potentially signifying a protective effect against muscle strains during actions with a high eccentric loading demand (Brughelli et al., 2010).

Eccentric quasi-isometric contractions, also known as holding, yielding, or eccentric isometrics, require holding a position until isometric failure and maximally resisting the subsequent eccentric phase (Oranchuk et al., 2019b). This type of isometric exercise is effective in generating mechanical tension (i.e. force and active stretch) required to promote muscle and connective tissue structural adaptations, with less acute muscle soreness than dynamic eccentric muscle actions (Oranchuk et al., 2019b, 2020). They have also been shown to require a rapid motor-unit pool recruitment in order to sustain force requirements, resulting in quicker time to fatigue than overcoming ('pushing' or 'pulling') isometrics (Baudry et al., 2009). Therefore, by increasing the activated motor units force sustaining capacity (Schaefer & Bittmann, 2017), it could be concluded that neuromuscular coordination will be enhanced when resisting loads eccentrically resulting in an enhanced braking force endurance capacity (Oranchuk et al., 2019b). Eccentric quasi-isometrics may also help to optimise gains in muscle hypertrophy, strength, and muscle connective tissue stiffness that is essential for the effective transmission and attenuation of deceleration forces (Balshaw et al., 2016; Massey et al., 2018). Therefore, eccentric quasi-isometric exercises that challenge the ability to resist flexion (yielding) of each lower-limb joint, whilst adopting similar postural positions seen when decelerating, should be selected and used within the general preparatory period (Oranchuk et al., 2019b).

Finally, eccentric landing control exercises aim to develop the neuromuscular abilities to safely attenuate forces when landing from various movement tasks (e.g. jumping, hopping, and bounding). The difficulty can be manipulated through changing task constraints, such as drop height, landing technique, surface, time to stabilisation, additional resistance, movement velocity (e.g. band assistance), or holding external objects (e.g. broom stick, medicine ball). These exercises should also be incorporated in the horizontal plane to increase specificity to the forces and postural control demands experienced when braking. Demands can also be augmented using assisted load through cable machines, electro-motor devices, or band resistance. For example, a unilateral horizontal hop and hold performed with progressive cable assisted loads of 4, 8, 12, and 16% BM progressively increased eccentric braking GRF demands, in addition to challenging postural control (Cronin et al., 2016). These exercises should complement other cyclic deceleration exercises (i.e. pre-planned or reactive horizontal decelerations) to enhance horizontal deceleration ability and for injury-risk reduction and rehabilitation purposes.

Braking Development Exercises

Braking developmental exercises aim to increase the ability to generate braking forces in less time (i.e. braking impulse). Training interventions that can increase eccentric and concentric joint angular velocities and RFD are important inclusions within this category. Furthermore, given the increased focus on global specificity, exercises within this category have increased focus on replicating the specific movement demands of rapid horizontal decelerations. Training solutions include fast eccentric loading methods (including accelerated eccentrics, which perform eccentric phase at an increased velocity, determined by eccentric phase execution strategies), overspeed eccentrics (addition of resistance bands to allow faster eccentric phase execution), accelerated eccentric loading (resistance bands used to accelerate eccentric phase before bands are released before concentric phase) and accentuated eccentric loading (eccentric load in excess of concentric load exercises [Handford et al., 2022]), plyometrics, assisted horizontal decelerations, pre-planned COD, fast concentric loading, overcoming isometrics, and oscillatory isometrics.

Some of the fast eccentric loading methods can also be performed with an eccentric-only option where load is moved rapidly through the desired eccentric range of motion before decelerating to an isometric position. Using this approach, fast eccentric (~1 s) squat training performed with a load (~70% 1 RM) that optimised eccentric RFD resulted in greater fascicle lengths (10%) and isometric RFD (10–19%), compared to performed slow velocity (~4 s) eccentric-only squats training. Furthermore, utilising fast eccentric-only squats, in combination with unloaded CMJs in a six-week low-volume (6 × 2 fast eccentric half-squats with CMJ performed on each minute of a four-minute inter-set rest period) fast eccentric complex training programme, resulted in greater eccentric RFD (40–107%), CMJ concentric peak power (20–36%), and slow and fast (IIA and IIX) twitch muscle fibre hypertrophy (8.6–11.6%) (Bogdanis et al., 2018).

Utilisation of accelerated or accentuated eccentric loading through elastic bands or free-weights, respectively, can provide an effective training solution for fast eccentric loading. For example, using band resistance equivalent to 20 and 30% BM during the eccentric phase of a drop jump (35 or 50 cm heights) increased eccentric impulse and RFD, with earlier quadriceps and soleus muscle activity onsets prior to impact compared to unloaded drop jump (Aboodarda et al., 2014). Interestingly, a short four-week training block with accentuated eccentric loaded drop jumps (52 cm height) with an additional 20% BM load, resulted in greater improvements in CMJ eccentric peak force, drop jump-reactive strength index, and 180° COD performance, compared to a unloaded drop jump training from the same height (Bridgeman et al., 2020). All of which are key determinants of deceleration ability (Figure 5.5), thus highlighting the potential benefits of fast eccentric load training for improving deceleration ability. Furthermore, low-volume drop-jump accentuated eccentric loading through mechanisms aligned to the repeated bout effect could also be used as an effective strategy to protect players from eccentric exercise induced muscle damage and associated declines in eccentric and concentric peak force capabilities (Bridgeman et al., 2017).

Fast concentric loading aims to enhance concentric force generation capabilities at faster joint angular velocities – important factors associated with horizontal deceleration ability (Figure 5.5). One strategy could be assisted jump training that facilitates higher lower-limb-joint angular velocities compared to using loads equal to BM or above (Samozino et al., 2018). For example, a training programme consisting of specific high-velocity training exercises (i.e. assisted squats and CMJs) can result in extremely large changes in maximal lower-limb velocity and jump performance capabilities (Jiménez-Reyes et al., 2019).

Overcoming isometrics ('pushing' or 'pulling' isometric muscle actions) require athletes to push or pull actively against a stable object using specific postures and joint angle configurations (Schaefer & Bittmann, 2017). There are two distinct types: (1) explosive contraction training involves very short (~1 s) explosive contractions interspersed with short (~5 s) relaxation periods and (2) sustained contraction training involving longer (~4 s) contraction durations interspersed with varied (2 to 20 s) relaxation periods (Balshaw et al., 2016; Lanza et al., 2019; Massey et al., 2018). Explosive contraction training can be a potent stimulus for enhancing early RFD and free-tendon stiffness, whilst sustained contraction training can be more beneficial for muscle hypertrophy and tendon-aponeurosis complex stiffness (Massey et al., 2018). The neural and connective tissue adaptations unique to explosive and sustained contraction training can be seen as crucial for intense braking actions were rapid forces need to be generated and attenuated in very short time frames. Indeed, ten weeks of explosive contraction training of the ankle plantar flexors increased

Achilles tendon stiffness and muscle strength, with reductions in active fascicle lengthening and lengthening velocity during a high-impact single-leg braking task, potentially mitigating muscle damage caused by fast eccentric muscle actions (Werkhausen et al., 2018).

Since overcoming isometric training adaptations are deemed more effective at the specific joint angles that are trained, practitioners looking to enhance deceleration ability should select postures and joint positions that closely mimic those seen when performing horizontal decelerations (Oranchuk et al., 2019a). For example, an overcoming isometric multi-joint deceleration exercise targeting the lead limb ankle and knee extensor muscles is illustrated in Figure 5.6. Practitioners may also attempt to perform overcoming isometrics by targeting specific muscles and tendons known to be important for enhancing deceleration-specific qualities. For example, ankle plantar-flexor muscles (i.e. soleus and gastrocnemius) and their associated connective tissue structures are important for attenuating forces upon ground contact and for generating ankle extensor moments to help prevent forward excursion of the centre of mass.

Oscillatory isometrics involve an active, intense, oscillatory pushing and pulling component. These exercises also aim to target specific deceleration joint positions and involve a rapid motor unit pool recruitment (Schaefer & Bittmann, 2017). The active pushing and pulling motion in oscillatory isometrics generates impulse-like contractions that could help to prevent fatigue by maintaining the transport of substrates that are thought to be a cause of fatigue in holding isometrics (Schaefer & Bittmann, 2017) whilst also necessitating a higher motor unit discharge rate that influences the maximal RFD (Baudry et al., 2009). Furthermore, by performing the oscillations at long muscle lengths, a contractile disadvantage, higher neural activations, and stress and strain to passive elastic structures are achieved (Desbrosses et al., 2006). As decelerations require rapid

FIGURE 5.6 Overcoming braking multi-joint isometric exercise, which can be implemented with explosive or sustained contraction-type durations. Emphasis is placed on pushing away with lead limb braking foot, thereby generating a horizontal force vector component.

muscle activation and relaxation rates and connective tissues to help buffer forces, oscillatory isometrics provide a useful training option to target these specific neural and mechanical qualities.

Braking Performance Exercises

Braking performance exercises aim to maximise braking skills under constraints specific to the competitive environment (i.e. game-representative braking) (Woods et al., 2020). Training options include unanticipated decelerations, contextual position-specific decelerations, and game-specific decelerations. During these exercises players are required to utilise an array of changing perceptual information to make high-speed decisions on the braking strategies that should be deployed to maximise performance outcomes of the task.

Unanticipated horizontal decelerations are designed with multidirectional, linear, or curvilinear movement challenges, or combinations of these, with either or both offensive (i.e. to create space/evade) and defensive (i.e. to reduce space/pursue) goals. Anticipating and responding to human stimuli is a key feature. Therefore, athletes will have to precisely regulate braking and deceleration magnitudes against constantly changing movement speeds and spatial and temporal constraints. Additionally, these tasks aim to enhance decision-making speed to afford greater preparation times to generate higher horizontally oriented braking forces, thereby enabling faster horizontal decelerations (Spiteri, Hart, et al., 2014).

Contextual position-specific horizontal decelerations aim to recreate movement patterns that incorporate game-specific deceleration actions combined with position-specific technical and tactical outcomes that are encountered both in- and out-of-possession. These can be designed using either an isolated position-specific format or a combined format where all positions are worked in unison (Ade et al., 2016). Furthermore, to optimise match-play specificity and ensure players are optimally prepared to perform the magnitude ($m \cdot s^{-2}$) and density ($n \cdot min^{-1}$) of decelerations, practitioners should ensure deceleration demands replicate or progressively overload those experienced during match play. For example, in soccer, all positional roles may be required to perform 4 to 5 high-intensity decelerations per minute during the most demanding passages of play (Martin-Garcia et al., 2018). Using this data and the common technical and tactical actions performed by wide midfielders whilst in and out of possession of the ball (Ade et al., 2016), an example contextual position-specific drill is illustrated in Figure 5.7.

Finally, game-specific decelerations are 'modified' versions of the formal competitive game (i.e. small-sided games [SSGs]) (Ometto et al., 2018), with the aim to develop players' game-specific deceleration capabilities in game-representative tasks. Accordingly, dynamic sport-specific information sources and individual action capabilities will be utilised to inform player deceleration actions, with the intention of enhancing sport-specific technical and tactical outcomes. By manipulating task constraints, practitioners can target different horizontal deceleration capabilities known to be important for match play. For example in soccer, SSGs designed with smaller player numbers (e.g. 4 vs 4, 5 vs 5 or 6 vs 6) and playing areas (lower space per player) can overload the high-intensity ($<-3\ m \cdot s^{-2}$) deceleration frequencies and associated technical actions compared to the average and most demanding passages of competitive matches (Martin-Garcia et al., 2019; Martín-García et al., 2020). However, SSGs might not provide an adequate opportunity for players to attain near-to-maximal horizontal deceleration magnitudes that are possible when performing pre-planned maximal horizontal decelerations from higher running velocities (Harper et al., 2020; Oliva-Lozano et al., 2020). Accordingly, large-sided games (LSG; e.g. 9 vs 9, 10 vs 10) with larger playing areas can allow players to attain higher and more frequent

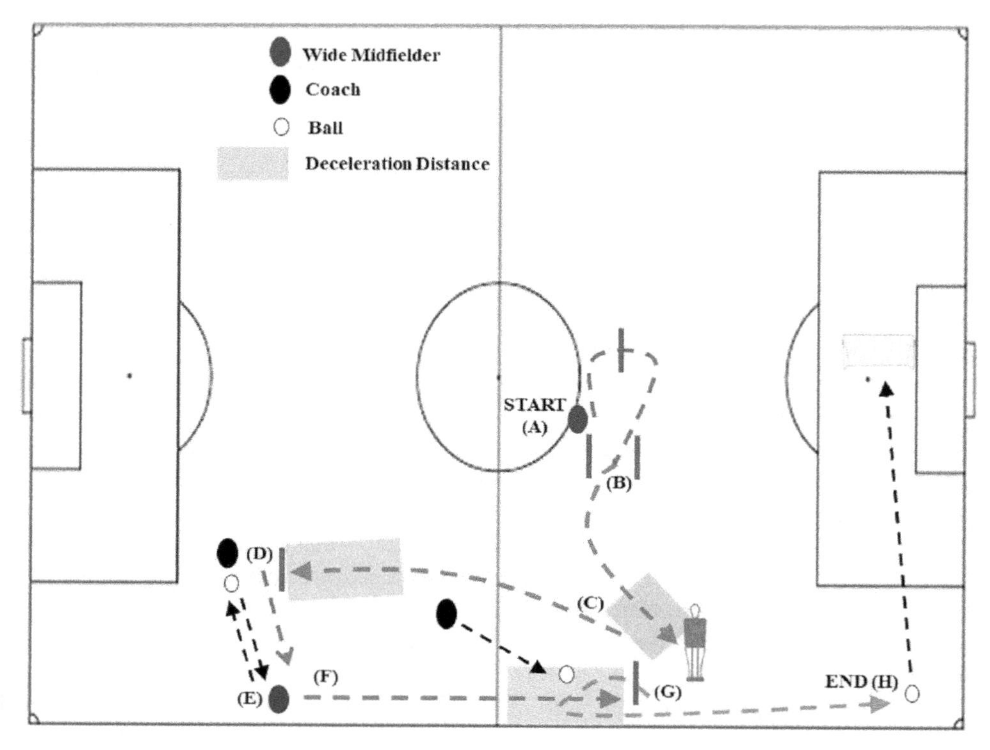

FIGURE 5.7 Contextual position specific for a wide midfielder. Movement sequences A, B, and C performed when out of possession, and D, E, F, G, and H are performed when in possession of the ball. A = start in middle-third of pitch with slow jog to side-shuffle, B = ~90° turn with curvilinear sprint to high-intensity deceleration (tactical aim: close down opposition player), C = ~90–180° turn to curvilinear sprint to high-intensity deceleration (tactical aim: track opposition players drive through middle), D = ~90–180° turn to backpedal, E = quick one-touch pass, F = ~90–180° turn to sprint down channel to high-intensity deceleration (tactical aim: overlapping run), G = ~90–180° turn to receive pass and dribble down line, and H = end with cross into mini-goal.

maximal decelerations values than SSGs (Abbott et al., 2018; Gaudino et al., 2014). An alternative strategy to target higher maximal horizontal decelerations using SSGs is to increase the playing area, thereby allowing players greater distances to attain higher running velocities and maximal deceleration values (Hodgson et al., 2014). Furthermore, practitioners should also carefully consider work-to-rest ratios and number of sets performed since longer continuous durations and a higher number of sets can reduce high-intensity deceleration frequencies (Clemente et al., 2019).

Conclusion

This chapter has provided new insights into the biomechanical and physiological demands of deceleration. Deceleration has major performance and injury-risk implications for athletes involved in multidirectional sports. Therefore, careful attention should be given to training solutions that can enhance an athlete's deceleration ability. The braking performance framework provides coaches and sports science and medicine practitioners with training solutions that could be used to enhance an athlete's deceleration ability. Further research is needed to investigate the implications of these training approaches on an athlete's deceleration ability, including their performance and resilience to repeated intense decelerations that are required to be performed during match play.

References

Abbott, W., Brickley, G., & Smeeton, N. J. (2018). Positional differences in GPS outputs and perceived exertion during soccer training games and competition. *Journal of Strength and Conditioning Research, 32*(11), 3222–3231. https://doi.org/10.1519/JSC.0000000000002387

Aboodarda, S. J., Byrne, J. M., Samson, M., Wilson, B. D., Mokhtar, A. H., & Behm, D. G. (2014). Does performing drop jumps with additional eccentric loading improve jump performance? *Journal of Strength and Conditioning Research/National Strength & Conditioning Association, 28*(8), 2314–2323. https://doi.org/10.1519/JSC.0000000000000498

Ade, J., Fitzpatrick, J., & Bradley, P. S. (2016). High-intensity efforts in elite soccer matches and associated movement patterns, technical skills and tactical actions. Information for position-specific training drills. *Journal of Sports Sciences, 34*(24), 2205–2214. https://doi.org/10.1080/02640414.2016.1217343

Arjol-Serrano, J. L., Lampre, M., Díez, A., Castillo, D., Sanz-López, F., & Lozano, D. (2021). The influence of playing formation on physical demands and technical-tactical actions according to playing positions in an elite soccer team. *International Journal of Environmental Research and Public Health, 18*(8), 1–12. https://doi.org/10.3390/ijerph18084148

Balshaw, T. G., Massey, G. J., Maden-Wilkinson, T. M., Tillin, N. A., & Folland, J. P. (2016). Training-specific functional, neural, and hypertrophic adaptations to explosive- vs. sustained-contraction strength training. *Journal of Applied Physiology, 120*(11), 1364–1373. https://doi.org/10.1152/japplphysiol.00091.2016

Baudry, S., Rudroff, T., Pierpoint, L. A., & Enoka, R. M. (2009). Load type influences motor unit recruitment in biceps brachii during a sustained contraction. *Journal of Neurophysiology, 102*(3), 1725–1735. https://doi.org/10.1152/jn.00382.2009

Behan, F. P., Pain, M. T. G., & Folland, J. P. (2018). Explosive voluntary torque is related to whole-body response to unexpected perturbations. *Journal of Biomechanics, 81*, 86–92. https://doi.org/10.1016/j.jbiomech.2018.09.016

Bezodis, I. N., Kerwin, D. G., & Salo, A. I. T. (2008). Lower-limb mechanics during the support phase of maximum-velocity sprint running. *Medicine and Science in Sports and Exercise, 40*(4), 707–715. https://doi.org/10.1249/MSS.0b013e318162d162

Bloomfield, J., Polman, R., & O'Donaghue, P. (2007). Deceleration movements performed during FA Premier League soccer matches. *Journal of Sports Science and Medicine, Supplement*, 6–11. http://books.google.com/books?hl=en&lr=&id=wfv0_PiqGGcC&oi=fnd&pg=PA174&dq=Deceleration+movements+performed+during+FA+Premier+League+soccer+matches&ots=IMfMRcxHL3&sig=sa_aOiJ-gqmkFEOAeHxV5jvS4ro

Bogdanis, G. C., Tsoukos, A., Brown, L. E., Selima, E., Veligekas, P., Spengos, K., & Terzis, G. (2018). Muscle fiber and performance changes after fast eccentric complex training. *Medicine and Science in Sports and Exercise, 50*(4), 729–738. https://doi.org/10.1249/MSS.0000000000001507

Brearley, S., & Bishop, C. (2019). Transfer of training: How specific should we be? *Strength and Conditioning Journal, 41*(3), 97–109. https://doi.org/10.1519/SSC.0000000000000450

Bridgeman, L. A., Gill, N. D., Dulson, D. K., & McGuigan, M. R. (2017). The effect of exercise-induced muscle damage after a bout of accentuated eccentric load drop jumps and the repeated bout effect. *Journal of Strength and Conditioning Research, 31*(2), 386–394. https://doi.org/10.1519/JSC.0000000000001725

Bridgeman, L. A., Mcguigan, M. R., & Gill, N. D. (2020). A case study investigating the effects of an accentuated eccentric load drop jump training program on strength, power, speed and change of direction. *Sport Performance & Science Reports, cm*, 1–4.

Brown, M. A., Howatson, G., Keane, K. M., & Stevenson, E. J. (2016). Adaptation to damaging dance and repeated-sprint activity in women. *Journal of Strength and Conditioning Research, 30*(9), 2574–2581. https://doi.org/10.1519/JSC.0000000000001346

Brughelli, M., Mendiguchia, J., Nosaka, K., Idoate, F., Arcos, A. L., & Cronin, J. (2010). Effects of eccentric exercise on optimum length of the knee flexors and extensors during the preseason in professional soccer players. *Physical Therapy in Sport, 11*(2), 50–55. https://doi.org/10.1016/j.ptsp.2009.12.002

Clemente, F. M., Nikolaidis, P. T., Rosemann, T., & Knechtle, B. (2019). Variations of internal and external load variables between intermittent small-sided soccer game training regimens. *International Journal of Environmental Research and Public Health, 16*(16). https://doi.org/10.3390/ijerph16162923

Cochrane, J. L., Lloyd, D. G., Buttfield, A., Seward, H., & McGivern, J. (2007). Characteristics of anterior cruciate ligament injuries in Australian football. *Journal of Science and Medicine in Sport, 10*(2), 96–104. https://doi.org/10.1016/j.jsams.2006.05.015

Colby, S., Francisco, A., Yu, B., Kirkendall, D., Finch, M., & Garrett, W. (2000). Electromyographic and kinematic analysis of cutting maneuvers implications for anterior cruciate ligament injury. *The American Journal of Sports Medicine, 28*(2), 234–240. https://doi.org/10.1016/S1440-2440(99)80066-8

Cronin, J. B., Ross, A., Bedford, C., Crosland, R., Birch, W., & Fathers, S. (2016). Deceleration forces associated with a novel cable pulling exercise. *Journal of Australian Strength and Conditioning, 24*(5), 16–19. http://search.ebscohost.com/login.aspx?direct=true&db=sph&AN=119317148&site=ehost-live

Cunningham, D. J., Shearer, D. A., Drawer, S., Pollard, B., Eager, R., Taylor, N., Cook, C. J., & Kilduff, L. P. (2016). Movement demands of elite under-20s and senior international rugby union players. *PLoS ONE, 11*(11), 1–13. https://doi.org/10.1371/journal.pone.0164990

Debenham, J., Travers, M., Gibson, W., Campbell, A., & Allison, G. (2015). Eccentric fatigue modulates stretch-shortening cycle effectiveness – a possible role in lower limb overuse injuries. *International Journal of Sports Medicine.* https://doi.org/10.1055/s-0035-1549923

Della Villa, F., Tosarelli, F., Ferrari, R., Grassi, A., Ciampone, L., Nanni, G., Zaffagnini, S., & Buckthorpe, M. (2021). Systematic video analysis of anterior cruciate ligament injuries in professional male rugby players: Pattern, injury mechanism, and biomechanics in 57 consecutive cases. *Orthopaedic Journal of Sports Medicine, 9*(11), 232596712110481. https://doi.org/10.1177/23259671211048182

Dempsey, G. M., Gibson, N. V., Sykes, D., Pryjmachuk, B. C., & Turner, A. P. (2018). Match demands of senior and junior players during international rugby league. *Journal of Strength and Conditioning Research, 32*(6), 1678–1684. https://doi.org/10.1519/JSC.0000000000002028

Desbrosses, K., Babault, N., Scaglioni, G., Meyer, J. P., & Pousson, M. (2006). Neural activation after maximal isometric contractions at different muscle lenghts. *Medicine and Science in Sports and Exercise, 38*(5), 937–944. https://doi.org/10.1249/01.mss.0000218136.58899.46

Dos'Santos, T., Thomas, C., Comfort, P., & Jones, P. A. (2018). The effect of angle and velocity on change of direction biomechanics: An angle-velocity trade-off. *Sports Medicine, 48*(10), 2235–2253. https://doi.org/10.1007/s40279-018-0968-3

Dos'Santos, T., Thomas, C., Comfort, P., & Jones, P. A. (2019). Role of the penultimate foot contact during change of direction: Implications on performance and risk of injury. *Strength and Conditioning Journal, 41*(1), 87–104. https://doi.org/10.1519/SSC.0000000000000395

Dos'Santos, T., Thomas, C., & Jones, P. A. (2021). How early should you brake during a 180° turn? A kinetic comparison of the antepenultimate, penultimate, and final foot contacts during a 505 change of direction speed test. *Journal of Sports Sciences, 39*(4), 395–405. https://doi.org/10.1080/02640414.2020.1823130

Dos'Santos, T., Thomas, C., Jones, P. A., & Comfort, P. (2017). Mechanical determinants of faster change of direction speed performance in male athletes. *Journal of Strength and Conditioning Research, 31*(3), 696–705. https://doi.org/10.1519/JSC.0000000000001535

Douglas, J., Pearson, S., Ross, A., & McGuigan, M. (2017). Chronic adaptations to eccentric training: A systematic review. *Sports Medicine, 47*(5), 917–941. https://doi.org/10.1007/s40279-016-0628-4

Edwards, W. B. (2018). Modeling overuse injuries in sport as a mechanical fatigue phenomenon. *Exercise and Sport Sciences Reviews, 46*(4), 224–231. https://doi.org/10.1249/JES.0000000000000163

Ellens, S., Carey, D., Gastin, P., & Varley, M. C. (2022). Changing the criteria applied to acceleration and deceleration efforts changes the types of player actions detected. *Science and Medicine in Football, 00*(00), 1–8. https://doi.org/10.1080/24733938.2022.2137575

Flanagan, E. P., & Comyns, T. M. (2008). The use of contact time and the reactive strength index to optimize fast stretch-shortening cycle training. *Strength and Conditioning Journal, 30*(5), 32–38. https://doi.org/10.1519/SSC.0b013e318187e25b

Gageler, W. H., Thiel, D., Neville, J., & James, D. A. (2013). Feasibility of using virtual and body worn inertial sensors to detect whole-body decelerations during stopping. *Procedia Engineering, 60*(0), 28–33. https://doi.org/10.1016/j.proeng.2013.07.040

Gaudino, P., Alberti, G., & Iaia, F. M. (2014). Estimated metabolic and mechanical demands during different small-sided games in elite soccer players. *Human Movement Science, 36*, 123–133. https://doi.org/10.1016/j.humov.2014.05.006

Graham-Smith, P., Rumpf, M., & Jones, P. A. (2018). Assessment of deceleration ability and relationship to approach speed and eccentric strength. *ISBS-Conference Proceedings Archive, 36*(1). https://doi.org/https://commons.nmu.edu/isbs/vol36/iss1/3/

Griffin, J., Horan, S., Keogh, J., Andreatta, M., & Minahan, C. (2021). Time to be negative about acceleration: A spotlight on female football players. *Journal of Strength and Conditioning Research*. https://doi.org/10.1519/JSC.0000000000004061

Gronwald, T., Klein, C., Hoenig, T., Pietzonka, M., Bloch, H., Edouard, P., & Hollander, K. (2022). Hamstring injury patterns in professional male football (soccer): A systematic video analysis of 52 cases. *British Journal of Sports Medicine, 56*(3), 165–171. https://doi.org/10.1136/bjsports-2021-104769

Hader, K., Mendez-Villanueva, A., Palazzi, D., Ahmaidi, S., & Buchheit, M. (2016). Metabolic power requirement of change of direction speed in young soccer players: Not all is what it seems. *PLoS ONE, 11*(3), e0149839. https://doi.org/10.1371/journal.pone.0149839

Handford, M. J., Bright, T. E., Mundy, P., Lake, J., Theis, N., & Hughes, J. D. (2022). The need for eccentric speed: A narrative review of the effects of accelerated eccentric actions during resistance-based training. *Sports Medicine, 52*(9), 2061–2083. https://doi.org/10.1007/s40279-022-01686-z

Harper, D. J., Carling, C., & Kiely, J. (2019). High-intensity acceleration and deceleration demands in elite team sports competitive match play: A systematic review and meta-analysis of observational studies. *Sports Medicine, 49*(12), 1923–1947. https://doi.org/10.1007/s40279-019-01170-1

Harper, D. J., Cohen, D. D., Rhodes, D., Carling, C., & Kiely, J. (2022). Drop jump neuromuscular performance qualities associated with maximal horizontal deceleration ability in team sport athletes. *European Journal of Sport Science, 22*(7), 1005–1016. https://doi.org/10.1080/17461391.2021.1930195

Harper, D. J., Jordan, A. R., & Kiely, J. (2021). Relationships between eccentric and concentric knee strength capacities and maximal linear deceleration ability in male academy soccer players. *Journal of Strength and Conditioning Research, 35*(2), 465–472. https://doi.org/10.1519/JSC.0000000000002739

Harper, D. J., & Kiely, J. (2018). Damaging nature of decelerations: Do we adequately prepare players? *BMJ Open Sport & Exercise Medicine, 4*, e000379. https://doi.org/10.1136/bmjsem-2018-000379

Harper, D. J., McBurnie, A. J., Santos, T. D., Eriksrud, O., Evans, M., Cohen, D. D., Rhodes, D., Carling, C., & Kiely, J. (2022). Biomechanical and neuromuscular performance requirements of horizontal deceleration: A review with implications for random intermittent multi-directional sports. *Sports Medicine, 52*(10), 2321–2354. https://doi.org/10.1007/s40279-022-01693-0

Harper, D. J., Morin, J. B., Carling, C., & Kiely, J. (2020). Measuring maximal horizontal deceleration ability using radar technology: Reliability and sensitivity of kinematic and kinetic variables. *Sports Biomechanics*, 1–17. https://doi.org/10.1080/14763141.2020.1792968

Harper, D. J., Sandford, G. N., Clubb, J., Young, M., Taberner, M., Rhodes, D., Carling, C., & Kiely, J. (2021). Elite football of 2030 will not be the same as that of 2020: What has evolved and what needs to evolve? *Scandinavian Journal of Medicine and Science in Sports, 31*, 493–494. https://doi.org/10.1111/sms.13876

Hewit, J., Cronin, J., Button, C., & Hume, P. (2011). Understanding deceleration in sport. *Strength and Conditioning Journal, 33*(1), 47–52. https://doi.org/10.1519/SSC.0b013e3181fbd62c

Hodgson, C., Akenhead, R., & Thomas, K. (2014). Time-motion analysis of acceleration demands of 4v4 small-sided soccer games played on different pitch sizes. *Human Movement Science*, *33*, 25–32. https://doi.org/10.1016/j.humov.2013.12.002

Howatson, G., & Milak, A. (2009). Exercise-induced muscle damage following a bout of sport specific repeated sprints. *Journal of Strength and Conditioning Research*, *23*(8), 2419–2424. https://doi.org/10.1519/JSC.0b013e3181bac52e

Hyldahl, R. D., Chen, T. C., & Nosaka, K. (2017). Mechanisms and mediators of the skeletal muscle repeated bout effect. *Exercise and Sport Sciences Reviews*, *45*(1), 24–33. https://doi.org/10.1249/JES.0000000000000095

Jakobsen, M. D., Sundstrup, E., Randers, M. B., Kjær, M., Andersen, L. L., Krustrup, P., & Aagaard, P. (2012). The effect of strength training, recreational soccer and running exercise on stretch-shortening cycle muscle performance during countermovement jumping. *Human Movement Science*, *31*(4), 970–986. https://doi.org/10.1016/j.humov.2011.10.001

James, C. A., Gibson, O. R., Dhawan, A., Stewart, C. M., & Willmott, A. G. B. (2021). Volume and intensity of locomotor activity in international men's field hockey matches over a 2-year period. *Frontiers in Sports and Active Living*, *3*(May), 1–11. https://doi.org/10.3389/fspor.2021.653364

Jiménez-Reyes, P., Samozino, P., & Morin, J. B. (2019). Optimized training for jumping performance using the force-velocity imbalance: Individual adaptation kinetics. *PLoS ONE*, *14*(5), 1–20. https://doi.org/10.1371/journal.pone.0216681

Johnston, J. T., Mandelbaum, B. R., Schub, D., Rodeo, S. A., Matava, M. J., Silvers-Granelli, H. J., Cole, B. J., ElAttrache, N. S., McAdams, T. R., & Brophy, R. H. (2018). Video analysis of anterior cruciate ligament tears in professional American football athletes. *American Journal of Sports Medicine*, *46*(4), 862–868. https://doi.org/10.1177/0363546518756328

Johnston, R. J., Watsford, M. L., Austin, D., Pine, M. J., & Spurrs, R. W. (2015). Player acceleration and deceleration profiles in professional Australian football. *The Journal of Sports Medicine and Physical Fitness*, *55*(9), 931–939. https://doi.org/26470636

Jones, P. A., Thomas, C., Dos'Santos, T., McMahon, J. J., & Graham-Smith, P. (2017). The role of eccentric strength in 180° turns in female soccer players. *Sports*, *5*(2), 42. https://doi.org/10.3390/sports5020042

Jordan, A. R., Carson, H. J., Wilkie, B., & Harper, D. J. (2021). Validity of an inertial measurement unit system to assess lower-limb kinematics during a maximal linear deceleration. *Central European Journal of Sport Sciences and Medicine*, *33*(1), 5–16. https://doi.org/10.18276/cej.2021.1-01

Kerin, F., Farrell, G., Tierney, P., McCarthy Persson, U., De Vito, G., & Delahunt, E. (2022). Its not all about sprinting: Mechanisms of acute hamstring strain injuries in professional male rugby union-a systematic visual video analysis. *British Journal of Sports Medicine*, *56*(11), 608–615. https://doi.org/10.1136/bjsports-2021-104171

Kovacs, M. S., Roetert, E. P., & Ellenbecker, T. S. (2015). Efficient deceleration: The forgotten factor in tennis-specific training. *Strength and Conditioning Journal*, *37*(2), 92–103. https://doi.org/10.1519/SSC.0b013e31818e5fbc

Lanza, M. B., Balshaw, T. G., & Folland, J. P. (2019). Is the joint-angle specificity of isometric resistance training real? And if so, does it have a neural basis? *European Journal of Applied Physiology*, *119*(11–12), 2465–2476. https://doi.org/10.1007/s00421-019-04229-z

Lazarczuk, S. L., Maniar, N., Opar, D. A., Duhig, S. J., Shield, A., Barrett, R. S., & Bourne, M. N. (2022). Mechanical, material and morphological adaptations of healthy lower limb tendons to mechanical loading: A systematic review and meta-analysis. *Sports Medicine*, *52*(10), 2405–2429. https://doi.org/10.1007/s40279-022-01695-y

Lockie, R. G., Schultz, A. B., Callaghan, S. J., & Jeffriess, M. D. (2014). The effects of traditional and enforced stopping speed and agility training on multidirectional speed and athletic function. *Journal of Strength and Conditioning Research*, *28*(6), 1538–1551. https://doi.org/10.1519/JSC.0000000000000309

Lorenzo-Martínez, M., Corredoira, F. J., Lago-Peñas, C., Campo, R. L. D., Nevado-Garrosa, F., & Rey, E. (2021). Effects of age on match-related acceleration and deceleration efforts in elite soccer players. *International Journal of Sports Medicine*, *42*(14), 1274–1280. https://doi.org/10.1055/a-1337-2961

Lozano-Berges, G., Clansey, A. C., Casajús, J. A., & Lake, M. J. (2021). Lack of impact moderating movement adaptation when soccer players perform game specific tasks on a third-generation artificial surface without a cushioning underlay. *Sports Biomechanics, 20*(6), 665–679. https://doi.org/10.1080/14763141.2019.1579365

Lucarno, S., Zago, M., Buckthorpe, M., Grassi, A., Tosarelli, F., Smith, R., & Della Villa, F. (2021). Systematic video analysis of anterior cruciate ligament injuries in professional female soccer players. *The American Journal of Sports Medicine, 49*(7), 1794–1802. https://doi.org/10.1177/03635465211008169

Mara, J. K., Thompson, K. G., Pumpa, K. L., & Morgan, S. (2016). The acceleration and deceleration profiles of elite female soccer players during competitive matches. *Journal of Science and Medicine in Sport*, 1–6. https://doi.org/10.1016/j.jsams.2016.12.078

Martin-Garcia, A., Casamichana, D., Diaz, A. G., Cos, F., & Gabbett, T. J. (2018). Positional differences in the most demanding passages of play in football competition. *Journal of Sports Science & Medicine, 17*(4), 563–570. www.ncbi.nlm.nih.gov/pubmed/30479524

Martin-Garcia, A., Castellano, J., Diaz, A. G., Cos, F., & Casamichana, D. (2019). Positional demands for various-sided games with goalkeepers according to the most demanding passages of match play in football. *Biology of Sport, 36*(2), 171–180. https://doi.org/10.5114/biolsport.2019.83507

Martín-García, A., Castellano, J., Méndez Villanueva, A., Gómez-Díaz, A., Cos, F., & Casamichana, D. (2020). Physical demands of ball possession games in relation to the most demanding passages of a competitive match. *Journal of Sports Science and Medicine, 19*(1), 1–9.

Martínez-Hernández, D., Quinn, M., & Jones, P. (2022). Linear advancing actions followed by deceleration and turn are the most common movements preceding goals in male professional soccer. *Science and Medicine in Football*. https://doi.org/10.1080/24733938.2022.2030064

Massey, G. J., Balshaw, T. G., Maden-Wilkinson, T. M., Tillin, N. A., & Folland, J. P. (2018). Tendinous tissue adaptation to explosive- vs. Sustained-contraction strength training. *Frontiers in Physiology, 9*(1170), 1–17. https://doi.org/10.3389/fphys.2018.01170

Mateus, R. B., Ferrer-Roca, V., João, F., & Veloso, A. P. (2020). Muscle contributions to maximal single-leg forward braking and backward acceleration in elite athletes. *Journal of Biomechanics, 112*, 110047. https://doi.org/10.1016/j.jbiomech.2020.110047

McBurnie, A. J., Harper, D. J., Jones, P. A., & Dos'Santos, T. (2022). Deceleration training in team sports: Another potential "vaccine" for sports-related injury? *Sports Medicine (Auckland, N.Z.), 52*(1), 1–12. https://doi.org/10.1007/s40279-021-01583-x

Mendiguchia, J., Alentorn-Geli, E., Idoate, F., & Myer, G. D. (2013). Rectus femoris muscle injuries in football: A clinically relevant review of mechanisms of injury, risk factors and preventive strategies. *British Journal of Sports Medicine, 47*, 359–366. https://doi.org/10.1136/bjsports-2012-091250

Nassis, G. P., Massey, A., Jacobsen, P., Brito, J., Randers, M. B., Castagna, C., Mohr, M., & Krustrup, P. (2020). Elite football of 2030 will not be the same as that of 2020: Preparing players, coaches, and support staff for the evolution. *Scandinavian Journal of Medicine & Science in Sports, 30*(6), 962–964. https://doi.org/10.1111/sms.13681

Nedergaard, N. J., Kersting, U., & Lake, M. (2014). Using accelerometry to quantify deceleration during a high-intensity soccer turning manoeuvre. *Journal of Sports Sciences, 32*(20), 1897–1905. https://doi.org/10.1080/02640414.2014.965190

Oliva-Lozano, J. M., Fortes, V., Krustrup, P., & Muyor, J. M. (2020). Acceleration and sprint profiles of professional male football players in relation to playing position. *PloS One, 15*(8), e0236959. https://doi.org/10.1371/journal.pone.0236959

Oliva-Lozano, J. M., Gómez-Carmona, C. D., Fortes, V., & Pino-Ortega, J. (2022). Effect of training day, match, and length of the microcycle on workload periodization in professional soccer players: A full-season study. *Biology of Sport, 39*(2), 397–406. https://doi.org/10.5114/biolsport.2022.106148

Oliva-Lozano, J. M., Rojas-Valverde, D., Gómez-Carmona, C. D., Fortes, V., & Pino-Ortega, J. (2021). Impact of contextual variables on the representative external load profile of Spanish professional soccer match-play: A full season study. *European Journal of Sport Science, 21*(4), 497–506. https://doi.org/10.1080/17461391.2020.1751305

Ometto, L., Vasconcellos, F. V. A., Cunha, F. A., Teoldo, I., Souza, C. R. B., Dutra, M. B., O'Sullivan, M., & Davids, K. (2018). How manipulating task constraints in small-sided and conditioned games shapes emergence of individual and collective tactical behaviours in football: A systematic review. *International Journal of Sports Science and Coaching, 13*(6), 1200–1214. https://doi.org/10.1177/1747954118769183
Oranchuk, D. J., Nelson, A., Storey, A., & Diewald, S. (2020). Short-term neuromuscular, morphological and architectural responses to eccentric quasi-isometric muscle actions. *European Journal of Applied Physiology, September.* https://doi.org/10.1007/s00421-020-04512-4
Oranchuk, D. J., Storey, A. G., Nelson, A. R., & Cronin, J. B. (2019a). Isometric training and long-term adaptations: Effects of muscle length, intensity, and intent: A systematic review. *Scandinavian Journal of Medicine and Science in Sports, August 2018,* 1–20. https://doi.org/10.1111/sms.13375
Oranchuk, D. J., Storey, A. G., Nelson, A. R., & Cronin, J. B. (2019b). Scientific basis for eccentric quasi-isometric resistance training: A narrative review. *Journal of Strength and Conditioning Research, 33*(10), 2846–2859. https://doi.org/10.1519/JSC.0000000000003291
Panduro, J., Ermidis, G., Røddik, L., Vigh-Larsen, J. F., Madsen, E. E., Larsen, M. N., Pettersen, S. A., Krustrup, P., & Randers, M. B. (2021). Physical performance and loading for six playing positions in elite female football: Full-game, end-game, and peak periods. *Scandinavian Journal of Medicine and Science in Sports, October 2020,* 1–12. https://doi.org/10.1111/sms.13877
Rago, V., Silva, J., Mohr, M., Randers, M., Barreira, D., Krustrup, P., & Rebelo, A. (2018). Influence of opponent standard on activity profile and fatigue development during preseasonal friendly soccer matches: A team study. *Research in Sports Medicine, 26*(4), 413–424. https://doi.org/10.1080/15438627.2018.1492400
Rennie, M. J., Kelly, S. J., Bush, S., Spurrs, R. W., Austin, D. J., & Watsford, M. L. (2020). Phases of match-play in professional Australian football: Distribution of physical and technical performance. *Journal of Sports Sciences, 38*(14), 1682–1689. https://doi.org/10.1080/02640414.2020.1754726
Rhodes, D., Valassakis, S., Bortnik, L., Eaves, R., Harper, D., & Alexander, J. (2021). The effect of high-intensity accelerations and decelerations on match outcome of an elite English league two football team. *International Journal of Environmental Research and Public Health, 18*(18), 9913. https://doi.org/10.3390/ijerph18189913
Roberts, T. J., & Konow, N. (2013). How tendons buffer energy dissipation by muscle. *Exercise and Sport Sciences Reviews, 41*(4), 186–193. https://doi.org/10.1097/JES.0b013e3182a4e6d5
Russell, M., Sparkes, W., Northeast, J., Cook, C. J., Love, T. D., Bracken, R. M., & Kilduff, L. P. (2016). Changes in acceleration and deceleration capacity throughout professional soccer match-play. *Journal of Strength and Conditioning Research, 30*(10), 2839–2844. https://doi.org/10.1519/JSC.0000000000000805
Samozino, P., Rivière, J. R., Rossi, J., Morin, J. B., & Jimenez-Reyes, P. (2018). How fast is a horizontal squat jump? *International Journal of Sports Physiology and Performance, 13*(7), 910–916. https://doi.org/10.1123/ijspp.2017-0499
Schaefer, L. V., & Bittmann, F. N. (2017). Are there two forms of isometric muscle action? Results of the experimental study support a distinction between a holding and a pushing isometric muscle function. *BMC Sports Science, Medicine and Rehabilitation, 9*(1), 1–13. https://doi.org/10.1186/s13102-017-0075-z
Schultz, B. J., Thomas, K. A., Cinque, M., Harris, J. D., Maloney, W. J., & Abrams, G. D. (2021). Tendency of driving to the basket is associated with increased risk of anterior cruciate ligament tears in national basketball association players: A cohort study. *Orthopaedic Journal of Sports Medicine, 9*(11), 1–8. https://doi.org/10.1177/23259671211052953
Smalley, B., Bishop, C., & Maloney, S. J. (2022). "Small steps, or giant leaps?" Comparing game demands of U23, U18, and U16 English academy soccer and their associations with speed and endurance. *International Journal of Sports Science and Coaching, 17*(1), 134–142. https://doi.org/10.1177/17479541211018771
Spiteri, T., Cochrane, J. L., Hart, N. H., Haff, G. G., & Nimphius, S. (2013). Effect of strength on plant foot kinetics and kinematics during a change of direction task. *European Journal of Sport Science, 13*(6), 646–652. https://doi.org/10.1080/17461391.2013.774053
Spiteri, T., Hart, N. H., & Nimphius, S. (2014). Offensive and defensive agility: A sex comparison of lower body kinematics and ground reaction forces. *J Appl Biomech, 30*(4), 514–520. https://doi.org/10.1123/jab.2013-0259

Spiteri, T., Nimphius, S., Hart, N. H., Specos, C., Sheppard, J. M., & Newton, R. U. (2014). Contribution of strength characteristics to change of direction and agility performance in female basketball athletes. *Journal of Strength and Conditioning Research/National Strength & Conditioning Association, 28*(9), 2415–2423. https://doi.org/10.1519/JSC.0000000000000547

Thomas, C., Comfort, P., Chiang, C.-Y., & A. Jones, P. (2015). Relationship between isometric mid-thigh pull variables and sprint and change of direction performance in collegiate athletes. *Journal of Trainology, 4*(1), 6–10. https://doi.org/10.17338/trainology.4.1_6

Tierney, P. J., Young, A., Clarke, N. D., & Duncan, M. J. (2016). Match play demands of 11 versus 11 professional football using Global Positioning System tracking: Variations across common playing formations. *Human Movement Science, 49*, 1–8. https://doi.org/10.1016/j.humov.2016.05.007

Turner, A. N., Read, P., Maestroni, L., Chavda, S., Yao, X., Papadopoulos, K., Virgile, A., Spiegelhalter, A., & Bishop, C. (2021). Reverse engineering in strength and conditioning. *Strength & Conditioning Journal*, 1–10. https://doi.org/10.1519/ssc.0000000000000681

Vázquez-Guerrero, J., Suarez-Arrones, L., Gómez, D. C., & Rodas, G. (2018). Comparing external total load, acceleration and deceleration outputs in elite basketball players across positions during match play. *Kinesiology, 50*(2), 228–234. https://doi.org/10.26582/K.50.2.11

Verheul, J., Nedergaard, N. J., Pogson, M., Lisboa, P., Gregson, W., Vanrenterghem, J., & Robinson, M. A. (2021). Biomechanical loading during running: Can a two mass-spring-damper model be used to evaluate ground reaction forces for high-intensity tasks? *Sports Biomechanics, 20*(5), 571–582. https://doi.org/10.1080/14763141.2019.1584238

Verheul, J., Warmenhoven, J., Lisboa, P., Gregson, W., Vanrenterghem, J., & Robinson, M. A. (2019). Identifying generalised segmental acceleration patterns that contribute to ground reaction force features across different running tasks. *Journal of Science and Medicine in Sport, 22*(12), 1355–1360. https://doi.org/10.1016/j.jsams.2019.07.006

Waldén, M., Krosshaug, T., Bjørneboe, J., Andersen, T. E., Faul, O., & Hägglund, M. (2015). Three distinct mechanisms predominate in noncontact anterior cruciate ligament injuries in male professional football players: A systematic video analysis of 39 cases. *British Journal of Sports Medicine, 49*(22), 1452–1460. https://doi.org/10.1136/bjsports-2014-094573

Werkhausen, A., Albracht, K., Cronin, N. J., Meier, R., Bojsen-Møller, J., & Seynnes, O. R. (2017). Modulation of muscle–tendon interaction in the human triceps surae during an energy dissipation task. *The Journal of Experimental Biology, 220*(22), 4141–4149. https://doi.org/10.1242/jeb.164111

Werkhausen, A., Albracht, K., Cronin, N. J., Paulsen, G., Bojsen-Møller, J., & Seynnes, O. R. (2018). Effect of training-induced changes in Achilles tendon stiffness on muscle-tendon behavior during landing. *Frontiers in Physiology, 9*(June), 1–11. https://doi.org/10.3389/fphys.2018.00794

Wellman, A. D., Coad, S. C., Goulet, G. C., & McLellan, C. P. (2015). Quantification of competitive game demands of NCAA division I college football players using global positioning systems. *Journal of Strength and Conditioning Research, 30*(1), 11–19. https://doi.org/10.1519/JSC.0000000000001206

Winter, E. M., Abt, G., Brookes, F. B. C., Challis, J. H., Fowler, N. E., Knudson, D. V, Knuttgen, H. G., Kraemer, W. J., Lane, A. M., van Mechelen, W., Morton, R. H., Newton, R. U., Williams, C., & Yeadon, M. R. (2016). Misuse of "power" and other mechanical terms in sport and exercise science research. *Journal of Strength and Conditioning Research, 30*(1), 292–300. https://doi.org/10.1519/JSC.0000000000001101

Winter, E. M., & Fowler, N. (2009). Exercise defined and quantified according to the Systeme International d'Unites. *Journal of Sports Sciences, 27*(5), 447–460. https://doi.org/10.1080/02640410802658461

Woods, C. T., McKeown, I., Rothwell, M., Araújo, D., Robertson, S., & Davids, K. (2020). Sport practitioners as sport ecology designers: How ecological dynamics has progressively changed perceptions of skill "acquisition" in the sporting habitat. *Frontiers in Psychology, 11*(654), 1–15. https://doi.org/10.3389/fpsyg.2020.00654

Young, W. B. (1995). Laboratory strength assessment of athletes. *New Studies in Athletics, 10*(1), 89–96.

Zhang, Q., Léam, A., Fouré, A., Wong, D. P., & Hautier, C. A. (2021). Relationship between explosive strength capacity of the knee muscles and deceleration performance in female professional soccer players. *Frontiers in Physiology, 12*(October), 1–9. https://doi.org/10.3389/fphys.2021.723041

PART 2

Assessment and Development of Multidirectional Speed

6

ASSESSMENT OF MULTIDIRECTIONAL SPEED QUALITIES

Paul A. Jones and Thomas Dos'Santos

Introduction

Evaluation of sports speed in land-based field and court sports has so often taken the form of a linear sprint test typically over a 20 m distance in test batteries. However, as outlined in Chapter 1, development of *multidirectional speed* (MDS) has so many facets that need evaluating to help individualise MDS training programmes and physically prepare the athlete for the often-chaotic multidirectional demands of sport. Figure 6.1 highlights that whilst expressing speed running in a straight line is important, evaluating other qualities related to actions often seen in expressions of agility in sport, such as change of direction, deceleration, transitional movements, and curvilinear sprint running, is an important consideration. The assessment of such qualities is important to offer avenues for intervention for developing MDS with athletes. Furthermore, above all of this is the consideration of contextual speed (agility) (e.g. evaluating an athlete's ability to 'read' a situation and respond with and execute the most appropriate action), which is no mean feat and, as discussed later in this chapter, may actually be the holy grail of performance assessment.

To recognise the qualities that could be considered to evaluate MDS with athletes, Figure 6.2 is a flow chart of questions (black boxes) related to the typical time-motion demands of a chosen sport leading to test solutions (grey boxes) to be considered by the practitioner. It should be noted that evaluating any of the qualities mentioned in Figure 6.2, to inform a MDS programme more clearly for athletes, it is important to consider evaluating the technique of athletes performing the actions associated with the test, which can be simply done by filming the athlete(s) during the test (generally in the sagittal plane) for insight into an athlete's technique and movement strategy. This can be simply done using the high-speed recording capabilities on smart device technology. An evaluation of technique could offer avenue for intervention through technique modification training (Chapter 10) and is particularly pertinent for the rehabilitating athlete returning to play from injury (Buckthorpe, 2021). Furthermore, coupling assessments of MDS with physical performance tests associated with the movement actions involved, as outlined in Chapter 7, will also help the practitioner holistically evaluate the athlete regarding MDS and further individualise training programmes.

DOI: 10.4324/9781003267881-8

The remainder of this chapter discusses strategies to evaluate the components of MDS outlined in Figure 6.1. The chapter begins by outlining technologies to measure speed and time before discussing how such technologies can be used to assess linear speed, curvilinear speed, change of direction, deceleration, manoeuvrability, and finally, agility. The chapter attempts to offer suggestions for best practice in assessing these qualities.

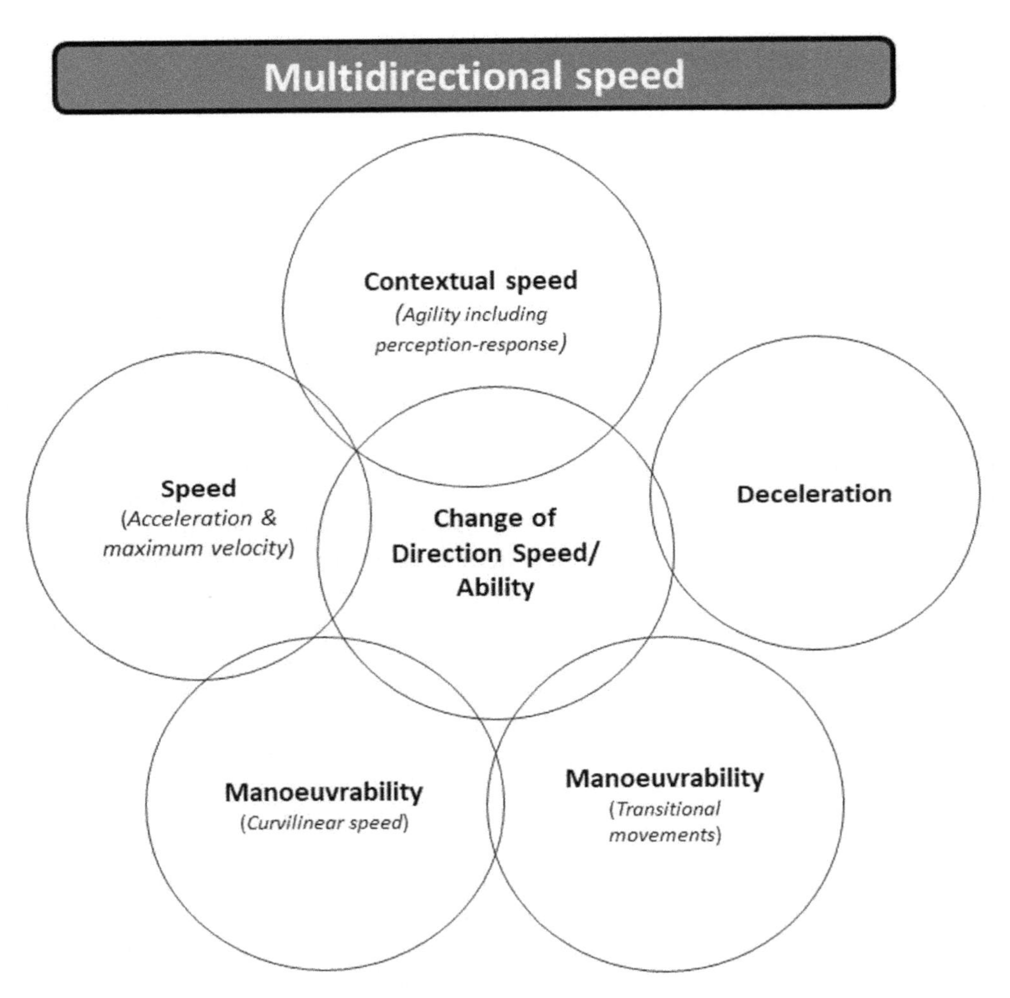

FIGURE 6.1 An outline of the components that make up multidirectional speed. Whilst assessment of contextual speed through well-designed agility tests that also assess perception-response time are important, underneath this quality is the consideration of the athlete's physical and mechanical ability to perform several movement actions (i.e. how). The diagram highlights how some tests of these qualities maybe linked such as sprinting and deceleration within a change-of-direction test and the fact that some so-called change-of-direction tests may also assess aspects of manoeuvrability (e.g. curvilinear speed, transitional movements).

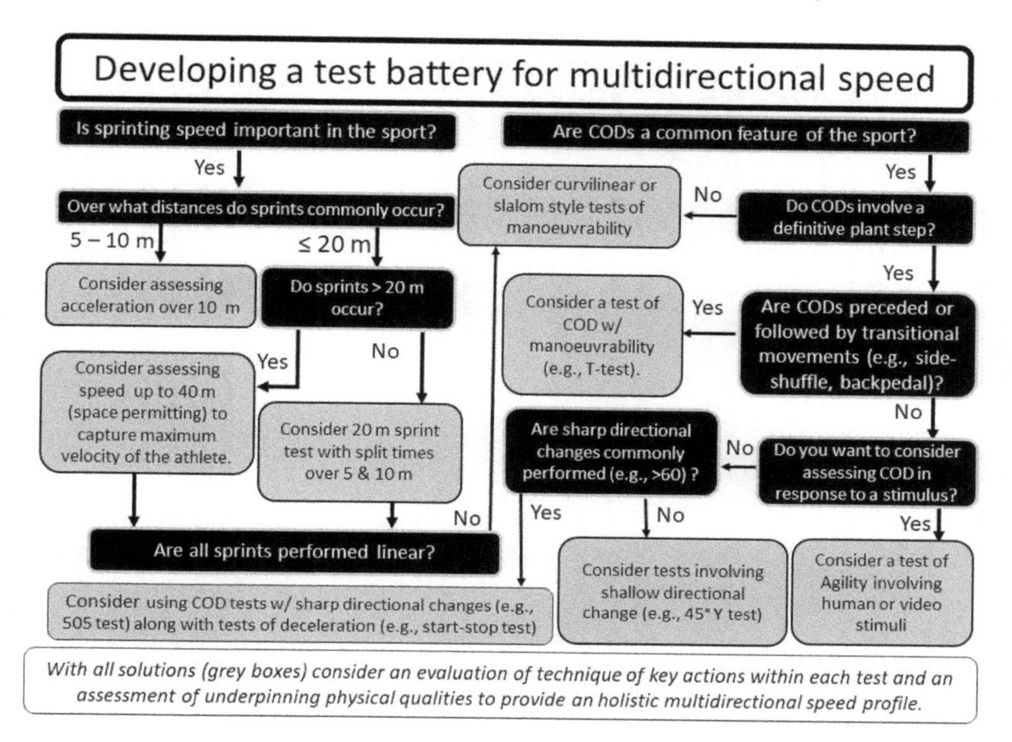

FIGURE 6.2 A flow chart to help design a battery of assessments for evaluating an athlete's multidirectional speed. By considering the sport's time-motion demands, answering the questions in the darker grey boxes leads to test solutions in the lighter grey boxes. It is important to note that in addition to assessing task completion times of some of the test solutions stated, practitioners should also consider evaluation of technique performing actions involved in these tests and consider assessing underpinning physical qualities.

Technologies Used To Assess Speed and Time

Fundamentally, as most sporting tasks require athletes to get to and from a specific location on the pitch or court as quickly as possible, assessments of MDS require devices to measure time and/or velocity. There is a variety of technologies to measure time and velocity, including hand-held devices, video, timing gates, laser devices, radar guns, global positioning systems, Optojump, and motorised resistance devices. The advantages and disadvantages of these devices are summarised in Table 6.1. The use of global positioning systems to monitor MDS development programmes is discussed in Chapter 15 and, thus, are not discussed here.

A popular choice for assessing sprint performance are *timing gates* (Lockie, 2018). Therefore, a dedicated section on important considerations for using timing gates follows. The cheapest and most accessible method to measure time is using *hand-held timing devices*. Experienced timekeepers can reliably record sprint time data (Hetzler et al., 2008; Mayhew et al., 2010; Mann et al., 2015). However, the accuracy of stopwatches or similar devices to record sprint times is influenced by reaction time of the timekeeper and result in greater measurement error compared to other devices (Haugen & Buchheit, 2016), and significant differences are often reported between

TABLE 6.1 A Summary of the Advantages and Disadvantages of Various Devices to Measure Time and/or Velocity for Athlete Assessment

Device	*Company/Source*	*Cost*	*Advantages*	*Disadvantages*
Stopwatches	Various sources	~≥£10	• Cheap, easily accessible • Perhaps more applicable for longer duration tasks such as manoeuvrability assessments of >10 s because the user error has less of an impact compared to linear sprint tasks	• Tester reaction time • Issues positioning the assessor (near start, middle, or finish?) • Errors are more problematic for times of shorter duration/speed at shorter distances. For example, a 0.1 s error is problematic for a 5 m sprint of 1 s, compared to a 0.1 s error for 40 m sprint of 5 s.
Timing gates	**Single-beam timing gates** Brower timing systems https://browertiming.com/ https://performbetter.co.uk/product/brower-timing-system/ **Dual-beam timing gates** Micrograte https://performbetter.co.uk/product/witty-dual-beam-system/ Swift http://swiftperformance.com https://performbetter.co.uk/product/swift-duo-wireless-timing-system/ **Post-processing timing gates** www.fusionsport.com	£1,410.00 (starter one gate system) Additional gates – £630 £3,028.80 (dual gates; additional gate – £1,141.20). £4,194.00 (2 gates) £9,714 (5 gates) $800 to $22,000 (1–8 gates)	• Can be used for multidirectional movement (e.g. COD and manoeuvrability tests).	• Only gives 'average speed' • Strict procedural considerations to ensure accurate data collection – although easy to implement • Accuracy can be influenced by type of device (e.g. single-beam vs dual-beam vs post-processing) and has resource implications.
Video analysis	Standard smartphone http://mysprint-app.com/	~£300	• Easy and readily available (e.g. high-speed video from an iPhone), possibly cheap given most people have a smartphone • Can be used to provide useful additional information (e.g. qualitative or quantitative technique evaluation)	• Accuracy influenced by available sample frequency • Time-consuming, although apps (e.g. COD Timer) and software (e.g. Quintic Biomechanics) can help speed up the process • Perhaps restricted to uniplanar tasks

Laser device	Muscle Lab www.musclelabsystem.com/ laser speed and distance sensor	£8,500	• Instantaneous measurement of speed; gives more detail on acceleration, maximum speed, and speed maintenance (e.g. velocities at key instances)	• Generally restricted to unidirectional movement, although a combination of one (Graham-Smith & Pearson, 2005; Ken-ichi et al., 2019) or two devices (Hader et al., 2015) have been used to provide approach and exit evaluations of COD manoeuvres • Accuracy compromised by 'absorbent' surfaces • Accuracy of measurement depends on experience of user. • Current models have lower sampling frequency (35 Hz) compared to discontinued devices commonly used in research such as the sport-LAVEG (50–100 Hz)
Radar	Applied Concepts, Inc. www.stalkerradar.com	$500–2,000	• Instantaneous measurement of speed; gives more detail on acceleration, maximum speed, and speed maintenance	• Measurement sensitive to reflections from objects close to the athlete when performing the sprint
GPS	Catapult Sports www.catapultsports.com/ STATSports https://statsports.com/	Single units (e.g. Catapult 1 or STATSports Apex Athlete Series) ≥£150 per athlete per year	• Can quantify in-game and practice running speed characteristics • Multiple units allow multiple players to be tested simultaneously. • Can enable in situ F-V profiling using training data from multiple football sessions over a training period (i.e. two-week period), without the requirement for isolated speed testing (Morin et al., 2021)	• Accuracy limited by sampling frequency of units (≤15 Hz) • Ensures athlete keeps the same unit on (longitudinally) in case of compromised inter-unit reliability • Signal strength dependent on weather, location, number of satellites, etc. • Difficulty quantifying COD movements • Limited to outdoors

(Continued)

TABLE 6.1 (Continued)

Device	*Company/Source*	*Cost*	*Advantages*	*Disadvantages*
Optojump system	Microgate https://performbetter.co.uk/product/optojump-next-modular-system/	10 m – £19,470 (additional metres – £1,947)	• Can obtain information on spatiotemporal characteristics during sprinting (e.g. flight and contact times, drive index)	• Only suitable to measure velocity/time over the maximum velocity phase of a sprint when step characteristics are more stable (Dolenc & Coh, 2009). • Not possible to determine the beginning and end of specific distances; thus, not comparable with timing gates (Dolenc & Coh, 2009) • Cost if needing to evaluate over longer sprint distances • Difficult to accurately measure step characteristics during acceleration due to changes in step kinematics over this phase (Lockie, 2018)
Motorised resistive device	1080motion https://1080motion.com/	$19,300	• Instantaneous measurement of speed; gives more detail on acceleration, maximum speed, and speed maintenance	• Ecological validity – tasks are performed with some resistance or assistance. • Effects on athletes' technique unknown • Use of wearable may restrict compliance.
Light detection and ranging laser technology (LiDAR)	Garmin LiDAR-Lite V3 laser ranging module and Arudinio Uno controller	$250	• Instantaneous measurement of speed; gives more detail on acceleration, maximum speed, and speed maintenance at 270 Hz	

electronic and manual timing (Ebben et al., 2009; Mann et al., 2015; Mayhew et al., 2010). Incorporating correction factors to manually recorded times may not be effective in improving the accuracy of hand-held times (Hetzler et al., 2008). If the only option for practitioners is to use hand-held timing devices, then clear instructions on the methods should be reported to ensure consistency (Hetzler et al., 2008; Lockie, 2018); however, due to the large error associated with hand-held timing, electronic devices such as timing gates are preferable (Hetzler et al., 2008; Haugen & Buchheit, 2016; Lockie, 2018) (see Table 6.1).

Given the evolution of high-speed *video*-recording capability (e.g. smartphone) makes assessment of time and velocity more accessible. Simply, by videoing an individual passing measured checkmarks during a sprint-related task, time to cover the known distance can be estimated by counting the number of frames and multiplying by 1 divided by the sampling frequency of the video. Smartphone applications such as the Sprint App or COD Timer can make light work of this or specialist video analysis software (e.g. Quintic Biomechanics) can be used to count the number of frames more accurately. However, the accuracy of sprint time or task completion time can be influenced by parallax error as an athlete passes a check mark (so careful video camera set-up is required (*see* Stenroth et al., 2020) and may remain time-consuming (requires post-processing). As shown in Box 6.1, video maybe a useful option to provide phase-specific information regarding COD manoeuvres in the field.

Laser devices or *radar guns* are electronic timing devices that have the advantage of tracking an athlete throughout a sprint, which can provide measurement of a variety of characteristics to describe an athlete's sprint performance (e.g. maximum velocity and where this occurs, velocity at pre-set distances). In contrast, timing gates do not provide instantaneous speed but average speed to complete a split distance. For example, two athletes may cover the distance at the same time but display different velocity profiles during the tests and their velocity at the end of the task could be different. Laser devices measure time delays of reflected pulsed infrared light. Radar guns use the Doppler effect; the gun transmits an electromagnetic signal that interact with the athlete before returning to the device at a different frequency (Chen et al., 2006). Changes in the properties of the returned signal are detected by the radar gun and converted to speed measurement (Lockie, 2018). Radar guns are sensitive to reflections from objects extraneous to the athlete, which can affect measurement, unlike laser devices. Typically, both devices work in the same way, set up on a tripod either in front or behind (behind is easier) the athlete. The tester tracks the athlete's lower torso as they run away or towards the device. Whilst laser (and radar devices) has been used with a variety of sports performers, found to agree with sprint velocities derived from video analysis and Optojump (Bezodis et al., 2012; Sides, 2014) and to be reliable (Bullock et al., 2008; Comfort et al., 2011; Schuster & Jones, 2016), there are limitations to their use. Testers must ensure a consistent target on the athlete to track. Laser devices have reported high levels of random error in the first 5 m of a maximal sprint, owing to the changing position of the trunk as the athletes accelerates from a stationary position (Bezodis et al., 2012). Thus, laser devices and radar guns are better suited for assessing characteristics of maximum velocity rather than initial acceleration (Lockie, 2018).

Considerations for Linear Sprint Testing and Using Timing Gates

Timing gates (Figure 6.3) are probably the most common apparatus used for sprint testing. Therefore, this section focuses on important considerations for sprint testing using timing cells and is also relevant to a later discussion of assessing *change-of-direction speed*. Timing cells will operate if the transmitter and reflector are aligned (Figure 6.3). However, this does not guarantee accurate

FIGURE 6.3 Timing gates consist of a least one transmitter and one reflector unit that are placed on adjustable tripods that form a gate along with a hand-held device to record times (a). When the transmitter and reflector are positioned opposite each other, the light beam from the transmitter hits the reflector and is bounced back to the transmitter where it is detected to form a 'gate' (d). When sets of transmitters and reflectors are arranged a known distance along a track (b), a series of beams are produced, which are interrupted when an athlete runs through. If the voltage output for each is logged, a pulse wave is produced, which rises on beam interruption and falls when the beam is reinstated (Yeadon et al., 1999). Subsequently, the time between the athlete passes each gate can be recorded on a hand-held data recorder (a). Ideally, the tester should be positioned close to the first gate (c) to monitor the start of the athlete and ensure the hand-held device is in range of the timing gates.

and reliable timing information to provide meaningful data. There are four main factors that need to be considered.

1. *Timing Gate System*

Timing gate systems can be *single-* and *dual-beam* or can incorporate *post-processing* techniques to accurately identify the moment an athlete breaks the timing cells. The latter two systems are considered more accurate as they can reduce any timing errors associated with the recorded time (Haugen et al., 2014; Haugen & Buchheit, 2016). A major source of error from a timing gate system is a false signal, which may occur when the light beam is broken by an outstretched arm or leg rather than the torso of the athlete (Yeadon et al., 1999). Single-beam systems are more susceptible to false signals when a limb breaks the light between the gates rather than the torso (Yeadon et al., 1999). Hence, when using single-beam timing cells, the height of the transmitter and reflector is critical (Cronin & Templeton, 2008; Altmann et al., 2017) (see point 2), and thus, single-beam timing cells have shown to be reliable (Mann et al., 2015; McMahon et al., 2017; Webster et al., 2022). Dual-beam timing gates involve light beams positioned at two heights and, therefore, should limit the effects of a limb breaking a single-beam, as the gates are only triggered when both beams are broken (Lockie, 2018). The Smart Speed system (Fusion Sport, Sumner Park, Australia) are single-beam timing cells, but use post-processing techniques to recognise error detection (Stanton et al., 2016). In the event of multiple triggers (e.g. limbs and trunk breaking the beam), the systems algorithm identifies the longest trigger of the beam as the true break in the beam (e.g. the largest segment, the trunk, would cause the longest break of the beam), subsequently leading to reliable sprint times (Stanton et al., 2016).

2. The Height the Transmitter and Reflector Are Set

The purpose of timing gates is to give a measure of whole-body speed by recording an accurate time to cover a pre-set distance. The transmitter and reflector should therefore be set at a height which will detect the movements of the athlete's centre of mass – that is, lower torso/tummy button height, position A on Figure 6.4 (Yeadon et al., 1999). If the height of the transmitter and reflector is either too low (position B) or too high (position C), there is an increased risk of measurement error due to the legs or head breaking the beam earlier than the torso would have done or missing the beam entirely (e.g. forward inclination during acceleration if beams are too high or stepping over due to high knee lift if beams are too low) (Figure 6.4). This would effectively reduce the split time and exaggerate the athlete's speed between consecutive gates. These recommendations are of course based on using single-beam timing cells; if using a dual-beam system, then the second beam should be placed around an approximate chest height.

3. Positioning of the Timing Gates

When setting up the positions of the transmitters and reflectors on the track it is imperative that they are aligned 90° to each other. Simply measuring out the position of the transmitter units and then using the mal-alignment detector to give the correct position of the reflector, could introduce more error. For example, in Figure 6.5 (A and B), the measured distance between the two-timing gates is 10 m, but one timing gate is not aligned 90° to the track. The distance between the reflector units could therefore be less than or greater than 10 m. This means that the time recorded would be for an unknown distance. To be exact and consistent the positions of both transmitter and reflector units need to be measured on both sides, as shown in Figure 6.5 (C). It is useful to mark the distances on the ground in case the stand or tripod is knocked. In addition, shining a laser pen on top of the transmitter to reflector to ensure they are aligned may be beneficial.

4. Consistency

To better replicate sprint testing sessions, the transmitter and reflector units need to be placed in the same positions each time measurements are taken. Generally, the start line should be 0.3 to

FIGURE 6.4 The height that a timing gate is set to is critical when using single-beam timing cells to avoid a false trigger. In position A, the timing gates are set around hip height, which approximates the height of the centre of mass and avoids being triggered by the arms or legs, which may occur when the timing gates are set too low (B) or too high (C).

0.5 m (certainly no more than 1 m) behind the first gate (Figure 6.5A); this is to avoid the athlete prematurely breaking the beam to trigger the timing system, whilst avoiding too much distance of travel prior to the first gate (e.g. remove influence of a 'flying' start) (Altmann et al., 2015; Haugen et al., 2015). Furthermore, it is also essential to standardise start techniques, such as a two-point split stance without any prior 'rocking' forward and backward movements (Figure 6.6) (Haugen et al., 2012). Most initial accelerations in sport are initiated from an upright stance, so a two-point start in most cases is recommended. When preparing for the NFL combine or certain situations when athletes start from a very low acceleration position (defensive line in NFL, rugby league, etc.) a three-point stance might be recommended. This ensures inter-athlete and intra-athlete consistency. It is also important to ensure that testing takes place on the same surface (e.g. indoor sports hall with rubber surface) with similar running shoes used by the athlete to ensure a similar

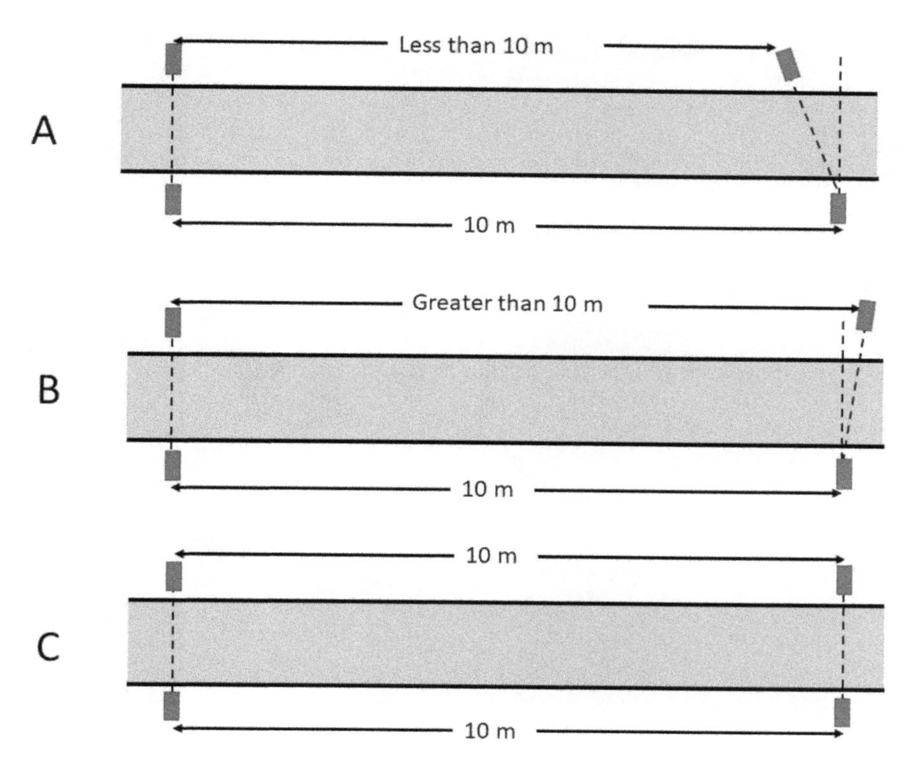

FIGURE 6.5 When using timing gates, it is essential to measure both sides of the runway to align timing cells (C). In scenarios A and B, one side has been measured, whereas the opposite side has been estimated, which potentially leads to a distance less than (A) or more than (B) the desired 10 m distance.

shoe-surface interface is used between sessions. Depending on how many pairs of transmitter and reflector units are available, the following set-ups for assessing early and mid-acceleration could be used, which may be appropriate for several field- and court-based sports. Typically, a 20 m sprint distance is used in such sports, but it should be noted that information regarding maximum velocity will not be attained without using sprint distances of around 40 m. Sprinters generally reach their maximum speed between 40 m and 60 m. In this case, four or five pairs of gates to attain realistic measures of maximum speed by positioning a final gate at 50 m would be required (Figure 6.7b). It would therefore be advisable with such athletes to use radar guns or laser devices to attain information regarding maximum velocity sprinting and not be restricted by the number of timing gates available. Other considerations include attempting to standardise environmental conditions (e.g. wind, temperature) which may ideally involve assessing indoors and adequate recovery between trials (e.g. rest periods 1 min for every 10 m). For more information regarding considerations for assessing speed, see Lockie et al. (2018).

Assessment of Curvilinear Sprint Ability (Manoeuvrability)

Whilst linear sprint tests are commonly conducted to evaluate players/athletes' 'speed', many sprints during field-based sports are curvilinear (Brice et al., 2004; Caldbeck, 2019; Fitzpatrick et al.,

FIGURE 6.6 A two-point 'split stance' starting position. The athlete starts 30 cm behind the timing cells and should be stationary.

2019), suggesting that curvilinear sprint performance (a sub-component of manoeuvrability) should be evaluated with athletes from such sports. Although curvilinear sprint performance is commonly associated with some track events (e.g. 200 and 400 m running), tests of such qualities are infrequently carried out in the literature. Fílter et al. (2020) developed a curvilinear sprint test for football, which used the D of the penalty area of a football pitch. Players were required to sprint in both a clockwise and anticlockwise manner around the D of the penalty area – a known length of 17 m and a radius of 9.15 m, with timing cells at the start and end of the D and at the mid-point (8.5 m). The authors reported acceptable reliability for each variable reported (ICC = 0.75–0.96; typical error = 0.03–0.06 s; CV = 0.5–1.97%). Interestingly, the authors reported low association between a linear 17 m sprint test and curvilinear sprints in either direction (R^2 = 0.35–0.37), suggesting that the curvilinear sprints are assessing different qualities to a linear sprint test. This offers avenues for performance testing in soccer to evaluate curvilinear sprint ability alongside linear sprint ability. Further research is required to adapt such protocols with other sports where curvilinear sprint ability is a prerequisite for performance and may require a multitude of different lengths and radii to be assessed to provide a curvilinear speed profile for an athlete in a specific field-based sport.

Assessment of Change-of-Direction Speed and/or Manoeuvrability

There are a variety of tests available to strength and conditioning coaches to evaluate athletes' COD speed. Well-known tests include the 505 (Draper & Lancaster, 1985; Barber et al., 2016),

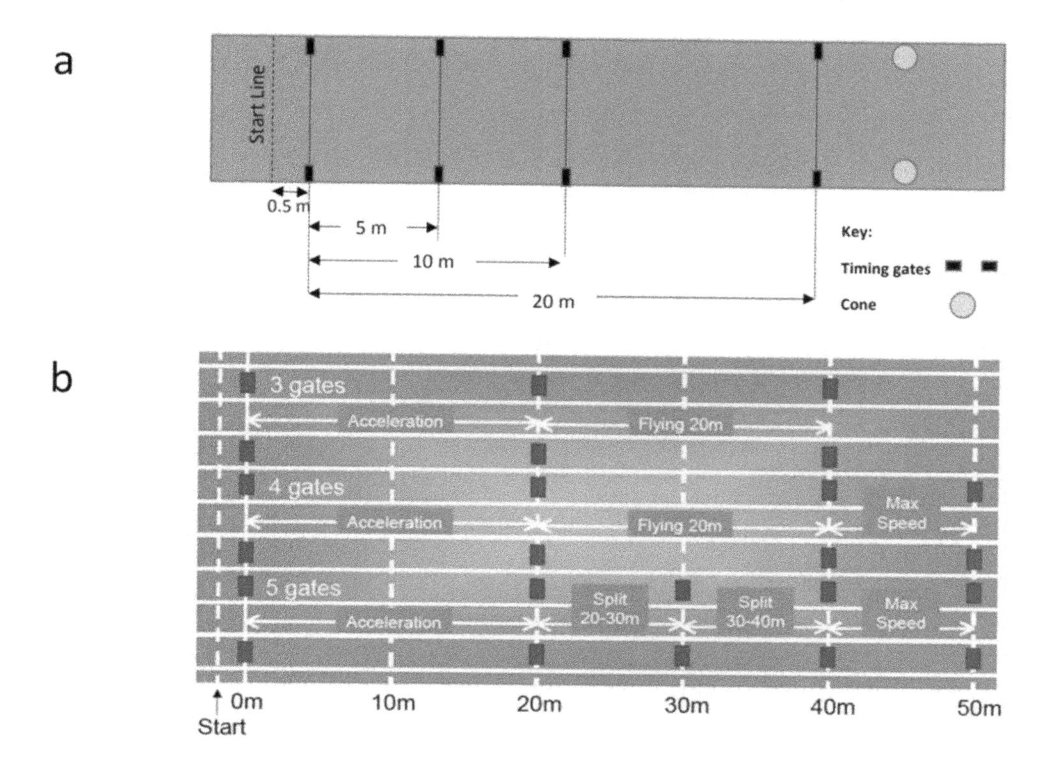

FIGURE 6.7 (a) Ideal to test set-ups for sprint testing using timing cells depending on information required. Cones are placed after the finish line to ensure the athlete runs through the final set of timing cells. The distance of the start line prior to the first set of timing gates is recommended to be 0.3 to 0.5 to prevent early triggering and a 'flying' start (0.3 m for children and athletes for smaller stature and 0.5 m for adults and taller youths). (b) When information regarding maximum velocity is required, then several sets of timing gates are required and could be set up as shown to provide information regarding acceleration and maximum velocity.

pro-agility (Sierer et al., 2008), the L-run/three-cone drill (Sierer et al., 2008; Gabbett et al., 2008), the T-test (Munro & Herrington, 2011) and the Illinois test (Vescovi & McGuigan, 2008). Furthermore, several tests designed for specific sports appear in the literature, such the arrowhead agility test in soccer (Rago et al., 2020), running a two or three in cricket (Foden et al., 2015), Australian (rules) football league agility test (Hart et al., 2014), an agility test for rugby league (Comfort et al., 2011), softball home to second base (Nimphius et al., 2010), and squash specific COD speed test (Wilkinson et al., 2009). A summary of several COD speed tests from the literature are presented in Table 6.2 with classifications previously described in Chapter 1 to assist in determining the sub-qualities of COD examined by the test. For an extensive overview of a range of COD speed tests, the interested reader should refer to the excellent article by Nimphius et al. (2018). For detailed descriptions of the common tests mentioned, see Jones and Nimphius (2018).

A limitation of many traditional COD speed tests often is the test duration (Table 6.2). A test of COD speed should be of short duration, as the longer the test is, then there is less emphasis

TABLE 6.2 Summary of Change-of-Direction and Manoeuvrability Tests

Test	*Description*	*COD*	*Manoeuvrability*		*Test Duration*	*Total Distance*	*References*
		With a definitive 'plant' step angle (number)	*Maintain velocity or curvilinear sprint path*	*Change in mode of travel*			
505 (modified and traditional)	The 505 test involves a 5 m approach and return separated by a single 180° turn and can be performed from a 15 m (traditional) or 5 m approach (modified). (*Adaptations for shallow directional changes [90°] have also been implemented – Cuthbert et al., 2019; Dos'Santos et al., 2019b*)	180° (1)	×	×	2–3 s	10 m	Draper & Lancaster, 1985; Barber et al., 2016; Nimphius et al., 2016a
Pro-agility	Athlete begins in a three-point stance, turns left, and sprints towards and touches the base of a cone, with the right hand 4.6 m away, and then turns 180° and sprints 9.2 m and touches the base of another cone, with the left hand 9.2 m away, then performs a 180° turn and sprints back through the start line.	180° (2)	×	×	4–5 s	18.4 m	Sierer et al., 2008; Nimphius et al., 2013
L-run	Athlete sprints 4.6 m to a cone (B), turns 180° and sprints back to the start line (cone A), turns 180° and sprints back and around cone B (turning 90°) and continues to sprint and run around another cone (C) 4.6 m away (turning 180°). The athlete then continues to sprint back around (90°) cone B and through the start line at cone A.	180° + [90° & 180° approx. around cones] (5)	✓	×	~7 s	~27 m	Gabbett et al., 2008; Sierer et al., 2008

T-test (and modified T-test)	Athlete sprints 9.1 m to a cone B (touching the base of the cone with the right hand) and then, 90° to the original direction, side-shuffles 4.6 m to another cone (C), touching the base of the cone with the left hand. The athlete then side-shuffles 9.1 m to another cone (D), touching the base of the cone with the right hand, and then side-shuffles back to cone B, touching base of the cone with the left hand, and then backpedals back to the start line. Modified involves a reduced distance of 5 m sprint approach and backpedal exit, 2.5 m between cones.	90° & 180° (4)	×	✓	7.5–13.5 s (modified 3–7 s)	36.56 m (modified 15 m)	Munro & Herrington, 2011; Sassi et al., 2009; Pauole et al., 2000
Illinois	Athlete begins in a press up position and, on 'go', sprints up and back along a 9.14 m track and then circles and runs in and out of four cones spaced along the same 9.14 m distance. The test is completed by performing two more sprints (up and back) along the 9.14 m course.	180° + (≥90° approx. around cones), (11)	✓	×	13–19 s	~60 m	Vescovi & McGuigan, 2008; Hachana et al., 2013
4 × 5 m sprint	Athlete sprints 5 m, turns 90° to the right (around cone), and then sprints 5 m before turning 90° left (around cone). The athlete then continues to sprint 5 m and turns 180° around a cone and sprints back 5 m through the finish line.	90° and 180° (3)	✓	×	5.5–6.5 s	20 m	Sporis et al. (2010)
9,6, 3, 6, 9 test	Athlete sprints 9 m, turns 180°, sprints 6 m, turns 180°, sprints 3 m, turns 180°, sprints 6 m, turns 180°, and then finally sprints 9 m through the finish line. An alternative version involves backpedalling the 6 m portions of the test (e.g. sprint 9 m, backpedal 6 m, sprint 3 m, backpedal 6 m, and sprint 9 m).	180° (4)	×	✓ *(if using backpedal on 6 m sprints)*	7–8 s	33 m	Sporis et al. (2010)

(*Continued*)

TABLE 6.2 (Continued)

Test	*Description*	*COD*	*Manoeuvrability*		*Test Duration*	*Total Distance*	*References*
		With a definitive 'plant' step angle (number)	*Maintain velocity or curvilinear sprint path*	*Change in mode of travel*			
Shuttle tests over various distances	Sprint, followed by a 180°, followed by another sprint of the same length; this has been widely used in the literature using a variety of distances, numbers of sprints, and directional changes ranging from 2 × 5 yards/metres to 10 × 5 metres.	180° (2–20)	×	×	2.5–22 s, depending on test design	10–50 m, depending on test design	Malisoux et al., 2006; Harris et al., 2000; Markovic et al., 2007
Slalom test	This involves sprinting up and down over a set distance (11 m), weaving around cones placed every 2 m long the sprint path. Variations may vary in the literature.	30–45° and 180° (11)	✓	×	7–8 s	22 m	Sporis et al., 2010
CODAT	5 m sprint, 45° COD at a cone, 3 m sprint, 90° COD at a cone, 3 m sprint, 90° COD at a cone, 3 m sprint, 45° COD, 10 m sprint to finish	45° and 90° (4)	✓ (possibly)	×	5.5–6.5 s	~24 m	Lockie et al., 2013; Lockie et al., 2014
Pre-planned Y (agility)	Pre-planned versions of the Y-agility tests involving video or human stimulus (see later section). Test involves sprinting 4–5 m then performing a 45° COD at a check mark and then sprinting another 4–5 m. Test administered to both left and right.	45° (1)	✓ (possibly)	×	2–3 s	8–10 m	Lockie et al. 2013; Serpell et al., 2010
Sprints with CODs embedded	Sprint with 90° COD – consists of a 21 m sprint separated by six 90° turns with 2 to 5 m between turns. 30 m sprint separated by 2–5 CODs Zig-zag test involves three 5 m sprints separated by three 100° CODs	90° (6) 45°, 80°, 120° (2–5) 100° (3)	✓	×	6–8 s 4–11 s 4–6 s	~21 m ~30 m ~20 m	Sporis et al., 2010 Young et al., 2001 Little & Williams, 2005

Stop 'n' go COD test	Course involves a 2 m distance from the start line to the centre point where four cones are placed 2 m away to left and right at 90° and 45° angles. After initially running to the first cone (left-hand side) and back to start line, an athlete would proceed to run to all four cones from the centre line before returning to the start line to complete the test.	45°, 90°, and 180° (13)	✓	×	8–10 s	28 m	Sekulic et al., 2014
Box test or AG test	Athletes follow a predetermined course within a 4 × 4 m box three times, touching the base of the cone at each directional change.	135° (11)	×	×	15–17 s	57.954 m	Tricoli et al., 2005
Hexagon test	The performer faces one direction and executes double-leg hops forward, sideways, and backwards around a hexagon (with 61 cm sides at 120° angles) from the centre three times (18 jumps and return).	60° (18)	×	×	8–16 s	21.6 m	Beekhuizen et al., 2009

on assessing COD speed, but more on anaerobic capacity and sprint ability as more time is spent running between COD actions (Nimphius et al., 2016a). For instance, typical test durations shown in Table 6.2 suggest performance on all these tests may be influenced by metabolic limitations (Vescovi & McGuigan, 2008) and sprint ability (Nimphius et al., 2016a) and less on COD ability. Furthermore, many of the mentioned tests, due to the involvement of transitional movements (e.g. T-test) or a curvilinear path of running (e.g. running around cones during an L-run or Illinois), are suggested to be more appropriate assessments of manoeuvrability rather than an isolated measure of COD ability (Nimphius, 2014; DeWeese & Nimphius, 2016; Nimphius et al., 2018). Therefore, careful consideration of test design is needed to ensure the required MDS quality is being assessed.

The 505 test avoids the limitation of test duration as the typical completion times last 2–3 s (Gabbett et al., 2008; Jones et al., 2009; Nimphius et al., 2016a). The 505 removes much of the task complexity of other tests as with only one turn involved it provides a measure of COD ability with a particular emphasis during the traditional 505 on deceleration ability prior to a COD. The tests clearly involve a change of direction as there is a definitive plant step at a turn line and does not involve running around cones, which would then effectively make it a test of manoeuvrability. However, the total completion time of a 505 test may not necessarily provide a measure of COD ability. For instance, Nimphius et al. (2013) found that only 31% of the time during a 505 test is spent turning, with the remainder of the time decelerating and accelerating. This is further supported by biomechanical studies with final contact time representing approximately 19.5–20% of completion times of 180° pivot tasks from various approaches (Jones et al., 2016; Graham-Smith et al., 2009), whereas Ken-ichi et al. (2019) found that COD time (termed *cutting time* – last 1 m of approach to first 1 m exit measured using a LAVEG) constituted a third (0.8 ± 0.08 s) of 505 completion times in a group (n = 24) of faster performers (2.45 ± 0.11 s). Therefore, linear sprinting ability may also influence 505 completion times and is perhaps more pronounced during traditional compared to modified 505 tests due to the greater entry velocity developed during the initial 10 m sprint. This notion is supported by several studies that have found a relationship between linear sprinting speed and 505 test performance (Gabbett et al., 2008; Jones et al., 2009; Nimphius et al., 2016a) despite the recognition that they are different physical qualities (Young et al., 2001). Furthermore, Sayers (2015), using 3D motion analysis to examine COD performance times over distances of 0.3, 0.5, and 1 m before and after the turn, measured as the time for the centre of mass to cover each distance before and after the turn, revealed strong relationships between 505 time and 5, 10, and 20 m sprint performance. However, the strength of these correlations reduced when COD ability was measured 0.5 m and 0.3 m before and after the turn, thus highlighting that 505 performance time is biased by linear sprinting ability.

Assessing COD ability over shorter approach and exit distances (i.e. less than 1 m before and after the turn) is not really an option due to compromised reliability associated with reduced distances (Sayers, 2015). An approach to overcome the limitation of linear sprinting speed influencing 505 test performance is to calculate the *COD deficit* (Nimphius et al., 2013; Nimphius et al., 2016a), whereby a 10 m sprint time is subtracted from the 505 time. The lower the value, the greater the COD ability. This concept was initially proposed and investigated in 66 collegiate American football players performing 40-yard sprints with a 10-yard split and pro-agility trials with a split time for the first 10 yards of the test (a single 180° turn) (Nimphius et al., 2013). COD deficit was determined by subtracting the 10-yard sprint split time from the 10-yard split time from the pro-agility test, with the resultant time providing an indication of the time taken to negotiate the 180° turn. Significant ($p < 0.001$) correlations were observed between pro-agility scores (total and split) time and 10-yard sprint performance. However, a low non-significant correlation was observed between COD deficit and 10-yard sprint time (r = 0.19), but significant moderate correlations were observed to pro-agility (r = 0.54) and pro-agility split times (r = 0.61). This data suggests that the COD deficit offers a measure of COD speed independent of linear sprinting speed. Subsequently, Nimphius et al. (2016a) investigated the application of the COD deficit within the 505 tests in 17 cricketers. The authors found that COD deficit correlated to 505 (r = 0.74–0.81) but not 10 m sprint time (r = -0.11–0.10), whilst 505 time correlated with sprint time (r = 0.52–0.70). Moreover, when Z scores were examined, 5 of the 17 subjects were classified differently in terms of COD ability when using 505 or COD deficit. The results support the use of the COD deficit to isolate and quantify an individual's COD ability, independent from their linear sprinting speed. The COD deficit has been further explored at various change-of-direction angles (Cuthbert et al., 2019; Nimphius et al., 2016b), transitioning between modes of travel (e.g. sprint to shuffle) (Nimphius et al., 2016b) and been shown to be more able to detect asymmetries in COD ability during a 505 test (Dos'Santos et al., 2019a). Thus, determining COD deficit should be a minimum requirement when assessing COD speed/ability.

Another important aspect to consider is whether the athlete applies a 'pacing strategy' during tests such as the 505 test. This could be evaluated by comparing the 10 m approach time from a traditional 505 test to that from a linear 10 m sprint time. If the approach time is slower than the 10 m sprint, it immediately tells the examiner that the athlete is adopting a pacing strategy (self-regulatory) to either, make the test slightly easier and/or to reduce the braking demands/load. A cut-off value could be an approach speed which is slower than a linear 10 m sprint time by a margin greater than the typical error, coefficient of variation or standard error of measurement associated with the 10 m linear sprint test.

Assessment of time to completion of any COD task may still provide an oversimplification of an athlete's COD ability. With available resources such as 3D motion analysis, force platforms, and high-speed cameras, additional information of approach (deceleration), contact times, and reacceleration phases can be provided. This would allow an evaluation of athlete's deceleration and reacceleration abilities. The associated costs and practicality (i.e. lab-based) often precludes application of such analyses. High-speed (>100 Hz) cameras are now more readily available and can be incorporated into the field. Whilst 2D analysis to derive centre-of-mass velocities to determine approach and exit velocities maybe too time consuming for a strength and conditioning coach and delay feedback to athletes, Box 6.1 outlines an approach to breakdown a 505 test into approach, execution, and reacceleration phases from video analysis. Additional information regarding step characteristics can also be provided. Alternative approaches could involve using additional timing gates or laser devices (Graham-Smith & Pearson, 2005; Hader et al., 2015; Ken-ichi et al., 2019). For instance, Hader et al. (2015) used 2 LAVEG speed guns to measure approach (10 m) speed toward and exiting (10 m) from 45° and 90° cuts, whereas others (Graham-Smith & Pearson, 2005; Ken-ichi et al., 2019) have used a LAVEG laser speed gun to examine the approach and exit velocity characteristics during a 180° COD task. The timing system has been shown to provide acceptable levels of validity and reliability to assess a range of movement characteristics (e.g. peak and minimum speed, distance at peak speed) during such tasks (Hader et al., 2015) and could also be used to identify time spent braking, change direction, and reaccelerate in a 505 test (Ken-ichi et al., 2019). Motorised resistance devices have also been used to quantify such variables during a 505 test (Eriksrud et al., 2022). Thus, may be options to practitioners with available resources.

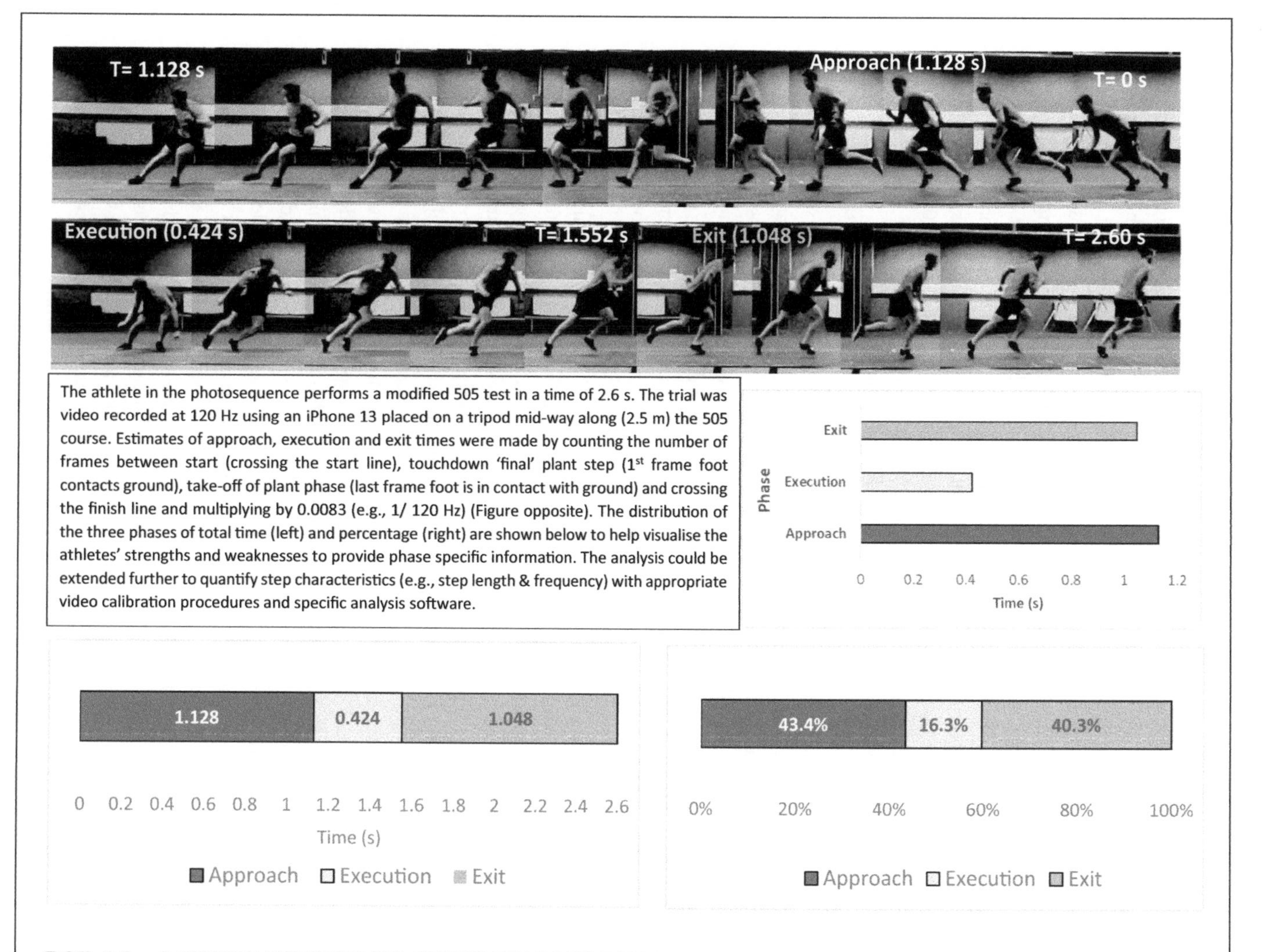

The athlete in the photosequence performs a modified 505 test in a time of 2.6 s. The trial was video recorded at 120 Hz using an iPhone 13 placed on a tripod mid-way along (2.5 m) the 505 course. Estimates of approach, execution and exit times were made by counting the number of frames between start (crossing the start line), touchdown 'final' plant step (1st frame foot contacts ground), take-off of plant phase (last frame foot is in contact with ground) and crossing the finish line and multiplying by 0.0083 (e.g., 1/ 120 Hz) (Figure opposite). The distribution of the three phases of total time (left) and percentage (right) are shown below to help visualise the athletes' strengths and weaknesses to provide phase specific information. The analysis could be extended further to quantify step characteristics (e.g., step length & frequency) with appropriate video calibration procedures and specific analysis software.

BOX 6.1 A SIMPLE METHOD TO EVALUATE EACH PHASE OF A CHANGE-OF-DIRECTION MANOEUVRE USING VIDEO ANALYSIS

Test selection

To decide on an appropriate test/assessment strategy for COD and/or manoeuvrability, it is important to ensure the 'why' of testing is considered (Nimphius et al., 2018). Practitioners need to make informed decisions as to which of the following is most beneficial:

- Considering if isolating the COD being assessed by shortening the length of the test (e.g. accomplished through calculating the COD deficit) and ensuring a definitive plant step is performed to change direction
- Considering the calculation of approach momentum (COM velocity × body mass) for contact sports and identify/consider the braking demand this places on the athlete
- Qualitative technique analysis of the movement to determine COD efficiency or movement quality/braking strategy upon return to play scenarios
- Considering if the test is intended to measure change in mode of travel or ability to maintain velocity (termed manoeuvrability) rather than intending to assess COD as defined in Chapter 1

Once these decisions are made, the selection of an appropriate test may in part depend on the common movement patterns involved within that sport. However, tests may be selected purely based on the physical demand the test elicits on an athlete for general athletic quality assessment or return to play evaluation (Nimphius, 2017). For instance, the 505 test from a sport perspective mimics running and turning between wickets in cricket, and thus, the test has a strong association to the movement patterns associated with that sport (Foden et al., 2015). However, whilst 180° turns are often observed in many different field- and court-based sports, they are often the least common compared to other angles of direction change (Bloomfield et al., 2007; Sweeting et al., 2017; Morgan et al., 2021; Talty et al., 2022). Nevertheless, practitioners in such sports may often use a test like the 505 test due to the deceleration/braking demand involved in the test. It should be recognised that changing direction to differing angles (also from different approach velocities) results in marked biomechanical differences (Schreurs et al., 2017; Dos'Santos et al., 2018; Dos'Santos et al., 2021); therefore, potentially practitioners may consider assessing performance and/or technique of athletes performing different directional changes given that multiple-directional changes may be performed in their sport. Box 6.2 outlines an approach to evaluate a 'change-of-direction angle profile' that maybe considered by practitioners.

The pre-planned structure of all the tests outlined in Table 6.2 often leads to questions regarding the ecological validity in relation to match or game performance. For instance, the pro-agility or L-run used in the NFL combine (Sierer et al., 2008) hardly matches the changing patterns of play for all positions on the field in American football. Realistically, the mentioned tests or any other tests designed to mimic movement patterns in a sport will not achieve an exact replication due to the constantly changing patterns of play on the field. Moreover, often strategies adopted by athletes to negotiate the manoeuvre often leads to breaks in posture and technique from what is achieved during similar manoeuvres during match play in 'open' situations (Figure 6.8), and thus, maybe rules should be implemented to negate any undesired movement mechanics in this regard. Ultimately, the test choice and associated methods must be determined with respect to the purpose of the assessment (e.g. is it to replicate common patterns, assess a specific aspect of athleticism, to evaluate confidence and physical capacity prior to return to play or transition to more open and demanding drills, tests or scenarios?) (Jones & Nimphius, 2018).

Change of direction angle profile

Most sports require athletes to be competent at changing direction from both limbs, across a spectrum of shallow, moderate and sharp COD angles, it would therefore be prudent to examine athletes' change of direction ability across a range of different angles.

Additionally because the biomechanical demands of COD are angle and velocity dependent (Dos'Santos et al., 2018), it would be erroneous to assume an athlete with sufficient shallow COD ability will also display superior COD ability to a task of greater angle, and vice versa.

Consequently, practitioners could build a COD angle profile by examining completion time and COD deficit during isolated COD tasks of 45, 90, 135 and 180° as illustrated in the image on the right. Typically this would involve athletes performing 2 trials per limb of each angle.

This allows practitioners to:

- Build an angle profile (bottom)– identify specific COD angles the athlete needs to work on – velocity (shallow), force (sharp)?
- Also identify directional dominance and asymmetries (bottom). For example, does that athlete have superior performance with left limb?

Test set-up

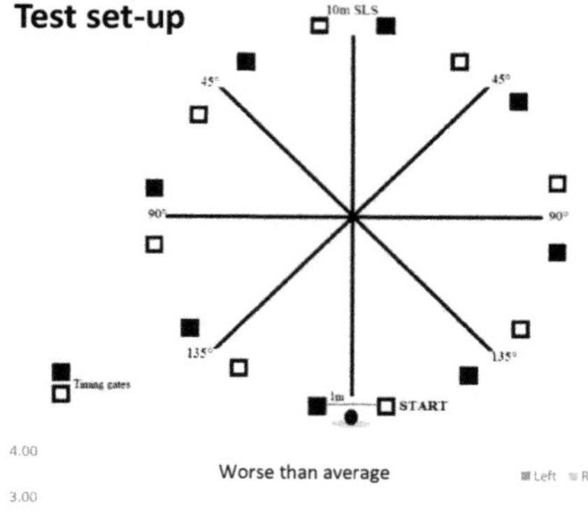

Evaluation

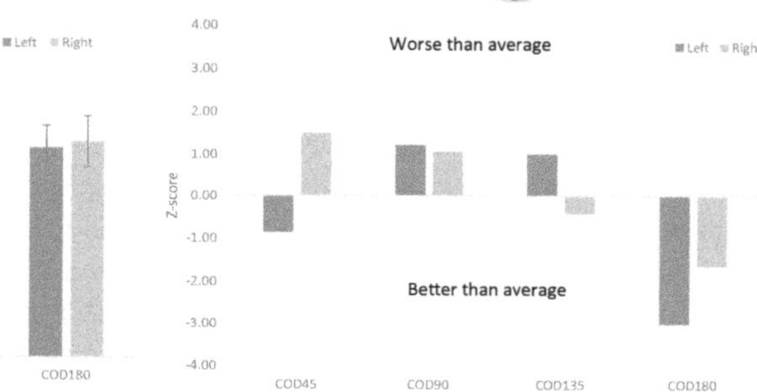

BOX 6.2 A POTENTIAL APPROACH TO ESTABLISH A CHANGE-OF-DIRECTION PROFILE WITH ATHLETES

Assessment of Deceleration Ability

As outlined in Chapters 1, 4, and 5, the ability to decelerate is an important component of COD speed besides being a vital action in sports match play. Until recently the ability to quantify deceleration ability has not been adequately considered. Early attempts to evaluate deceleration ability involved determining stopping distance from a 10 m maximal sprint using a standard tape measure to determine distance from the finishing line to the posterior heel of the stationary participant on the complete stop (Naylor & Greig, 2015). This test was used in a study to explore the interaction between a battery of physical and cognitive profiling tests against four common agility tests; thus, it did not report any validity or reliability of the method. Furthermore, the method lacks an objective quantification of entry velocity into the deceleration zone and the ability to measure further characteristics of deceleration. Harper et al. (2018) utilised video analysis using

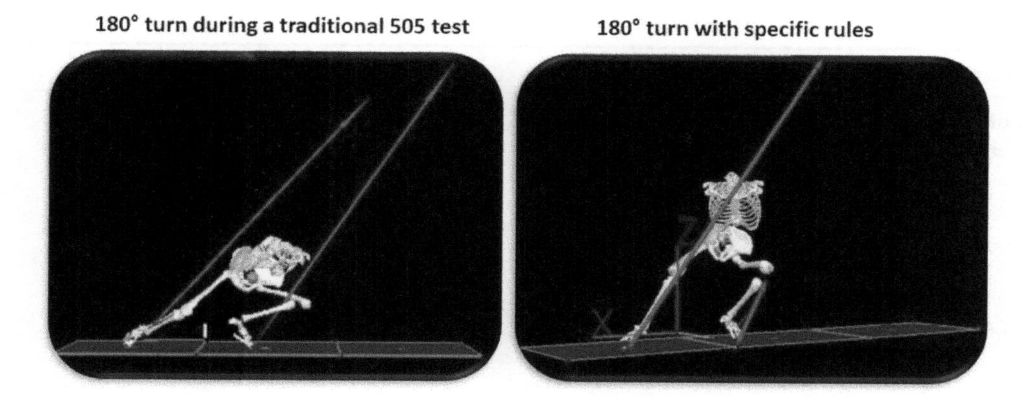

FIGURE 6.8 A photo sequence showing differences in posture and technique between a 505 test (left) compared to when specific rules (e.g., turn at the turn line, no hand placement on floor) are applied to a 505 test (right); the posture and technique moves closer to that during match play. The slightly greater trunk lean (lack of trunk control) here likely due to greater approach velocity involved with the 505 test.

a low sampling rate of 50 Hz to determine and calculate maximal linear deceleration distance and time to stop from a 20 m maximal sprint. They determined approach velocity by calculating the velocity within the final 1 m of the approach to the deceleration zone. The mentioned laser devices (LAVEG) have been used to quantify stopping distance following a maximal sprint. Ashton and Jones (2019) explored within and between session reliability of determining stopping distances following a 15 m sprint in rugby union players, finding that 'stopping distance' could be reliably determined (ICC = 0.91; SEM = 6.54%; SDD = 9.11%). However, a limitation of this approach pointed out by the authors is that even though participants were instructed to stop after hearing the 'audible bleep' after passing through a set of timing cells at the finish of the 15 m sprint, velocity profile data revealed a slight drop-off in velocity prior to the finish of the 15 m sprint, which is difficult to account for and may influence the accuracy of determining true stopping distance. This finding also questions the accuracy of determining stopping distance using tape measure and video-based methods mentioned earlier. Harper et al. (2020) used a similar test design involving a 20 m sprint to a complete stop followed by a backpedal, but the use of a radar device to determine deceleration characteristics found poor to moderate (particularly poor between session) reliability for deceleration variables, such as time and distance, to stop and early and late deceleration. However, the authors found estimated kinetic characteristics (e.g. braking force and impulse) to have moderate to good reliability, despite such variables being determined from the previously mentioned velocity- and time-derived variables. Again, the approach by Harper et al. (2020) may lead to an anticipatory drop-off in velocity prior to the end of the 20 m sprint in this case and is a drawback in determining deceleration characteristics for such test designs.

An alternative approach by Graham-Smith et al. (2018) involved subjects performing a 30 m sprint, followed by start-stop drills over 5, 10, 15, and 20 m (subjects having to accelerate maximally and stop within the pre-set distance). This approach allows the practitioner

TABLE 6.3 An Overview of Metrics to Consider When Examining COD Speed and Agility

Measure	*Description*	*Interpretation*
Completion time	Total time to complete the task	Completion time represents the duration it takes the athlete get from A to B but can be biased towards athletes with superior linear speed and provides limited information regarding COD ability or technique. It can be simply assessed using a stopwatch or electronic timing gates.
COD deficit	Difference in time between a maximal effort straight-line (linear) sprint and a COD speed test of equal length	COD deficit provides an isolated measure of COD ability, which is generally not biased to athletes with superior linear speed. It provides insight into the additional time required to change direction in light of their linear speed capacity. It can be simply assessed using a stopwatch or electronic timing gates.
Ground contact time	Duration of ground contact from initial contact to toe-off during the main execution plant foot contact	Shorter ground contacts times are generally associated with faster COD performance and indicates the athlete is spending less time performing the COD (as long as the athlete deflects their COM at the same angle). Insight into GCT can establish whether the athlete is actually improving their COD ability irrespective of total time. GCT can be measured using a built-in force plate or contact mat or verified using 2D analysis.
Exit velocity	Horizontal COM velocity of the athlete at the end of the toe-off during the main execution foot contact or first step of reacceleration	Exit velocity is a strong determinant of COD completion time, and high exit velocity is generally the overarching aim when executing agility actions. Insight into COM velocity profiles actually provides insight into COD ability to establish whether COD velocity is actually improving. It can be assessed using 3D motion analysis, 2D analysis tracking a pelvis/hip marker, or a laser/radar speed gun (but reliability of laser speed is gun is questionable). Again, please note that athletes should deflect their COM at the same angle due to the angle-velocity trade-off.
Entry velocity	Horizontal COM velocity of the athlete prior to the main execution foot contact. This could be several steps prior or the velocity during the PFC.	Entry velocity is a strong determinant of COD completion time, and the ability to enter the COD with high velocity can be advantageous for COD actions. Insight into entry velocity can be used to establish whether any pacing or self-regulatory strategies are adopted. Exit velocity can also be determined in a similar manner.

Measure	*Description*	*Interpretation*
Decision-making time	Measurement of the time between two events is considered decision-making time and can either be a positive or a negative value (anticipation). Decision-making time can be broken down into two different orientations to comprehensively assess how athletes respond during game scenarios: (1) defensive (move in the same direction as the stimulus) and (2) offensive (move in the opposite direction to the stimulus).	Similar to the measurement of entry and exit velocity, a high-speed camera can be positioned to the side of the directional change to capture both the stimulus and the athlete's first definitive foot plant to change direction in response. If the decision-making time is negative, this indicates that the athlete anticipated the directional change before the stimulus finalised the movement. Negative decision-making time is observed only during response to movements of another person (video or human stimulus), highlighting the importance of stimulus specificity during agility protocols. The measurement of decision-making time in both defensive and offensive situations allows coaches to identify whether athletes need to develop their perceptual-cognitive ability in a specific game scenario.

to determine maximum velocity attained in each start-stop trial and relate that to maximum velocity achieved in the 30 m sprint, and then determine the stopping distance, time, and deceleration involved within each task. This approach overcomes the limitation of the 'anticipatory' reduction in velocity involved with other approaches (e.g. set sprint distance and the stopping zone) but would require the athletes having sufficient familiarity with the start-stop tests/drills. Another approach used in the literature to determine deceleration ability was developed by Clarke et al. (2022) to quantify deceleration within a typical 505 test. The authors used a contact mat linked to timing cells placed at the turning point of a typical 505 test, and the approach and reacceleration phases of the 505 test were based on the time to and from 50% of the ground contact time attained from the contact mat. The authors quantified a deceleration deficit, the time to complete the full 15 m approach of a traditional 505 test minus a linear 15 m sprint time, to quantify the time lost due to decelerating. The authors found that the deceleration deficit was unrelated to change-of-direction deficit suggesting an isolated measure of deceleration ability. However, the authors did not consider whether participants used a pacing strategy during the 10 m approach prior to the 505, which could account for the time lost due to decelerating and may reflect their psychological approach to the tests rather than the physical capacity to decelerate. As mentioned earlier, a cheaper option of using video analysis (Box 6.1) or incorporating specialist devices (e.g. Optojump, incorporating participant tracking devices (Graham-Smith & Pearson, 2005; Hader et al., 2015] or motorised resistance devices [Eriksrud et al., 2022]) during change-of-direction tests could be used to provide phase specific information during change-of-direction tests and more effectively quantify task-specific deceleration performance.

Assessment of Agility

Assessments of agility, essentially requires tests of COD and/or manoeuvrability in response to stimuli, whereby the athlete's perceptual-cognitive abilities along with their ability to move quickly (perceptual-motor ability) are evaluated. Whilst calls to move away from assessing pre-planned COD tests and incorporating true agility tests have been made (Young et al., 2021), limited options are currently available to assess agility and as discussed in the remainder of this chapter current approaches may not fully evaluate athletes' ability to read and appropriately react to the often-chaotic environment of match play. There are currently three options for evaluating agility: (1) light or arrow systems, (2) video stimulus, and (3) human stimulus. A summary of the advantages and disadvantages are summarised in Table 6.4.

TABLE 6.4 Overview Along With Advantages and Disadvantages of Methods to Assess Agility

Method	*Light/Arrow*	*Video*	*Human Stimulus*
Measures	• Simple reaction time • Response accuracy	• Visual search • Perception-response (decision) time • Movement time • Response accuracy	• Visual search • Perception-response (decision) time • Movement time • Response accuracy
Location	Lab and field	Lab	Lab and field
Advantages	• Simple to administer • Easy to standardise timing of stimulus consistently for athletes	• Easy to standardise timing of stimulus consistently for athletes • Greater sports specificity	• Increased sports specificity over light/arrow • Involves true perception-action coupling • Permits anticipatory evaluation • Less equipment requirements (e.g. timing cells and high-speed video)
Disadvantages	• Specialist equipment required • Lacks ecological validity due to lack of sport-specific stimulus • Purely reactive with no anticipation skills such as advanced cue utilisation	• Difficult to coordinate video • Software and hardware requirements • Preparation time (e.g. creation of video library to include a variety of sports-specific events) • 2D image, so no depth perception during visual scanning • Generally restricted to lab environments • High number of trials needed to cater for variability	• Lower reliability • Adequate training and familiarisation of tester needed. • Need to control and quantify tester movement time • Difficult to standardise timing of stimulus, which subsequently affects preparation times • Limited to 1 vs 1 scenarios, lacking wider sports specificity; perhaps limited to shallow cutting angles/low velocity • High number of trials needed to cater for variability

Light or Arrow Systems

For several years, light systems have been used in biomechanical studies (Besier et al., 2001) to compare between pre-planned and unanticipated COD tasks. Furthermore, commercially available systems with light stimuli or triggers have been available for some time (Smart Speed, Fusion Sport). Oliver and Meyers (2009) found such systems to be reliable measures of agility; however, light systems do not allow assessment of the 'anticipatory (perceptual-cognitive) skills', such as visual scanning, pattern recognition, and knowledge of situations (Sheppard & Young, 2006). Further, the use of a light-based system has been shown to result in different postural adjustments and knee moments than the more ecologically valid video-based systems (Lee et al., 2013a), which will be discussed later in the chapter.

Research has shown that expert soccer players (Helsen & Pauwels, 1993; Williams et al., 1994; Williams & Davids, 1998) display superior anticipatory skills than less-skilled players. Moreover, expert soccer players are better able to recognise and recall typical patterns of play from memory (Williams et al., 1993) and have more effective visual search strategies than non-experts (Helsen & Pauwels, 1993; Williams et al., 1994; Williams & Davids, 1998), leading to an improved ability to anticipate situations. It has been established those expert performers have a superior ability to identify useful anticipatory information from early in their opponents' movement patterns, referred to as 'advanced cue utilisation' (Williams et al., 1994; Williams, 2000; Vaeyens et al., 2007a). Moreover, skilled performers use their superior knowledge to control eye movement patterns (i.e. number of fixations, duration of fixations) to find and retrieve important sources of information (Williams, 2000). Such eye movement patterns may be influenced by the task (e.g. offensive vs defensive situations) (Helsen & Pauwels, 1993; Williams et al., 1998), field of view (e.g. 11 vs 11 compared to 1 vs 1 and 3 vs 3 situations) (Williams et al., 1994; Williams et al., 1998) and situations (e.g. 4 vs 3 or 5 vs 3 offensive scenarios) (Vaeyens et al., 2007a, 2007b). Hence, increasing the number of defenders or the type of stimulus presented (arrow versus single-defender versus two-defenders) results in significant changes in knee moments and posture in athletes (Lee et al., 2013a). Given the differences that exist between expert and non-expert sports performers, an effective agility test needs to be able to discriminate between sport ability levels, as higher-level players should theoretically have superior perceptual-cognitive abilities than lower-level players. To assess this quality, athletes need to respond to actions of an opponent or passages of play within an agility test (i.e. sport-specific vs generic stimuli), which can be achieved by responding to (1) video images (Farrow et al., 2005) or (2) human stimuli (Sheppard et al., 2006).

Previous research has illustrated the effectiveness of such tests compared to signals (e.g. arrow or light to indicate a direction change). Young et al. (2011) compared 'reactive' agility tests using video images (RAT_{VIDEO}) or arrows displayed (RAT_{ARROW}) on a screen in front of an approaching athlete to indicate the direction change. The RAT_{VIDEO} revealed significant differences between different ability levels of Australian rules football players, whereas the RAT_{ARROW} revealed only trivial differences between ability levels, suggesting that to assess perceptual-cognitive elements within an agility test and discriminate between ability levels, a stimulus involving actual movements of an opponent is required as the response stimulus. In support of this, Henry et al. (2011) compared RAT_{VIDEO} and light-based tests (RAT_{LIGHT}) with high- and low-level Australian rules footballers and a group of non-footballers. The authors found a certain degree of commonality between RAT_{LIGHT} and RAT_{VIDEO} ($r = 0.75$), but the faster (shorter) decision times associated with the RAT_{LIGHT} suggested that a light stimulus does not allow enough cognitive demand and, thus, is a less valid measure of (reactive) agility than tests involving a stimulus from actual movement of an opponent.

Video-based Systems

Video-based systems offer a solution to assess an athlete's perceptual-cognitive ability in relation to agility. Farrow et al. (2005) developed a video-based system to evaluate agility of netball players. The authors examined the performance of three groups of netball players (high- [n = 12], moderate- [n = 12], and low-skilled [n = 8] players) during a pre-planned and unanticipated test. The test involved players side-shuffling through a start gate (gate 1) 4 m, then back 2 m, before sprinting forward 1 m through a second timing gate (gate 2). Gate 2 was linked to a laptop which triggered the playing of a netball-specific video clip, which was projected on a screen in front of the athlete (approximately >5 m away). The players had to respond to the visual stimulus and run through a third gate (4.1 m away) in either a left or right direction, dependent on the visual cues from the video stimulus. Five measures were recorded: shuffle time (gate 1 to gate 2), sprint time (gate 2 to gate 3), total time (gate 1 to gate 3), perception-response time from a 50 Hz video (time of display occlusion to first definitive foot contact initiating the direction change), and response accuracy. Pre-planned trials removed the video stimulus recording the same completion times. Significant differences in sprint time, total time, and perception-response time were observed between high- and low-skilled players for unanticipated trials, with moderately skilled players significantly having faster sprint times than low-skilled ones. No differences were observed between groups in pre-planned trials, suggesting that the unanticipated protocol was able to discriminate between high- and low-skilled players, whereas COD ability (pre-planned trials) did not discriminate between player ability levels. Unanticipated and pre-planned sprint times shared 49% (R = 0.7) common variance, suggesting that each test assessed independent qualities.

Similar approaches have been carried out in rugby league (Serpell et al. 2010), Australian rules football (Young et al., 2011; Henry et al., 2011), and basketball (Spiteri et al., 2014). Serpell et al. (2010) using 15 NRL and 15 National Youth Rugby League players involved a similar approach to Farrow with the removal of the initial side-shuffling component and slightly longer sprint distances (~10 m). Each player performed 8 trials with 8 videos randomly selected from 12 available, whilst pre-planned trials were performed removing the video stimulus. No correlation was found between COD (pre-planned trials) and unanticipated trials ($\rho = -0.08$; $P > 0.05$). Furthermore, significant differences were observed between unanticipated sprint and response times between NRL and Youth players, suggesting the video-based protocol could discriminate between ability levels and that unanticipated and pre-planned versions of the test assessed different qualities. Henry et al. (2011) used a similar approach in Australian rules football players, finding higher-level players produced significantly faster agility and movement (time from response initiation to triggering the finish gate) times than non-players. This time a moderate correlation ($r = 0.68$) was found between agility time on the video-based and pre-planned tests.

A possible drawback of the video-based approach is perhaps the time-consuming preparation required to develop and update a video library to carry out regular assessment and monitoring of agility performance. Moreover, the development of video clips requires careful consideration to develop true match-like scenarios to present to the athlete. Other factors to consider are the cost of additional hardware and software and expertise to develop the protocol. Moreover, whilst the stimulus in each study was displayed as a life-sized image on a screen, the 2D presentation of the image may limit the amount and specificity (i.e. lack of depth) of the cues for which the athlete must react to (Farrow et al., 2005), which may not affect the reaction time but does change the visual search strategy used to complete the task in comparison to a 3D stimulus (Lee et al., 2013b).

Another potential limitation of video-based systems is that due to the large potential response variability associated with different scenarios presented to athletes often mixed reliability of the protocols is reported. For instance, Farrow et al. (2005) reported an ICC of 0.83 for completion time in their video-based protocol in netball players. Whilst Young et al. (2011) reported poor reliability for their video-based test (ICC = 0.33; CV = 2.7%; TE = 0.07 s) in 50 junior Australian rules football players. However, the authors did report that the reliability was better than the arrow-based test (ICC = 0.1; CV = 3.4%; TE = 0.09 s) used in that study. Spiteri et al. (2014) reported good reliability (ICC = 0.81; CV = 3.3%), despite using a more complex protocol that involved two CODs in response to two different video stimuli. Serpell et al. (2010) reported good reliability for completion times (ICC = 0.82; SEM = 0.01) but poor reliability for perception-response time (ICC = 0.31; SEM = 0.01) perhaps due to the low sampling rate of video (50 Hz) used to evaluate perception-response times. Moreover, Farrow et al. (2005) also collected video at 50 Hz to measure perception-response time in their study, which may have impacted on the ability to discriminate between moderate- and low-skilled netball players in that study. For instance, the precision in determining the time difference between video occlusion and the athlete's definitive foot contact prior to initiating the direction change maybe influenced by the video sampling rate. Therefore, high-speed video (>100 Hz) is recommended to accurately determine perception-response time.

Human Stimulus

An alternative approach to video-based systems involves using the movements of a tester to provide the stimulus for athletes to react to. The reactive agility test (RAT_{HS}), developed by Sheppard et al. (2006), involves the tester beginning on a timing mat whilst an athlete begins on a start line (5 m apart). Timing cells are placed 5 m on either side of the athlete, and the tester is 2 m in front of the athlete. Once the tester leaves the timing mat and runs to one side, the athlete needs to respond to the direction of the tester and sprint through the timing cells to the side the tester turned to (i.e. mimicking a defensive situation; Figure 6.9). The athlete responds to one of four scenarios: (1) Step forward with right foot and change direction to the left. (2) Step forward with the left foot and change direction to the right. (3) Step forward with the right foot, then left, and change direction to the right. Or (4) step forward with the left foot, then right, and change direction to the left. The authors found that elite athletes recorded faster times than sub-elite athletes ($d = 1.23$), which was not the case for the sprint and pre-planned COD tests. Furthermore, low association between sprint and RAT_{HS} ($r = 0.333$) and pre-planned COD and RAT_{HS} ($r = 0.331$) suggested the RAT_{HS} could discriminate between athletes of different performance levels and is an independent quality from a pre-planned COD test. The RAT_{HS} requires less preparation time and is easier to administer than video-based systems. RAT_{HS} protocols have been widely used in rugby league (Gabbett et al., 2008; Gabbett & Benton, 2009; Gabbett et al., 2011a; Gabbett et al., 2011b), basketball (Scanlan et al., 2014a; Scanlan et al., 2014b), Australian rules football (Veale et al., 2010), and soccer (Trajkovic et al., 2020). As with video-based tests, the RAT_{HS} and variations (completion time and/or perception-response time) has repeatedly shown to be able to discriminate between different athlete performance standards (Gabbett et al., 2008; Gabbett & Benton, 2009; Veale et al., 2010; Trajkovic et al., 2020). Moreover, Gabbett et al. (2011b) found that reactive agility was one factor significantly associated (although low; $r = 0.29$) with the number of line break assists (an offensive match statistic) in professional rugby league match play.

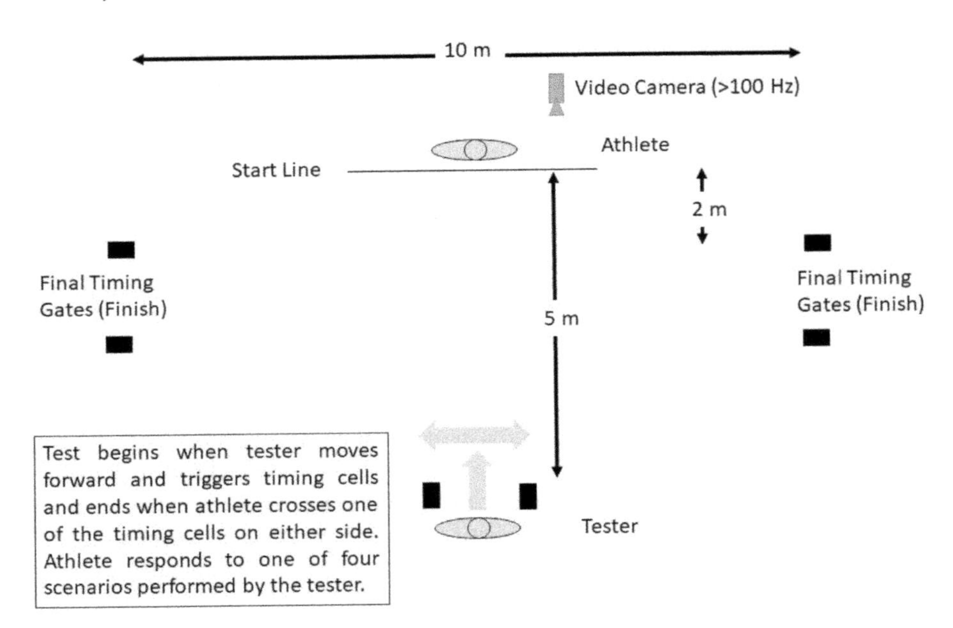

FIGURE 6.9 An outline of the reactive agility test with human stimulus. The athlete responds to one of four scenarios performed by the tester: (1) Step forward with the right foot and change direction to the left. (2) Step forward with the left foot and change direction to the right. (3) Step forward with the right foot, then the left, and change direction to the right. Or (4) step forward with the left foot, then the right, and change direction to the left. Total time described in the figure should be accompanied with estimates of perception-response time and tester movement time from the video camera to the rear of the athlete.

Again, an important element to assess is *perception-response time* (which was not initially evaluated in Sheppard's original protocol). Furthermore, *tester movement time* should be factored into overall RAT_{HS} time. Using a high-speed camera to the rear of the athlete, the athlete's response time between definitive footfalls prior to initiating the COD between the tester and the athlete (Gabbett et al., 2008; Young & Wiley, 2010) can be determined as with video-based protocols. Using high-speed video during the RAT_{HS} in semi-professional Australian rules footballers, Young and Willey (2010) measured the *tester's movement time* (first forward movement [trigger timer] of tester to their definitive foot plant to initiate COD), the *athlete's perception-response time* (time from tester definitive foot plant to initiate COD to athlete definitive foot plant to initiate COD), and *response-movement time* (athlete definitive foot plant to initiate COD to crossing the gates [stop timer]). Large associations were observed between total time and perception-response time (r = 0.77) and total time and response-movement time (r = 0.59). Whilst tester time reported a low coefficient of variation (5.1%), total time and tester time showed a significant low association (r = 0.37). In another version of the $RAT_{HS,}$ Scanlan et al. (2014a) reported large associations between *response* (duration from movement initiation of tester until the participant crossed timing gates that were added in at the start) (r = 0.76) and *perception-response* time (referred to as decision time) (r = 0.58) with total RAT movement time. Furthermore, response time was identified as the sole predictor (r^2 = 0.58) of RAT time, although it should be noted that inappropriate statistics were performed for the latter finding given the low sample size (N = 12 male basketball players). As with the video-based tests mentioned earlier, the perception-response time is an important component of the RAT_{HS} and should be evaluated, whilst the tester time needs to be controlled by evaluating to isolate its influence.

The RAT_{HS} method is not without limitations. Firstly, in the RAT_{HS}, athletes respond to stimuli under low velocity of approach conditions (Sheppard et al., 2006; Gabbett et al., 2008; Gabbett & Benton, 2009). Using a slightly modified version (Veale et al., 2010) that involved an initial 2 m sprint (between the first and second timing gates), a 45° cut in response to unanticipated human stimuli (as with other RAT_{HS}), then sprinting 5 m to another (third) timing gate where a pre-planned 45° COD was performed before sprinting 5 m through a fourth timing gate. This test set-up allows a response to stimuli under slightly higher approach velocity conditions. The authors found that the modified version of the RAT_{HS} was able to discriminate between different ability levels of U18 Australian rules football players. Research has shown the RAT_{HS} to be reliable and perhaps more so than the video-based systems reported earlier (Sheppard et al., 2006; Gabbett et al., 2008; Scanlan et al., 2014b), despite the large potential response variability associated with different scenarios presented to athletes during the RAT_{HS}. The reliability of tester and athlete movements have been investigated (Spiteri et al., 2012) during a modified version of the RAT_{HS}, whereby an athlete moves forward to a line 3 m away, where they respond by moving 2 m to either the left or right to movements of a tester, who is situated 6 m in front of the athlete. Spiteri et al. (2012) reported good reliability for movements performed by the human stimulus (ICC = 0.71–0.99; CV = 1.11–4.77%) and athlete running times (offensive: ICC = 0.91; CV = 3.30%; TE = 0.06, defensive: ICC = 0.90; CV = 3.60%; TE = 0.05). These findings support the implementation of a human stimulus to evoke athlete responses for agility testing, providing the tester is experienced with such protocols, which may require adequate training and familiarisation prior to administration. A final limitation of the RAT_{HS} is that such approaches may not truly assess the athlete's ability to respond in game like scenarios with only 1 vs. 1 scenarios with 4 distinct movement patterns of the tester considered. This may have limited application across several field- and court-based sports and does not fully cater to the 'chaos' of match play. For instance, Rayner (2020) found that 50% of the time, defenders were to the side or behind attackers in Australian rules football. Further research is required to develop the RAT_{HS} to provide more game-like scenarios which incorporate match implements. That said, the consistency of testers to replicate such scenarios to ensure reliable performance testing is a major barrier to this. Currently, the assessment of agility remains the holy grail of performance testing; on the one hand, researchers and practitioners know that the quality needs to be assessed, but satisfying the need to standardise, be reliable, and remain ecologically valid may remain elusive.

Summary

Evaluating MDS with athletes requires a multifactorial approach whereby both the physical and technical (speed, COD speed, and manoeuvrability) and the perceptual-cognitive (agility) elements are evaluated. This chapter provides an overview of the means and methods to evaluate MDS with athletes, and there are many important considerations outlined to ensure that accurate, reliable, and ecologically valid data collection takes place. When developing MDS assessment strategies, it is important for practitioners to establish what information is required from testing (e.g. general evaluation of qualities, mimic sport demands, return to play) through identifying exactly the qualities (e.g. speed, COD speed, manoeuvrability, perceptual-cognitive) that need to be assessed and whether the test(s) design effectively enables this. Given the multifactorial underpinning of several MDS qualities, practitioners need to decide whether additional information from testing (e.g. technical evaluation, consideration of momentum, phase evaluation) could be attained to better inform the design of intervention programmes.

References

Altmann, S., Hoffmann, M., Kurz, G., Neumann, R., Woll, A., & Haertel, S. (2015). Different starting distances affect 5-m sprint times. *Journal of Strength & Conditioning Research, 29*, 2361–2366.

Altmann, S., Spielmann, M., Engel, F.A., Neumann, R., Ringhof, S., Oriwol, D., & Haertel, S. (2017). Validity of single-beam timing lights at different heights. *Journal of Strength & Conditioning Research, 31*, 1994–1999.

Ashton, J., & Jones, P.A. (2019). The reliability of using a laser device to assess deceleration ability. *Sports (Basel), 7*, 191. doi:10.3390/sports7080191

Barber, O.R., Thomas, C., Jones, P.A., Mcmahon, J.J., & Comfort, P. (2016). Reliability of the 505 Change-of-direction test in Netball Players. *International Journal of Sports Physiology & Performance, 11*, 377–380.

Beekhuizen, K.S., Davis, M.D., Kolbe, R.M.J., & Cheng, M.S.S. (2009). Test-retest reliability and minimal detectable change of the hexagon agility test. *Journal of Strength & Conditioning Research, 23*, 2167–2171.

Besier, T.F., Lloyd, D.G., Ackland, T.R., & Cochrane, J.L. (2001). Anticipatory effects on knee joint loading during running and cutting maneuvers. *Medicine & Science in Sports & Exercise, 33*, 1176–1181.

Bezodis, N.E., Kerwin, D.G., & Salo, A. (2012). Measurement error in estimates of sprint velocity from a laser displacement measurement device. *International Journal of Sports Medicine, 33*, 439–444.

Bloomfield, J., Polman, R., & O'Donoghue, P. (2007). Physical demands of different positions in FA Premier League soccer. *Journal of Sports Science & Medicine, 6*, 63.

Brice, P., Smith, N., & Dyson, R. (2004). Frequency of curvilinear motion during competitive soccer play. *Journal of Sports Sciences, 22*, 485–593.

Buckthorpe, M. (2021). Recommendations for movement re-training after ACL reconstruction. *Sports Medicine, 51*, 1601–1618.

Bullock, N., Martin, D.T., Ross, A., Rosemood, C.D., Jordan, M.J., & Marino, F.E. (2008). Acute effect of whole-body vibration on sprint and jumping performance in elite skeleton athletes. *Journal of Strength & Conditioning Research, 22*, 1371–1374.

Caldbeck, P. (2019). *Contextual Sprinting in Football* [thesis]. Liverpool John Moores University, Liverpool, UK.

Chen, V.C., Li, F., Ho, S.S., & Wechsler, H. (2006). Micro-doppler effect in radar: Phenomenon, model and simulation study. *IEEE Transactions Aerospace and Electronic Systems, 42*, 2–21.

Clarke, R., Read, P.J., De Ste Croix, M.B.A., & Hughes, J.D. (2022). The deceleration deficit. *Journal of Strength & Conditioning Research, 36*, 2434–2439.

Comfort, P., Graham-Smith, P., Matthews, M.J., & Bamber, C. (2011). Strength and power characteristics in English elite rugby league players. *Journal of Strength & Conditioning Research, 25*, 1374–1384.

Cronin, J.B., & Templeton, R.L. (2008). Timing light height affects sprint times. *Journal of Strength & Conditioning Research, 22*, 318–320.

Cuthbert, M., Thomas, C., Dos'Santos, T., & Jones, P.A. (2019). The application of change of direction deficit to evaluate cutting ability. *Journal of Strength & Conditioning Research, 33*, 2138–2144.

DeWeese, B.H., & Nimphius, S. (2016). Program design and technique for speed and agility training. In *Essentials of Strength Training and Conditioning* (4th editions) (Eds. G.G. Haff & N.T. Triplett). Champaign, IL: Human Kinetics, 521–557.

Dolenc, A., & Coh, M. (2009). Comparison of photocell and optojump measurements of maximum running velocity. *Kinesiologia Slovenica, 15*, 16–24.

Dos'Santos, T., Thomas, C., Comfort, P., & Jones, P.A. (2018). The effect of angle and velocity on change of direction biomechanics: An angle-velocity trade-off. *Sports Medicine, 48*, 2235–2253. doi:10.1007/s40279-018-0968-3

Dos'Santos, T., McBurnie, A., Comfort, P., & Jones, P.A. (2019b). The effects of six-weeks change of direction speed and technique modification training on cutting performance and movement quality in male youth soccer players. *Sports, 7*, 205. doi:10.3390/sports7090205

Dos'Santos, T., Thomas, C., & Jones, P.A. (2021). The effect of angle on change of direction biomechanics: Comparison and inter-task relationships. *Journal of Sports Sciences, 39*(22), 2618–2631. DOI: doi.org/10.1080/02640414.2021.1948258

Draper, J.A., & Lancaster, M.G. (1985). The 505 test: A test for agility in the horizontal plane. *Australian Journal of Science & Medicine in Sport, 17*(1), 15–18.

Ebben, W.P., Petushek, E.J., & Clewein, R. (2009). A comparison of manual and electronic timing during 20 and 40 yards sprints. *Journal of Exercise Physiology Online, 12*(5), 34–38.

Eriksrud, O., Ahlbeck, F., Harper, D., & Gloresen, O. (2022). Validity of velocity measurements of motorised resistance device during change of direction. *Frontiers in Physiology, 13*, 824606. doi:10.3389/fphys.2022.824606

Farrow, D., Young, W., & Bruce, L. (2005). The development of a test of reactive agility for netball: A new methodology. *Journal of Science & Medicine in Sport, 8*(1), 52–60.

Fílter, A., Olivares, J., Santalla, A., Nakamura, F.Y., Loturco, I., & Requena, B. (2020). New curve sprint test for soccer players: Reliability and relationship with linear sprint. *Journal of Sports Sciences, 38*, 1320–1325. doi:10.1080/02640414.2019.1677391.

Fitzpatrick, J.F., Linsley, A., & Musham, C. (2019). Running the curve: A preliminary investigation into curved sprinting during football match-play. *Sport Performance & Science Reports, 55*, 1–3.

Foden, M., Astley, S., McMahon, J.J., Comfort, P., Matthews, M.J., & Jones, P.A. (2015). Relationships between speed, change of direction and jump performance with cricket specific speed tests in male academy cricketers. *Journal of Trainology, 4*(2), 37–42.

Gabbett, T., & Benton, D. (2009). Reactive agility of rugby league players. *Journal of Science & Medicine in Sport, 12*, 212–214.

Gabbett, T.J., Jenkins, D.G., & Abernethy, B. (2011a). Relative importance of physiological, anthropometric and skill qualities to team selection in professional rugby league. *Journal of Sports Sciences, 29*, 1453–1461.

Gabbett, T.J., Jenkins, D.G., & Abernethy, B. (2011b). Relationships between physiological, anthropometric and skill qualities and playing performance in professional rugby league players. *Journal of Sports Sciences, 29*(15), 1655–1664.

Gabbett, T.J., Kelly, J.N., & Sheppard, J.M. (2008). Speed, change of direction speed, and reactive agility of rugby league players. *Journal of Strength & Conditioning Research, 22*, 174–181.

Graham-Smith, P., Atkinson, L. Barlow, R., & Jones, P. (2009). Braking characteristics and load distribution in 180° turns. *Proceedings of the 5th Annual UK Strength and Conditioning Association Conference*, Wyboston Lakes, Bedfordshire. 5–7 June 2009, 6–7.

Graham-Smith, P., & Pearson, S.J. (2005). An investigation into the determinants of agility performance. *Proceedings of the 3rd International Biomechanics of the Lower Limb in Health, Disease and Rehabilitation*, Manchester, UK, 5–7 September 2005.

Graham-Smith, P., Rumpf, M., & Jones, P.A. (2018). Assessment of deceleration ability and relationship to approach speed and eccentric strength. *Proceedings of the International Society of Biomechanics in Sport Conference*, Auckland, New Zealand, 10–14 September 2018, 8–11.

Hachana, Y., Chaabène, Nabli, M.A., Attia, A., Moualhi, J., Farhat, N., & Elloumi, M. (2013). Test-retest reliability, criterion-related validity, and minimal detectable change of the Illinois agility test in male team sports athletes. *Journal of Strength & Conditioning Research, 27*(10), 2752–2759.

Hader, K., Palazzi, D., & Buchheit, M. (2015). Change of direction speed in soccer: How much braking is enough? *Kinesiology, 47*(1), 67–74.

Harper, D., Jordan, A., & Kiely, J. (2018). Relationships between eccentric and concentric knee strength capacities and maximal linear deceleration ability in male academy soccer players. *Journal of Strength & Conditioning Research, 9*, 1–8.

Harper, D.J., Morin, J.B., Carling, C., & Kiely, J. (2020). Measuring maximal horizontal deceleration ability using radar technology: Reliability and sensitivity of kinematic and kinetic variables. *Sports Biomechanics*, Epub Ahead of Print. doi:10.1080/14763141.2020.1792968.

Harris, G.R., Stone, M.H., O'Bryant, H.S., Proulx, C.M., & Johnson, R.L. (2000). Short-term performance effects of high power, high force, or combined weight-training methods. *Journal of Strength & Conditioning Research, 14*, 14–20.

Hart, N.H., Spiteri, T., Lockie, R.G., Nimphius, S., & Newton, R.U. (2014). Detecting deficits in change of direction performance using the preplanned multidirectional Australian football league agility test. *Journal of Strength & Conditioning Research, 28*, 3552–3556.

Haugen, T., & Buchheit, M. (2016). Sprint running performance monitoring: Methodological and practical considerations. *Sports Medicine, 46*, 641–656.

Haugen, T., Svendsen, I.S., & Seiler, S. (2014). Sprint time differences between single and dual beamed timing systems. *Journal of Strength & Conditioning Research, 28*(8), 2376–2379.

Haugen, T., Tønnessen, E., & Seiler, S. (2015). Correction factor for photocell sprint timing with flying start. *International Journal of Sports Physiology & Performance, 10*, 1055–1057.

Haugen, T.A., Tonnessen, E., & Seiler, S.K. (2012). The difference is in the start: Impact of timing and start procedure on sprint running performance. *Journal of Strength & Conditioning Research, 26*, 473–479.

Helsen, W.F., & Pauwels, J.M. (1993). The relationship between expertise and visual information processing in sport. In *Cognitive Issues in Motor Expertise* (Eds. J.L. Starkes & F. Allard). Amsterdam: Elsevier, 109–134.

Henry, G., Dawson, B., Lay, B., & Young, W. (2011). Validity of a reactive agility test for Australian football. *International Journal of Sports Physiology & Performance, 6*(4), 534–545.

Hetzler, R.K., Stickley, C.D., Lundquist, K.M., & Kimura, I.F. (2008). Reliability and accuracy of handheld stopwatches compared with electronic timing in measuring sprint performance. *Journal of Strength & Conditioning Research, 22*(6), 1969–1976.

Jones, P., Bampouras, T., & Marrin, K. (2009). An investigation into the physical determinants of change of direction speed. *Journal of Sports Medicine & Physical Fitness, 49*(1), 97–104.

Jones, P.A., Herrington, L.C., & Graham-Smith, P. (2016). Braking characteristics during cutting and pivoting in female soccer players. *Journal of Electromyography & Kinesiology. 30*, 46–54.

Jones, P.A., & Nimphius, S. (2018). Change of direction and agility. In *Performance Assessment in Strength and Conditioning* (Eds. P. Comfort, P.A. Jones, & J.J. McMahon). London: Routledge, 140–165.

Ken-ichi, K., Tomoya, H., Michio, Y., Yu, K., Noriko, H., Takahito, T., & Kazuo, F. (2019). Factors affecting the 180-degree change-of-direction speed in youth male soccer players. *Human Performance Measurement, 16*, 1–10.

Lee, M.J., Lloyd, D.G., Lay, B.S., Bourke, P.D., & Alderson, J.A. (2013a). Effects of different visual stimuli on postures and knee moments during sidestepping. *Medicine & Science in Sports & Exercise. 45*(9), 1740–1748.

Lee, M.J., Tidman, S.J., Lay, B.S., Bourke, P.D., Lloyd, D.G., & Alderson, J.A. (2013b). Visual search differs but not reaction time when intercepting a 3D versus 2D videoed opponent. *Journal of Motor Behaviour, 45*, 107–115.

Little, T., & Williams, A.G. (2005). Specificity of acceleration, maximum speed, and agility in professional soccer players. *Journal of Strength & Conditioning Research, 19*(1), 76–78.

Lockie, R.G. (2018). Sprint testing. In *Performance Assessment in Strength and Conditioning* (Eds. P. Comfort, P.A. Jones, & J.J. McMahon). London: Routledge, 117–139.

Lockie, R.G., Schultz, A.B., Callaghan, S.J., & Jeffriess, M.D. (2014). The effects of traditional and enforced stopping speed and agility training on multidirectional speed and athletic function. *Journal of Strength & Conditioning Research, 28*(6), 1538–1551.

Lockie, R.G., Schultz, A.B., Callagahan, S.J., Jeffriees, M.D., & Berry, S.P. (2013). Reliability and validity of a hew test of change of direction speed for field-based sports: The change of direction and acceleration test (CODAT). *Journal of Sports Science & Medicine, 12*, 88–96.

Malisoux, L., Francaux, M., Nielens, H., & Theisen, D. (2006). Stretch-shortening cycle exercises: An effective training paradigm to enhance power output of human single muscle fibers. *Journal of Applied Physiology, 100*, 771–779.

Mann, J.B., Ivey, P.J., Brechue, W.F., & Mayhew, J.L. (2015). Validity and reliability of hand and electronic timing for 40-yd sprint in college football players. *Journal of Strength & Conditioning Research, 29*(6), 1509–1514.

Markovic, G., Jukic, I., Milanovic, D., & Metikos, D. (2007). Effects of sprint and plyometric training on muscular function and athletic performance. *Journal of Strength & Conditioning Research, 21*, 543–549.

Mayhew, J.L., Houser, J.J., Briney, B.B., Williams, T.B., Piper, F.C., & Brechue, W.F. (2010). Comparison between hand and electronic timing of 40-yd dash performance in college football players. *Journal of Strength & Conditioning Research, 24*(2), 447–451.

McMahon, J.J., Kyriakidou, I., Murphy, S., Rej, S., Young, A., & Comfort, P. (2017). Reliability of five-, ten- and twenty metre sprint times in both sexes using single-photocell electronic timing gates. *Professional Strength & Conditioning. 45*, 17–21.

Morgan, O.J., Drust, B., Ade, J.D., & Robinson, M.A. (2021): Change of direction frequency off the ball: New perspectives in elite youth soccer. *Science and Medicine in Football.* doi:10.1080/24733938.2021.1986635

Morin, J.B., Le Mat, Y., Osgnach, C., Barnabò, A., Pilati, A., Samozino, P., & di Prampero, P.E. (2021). Individual acceleration-speed profile in-situ: A proof of concept in professional football players. *Journal of Biomechanics, 123*, 110524. https://doi.org/10.1016/j.jbiomech.2021.110524

Munro, A.G., & Herrington, L.C. (2011). Between session reliability of four hop tests and the agility t-test. *Journal of Strength & Conditioning Research, 25*, 1470–1477.

Naylor, J., & Greig, M.A. (2015). Hierarchical model of factors influencing a battery of agility tests. *Journal of Sports Medicine & Physical Fitness, 55*, 1329–1335.

Nimphius, S. (2014). Increasing agility. In *High-performance Training for Sports* (Eds. D. Joyce & D. Lewindon). Champaign, IL: Human Kinetics, 185–198.

Nimphius, S. (2017). Training change of direction and agility. In *Advanced Strength and Conditioning: An Evidence-based Approach* (Eds. A. Turner & P. Comfort). Abingdon, Oxon: Routledge, 291–309.

Nimphius, S., Callaghan, S.J., Bezodis, N.E., & Lockie, R.G. (2018). Change of direction and agility tests: Challenging our current measures of performance. *Strength & Conditioning Journal, 40*, 26–38.

Nimphius, S., Callaghan, S.J., & Lockie, R. (2016a). Change of direction deficit: A more isolated measure of change of direction performance than total 505 time. *Journal of Strength & Conditioning Research, 30*, 3024–3032.

Nimphius, S., Callaghan, S.J., & Hawser, A. (2016b). Comparison of simplified change of direction tests. *Journal of Strength & Conditioning Research, 30*(Supplement 2), S155–S156.

Nimphius, S., Geib, G., Spiteri, T., & Carlisle, D. (2013). "Change of direction" deficit measurement in division I American football players. *Journal of Australian Strength & Conditioning, 21*, 115–117.

Nimphius, S., McGuigan, M.R., & Newton, R.U. (2010). Relationship between strength, power, speed, and change of direction performance of female softball players. *Journal of Strength & Conditioning Research, 24*, 885–895.

Oliver, J.L., & Meyers, R.W. (2009). Reliability and generality of measures of acceleration, planned agility and reactive agility. *International Journal of Sports Physiology & Performance, 4*, 345–354.

Pauole, K., Madole, K., Garhammer, J., Lacourse, M., & Rozenek, R. (2000). Reliability and validity of the T-test as a measure of agility, leg power and leg speed in college-aged men and women. *Journal of Strength & Conditioning Research, 14*(4), 443–450.

Rago, V., Brito, J., Figueiredo, P., Ermidis, G., Barreira, D., & Rebelo, A. (2020). The arrowhead agility test: Reliability, minimum detectable change, and practical applications in soccer players. *Journal of Strength & Conditioning Research, 34*(2), 483–494. doi:10.1519/JSC.0000000000002987.

Rayner, R. (2020). *Training and Testing of 1V1 Agility in Australian Football* [PhD thesis]. School of Health Sciences, Victoria Australia Federation University, Australia.

Sassi, R.H., Dardouri, W., Yahmed, M.H., Gmada, N., Mahfoudhi, M.E., & Gharbi, Z. (2009). Relative and absolute reliability of a modified agility T-test and its relationship with vertical jump and straight sprint. *Journal of Strength & Conditioning Research, 23*, 1644–1651.

Sayers, M.G.L. (2015). Influence of test distance on change of direction speed test results. *Journal of Strength & Conditioning Research, 29*, 2412–2416.

Scanlan, A., Humphries, B., Tucker, P.S., & Dalbo, V. (2014a). The influence of physical and cognitive factors on reactive agility performance in men basketball players. *Journal of Sports Sciences, 32*, 367–374.

Scanlan, A., Tucker, P.S., & Dalbo, V.J. (2014b). A comparison of linear speed, closed-skill agility, and open-skill agility qualities between backcourt and front court adult semi-professional male basketball players. *Journal of Strength & Conditioning Research, 28*(5), 1319–1327.

Schreurs, M.J., Benjaminse, A., & Lemmink, K.A. (2017). Sharper angle, higher risk? The effect of cutting angle on knee mechanics in invasion sport athletes. *Journal of Biomechanics, 63*, 144–150.

Schuster, D., & Jones, P.A. (2016). Relationships between unilateral horizontal and vertical drop jumps and 20 metre sprint performance. *Physical Therapy in Sport. 21*, 20–25. doi:10.1016/j.ptsp.2016.02.007

Sekulic, D., Krolo, A., Spasic, M., Uljevic, O., & Peric, M. (2014). The development of a new stop "n" go reactive-agility test. *Journal of Strength & Conditioning Research, 28*, 3306–3312.

Serpell, B.G., Ford, M., & Young, W.B. (2010). The development of a new test of agility for rugby league. *Journal of Strength & Conditioning Research, 24*, 3270–3277.

Sheppard, J.M., & Young, W.B. (2006). Agility literature review: Classifications, training and testing. *Journal of Sports Sciences, 24*, 919–932.

Sides, D.L. (2014). *Kinematics and Kinetics of Maximal Velocity Sprinting and Specificity of Training in Elite Athletes* [PhD thesis]. University of Salford.

Sierer, S.P., Battaglini, C.L., Mihalik, J.P., Shields, E.W., & Tomasini, N.T. (2008). The National Football League combine: Performance differences between drafted and non-drafted players entering the 2004–2005 drafts. *Journal of Strength & Conditioning Research, 22*, 6–12.

Spiteri, T., Cochrane, J.L., & Nimphius, S. (2012). Human stimulus reliability during an offensive and defensive agility protocol. *Journal of Australian Strength & Conditioning 20*, 14–21.

Spiteri, T., Nimphius, S., Hart, N.H., Specos, C., Sheppard, J.M., & Newton, R.U. (2014). Contribution of strength characteristics to change of direction and agility performance in female basketball players. *Journal of Strength & Conditioning Research, 28*, 2415–2423.

Sporis, G., Jukic, I., Milanovic, L., & Vucetic, V. (2010). Reliability and factorial validity of agility tests for soccer players. *Journal of Strength & Conditioning Research, 24*, 679–686.

Stanton, R., Hayman, M., Humphris, N., Borgelt, H., Fox, J., Del Vecchio, L., & Humprhries, B. (2016). Validity of a smartphone-based application for determining sprint performance. *Journal of Sports Medicine.* doi:10.1155/2016/7476820

Stenroth, L., Vartiainen, P., & Karjalainen, P.A. (2020). Force-velocity profiling in ice hockey skating: reliability and validity of a simple, low-cost field method. *Sports biomechanics*, 1–16. https://doi.org/10.1080/14763141.2020.1770321

Sweeting, A. J., Aughey, R. J., Cormack, S. J., & Morgan, S. (2017). Discovering frequently recurring movement sequences in team-sport athlete spatiotemporal data. *Journal of Sports Sciences, 35*, 2439–2445.

Talty, P.F., Mcguigan, K., Quinn, M., & Jones, P.A. (2022). Agility demands of Gaelic football match-play: A time-motion analysis. *International Journal of Performance Analysis in Sport.* doi:10.1080/24748668.2022.2033519

Trajkovic, N., Sporis, G., Kristicevic, T., Madic, D.M., & Bogataj, S. (2020). The importance of reactive agility tests in differentiating adolescent soccer players. *International Journal of Environmental Research and Public Health. 17*, 3839. doi:10.3390/ijerph17113839

Tricoli, V., Lamas, L., Carnevale, R., & Ugrinowitsch, C. (2005). Short-term effects on lower-body functional power development: Weightlifting vs. vertical jump training programs. *Journal of Strength & Conditioning Research, 19*, 433–437.

Vaeyens, R., Lenoir, M., Williams, A.M., Mazyn, L., & Philippaerts, R.M. (2007a). The effects of task constraints on visual search behavior and decision-making skill in youth soccer players. *Journal of Sport Exercise Psychology, 29*, 147–169.

Vaeyens, R., Lenoir, M., Williams, A.M., & Philippaerts, R.M. (2007b). Mechanisms underpinning successful decision marking in skilled youth soccer players: An analysis of visual search behaviours. *Journal of Motor Behaviour, 39*(5), 395–408.

Veale, J.P., Pearce, A.J., & Carlson, J.S. (2010). Reliability and validity of a reactive agility tests for Australian football. *International Journal of Sports Physiology & Performance, 5*, 239–248.

Vescovi, J.D., & Mcguigan, M.R. (2008). Relationships between sprinting, agility, and jump ability in female athletes. *Journal of Sports Sciences, 26*(1), 97–107.

Webster, T.M., Comfort, P., & Jones, P.A. (2022). Relationship between physical fitness and the physical demands of 50-over cricket in fast bowlers. *Journal of Strength & Conditioning Research, 36*(3), e66–e72. doi:10.1519/JSC.0000000000003542

Wilkinson, M., Leedale-Brown, D., & Winter, E.M. (2009). Validity of a squash-specific test of change-of-direction speed. *International Journal of Sports Physiology & Performance, 4*, 176–185.

Williams, A.M. (2000). Perceptual skill in soccer: Implications for talent identification and development. *Journal of Sports Sciences, 18*(9), 737–750.

Williams, A.M., & Davids, K. (1998). Visual search strategy, selective attention, and expertise in soccer. *Research Quarterly for Exercise & Sport, 69*, 111–128.

Williams, A.M., Davids, K., Burwitz, L., & Williams, J.G. (1993). Cognitive knowledge and soccer performance. *Perceptual Motor Skills, 76*, 579–593.

Williams, A.M., Davids, K., Burwitz, L., & Williams, J.G. (1994). Visual search strategies of experienced and inexperienced soccer players. *Research Quarterly for Exercise & Sport, 65*, 127–135.

Yeadon, M.R., Kato, T., & Kerwin, D.G. (1999). Measuring running speed using photocells. *Journal of Sports Sciences, 17*, 249–257.

Young, W., Farrow, D., Pyne, D., Mcgregor, W., & Handke, T. (2011). Validity and reliability of agility tests in junior Australian football players. *Journal of Strength & Conditioning Research, 25*, 3399–3403.

Young, W.B., Mcdowell, M.H., & Scarlett, B.J. (2001). Specificity of sprint and agility training methods. *Journal of Strength & Conditioning Research, 15*, 315–319.

Young, W.B., Rayner, R., & Talpey, S. (2021). It's time to change direction on agility: A call to action. *Sports Medicine Open*, 7, 12.

Young, W.B., & Willey, B. (2010). Analysis of a reactive agility tests. *Journal of Science & Medicine in Sport, 13*, 376–378.

7

ASSESSMENT OF PHYSICAL QUALITIES ASSOCIATED WITH MULTIDIRECTIONAL SPEED

Christopher Thomas

Introduction

Although multidirectional speed (MDS) may be a global concept, the classification of sub-components (e.g. perceptual and decision-making factors and change-of-direction speed) allows us to break down and isolate the specific cognitive, biomechanical, technical, and physical requirements of each task, enabling a more precise application of targeted training methods. With reference to the physical component, practitioners may employ a wide variety of training methods that aim to develop key underpinning strength- and power-related characteristics (e.g. reactive strength, rate of force development [RFD], peak force [PF]). These are fundamental physical qualities which are necessary to achieve high and rapid magnitudes of braking and propulsive impulse, thus change in momentum, which are central to changing direction, sprinting, decelerating, and the performance of MDS actions. Unsurprisingly, these physical qualities have been shown to underpin key MDS components (McBurnie and Dos'Santos, 2022), such as deceleration capacity, acceleration, and top-end speed capabilities, which may provide an athlete with a wide range of physical affordances, thereby increasing their likelihood of outmanoeuvring their opponents and closing/creating time and space to bring about positive opportunities for their team. The remainder of the chapter will discuss the assessment of underpinning physical capacities which characterise MDS for evaluation and monitoring purposes. This may allow a reverse-engineered approach based on the requirements of the task and determine underpinning technique, biomechanical, and physical factors that contribute to performance.

Physical Capacities Underpinning Change of Direction

A detailed evaluation of the biomechanical and physical demands of COD is provided in Chapter 4, leading to the identification of important muscle strength qualities that should be considered for profiling the MDS athlete. These physical qualities are summarised by phase of a COD task in Table 7.1.

DOI: 10.4324/9781003267881-9

TABLE 7.1 A Summary of the Underpinning Muscle Strength Qualities Associated with Each Phase of a Change-of-Direction Task

Phase	*Rationale*	*Recommended Tests*
Initiation/approach (This assumes sprint running as the approach action.)	• Key variables associated with ground reaction force characteristics during ground contact, notably horizontal and vertical impulse (i.e. magnitude and orientation of force). • The hip extensors (hamstrings and glutes) appear to help facilitate this orientation of force. It is therefore likely that such connections exist between the ability of the hamstring muscles to produce horizontally oriented force during ground contact and their ability to produce high levels of *eccentric force*, specifically at the end of the swing phase (combined hip flexion and knee extension). • The hamstrings and glutes (hip extensors) have a key role here in facilitating a high early RFD, without excessive braking force. • As the gluteals are shortening throughout ground contact, RFD rather than maximum force is a key quality for development.	• IMTP/ISQT (*See section on assessing isometric strength.*) • Eccentric knee flexor strength (*See section on assessing isokinetic dynamometry.*)
Preparation (Steps prior to the 'plant' step [e.g. penultimate foot contact] and potentially steps prior)	• Eccentric overload training of the hamstrings produced substantial improvements in contact time, time spent braking, and braking force during 45–60° COD tasks (de Hoyo et al., 2016), suggesting eccentric strength to be an underpinning factor of efficient preliminary deceleration (McBurnie et al., 2022). • *Eccentrically (knee flexor and extensor)* stronger female soccer players were shown to approach faster and display greater reductions in velocity and braking forces during 180° turns (Jones et al., 2017). • *Eccentrically stronger (knee flexor and extensor)* soccer players were able to maintain velocity, attain higher minimum speeds, and tolerate greater loads during a 90° cutting task (Jones et al., 2022). • *Eccentric knee flexor strength* helps to generate hip extensor moment to help maintain trunk position (reduce trunk flexion and hamstring stretch load) in transition to the 'plant' step and assist with knee joint stability (co-contraction). • The combined need for high peak eccentric force and a high eccentric RFD will be critical for sustaining rapid reductions in whole-body momentum alongside the maintenance of neuromuscular control and stability of the knee joint when decelerating over rapid time frames.	• Isokinetic dynamometry: eccentric knee extensor and flexor strength (*See section on isokinetic dynamometry.*)

(*Continued*)

TABLE 7.1 (Continued)

Phase	*Rationale*	*Recommended Tests*
Execution ('Plant' step)	• Due to the dual-support nature of sharper-angle COD, the *eccentric strength of the knee extensors and flexors and hip extensors* will aid in an athlete's stability from touchdown to maximum knee flexion, allowing a safer execution and firm base to push from (propulsion). • Due to longer ground contact times ≥0.40 s (increased braking), the propulsion (maximum knee flexion to take-off) sub-phase of the execution phase may be facilitated by use of the *slow stretch-shorten cycle (concentric strength of the lower-limb extensors)* as the athlete extends at the hip, knee, and ankle into the first reacceleration step. However, ground contact times during the 'plant' step depend on the approach velocity and angle of direction change and, thus, influence the categorisation of the stretch-shorten cycle function (Dos'Santos et al., 2018). • The gastrocnemius and soleus help to contribute to displace the centre of mass forward by storing and releasing elastic energy to aid the body's forward projection out of the COD due to the eccentric-concentric coupling typically associated with COD manoeuvres and sprinting tasks; thus, *reactive strength* is also key physical quality for multidirectional speed performance (Jarvis et al., 2022).	• Isokinetic dynamometry: eccentric knee extensor and flexor strength. (*See section on isokinetic dynamometry.*) • Slow (e.g. CMJ)/ fast SSC/reactive strength (e.g. DJ, 10/5 RJT) (*See section on stretch-shorten cycle function.*)
Reacceleration	• Application of force through a greater range, combined with a longer ground contact time, supports the increase of horizontal impulse, resulting in an increased rate of change in horizontal velocity (impulse-momentum relationship/work-energy principle). • *Concentric strength of the ankle, knee, and hip extensors* (gastrocnemius, soleus, quadriceps, and glutes) will be strength qualities important for technical execution of the reacceleration phase.	• IMTP/ISQT/1 RM testing (*See section on assessing isometric and dynamic strength.*)

Key: COD: change of direction; RFD: rate of force development; IMTP: isometric mid-thigh pull; ISQT: isometric squat; RM: repetition maximum; SSC: stretch-shorten cycle; CMJ: countermovement jump; DJ: drop jump; 10/5 RJT: 10/5 repeated jump test

Best Practice

To determine an athlete's current fitness and monitor the progression made during both training and rehabilitation, specific fitness components must be assessed. Fitness testing allows practitioners to identify an athlete's strengths and weaknesses, enabling them to tailor and adjust training and rehabilitation according to the athlete's greatest need(s). This optimises the use of training time and resources, helping to achieve maximal performance gains and enhance rehabilitation efficiently. Regular fitness testing provides vital information to athletes and their support teams and should therefore form part of any athlete's development programme. Moreover, fitness testing is used to monitor the effectiveness of training programmes, establish a baseline that may be used to monitor the progress of rehabilitation post-injury, and provide a motivational tool for athletes and for talent identification. Without fitness testing, it is impossible to accurately monitor an athlete's progress and objectively assess neuromuscular preparedness and readiness to return to sport post-injury. For tests to be effective and reflect the changes in an athlete's fitness, they must be valid, reliable, and repeatable and be conducted at regular intervals using carefully controlled and standardised procedures. Consequently, the principles of validity, reliability, and objectivity must be considered.

Validity

Validity refers to whether the test measures what it intends to measure. Some tests directly measure that which is required: what you see is what you get. For example, a 1 RM (repetition maximum) back squat provides an overall measure of maximal dynamic strength, whereas performing a 20 RM would a reflect muscular endurance. Both examples use the same test but manipulating the number of repetitions will change the physical quality tested. Therefore, practitioners should ensure that the test they are using is measuring the physical quality of interest.

Several types of validity can be considered by the tester when implementing a testing battery. Content validity is indicative of the appearance of an instrument to test what it is meant to test (Thomas et al., 2010). Ecological validity is the applicability of the test in a real-world setting (Thomas et al., 2010). Criterion validity refers to how the scores on a test relate to a recognised standard or criterion (Thomas et al., 2010). Comparing equipment against a gold standard can help to establish the validity of that technology. This process will help in deciding which types of equipment and technology are most appropriate for assessment and monitoring.

Reliability

Reliability is the extent to which scores are consistent and repeatable across time or between testers and, therefore, reflects the ability to detect actual changes with time. The measurement instrument, athlete, and tester are sources of potential error. The observed measure always consists of the true error inclusive of some measurement error. Two error types include systematic bias and random error (Atkinson and Nevill, 1998). Systematic bias includes the trend for measures to be different due to learning effects, motivation, or fatigue. Random error refers to the 'noise' typically seen as within-subject variation, inconsistencies in the measurement protocol, or the examiner's measurements. The common measures of reliability include intraclass correlation coefficient, coefficient of variation, typical error, standard error of measurement, and smallest detectable difference.

The intraclass correlation coefficient is used to provide a measure of between-subject variation and is the measure of the ratio between the subjects and the total variance (Koo and Li, 2016). The coefficient of variation is calculated as standard deviation/mean × 100 and can be calculated individually or averaged between athletes. This method is used to indicate the degree of within-subject variation in a test. The typical error is another way of expressing the error associated with the test in its raw value (Hopkins, 2000). The standard error of measurement (SEM) refers to the amount of error associated with the test and can be calculated as the standard deviation × √1 minus the intraclass correlation coefficient (Atkinson and Nevill, 1998). It is related to the CV, which is this value expressed as the percentage of the athlete's mean variation. Thus, it reflects the within-athlete variation and calculates the variability of the measure at the individual level. The smallest detectable difference (SEM × √(2) × 1.96) is the ability of a test to detect the smallest meaningful or practically worthwhile change in performance (Drake et al., 2018) and is an important reference value to establish 'real' and 'true' changes in performance.

Deciding on Tests

The choice of tests should reflect the characteristics of both the sport and individual player position. When designing a fitness testing battery, several factors must be considered:

- How many tests? The number of athletes and the amount of time allowed will determine how many tests are feasible.
- What tests? The decision will be based on the needs analysis of the sport and the available equipment.
- What order? When conducting several tests, the performance of a previous test can impact the performance of a subsequent one.
- What equipment? The equipment should allow tests to be accurately reproduced and limit tester objectivity.

Laboratory Versus Field Testing

Historically, exercise science has divided testing into two categories: laboratory-based tests and field-based tests. This categorisation has grown less well-defined as more portable technology to evaluate strength and power attributes have emerged. For example, testing previously conducted in laboratories (e.g. in-ground force platforms) are now common in the field (e.g. portable, lightweight force platforms) due to the tester being able to transport the equipment relatively easily. Likewise, wearable technologies now allow for assessment of many metrics that previously required expensive equipment. In these scenarios, there may be trade-offs due to perceived lack of control, but there are significant advantages for ecological validity. Test robustness remains important, and practitioners need to know that the data they collect is valid and reliable.

Standardisation of Testing

Ideally, test conditions should be standardised each session. This will increase the validity and reliability of the test, and as such, retesting should be conducted under the same conditions as the original test. This can be challenging for practitioners. Although it may not be possible to control for all factors, testers should be aware of their potential impact on test results and should be acknowledged when making longitudinal assessments of physical attributes and subsequent decisions. Nonetheless, athletes must be provided with a testing environment that allows them to perform at their best. Therefore, several factors should be considered when standardising test sessions (Table 7.2).

Meaningful Metrics

After selecting the right assessments for the sport, the next challenge is to identify meaningful metrics to analyse and inform training. Many software packages return countless variables to

TABLE 7.2 Factors to Consider When Standardising Testing Sessions (Adapted from McGuigan, 2019)

Testing Factor	*Rationale*
Time of day	Body temperature and appropriate warm-up prior to testing appear to impact time-of-day effects (Taylor et al., 2011; West et al., 2014). To reduce the effects of variability throughout the day, we recommend performing all strength and power tests at approximately the same time of the day whenever possible and performing appropriate warm-up exercises prior to testing.
Instructions	Verbal encouragement has been shown to increase strength and power performance (Binboğa et al., 2013; McNair et al., 1996). Therefore, testing should begin with a description of the testing procedure so that the athlete or client understands these details. Personal preference for verbal encouragement should also be considered. Ultimately, test conditions should allow athletes/clients to perform at their best and reduce the risk of injury.
Attentional focus	Externally focused instruction results in different results on jump (Wulf and Dufek, 2009) and strength tests (Halperin et al., 2016). Swearing has been shown to have a significant impact on muscle strength and power output (Stephens et al., 2018) by appearing to increase pain tolerance. Practitioners should consider professional criteria typically employed in their organisations, particularly when working with youth athletes.
Test order	Testers should consider the impact of one test on another. Post-activation potentiation (PAP) is a potential confounding factor when performing strength and power tests. Performing a maximal strength test may improve performance on subsequent power tests (Suchomel et al., 2016). Alternate scenarios, such as performing tests on separate days, should be considered. Test order should be standardised, and there should be rest periods between tests when running multiple tests in one session.
Fatigue	Fatigue must be considered when conducting several tests within a session, as any subsequent tests performed whilst the athlete is still fatigued will still be impaired. Ideally, athletes should perform testing in a non-fatigued state, perhaps with 48 hours' rest, which may coincide with a deload week in a periodised training programme. Performing the most fatiguing tests at the end of the testing session is advised (i.e. aerobic capacity). Tests can be performed in randomised fashion to control for the order effect. Practitioners need to consider the context of the testing session, considering any prior training.
Environmental conditions	Ideally, conditions within a test session should be controlled and standardised as much as possible. Testers must keep records of the conditions and circumstances under which the tests were conducted. If possible, room temperature and humidity should be kept the same between tests.
Nutritional status	Pretest conditions, such as food intake, nutritional supplements, and fluid status, can also influence test performance (Savoie et al., 2015; Grgic et al., 2018). The effects of caffeine on force generation are well documented (Grgic et al., 2018; Warren et al., 2010); thus, a common approach in research is to have athletes refrain from taking caffeine for a set period before testing.
Warm-up	General and test-specific warm-ups should be followed prior to testing, including a pulse raiser, specific dynamic stretching, and submaximal trials of the test. The effects of stretching and dynamic movement on test performance should be standardised each session.

feedback to the athlete, but practitioners should be mindful as to which variables are used to ultimately improve their athletes' performance. These include the following:

- Relationship of the metric to performance (validity).
- Selecting a variable which has high reliability (low error) and is sensitive enough to detect 'real' changes in performance.
- Variables which have good predictive capabilities (i.e. surrogate) or can discriminate between different playing standards/levels.
- The needs of the sport and athlete. This requires gathering accurate, precise, and reliable data, ideally from the published literature, combined with detailed observation of training and competition. Subsequently, comparisons are made to determine individual strengths and weaknesses that inform the implementation of appropriate training that focuses on the sport, the athlete, and any identified injury risk.

Practitioners should ensure that selected tests and their associated metrics help to inform practice. Figure 7.1 shows a summary of factors to consider for standardisation of testing physical qualities associated with MDS.

Assessment of Physical Qualities

Stretch-shorten Cycle Function

Vertical jump tasks are commonly used to assess and monitor the capacity of the lower body to produce impulse in team and individual sports. Some widely used tests include the countermovement jump (CMJ), drop jump (DJ), and 10/5 repeated jump test (10/5 RJT).

Stretch-shortening cycle (SSC) performance is a common component of testing protocols for athletes (McGuigan et al., 2013; McMaster et al., 2014; Suchomel et al., 2016). Typically, SSC movements are classified as slow (ground contact >250 ms) or fast (ground contact <250 ms) (Verkhoshansky and Siff, 2009), and thus, appropriate tests need to be selected to effectively assess and monitor the physical qualities associated with MDS. In this section, we will provide guidelines including different equipment that can be used to assess SSC function, the protocols that should be considered, and how best the practitioner can use this information to inform their athletes' training.

CMJ movement time is ~800 ms (Suchomel et al., 2015) and is therefore classed as a slow-SSC movement. Likewise, the SJ test is another common test used to measure concentric-only aspects of performance (Hughes et al., 2021). Different methods have been used to compare CMJ and SJ performance as an indication of SSC performance (Suchomel et al., 2016), including the reactive strength index (RSI), eccentric utilisation ratio (EUR), and the percentage of pre-stretch augmentation (PSA). The RSI is calculated by subtracting the SJ height from CMJ height, which is considered a measure of the SSC ability during the CMJ (Young, 1995). The EUR is calculated by dividing the CMJ height by SJ height and considered an indicator of SSC performance (McGuigan et al., 2006). The PSA is calculated by subtracting the SJ height from CMJ height, dividing by SJH, then multiplying by 100, and is considered a measure of the ability to utilise the muscles pre-stretch during a CMJ (Kubo et al., 2007). Little differences have been observed between the methods tested, including RSI, EUR, and PSA (Suchomel et al., 2016)

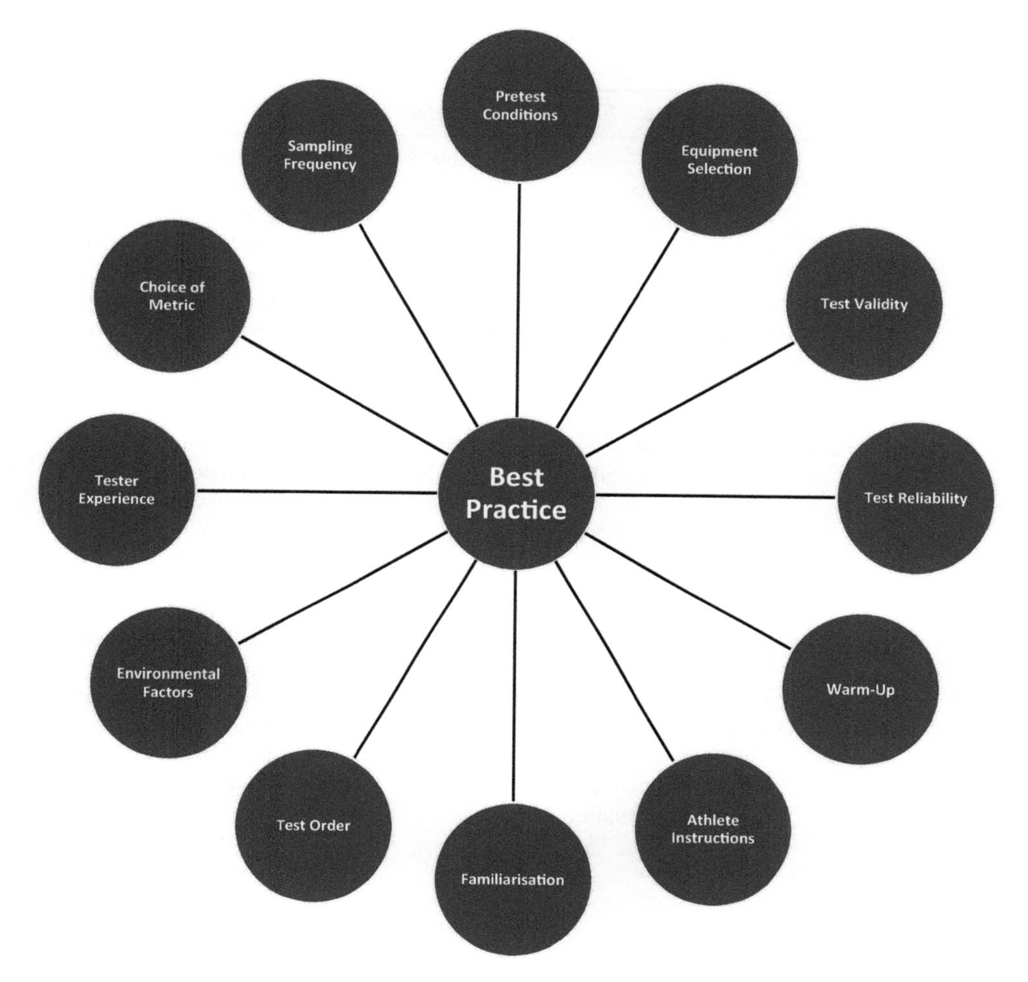

FIGURE 7.1 Key factors to consider when standardising tests (adapted from McGuigan, 2019).

Equipment

Many options are available to assess SSC function, yet the choice will depend on the level of information required by the practitioner. Force platforms are considered the gold standard method to assess SSC function. Affordable and valid commercial force platforms have been recently developed, demonstrating high reliability (Lake et al., 2018). The use of force platforms has been reported previously (Beckham et al., 2014; McMahon et al., 2018b); thus, a brief overview is provided here. Other alternative (field-based) methods that are commercially available to practitioners are outlined in Table 7.3.

Force Platforms

The fundamental mechanical principle which force platforms adhere to is Newton's third law of motion, and this helps to associate the measured force with the force applied by the athlete

TABLE 7.3 Overview of Field-Based Methods to Quantify SSC Function (Adapted from McMahon et al., 2018b)

Ranking	*Equipment*	*Main Variables*	*Main Benefits*	*Main Limitations*
Gold	Jump mats	• Jump height • Contact time • Flight time • Reactive strength index	• Reliable • Portable • Instantaneous results • Affordable	• Sometimes inaccurate in overestimating jump height (flight time) due to change in take-off and landing positions
	Optoelectric devices	• Jump height • Contact time • Flight time • Reactive strength index	• Reliable • Valid • Portable • Instantaneous results	• Underestimates jump height due to shorter flight times • No insight into jump strategy metrics
	Video cameras	• Jump height • Reactive strength index • Force-velocity profile	• Highly accessible • Affordable • Reliable • Valid	• Can require anthropometric measures • Incorrectly identifies moment of take-off and landing if using lower video-recording frequencies • Can lead to reduced inter-rater reliability
Silver	Accelerometers	• Jump height • Peak and mean velocity • Peak and mean power • Reactive strength index	• Reliable • Portable • Instantaneous results	• Overestimates jump height (particularly when using the take-off velocity method) • Consider attachment point versus GRF
	Linear position transducers	• Jump height • Peak power • Peak force • Peak velocity	• Reliable • Portable • Instantaneous results	• Consider attachment point versus GRF • Overestimates jump height
Bronze	Jump and reach devices	• Jump height	• Reliable • Portable • Instantaneous results • Can simulate sport-specific jumps (e.g. volleyball)	• Influenced by shoulder range of motion and elbow extension • Coordination of countermovement and arm swing • Overestimates jump height due to its calculation (difference between height reached whilst standing and height during the jump) • Only provides insight into jump height

Key: GRF: ground reaction force

(i.e. ground reaction force). Dependent on the manufacturer, forces are measured directly in three planes (vertical, anterior-posterior, and medio-lateral). Inexpensive portable force plate systems have shown to record accurate measures of CMJ force-time variables, compared to laboratory-based systems (Lake et al., 2018). A possible limitation of such systems is that each platform is relatively small compared to laboratory-based platforms and may affect some athletes for some movements. Regardless of the type of force platform used to assess SSC function, there are common considerations which must be given to their set-up to increase the validity and reliability of resultant force-time data (Table 7.4).

TABLE 7.4 Basic Considerations When Using Force Platforms for Jump and Isometric Tests

Sampling rates	• When performing jump and isometric assessments, it is generally recommended that sampling frequencies ≥1,000 Hz are used in order to ensure accuracy (Owen et al., 2014; Street et al., 2001), especially for time-dependent variables, such as RFD and impulse (Maffiuletti et al., 2016).
Thresholds	• Different approaches have been suggested for detecting movement or muscle action onset that use absolute or relative thresholds in both jump (Donahue et al., 2021; Meylan et al., 2011; Owen et al., 2014; Pérez-Castilla et al., 2019a) and isometric tests (Dos'Santos et al., 2017a). • Five times the standard deviation of bodyweight has been recommended by several authors (−30 ms for CMJ) as it accounts for signal/participant noise (Donahue et al., 2021; Dos'Santos et al., 2017a; McMahon et al., 2018c; Owen et al., 2014). • Errors in identifying the onset threshold may have little effect on global measures of performance (i.e. jump height or PF) but will impact time-related measures, such as RFD and force at time epochs (Eagles et al., 2015) and reactive strength index modified. • Based on current evidence, there is no general agreement on which starting threshold to use (Eagles et al., 2015).
Filtering techniques	• Unfiltered force-time data should be analysed due to various filters (and their varying cut-off frequencies) leading to underestimations of CMJ height (Street et al., 2001). • If filtering must be applied, then a zero-lag, low-pass filter, such as a fourth-order Butterworth filter with the highest possible cut-off frequency should be used to minimise the potential for time shifts (Maffiuletti et al., 2016).
Warm-up	• Prior to commencing testing (jump or isometric assessment), a warm-up should be performed. The warm-up does not need to be extensive and can consist of body weight exercises (e.g. squats, lunges, walking Romanian deadlifts), along with some dynamic stretching. Several submaximal trials should also be performed prior to the testing to increase reliability.
Weighing period	• When using the forward dynamics approach to establish squat and countermovement jump variables, it is essential that the jump is preceded by a 'weighing' period. Here, the athlete should remain still for at least one second to enable an accurate estimate of the subject's bodyweight to avoid errors in the calculation of jump variables (McMahon et al., 2018b). The inability to remain still during single-limb standing is one reason that may preclude the use of unilateral countermovement jump tests in test batteries. A one-second weighing period is also recommended for isometric strength tests.

Key: RFD: rate of force development; PF: peak force; CMJ: countermovement jump

Squat jump assessments (referred to as either squat or static jumps) have been shown to be highly reliable (Markovic et al., 2004; Petronijevic et al., 2018). Moir and colleagues (Moir et al., 2005) found limited SJ familiarisation is required with trained adult populations, with force variables showing reasonably good levels of test-retest reliability (ICC: 0.75–0.99; CV: 1.2–7.6%). The test begins by an athlete performing a countermovement that is held for 2–3 seconds before vertically jumping. One issue with SJ testing is controlling for a further countermovement that can occur during the 2-to-3-second static period (Sheppard et al., 2006). A set position of 90° has been used to standardise the testing protocol, assuming that variations in squat depth could affect the magnitude of the mechanical outputs. Other authors have utilised a self-selected depth for SJ testing (Janicijevic et al., 2020; McBride et al., 2010; Petronijevic et al., 2018), indicating it could provide a simpler and more ecologically valid procedure than the set 90° position. For instance, Petronijevic and colleagues (Petronijevic et al., 2018) compared self-selected (93–97° knee angle) and standardised (90° knee angle) SJ starting positions in handball players and physical education students and found no differences in jump height between positions, with both highly reliable. Whereas McBride and colleagues (McBride et al., 2010) showed jump heights increased with greater squat depths, yet the time needed to complete the jump from a deeper position was longer and thus might make it impractical for certain athletic populations.

CMJ testing for jump height has excellent reliability (Cormack et al., 2008b). Limited familiarisation is required for CMJ testing, particularly with athletes (Nibali et al., 2015). Instructions have been shown to be vital during jump testing (Kershner et al., 2019; Talpey et al., 2016). Instructing to 'jump for maximum height' resulted in great jump height and velocity, whereas instructing to 'extend the legs as fast as possible to maximise explosive force' produced greater peak force (Talpey et al., 2016). A follow-up study examined additional cues (Kershner et al., 2019). Alongside the standardised instruction of 'jump as high as possible', internal focus instruction of 'extending your knees and hips as explosively as possible' and external focus instruction of 'push away from the ground as explosively as possible' were investigated. Jump height, peak velocity, and mean concentric velocity were greater when using an external focus compared to an internal focus. Furthermore, recently, reactive strength index modified was found to be higher with instructions to 'jump as fast as possible' compared to 'jump as high and as fast as possible' (Sánchez-Sixto et al., 2021). Likewise, higher reactive strength index modified values were found when athletes were instructed to perform a faster countermovement in comparison to a self-selected speed during the CMJ (Pérez-Castilla et al., 2019). Therefore, researchers and practitioners need to take instructions into account when performing jump testing.

Jumping with or without the use of the arms will impact on the results, with higher vertical jump height with arm swing (13–19% higher) (Lees et al., 2004; Mosier et al., 2019). It may be the case that jump tests that utilise arm swing may be appropriate for certain sports (e.g. volleyball) and could increase the specificity of the test (Sheppard et al., 2012).

The depth of the countermovement is another testing consideration which can affect force-time variables (Gheller et al., 2015; Mandic et al., 2015, 2016; Pérez-Castilla et al., 2019). Higher jump heights are observed in jumps that start from a deeper squat position (or larger range of countermovement) compared to jumps performed from a smaller squat depth (Gheller et al., 2015). In contrast, maximum force and power output are higher in jumps with a smaller squat depth. Taken together, maximum force and power assessed through vertical jumps should be taken with caution since both of them could be markedly confounded by the depth of the countermovement (Mandic et al., 2015). Based on the available evidence, encouraging the athlete to adopt their preferred countermovement depth appears to be best practice from a reliability perspective (Petronijevic et al., 2018) and will provide the practitioner with an opportunity to quantify the athlete's natural jump strategy (and possible changes to said strategy thereafter).

Several trials should be conducted with jump assessments. Increasing trial size will, in most cases, reduce the typical error associated with a test variable. Recent work found taking the average of multiple trials resulted in lower CVs when compared to the best value of eight CMJs (Kennedy and Drake, 2021), but it may be best to take the average from two to three trials to save on additional testing time. Al Haddad and colleagues (Al Haddad et al., 2015) recommended using either the best or average performance may have a similar ability to monitor changes in jump performance. A meta-analysis found that using average CMJ height was more sensitive than the highest CMJ height in monitoring neuromuscular status (Claudino et al., 2017).

Drop jump testing can be used to measure reactive strength and ability to tolerate rapid SSC movements. The RSI is commonly assessed (Flanagan et al., 2008; Markwick et al., 2015) and is expressed as contact time relative to flight time (or jump height), which requires some type of measurement device (e.g. force platform or jump/contact mat). The modified RSI determined from a CMJ has also been proposed (Suchomel et al., 2015, 2016). This is calculated using jump height and time to take-off. The flight-time-to-contraction-time ratio has also been used for athlete assessment (Cormack et al., 2008a). The flight-time-to-contraction-time ratio been shown to provide the same information as the modified RSI (McMahon et al., 2018a). Whichever method is chosen, it should be used consistently, and practitioners need to be aware of differences that may exist with other approaches. Acceptable within-session reliability of DJ RSI has been shown in track and field athletes (0.3 m drop height) (Flanagan et al., 2008) and professional basketball players (0.20–0.50 m drop heights) (Markwick et al., 2015), whereas acceptable between-session reliability of DJ RSI from 0.40 m has been shown in junior international rugby players (Beattie and Flanagan, n.d.).

A single drop height (e.g. 0.30 m or 0.40 m) or a profile of several heights, such as 0.30–0.80 m can be used (Byrne et al., 2017; Moir et al., 2018). Using several heights allows coaches to build a reactive strength profile for each individual athlete and evaluates their stretch-load tolerance. This profile can provide information such as the best RSI and the optimal drop height, which may help future training prescription. However, the coach's assessment of technical competency should remain the primary determining factor for the selection of an appropriate drop height during training.

Different verbal instructions can acutely affect DJ performance outcomes (Young et al., 1995). For example, when given specific instructions to maximise their reactive strength index (e.g. 'jump as high as possible while minimising ground contact time'), athletes do indeed decrease their contact time, but their maximum jump height also decreases (Young et al., 1995). One study found no difference in jump height when instructed to either 'focus on simultaneously extending your hips, knees, and ankles when jumping' or 'focus on jumping as high as you can' (Khuu et al., 2015). In contrast, RSI was largest when instructed to 'focus on getting-off the ground as fast as you can after landing'. Practitioners frequently instruct athletes to jump as high as possible while minimising the time spent on the ground. This focus on ground-contact time invariably leads to a reduction in jump height, greater peak vertical ground reaction force, and greater loading rates because of the stiffer landings usually observed (Khuu et al., 2015).

An important factor to consider is when performing the DJ athletes drop from the same height of the box. In fact, drop heights have been reported to be 28.6–39.5% different to box height (Costley et al., 2017; Geraldo et al., 2019). Athletes should be instructed to step out from the box and not step down or jump off the box. This is problematic when assessing DJ performance because the testing conditions will be different for each athlete as variations in drop height will change the mechanical demands of the test. Resultantly, data accuracy may be questionable due to athletes dropping from different heights trial to trial (McMahon et al., 2021). To overcome the issue of standardising height, repeated jump tests such as the 10/5 can be used to evaluate reactive strength qualities (Stratford et al., 2021).

Testing Isometric Strength

Isometric or static contractions are muscle actions which result in no change in joint angle. Typically, the muscle's maximal and rapid force-production capabilities are assessed via isometric strength tests which require subjects to produce maximal force against an immovable object or resistance. Various methodologies are available with strain gauge, cable tensiometer, force plates, or other devices used to measure the applied force. Some authors have suggested that isometric tests not to be used for the purposes of athletic assessment, based on research showing low relationships between single-joint isometric tests and athletic tasks (Wilson and Murphy, 1996a, 1996b; Young et al., 2002). Conversely, there is increasing evidence showing strong relationships between isometric force-time characteristics and sprint and change-of-direction performance (Comfort et al., 2019). Additionally, isometric tests can be easily administered, are highly reliable, require little familiarisation, are faster and less fatiguing versus dynamic 1 RM tests, and correlate with RM performance across various dynamic strength tests. Thus, the diagnostic ability of isometric tests may be of importance when considering time constrained tasks within MDS actions.

Commonly reported metrics during isometric tests include peak force (PF) and force at a variety of epochs (Beckham et al., 2013), as well as RFD (Maffiuletti et al., 2016). Additionally, RFD can be quantified at specific epochs (50, 100, 150, 200, and 250 ms) or consecutive periods (e.g. 100–200 ms) (Peñailillo et al., 2015) relative to force onset. Additionally, impulse values across similar epochs (0–100, 0–200, and 0–300 ms) have been associated with MDS performance. Impulse is the integral beneath the force-time recording (Folland et al., 2014) and provides information about the time history of the contraction including the overall influence of all the examined RFD measurements (Aagaard et al., 2002). Ultimately, the ability to dissect the force-time curve allows for various aspects of strength to be quantified and monitored.

The isometric mid-thigh pull (IMTP) and isometric squat (ISQT) are common multi-joint tasks to evaluate isometric force-time characteristics. More recently, the isometric leg press (ILP) has emerged as another method for quantifying lower-limb force-time characteristics (Zaras et al., 2016).

Isometric Mid-thigh Pull

The most common isometric test used with athletes is the IMTP (Comfort et al., 2019; Stone et al., 2019, p. 25). An adjustable isometric rack is used to mimic the second-pull weightlifting position (i.e. 'power position') (Haff et al., 1997). This position is where the highest forces and velocities (and subsequently power) are achieved in the clean and snatch in weightlifters (Garhammer, 1993). Since its origin, the IMTP has subsequently been used by researchers and practitioners across a range of sports (Brady et al., 2020).

The IMTP PF has consistently been shown to be highly reliable with ICCs ≥ 0.92 and CVs ≤ 5% (Comfort et al., 2020). Likewise, force at specific epochs are highly reliable during the IMTP (Comfort et al., 2020; Haff et al., 2015); however, RFD and other time-related variables are generally less reliable (Haff et al., 2015). When examining the literature, it appears RFD has been quantified as a peak measure or through time-dependent epochs. Quantifying peak RFD, which occurs within a predefined window (2 ms), may be too sensitive to unsystematic variability, with Haff et al. (2015) reporting a sampling window of 20 ms to produce the best reliability (ICC = 0.90, CI = 0.73–0.97, CV = 12.9%, CI = 0.5–20.7). The use of time-dependent epochs (0–200 ms) to assess RFD has shown to produce much more reliable results (Haff et al., 2015) and better relationships to dynamic performance measures. As such, it is now common to examine RFD measures in specific time bands. Recently, it has been suggested practitioners should select specific testing protocols depending on the component of an athlete's force-generating capacity they wish to assess (PF versus RFD) (Guppy et al., 2022). Specifically, performing five ~1-second IMTP trials resulted in more reliable RFD measures compared to five 5-second traditional trials. Also, ~1-second trials resulted in greater force at various epochs, RFD, and impulse compared to traditional trials, suggesting practitioners should potentially separate the assessment of maximal force and time-specific force during IMTP testing. While shortening the duration of the overall testing protocol may represent a more time-efficient and less fatiguing assessment than previously suggested, more research is needed to understand how best to utilise this assessment in a sports performance monitoring programme.

Haff et al. (1997) originally identified the position for testing should reflect the power position (i.e. start of the second pull) in the clean rather than the mid-thigh. One study reported that body position had no effect on PF or RFD during the IMTP (Comfort et al., 2015). However, several studies suggest that IMTP force-time measures are dependent on the body position adopted during the test (Dos'Santos et al., 2017b; Beckham et al., 2018; Guppy et al. 2018, 2019). Based on the aforementioned research, it appears that (1) measures of PF and time-specific force are reliable regardless of position used, (2) RFD measures are less reliable and should be interpreted accordingly, and (3) a barbell position matching the second pull of the clean and an upright torso appears to allow for the maximum force to be produced in the majority of individuals (Beckham et al., 2018; Guppy et al., 2019). A recent review recommended a standardised posture of hip angle 140–150° and knee angle 125–145° (Comfort et al., 2020), whereby, depending on the athlete, the exact knee and hip angle may vary and some angle adjustments may be necessary to optimise the individual athletes pulling position. Like teaching the power position to an athlete, posture should be individualised; however, an athlete's IMTP position should be consistent between testing sessions.

IMTP force-time data has been compiled accurately with a sampling frequency as low as 500 Hz (Haff et al., 1997), while others have opted for higher sampling frequencies, such as 2,000 Hz (Guppy et al., 2022), and these differences may simply be due to the choice of sampling frequency available with certain force platforms. Three review articles suggest that a minimum sampling frequency of 1,000 Hz should be used when performing isometric assessments to ensure accuracy, especially in time-dependent variables, such as time-specific force, RFD, and impulse (Comfort et al., 2019; Maffiuletti et al., 2016; McMaster et al., 2014). Sampling frequency of 1,000 Hz may also be used to accurately identify contraction onset. Therefore, a minimum force platform sample frequency of 1,000 Hz is recommended (if the force platform used has this capability) when conducting IMTP testing, but sampling as low as 500 Hz is sufficient when measuring peak force, time-specific force values, and RFD at predetermined time bands (Dos'Santos et al., 2019). If higher sampling frequencies can be used, then they are preferred as they may increase the accuracy of time-dependent measures. What appears to be most critical is to maintain the sampling frequency at the same level between testing sessions.

The effect of the type of instruction can also affect IMTP outputs (Halperin et al., 2016). The typical instruction given is to 'pull as hard and as fast as possible' (Halperin et al., 2016). Specifically, an externally focused instruction of 'focus on pushing the ground as hard and as fast as you possibly can' produced greater PF compared to an internally focused and control instruction. Likewise, the instruction 'pull as hard and as fast as you can, push the ground away, drive your feet into the ground and the bar from the floor' has been used (Brady et al., 2018). Indeed, strong verbal encouragement during testing ensures that athletes give a maximum effort (Belkhiria et al., 2018). Recent standardisation and methodological considerations for the IMTP recommend to instruct athletes to 'push your feet into the ground as fast and as hard as possible', followed by the countdown of 'three, two, one – *push*' (Comfort et al., 2019). It is also recommended that athletes understand that the focus is to drive the feet directly into the force platform and not attempt to pull the bar with their arms. A recent study showed no impact on PF or impulse over various epochs when instructing athletes to (1) 'pull as hard and fast as possible', (2) 'pull as fast as possible', or (3) 'pull as hard as possible' (McCormick et al., 2022). The most critical factor is to apply the methods consistently between and within testing sessions to increase reliability and validity. Testers should also be mindful of an individual's preference, as some may not respond as positively to excessive verbal encouragement.

Researchers have utilised various set-ups for isometric testing and have developed portable systems which allow for cheaper alternatives to force plates, such as load cells (James et al., 2017) and custom-built dynamometers (Dobbin et al., 2018; Till et al., 2018). The reliability of some of these systems has been shown to be acceptable for measures of PF but uncertain for RFD and force at selected epochs (James et al., 2017), questioning the validity of such systems compared to a criterion (force platform) (Till et al., 2018). Isometric strength is commonly assessed in bilateral conditions (Brady et al., 2018; Comfort et al., 2019); unilateral testing, however, has shown to be reliable with both bilateral (Bailey et al., 2015) and unilateral methods (Dos'Santos et al., 2016).

Isometric Squat

The isometric squat is also commonly used to assess isometric strength in a range of populations (Bazyler et al., 2014; Brady et al., 2018; Drake et al., 2018). Yet research on the reliability of the isometric squat variables is limited compared to the IMTP. Isometric squat peak force has consistently shown to be highly reliable (ICCs ≥ 0.97 and CVs ≤ 4.0%) (Brady et al., 2018). Likewise, impulse at specific epochs are highly reliable (ICCs ≥ 0.92 and CVs ≤ 10%) (Brady et al., 2018); however, RFD and other time-related variables have shown greater variability (Bazyler et al., 2015; Drake et al., 2019; Palmer et al., 2018). Peak RFD determined as the highest RFD produced within a 30 ms window between the onset of contraction and the PF value was only reported to be reliable under one criteria of reliability in bilateral isometric squat (ICC = 0.94 and CV = 15.2%) but not in a unilateral variation (ICC = 0.36 and CV = 45.5%) (Hart et al., 2012). The use of time-dependent epochs (0–200 ms) to assess RFD have shown to produce much more reliable results (Bazyler et al., 2015; Brady et al., 2018; Palmer et al., 2018) and better relationships to dynamic performance measures. Furthermore, practitioners assessing multi-joint RFD should potentially employ an explosive isometric squat test as opposed to the traditional isometric squat test (Drake et al., 2019). Specifically, when assessing RFD, performing three ~1-second isometric squat trials with the primary goal to produce the highest force as fast as possible resulted in more reliable RFD measures (over 150, 200, and 250 ms) compared to the traditional isometric squat test (produce the highest force possible) (Drake et al., 2019). Despite common use of instantaneous RFD variables, several studies (Brady et al., 2018; Drake et al., 2019; Haff et al., 2015) question the reliability of this measure, as this may be an inconsistent point on the force-time trace. Therefore, the application of instantaneous RFD may be problematic using existing protocols, and further work may be required to explore the usefulness of this measure when assessing a sports performance monitoring programme. Researchers have compared the isometric squat and IMTP performed at the same knee and hip angles (Brady et al., 2018; Nuzzo et al., 2008). Participants produced greater peak force and impulse (0–300 ms) in the isometric squat compared to the IMTP. The authors suggested that if researchers and practitioners are interested in determining the true maximum lower-body force capacity of athletes, then the isometric squat should be preferred (Brady et al., 2018). Similar to IMTP, joint angle can also affect resultant isometric squat metrics and reliability (Brady et al., 2018; Lynch et al., 2021; Palmer et al. 2018) and thus need to be standardised.

The isometric squat may require more familiarisation compared to the IMTP (Drake et al., 2018). As with the IMTP, constant tension should be applied to the bar prior to the initiation of the test (Bazyler et al., 2015). Excessive force production prior to the start of the test should be avoided as this will impact RFD values. Taken together, it is important that researchers and practitioners not use these tests interchangeably. Both tests are useful to be performed, yet practitioners should consider the demands of the sport and adopt a test that provides consistency in joint angles and subsequent reliability of key metrics to evaluate maximum isometric strength.

Isometric Leg Press

While the IMTP and isometric squat have commonly been used to assess maximum isometric strength, the anatomical position required may compromise the trunk and spinal column due to high levels of compression, increasing the potential for injury. Alternatively, an isometric assessment performed on an incline leg press provides overcomes these issues. Peak force has shown to be highly reliable (ICCs ≥ 0.93, CV ≤ 5.6%) at both 90° and 120° knee angles (Harden et al., 2018), with the greatest force produced at 120° compared to 90°. Compared to other movements, the isometric leg press has not been studied as extensively, so more work is required to determine the reliability of the test across a range of populations.

Testing Dynamic Strength

Another method for evaluating muscular strength is determining the maximum weight that can be lifted for a prescribed number of repetitions. When attempting to evaluate strength either the 1 RM, 3 RM, or 5 RM tests are employed (McGuigan et al., 2013; Nimphius et al., 2012). If strength endurance is being evaluated the maximum weight that can be lifted for 8–12 RM tests may be evaluated. All tests are measures of the maximum amount of load lifted according to the correct technical specifications. The most common lower-body exercises tested are the back squat and power clean. When conducting these types of tests, it is important to consider the movement pattern, contraction type (i.e. eccentric-concentric, concentric-only, eccentric-only) and the warm-up strategy employed to prepare the athlete to give a maximal effort as these may impact the reliability of the test. Basic considerations for lower-body repetition maximum testing are presented in Table 7.5, whilst specific methods and protocols for conducting RM testing have been described previously (Haff, 2018; McGuigan, 2019).

TABLE 7.5 Basic Considerations for Lower-Body Repetition Maximum Testing

Reliability	• Repetition maximum testing has been shown to be a reliable method of assessing maximum dynamic strength in a range of populations and exercises. • Reliability can also be increased by incorporating the exercises tested in training via enhanced familiarisation. • It appears that RM testing can produce reliable results in individuals with some training experience after as little as three to four familiarisation sessions.
Advantages	• RM testing provides a direct measure of maximal strength. From this, it can also be used as an effective guide for programming based on estimates from other training load zones. • RMs are not goals. RMs serve more of a prescriptive role rather than descriptive for strength and power training. • Testing of the RM is very safe if the technique is sound.
Disadvantages	• Concerns are sometimes raised about the issue of injury, particularly with novice or inexperienced individuals. • Athletes tested should have stable technique to reduce potential injury risk and maximise the diagnostic capacity of the test. • These risks are further minimised with adequate familiarisation with resistance training and testing and supervision by an experienced and qualified tester, alongside clear instructions for testing.
Estimation equations	• Several equations been presented in the literature to estimate RM without the need to test directly. • The practical application of the methods needs to be weighed against the scientific rigour of the methods. • The validity, reliability, and accuracy of these equations warrant further investigation. • The choice of equation will impact the overall RM value, but it should be applied consistently, and practitioners should be aware of the error associated with it.

Isokinetic Dynamometry

Isokinetic dynamometry allows the measurement of muscle strength (net muscle torque) for all joints of the body in most of their planar movements, at controlled speeds of movement (constant angular velocity), and in different modes of contraction (concentric, eccentric, and isometric). A main advantage of isokinetic assessment in relation to MDS is that eccentric knee extensor and flexor strength can be isolated and assessed linked to its role in the phases of COD and subsequent profiling of the athlete (see Table 7.1). With the exception of Nordic curls (Opar et al., 2013), there is a paucity of tests to assess lower-body eccentric strength. Yet Nordic curls are bilateral and do not quantify the maximal torque a hamstring group can produce (Wiesinger et al., 2020). It is beyond the scope of this chapter to discuss the use of isokinetics at length; therefore, key considerations are summarised in Table 7.6 and can apply to assessment of other muscle groups (e.g. hip strength assessments). The authors recommend reading the chapter by Baltzopoulos (2007) for a more detailed review.

Conclusion

The assessment of muscle strength qualities that underpin MDS is essential to identify strengths and weaknesses in an athlete's physical profile to help individualise MDS development programmes. Several muscle strength qualities, such as SSC function, maximal force, RFD, and concentric and

TABLE 7.6 Summary of the Key Considerations for Conducting Isokinetic Assessment (Taken from Herrington et al., 2018)

Key variables	Strength during isokinetic assessment is quantified by the maximum moment and should be achieved within three to six repetitions (Baltzopoulos, 2007). An average moment (peak) from a number of trials should not be reported, as an average may be taken from different joint positions and thus does not provide information about the joint–moment position relationship (Baltzopoulos, 2007).
Angular velocity	Aside from the muscle group and mode of assessment (i.e. concentric vs eccentric), practitioners need to decide on an appropriate angular velocity at which to assess. To assess strength, angular velocities <60°/s should be considered. Many practitioners may consider assessing at faster speeds >180°/s to provide an assessment at more functional sports-specific speeds. However, the measurement limits of many dynamometers (e.g. Biodex System 4, concentrically 500°/s, eccentrically 300°/s; Cybex Humac Norm 500°/s) fail to reach typical angular velocities achieved during many sports-specific movements (knee angular velocity during maximal instep kick in soccer: 1,134 ± 257 [Lees and Nolan, 2002]; maximum velocity sprinting −460 ± 86 to 601 ± 143°/s [Bezodis et al., 2008]).
Joint alignment	Practitioners should ensure that the dynamometer axis is aligned to the best approximation of the joint axis, as any errors here could lead to (1) incorrect lever arm length of the limb in determining joint moment and (2) the force vector from the limb to the dynamometer not applied perpendicular to the lever. Practitioners should thoroughly ensure that the joint aligns to the dynamometer around the expected position of the angle of peak moment and ensure that compression of the subject's soft tissues and cushion of the dynamometer seat do not affect the alignment of the joint axis (Baltzopoulos, 2007).
Inspection of isokinetic range	Measurement at greater angular velocities reduces the available 'isokinetic range' as greater ranges of movement are required to reach and decelerate from greater velocities. Thus, careful examination of the moment–angular velocity profiles is essential to ensure that the peak moment at these greater velocities is achieved within isokinetic range, and reliability of such measures may also be compromised.
Gravity correction	Data should be gravity-corrected to ensure that the peak moments of muscle groups working against gravity are not underestimated and those working with gravity are not overestimated. Most dynamometers include a function to assess the weight of the limb at a set position, and this is then gravity-corrected throughout the full range of motion to ensure the gravity correction considers the changes in the gravitational lever arm throughout the full range of motion. It is recommended in the case of knee extensor and flexor strength assessment that the weight of the limb is measured at 30° of flexion (0° full extension of the knee) to ensure that tension from the hamstring muscle-tendon complex does not add to the weight of the limb if this was measured nearer to full knee extension (Baltzopoulos, 2007).

eccentric strength may be considered important underpinning physical qualities for MDS actions and should be considered for assessment. Test options for these qualities have been outlined in this chapter, which is by no means an exhaustive list, and other test options for these qualities may be available to better serve practitioners. Nevertheless, in designing and implementing a test battery, practitioners *must* carefully consider the standardisation, reliability, and validity of test protocols to ensure that the tests can precisely identify the athlete's physical abilities and enable monitoring of these abilities against the goals of the training programme.

References

Aagaard, P., Simonsen, E.B., Andersen, J.L., Magnusson, P., Dyhre-Poulsen, P., (2002). Increased rate of force development and neural drive of human skeletal muscle following resistance training. *Journal of Applied Physiology 93*(4), 1318–1326.

Al Haddad, H., Simpson, B.M., Buchheit, M., (2015). Monitoring changes in jump and sprint performance: Best or average values? *International Journal of Sports Physiology and Performance 10*, 931–934.

Atkinson, G., Nevill, A.M., (1998). Statistical methods for assessing measurement error (reliability) in variables relevant to sports medicine. *Sports Medicine 26*, 217–238.

Bailey, C.A., Sato, K., Burnett, A., Stone, M.H., (2015). Force-production asymmetry in male and female athletes of differing strength levels. *International Journal of Sports Physiology & Performance 10*, 504–508. https://doi.org/10.1123/ijspp.2014-0379

Baltzopoulos, V., (2007). Isokinetic dynamometry. In *Biomechanical Evaluation of Movement in Sport and Exercise*. London: Routledge, pp. 117–142.

Bazyler, C.D., Bailey, C.A., Chiang, C.-Y., Sato, K., Stone, M.H., (2014). The effects of strength training on isometric force production symmetry in recreationally trained males. *Journal of Trainology 3*, 6–10.

Bazyler, C.D., Beckham, G.K., Sato, K., (2015). The use of the isometric squat as a measure of strength and explosiveness. *Journal of Strength & Conditioning Research 29*, 1386–1392.

Beattie, K., Flanagan, E.P., (n.d.). Establishing the reliability & meaningful change of the drop-jump reactive-strength index. *Journal of Australian Strength & Conditioning 23*, 12–18.

Beckham, G., Mizuguchi, S., Carter, C., Sato, K., Ramsey, M., Lamont, H., Hornsby, G., Haff, G., Stone, M., (2013). Relationships of isometric mid-thigh pull variables to weightlifting performance. *Journal of Sports Medicine & Physical Fitness 53*(5), 573–581.

Beckham, G., Suchomel, T., Mizuguchi, S., (2014). Force plate use in performance monitoring and sport science testing. *New Studies in Athletics* 25.

Beckham, G.K., Sato, K., Santana, H.A., Mizuguchi, S., Haff, G.G., Stone, M.H., (2018). Effect of body position on force production during the isometric midthigh pull. *The Journal of Strength & Conditioning Research 32*, 48–56.

Belkhiria, C., De Marco, G., Driss, T., (2018). Effects of verbal encouragement on force and electromyographic activations during exercise. *Journal of Sports Medicine and Physical Fitness 58*, 750–757.

Binboğa, E., Tok, S., Catikkas, F., Guven, S., Dane, S., (2013). The effects of verbal encouragement and conscientiousness on maximal voluntary contraction of the triceps surae muscle in elite athletes. *Journal of Sports Sciences 31*, 982–988.

Brady, C.J., Harrison, A.J., Comyns, T.M., (2020). A review of the reliability of biomechanical variables produced during the isometric mid-thigh pull and isometric squat and the reporting of normative data. *Sports Biomechanics 19*(1), 1–25.

Brady, C.J., Harrison, A.J., Flanagan, E.P., Haff, G.G., Comyns, T.M., (2018). A comparison of the isometric midthigh pull and isometric squat: Intraday reliability, usefulness, and the magnitude of difference between tests. *International Journal of Sports Physiology and Performance 13*, 844–852.

Byrne, D.J., Browne, D.T., Byrne, P.J., Richardson, N., (2017). Interday reliability of the reactive strength index and optimal drop height. *Journal of Strength and Conditioning Research 31*, 721–726.

Claudino, J.G., Cronin, J., Mezêncio, B., McMaster, D.T., McGuigan, M., Tricoli, V., Amadio, A.C., Serrão, J.C., (2017). The countermovement jump to monitor neuromuscular status: A meta-analysis. *Journal of Science and Medicine in Sport 20*, 397–402.

Comfort, P., Dos'Santos, T., Beckham, G.K., Stone, M.H., Guppy, S.N., Haff, G.G., (2019). Standardization and methodological considerations for the isometric midthigh pull. *Strength & Conditioning Journal 41*, 57–79.

Comfort, P., Jones, P.A., McMahon, J.J., Newton, R., (2015). Effect of knee and trunk angle on kinetic variables during the isometric midthigh pull: Test-retest reliability. *International Journal of Sports Physiology and Performance 10*, 58–63.

Comfort, P., Jones, P.A., Thomas, C., Dos'Santos, T., McMahon, J.J., Suchomel, T.J., (2020). Changes in early and maximal isometric force production in response to moderate-and high-load strength and power training. *Journal of Strength and Conditioning Research*. https://doi.org/10.1519/JSC.0000000000003544

Cormack, S.J., Newton, R.U., McGuigan, M.R., Cormie, P., (2008a). Neuromuscular and endocrine responses of elite players during an Australian rules football season. *International Journal of Sports Physiology and Performance 3*, 439–453.

Cormack, S.J., Newton, R.U., McGuigan, M.R., Doyle, T.L., (2008b). Reliability of measures obtained during single and repeated countermovement jumps. *International Journal of Sports Physiology and Performance 3*(2), 131–144. https://doi.org/10.1123/ijspp.3.2.131

Costley, L., Wallace, E., Johnston, M., Kennedy, R., (2017). Reliability of bounce drop jump parameters within elite male rugby players. *The Journal of Sports Medicine and Physical Fitness 58*, 1390–1397.

de Hoyo, M., Sañudo, B., Carrasco, L., Mateo-Cortes, J., Domínguez-Cobo, S., Fernandes, O., Del Ojo, J.J., Gonzalo-Skok, O., (2016). Effects of 10-week eccentric overload training on kinetic parameters during change of direction in football players. *Journal of Sports Sciences 34*(14), 1380–1387.

Dobbin, N., Hunwicks, R., Jones, B., Till, K., Highton, J., Twist, C., (2018). Criterion and construct validity of an isometric midthigh-pull dynamometer for assessing whole-body strength in professional rugby league players. *International Journal of Sports Physiology and Performance 13*, 235–239.

Donahue, P.T., Hill, C.M., Wilson, S.J., Williams, C.C., Garner, J.C., (2021). Squat jump movement onset thresholds influence on kinetics and kinematics. *International Journal of Kinesiology and Sports Science 9*(3), 1–7.

Dos'Santos, T., Jones, P.A., Comfort, P., Thomas, C., (2017a). Effect of different onset thresholds on isometric midthigh pull force-time variables. *The Journal of Strength & Conditioning Research 31*(12), 3463–3473.

Dos'Santos, T., Jones, P.A., Kelly, J., McMahon, J.J., Comfort, P., Thomas, C., (2019). Effect of sampling frequency on isometric midthigh-pull kinetics. *International Journal of Sports Physiology and Performance* 14, 525–530.

Dos'Santos, T., Thomas, C., Comfort, P., Jones, P.A., (2018). The effect of angle and velocity on change of direction biomechanics: An angle-velocity trade-off. *Sports Medicine 48*, 2235–2253.

Dos'Santos, T., Thomas, C., Jones, P.A., Comfort, P., (2016). Assessing muscle strength asymmetry via a unilateral stance isometric mid-thigh pull. *International Journal of Sports Physiology & Performance 12*, 505–511. https://doi.org/10.1123/ijspp.2016-0179

Dos'Santos, T., Thomas, C., Jones, P.A., McMahon, J.J., Comfort, P., (2017b). The effect of hip joint angle on isometric midthigh pull kinetics. *The Journal of Strength & Conditioning Research 31*(10), 2748–2757.

Drake, D., Kennedy, R.A., Wallace, E.S., (2018). Familiarization, validity and smallest detectable difference of the isometric squat test in evaluating maximal strength. *Journal of Sports Sciences 36*, 2087–2095.

Drake, D., Kennedy, R.A., Wallace, E.S., (2019). Multi-joint rate of force development testing protocol affects reliability and the smallest detectible difference. *Journal of Sports Sciences 37*, 1570–1581.

Eagles, A.N., Sayers, M.G.L., Bousson, M., Lovell, D.I., (2015). Current methodologies and implications of phase identification of the vertical jump: A systematic review and meta-analysis. *Sports Medicine 45*, 1311–1323.

Flanagan, E.P., Ebben, W.P., Jensen, R.L., (2008). Reliability of the reactive strength index and time to stabilization during depth jumps. *Journal of Strength & Conditioning Research 22*, 1677–1682.

Folland, J.P., Buckthorpe, M.W., Hannah, R., (2014). Human capacity for explosive force production: neural and contractile determinants. *Scandinavian Journal of Medicine & Science in Sports 24*(6), 894–906.

Garhammer, J., (1993). A review of power output studies of Olympic and powerlifting: Methodology, performance prediction, and evaluation tests. *Journal of Strength & Conditioning Research* 7, 76–89.

Geraldo, G. de F., Bredt, S. da G.T., Menzel, H.-J.K., Cançado, G.H. da C.P., Carvalho, L.A.C.M., Lima, F.V., Soares, J. da S., Andrade, A.G.P. de, (2019). Drop height is influenced by box height but not by individual stature during drop jumps. *Journal of Physical Education* 30.

Gheller, R.G., Dal Pupo, J., Ache-Dias, J., Detanico, D., Padulo, J., dos Santos, S.G., (2015). Effect of different knee starting angles on intersegmental coordination and performance in vertical jumps. *Human Movement Science 42*, 71–80.

Grgic, J., Trexler, E. T., Lazinica, B., Pedisic, Z., (2018). Effects of caffeine intake on muscle strength and power: a systematic review and meta-analysis. *Journal of the International Society of Sports Nutrition 15*, 11. https://doi.org/10.1186/s12970-018-0216-0

Guppy, S.N., Brady, C.J., Kotani, Y., Stone, M.H., Medic, N., Haff, G.G., (2018). The effect of altering body posture and barbell position on the between-session reliability of force-time curve characteristics in the isometric mid-thigh pull. *Sports 6*(4), 162.

Guppy, S.N., Brady, C.J., Kotani, Y., Stone, M.H., Medic, N., Haff, G.G., (2019). Effect of altering body posture and barbell position on the within-session reliability and magnitude of force-time curve characteristics in the isometric midthigh pull. *The Journal of Strength & Conditioning Research 33*, 3252–3262.

Guppy, S.N., Kotani, Y., Brady, C.J., Connolly, S., Comfort, P., Haff, G.G., (2022). The reliability and magnitude of time-dependent force-time characteristics during the isometric midthigh pull are affected by both testing protocol and analysis choices. *Journal of Strength and Conditioning Research 36*, 1191–1199.

Haff, G.G., (2018). Strength–isometric and dynamic testing. In *Performance Assessment in Strength and Conditioning* (Eds. Comfort, P., Jones, P.A., McMahon, J.J.). London: Routledge, 166–192.

Haff, G.G., Ruben, R.P., Lider, J., Twine, C., Cormie, P., (2015). A comparison of methods for determining the rate of force development during isometric midthigh clean pulls. *Journal of Strength & Conditioning Research 29*, 386–395.

Haff, G.G., Stone, M., O'Bryant, H.S., Harman, E., Dinan, C., Johnson, R., Han, K.-H., (1997). Force-time dependent characteristics of dynamic and isometric muscle actions. *Journal of Strength & Conditioning Research 11*, 269–272.

Halperin, I., Williams, K.J., Martin, D.T., Chapman, D.W., (2016). The effects of attentional focusing instructions on force production during the isometric midthigh pull. *Journal of Strength & Conditioning Research 30*, 919–923.

Harden, M., Wolf, A., Hicks, K.M., Howatson, G., (2018). Familiarisation, reproducibility, sensitivity and joint angle specificity of bilateral isometric force exertions during leg press. *Isokinetics and Exercise Science 26*, 291–298.

Hart, N., Nimphius, S., Wilkie, J., Newton, R., (2012). Reliability and validity of unilateral and bilateral isometric strength measures using a customised, portable apparatus. *Journal of Austrailan Strength and Conditioning 20*(1), 61–67.

Herrington, L.C., Munro, A.G., and Jones, P.A., (2018). Assessment of factors associated with injury risk. In *Performance Assessment in Strength and Conditioning*. (Eds. Comfort, P., McMahon, P.A., Jones, P.A.). Abingdon, Oxon, United Kingdom: Routledge, 53–95.

Hopkins, W.G., (2000). Measures of reliability in sports medicine and science. *Sports Medicine 30*, 1–15.

Hughes, S., Warmenhoven, J., Haff, G.G., Chapman, D.W., Nimphius, S., (2021). Countermovement jump and squat jump force-time curve analysis in control and fatigue conditions. *The Journal of Strength & Conditioning Research 36*(10), 2752–2761.

James, L.P., Roberts, L.A., Haff, G.G., Kelly, V.G., Beckman, E.M., (2017). Validity and reliability of a portable isometric mid-thigh clean pull. *The Journal of Strength & Conditioning Research 31*, 1378–1386.

Jarvis, P., Turner, A., Read, P., Bishop, C., (2022). Reactive strength index and its associations with measures of physical and sports performance: A systematic review with meta-analysis. *Sports Medicine 52*(2), 301–330.

Jones, P.A., Dos'Santos, T., McMahon, J.J., Graham-Smith, P., (2022). Contribution of eccentric strength to cutting performance in female soccer players. *Journal of Strength and Conditioning Research 36*(2), 525–533.

Jones, P.A., Thomas, C., Dos' Santos, T., McMahon, J.J., Graham-Smith, P., (2017). The role of eccentric strength in 180 turns in female soccer players. *Sports 5*(2), 42.

Janicijevic, D., Knezevic, O.M., Mirkov, D.M., Pérez-Castilla, A., Petrovic, M., Samozino, P., Garcia-Ramos, A., (2020). Assessment of the force-velocity relationship during vertical jumps: Influence of the starting position, analysis procedures and number of loads. *European Journal of Sport Science 20*, 614–623.

Kennedy, R.A., Drake, D., (2021). Improving the signal-to-noise ratio when monitoring countermovement jump performance. *The Journal of Strength & Conditioning Research 35*, 85–90.

Kershner, A.L., Fry, A.C., Cabarkapa, D., (2019). Effect of internal vs. external focus of attention instructions on countermovement jump variables in NCAA Division I student-athletes. *The Journal of Strength & Conditioning Research 33*, 1467–1473.

Khuu, S., Musalem, L.L., Beach, T.A., (2015). Verbal instructions acutely affect drop vertical jump biomechanics – implications for athletic performance and injury risk assessments. *The Journal of Strength & Conditioning Research 29*, 2816–2826.

Koo, T.K., Li, M.Y., (2016). A guideline of selecting and reporting intraclass correlation coefficients for reliability research. *Journal of Chiropractic Medicine 15*(2), 155–163. https://doi.org/10.1016/j.jcm.2016.02.012

Kubo, K., Morimoto, M., Komuro, T., Tsunoda, N., Kanehisa, H., Fukunaga, T., (2007). Influences of tendon stiffness, joint stiffness, and electromyographic activity on jump performances using single joint. *European Journal of Applied Physiology 99*, 235–243.

Lake, J., Mundy, P., Comfort, P., McMahon, J.J., Suchomel, T.J., Carden, P., (2018). Concurrent validity of a portable force plate using vertical jump force–time characteristics. *Journal of Applied Biomechanics 34*, 410–413.

Lees, A., Nolan, L., (2002). *Three-Dimensional Kinematic Analysis of the Instep Kick under Speed and Accuracy Conditions, in Science and Football IV* (Eds. Spinks, W., Reilly, T., Murphy, A.). London: Routledge, 16–21.

Lees, A., Vanrenterghem, J., Clercq, D.D., (2004). Understanding how an arm swing enhances performance in the vertical jump. *Journal of Biomechanics 37*, 1929–1940.

Lynch, A.E., Davies, R.W., Jakeman, P.M., Locke, T., Allardyce, J.M., Carson, B.P., (2021). The influence of maximal strength and knee angle on the reliability of peak force in the isometric squat. *Sports 9*(10), 140.

Maffiuletti, N.A., Aagaard, P., Blazevich, A.J., Folland, J., Tillin, N., Duchateau, J., (2016). Rate of force development: Physiological and methodological considerations. *European Journal of Applied Physiology 116*, 1091–1116.

Mandic, R., Jakovljevic, S., Jaric, S., (2015). Effects of countermovement depth on kinematic and kinetic patterns of maximum vertical jumps. *Journal of Electromyography and Kinesiology 25*, 265–272.

Mandic, R., Knezevic, O.M., Mirkov, D.M., Jaric, S., (2016). Control strategy of maximum vertical jumps: The preferred countermovement depth may not be fully optimized for jump height. *Journal of Human Kinetics 52*, 85–94.

Markovic, G., Dizdar, D., Jukic, I., Cardinale, M., (2004). Reliability and factorial validity of squat and countermovement jump tests. *Journal of Strength & Conditioning Research 18*, 551–555. https://doi.org/10.1519/1533-4287(2004)18<551:RAFVOS>2.0.CO;2 [doi]

Markwick, W.J., Bird, S.P., Tufano, J.J., Seitz, L.B., Haff, G.G., (2015). The intraday reliability of the Reactive Strength Index calculated from a drop jump in professional men's basketball. *International Journal of Sports Physiology and Performance 10*(4), 482–488. https://doi.org/10.1123/ijspp.2014-0265

McBride, J.M., Kirby, T.J., Haines, T.L., Skinner, J., (2010). Relationship between relative net vertical impulse and jump height in jump squats performed to various squat depths and with various loads. *International Journal of Sports Physiology & Performance 5*, 484–496.

McBurnie, A.J., Dos'Santos, T., (2022). Multidirectional speed in youth soccer players: Theoretical underpinnings. *Strength and Conditioning Journal 44*, 15–33.

McCormick, B., MacMahon, C., Talpey, S., James, L., (2022). The influence of instruction on isometric mid-thigh pull force-time variables. *International Journal of Strength and Conditioning* 2.

McGuigan, M., (2019). *Testing and Evaluation of Strength and Power*. London: Routledge.

McGuigan, M.R., Cormack, S.J., Gill, N.D., (2013). Strength and power profiling of athletes: Selecting tests and how to use the information for program design. *Strength & Conditioning Journal 35*, 7–14.

McGuigan, M.R., Doyle, T.L., Newton, M., Edwards, D.J., Nimphius, S., Newton, R.U., (2006). Eccentric utilization ratio: Effect of sport and phase of training. *The Journal of Strength & Conditioning Research 20*, 992–995.

McMahon, J.J., Lake, J.P., Comfort, P., (2018a). Reliability of and relationship between flight time to contraction time ratio and reactive strength index modified. *Sports 6*, 81.

McMahon, J.J., Lake, J.P., Stratford, C., Comfort, P., (2021). A proposed method for evaluating drop jump performance with one force platform. *Biomechanics 1*, 178–189.

McMahon, J.J., Lake, J.P., Suchomel, T.J., (2018b). Vertical jump testing. In *Performance Assessment in Strength and Conditioning* (Eds. Comfort, P., Jones, P.A., McMahon, J.J.). London: Routledge, pp. 96–116.

McMahon, J.J., Suchomel, T.J., Lake, J.P., Comfort, P., (2018c). Understanding the key phases of the countermovement jump force-time curve. *Strength & Conditioning Journal 40*(4), 96–106.

McMaster, D.T., Gill, N., Cronin, J., McGuigan, M., (2014). A brief review of strength and ballistic assessment methodologies in sport. *Sports Medicine 44*, 603–623.

McNair, P.J., Depledge, J., Brettkelly, M., Stanley, S.N., (1996). Verbal encouragement: Effects on maximum effort voluntary muscle action. *British Journal of Sports Medicine 30*, 243–245.

Meylan, C.M., Nosaka, K., Green, J., Cronin, J.B., (2011). The effect of three different start thresholds on the kinematics and kinetics of a countermovement jump. *The Journal of Strength & Conditioning Research 25*(4), 1164–1167.

Moir, G., Sanders, R., Button, C., Glaister, M., (2005). The influence of familiarization on the reliability of force variables measured during unloaded and loaded vertical jumps. *Journal of Strength & Conditioning Research 19*, 140–145.

Moir, G.L., Snyder, B.W., Connaboy, C., Lamont, H.S., Davis, S.E., (2018). Using drop jumps and jump squats to assess eccentric and concentric force-velocity characteristics. *Sports 6*, 125.

Mosier, E.M., Fry, A.C., Lane, M.T., (2019). Kinetic contributions of the upper limbs during countermovement vertical jumps with and without arm swing. *The Journal of Strength & Conditioning Research 33*, 2066–2073.

Nibali, M.L., Tombleson, T., Brady, P.H., Wagner, P., (2015). Influence of familiarization and competitive level on the reliability of countermovement vertical jump kinetic and kinematic variables. *The Journal of Strength & Conditioning Research 29*, 2827–2835.

Nimphius, S., McGuigan, M.R., Newton, R.U., (2012). Changes in muscle architecture and performance during a competitive season in female softball players. *Journal of Strength & Conditioning Research 26*, 2655–2666.

Nuzzo, J.L., McBride, J.M., Cormie, P., McCaulley, G.O., (2008). Relationship between countermovement jump performance and multijoint isometric and dynamic tests of strength. *Journal of Strength & Conditioning Research 22*, 699–707.

Opar, D.A., Piatkowski, T., Williams, M.D., Shield, A.J., (2013). A novel device using the Nordic hamstring exercise to assess eccentric knee flexor strength: A reliability and retrospective injury study. *Journal of Orthopaedic & Sports Physical Therapy 43*, 636–640.

Owen, N.J., Watkins, J., Kilduff, L.P., Bevan, H.R., Bennett, M.A., (2014). Development of a criterion method to determine peak mechanical power output in a countermovement jump. *The Journal of Strength & Conditioning Research 28*(6), 1552–1558.

Palmer, T.B., Pineda, J.G., Durham, R.M., (2018). Effects of knee position on the reliability and production of maximal and rapid strength characteristics during an isometric squat test. *Journal of Applied Biomechanics 34*, 111–117.

Peñailillo, L., Blazevich, A., Numazawa, H., Nosaka, K., (2015). Rate of force development as a measure of muscle damage. *Scandinavian Journal of Medicine & Science in Sports 25*(3), 417–427.

Pérez-Castilla, A., Rojas, F.J., Gómez-Martínez, F., García-Ramos, A., (2019). Vertical jump performance is affected by the velocity and depth of the countermovement. *Sports Biomechanics* 1–16.

Petronijevic, M.S., Ramos, A.G., Mirkov, D.M., Jaric, S., Valdevit, Z., Knezevic, O.M., (2018). Self-preferred initial position could be a viable alternative to the standard squat jump testing procedure. *The Journal of Strength & Conditioning Research 32*, 3267–3275.

Savoie, F.A., Kenefick, R.W., Ely, B.R., Cheuvront, S.N., Goulet, E.D., (2015). Effect of hypohydration on muscle endurance, strength, anaerobic power and capacity and vertical jumping ability: A meta-analysis. *Sports Medicine 45*, 1207–1227.

Sánchez-Sixto, A., McMahon, J.J., Floría, P., (2021). Verbal instructions affect reactive strength index modified and time-series waveforms in basketball players. *Sports Biomechanics* 1–11. Advance online publication. https://doi.org/10.1080/14763141.2020.1836252

Sheppard, J.M., Nolan, E., Newton, R.U., (2012). Changes in strength and power qualities over two years in volleyball players transitioning from junior to senior national team. *Journal of Strength & Conditioning Research 26*, 152–157.

Sheppard, J.M., Young, W.B., Doyle, T.L.A., Sheppard, T.A., Newton, R.U., (2006). An evaluation of a new test of reactive agility and its relationship to sprint speed and change of direction speed. *Journal of Science & Medicine in Sport 9*, 342–349.

Stephens, R., Spierer, D.K., Katehis, E., (2018). Effect of swearing on strength and power performance. *Psychology of Sports & Exercise 35*, 111–117.

Stone, M.H., O'Bryant, H.S., Hornsby, G., Cunanan, A., Mizuguchi, S., Suarez, D.G., South, M., Marsh, D., Haff, G.G., Ramsey, M.W., (2019). Using the isometric mid-thigh pull in the monitoring of weighlifters: 25+ years of experience. *UKSCA Journal: Professional Strength and Conditioning* (54), 19–26.

Stratford, C., Dos'Santos, T., McMahon, J.J., (2021). The 10/5 repeated jumps test: Are 10 repetitions and three trials necessary? *Biomechanics 1*(1), 1–14.

Street, G., McMillan, S., Board, W., Rasmussen, M., Heneghan, J.M., (2001). Sources of error in determining countermovement jump height with the impulse method. *Journal of Applied Biomechanics 17*(1), 43–54.

Suchomel, T.J., Lamont, H.S., Moir, G.L., (2016). Understanding vertical jump potentiation: a deterministic model. *Sports Medicine 46*, 809–828.

Suchomel, T.J., Sole, C.J., Bailey, C.A., Grazer, J.L., Beckham, G.K., (2015). A comparison of reactive strength index-modified between six US collegiate athletic teams. *Journal of Strength & Conditioning Research 29*, 1310–1316.

Suchomel, T.J., Sole, C.J., Stone, M.H., (2016). Comparison of methods that assess lower-body stretch-shortening cycle utilization. *The Journal of Strength & Conditioning Research 30*, 547–554.

Talpey, S.W., Young, W.B., Beseler, B., (2016). Effect of instructions on selected jump squat variables. *Journal of Strength and Conditioning Research 30*, 2508–2513.

Taylor, K., Cronin, J.B., Gill, N., Chapman, D.W., Sheppard, J.M., (2011). Warm-up affects
diurnal variation in power output. *International Journal of Sports Medicine 32*, 185–189.

Thomas, J.R., Nelson, J.K., Silverman, S.J., (2010). *Research Methods in Physical Activity*. Human Kinetics, Champaign, IL.

Till, K., Morris, R., Stokes, K., Trewartha, G., Twist, C., Dobbin, N., Hunwicks, R., Jones, B., (2018). Validity of an isometric midthigh pull dynamometer in male youth athletes. *The Journal of Strength & Conditioning Research 32*, 490–493.

Verkhoshansky, Y., Siff, M.C., (2009). *Supertraining*. Verkhoshansky SSTM Moscau, Russia.

Warren, G.L., Park, N.D., Maresca, R.D., McKibans, K.I., Millard-Stafford, M.L. (2010). Effect of caffeine ingestion on muscular strength and endurance: A meta-analysis. *Medicine & Science in Sports & Exercise 42*, 1375–1387.

Wiesinger, H.P., Gressenbauer, C., Kösters, A., Scharinger, M., Müller, E., (2020). Device and method matter: A critical evaluation of eccentric hamstring muscle strength assessments. *Scandinavian Journal of Medicine & Science in Sports 30*(2), 217–226.

Wilson, G.J., Murphy, A.J., (1996a). The use of isometric tests of muscular function in athletic assessment. *Sports Medicine 22*, 19–37.

Wilson, G.J., Murphy, A.J., (1996b). Strength diagnosis: The use of test data to determine specific strength training. *Journal of Sports Sciences 14*, 167–173.

Wulf, G., Dufek, J.S., (2009). Increased jump height with an external focus due to enhanced lower extremity joint kinetics. *Journal of Motor Behavior 41*, 401–409.

Young, W., (1995). Laboratory strength assessment of athletes. *New Studies in Athletics 10*, 89–89.

Young, W.B., James, R., Montgomery, I., (2002). Is muscle power related to running speed with changes of direction? *Journal of Sports Medicine & Physical Fitness 42*, 282–288.

Young, W.B., Pryor, J.F., Wilson, G.J., (1995). Effect of instructions on characteristics of countermovement and drop jump performance. *The Journal of Strength & Conditioning Research 9*, 232–236.

Zaras, N.D., Stasinaki, A.N., Methenitis, S.K., Krase, A.A., Karampatsos, G.P., Georgiadis, G.V., Spengos, K.M., Terzis, G.D., (2016). Rate of force development, muscle architecture, and performance in young competitive track and field throwers. *Journal of Strength & Conditioning Research 30*, 81–92.

8

DEVELOPMENT OF PHYSICAL QUALITIES RELATED TO MULTIDIRECTIONAL SPEED

Paul Comfort

Introduction

Maximising multidirectional speed (MDS) requires athletes not only to be highly skilled and competent at the required movement patterns but also to have developed the physical qualities required for rapid acceleration, deceleration, and change of direction while reducing the associated injury risk (Dos'Santos et al., 2021b). As such, it is essential that appropriate strength levels are developed that are sufficient to effectively decelerate their momentum (i.e. body mass × velocity) based on their running velocity and body mass. However, in addition to a high relative force production capability, rapid force development is also essential for acceleration and deceleration due to decreases in ground contact times with an increasing running velocity. It is relative net impulse (net impulse/body mass [impulse = mean force × time]) that determines the acceleration or deceleration of an object (i.e. the individual's mass during change-of-direction or MDS tasks). If the individual's body mass does not change notably and the movement duration is constrained, increased net force production over the given duration (i.e. the ground contact time) is essential. While linear speed (i.e. approach and exit velocity) makes up a large component of any assessment of change of direction, the time taken to change direction is of great importance (Nimphius et al., 2016; Cuthbert et al., 2019), and an increase in velocity or mass will result in greater momentum and therefore an increased requirement for rapid force production (i.e. net impulse) during any change of direction. This is an important point to consider, especially during pre-season where improvements in sprint speeds are commonly observed, which may initially result in decreased change-of-direction performance, due to the increased momentum.

Interestingly, while strength characteristics have been shown to demonstrate strong associations with change-of-direction performance (Nimphius et al., 2010; Spiteri et al., 2013; Spiteri et al., 2014; Spiteri et al., 2015; Thomas et al., 2015), Brughelli et al. (2008) previously reported that most strength-training investigations have failed to demonstrate improvements in change-of-direction performance. In contrast, training interventions, including tasks which more closely mimic change-of-direction performance (e.g. horizontal and lateral jump training), have elicited improvements in change-of-direction performance (Brughelli et al., 2008). It is possible, however, that the more traditional strength-training methods resulted in improvements in running velocity

DOI: 10.4324/9781003267881-10

(Comfort et al., 2012a; Styles et al., 2015), resulting in increased momentum and therefore a more challenging change of direction, which may also elicit a lag effect (as with the pre-season example earlier). In contrast, Kaabi et al. (2022) recently reported that eight weeks of weightlifting training resulted in greater improvements in change-of-direction performance compared to plyometric training; however, the plyometric training was actually unloaded jump training focusing on the slow stretch-shortening cycle (SSC) rather than the fast SSC, which usually differentiates between ballistic and plyometric training. Interestingly, Dos'Santos et al. (2021c) demonstrated that six weeks of technique modification training, with no focused strength or plyometric training, resulted in improvements in technique and an increase in change-of-direction speed (i.e. reduced time to complete the change-of-direction task), with the results of a subsequent study highlighting that a technique modification intervention also reduces injury risk (Dos'Santos et al., 2021a).

It is clear that no single training intervention will optimise change-of-direction performance while also reducing associated injury risks, with increases in performance exposing the athlete to greater mechanical demands in positions associated with elevated risks of anterior cruciate ligament injury (Dos'Santos et al., 2021b). As such, it is essential that practitioners employ a multimodal approach to improving change-of-direction performance while reducing the associated risk of injury. As mentioned earlier, there is evidence that maximal strength, rapid and ballistic force production, and technique modification can all enhance change-of-direction performance and reduce injury risk, but it is important that each of these interventions is employed appropriately, with a changing emphasis placed on the development of these characteristics in a phased and sequential approach (Figure 8.1). There are key points that need to be considered when planning and implementing such a sequential approach:

- How long should each phase last? How long will it take for a meaningful change in the emphasised characteristic (e.g. increase in force production, improved movement mechanics) to occur?
- Should the resistance training emphasise bilateral or unilateral exercises? Where is the athlete's greatest deficit? (For example, are they strong during a back squat but disproportionately weak during a split squat/step-up?) Is the athlete stable during unilateral/split stand exercises, or does this need to be developed for better transference to sports performance? Note: if they are generally weak, they will adapt to any progressive overload irrespective of stance.
- Does the athlete demonstrate the required physical capacity to be able to perform the task in the desired way, or is their technique a result of a deficiency in a specific physical quality (e.g. weak posterior chain muscles resulting in excessive forward lean of the trunk)?
- Should the technique modification emphasise high volumes of controlled, moderate intensity tasks (i.e. if they do not yet possess the physical capacity to perform the tasks with near maximal intent), or should near-maximal-intensity, low-volume practice be performed (i.e. they have the physical capacity and can perform the task well at a moderate intensity)?
- How does all of this fit in with the rest of the athlete's training schedule? (For example, are dedicated sessions required, or can this be integrated into the warm-ups?)
- How much should each component (e.g. maximal strength, rapid force production, technique modification) be emphasised at each time point? Note: ideally each is trained, but the level of emphasis changes depending on the needs of the athlete.

From an injury-risk perspective, it is important to ensure that the appropriate musculature can generate sufficient force, over short durations, to ensure that the athlete can avoid postures that

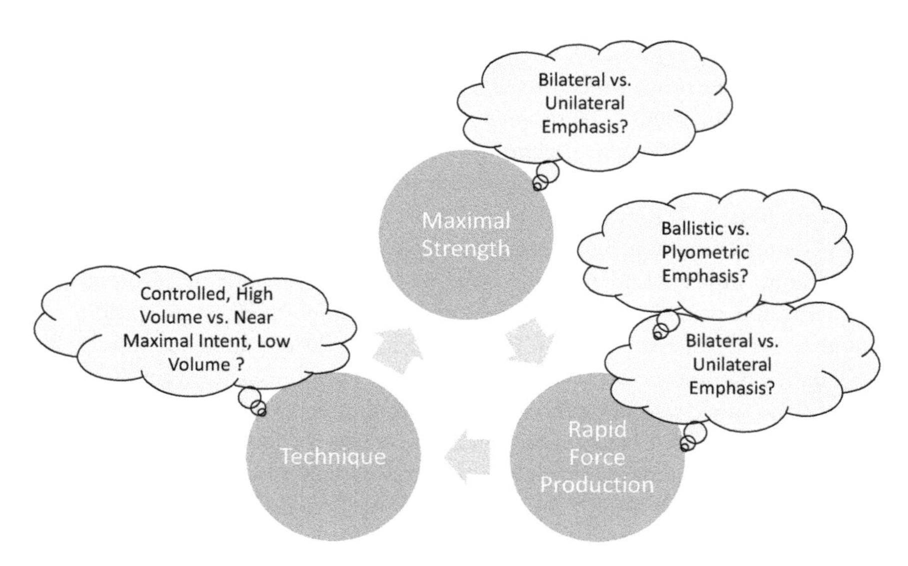

FIGURE 8.1 Holistic, sequential approach to enhance change-of-direction performance and reduce injury risk.

may elevate injury risk. At the same time, the development of such force production capability should increase the ability of the associated tissues (e.g. muscle, tendon, ligament, and bone) to tolerate the loads associated with rapid decelerations and changes of direction. This is of great importance as there is a conflict between performance and injury risk, with faster performances associated with increased injury risk due to increased ground reaction forces, shorter ground contact times, and increased multiplanar knee moments (Dos'Santos et al., 2021b).

In the subsequent sections, different modes of training (e.g. traditional strength training, ballistic training, weightlifting, and plyometrics) will be explored, with explanation regarding how each mode may be best suited to the development of specific force production qualities to enhance MDS. For more detail regarding technique, technique development, and coaching of change-of-direction technique, see Chapters 10 and 11.

Strength Training

Muscular strength is defined as the ability to exert force on an external object or resistance (Stone, 1993; Stone et al., 1981; Stone et al., 1982) and underpins rate of force development (RFD) and power development (Cormie et al., 2007; Cormie et al., 2011a; Cormie et al., 2011b; Aagaard et al., 1994; Aagaard et al., 2002; Andersen and Aagaard, 2006; Andersen et al., 2010). With strong associations between strength, power, and performance in athletic tasks (Hori et al., 2008; McBride et al., 2009; Nimphius et al., 2012; Secomb et al., 2015; Comfort et al., 2014), it is not surprising that strength training is commonly used to enhance performance in athletic tasks. Correlations, however, should be treated with caution as they do not infer cause and effect, although there is strong evidence to support that increases in strength, via traditional strength training (Seitz et al., 2014; Styles et al., 2015) and mixed-methods approaches (e.g. strength, ballistic, and weight training) (Comfort et al., 2012a; Comfort et al., 2018; Suchomel et al., 2020a; Suchomel et al., 2020b), improve performance in athletic tasks (Suchomel et al., 2016a; Suchomel et al., 2018).

Some individuals believe that training with lighter loads, resulting in higher movement velocities, will enhance rapid force development; however, it is the intent to move rapidly rather than the actual movement velocity that results in high RFD and the recruitment of high threshold motor units (Behm and Sale, 1993). As such, the actual movement velocity of a resistance exercise should not be of concern, as long as maximal intent is used, ideally using a mixed-methods approach (e.g. a combination of high-load [≥80% 1 RM] low-velocity tasks and low-to-moderate-load [≤60% 1 RM], high-velocity tasks) to enhance rapid force production (Newton and Kraemer, 1994; Stone et al., 2021; Haff and Nimphius, 2012; Harris et al., 2000). Interestingly, the results of a recent training intervention indicate that high-load (80–90% 1 RM) multi-joint resistance training, which follows moderate-load training (60–82.5% 1 RM), results in superior increases in rapid force production (force at 50, 100, 150, 200, and 250 ms), compared to the changes observed after moderate-load, higher-velocity resistance training (Comfort et al., 2022).

Strength training should be performed in a phased and sequential manner (i.e. phase potentiation), progressing from strength endurance to general strength to maximal strength (Table 8.1) (Stone et al., 1982; Stone et al., 2021; DeWeese et al., 2015; Haff, 2016). It is also possible to emphasise different characteristics during strength training, such as *strength*-speed and *speed*-strength (also referred to as power training), with the later including more ballistic exercises or semi-ballistic weightlifting exercises (Table 8.1). It is important to note that training to momentary muscle failure is not necessary for adaptation and is likely detrimental for the development of maximal strength and rapid force production (Vieira et al., 2022), where the set should be terminated with one to two repetitions in reserve (Suchomel et al., 2021), but with each repetition performed with maximal intent (Behm and Sale, 1993). However, while this should be a sequential process, it is not always essential to revisit each of the physical qualities. For example, in team sports during the competitive season, it would not be advisable to perform the higher-volume strength-endurance phase with athletes who are competing regularly, especially in sports such as soccer where two games per week are commonly played, as this would induce additional and unnecessary fatigue (Haff, 2016; Stone et al., 2021). In such a scenario, alternating between periods of *strength*-speed and *speed*-strength would be advisable, to increase both maximal and rapid force production characteristics while minimising localised muscular fatigue. Due to the

TABLE 8.1 Common Set, Repetition, and Loading Ranges for the Development of Different Strength Qualities

Emphasis/Quality	*Sets*	*Repetitions*	*Load (% 1 RM)*	*Repetitions in Reserve*
Strength endurance	3	10–15	60–75	1
General strength	3–5	4–6	80–90	1–2
Maximal strength	4–6	1–3	90–97.5	1
Strength-speed	3–6	2–6	80–95	1–2
Speed-strength*	4–6	2–6**	30–80***	2–3

* Usually includes ballistic exercise (e.g. loaded jumps) and semi-ballistic exercises (e.g. weightlifting exercises and their derivatives).

** Repetitions usually low to minimise fatigue and emphasise movement velocity. More complex and demanding exercises (e.g. split jerk) also tend to be performed using lower repetitions.

*** The load varies depending on the exercises (e.g. ballistic exercises, such as loaded jumps at 20–60% 1 RM; power cleans/snatches 60–80% 1 RM). Additionally, please note that load can alter the force-velocity characteristics and subsequent training stimulus.

force production requirements for multidirectional speed, multi-joint exercises specifically targeting the ankle, knee, and hip extensors and the entire posterior chain are essential, although single-joint exercises may be advantageous if there is a specific strength deficit in a muscle group.

Ballistic Training

One drawback of traditional strength training is the fact that during the last ~45% of the range-of-motion deceleration, rather than acceleration, occurs (Newton et al., 1996). This makes sense, as if the individual were to continue to accelerate during the extension phase of a squat, they would jump, unless using near maximal loads. As such, ballistic exercises permit acceleration throughout most of the extension phase; in fact, during jumping tasks, deceleration does not commence until plantar flexion commences. As a result, ballistic training emphasises acceleration throughout the range of motion that acceleration commonly occurs during athletic tasks, such as jumping and sprinting; however, it must be noted that the loads, and therefore forces, are not as high as those observed during traditional strength training. These advantages and disadvantages may explain why the mixed-methods approach is advantageous when aiming to maximise rapid force production during *speed*-strength phases of training (Newton et al., 2002; Newton and Kraemer, 1994; Stone et al., 2021; Haff, 2016; Haff and Nimphius, 2012; Toji and Kaneko, 2004; Toji et al., 1997; Harris et al., 2000).

Ballistic training is effective at enhancing rapid force production capability during both concentric and eccentric phases of slow stretch-shortening cycle tasks (e.g. loaded countermovement jumps) (Cormie et al., 2007; Cormie et al., 2010b; Cormie et al., 2010a; Cormie et al., 2011b; Newton et al., 1999; Oranchuk et al., 2019) and short sprint performance (Cormie et al., 2010a; Harris et al., 2008). However, it should be noted that similar improvements in performance have been reported from heavy strength training and ballistic training (Harris et al., 2008; Cormie et al., 2010b; Cormie et al., 2010c), with Cormie et al. (2010a) suggesting that strength training would be a more effective training modality in weaker individuals due to the long-term benefits associated with heavy strength training.

While there may be some concern over the forces associated with landing from loaded jumps, it should be noted that the landing forces do not progressively increase with an increase in external load, as may be expected. Due to the increase in external load, the height jumped progressively decreases, as such the duration for acceleration, due to gravity, is therefore reduced, resulting in no substantial change in landing forces across a range of barbell loads (Lake et al., 2021; Suchomel et al., 2016b). During such training, it is important, however, for the coach to monitor landing mechanics to ensure that there is minimal knee valgus and appropriate combined flexion of the hips, knees, and ankle. It is probably most appropriate to utilise training loads ≤60% 1 RM during ballistic tasks (e.g. hexagonal barbell jumps, jump squats), to take advantage of the higher movement velocities and the rapid force production associated with such tasks while using the more traditional strength training approaches (e.g. bilateral squat and split squat variations) to emphasise the development of maximal force production.

Weightlifting

While ballistic training may emphasise the development of rapid force production via high-velocity, lower-load tasks and traditional strength-training approaches emphasise force production using high to near-maximal loads, at relatively low velocities, weightlifting exercises and their derivatives can be used to train across a broad spectrum of loads and velocities and subsequent force-velocity characteristics. Additionally, there is minimal deceleration toward the end of the range of motion, unlike traditional strength training, while landing mechanics are less of an issue, although appropriate mechanics are essential when catching or decelerating the barbell. Some coaches express concerns that it can take a long time to coach an athlete to be competent in the performance of weightlifting exercises; however, Haug et al. (2015) reported that four weeks of learning the hang power clean (two sessions per week for 20–30 minutes) resulted in improvements in weightlifting technique and jump performance. Exercises such as the jump shrug, mid-thigh pull, and hang pull can be taught to athletes who are inexperienced in performing weightlifting exercises in one or two sessions. In addition, if the athletes are not competent in performing the full lifts, selecting less complex weightlifting derivatives (e.g. power variations, pulling variations, push press) to suit the individual's goals while learning the more complex variations (e.g. snatch, split jerk) is feasible. Recently, researchers have demonstrated that using less complex weightlifting pulling derivatives resulted in similar adaptations compared to comparable catching derivatives (Comfort et al., 2018).

Some weightlifting derivatives (e.g. jump shrug, hang high pull [30–60% 1 RM hang power clean]) permit emphasis of movement velocity (Suchomel et al., 2013; Suchomel et al., 2014; Suchomel et al., 2015a; Suchomel et al., 2017), while the pulling variations (e.g. hang pull, mid-thigh pull) permit emphasis of rapid force production using very heavy loads (e.g. ≥100% 1 RM of the catching derivative due to the exclusion of the catch) (Comfort et al., 2012b; Comfort et al., 2015; Meechan et al., 2020a; Meechan et al., 2020b; Suchomel et al., 2017). As such, the appropriate selection of weightlifting exercises and loads can permit the athlete to effectively train the appropriate areas of the force-velocity curve during the relevant phases of their periodised training plan, especially when used appropriately in conjunction with traditional strength training methods, ballistic training, and plyometric training. In fact, in a recent study, Suchomel et al. (2020a) demonstrated greater improvements in 5–0–5 change-of-direction performance when force (>100% 1 RM for pulling derivatives) and velocity (30–45% 1 RM for jump shrugs) were emphasised with exercise and load manipulation, compared to more traditional loading paradigms (65–95% 1 RM) for weightlifting exercises. It is likely that each of these modes of training will be incorporated in a comprehensively planned mesocycle, with an increased or decreased emphasis on specific exercises and loading paradigms, depending on the training status of the athlete, the point in the season, and their individual goals and competency (Soriano et al., 2019; Suchomel et al., 2015b; Suchomel et al., 2017; Suchomel et al., 2018; Stone et al., 2021).

Plyometric Training

Plyometric exercises are usually implemented to develop rapid and reactive force production capability and should utilise the fast SSC (<250 ms contact time) and include a reactive or rebound component (Sole et al., 2022). The results of numerous studies indicate that plyometric type training can effectively enhance change-of-direction performance (Davies et al., 2021; Chaabene et al., 2021; Singh et al., 2018; Asadi et al., 2016); however, it is unclear if this is due to enhanced short-sprint ability or change-of-direction ability with limited research that has investigated the biomechanical mechanisms responsible for enhanced change-of-direction performance.

Chaabene et al. (2021) reported that a simple (bilateral ankle hops) and progressive (80–120 foot contacts over eight weeks) plyometric training programme enhanced short-sprint and change-of-direction ability in adolescent youth handball players. However, based on the performances of these athletes' pre-intervention, it is likely that most interventions that appropriately applied progressive overload would have been effective. Davies et al. (2021) also recently reported that plyometric training enhanced countermovement jump, reactive jump, and change-of-direction performance in youth female athletes, albeit that jump performance increased to a greater extent than the change-of-direction performance, which is likely due to specificity. Interestingly, the authors of a meta-analysis report that plyometric training improves change-of-direction performance but that the magnitude of improvement tends to vary (effect size = 0.28 [small] to 0.96 [large]), depending on the method used to assess change-of-direction performance. Interestingly, it appears that higher intensity plyometric activities likely result in greater improvements in performance than lower-intensity plyometric tasks (Asadi et al., 2016; de Villarreal et al., 2009; Saez de Villarreal et al., 2012; Váczi et al., 2013), although it is essential to ensure that the athlete is capable of performing such tasks, based on their existing plyometric ability, landing mechanics, and strength levels. In addition, based on the results of their meta-analysis, Asadi et al. (2016) recommended a combination of vertical (e.g. drop jumps) and horizontal plyometric tasks (e.g. bounding, horizontal hopping) to enhance MDS. As with any exercise, it is important to ensure appropriate progressions in terms of technique and loading prior to performing highly demanding tasks (Lievens et al., 2021; Suchomel et al., 2018).

Eccentric Training

Numerous eccentric training modalities can be used to enhance force production, each of which has unique characteristics that can stimulate physiological adaptations. It is well documented that the habitual use of eccentric exercise, usually with isolated single-joint tasks, can result in a larger and stronger muscle that has the potential to generate higher power outputs when compared to traditional isotonic training (Higbie et al., 1996; Franchi et al., 2014; Franchi et al., 2015; Narici et al., 1989). During traditional strength training, the load lifted is usually determined by the maximal concentric strength, based on the assessment of the 1 RM in that exercise; however, this limits the ability to take advantage of the increased force generation capacity during eccentric muscle actions. While both concentric and eccentric strengths increase in response to traditional strength training, the eccentric phase can permit loads up to 150% of the load used during the concentric phase (Hortobágyi and Katch, 1990; Dufour et al., 2004; Harden et al., 2019). It is important to note that this higher level of eccentric force production varies notably between individuals, likely due to familiarity with the task and the athlete's relative strength levels (Hody et al., 2019; Harden et al., 2018), and therefore, eccentric loads ≥100% should be progressed cautiously and incrementally. Interestingly, strong athletes (world-class power lifters) tolerate lower eccentric loads 105–110% 1 RM, while lower-level athletes were reported to tolerate loads of 120–130% 1 RM (Refsnes, 1999).

During such eccentric exercise, muscles experience unique strain, which stimulates a cascade of distinct physiological events resulting in increased fascicle length (Franchi et al., 2014; Franchi et al., 2015; Geremia et al., 2019), leading to higher maximal shortening velocity and therefore increased potential for rapid force development (Narici, 1999; Lieber and Fridén, 2000), which is essential during the deceleration and acceleration phases of a change-of-direction and MDS movements. Unfortunately, many of the eccentric training methods utilised in published studies lack ecological validity (e.g. the equipment is not commercially available or, in the case of single-joint training on an isokinetic dynamometer, the training protocols would take too long in most sports setting) and are therefore not easily applied to normal isotonic multi-joint resistance-training exercises. It is important to note that when high eccentric loads are used, muscle soreness is common; fortunately, a clear repeated bout effect is evident with eccentric training, whereby myofibrillar disruption, swelling, and muscle soreness are reduced in subsequent bouts of the same activity, even after an initial single bout of eccentric exercise (McHugh et al., 1999; Nosaka and Aoki, 2011).

Numerous methods are available to emphasise eccentric muscle actions during training, with tempo training (i.e. decreasing the speed and increasing the duration of the eccentric phase) being the easiest to implement, although this does not take advantage of the increased force production capability during eccentric muscle actions (i.e. supramaximal eccentrics); instead, it increases the time under tension during the eccentric phase. As such, this method is not the most effective at increasing eccentric strength versus other methods; however, as time under tension-associated muscle hypertrophy and the fact that eccentric muscle actions may stimulate greater muscle hypertrophy than training biased towards concentric muscle actions (Marzilger et al., 2019; Marzilger et al., 2020; Burd et al., 2012), tempo training could prove beneficial for muscle growth. Additionally, adaptations in the tendons may also be enhanced due to increased time under tension (Arampatzis et al., 2010).

Equipment that facilitates the ability to perform eccentric training is now becoming more accessible, such as flywheel devices (Petré et al., 2018; Beato et al., 2021a; Beato et al., 2021b) and weight releasers for accentuated eccentric loading (AEL) (Merrigan et al., 2020a; Merrigan et al., 2020b; Doan et al., 2002). It is worth noting, however, that flywheel devices appear to result in forces during the eccentric phase that are comparable to those during the concentric phase, although not greater than the concentric phase (Suchomel et al., 2019). Interestingly, flywheel exercises have been shown to acutely enhance change-of-direction performance, likely through a post-activation performance enhancement response (Beato et al., 2021a; Beato et al., 2021b). The authors of a meta-analysis evaluating the chronic effects of flywheel training reported that meaningful increases in hypertrophy, strength, and power can be achieved over 4-to-24-week interventions, with shorter more intensive blocks, likely most beneficial (Petré et al., 2018). However, there is currently no consensus on the programming of such exercises, and therefore, it is recommended that progressive overload is applied in a conservative manner to avoid excessive muscle soreness in the initial stages of implementation.

The primary purpose of AEL is to permit loads >100% 1 RM to be used during the eccentric phase, to take advantage of the higher forces associated with eccentric muscle actions (Walker et al., 2016; Walker et al., 2017). Due to the high loads involved, it is essential that athletes demonstrate excellent technique on any exercise where such loading is implemented. The eccentric phase should be prolonged (i.e. low velocity lasting 3–5 seconds, as with tempo training) and the concentric phase performed with maximal intent to ensure optimal motor unit recruitment (Behm and Sale, 1993), albeit with a sufficient load to stimulate strength adaptations during the concentric portion of the movement (e.g. ≥80% 1 RM), resulting in a relatively low velocity (Figures 8.2 and 8.3). Figure 8.2 illustrates how this approach may be utilised within a set, with the additional eccentric load only used during the initial repetition (the weight releasers will fall off at the bottom of the initial repetition), providing a novel stimulus, which should not be excessive and permit the subsequent repetitions within the set to be performed unimpeded. In contrast, Figure 8.3 illustrates the use of additional eccentric load during each repetition, with a brief pause between repetitions where the bar is placed back on the squat rack and the weight releasers reloaded on to the bar, effectively resulting in a cluster set and a higher total volume of eccentric load. It may be advantageous to start with the format illustrated in Figure 8.2 and then progressing to the format in Figure 8.3 as

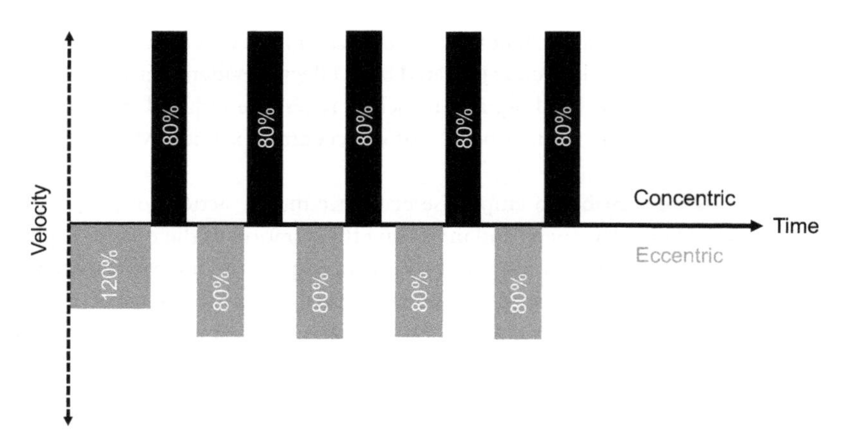

FIGURE 8.2 A schematic diagram illustrating accentuated eccentric training using weight releasers. During the first repetition, a total of 120% 1 RM is used resulting in a relatively low-velocity, prolonged, eccentric phase in an attempt to enhance the lower-load (80% 1 RM) concentric phase once the weight releasers (holding a total of 40% 1 RM) fall off the bar. The subsequent four repetitions are performed using a constant load of 80% 1 RM to avoid the time delays of reloading the weight releasers.

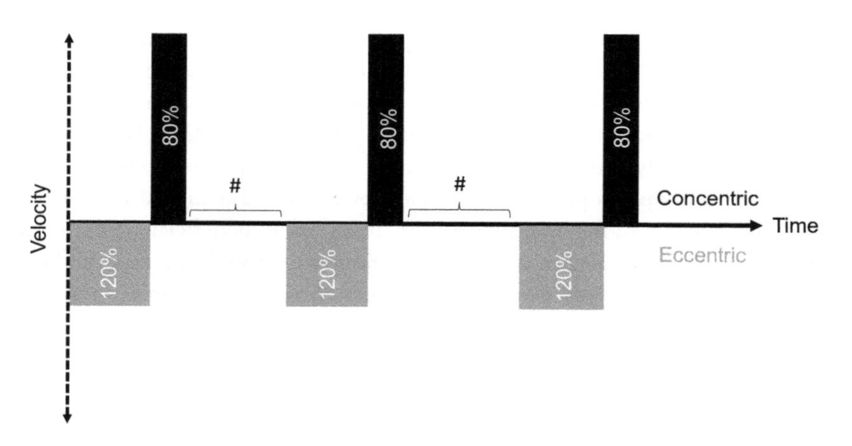

FIGURE 8.3 A schematic diagram illustrating accentuated eccentric training using weight releasers. 120% 1 RM is used during a relatively low-velocity, prolonged, eccentric phase in an attempt to enhance the lower-load (80% 1 RM) concentric phase once the weight releasers (holding a total of 40% 1 RM) fall off the bar. # period required to reload the weight releasers on to the barbell, effectively resulting in a cluster set.

a logical progression, which may also take advantage of the repeated bout effect and minimise any unwanted muscle soreness. Additionally, it would be sensible to start at a load of ~105% 1 RM (e.g. 80% 1 RM on the barbell and 25% on the weight releasers [12.5% for each weight releaser]) and then add an addition 5% 1 RM to the weight releasers during each training session until 120% is reached, especially in individuals unfamiliar with such training methods. For more detail on eccentric training approaches, please see Harden et al. (2022).

Bilateral and Unilateral Training

There is considerable debate among practitioners regarding the advantages and disadvantages of unilateral and bilateral training and the resulting transfer to performance in athletic tasks. Part of this debate is focused on the fact that the majority of sporting tasks occur in a unilateral or split (staggered) stance rather than in a symmetrical bilateral stance. As such, unilateral or split-stance exercises may demonstrate greater specificity and result in greater improvements in force production capabilities in the stabilising muscles. Alternatively, when athletes exercise using a bilateral stance, they are more stable, resulting in the ability to use greater external loads, which may result in greater increases in strength. McCurdy et al. (2005) demonstrated comparable improvements in leg strength and power, other than when assessed during a unilateral task, after eight weeks of bilateral (e.g. back squat, bilateral jumps) versus unilateral training (e.g. rear-foot-elevated split squat [RFES] and unilateral jumps). Similarly, Speirs et al. (2016) demonstrated comparable improvements in strength, short-sprint, and change-of-direction performance after five weeks of unilateral (e.g. RFES) versus bilateral (e.g. back squat) training in academy rugby union players. Rather than using a split stance exercise, Appleby et al. (2020) compared the step-up to the back squat, ensuring that volume and system mass were comparable. While both groups demonstrated similar improvements in 20 m sprint performance, the bilateral group demonstrated greater improvements in change-of-direction performance (Appleby et al., 2020) even though the increase in step-up strength was greater than the increase in squat strength (Appleby et al., 2019), which may be due to the subject being less familiar with the step-up.

Both bilateral and unilateral exercises clearly have a place during strength development, especially if the athlete is notably weaker during unilateral and split stance exercises. It is recommended that a combination of both bilateral and unilateral exercise should be incorporated, but practitioners should be aware of the advantages and disadvantages of both, with the more stable bilateral exercises permitting higher loads and higher movement velocities, but the unilateral exercises result in greater stimulation of the stabilising muscles, which may further aid with lower-limb control during athletic tasks.

Practical Application

The following is a case study of a rugby league full-back through pre-season (seven weeks) and the start of the competitive season (four weeks). Baseline performance at the start of pre-season was considered adequate (Table 8.2), with the primary training focus on enhancing maximal and rapid force production to improve acceleration (short sprint performance) and change-of-direction performance.

The focus of the gym-based training during the first four weeks of pre-season was to maximise force production and ensure good movement quality during the lower-limb-control-focused exercises and the ballistic and plyometric (reactive) tasks. To ensure that the sessions could be completed in the allotted time frame, strength exercises were paired (using supersets) with some lower-limb-control tasks, which were deemed not to be fatiguing, or ballistic and plyometric exercises, which may have a potentiating effect on the subsequent strength exercise based using a maximal intent and a low volume (Bullock and Comfort, 2011), with ~90 seconds between paired exercises and athletes providing peer feedback regarding lower limb control and performance (e.g. jump height/hop distance). The second session in the week is a slightly lower volume, with intensity (% 1 RM) progressing across the first three weeks for the primary strength

TABLE 8.2 Changes in Physical Characteristics of a Rugby League Player over Two Phases of Training

		Start of Pre-Season (W0)	*End of Pre-Season (W7)*	*In-Season (W11)*
Body mass (kg)		94.5	94.0	94.0
Body fat (%)		10.2	8.1	8.3
Sprint	5 m (s)	1.09	0.95	0.96
	10 m (s)	1.78	1.69	1.65
	20 m (s)	3.12	2.98	2.89
5–0–5 COD (s)		2.78	2.75	2.62
5–0–5 CODD (s)		1.00	1.06	0.97
1 RM back squat (kg/kg)		1.71	1.95	/
IMTP	PF (N/kg)	39.1	47.0	47.2
	F150 (N/kg)	24.8	27.3	29.0
	F250 (N/kg)	32.9	35.6	36.5

COD = change of direction (modified 5–0–5); CODD = change-of-direction deficit (5–0–5 time – 10 m sprint time); RM = repetition maximum; IMTP = isometric mid-thigh pull; PF = peak force; F150 = force at 150 ms; F250 = force at 250 ms

TABLE 8.3 Lower-Body Gym-Based Training During the First Four Weeks of Pre-season

	Notes	*Week*	*1*	*2*	*3*	*4*
		Exercise	*Sets/Reps/Load*	*Sets/Reps/Load*	*Sets/Reps/Load*	*Sets/Reps/Load*
Session 1	Superset	**Clean pulls**	**4 / 5 / 90%***	**4 / 5 / 100%***	**4 / 5 / 110%***	**3 / 3 / 90%***
		Triple hop and hold	4 / 3 / BM	4 / 3 / BM	4 / 3 / BM	3 / 3 / BM
	Superset	**Back squats**	**5 / 5 / 80%**	**5 / 5 / 82.5%**	**5 / 5 / 85%**	**3 / 3 / 80%**
		Depth jumps	5 / 3 / BM (30 cm)	5 / 3 / BM (30 cm)	5 / 3 / BM (30 cm)	5 / 3 / BM (30 cm)
	Superset	**RFESs**	**3 / 5 / 80%**	**3 / 5 / 84%**	**3 / 5 / 88%**	**3 / 3 / 80%**
		Bilateral ankle hops	3 / 10 / BM	3 / 10 / BM	3 / 10 / BM	3 / 10 / BM
		NHE	3 / 3 / BM	3 / 4 / BM	3 / 5 / BM	3 / 3 / BM
Session 2	Superset	**Hang clean pulls**	**3 / 5 / 115%***	**3 / 5 / 120%***	**3 / 5 / 125%***	**3 / 3 / 115%***
		Hop and hold	3 / 3 / BM	3 / 3 / BM	3 / 3 / BM	3 / 3 / BM
	Superset	**Front squats**	**3 / 5 / 80%**	**3 / 5 / 82.5%**	**3 / 5 / 85%**	**3 / 3 / 80%**
		Drop jumps	3 / 3 / BM (30 cm)	3 / 3 / BM (30 cm)	3 / 3 / BM (30 cm)	3 / 3 / BM (30 cm)
	Superset	**Step-ups**	**3 / 3 / 75%**	**3 / 3 / 80%**	**3 / 3 / 85%**	**3 / 3 / 75%**
		SL Romanian deadlifts	**3 / 3 / 75%**	**3 / 3 / 80%**	**3 / 3 / 85%**	**3 / 3 / 75%**
		NHE	3 / 3 / BM	3 / 3 / BM	3 / 3 / BM	3 / 3 / BM

RFES = rear-foot-elevated split squat; NHE = Nordic hamstring exercise; SL = single leg; % = percentage of one repletion maximum; * = based off 1 RM power clean; BM = body mass; exercises in bold = primary strength exercises; shaded areas = lower limb control, ballistic, or reactive focus

TABLE 8.4 Lower-Body Gym-Based Training During the Final Three Weeks of Pre-season

	Notes	*Week*	*1*	*2*	*3*
		Exercise	*Sets/Reps/Load*	*Sets/Reps/Load*	*Sets/Reps/Load*
Session 1	Superset	**Hang power clean**	**3 / 6 / 70%¥**	**3 / 6 / 75%¥**	**3 / 6 / 80%¥**
		20 m bounding	3 / 1 / BM	3 / 1 / BM	3 / 1 / BM
	Superset	**Split jerks**	**3 / 6 / 70%**	**3 / 6 / 72.5%**	**3 / 6 / 75%**
		Drop jumps	3 / 5 / BM (45 cm)	3 / 5 / BM (45 cm)	3 / 5 / BM (45 cm)
	Superset	**Back squats**	**3 / 3 / 80%**	**3 / 3 / 82.5%**	**3 / 3 / 85%**
		Bilateral ankle hops	3 / 10 / BM	3 / 10 / BM	3 / 10 / BM
		NHE	3 / 3 / BM	3 / 4 / BM	3 / 5 / BM
Session 2	Superset	**Countermovement shrugs**	**3 / 5 / 110%★**	**3 / 5 / 120%★**	**3 / 5 / 130%★**
		CMJs	3 / 5 / BM	3 / 5 / BM	3 / 5 / BM
	Superset	**Jump shrugs**	**3 / 5 / 30%★**	**4 / 5 / 30%★**	**5 / 5 / 30%★**
		Drop jumps	3 / 5 / BM (30 cm)	4 / 5 / BM (30 cm)	5 / 5 / BM (30 cm)
	Superset	**Split squats**	**3 / 3 / 80%**	**3 / 3 / 82.5%**	**3 / 3 / 85%**
		Split squat jumps	**3 / 5 / BM**	**3 / 5 / BM**	**3 / 5 / BM**
		NHE	3 / 3 / BM	3 / 3 / BM	3 / 3 / BM

¥ = cluster sets (2 reps × 3 with 15 s rest between clusters); NHE = Nordic hamstring exercise; CMJ = countermovement jump; % = percentage of one repletion maximum; ★ = based off 1 RM power clean; BM = body mass; exercises in bold = primary strength exercises; shaded areas = lower limb control, ballistic, or reactive focus

exercises, and then the volume and load reducing, where appropriate, during week 4 to create a deload week prior to the start of the final three weeks of pre-season. Sprint and change-of-direction technique drills was included in all pitch-based warm-up sessions prior to technical and tactical sessions and field-based conditioning sessions.

During the final three weeks of pre-season (Table 8.4) a mixed-methods approach was used to alter focus to *speed*-strength. The most demanding and explosive exercises were performed at the start of the session, with a strength exercise toward the end of the sessions, to ensure that strength is maintained. The subsequent superset exercises emphasise plyometric performance which complement the loaded ballistic exercise that they are paired with. Total volumes are reduced compared to the first four weeks of pre-season, as such, no deload was provided prior to the next training phase. Based on the results of testing at the end of pre-season (Table 8.2), it is clear that strength and short sprint performance had improved, but the improvements in change-of-direction performance were minimal likely due to the increased momentum from the higher approach speeds.

The first four weeks in-season continued the focus on *speed*-strength, but with a slight decrease in total volume to ensure that each exercise was performed with maximal intent, with minimal residual fatigue due to the demands of the start of the competitive season. In addition, the second lower-body training session of the week has a lower volume due to this being in close proximity

TABLE 8.5 Lower-Body Gym-Based Training During the First Four Weeks In-season

	Notes	*Week*	*1*	*2*	*3*	*4*
		Exercise	*Sets/Reps/Load*	*Sets/Reps/Load*	*Sets/Reps/Load*	*Sets/Reps/Load*
Session 1	Superset	**Hang power clean**	**3 / 6 / 70%¥**	**3 / 6 / 75%¥**	**3 / 6 / 80%¥**	**3 / 3 / 90%★**
		20 m bounding	3 / 2 / BM	3 / 2 / BM	3 / 2 / BM	3 / 1 / BM
	Superset	**Split jerks**	**3 / 6 / 70%**	**3 / 6 / 72.5%**	**3 / 6 / 75%**	**3 / 3 / 80%**
		Drop jumps	3 / 6 / BM (45 cm)	3 / 6 / BM (45 cm)	3 / 6 / BM (45 cm)	5 / 3 / BM (45 cm)
		Front squats	**3 / 3 / 80%**	**3 / 3 / 82.5%**	**3 / 3 / 85%**	**3 / 3 / 75%**
		NHE	3 / 3 / BM	3 / 4 / BM	3 / 5 / BM	3 / 3 / BM
Session 2	Superset	**Power snatch**	**3 / 3 / 75%**	**4 / 3 / 75%**	**5 / 3 / 75%**	**3 / 3 / 70%**
		SL CMJ	3 / 5 / BM	3 / 5 / BM	3 / 5 / BM	3 / 3 / BM
	Superset	**Jump shrug**	**3 / 5 / 30%★**	**4 / 5 / 30%★**	**5 / 5 / 30%★**	**3 / 3 / 30%**
		Drop jumps	3 / 5 / BM (45 cm)	4 / 5 / BM (45 cm)	5 / 5 / BM (45 cm)	3 / 3 / BM (30 cm)
		Step-ups	**3 / 3 / 80%**	**3 / 3 / 82.5%**	**3 / 3 / 85%**	**3 / 3 / 75%**

RFES = rear-foot-elevated split squat; NHE = Nordic hamstring exercise; SL = single leg; % = percentage of one repletion maximum; ★ = based off 1 RM power clean; BM = body mass; exercises in bold = primary exercises; shaded areas = ballistic or plyometric focus

to match day. Table 8.2 illustrates that slight increases in short sprint performance and rapid force production have occurred, with larger improvements in change-of-direction performance. The focus of the subsequent four-week phase in-season was strength once the athlete was once again familiar with the demands of the competition and able to tolerate increase training volumes and intensities.

References

Aagaard, P., Simonsen, E. B., Andersen, J. L., Magnusson, P. & Dyhre-Poulsen, P. (2002). Increased rate of force development and neural drive of human skeletal muscle following resistance training. *Journal of Applied Physiology*, *93*, 1318–1326.

Aagaard, P., Simonsen, E. B., Trolle, M., Bangsbo, J. & Klausen, K. (1994). Effects of different strength training regimes on moment and power generation during dynamic knee extensions. *European Journal of Applied Physiology and Occupational Physiology*, *69*, 382–386.

Andersen, L. L. & Aagaard, P. (2006). Influence of maximal muscle strength and intrinsic muscle contractile properties on contractile rate of force development. *European Journal of Applied Physiology*, *96*, 46–52.

Andersen, L. L., Andersen, J. L., Zebis, M. K. & Aagaard, P. (2010). Early and late rate of force development: Differential adaptive responses to resistance training? *Scandinavian Journal of Medicine & Science in Sports*, *20*, e162–169.

Appleby, B. B., Cormack, S. J. & Newton, R. U. (2019). Specificity and transfer of lower-body strength: Influence of bilateral or unilateral lower-body resistance training. *Journal of Strength & Conditioning Research*, *33*, 318–326.

Appleby, B. B., Cormack, S. J. & Newton, R. U. (2020). Unilateral and bilateral lower-body resistance training does not transfer equally to sprint and change of direction performance. *Journal of Strength & Conditioning Research*, *34*, 54–64.

Arampatzis, A., Peper, A., Bierbaum, S. & Albracht, K. (2010). Plasticity of human Achilles tendon mechanical and morphological properties in response to cyclic strain. *Journal of Biomechanics*, *43*, 3073–3079.

Asadi, A., Arazi, H., Young, W. B. & Sáez De Villarreal, E. (2016). The effects of plyometric training on change-of-direction ability: A meta-analysis. *International Journal of Sports Physiology & Performance*, *11*, 563–573.

Beato, M., De Keijzer, K. L., Leskauskas, Z., Allen, W. J., Dello Iacono, A. & Mcerlain-Naylor, S. A. (2021a). Effect of postactivation potentiation after medium vs. high inertia eccentric overload exercise on standing long jump, countermovement jump, and change of direction performance. *Journal of Strength & Conditioning Research*, 35.

Beato, M., Madruga-Parera, M., Piqueras-Sanchiz, F., Moreno-Pérez, V. & Romero-Rodriguez, D. (2021b). Acute effect of eccentric overload exercises on change of direction performance and lower-limb muscle contractile function. *Journal of Strength & Conditioning Research*, 35.

Behm, D. G. & Sale, D. G. (1993). Intended rather than actual movement velocity determines velocity-specific training response. *Journal of Applied Physiology*, *74*, 359–368.

Brughelli, M., Cronin, J., Levin, G. & Chaouachi, A. (2008). Understanding change of direction ability in sport. *Sports Medicine*, *38*, 1045–1063.

Bullock, N. & Comfort, P. (2011). An investigation into the acute effects of depth jumps on maximal strength performance. *Journal of Strength & Conditioning Research*, *25*, 3137–3141.

Burd, N. A., Andrews, R. J., West, D. W. D., Little, J. P., Cochran, A. J. R., Hector, A. J., Cashaback, J. G. A., Gibala, M. J., Potvin, J. R., Baker, S. K. & Phillips, S. M. (2012). Muscle time under tension during resistance exercise stimulates differential muscle protein sub-fractional synthetic responses in men. *Journal of Physiology*, *590*, 351–362.

Chaabene, H., Negra, Y., Moran, J., Prieske, O., Sammoud, S., Ramirez-Campillo, R. & Granacher, U. (2021). Plyometric training improves not only measures of linear speed, power, and change-of-direction speed but also repeated sprint ability in young female handball players. *Journal of Strength & Conditioning Research*, 35.

Comfort, P., Dos'Santos, T., Thomas, C., McMahon, J. J. & Suchomel, T. J. (2018). An Investigation into the effects of excluding the catch phase of the power clean on force-time characteristics during isometric and dynamic tasks: An intervention study. *Journal of Strength & Conditioning Research*, *32*, 2116–2129.

Comfort, P., Haigh, A. & Matthews, M. J. (2012a). Are changes in maximal squat strength during preseason training reflected in changes in sprint performance in rugby league players? *Journal of Strength & Conditioning Research*, *26*, 772–776.

Comfort, P., Jones, P. A., Thomas, C., Dos'Santos, T., McMahon, J. J. & Suchomel, T. J. (2022). Changes in early and maximal isometric force production in response to moderate- and high-load strength and power training. *Journal of Strength & Conditioning Research*, *36*, 593–599.

Comfort, P., Jones, P. A. & Udall, R. (2015). The effect of load and sex on kinematic and kinetic variables during the mid-thigh clean pull. *Sports Biomechanics*, *14*, 139–156.

Comfort, P., Stewart, A., Bloom, L. & Clarkson, B. (2014). Relationships between strength, sprint, and jump performance in well-trained youth soccer players. *Journal of Strength & Conditioning Research*, *28*, 173–177.

Comfort, P., Udall, R. & Jones, P. (2012b). The affect of loading on kinematic and kinetic variables during the mid-thigh clean pull. *Journal of Strength & Conditioning Research*, *26*, 1208–1214.

Cormie, P., McCaulley, G. O. & McBride, J. M. (2007). Power versus strength-power jump squat training: Influence on the load-power relationship. *Medicine & Science in Sports & Exercise*, *39*, 996–1003.

Cormie, P., McGuigan, M. R. & Newton, R. U. (2010a). Adaptations in athletic performance after ballistic power versus strength training. *Medicine & Science in Sports & Exercise, 42*, 1582–1598.

Cormie, P., McGuigan, M. R. & Newton, R. U. (2010b). Influence of strength on magnitude and mechanisms of adaptation to power training. *Medicine & Science in Sports & Exercise, 42*, 1566–1581.

Cormie, P., McGuigan, M. R. & Newton, R. U. (2010c). Influence of training status on power absorption & production during lower body stretch-shorten cycle movements. *Journal of Strength & Conditioning Research, 24*, 1.

Cormie, P., McGuigan, M. R. & Newton, R. U. (2011a). Developing maximal neuromuscular power: Part 1 – biological basis of maximal power production. *Sports Medicine, 41*, 17–38.

Cormie, P., McGuigan, M. R. & Newton, R. U. (2011b). Developing maximal neuromuscular power: Part 2 – training considerations for improving maximal power production. *Sports Medicine, 41*, 125–146

Cuthbert, M., Thomas, C., Dos'Santos, T. & Jones, P. A. (2019). Application of change of direction deficit to evaluate cutting ability. *Journal of Strength & Conditioning Research*, 33.

Davies, M. J., Drury, B., Ramirez-Campillo, R., Chaabane, H. & Moran, J. (2021). Effect of plyometric training and biological maturation on jump and change of direction ability in female youth. *Journal of Strength & Conditioning Research*, 35.

de Villarreal, E. S.-S., Kellis, E., Kraemer, W. J. & Izquierdo, M. (2009). Determining variables of plyometric training for improving vertical jump height performance: A meta-analysis. *Journal of Strength & Conditioning Research, 23*, 495–506.

DeWeese, B. H., Hornsby, G., Stone, M. & Stone, M. H. (2015). The training process: Planning for strength–power training in track and field. Part 1: Theoretical aspects. *Journal of Sport and Health Science, 4*, 308–317.

Doan, B. K., Newton, R. U., Marsit, J. L., Triplett-McBride, N. T., Koziris, L. P., Fry, A. C. & Kraemer, W. J. (2002). Effects of increased eccentric loading on bench press 1RM. *Journal of Strength & Conditioning Research, 16*, 9–13.

Dos'Santos, T., Thomas, C., Comfort, P. & Jones, P. A. (2021a). Biomechanical effects of a 6-week change-of-direction technique modification intervention on anterior cruciate ligament injury risk. *Journal of Strength & Conditioning Research, 35*, 2133–2144.

Dos'Santos, T., Thomas, C., McBurnie, A., Comfort, P. & Jones, P. A. (2021b). Biomechanical determinants of performance and injury risk during cutting: A performance-injury conflict? *Sports Medicine, 51*, 1983–1998.

Dos'Santos, T., Thomas, C., McBurnie, A., Comfort, P. & Jones, P. A. (2021c). Change of direction speed and technique modification training improves 180 degrees turning performance, kinetics, and kinematics. *Sports (Basel)*, 9.

Dufour, S. P., Lampert, E., Doutreleau, S., Lonsdorfer-Wolf, E., Billat, V. L., Piquard, F. & Richard, R. (2004). Eccentric cycle exercise: Training application of specific circulatory adjustments. *Medicine & Science in Sports & Exercise, 36*, 1900–1906.

Franchi, M. V., Atherton, P. J., Reeves, N. D., Flück, M., Williams, J., Mitchell, W. K., Selby, A., Beltran Valls, R. M. & Narici, M. V. (2014). Architectural, functional and molecular responses to concentric and eccentric loading in human skeletal muscle. *Acta Physiologica, 210*, 642–654.

Franchi, M. V., Wilkinson, D. J., Quinlan, J. I., Mitchell, W. K., Lund, J. N., Williams, J. P., Reeves, N. D., Smith, K., Atherton, P. J. & Narici, M. V. (2015). Early structural remodeling and deuterium oxide-derived protein metabolic responses to eccentric and concentric loading in human skeletal muscle. *Physiological Reports*, 3, e12593.

Geremia, J. M., Baroni, B. M., Bini, R. R., Lanferdini, F. J., De Lima, A. R., Herzog, W. & Vaz, M. A. (2019). Triceps surae muscle architecture adaptations to eccentric training. *Frontiers in Physiology*, 10.

Haff, G. G. (2016). Periodization. *In:* Haff, G. G. & Triplett, N. T. (eds.) *Essentials of Strength Training and Conditioning*. Champaign, IL: Human Kinetics.

Haff, G. G. & Nimphius, S. (2012). Training principles for power. *Strength Cond J, 34*, 2–12

Harden, M., Comfort, P. & Haff, G. G. (2022). Eccentric training: Scientific background and practical applications. *In:* Turner, A. N. & Comfort, P. (eds.) *Advanced Strength and Conditioning: An Evidence-based Approach*. 2nd ed. New York: Routledge.

Harden, M., Wolf, A., Haff, G. G., Hicks, K. M. & Howatson, G. (2019). Repeatability and specificity of eccentric force output and the implications for eccentric training load prescription. *Journal of Strength & Conditioning Research, 33*, 676–683.

Harden, M., Wolf, A., Russell, M., Hicks, K. M., French, D. & Howatson, G. (2018). An Evaluation of supramaximally loaded eccentric leg press exercise. *Journal of Strength & Conditioning Research, 32*, 2708–2714.

Harris, G. R., Stone, M., O'Bryant, H. S., Proulx, C. M. & Johnson, R. (2000). Short-term performance effects of high power, high force or combined weight training methods. *Journal of Strength & Conditioning Research, 14*, 14–20.

Harris, N. K., Cronin, J. B., Hopkins, W. G. & Hansen, K. T. (2008). Squat jump training at maximal power loads vs. heavy loads: Effect on sprint ability. *Journal of Strength & Conditioning Research, 22*, 1742–179.

Haug, W. B., Drinkwater, E. J. & Chapman, D. W. (2015). Learning the hang power clean: Kinetic, kinematic, and technical changes in four weightlifting naive athletes. *Journal of Strength & Conditioning Research, 29*, 1766–1779.

Higbie, E. J., Cureton, K. J., Warren, G. L. & Prior, B. M. (1996). Effects of concentric and eccentric training on muscle strength, cross-sectional area, and neural activation. *Journal of Applied Physiology, 81*, 2173–2181.

Hody, S., Croisier, J.-L., Bury, T., Rogister, B. & Leprince, P. (2019). Eccentric muscle contractions: Risks and benefits. *Frontiers in Physiology*, 10.

Hori, N., Newton, R. U., Andrews, W. A., Kawamori, N., McGuigan, M. R. & Nosaka, K. (2008). Does performance of hang power clean differentiate performance of jumping, sprinting, and changing of direction? *Journal of Strength & Conditioning Research, 22*, 412–418

Hortobágyi, T. & Katch, F. I. (1990). Eccentric and concentric torque-velocity relationships during arm flexion and extension. *European Journal of Applied Physiology, 60*, 395–401.

Kaabi, S., Mabrouk, R. H. & Passelergue, P. (2022). Weightlifting is better than plyometric training to improve strength, counter movement jump, and change of direction skills in tunisian elite male junior table tennis players. *Journal of Strength & Conditioning Research*, Published ahead of print.

Lake, J. P., Mundy, P. D., Comfort, P., McMahon, J. J., Suchomel, T. J. & Carden, P. (2021). Effect of barbell load on vertical jump landing force-time characteristics. *Journal of Strength & Conditioning Research*, 35.

Lieber, R. L. & Fridén, J. (2000). Functional and clinical significance of skeletal muscle architecture. *Muscle & Nerve, 23*, 1647–1666.

Lievens, M., Bourgois, J. G. & Boone, J. (2021). Periodization of plyometrics: Is there an optimal overload principle? *Journal of Strength & Conditioning Research*, 35.

Marzilger, R., Bohm, S., Mersmann, F. & Arampatzis, A. (2019). Effects of lengthening velocity during eccentric training on vastus lateralis muscle hypertrophy. *Frontiers in Physiology*, 10.

Marzilger, R., Bohm, S., Mersmann, F. & Arampatzis, A. (2020). Modulation of physiological cross-sectional area and fascicle length of vastus lateralis muscle in response to eccentric exercise. *Journal of Biomechanics, 111*, 110016.

McBride, J. M., Blow, D., Kirby, T. J., Haines, T. L., Dayne, A. M. & Triplett, N. T. (2009). Relationship between maximal squat strength and five, ten, and forty yard sprint times. *Journal of Strength & Conditioning Research, 23*, 1633–1636.

McCurdy, K. W., Langford, G. A., Doscher, M. W., Wiley, L. P. & Mallard, K. G. (2005). The effects of short-term unilateral and bilateral lower-body resistance training on measures of strength and power. *Journal of Strength & Conditioning Research, 19*, 9–15.

McHugh, M. P., Connolly, D. A. J., Eston, R. G. & Gleim, G. W. (1999). Exercise-induced muscle damage and potential mechanisms for the repeated bout effect. *Sports Medicine, 27*, 157–170.

Meechan, D., McMahon, J. J., Suchomel, T. J. & Comfort, P. (2020a). A comparison of kinetic and kinematic variables during the pull from the knee and hang pull, across loads. *Journal of Strength & Conditioning Research, 34*, 1819–1829.

Meechan, D., Suchomel, T. J., McMahon, J. J. & Comfort, P. (2020b). A comparison of kinetic and kinematic variables during the midthigh pull and countermovement shrug, across loads. *Journal of Strength & Conditioning Research, 34*, 1830–1841.

Merrigan, J. J., Tufano, J. J., Falzone, M. & Jones, M. T. (2020a). Effectiveness of accentuated eccentric loading: Contingent on concentric load. *International Journal of Sports Physiology & Performance*, 1–7.

Merrigan, J. J., Tufano, J. J. & Jones, M. T. (2020b). Potentiating effects of accentuated eccentric loading are dependent upon relative strength. *Journal of Strength & Conditioning Research*, Publish Ahead of Print.

Narici, M. (1999). Human skeletal muscle architecture studied in vivo by non-invasive imaging techniques: Functional significance and applications. *Journal of Electromyography & Kinesiology*, *9*, 97–103.

Narici, M. V., Roi, G. S., Landoni, L., Minetti, A. E. & Cerretelli, P. (1989). Changes in force, cross-sectional area and neural activation during strength training and detraining of the human quadriceps. *European Journal of Applied Physiology & Occupational Physiology*, *59*, 310–319.

Newton, R. U., Hakkinen, K., Häkkinen, A., Mccormick, M., Volek, J. & Kraemer, W. J. (2002). Mixed-methods resistance training increases power and strength of young and older men. *Medicine & Science in Sports & Exercise*, *34*, 1367–1375.

Newton, R. U. & Kraemer, W. J. (1994). Developing explosive muscular power: Implications for a mixed methods training strategy. *Strength & Conditioning Journal*, *16*, 20–31.

Newton, R. U., Kraemer, W. J. & Hakkinen, K. (1999). Effects of ballistic training on preseason preparation of elite volleyball players. *Medicine & Science in Sports & Exercise*, *31*, 323–330.

Newton, R. U., Kraemer, W. J., Häkkinen, K., Humphries, B. & Murphy, A. J. (1996). Kinematics, kinetics and muscle activation during explosive upper body movements. *Journal Applied Biomechanics*, *22*, 31–43.

Nimphius, S., Callaghan, S. J., Spiteri, T. & Lockie, R. G. (2016). Change of direction deficit: A more isolated measure of change of direction performance than total 505 time. *Journal of Strength Conditioning Research*, *30*, 3024–3032.

Nimphius, S., McGuigan, M. R. & Newton, R. U. (2010). Relationship between strength, power, speed, and change of direction performance of female softball players. *Journal of Strength Conditioning Research*, *24*, 885–895.

Nimphius, S., McGuigan, M. R. & Newton, R. U. (2012). Changes in muscle architecture and performance during a competitive season in female softball players. *Journal of Strength Conditioning Research*, *26*, 2655–2666.

Nosaka, K. & Aoki, M. (2011). Repeated bout effect: Research update and future perspective. *Brazilian Journal of Biomotricity*, *5*, 5–15.

Oranchuk, D. J., Robinson, T. L., Switaj, Z. J. & Drinkwater, E. J. (2019). Comparison of the hang high-pull and loaded jump squat for the development of vertical jump and isometric force-time characteristics. *Journal of Strength & Conditioning Research*, *33*, 17–24.

Petré, H., Wernstål, F. & Mattsson, C. M. (2018). Effects of flywheel training on strength-related variables: A meta-analysis. *Sports Medicine – Open*, *4*, 55–55.

Refsnes, P. E. (1999). Testing and training for top Norwegian athletes. *In:* Mueller, E., Ludescher, F. & Zallinger, G. (eds.) *Science in Elite Sport*. London: E & FN Spon.

Saez de Villarreal, E., Requena, B. & Cronin, J. B. (2012). The effects of plyometric training on sprint performance: A meta-analysis. *Journal of Strength Conditioning Research*, *26*, 575–584

Secomb, J. L., Farley, O. R. L., Lundgren, L., Tran, T. T., King, A., Nimphius, S. & M., S. J. (2015). Association between the performance of scoring manoeuvres and lower-body strength and power in elite surfers. *International Journal of Sports Science & Coaching*, *10*, 911–918.

Seitz, L. B., Reyes, A., Tran, T. T., De Villarreal, E. S. & Haff, G. G. (2014). Increases in lower-body strength transfer positively to sprint performance: A systematic review with meta-analysis. *Sports Medicine*, *44* 1693–1702.

Singh, J., Appleby, B., Netto, K. & Lavender, A. (2018). Effect of plyometric training on change of direction ability in elite field hockey players. *Journal of Science &Medicine in Sport*, *21*, S88.

Sole, C. J., Bellon, C. R. & Beckham, G. K. (2022). Plyometric training. *In:* Turner, A. & Comfort, P. (eds.) *Advanced Strength and Conditioning: An Evidence-based Approach*. 2nd ed. New York: Routledge.

Soriano, M. A., Suchomel, T. J. & Comfort, P. (2019). Weightlifting overhead pressing derivatives: A review of the literature. *Sports Medicine*, *49*, 867–885.

Speirs, D. E., Bennett, M. A., Finn, C. V. & Turner, A. P. (2016). Unilateral vs. bilateral squat training for strength, sprints, and agility in academy rugby players. *Journal of Science & Medicine in Sport*, 30.

Spiteri, T., Cochrane, J. L., Hart, N. H., Haff, G. G. & Nimphius, S. (2013). Effect of strength on plant foot kinetics and kinematics during a change of direction task. *European Journal of Sport Science, 13*, 646–652.

Spiteri, T., Newton, R. U., Binetti, M., Hart, N. H., Sheppard, J. M. & Nimphius, S. (2015). Mechanical determinants of faster change of direction and agility performance in female basketball athletes. *Journal of Strength Conditioning Research, 29*, 2205–2214.

Spiteri, T., Nimphius, S., Hart, N. H., Specos, C., Sheppard, J. M. & Newton, R. U. (2014). Contribution of strength characteristics to change of direction and agility performance in female basketball athletes. *Journal of Strength Conditioning Research, 28*, 2415–2423.

Stone, M. H. (1993). Explosive exercise and training. *Strength & Conditioning Journal*, 15.

Stone, M. H., Hornsby, W. G., Haff, G. G., Fry, A. C., Suarez, D. G., Liu, J., Gonzalez-Rave, J. M. & Pierce, K. C. (2021). Periodization and block periodization in sports: Emphasis on strength-power training-a provocative and challenging narrative. *Journal of Strength Conditioning Research, 35*, 2351–2371.

Stone, M. H., O'Bryant, H. & Garhammer, J. (1981). A hypothetical model for strength training. *Journal of Sports Medicine & Physical Fitness, 21*, 342–351.

Stone, M. H., O'Bryant, H., Garhammer, J., McMillan, J. & Rozenek, R. (1982). A theoretical model of strength training. *Strength & Conditioning Journal, 4*, 36–39.

Styles, W. J., Matthews, M. J. & Comfort, P. (2015). Effects of strength training on squat and sprint performance in soccer players. *Journal of Strength Conditioning Research, 30*, 1534–1539.

Suchomel, T. J., Beckham, G. K. & Wright, G. A. (2013). Lower body kinetics during the jump shrug: Impact of load. *Journal of Trainology, 2*, 19–22.

Suchomel, T. J., Beckham, G. K. & Wright, G. A. (2015a). The effect of various loads on the force-time characteristics of the hang high pull. *Journal of Strength Conditioning Research, 29*, 1295–301.

Suchomel, T. J., Comfort, P. & Lake, J. P. (2017). Enhancing the force-velocity profile of athletes using weightlifting derivatives. *Strength & Conditioning Journal, 39*, 10–20.

Suchomel, T. J., Comfort, P. & Stone, M. (2015b). Weightlifting pulling derivatives: Rationale for implementation and application. *Sports Medicine, 45*, 823–839.

Suchomel, T. J., McKeever, S. M. & Comfort, P. (2020a). Training with weightlifting derivatives: The effects of force and velocity overload stimuli. *Journal of Strength Conditioning Research, 34*, 1808–1818.

Suchomel, T. J., McKeever, S. A., Mcmahon, J. J. & Comfort, P. (2020b). The effect of training with weightlifting catching or pulling derivatives on squat jump and countermovement jump force-time adaptations. *Journal of Functional. Morphology & Kinesiology*, 5.

Suchomel, T. J., Nimphius, S., Bellon, C. R., Hornsby, W. G. & Stone, M. H. (2021). Training for muscular strength: Methods for monitoring and adjusting training intensity. *Sports Medicine, 51*, 2051–2066.

Suchomel, T. J., Nimphius, S., Bellon, C. R. & Stone, M. H. (2018). The importance of muscular strength: Training considerations. *Sports Medicine, 48*, 765–785.

Suchomel, T. J., Nimphius, S. & Stone, M. H. (2016a). The importance of muscular strength in athletic performance. *Sports Medicine, 46*, 1419–1449.

Suchomel, T. J., Taber, C. B. & Wright, G. A. (2016b). Jump shrug height and landing forces across various loads. *International Journal of Sports Physiology & Performance, 11*, 61–65.

Suchomel, T. J., Wagle, J. P., Douglas, J. H., Taber, C. B., Harden, M., Haff, G. G. & Stone, M. (2019). Implementing eccentric resistance training. part 1: A brief review of existing methods. *Journal of Functional Morphology & Kinesiology, 4*, 38.

Suchomel, T. J., Wright, G. A., Kernozek, T. W. & Kline, D. E. (2014). Kinetic comparison of the power development between power clean variations. *Journal of Strength Conditioning Research, 28*, 350–360.

Thomas, C., Comfort, P., Chiang, C. & Jones, P. A. (2015). Relationship between isometric mid-thigh pull variables and sprint and change of direction performance in collegiate athletes. *Journal of Trainology, 4*, 6–10.

Toji, H. & Kaneko, M. (2004). Effect of multiple-load training on the force-velocity relationship. *Journal of Strength Conditioning Research, 18*, 792–795.

Toji, H., Suei, K. & Kaneko, M. (1997). Effects of combined training loads on relations among force, velocity, and power development. *Journal of Applied Physiology, 22*, 328–336.

Váczi, M., Tollár, J., Meszler, B., Juhász, I. & Karsai, I. (2013). Short-term high intensity plyometric training program improves strength, power and agility in male soccer players. *Journal of Human Kinetics*, *36*, 17–26.
Vieira, J. G., Sardeli, A. V., Dias, M. R., Filho, J. E., campos, Y., Sant'ana, L., Leitao, L., Reis, V., Wilk, M., Novaes, J. & Vianna, J. (2022). Effects of resistance training to muscle failure on acute fatigue: A systematic review and meta-analysis. *Sports Medicine*, *52*, 1103–1125.
Walker, S., Blazevich, A. J., Haff, G. G., Tufano, J. J., Newton, R. U. & Häkkinen, K. (2016). Greater strength gains after training with accentuated eccentric than traditional isoinertial loads in already strength-trained men. *Frontiers in Physiology*, 7, 149.
Walker, S., Häkkinen, K., Haff, G. G., Blazevich, A. J. & Newton, R. U. (2017). Acute elevations in serum hormones are attenuated after chronic training with traditional isoinertial but not accentuated eccentric loads in strength-trained men. *Physiological Reports*, *5*, e13241.

9

STRATEGIES TO DEVELOP LINEAR AND CURVILINEAR SPRINTING TECHNIQUE

James Wild and Jon Goodwin

Linear and curvilinear sprinting, including acceleration, are key activities within many sports. Whilst they are a small component as measured by volume, they can be differentiating factors in pivotal game moments (see Chapter 2). Technique exhibited in these tasks is considered by many to be fundamentally important to performance and injury risk reduction. Technique, however, is not an end in itself but supports the external force expression necessary to drive motion of the whole body that fits with the performance objective. Changes in technique can enhance force outcomes whilst at the same time force-generating capabilities provide the opportunity for changes in technique. Similarly, technique can modify injury risk and pain, whilst past injury and pain can also drive technical modification as a coping strategy. These factors need to be considered together in trying to understand an athlete's emergent movement and provide strategies to enhance performance (Figure 9.1).

In developing programmes to enhance linear and curvilinear sprinting, several steps can be defined that will guide this chapter from understanding the general demands of the task to analysing athletes' emergent movement strategy and hypothesising individual needs. Iterative cycles of interventions can include the modification of internal athlete constraints as well as the progression of specific practices that allow exploration of movement options under progressively more ecologically valid conditions. This chapter explores this process through a case study approach.

Understanding the Task

(Please see Chapters 3 and 4 for additional detail.)

Acceleration, high-speed running, and curved running are related tasks. This is highlighted by large ($r = 0.56$; Mendez-Villanueva et al., 2011) to practically perfect relationships ($r = 0.85$ to 0.97; Clark et al., 2019) between acceleration and high-speed running, and large ($r = 0.58$ to 0.61; Fílter et al., 2020) to practically perfect ($r = 0.93$ to 0.95; Kobal et al., 2021) relationships between linear and curved sprint performance across different radii curves. However, marked differences in the mechanical demands imposed by these tasks mean that material differences in ability across these skills can emerge, particularly within homogenous sporting groups. For example, most coaches will be familiar with seeing players who are fast over 10 m from static scenarios but seem to be nowhere when a 20 m race opens up on field from a fast rolling-start.

DOI: 10.4324/9781003267881-11

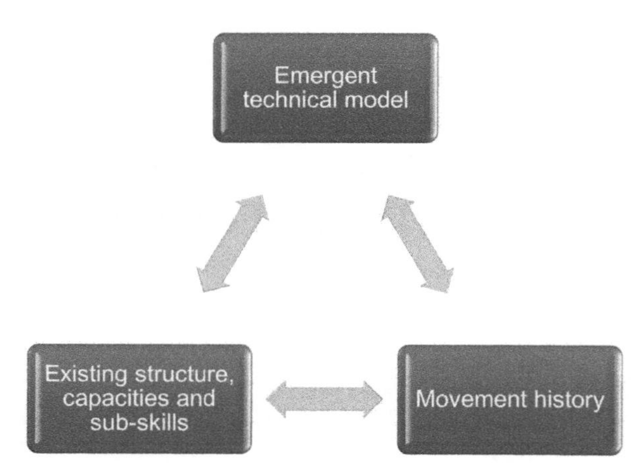

FIGURE 9.1 Bidirectional relationships existing between an athlete's current movement strategy, their existing physical qualities, and their movement history.

Acceleration and Maximum Velocity

During early acceleration, the ability to produce large ground reaction forces (GRF) (e.g. Morin et al., 2015) in short time periods (e.g. von Lieres Und Wilkau et al., 2020), whilst directing the GRF vector in a more horizontal direction (e.g. Rabita et al., 2015) are associated with better performance (see Figure 9.2). Although the time available is short during the initial steps, these time frames are at their longest compared with later sprint phases (Wild et al., 2011). Combined with a flexed lower limb at touchdown and a forward inclined body position, this provides athletes with access to greater leg extension ranges compared with later sprint phases and the ability to 'push' for longer during the stance phase in a more forwards direction.

Our ability to accelerate diminishes as we are exposed to a concomitant reduction in ground time and increase in relative ground speed such that rapid access to limb extension force plateaus (Colyer et al., 2018). Straight-line sprinting sits somewhere between bouncing and vaulting on a stiff limb, limited by our ability to rapidly access GRF sufficient to return us to a flight phase (Weyand et al., 2000). These constraints are managed with a swiftly retracting stance limb, which is straighter and stiffer on contact than earlier acceleration.

Collectively, the differences in constraints and associated technical outcome across these sprint phases explain the shift in emphasis from a greater power generation 'pushing' demand during early acceleration towards a more time-sensitive power dissipation 'bouncing' demand as a sprint progresses (Wild et al., 2011). They also align with research findings that higher maximum relative strength (back squat) and higher ballistic jumping performance (e.g. countermovement jump height and power) is more closely associated with acceleration performance, whereas higher vertical stiffness during rebound jumping more with maximum velocity performance (e.g. Chelly & Denis, 2001; Cunningham et al., 2013).

Curved vs Linear Running

Achieving high-speed outcomes on a curved path exposes the athlete to new constraints that lead to a suppression of running speeds. Curved running requires a continuous acceleration to take the athlete away from a straight-line path towards the arc of the curve. The most obvious adaptation to

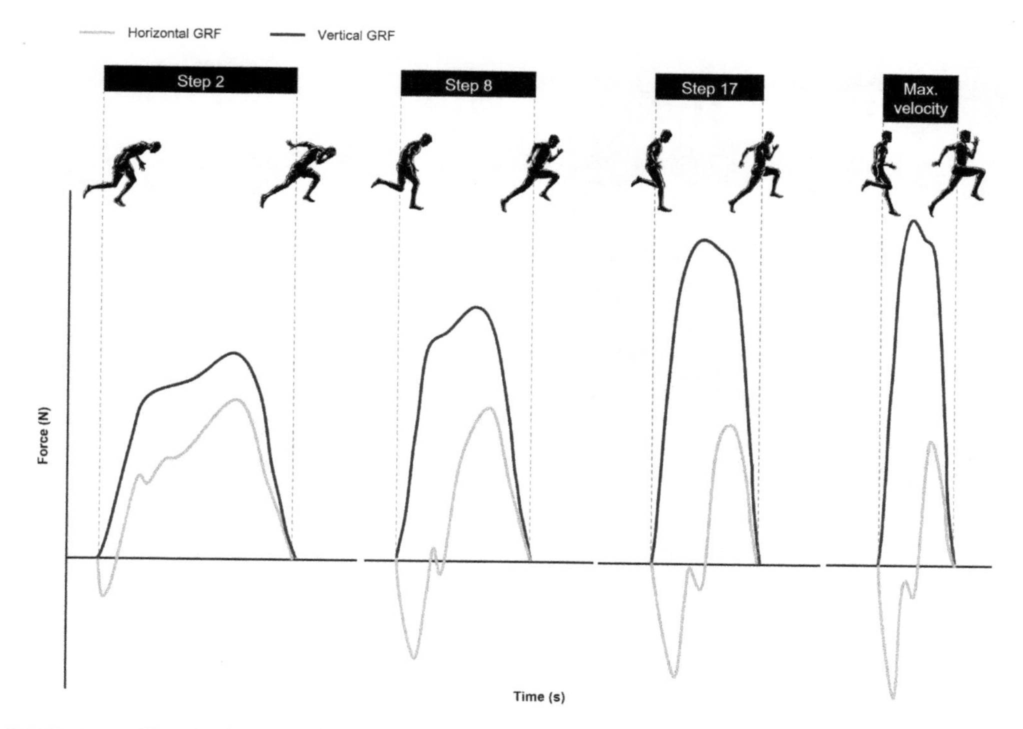

FIGURE 9.2 Changes in ground reaction force characteristics and the touchdown and toe-off positions observed during different phases of a sprint.

this demand is to incline the body towards the centre of the curve radius (see Figures 9.3 and 9.4). However, this imposes asymmetric demands on the limbs that limit performance (Figures 9.3, 9.4, and 9.5 – blue represents outside leg and orange represents inside leg performance). A combination of EMG changes (Filter et al., 2020) and kinematic changes (Churchill et al., 2015; Judson et al., 2020) indicates the muscles of the inside leg likely act to adduct and internally rotate the hip, whereas the muscles of the outside leg act to abduct and externally rotate the hip. As the mediolateral demands on the inside leg increase with curvature, along with a more everted foot position, vertical force potential diminishes (Figure 9.4), leading to increased contact and decreased flight times (Figure 9.5). This is particularly evident in the first half of stance where the ability of the foot to utilise a high-impact landing is lacking in this orientation. This analysis is supported by data showing increases in plantar-flexor moments and curved running speed with wedged footwear that facilitated a neutral foot position (Luo & Stefanyshyn, 2012). Overall, curved running represents a substantial altered demand on the lower limbs in terms of both performance and injury risk, notwithstanding other changes that are evident through the rest of the body but are less well researched.

Understanding the Current Technical Model

There Is No Fixed Technical Model

Whilst the use of generalised technical models is useful for coaches, research findings are mixed. For example, 'pushing' the centre of mass further forward of the stance foot during the stance phase

FIGURE 9.3 The 'inwards' lean during curved sprinting associated with altered stance foot orientation and global kinematics (Churchill et al., 2015; Judson et al., 2020).

has been shown by some to relate to better early acceleration performance (e.g. Kugler & Janshen, 2010; Wild et al., 2018) but not by others (e.g. Walker et al., 2021; Wild, 2022). The route to performance enhancement can also differ between individuals. For instance, faster groups have been shown to produce shorter contact times than slower groups during acceleration (e.g. Murphy et al., 2003), and yet contact times have also been shown to increase following training interventions, which have resulted in better acceleration performance (e.g. Lockie et al., 2014). Acceleration performance can also improve with different combinations of changes to spatiotemporal variables following different training programmes (Lockie et al., 2012; Lockie et al., 2014; Spinks et al., 2007), and changes in acceleration performance are observable without any meaningful changes to the spatiotemporal variables (e.g. Lahti et al., 2020). This suggests that whilst fundamental movements are broadly similar across individuals, a precise one-size-fits-all movement template may not exist and changes in technique may not be consistently necessary to deliver performance change.

So what should a technical model be? We define it here as a set of common positions and movements relating to efficient and safe skill execution, directed at management of the principal external constraints that limit performance. It comes with a range, more or less explicitly defined, of acceptable variation across different anatomical, capacity, and skill-based constraints within the athlete. Common technical elements proposed to support the GRF outcomes for sprinting can be inferred from research demonstrating the technical features related to better sprinting performance (e.g. Walker et al., 2021), separating faster from slower athlete groups (e.g. Wild et al., 2018; Clark et al., 2014), and emphasised in the technical models of elite sprinters (e.g. Mann & Murphy, 2015). Of course, technical models most frequently originate from the experience of coaches with generations of shared wisdom.

Understanding an athlete's current movement requires both data and some thoughtful consideration of context and history. Whilst data collection through observation, video, force plates, and other tools is common in the modern sport environment, less consideration is often given to context and history since their qualitative application is more challenging to justify in the workplace, more prone to biases in interpretation, and more subject to charlatanism. Coaches should not avoid this qualitative analysis though as de-skilling in this domain, with an expectation of data providing all the answers, is almost certain to do a disservice to the athlete. Once we understand an individual

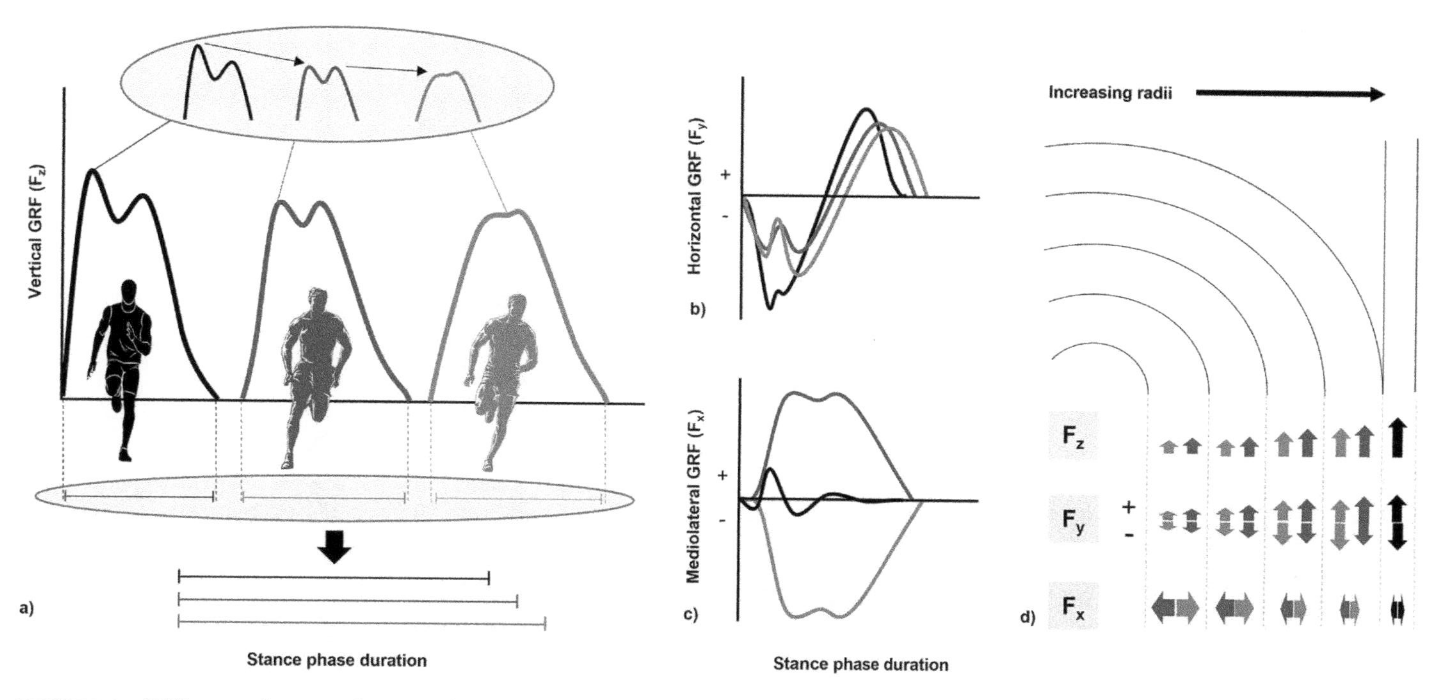

FIGURE 9.4 Differences between linear and curved sprinting ground reaction force characteristics. Steps during linear sprinting (black) and curved sprinting (radii like that of the curved path on a 400 m athletics track; blue = outside leg; orange = inside leg) at maximum or close to maximum velocity (a–c). Typical changes to GRF characteristics in response to changes in radii of a curved sprint path (d) (Chang & Kram, 2007; Churchill et al., 2016).

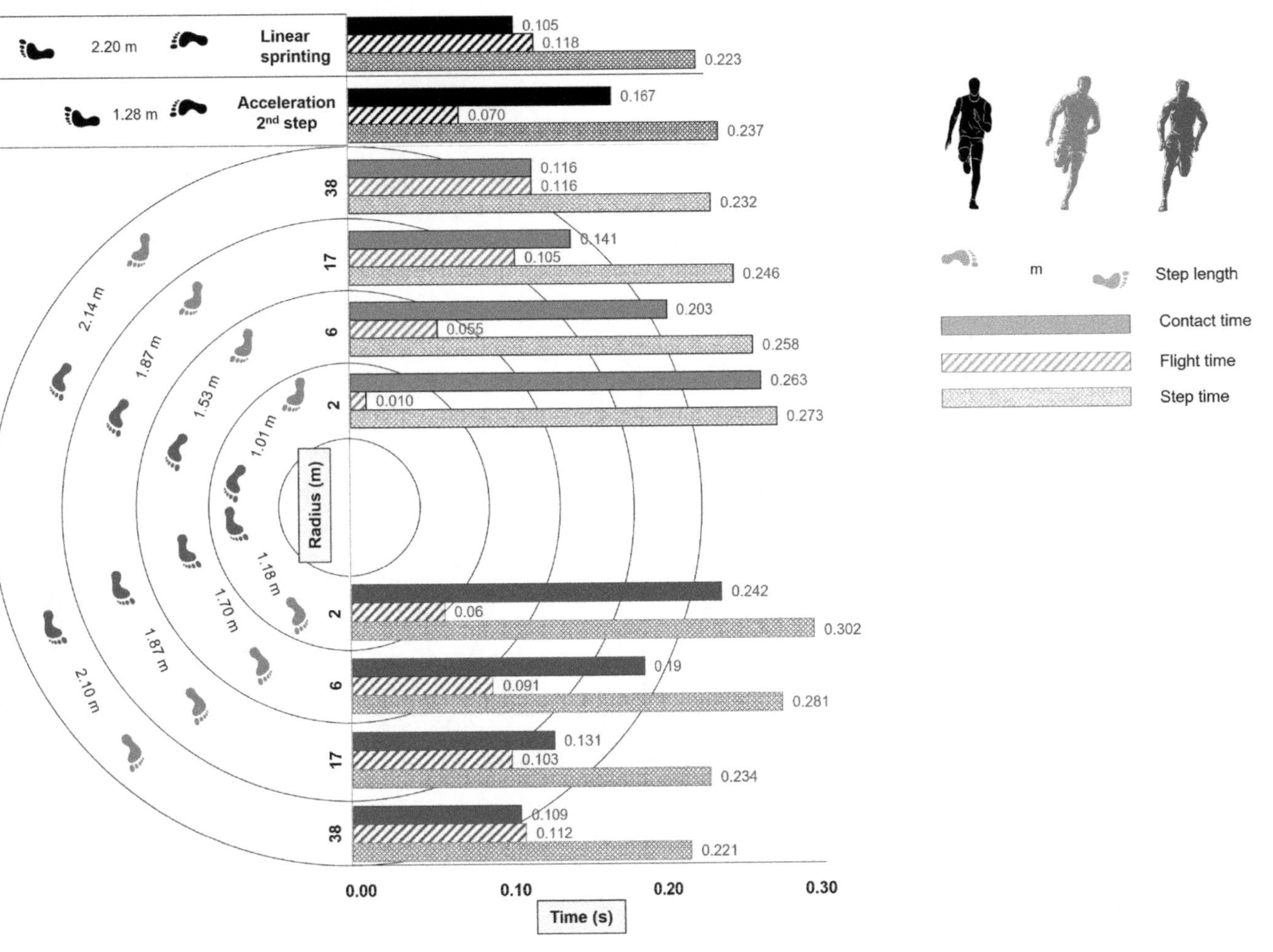

FIGURE 9.5 Changes in spatiotemporal step characteristics with changing radii of curved sprinting. Data presented are from 2–6 m radii (Chang & Kram, 2007), 17 m radius (Taboga et al., 2016), 38 m radius, linear sprinting (Churchill et al., 2016), and acceleration (Wild et al., 2018). Note: step length values for a 17 m radius curve are an estimate since inside and outside leg were not reported separately.

athlete's needs, directing training interventions at those needs can at times be more meaningful than correspondence with the task. The most specific tools might provide great benefit for one athlete, but with another, they can fall short if they do not relate (either to support it or work to change it) to the individual athlete's movement solution and current barriers to progression.

The Basic Template – Why Have Any Technical Care at All?

Table 9.1 highlights technical model elements for acceleration and sprinting. It is valuable to justify the contribution technical elements make to performance as the acceptable technical variance is qualitatively based on trade-offs between the value of the technical element and the downsides of technical change for the individual athlete (e.g. other conflicting technical demands of the sport; time investment required for changes vs other performance factors).

TABLE 9.1 Basic Technical Model Elements for Acceleration and Linear Sprinting

Acceleration	
Forward inclination	Facilitates forward inclination of the ground reaction force, maximising propulsive contribution and limiting flight time progression, supporting more step cycle time for force production. The degree of forward inclination is limited by the absolute magnitude of force available.
Thigh separation	Rapid, large split of the thighs through the stance phase enhances leg extension force, whilst preparing the swing limb (front-side catch) for rapid acceleration back down to the ground, optimising foot-ground touchdown interaction.
Back-side catch in late stance	Rapidly decelerating backwards limb rotation late in the stance phase to control hip extension and 'pull' the leg forward at take-off. Prevents 'over-pushing' when late stance phase impulse offers less performance benefits than moving to the next step.
Active ground strike	Forceful thigh retraction during late swing. Supports a point of contact approximately beneath the hip and rapid rotation of the stance leg around the foot, more quickly positioning the centre of mass ahead of the foot during the stance phase. Enhances the application of force in a more horizontal direction.
Heel-drop attenuation	Stable foot position during the early stance phase provides a foundation for the hip extensors to contribute more effectively to forwards acceleration whilst contributing to a more effective storage and release of elastic energy at the ankle.
High-speed running	
Back-side catch in late stance	Early hip flexor activation decelerates extending limb at end of stance phase. Prevents lower leg cycling behind the body after toe-off. Supports recovery leg forward acceleration. Enables both the timing of knee drive with peak stance support force and the achievement of effective front-side positions to set up strike.
Passive limb folding	Effective timing allows passive limb folding during recovery phase. Optimises efficiency and speed of motion.
Front-side catch	Delivers tibia to a high, forward position, effectively pre-loading/activating hamstrings. Provides space for rearward acceleration of the thigh, setting up stance force production.
Stiff fast-retracting limb into stance	High retraction rate reduces the propensity for braking forces, which in turn facilitates use of a stiffer leg spring.
Relaxation and rhythm	Efficient rapid switching of limb directions requires effective timing. Enabled by rapid switching *off* of key musculature. Allows limbs to swing and fold freely. Inappropriate continuous or mistimed co-contraction can drive higher energy consumption or slower joint accelerations and increase the risk.

Taking Information From Technique Directly

Strategies to analyse technique are common with tools like video, radar, timing systems, and force plates. Ultimately, the most holistic view of the athlete's movement comes from the coach's observation, and often these observations serve as the driver for questions around the athlete's movement that can be answered with access to data. Any further proactive reduction of the system to sets of data needs to be consolidated with the coach's view of the athlete to enable decision-making and coaching intervention. Case study 1 offers an example of applications of raw data in supporting interpretation of an athlete's challenges.

CASE STUDY 1A – HIGH-SPEED RUNNING

Athlete: Professional male rugby union (back) player

Coaching analysis: Athlete with a history of repeated left-side hamstring strain with a noticeable 'galloping' running action and reduced front-side action on the left leg. The athlete requires frequent modifications to rugby training owing to left-side hamstring complaints.

Data confirmation

Assessment	*Result*	*Analysis*
Maximum sprint velocity	*9.80 m/s*	*Top 15% of the group*
Step length	Left/right = 2.15 / 2.32 m	Between step difference = 8%
Contact time	Left/right = 0.113 / 0.105 s	Between step difference = 7%
Fight time	Left/right = 0.111 / 0.127 s	Between step difference = 14%
NordBord (eccentric knee flexor strength)	Left/right = 4.37 / 5.12 N/kg	Middle (left) and top 20% of the group (right), respectively. Between limb difference = 15%
Peak single-leg isometric hip-thrust torque	Left/right = 4.54 / 5.24 N/kg	13% difference (bottom 15% [left] and middle of group [right], respectively)

Interpretation: The asymmetric 'galloping' pattern observed were evident in the data as longer contact times and shorter flight times on the left side. Avoidance of a high front-side catch on the left leg appeared to be a protective mechanism, guarding the limb from loading during the late swing. In turn, the foot was not being accelerated into the ground at the same rate as the right side, so more time was needed on the left side to accrue vertical impulse sufficient to produce required flight time for the next step.

Between limb asymmetries alone are not necessarily a problem during sprinting, but when pieced together with a history of injury and related between limb strength differences, it suggests that one-sided hamstring injury recurrence is likely to continue if the deficits are not reduced.

A data-*led* strategy to addressing an individual's technical needs is to determine the technical features on which they are 'reliant' for performance. For example, Salo et al. (2011) observed that elite sprinters were typically individually reliant on the production of either higher step length or higher step frequency for better 100 m race performance. That is to say that athletes' best performances emerged with a strategy preferring either step length or step rate. Further individual insight can then be offered by considering the combinations of spatiotemporal variables that emerge, informing technical interventions (Wild, 2022). For example, for an athlete whose better sprinting performances are produced with higher step frequencies, it would be possible to determine whether this is achieved through a reduction in contact or flight time or a combination of both.

CASE STUDY 2A – ACCELERATION

Athlete: Professional male rugby union (back) player

Coaching analysis: Athlete generally excelled during acceleration. Despite this, enhancing 'speed off the mark' was deemed a priority at the time. Visually, there were no marked deviations from the basic technical model elements during acceleration.

Data confirmation

Assessment	*Result*	*Analysis*
5 m sprint time	*1.017 s*	*Top 10% of the group*
Step frequency	4.00 Hz ($r = -0.73$)[a]	Meaningful negative relationship
Step length	1.44 m ($r = -0.03$)[a]	Relationship not meaningful
Contact time	0.176 s ($r = 0.05$)[a]	Relationship not meaningful
Fight time	0.074 s ($r = 0.55$)[a]	Meaningful positive relationship
Peak single-leg isometric hip-thrust torque (average of both sides)	6.04 Nm/kg	Top 20% of the group
Squat jump P_{max}	31.8 W/kg	Top 25% of the group
Single-leg RSI (average of both sides)	0.75 (height/time)	Top 15% of the group

[a] Mean across the first four steps. Within-individual relationship between spatiotemporal variable and 5 m time are shown in brackets (quantified over 12 sprint trials).

Interpretation: No obvious 'strength deficits', 'technical issues', or indicators in the athlete's history to warrant further investigation. The athlete was seemingly reliant on producing higher step frequency for better acceleration performance, underpinned by shorter flight times. This indicated, despite no other problematic markers, that technical change to increase step frequency led by consistent flight time reduction may create an opportunity for improved acceleration performance.

Technical Model Defined by Movement History

Factors influencing the technical patterns of athletes extend beyond anatomical or strength-related differences. In particular, their learning history and current intentions within their movement can be important in interpreting their current movement outcomes and needs. Movement choices form and can become sticky, dependent on when and where they emerged or were learned. Take the example of a young athlete sprinting who, due to any combination of genetics/lifestyle/injury history, had a relatively underperforming lower-limb segment (you can choose wherever you like) – a weak link. If they are tasked with running fast on a regular basis, they will find the best way they can to solve this problem. If they do this enough, they can develop a profile of qualities that supports their strategy, and even though this strategy might place restrictions on their long-term development, they can get stuck there, 'dead-ending' their development. They have found a strong attractor state (e.g. Van Hooren et al., 2019) that we (the coaches) might not believe is optimal for them in the long term. This is the basis of technical errors. Coaches need to be careful here. Individual athletes have peculiarities for all sorts of reasons, managing all sorts of limitations. Bowling in with a drive towards the 'correct' technique can be harmful as often as not, creating new risks and no guarantee of performance gains. The 'error' in technique is often not an issue to be fixed in and of itself but rather a *signal*, a data point in the analysis of the athlete's needs. It is providing information as to what limitations the athlete is working with rather than awaiting a cue to make a fix. In a similar way, movement errors are often a sign of the athlete's intentions tied to their perception of the task. Athletes take these intentions from their peers, other coaches, and their own interrogation of the task. If we can capture misaligned intentions, then a technical correction might offer less of the answer compared to a modification of their perception and associated intention.

Technical Model Defined by Strength Qualities

Although methodological differences may account for some of the inconsistent results observed in technique-focused research, it is also likely that differences in the performer constraints (Newell, 1986) between and within athlete groups will affect the movement preferences they exhibit. From a physical standpoint, inter-individual differences in anatomy (e.g. leg and segment lengths, body mass, skeletal structure, tendon-bone attachment sites) will influence movement solutions. Even when some of these constraints are controlled for (e.g. leg length and body mass), different successful movement strategies still emerge (e.g. Wild et al., 2022). Other factors then, including the strength characteristics of individuals, will also influence the movement solutions available to them (e.g. Wild, 2022; Wild et al., 2022).

The body is a remarkable adaptive system. However, reorganisation within regular cyclical tasks or high-speed/force/complexity tasks, either chronically around weak links or in response to pain, progressively shunts demands around the system. Whilst such adaptability makes the system resilient, it is built on spending available movement options. Closing off options, due to weakness or pain, diminishes the number of available organisational outcomes (e.g. Homs et al., 2022). In general, the body has adequate movement options and tissue resilience for this not to cause problems, but this is not always the case. Periodically the resultant movement narrows the remaining movement options so much as to cause marked increase in acute or chronic risk. As such, part of the objective of athletic preparation is to both remove weak links that might narrow movement options and over-engineer relevant

CASE STUDY 3A – HIGH-SPEED RUNNING

Athlete: Female international lacrosse player

Coaching analysis: An ex-gymnast turned lacrosse player with a marked 'butt-kicking' sprinting action and seemingly poor lumbo-pelvic control during upright running. Arms swing across the body with limited shoulder range.

Data confirmation

Assessment	*Result*	*Analysis*
Maximum sprint velocity	*7.48 m/s*	*Bottom 15% of the group*
Visual inspection during assessment	Marked early and excessive lumbar extension and marked mid-thoracic restriction	Poor lumbo-pelvic control exacerbated by 'overactive' erector spinae and hip flexors and limited thoracic extension/ rotation
Thomas test	Marked restricted hip extension	Iliopsoas and rectus femoris 'tightness'
Peak single-leg isometric hip-thrust torque (average of both sides)	3.45 Nm/kg	Bottom 25% of the group
Squat jump P_{max}	24.0 W/kg	Top 20% of the group
Single-leg RSI (average of both sides)	0.60 (height/contact)	Top 15% of the group

Interpretation: Patterns observed (i.e. early lumbar extension, anterior pelvic tilt and associated muscle tightness and poor motor control of the lumbo-pelvic region) were consistent with those frequently found in gymnasts (e.g. Ambegaonkar et al., 2014) and likely borne out of her prior movement history. The athlete was 'locked' into this pattern, resulting in excessive leg cycling behind the body and an inability to execute an effective front-side catch, resulting in a 'flicking out' of the foot during the late swing phase due to reduced space/time for backwards acceleration of the thigh. Hip extension force capabilities were poor as indicated by her low hip torque strength score. Mid-thoracic restrictions likely contribute to a transverse-plane dominant-arm action.

TABLE 9.2 Partial Correlation Coefficients Between Strength-Based Variables in Their Absolute Form and Normalised Kinematic Variables (Hof, 1996) over the Initial Four Steps of Sprinting, Controlling for Body Mass

Strength-based assessment	*Strength variable*	*Spatiotemporal variables*	*Linear kinematics*	*Touchdown and stance phase angular kinematics*	*Toe-off angular kinematics*
Peak unilateral hip extensor isometric torque, adapted from Goodwin and Bull (2021)	**Hip torque**	Contact time (−0.42)	Touchdown distance (−0.51)	Shank angle (−0.46)	Shank angle (0.42)
		-	Contact length (−0.49)	-	-
Maximum leg extension power obtained during a squat jump profiling assessment, adapted from Samozino et al. (2013)	$\mathbf{P_{max}}$	-	-	Ankle angle (−0.46)	-
		-	-	Peak ankle DF angle (−0.56)	-
		-	-	Knee angle (−0.50)	-
		-	-	Hip touchdown angular velocity (−0.47)	-
		-	-	Stance mean hip angular velocity (0.57)	-
Repeated unilateral in-place jump test aiming for maximum height and minimum contact times, adapted from Comyns et al. (2019); CT = contact time, RSI = reactive strength index (jump height/contact time)	**Repeated CT**	Step rate (−0.47)	Touchdown distance (0.45)	Peak angle DF angle (−0.40)	-
		Contact time (0.43)	Contact length (0.46)	-	-
	Repeated jump height	-	-	Stance mean hip angular velocity (0.49)	Ankle angle (−0.43)
	RSI	Contact time (−0.42)	-	-	-
Ratio of peak unilateral hip extensor isometric torque to the mean contact times achieved in the repeated unilateral in-place jump	**Hip torque/ CT ratio**	Contact time (−0.55)	Touchdown distance (−0.64)	Foot angle (−0.41)	-
		-	Toe-off distance (0.48)	Shank angle (−0.55)	-
		-	Contact length (−0.63)	Thigh angle (−0.48)	Shank angle (0.44)

Strength of relationships are shown in brackets. All relationships are statistically significant ($p < 0.05$) and greater than the smallest clinically important correlation coefficient ($r = \pm 0.26$). Data from Wild (2022)

structures to improve tolerance for unanticipated loading. Such a strategy should complement a plan to enhance athletes' key performance drivers, reduce risk, and enhance future consistency of training.

Curve running is an example of gradually losing options. Running the curve requires lateral force. The best way to do this tips the system over and everts the inside foot, which takes away the option to rebound effectively. Having a foot that can evert serves many benefits, but importantly, it is not essential for locomotion. In this situation the 'choice' to have a foot that 'everts' combined with the 'choice' to lean into the curve progressively causes speed loses during curved running. The body runs out of options to enable speed. Every decision made in a complex system necessarily reduces future available options.

Knowledge of the way that strength-based qualities relate to technical features adopted during sprinting provides some insight into how the different movement strategies observed in athletes may be influenced. Table 9.2 provides a summary of the relationships between the strength characteristics of professional rugby union backs and their initial acceleration performance.

CASE STUDY 4A – HIGH-SPEED RUNNING

Athlete: Professional football player

Coaching analysis: A hip dominant runner getting nothing out of the foot and ankle. Unable to tolerate a stiff leg ground contact and as such sat low through stance on a 'soft' spring.

Data confirmation

Assessment	*Result*	*Analysis*
Maximum sprint velocity	*9.4 m/s*	*Top 20% of the group*
Hip sweep during stance	64°	Widest in the group
Hex bar deadlift 1 RM	230 kg	Top 10% of the group
10–5 pogo	2.18	Bottom 10% of the group
Vertical jump height	44.4 cm	Bottom 25%

Interpretation: Despite apparently good hip strength, it seemed the ability to tolerate a rapid stretch-shortening cycle at the knee was poor, and particularly the ability to tolerate impact landing at the ankle was very poor. As a result, during sprinting, the athlete extended in front to a long contact distance, reducing the impact demands and spreading the achievement of vertical impulse across a large hip sweep range through stance. This aligned with cohort data highlighting a high ratio of function between the hip and ankle/knee was correlated with increased contact lengths and touchdown distances (Wild, 2022).

CASE STUDY 5A – ACCELERATION

Athlete: Professional male rugby union (back) player
Coaching analysis: Sluggish during acceleration – passive, flat-foot landing with an excessive forward trunk lean, vaulting (slowly) over a stance leg positioned far forward relative to the centre of mass.

Data confirmation

Assessment	*Result*	*Analysis*
10 m sprint time	*1.79 s*	*Bottom 5% of group*
Contact time	0.174 s ($r = 0.62$)[a]	Meaningful positive relationship
Contact length	1.01 m	Top (i.e. longest) 5% of the group
Peak single-leg isometric hip-thrust torque (average of both sides)	4.98 Nm/kg	Bottom 15% of the group
Squat jump P_{max}	30.5 W/kg	Top 25% of the group
Contact time during a repeated unilateral in-place jump assessment (average of both sides)	0.294 s	Bottom 10% of the group

[a] Mean value of variable across the first six steps. Within-individual relationship between contact time and 10 m time are shown in brackets (quantified over 12 sprint trials).

Interpretation: The combination of weak hip extensors and poor vertical stiffness qualities had seemingly negatively influenced the ability of the athlete to transmit force effectively through the ankle or use his hip to achieve rapid horizontal acceleration of the centre of mass. This manifested in a large touchdown distance, a rapid and excessive heel-drop at touchdown, and a long contact time.

Technical Change Through Modification of Internal Constraints

(See Chapter 8 for additional details.)
General interventions directed at modifying technical affordances and latterly performance outcomes are secondary or tertiary in their potential transfer (Goodwin & Cleather, 2016) and different in their mechanism of action to tools used for primary transfer (for example, cohort-wide impact of plyometrics on sprint performance). As such, the coach should envision a multistep process in supporting transfer to performance. This requires consistency of application and patience, along with effective data collection to understand the responsiveness to capacity development and associated emergence of technical progression. Following the development of identified capacities, the exploration of the skill is necessary, and possibly the disruption of the existing movement, to support recognition of new affordances. Iteration of this process, along with more contextualised stress testing of movement outcomes, all become important in understanding the developing technical model and its stability.

The case studies that follow highlight some successful examples of secondary transfer outcomes, where improvements in general capacity supported changes in technical outcomes alongside improved performance.

CASE STUDY 4B – HIGH-SPEED RUNNING

Intervention: The athlete was already, for the previous year, exposed to weekly sprint practice, periodic technical running sessions, and regular wicket runs as part of warm-ups. The programme change was to include a 12-week progressive programme of calf strength, skipping, hopping, and jumping, largely in addition to the player's regular programme.

Outcome

Assessment	*Result*	*Change*
Maximum sprint velocity	*9.9 m/s*	*+5.3%*
Hip sweep during stance	53°	–14%
Hex bar deadlift	240 kg	+4%
10–5 pogo	2.65	+22%
Vertical jump height	52.4 cm	+18%

Interpretation: Tracking data highlighted a change in technical movement strategy emerging around the tenth week, with the athlete additionally showing qualitative improvements in ankle stiffness through acceleration phase, improved front-side position at maximum velocity and a shorter hip range through stance, almost entirely explained with a reduced touchdown distance during sprinting. The change in max velocity capability emerged at the end of the 12-week period described here, with no prior maximum velocity variance in the weeks preceding. Relevant gym-based metrics had increased steadily over the period. It would appear that the improved tolerance to a stiff landing at the ankle and knee permitted a phase shift in the technical model and a resultant improvement in maximal speed capability.

Differences in touchdown and toe-off positions achieved by the athlete pre (left) and post (right) intervention.

CASE STUDY 5B – ACCELERATION

Intervention: Over 21 weeks of programming additions included specific plantar-flexor isometric training and a higher volume of plyometric training with a view to enhance muscle-tendon stiffness qualities. Hip extensor strength was targeted using exercises, placing greater demands on the hip compared to the knee and ankle (e.g. hip thrust, glute-ham, RDL). The athlete continued to sprint on a weekly basis as before.

Outcome

Assessment	*Result*	*Change*
10 m sprint time	*1.73 s*	*–3% (large effect, d = –1.35)*
Contact time	0.161 s	–8% (very large effect, *d* = –3.12)
Contact length	0.95 m	–6% (large effect, *d* = –1.39
Peak single-leg isometric hip-thrust torque (average of both sides)	5.33 Nm/kg	+7% (very large effect, *d* = 3.33)
Contact time during a repeated unilateral in-place jump assessment (average of both sides)	0.263 s	–11% (very large effect, *d* = –3.97)

Interpretation: Changes in hip torque and repeated contact time were first observed at weeks 4 and 9, respectively. Decreases in contact time and contact length (objectively measured) and decreases in touchdown distance, as well as a more 'stable' stance foot, occurred after 14 weeks. Acceleration improvements began by week 17. The changes made to the physical capacities of the athlete, whilst sprinting regularly, seemingly led to changes in their movement outcomes in the absence of specific 'technical' training. Visually the most notable differences could be observed at touchdown.

Pre (left) and post (right) positions at touchdown during the second step. Note the changes in stance foot and shank orientation and the distance required for the centre of mass to pass beyond the stance foot.

Practices To Allow Exploration of Movement Technique

For many athletes, substantial local detriments might not be the driver for technical and performance deficiencies. For example, athletes' wider movement history and task perceptions might simply have led to movement solutions that the coach believes are sub-optimal for long-term development. Under such conditions, more specific exploration and specific practice form the foundational tools to encouraging exploration of the task, disruption of an existing model, and in situ development of relevant physical capacities. This is not a journey to enforce a tight technical model deemed necessary by the coach. Some practices might expose athletes to new shapes or more flowing rhythm; some practices might encourage earlier hip flexor activation in late stance; some practices might encourage the athlete to feel what a stiffer ground strike is like; some cues might alter an athlete's perception of the task and disrupt a stubborn old pattern. The construction of purposeful practices around the individual, alongside the simple demand to practise the target skill of sprinting itself, are the basis of technical and performance development.

Numerous coaching strategies can contribute in different ways to finding or reinforcing technical change in an athlete. For instance, the amplification of errors (Milanese et al., 2008), targets internal feedback processes, encouraging self-detection of movement issues. When an athlete recognises the change in strategy being sought and is able to execute the movement within reasonable bandwidths, contrasting between their habitual and alternative sprinting actions within and between sessions can help transition the previous automatised movement pattern towards a new one (Hanin et al., 2002). At some point, removing interference is necessary, and directly 'forgetting' the previous action, by focusing solely on the 'new' action, (Bjork, 1970) may be required as part of the intervention to facilitate the shift in sprinting strategy being sought. It is also important that such approaches are dovetailed with opportunities to sprint under more game-specific scenarios to help 'put a lid' on the movement changes and offer the opportunity for them to be stress tested and manifest optimally for competition.

For some athletes, the exploration of a range of activities may be required to find advantageous shifts in technique. Some examples are highlighted in Table 9.3 and Figure 9.6. Drills involve

TABLE 9.3 A Selection of Sprint-Based Drills and Constrained Sprinting Tasks

Activity (see Figure 9.6)	*Primary technical element(s) emphasised (see Table 9.1)*
Drills	
Switches	Emphasises rapid limb switching and ground strike. More linear path of the foot lends closer similarity to acceleration phase. Can be completed with a hold between each rep or as a more rhythmic pattern with a multiple contact bounce on each side.
Resisted acceleration bound	Closest similarity to acceleration phase. Can be used to emphasise almost any technical aspect and also to overload all limb extension components.
Straight leg bound	The rapid retraction of a stiff limb offers some similarity to high-speed running. The long limb position retained on flexion demands high hip flexor activation from the back-side catch position.
Dead leg A drill	Rhythmic folding of the lower limb demands vastus group relaxation coordinated with hip flexor activation during recovery. Typically, a more circular path of the foot brings the pattern closer to high-speed running.
Dribbles	A scaled running practice popularised by Altis, enabling emphasis or focus on almost any aspect of the technical model. The foot path is typically circular, making this drill closer in correspondence to high-speed running.
Constrained sprinting	
Resisted sprinting	With manipulation of resistance, these runs can be moved to correspond more closely to acceleration or high-speed running mechanics. They can be considered a tool for overload (capacity focus) or an opportunity to explore technical aspects with slightly more time available.
Wicket run	These runs can constrain the athlete both vertically (encouraging a high foot recovery) and horizontally (manipulating step length and symmetry). Along with changes in speed, this run can allow focus on almost any technical aspect.

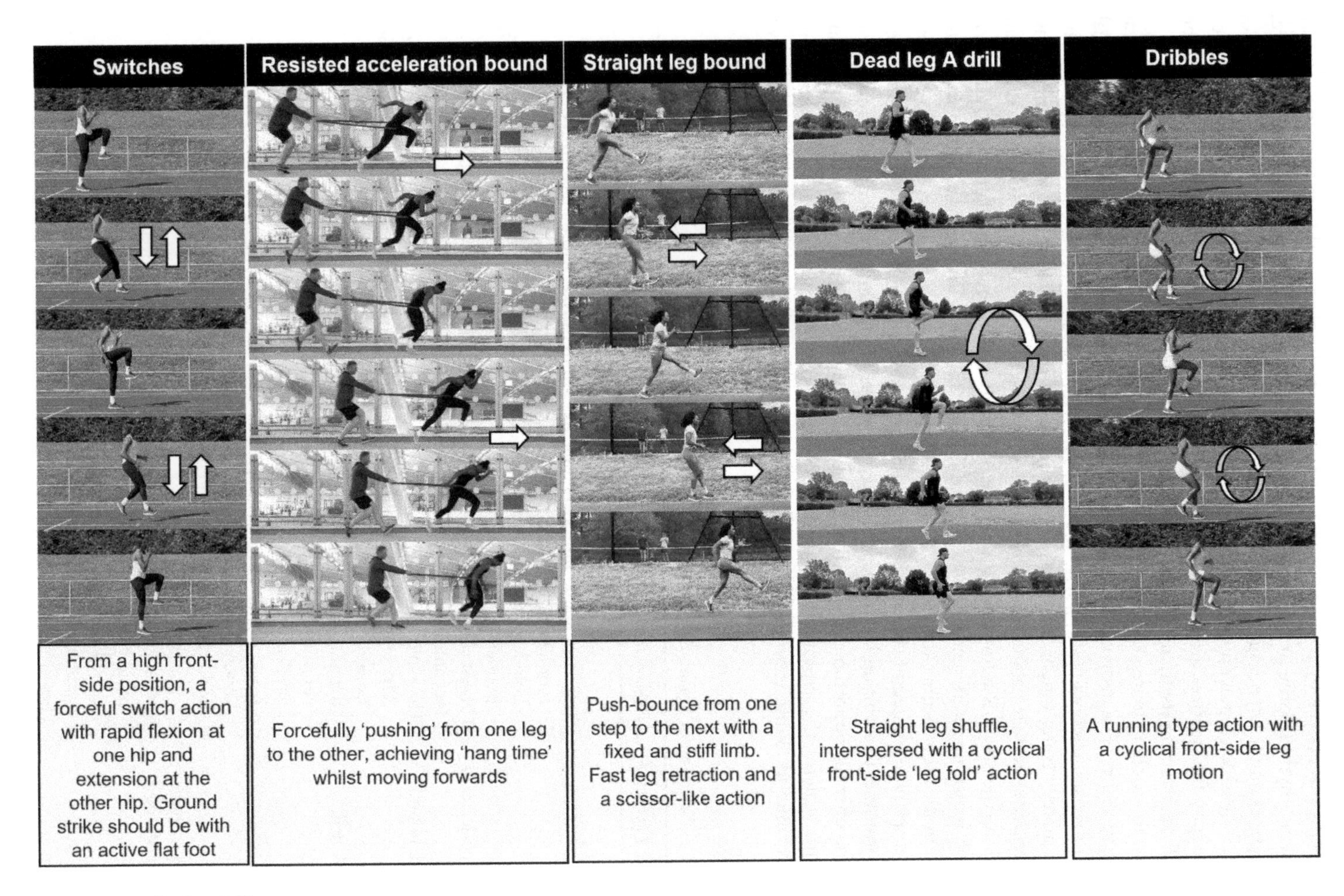

FIGURE 9.6 Sprint drills.

FIGURE 9.7 Constrained sprinting.

relatively low-intensity cyclic activities resembling the sprinting action and are considered favourable in terms of body position, rhythm, and tissue tolerance. Sprinting with constraints involves activities in which the sprinting action in its entirety is executed often at or close to the velocities achieved during free sprinting (e.g. resistance, assistance, obstacles, change of surface, technical instruction at submax sprinting intensities). Drills and running practices provide opportunities to embody technical ideas and therefore can contribute not just to physical changes but also to athlete's perception of the task. Coaches need to think critically about the technical aspects requiring exploration, reinforcement, disruption, or overload. This enables appropriate activity selection, execution strategy, description, and ongoing coaching to enable selected tools to impact individuals meaningfully. In this way, it is likely that athletes will move between progressions and regressions of simple closed and complexed drills, challenged drills and practices, and game scenarios.

CASE STUDY 1B – HIGH-SPEED RUNNING

Intervention: Over 14 weeks, a series of drills requiring rapid leg extension in similar positions to the late swing phase of sprinting (e.g. B-skip and 'kick-out' drills) were incorporated into the training week. The objective was structural adaptation to fast front-side 'catching', as well as increased confidence in being able to rapidly load the hamstrings in hip flexion. The athlete was removed from maximal sprinting (beyond 20 m), other than during rugby training and matches, whilst additional time was spent on submaximal running tasks (i.e. wicket runs and tempo-based running with a front-side technical focus). Technically focused near maximal sprint efforts progressively returned to the programme after six weeks. Simultaneously, eccentric knee flexor strength (Nordic curls and glute-ham raise variations) and hip extensor strength were targeted to address the deficits evident in these qualities.

Outcome

Assessment	*Result*	*Change*
Maximum sprint velocity	*9.67 m/s*	*–2% (no meaningful change)*
Step length	Left/right = 2.20 / 2.27 m	Between step difference = 3% (reduced by 5%)
Contact time	Left/right = 0.109 / 0.105 s	Between step difference = 4% (reduced by 3%)
Fight time	Left/right = 0.119 / 0.129 s	Between step difference = 8% (reduced by 6%)
NordBord (eccentric knee flexor strength)	Left/right = 4.99 / 5.37 N/kg	12% increase (L side now top 20% of group); between limb difference 7% (reduced by 8%)
Peak single-leg isometric hip-thrust torque	Left/right = 5.07 / 5.63 N/kg	10% increase (left side, now middle of the group); between limb difference 10% (reduced by 3%)

Interpretation: Although maximum sprint velocity did not change meaningfully (a –2% difference was within the normal biological range for the athlete), the athlete had no hamstring complaint during the final six weeks of the programme. This was the longest period he had gone without some kind of symptom requiring modification to training.

A visual representation of changes in the athlete's spatiotemporal variables pre and post intervention.

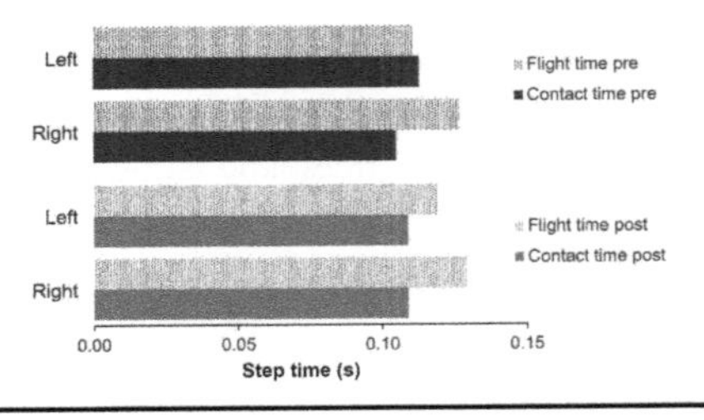

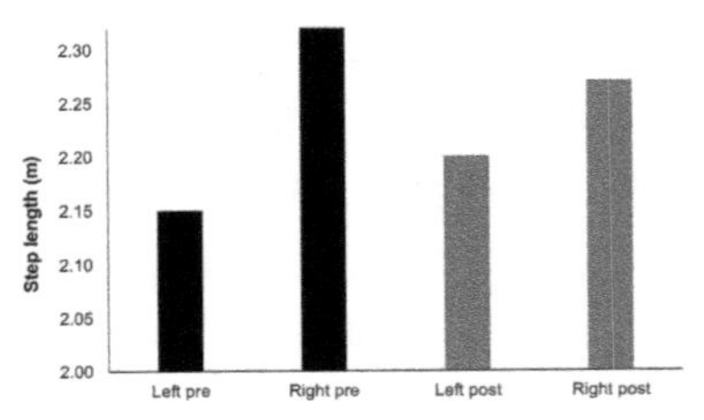

CASE STUDY 2B – ACCELERATION

Intervention: An exploratory session was carried out with the athlete to describe the results of the analysis and to spend time exploring the movement technique being sought (i.e. higher step frequency, driven predominantly by decreased flight time). A technical prompt ('skating') was self-generated by the athlete based on their perception of the task. A quality check was completed to determine whether the change in technique was effective when using the technical prompt.

Over an 18-week period, the athlete used opportunities in the week (during standalone speed sessions and during warm-ups prior to rugby training and matches) to focus on their technical prompt. The 'old way, new way' and 'direct forgetting' approaches were used at different times during the intervention period. No other changes were made to the athlete's programme.

Outcome

Assessment	*Result*	*Change*
5 m sprint time	*0.986 s*	*−3% (large effect, d = −1.28)*
Step frequency	4.18 Hz	+4% (very large effect, *d* = 2.43)
Fight time	0.065 s	−13% (large effect, *d* = 1.80)

Interpretation: Changes in acceleration strategy and acceleration performance simultaneously occurred after week 10 of the intervention and stabilised from week 15 onwards. The consistency of technically focused sprint efforts accumulated across 18 weeks appeared sufficient to bias the athlete's movement tendencies in the direction desired. It is possible that these changes emerged through use-dependent learning (e.g. Diedrichsen et al., 2010; Mawase et al., 2017).

The figure to the right shows the change in whole-body acceleration strategy of the athlete. The data points (circles) and covariance (ellipses) depict the distribution of the athlete's individual acceleration strategy pre (black) and post (red) intervention. The size of each data point represents the sprinting performance during that sprint trial (the larger the marker, the better the sprint performance). Data points higher or lower on the vertical axis represent greater step length or step rate, respectively, whereas data points further to the left or right represent shorter relative contact time or flight time, respectively, in each sprint.

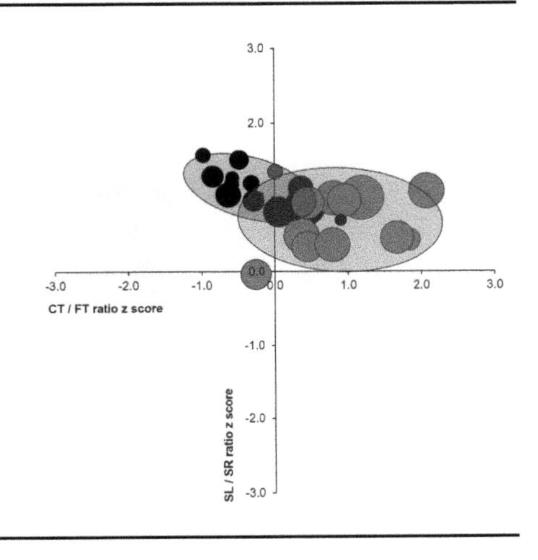

CASE STUDY 3B – HIGH-SPEED RUNNING

Intervention: Over 20 weeks, the athlete received weekly soft tissue treatment focusing on their anterior hip and lumbar musculature. They underwent a daily routine set by the physiotherapist, including lumbo-pelvic control exercises and hip and thoracic mobility work. A greater focus was placed on the development of hip extensor strength in their gym-based work, and several high-velocity drills, running tasks (e.g. wicket runs), and submaximal sprinting with a technical (front-side) focus were incorporated into their existing training, alongside maximal sprint efforts.

Outcome

Assessment	*Result*	*Change*
Maximum sprint velocity	*7.86 m/s*	*+5% (large effect, d* = 1.90)
Visual inspection during assessment	Moderate early and large lumbar extension and moderate mid-thoracic restriction	Some qualitative improvements in lumbo-pelvic control and thoracic mobility evident
Thomas test	Moderately restricted hip extension	Reduced iliopsoas and rectus femoris 'tightness'
Peak single-leg isometric hip-thrust torque (average of both sides)	4.59 Nm/kg	+25% (very large effect, $d = 3.56$)

Interpretation: The postural and movement tendencies seemed well embedded. After 18 weeks, notable changes arose during physio assessment. Changes in the athlete's maintenance of pelvic alignment, reduction in backside action, more effective front-side positions, and a more linear arm action emerged gradually after approximately ten weeks (qualitative visual inspection). Hip torque and linear sprint performance changes were notable after 4 and 15 weeks, respectively.

Notable visual changes were evident at touchdown and toe-off during high-speed running shown here pre (left) and post (right) intervention.

Curved running represents a progressive departure from linear running in terms of technique, tissue stress, and contextual application as the curve radius diminishes. Notwithstanding the prior existence of curved-running demands in athletes regular sport practice, the addition of specific volumes of high-intensity curved-running practice should ideally be preceded by targeted physical preparation. Foot and Achilles preparation for everted foot positions, hip adduction/abduction and rotation management, and trunk lateral flexion and rotational control would all represent sensible upregulated elements to programming for curved running. Following this, curved-running practices can be considered a form of constrained sprinting, and some examples are listed in Figure 9.8.

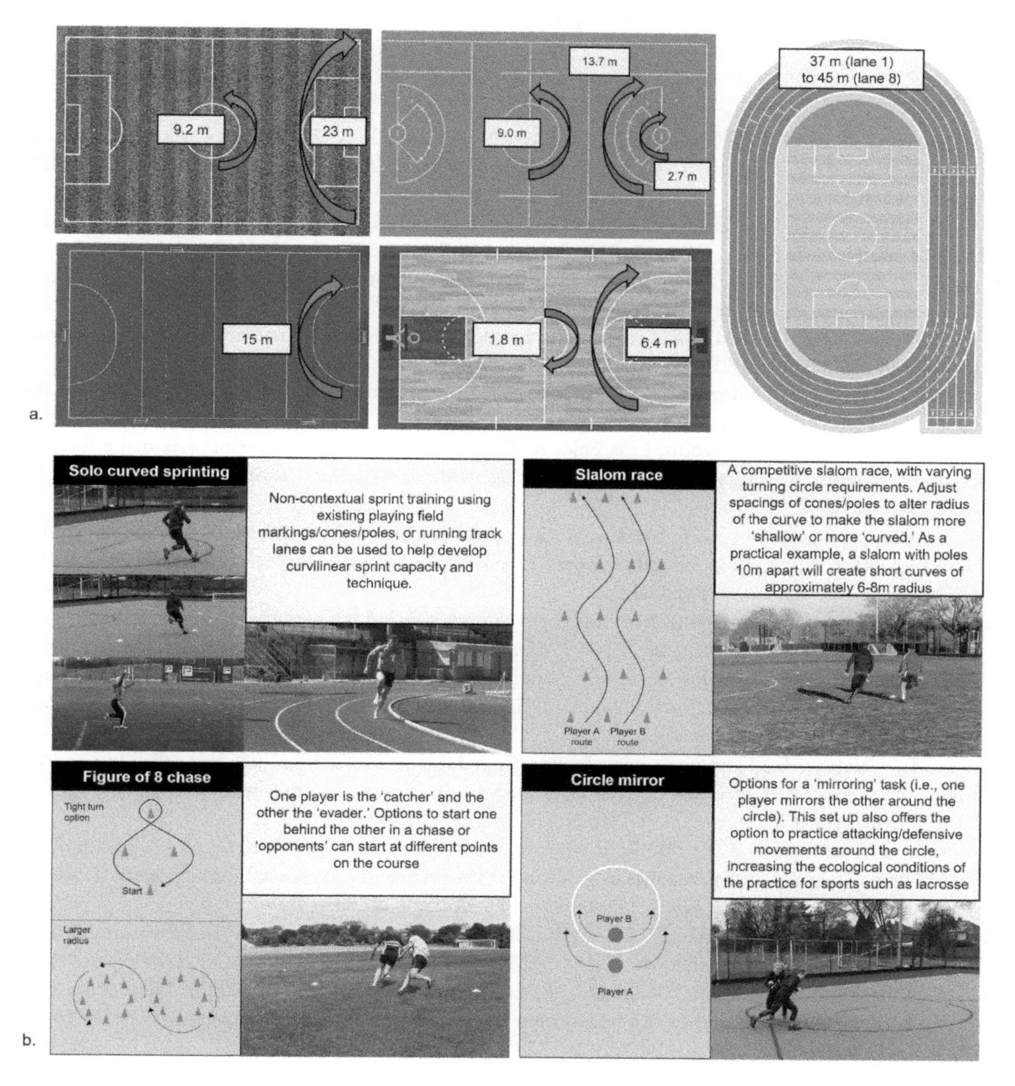

FIGURE 9.8 The radii of curved markings on different playing fields/courts and on a running track (a), with examples of curved sprint training under varying levels of game-based context.

Conclusion

Movement technique in sprinting exists in a complex relationship with performance and injury risk. Changes in physical capacity, movement history, and athletes' task perception can modify technical expression, whilst technique can provide information on developmental needs. In this chapter, a case study approach was taken to illustrate the individual nature of a process to intervene in these interrelations for the benefit of performance. Qualitative history, objective data, and coaches' interpretation were combined to understand individual needs and a flexible identification of technical improvement associated with performance change in the medium term. Longstanding performance change and performance transfer then become the objective of performance stabilisation and realistic ongoing practice.

References

Ambegaonkar, J., Caswell, A., Kenworthy, K., Cortes, N., & Caswell, S. (2014). Lumbar lordosis in female collegiate dancers and gymnasts. *Medical Problems of Performing Artists, 29*(4), 189–192. doi:10.21091/mppa.2014.4039

Bjork, R. (1970). Positive forgetting: The noninterference of items intentionally forgotten. *Journal of Verbal Learning and Verbal Behavior, 9*(3), 255–268. doi:10.1016/S0022-5371(70)80059-7

Chang, Y., & Kram, R. (2007). Limitations to maximum running speed on flat curves. *Journal of Experimental Biology, 210*(6), 971–982. doi:10.1242/jeb.02728

Chelly, M. S., & Denis, C. (2001). *Leg power and hopping stiffness: Relationship with sprint running performance.* doi:10.1097/00005768-200102000-00024

Churchill, S., Salo, A., & Trewartha, G. (2015). The effect of the bend on technique and performance during maximal effort sprinting. *Sports Biomechanics, 14*(1), 106–121. doi:10.1080/14763141.2015.1024717

Churchill, S., Trewartha, G., Bezodis, I., & Salo, A. (2016). Force production during maximal effort bend sprinting: Theory vs reality. *Scandinavian Journal of Medicine & Science in Sports, 26*(10), 1171–1179. doi:10.1111/sms.12559

Clark, K., Rieger, R., Bruno, R., & Stearne, D. (2019). The national football league combine 40-yd dash: How important is maximum velocity? *Journal of Strength and Conditioning Research, 33*(6), 1542–1550. doi:10.1519/JSC.0000000000002081

Clark, K. P., & Weyand, P. G. (2014). Are running speeds maximized with simple-spring stance mechanics? *Journal of Applied Physiology (Bethesda, Md.: 1985), 117*(6), 604. doi:10.1152/japplphysiol.00174.2014

Colyer, S., Nagahara, R., & Salo, A. (2018). Kinetic demands of sprinting shift across the acceleration phase: Novel analysis of entire force waveforms. *Scandinavian Journal of Medicine & Science in Sports, 28*(7), 1784–1792. doi:10.1111/sms.13093

Comyns, T., Flanagan, E., Fleming, S., Fitzgerald, E., & Harper, D. (2019). Inter-day reliability and usefulness of reactive strength index derived from two maximal rebound jump tests. *International Journal of Sports Physiology and Performance*, 1–17. doi:10.1123/ijspp.2018-0829

Cunningham, D. J., West, D. J., Owen, N. J., Shearer, D. A., Finn, C. V., Bracken, R. M., . . . Kilduff, L. P. (2013). Strength and power predictors of sprinting performance in professional rugby players. *The Journal of Sports Medicine and Physical Fitness, 53*(2), 105–111. doi:R40133635 [pii]

Diedrichsen, J., White, O., Newman, D., & Lally, N. (2010). Use-dependent and error-based learning of motor behaviors. *The Journal of Neuroscience, 30*(15), 5159–5166. doi:10.1523/JNEUROSCI.5406-09.2010

Fílter, A., Olivares, J., Santalla, A., Nakamura, F., Loturco, I., & Requena, B. (2020). New curve sprint test for soccer players: Reliability and relationship with linear sprint. *Journal of Sports Sciences, 38*(11–12), 1320–1325. doi:10.1080/02640414.2019.1677391

Goodwin, J., & Bull, A. M. (2021). Novel assessment of isometric hip extensor function: Reliability, joint angle sensitivity, and concurrent validity. *Journal of Strength and Conditioning Research, Publish Ahead of Print.* doi:10.1519/JSC.0000000000004012

Goodwin, J., & Cleather, D. (2016). The biomechanical principles underpinning strength and conditioning. In *Strength and conditioning for sports performance* (pp. 78–108). Routledge. doi:10.4324/9780203852286-16

Hanin, Y., Korjus, T., Jouste, P., & Baxter, P. (2002). Rapid technique correction using old way/new way: Two case studies with Olympic athletes. *The Sport Psychologist, 16*(1), 79–99. doi:10.1123/tsp.16.1.79

Hof, A. L. (1996). Scaling gait data to body size. *Gait & Posture, 4*(3), 222–223. doi:10.1016/0966-6362(95)01057-2

Homs, A., Dupeyron, A., & Torre, K. (2022). Relationship between gait complexity and pain attention in chronic low back pain. *Pain (Amsterdam), 163*(1), e31-e39. doi:10.1097/j.pain.0000000000002303

Judson, L., Churchill, S., Barnes, A., Stone, J., Brookes, I., & Wheat, J. (2020). Kinematic modifications of the lower limb during the acceleration phase of bend sprinting. *Journal of Sports Sciences, 38*(3), 336–342. doi:10.1080/02640414.2019.1699006

Kobal, R., Freitas, T., Fílter, A., Requena, B., Barroso, R., Rossetti, M., . . . Loturco, I. (2021). Curve sprint in elite female soccer players: Relationship with linear sprint and jump performance. *International Journal of Environmental Research and Public Health, 18*(5), 2306. doi:10.3390/ijerph18052306

Kugler, F., & Janshen, L. (2010). Body position determines propulsive forces in accelerated sprinting. *Journal of Biomechanics, 43*, 343–348.

Lahti, J., Huuhka, T., Romero, V., Bezodis, I., Morin, J., & Häkkinen, K. (2020). Changes in sprint performance and sagittal plane kinematics after heavy resisted sprint training in professional soccer players. *PeerJ, 8*, e10507. doi:10.7717/peerj.10507

Lockie, R., Murphy, A., Callaghan, S., & Jeffriess, M. (2014). Effects of sprint and plyometrics training on field sport acceleration technique. *Journal of Strength and Conditioning Research, 28*(7), 1790–1801. doi:10.1519/JSC.0000000000000297 [doi]

Lockie, R., Murphy, A., Schultz, A., Knight, T., & Janse de Jonge, X. (2012). The effects of different speed training protocols on sprint acceleration kinematics and muscle strength and power in field sport athletes. *Journal of Strength and Conditioning Research, 26*(6), 1539–1550. doi:10.1519/JSC.0b013e318234e8a0

Luo, G., & Stefanyshyn, D. (2012). Ankle moment generation and maximum-effort curved sprinting performance. *Journal of Biomechanics, 45*(16), 2763–2768. doi:10.1016/j.jbiomech.2012.09.010

Mann, R., & Murphy, A. (2015). *The mechanics of sprinting and hurdling*. Las Vegas: CreateSpace.

Mawase, F., Uehara, S., Bastian, A., & Celnik, P. (2017). Motor learning enhances use-dependent plasticity. *The Journal of Neuroscience, 37*(10), 2673–2685. doi:10.1523/JNEUROSCI.3303-16.2017

Mendez-Villanueva, A., Buchheit, M., Kuitunen, S., Douglas, A., Peltola, E., & Bourdon, P. (2011). Age-related differences in acceleration, maximum running speed, and repeated-sprint performance in young soccer players. *Journal of Sports Sciences, 29*(5), 477–484. doi:10.1080/02640414.2010.536248

Milanese, C., Facci, G., Cesari, P., & Zancanaro, C. (2008). "Amplification of error": A rapidly effective method for motor performance improvement. *The Sport Psychologist, 22*(2), 164–174. doi:10.1123/tsp.22.2.164

Morin, J., Slawinski, J., Dorel, S., de villareal, E. S., Couturier, A., Samozino, P., . . . Rabita, G. (2015). Acceleration capability in elite sprinters and ground impulse: Push more, brake less? *Journal of Biomechanics, 48*(12), 3149–3154. doi:10.1016/j.jbiomech.2015.07.009

Murphy, A., Lockie, R., & Coutts, A. (2003). Kinematic determinants of early acceleration in field sport athletes. *Journal of Sports Science & Medicine, 2*(4), 144–150.

Newell, K. (1986). Constraints on the development of coordination. In Wade, M., & Whiting, H. (Ed.), *Motor development in children: Aspects of coordination* (pp. 341–361). Amsterdam: Martinus Nijhoff Publishers.

Rabita, G., Dorel, S., Slawinski, J., Saez-de-Villarreal, E., Couturier, A., Samozino, P., & Morin, J. B. (2015). Sprint mechanics in world-class athletes: A new insight into the limits of human locomotion. *Scandinavian Journal of Medicine & Science in Sports, 25*(5), 583–594. doi:10.1111/sms.12389

Salo, A., Bezodis, I., Batterham, A., & Kerwin, D. (2011). Elite sprinting: Are athletes individually step-frequency or step-length reliant? *Medicine and Science in Sports and Exercise, 43*(6), 1055. doi:10.1249/MSS.0b013e318201f6f8

Samozino, P., Edouard, P., Sangnier, S., Brughelli, M., Gimenez, P., & Morin, J. (2013). Force-velocity profile: Imbalance determination and effect on lower limb ballistic performance. *International Journal of Sports Medicine, 35*(6), 505–510. doi:10.1055/s-0033-1354382

Spinks, C., Murphy, A., Spinks, W., & Lockie, R. (2007). The effects of resisted sprint training on acceleration performance and kinematics in soccer, rugby union, and Australian football players. *Journal of Strength and Conditioning Research, 21*(1), 77–85. doi:R-18145 [pii]

Taboga, P., Kram, R., & Grabowski, A. M. (2016). Maximum-speed curve-running biomechanics of sprinters with and without unilateral leg amputations. *Journal of Experimental Biology, 219*(Pt 6), 851–858. doi:10.1242/jeb.133488

Van Hooren, B., Meijer, K., & Mccrum, C. (2019). Attractive gait training: Applying dynamical systems theory to the improvement of locomotor performance across the lifespan. *Frontiers in Physiology, 9*, 1–5. doi:10.3389/fphys.2018.01934

von Lieres Und Wilkau, H, Bezodis, N., Morin, J. B., Irwin, G., Simpson, S., & Bezodis, I. (2020). The importance of duration and magnitude of force application to sprint performance during the initial acceleration, transition and maximal velocity phases. *Journal of Sports Sciences, 38*(20), 2359–2366. doi:10.1080/02640414.2020.1785193

Walker, J., Bissas, A., Paradisis, G., Hanley, B., Tucker, C., Jongerius, N., . . . Bezodis, I. N. (2021). Kinematic factors associated with start performance in world-class male sprinters. *Journal of Biomechanics, 124*, 110554. doi:10.1016/j.jbiomech.2021.110554

Weyand, P. G., Sternlight, D. B., Bellizzi, M. J., & Wright, S. (2000). Faster top running speeds are achieved with greater ground forces not more rapid leg movements. *Journal of Applied Physiology, 89*(5), 1991–1999.

Wild, J. (2022). *Biomechanics and motor control of early acceleration: Enhancing the initial sprint performance of professional rugby union backs*, PhD thesis, University of Surrey.

Wild, J., Bezodis, N., Blagrove, R., & Bezodis, I. (2011). A biomechanical comparison of accelerative and maximum velocity sprinting: Specific strength training considerations. *Professional Strength and Conditioning Journal, 21*, 23–36.

Wild, J., Bezodis, I., North, J., & Bezodis, N. (2018). Differences in step characteristics and linear kinematics between rugby players and sprinters during initial sprint acceleration. *European Journal of Sport Science, 18*(10), 1327–1337. doi:10.1080/17461391.2018.1490459 [doi]

Wild, J., Bezodis, I., North, J., & Bezodis, N. (2022). Characterising initial sprint acceleration strategies using a whole-body kinematics approach. *Journal of Sports Sciences, 40*(2), 203–214. doi:10.1080/02640414.2021.1985759

10

DEVELOPING CHANGE OF DIRECTION AND AGILITY TECHNIQUE AND MOVEMENT SOLUTIONS

Thomas Dos'Santos and Paul A. Jones

Introduction

Agility actions, such as side-steps, shuffle-steps, crossover cutting, split-steps, spins, sharp turns, and decelerations are important manoeuvres in multidirectional sports, often linked with decisive, match-winning moments (Dos'Santos, McBurnie et al., 2022; Martínez-Hernández et al., 2022; Zahidi & Ismail, 2018). Generally, the aims of these actions are to (1) evade and create separation from an opponent(s) for attacking purposes (i.e. usually penetrating defensive lines to gain territorial advantage); (2) reduce space, channel opposition players, and make important blocks, tackles, or interceptions for defensive purposes (i.e. to limit territory loss and regaining possession); (3) generate high exit velocities and momentums; or (4) facilitate a sharp redirection (Dos'Santos, McBurnie et al., 2022; Young et al., 2022). However, importantly, these actions are also inciting movements associated with lower-limb injury (i.e. ACL, adductor and hamstring strains, ankle sprains, and patellofemoral pain) (Dos'Santos, McBurnie et al., 2022) due to the propensity to generate potentially hazardous mechanical loads, which can result in tissue failure (Beaulieu et al., 2021; Kalkhoven et al., 2021). Given the importance of agility actions for sports performance and potential injury risk, in this chapter, the importance of technique development for performance enhancement and injury risk mitigation will be discussed, in addition to presenting an agility development framework (ADF) to best mediate the performance-injury risk conflict in the field.

A plethora of different agility actions are available, which have their own unique technical characteristics, advantages, and applications. These are summarised in Table 4.1, and the readers are encouraged to read (Dos'Santos, McBurnie et al., 2022) for a comprehensive overview of these actions. Briefly, however, due to the random, chaotic, and unpredictable nature of most multidirectional sports, movement adaptability (i.e. the ability to produce and coordinate an appropriate ratio of stable and unstable movement behaviours when required) (Otte et al., 2019) and avoiding a unidimensional approach (i.e. limited movement skills and movement solutions) has been recommended when preparing athletes for sports performance (Dos'Santos, McBurnie et al., 2022), with developing athletes' movement literacy to afford them a range of movement solutions to solve the potential problems they encounter in sport integral (Dos'Santos et al.,

DOI: 10.4324/9781003267881-12

2019b; McBurnie et al., 2022; Myszka, 2018). Strategies to develop athletes' movement solutions through the ADF will be discussed later.

The Importance of Technique in Agility Development

Agility, defined as 'a rapid, accurate whole-body movement with a change of direction (COD), velocity, or movement pattern in response to a stimulus' (Jones & Nimphius, 2018; Young & Farrow, 2006) is a highly important component of fitness to develop in team-sport players, importantly linking to the technical and tactical requirements associated with sport (Jeffreys, 2010; Young et al., 2022). Agility movements are a skill (Myszka, 2018), and they involve perception-action coupling (i.e. recognising and processing information to then execute an accurate motor response to achieve an outcome) in response to dynamic, constantly changing scenarios that occur within the game (Dos'Santos, McBurnie et al., 2022; Myszka, 2018; Young et al., 2022). While the determinants of agility are multifactorial (Young et al., 2022), it is underpinned by the interaction of technique (i.e. the relative position and orientation of body segments when performing a task effectively), mechanical (i.e. impulsive capabilities), physical (i.e. strength and speed capabilities) and perceptual-cognitive (i.e. rapid and accurate decision-making) factors (DeWeese & Nimphius, 2016; Nimphius, 2017). In theory, enhancing one of previously mentioned qualities could be developed in isolation to enhance agility, although a mixed-methods approach has been recently advocated to better optimise agility performance (Dos'Santos, McBurnie et al., 2022) and discussed in Chapters 4 and 8. Nonetheless, given the roles of sports science, medicine, and conditioning staff to prepare athletes for the demands of sport, to enhance performance and mitigate injury risk, developing an athlete's technique and mechanical abilities to perform the action (i.e. movement skill and quality) in a rapid, controllable, and efficient manner is an integral component for improving agility performance and mitigating injury risk (Dos'Santos, McBurnie et al., 2022; Myszka, 2018). Practitioners have a duty of care not only to enhances their athletes' physical capacity, but it could be argued what separates the exceptional from the average practitioners is the appreciation and ability to develop athlete's technique by exploring motor control, motor skill, and skill acquisition principles.

Technique, which is defined as 'the relative position and orientation of body segments as they change during the performance of a sport task to perform that task effectively' (Bober et al., 1981; Lees, 2002), is a crucial component for successful agility performance (Dos'Santos, McBurnie et al., 2022; Young et al., 2022). Specifically, the way that an athlete technically executes the movement (i.e. technical characteristics and postures) to optimise and facilitate effective braking, propulsion, and deflection of the centre of mass (COM) is integral for optimising team-sport performance (i.e. wide lateral foot placement, firm base of support [BOS], rapid triple extension, trunk control), with a plethora of literature highlighting key technical determinants of side-step cutting (Dos'Santos et al., 2019b; Dos'Santos, Thomas, McBurnie, Comfort, et al., 2021a; McBurnie, Dos'Santos, et al., 2021) and turning performance (Dos'Santos, McBurnie et al., 2022; Dos'Santos et al., 2020; Freitas et al., 2021). However, from an injury-risk perspective, sub-optimal technique (i.e. poor movement quality, biomechanical and neuromuscular control deficits such as knee valgus, lateral trunk flexion) is a critical factor which can amplify potentially hazardous mechanical loading, which can result in tissue injury (such as ACL injury) (Donelon et al., 2020; Dos'Santos, Thomas, McBurnie, Donelon, et al., 2021; Fox, 2018). Importantly, however, researchers have shown that in as little as six weeks, technique modification training can improve cutting movement quality and performance times (Dos'Santos et al., 2019a); improve cutting ground contact times, exit velocities, and propulsive forces and lower-limb kinematics (Dos'Santos, Thomas, Comfort, et al., 2021b); reduce cutting knee joint loads (Dempsey et al., 2009; Dos'Santos, Thomas, Comfort, et al., 2021a); improve turning performance (Dos'Santos, Thomas, McBurnie, Comfort, et al., 2021b; Jones et al., 2015); and reduce knee joint loads (Jones et al., 2015). However, currently, it is unknown if longer or shorter interventions could be equally or more effective, and it is unknown how long the technical modifications can be maintained for (Dos'Santos et al., 2019c). Thus, further research is necessary to examine the effect of different training dosages (e.g. volume, frequency, and duration) with follow-up retention testing to better understand agility and technique development training.

A *'one size fits all' approach* is unlikely to exist for all attacking agility actions, with athletes' optimal technique influenced by contextual factors, such as intended movement, angle of directional change (if applicable), entry velocity, sporting scenario, and contextual demands, in addition to unique factors related to the athlete, such as training age, mobility, physical capacity, and anthropometrics (Dos'Santos et al., 2019b; Dos'Santos et al., 2018; McBurnie & Dos'Santos, 2022; Nimphius, 2017; Rayner et al., 2022). Movement variability (i.e. increased unpredictability and multidimensionality) and a dynamic coordinative approach may provide an athlete with greater flexibility and adaptability to environmental constraints and perturbations, potentially resulting in a greater capacity for task execution (Hamill et al., 2012; Preatoni et al., 2013). Furthermore, although an optimal zone of movement variability will likely exist (e.g. inverted U – 'Goldilocks effect') (Hamill et al., 2012; Herrington et al., 2018), in the context of injury risk mitigation, movement and coordinative variability (i.e. within-skill variability) (Otte et al., 2019) may enable a more variable distribution of loading and stresses across the different joints and tissues, potentially reducing the cumulative loading on internal structures (Bartlett et al., 2007; Hamill et al., 1999; Hamill et al., 2012). Additionally, creating athletes who possess adaptable movement strategies and multiple movement solutions (i.e. between-skill variability) (Otte et al., 2019) to solve the problems they encounter during the unpredictable and chaotic nature of multidirectional invasion sports will therefore be imperative from both performance and injury risk mitigation perspectives (Dos'Santos et al., 2019b; McBurnie & Dos'Santos, 2022; Orangi et al., 2021). As such, in the case of most multidirectional sports and developing general athleticism and movement literacy, the underlying agility philosophy is to create fast, robust, effective 360° athletes who are equally proficient at changing direction rapidly and controllably from both left and right limbs, across a range of velocities (i.e. low, moderate, and high velocities), with an arsenal of movement solutions (i.e. well-developed agility movement literacy) to perform a variety of agility actions within the contextual demands of the sport (Dos'Santos, McBurnie et al., 2022; McBurnie & Dos'Santos, 2022). This will ensure that athletes can meet the physical demands of match play, resulting in a more skilful and adaptable performer, while potentially mitigating injury risk.

A perfect agility technique model is unlikely to exist, as agility techniques will differ across individuals of different anthropometrics, mobility, physical capacity, perceptual-cognitive ability, skill level, and training history (Dos'Santos et al., 2019b; Nimphius, 2017). However, it cannot be disputed there are key, fundamental technique characteristics which conform to biomechanical and movement principles that can optimise performance and mitigate injury risk and ultimately facilitate rapid, controllable, and effective movement, which are discussed in Chapter 4 (Dos'Santos, McBurnie et al., 2022; Jones et al., 2021; Lees, 2002). Technical models for the different attacking movements are presented in a previously published article (Dos'Santos, McBurnie et al., 2022); thus, the premise of the next section is how to construct an ADF, to provide a representative learning environment with recommendations for instruction and feedback to develop athletes' multidirectional speed technique.

Agility Training Philosophy and Development Framework

The overarching aim of the *agility development framework (ADF)* should be to create athletes who possess adaptable movement strategies and multiple movement solutions to solve the problems they encounter during the unpredictable and chaotic nature of multidirectional sports (Dos'Santos et al., 2019b; McBurnie & Dos'Santos, 2022). Skill training is where athletes are able to 'seek, explore, discover, assemble, and stabilise the coordination of movement patterns' (Davids et al., 2008). Thus, the ADF (Figure 10.1), to develop game-related movement skill, focuses on three phases (mesocycles) adapted from previous work (DeWeese & Nimphius, 2016; Dos'Santos et al., 2019d; Jones et al., 2015; Nimphius, 2017), and a similar approach to the Periodisation of Skill Training Framework (PoST) (Otte et al., 2019), Taberner et al. (2019) 'control to chaos' continuum approach, and the Skill Acquisition Periodisation Framework (Farrow & Robertson, 2017): (1) technique acquisition, (2) technique retention and integrity, and (3) movement solutions. Initially, this approach (phase 1) aims to develop pre-planned COD and deceleration technique and develop the athlete's movement literacy (i.e. between-skill variability) in a controlled environment, before exposing the athletes to higher intensity, task complexity and mechanical loading, reinforcing optimal mechanics and exploring 'repetition without repetition' and movement adaptability with the introduction of stimulus and information (low task complexity) (phase 2). Finally, this leads to increases in task complexity with multiple stimuli (and sports-specific information), application in open, unanticipated, and sports-specific activities with representative learning environments to improve the athlete's ability to select appropriate movement solutions under differing task and constraints (perceptual-motor ability) for emergent behaviours and solutions to emerge (McCosker et al., 2019).

Prior to applying the ADF model, practitioners are encouraged to conduct a needs analysis for the sport and perform qualitative and quantitative assessments of athletes' COD speed (see Chapter 6), deceleration (see Chapters 5 and 6), and agility (see Chapter 6), while also creating a strength/power diagnostic profile (see Chapter 7) for the athlete and taking into account the athletes' training and injury history before individualising the programme based on the ADF presented (Dos'Santos et al., 2019b). For instance, the Cutting Movement Assessment Score (Dos'Santos, Thomas, McBurnie, Donelon, et al., 2021), a qualitative screening tool, could be used to evaluate athlete's cutting technique during pre-planned and unplanned cutting tasks to potentially identify technique deficits, which could help inform technique modification training and the specific verbal cues to modify technique (Donelon et al., 2020; Dos'Santos, Thomas, McBurnie, Donelon, et al., 2021). Specific attention should also be placed on sporting and gameplay demands: (1) identify the common actions and MDS characteristics (e.g. typical angles, entry and exit speeds, frequency) performed in the sport and how they may be combined during match play; (2) identify the important technique characteristics of these actions to guide technique development; (3) examine the context by which the actions are performed in the sport (i.e. 'offensive/attacking' or 'defensive' situations); and (4) identify the type of visual (and other stimuli/information) stimuli athletes respond to (e.g. improve ability to use advanced cue utilisation in 1 vs 1 [and other] situations). Collectively, this information can then be used to identify strengths and deficiencies to subsequently better inform future training prescription for that athlete in context of the sporting demands (Nimphius, 2014, 2017).

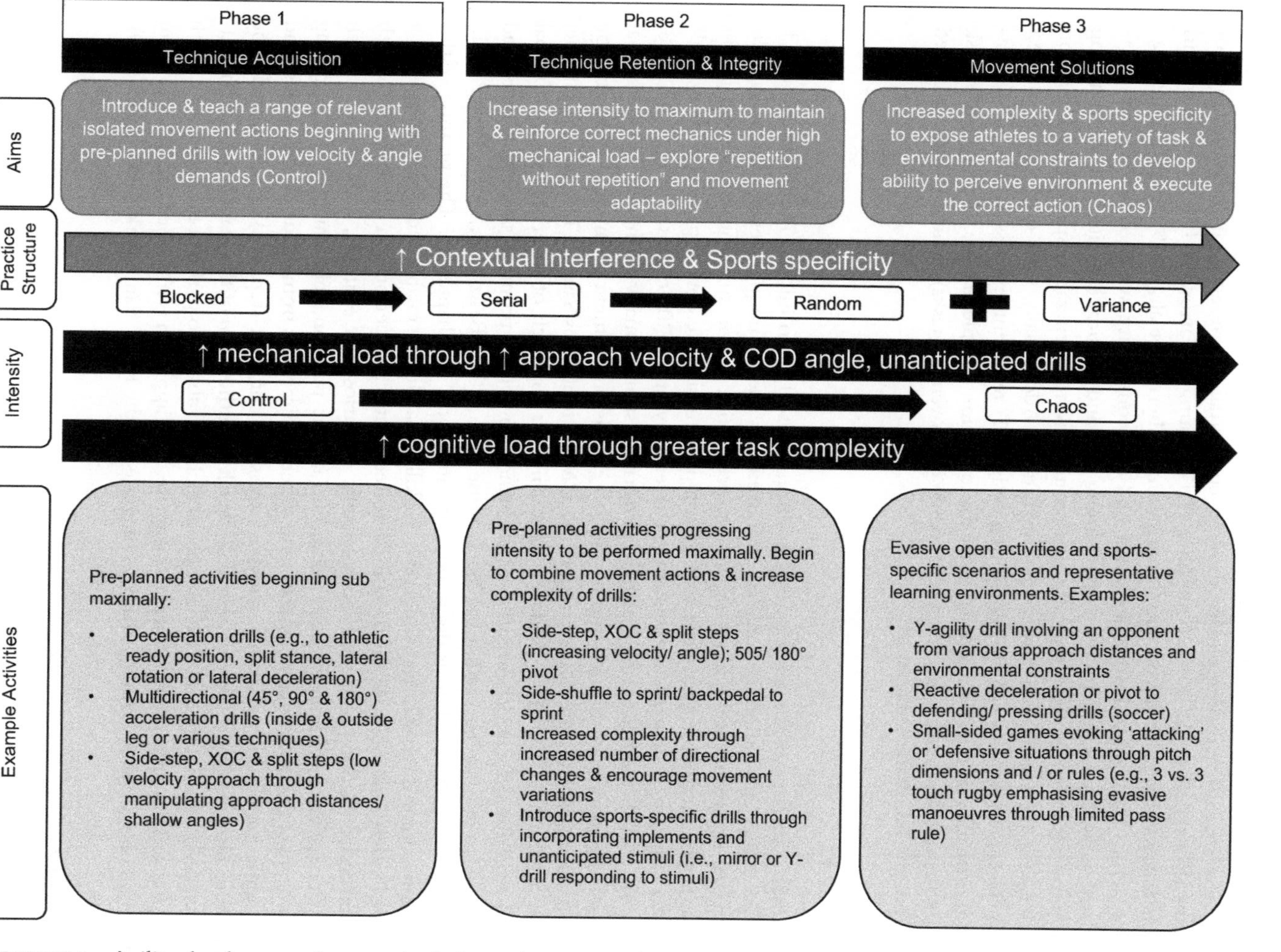

FIGURE 10.1 Agility development framework. A three-phase approach to developing agility and movement solutions: COD: change of directions; XOC: Crossover cut.

The three phases of the ADF shift from block to serial to random (with variance) practice structure (Farrow & Robertson, 2017; Nimphius, 2017), with progressive increases in intensity (via approach velocity and COD angle) (Dos'Santos et al., 2018), specificity (introduction of sport-specific stimuli), task complexity through contextual interference, and manipulation of constraints (Bourgeois et al., 2017; Nimphius, 2017; Young & Farrow, 2013). In addition, this approach follows the 'control to chaos' continuum (Taberner et al., 2019), with a conservative approach to mechanical loading exposure and task complexity, which is particularly pertinent when working with athletes with low training ages and physical capacity, athletes returning to play from rehabilitation, and typically transitioning from a general to specific periodisation approaches (e.g. off-season, pre-season to competition). Additionally, Otte et al. (2019) suggest three key factors to be aware of in skill training design: (1) representativeness of training, (2) stability and instability in training, and (3) level of information complexity (i.e. as managed by task constraint manipulations and the practice schedule of movement tasks), which will be discussed throughout the following paragraphs.

ADF: Phase 1

The primary objective of the technique acquisition (phase 1) is to initially introduce and coach the various agility and multidirectional speed movements and techniques, reinforcing and modifying optimal mechanics using block-practice structure (i.e. performing consecutive repetitions of the same task) and closed activities that are low in intensity (i.e. low approach velocity, shallow COD angle) in a controlled environment (Dempsey et al., 2009; Dos'Santos et al., 2018; Jones et al., 2015). Activities are generally performed submaximally with one or two verbal cues which are externally directed and focused to establish movement technique, which can be informed via qualitative screening through the CMAS tool (Dos'Santos, Thomas, McBurnie, Donelon, et al., 2021). There is evidence indicating this approach of externally focused verbal cues and attentional focus can improve performance outcomes, promote safer mechanics, and improve skill acquisition and retention (Benjaminse et al., 2015; Benz et al., 2016; Porter et al., 2010; Winkelman, 2018). This is discussed in greater detail in Chapter 11. The premise of this phase is movement diversification and between-skill variability to enable the athlete to possess a breadth of movement solutions for the athlete to recall later and perform in latter phases, which will entail more chaotic, game-like sports-specific scenarios. For example, activities that teach athletes to decelerate to different body positions (athletic position, split stance, etc.), practising different deceleration strategies, accelerating to different directions from inside or outside leg, and teaching different cutting variations (side-step, crossover cut, split-step, etc.) are advocated. The overarching aim is to develop movement skill, developing the *action* of the perceptual-action coupling associated with agility, and mechanical and technical ability to perform the movement, with deliberate practice a prominent feature of this phase. This approach is modelled on the movement stability and coordination training phases as suggested in the PoST framework (Otte et al., 2019).

ADF: Phase 2

Once the movement pattern, technique, and coordination ability for each isolated action has been mastered (i.e. movement stability), phase 2 activities can be progressed by manipulating the intensity (i.e. physical or cognitive load) to reinforce movement patterns (retention) and challenge technique integrity under greater mechanical load (Dos'Santos et al., 2019b). Over time, intensity is increased via increases in approach velocity and COD angle (Bourgeois et al., 2017; Dos'Santos et al., 2018; Nimphius, 2017), with the primary objective of the technique retention and integrity phase (phase 2) to maintain optimal technique and effective mechanics under higher mechanical loading. The intensity of drills can be manipulated by increasing approach speed through increasing distance, changing COD angle, and combining movements to involve multiple directional changes or actions (sprint, side-shuffle, backpedal, drop-step, etc.) as suggested by Jeffreys (2010), and the use of manoeuvrability drills could be effective to increase volume and exposure to high-intensity COD and agility actions to increase task complexity. In accordance to 'repetition without repetition' (Myszka, 2018) and to create movement adaptability and a flexible coordinative approach (i.e. within-skill variability and movement instability), and also in accordance with skill adaptability training in the PoST framework (Otte et al., 2019), serial and random practice structure is more prevalent, and athletes are encouraged to explore movement solutions by manipulating technical characteristics subtly, such as braking strategy, stride placement and adjustment, lower-limb flexion, body lean, and foot placement. In addition, subtle variations in transitional (rolling, backpedal, lateral shuffle, etc) and initiation (drop-step, split-step, inside/outside leg, etc.) movements (Jeffreys, 2010) and altering constraints, such as space, distance, angle of run, and starting position, are all to encourage 'repetition without repetition' and variation (Spiteri et al., 2018).

Simple unanticipated drills could also be incorporated (e.g. visual/audio signals) to increase the cognitive and physical load, task complexity, with the addition of one stimulus or piece of information to process, before gradually increasing complexity and information in phase 3 (Farrow & Robertson, 2017; Otte et al., 2019; Young & Farrow, 2013). These activities, however, do not enhance sport-specific agility, as the athlete does not have to evaluate environmental stimuli or sport-specific information before processing and executing the most appropriate movement action (Young & Farrow, 2013). Generic stimuli (e.g. arrow or light), however, have been shown to elicit greater knee joint loads (Lee et al., 2013; Lee et al., 2017), thus reducing the time or space available for decisions and preparatory postural adjustments and appropriate muscle coordination strategies, which increase joint loading and challenges technique integrity (Hughes & Dai, 2021). Additionally, this approach of using generic stimuli from a screening perspective can be viewed as an indicator of an athlete's robustness and technique integrity before focusing a greater proportion of time towards chaotic sports-specific activities in phase 3.

ADF: Phase 3

Finally, the movement solutions phase (phase 3) is the most complex (i.e. mechanically and cognitively), with the use of open drills utilising sports-specific scenarios, stimuli, and implements (if applicable) (Nimphius, 2017; Young & Farrow, 2013). In this phase, there is progressive increases in stimuli and information (i.e. progressive increases in number of attackers/defenders), task complexity, gradually promoting a more chaotic and random environment typically associated with multidirectional sports (Taberner et al., 2019). This phase encourages athletes to improve their adaptability to tolerate unforeseen circumstances in the field; thus, activities now become unanticipated and more representative of a sport-specific environment (Young & Farrow, 2013). In order to understand the athletes' responses to the challenging environments and information complexity, the use of internal load measures, such as 'rating of perceived challenges' (Hendricks et al., 2019), could be used to receive feedback from the athletes regarding complexity and knowledge of performance. In addition, external measures of exercise volume/load and indicators of performance outcomes, such as evasion success, blocks, and interceptions, can be further used to stimulate feedback and conversations with athletes regarding their agility performance (Otte et al., 2020) (see Chapter 15).

The primary focus of this phase is to provide a random environment for athletes to identify and process sport-specific information before retrieving, selecting, and executing the different agility action and manoeuvres, under high cognitive load and constraints (i.e. time, environment, rule adjustment), to achieve a performance outcome and improve overall skill retention and transfer (Farrow & Robertson, 2017; Nimphius, 2017; Young & Farrow, 2013). This approach promotes movement degeneracy, where there is a plethora of options available to achieve the performance outcome, and thus, athletes are encouraged to explore these performance and movement solutions (Myszka, 2018; Otte et al., 2019; Seifert & Davids, 2017), coinciding with the team-based and performance stability training methods of the PoST framework (Otte et al., 2019).

It is expected that athletes will concurrently develop their perceptual-cognitive speed, making faster and more accurate decisions, and learning to execute the appropriate motor action from the variations in which they have taught in phases 1 and 2 (Young et al., 2022). Additionally, it is important here that the stimuli and information presented to athletes in these activities closely resemble those within the match play/competition in order for athletes to develop familiarity between the stimuli and required action (i.e. *perception-action coupling)* (Spiteri et al., 2018). Practitioners during this phase are encouraged to seek the advice and where possible work collaboratively with motor skill, motor control, and/or skill acquisition experts, in addition to the skills coach, to best design representative learning environments and skill development frameworks (Dos'Santos, McBurnie et al., 2022; Otte et al., 2019).

Representative task design and learning environments are strongly advocated during phase 3 (Otte et al., 2019; Seifert & Davids, 2017), while manipulating constraints (i.e. demands of the conditions placed on emergent actions [McCosker et al., 2019]) and factors related to the task, environment, and organism, to facilitate new behaviours and movement solutions to emerge. Representative learning environments (i.e. sport-specific) permit learners with specific perception-action coupling, enabling them to be better perceptually accustomed to critical information sources (Otte et al., 2019; Seifert & Davids, 2017). Gibson (1979) describes the process as 'learning to search for, and detect, information in an environment that individuals learn to exploit for solving (i.e. 'navigating') performance-related problems, situated as fields (regions) within an evolving landscape'. Hence, an emphasis is placed on discovery learning during phase 3, with the practitioners role shifting primarily to 'facilitator' (Myszka, 2018; Otte et al., 2019). Consequently, facilitating representative learning environments, manipulating constraints, and varying the agility sports-specific activities, combined with discovery learning for movement solutions to emerge, will increase athletes' exposure and develop new knowledge of situations and memory recall (Young et al., 2022), enabling them to develop visual scanning and pattern recognition, thus improving the athletes ability to 'read and react'/anticipate and overall perceptual-cognitive speed (Young et al., 2022).

Small-sided games (SSGs) have the potential to enhance agility (i.e. improve the ability to 'read and react') (Paul et al., 2016; Young et al., 2022) and are recommended strategies to provide a conditioning stimulus, with simultaneous technical and tactical development in a representative and potentially chaotic environment (Young et al., 2022). However, this might be more through expanding sport experience, as it may not be feasible during SSGs to reinforce aspects of technique or highlight visual cues to respond to with athletes, when the aim of SSGs is to condition athletes. Additionally, although effective, some challenges associated with designing and implementing SSGs and chaotic, unpredictable sports-specific agility activities and scenarios during phase 3 are (1) prescribing and regulating the number of high-intensity multidirectional speed actions from an exercise volume/training load perspective; (2) some athletes defaulting to their dominant movement patterns (i.e. type of agility action or limb preference) and thus not exploring movement solutions and not developing between-skill variability; and (3) ensuring that all athletes are actively engaged and challenged, and obtaining an equal stimuli/load for all participants/across directions can also be challenging.

Researchers have highlighted that a large proportion of agility actions during match play are performed at submaximal intensities in sports such as soccer (Dos'Santos, Cowling et al., 2022) and Australia rules football (Rayner et al., 2022). As such, practitioners are encouraged to still include a small proportion of pre-planned activities within phase 3 to avoid detraining and to ensure the athletes are exposed to tolerable, high mechanical loads between limbs (and to reinforce technique) during high-intensity actions (i.e. decelerations/COD) that they may not be receiving during match play or training (McBurnie, Harper, et al., 2021). A similar approach has been advocated for high-speed sprint weekly exposures where athletes may receive 'top-ups' to mitigate hamstring strain injury risk (Malone et al., 2017; McBurnie et al., 2022). This maintenance dose will ensure that athletes are still physically prepared to meet the requirements associated with the chaotic demands of sport and to maintain tissue homeostasis (Dos'Santos, McBurnie et al., 2022; Edwards, 2018; McBurnie, Harper, et al., 2021). Pre-planned activities can simply be integrated and progressed appropriately throughout a warm-up prior to the sports-specific, open activities to ensure the athletes are sufficiently prepared for these tasks, while receiving a targeted, high-intensity stimulus for maintenance purposes.

ADF: Programming and Session Plans

The recommended phases are not to be performed exclusively but are the primary focus for that phase (i.e. largest proportion of training volume/percentage dedicated) (Nimphius, 2017). Agility sessions within the ADF will contain activities from all phases but performed at different densities (intensities and volume) following an emphasis model. The phases of emphasis will depend on a multitude of factors within the overarching context of the individual (e.g. physical capacity, training age, COD needs analysis, qualitative and quantitative analysis of COD performance, time of season). An example (in-season) agility session for multidirectional invasion-based sport containing elements from the three phases of the ADF is presented in Figure 10.2. Although the optimal dosages are not well understood for agility or COD speed training, and thus a future direction of research, two 15-to-30-minute sessions a week (with 48 hours recovery between sessions) have been shown to be effective (Dempsey et al., 2009; Dos'Santos et al., 2019a; Dos'Santos, Thomas, Comfort, et al., 2021b; Falch et al., 2019). From our experience, a conservative approach should be adopted for isolated agility development sessions (Dos'Santos et al., 2019a; Dos'Santos, Thomas, Comfort, et al., 2021b; Dos'Santos, Thomas, McBurnie, Comfort, et al., 2021b), with gradual progressions in total distance per session (230–480 m), number of COD (20–40) and decelerations (2–40), and perceived intensity (50–100%). Additionally, practitioners are encouraged to monitor and limit week-to-week changes, or progressive increases, within 10% for the aforementioned variables (McBurnie et al., 2022) to avoid rapid spikes in training load and thus potential injury risk (Gabbett, 2016; Kalkhoven et al., 2021), with emphasis placed on *quality* rather than *quantity*. If practitioners have logistical

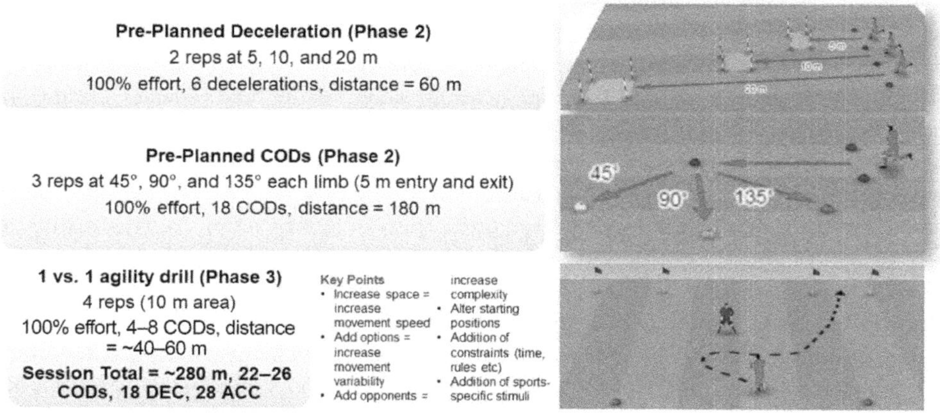

Pre-Planned Deceleration (Phase 2)
2 reps at 5, 10, and 20 m
100% effort, 6 decelerations, distance = 60 m

Pre-Planned CODs (Phase 2)
3 reps at 45°, 90°, and 135° each limb (5 m entry and exit)
100% effort, 18 CODs, distance = 180 m

1 vs. 1 agility drill (Phase 3)
4 reps (10 m area)
100% effort, 4–8 CODs, distance = ~40–60 m
Session Total = ~280 m, 22–26 CODs, 18 DEC, 28 ACC

Key Points
- Increase space = increase movement speed
- Add options = increase movement variability
- Add opponents = increase complexity
- Alter starting positions
- Addition of constraints (time, rules etc)
- Addition of sports-specific stimuli

45° 90° 135°

FIGURE 10.2 An example of (in-season) agility session for multidirectional invasion-based sport containing elements from the three phases of the agility development framework. COD: change of direction; DEC: deceleration; ACC: acceleration; XOC: crossover cut.

challenges incorporating isolated agility sessions within their microcycles, agility activities and technique modification can be easily integrated into field-based warm-ups prior to technical/tactical skill based sports sessions (Dos'Santos et al., 2019a; Dos'Santos, Thomas, McBurnie, Donelon, et al., 2021; McBurnie et al., 2022) or integrated in skill/tactical training activities in consultation with the skills coach. Practitioners should also be conscious of the other training units and sessions within the microcycle when designing their agility activities (i.e. intensive or extensive activities).

ADF: Practice Structure, Instruction and Feedback, and Learning Activities

Regarding practice structure, contextual interference (i.e. the ability for an athlete to predict the upcoming skill and select the appropriate motor programme) should be increased throughout the programme by shifting from blocked practice in phase 1 to random in phase 3 (drills executed in random order) and variance practice (variation of drills practised within a session) structures to enhance skill retention and transfer. This will enhance the athletes' ability to recall and adapt movement actions when required during match play (Spiteri et al., 2018). Additionally, practitioners should be mindful of the instruction and feedback techniques employed when facilitating agility training (Benjaminse et al., 2015; Chua et al., 2018; Otte et al., 2020), with readers encouraged to read the excellent overview by Otte et al. (2020) regarding the Skill Training Communication Model and Chapter 11. Specifically, external verbal cues focus on the environment and goal-relevant dimensions of the task, and in some cases, analogies are used (Benz et al., 2016; Winkelman, 2018). Regular cueing between repetitions has been suggested to be beneficial for performance (Benz et al., 2016), while regular feedback regarding COD technique has been reported to be beneficial in eliciting positive changes in technique (Dempsey et al., 2009; Dos'Santos, Thomas, Comfort, et al., 2021a, 2021b; Jones et al., 2015; Padua et al., 2018). However, it is strongly advised that coaches limit cues and instructions to one or two, and select cues relevant to the goal of the drill or technical element being emphasised (Winkelman, 2018). This approach will eliminate memory recall problems, permitting the athlete to concentrate on the one or two cues and technical elements to modify and to avoid 'overcoaching' (Winkelman, 2018).

Otte et al. (2020) presented the Skill Training Communication Model, and readers are encouraged to read this work for more information regarding appropriate feedback and instruction when coaching skill training with athletes. In addition, Chapter 11 provides a thorough overview regarding the coaching of multidirectional speed. Briefly, a variety of feedback and instruction methods are available (e.g. instructive, task-oriented, Q&A approach, trial and error, video feedback, model learning, and analogy-learning), which all have their own unique applications within the PoST framework and ADF. Practitioners will likely adopt a variety of different feedback and instruction methods when coaching agility. Dempsey et al. (2009) has previously used live video feedback and task-oriented constraints to modify side-step cutting technique and reduce knee joint loads in athletes. Conversely, video feedback may not always be feasible to implement in the field, particularly when working with large group sizes. As such, from our experience as practitioners and researchers, we have adopted a hybrid approach, utilising model learning, instructive (direct) feedback, and analogy learning (externally directed verbal coaching cues) to modify side-step cutting movement quality (Dos'Santos et al., 2019a), reduce knee joint loads (Dos'Santos, Thomas, Comfort, et al., 2021a), and improve cutting (Dos'Santos, Thomas, Comfort, et al., 2021b) and turning performance (Dos'Santos, Thomas, McBurnie, Comfort, et al., 2021b) in six weeks, following the ADF presented in Figure 10.1. Model learning is useful when working with novice athletes with low training ages, particularly when exposing athletes to unfamiliar and novel movement patterns (Otte et al., 2020). Cueing and analogies are particularly effective for redirecting attention externally (Winkelman, 2018) and can be scenario-based, constraint-based, and object-based (Otte et al., 2020). These cues are recommended to be used across all phases of the ADF and skill training frameworks. Finally, it is recommended that practitioners consider the timing, type, quality, and quantity of information provided, particularly paying attention to the emotional value and context of the feedback (Otte et al., 2020). For example, feedback which is supportive, motivating, and constructive should be prioritised, with praise rather than negative and critical feedback provided (Otte et al., 2020). Finally, Figure 10.3 provides an overview of example activities that can be used across different phases of the ADF, adapted from McBurnie et al. (2022).

Summary

In summary, there is a variety of different agility actions that have their own distinct technical differences, advantages, and applications in sport. Nevertheless, athletes may employ these different actions for attacking and defensive purposes to achieve a specific performance outcome. As such, it is encouraged that practitioners whose responsibility for the physical preparation of athletes to not neglect the importance of *technique* when developing multidirectional sports athletes' agility for performance and injury risk mitigation. Most athletes, irrespective of sport, will require the ability to perform agility actions within a 360° turning circle from both limbs. Therefore, it is integral that practitioners develop athletes who possess adaptable movement strategies and multiple movement solutions to solve the problems they encounter in the random, unpredictable, and chaotic sports, using the ADF presented in this chapter.

A. Deceleration activities (Phase 1 & 2)

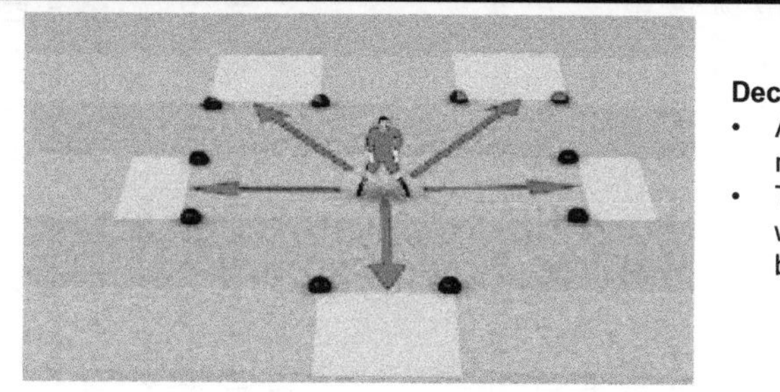

Deceleration Competency Drills

- Allows for control of desired deceleration angle and velocity through manipulation of cone distance and direction.
- Technical competency can also be developed through decelerations within a range movement planes and different finish positions (e.g., bilateral stance, split stance, rotated stance).

Deceleration Runways

- Building up deceleration capacity by progressively increasing the approach velocities.
- Multiple decelerations can be performed within the same 'runway' to increase the density of actions, but it should be noted that this may decrease movement speeds and therefore deceleration intensities.
- Method to increase eccentric strength?

'Stop at the Lights' Game

- Agility game-based drill in which the players must react to the green (accelerate) and red (decelerate) signals from the coach.
- A race to the end and players are disqualified if they are unable to stop on the coaches' command.
- Can be manipulated with auditory stimuli and partner / opponent stimuli.

FIGURE 10.3 Example deceleration, change-of-direction speed, and agility activities.

B. COD speed and manoeuvrability development (Phase 1 & 2)

A.

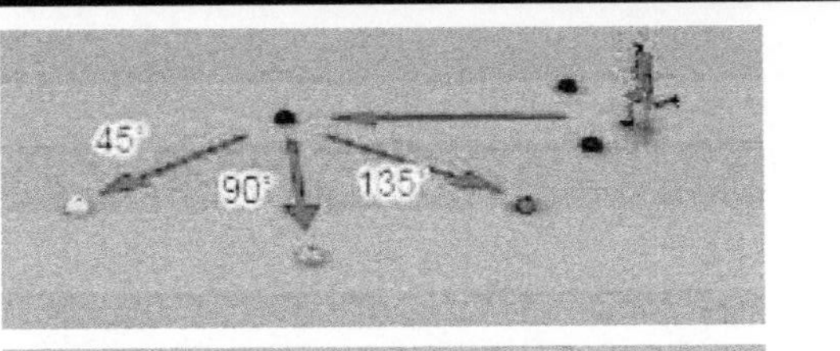

Three-Point Drills

- Allows for control of desired COD angle and velocity through manipulation of cone distance and direction.
- This is useful for embedding COD competency through technique emphasis.
- Simple for prescription, monitoring dosages, regulating intensity.

B.

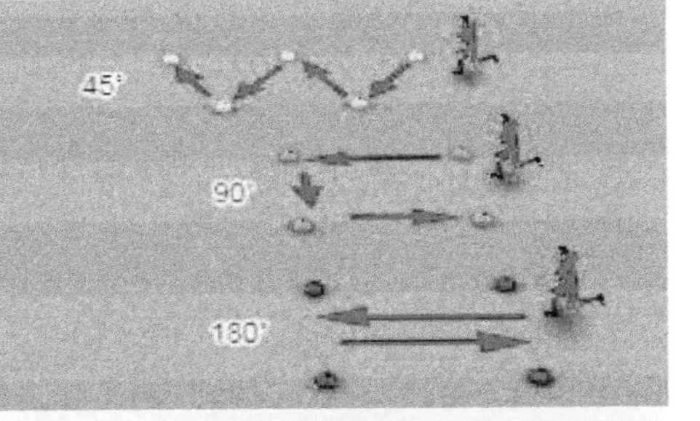

Zig-Zag / Combination Drills

- Increased repetition frequency with addition of multiple COD manoeuvres (typically the same) within the same drill.
- This is useful for developing COD capacity through increased density of COD actions.
- Practitioners should note the increased loading demands associated with sharper COD angles, and so repetition number should reflect this.

C.

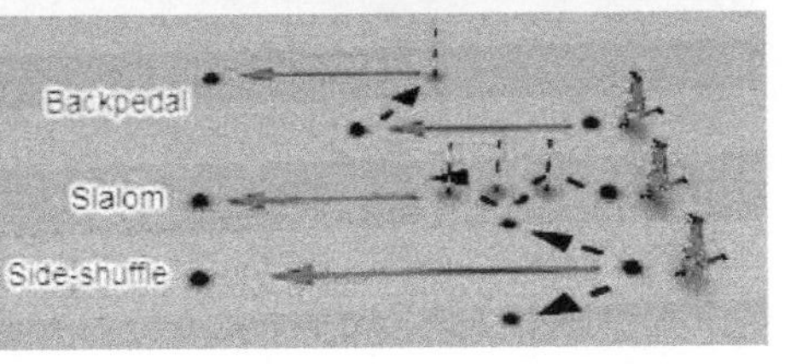

Manoeuvrability Drills

- A method for incorporating a variety of MDS elements within the same drill.
- This can be used to introduce more sports-specific actions (i.e., backpedal) in a sequence which can relate to an individual's playing position.

FIGURE 10.3 *(Continued)*

C. Agility development (Phase 3)

A.

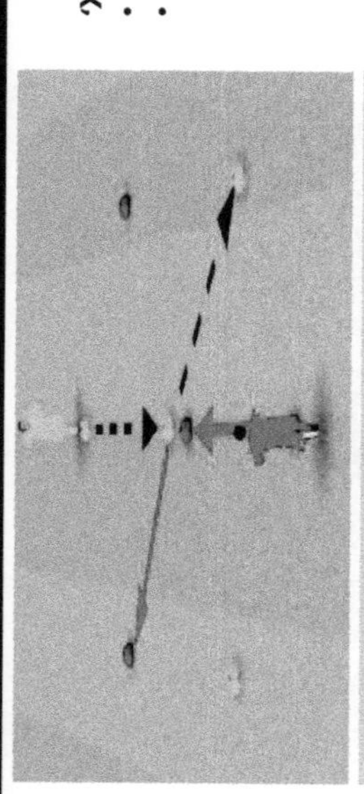

'X' and 'Y' Drills

- Incorporation of a reactive stimulus within COD or manoeuvrability.
- This can be achieved through a verbal or visual cue from the coach, or reacting to an opponent's movement.

B.

1 v 1 Drills

- An open, opposed drill where players have to evade their opponent(s) in order to pass through a gate.
- Manipulation of player numbers, distance and objectives can bring about different movement actions/COD angles and intensities.

C.

Agility games

- Inherently the most chaotic and cognitively demanding form of agility training, and can be effective for diversifying the programme through introducing multi-sports.
- Manipulation of player numbers, distance and objectives can bring about different outcomes.

FIGURE 10.3 *(Continued)*

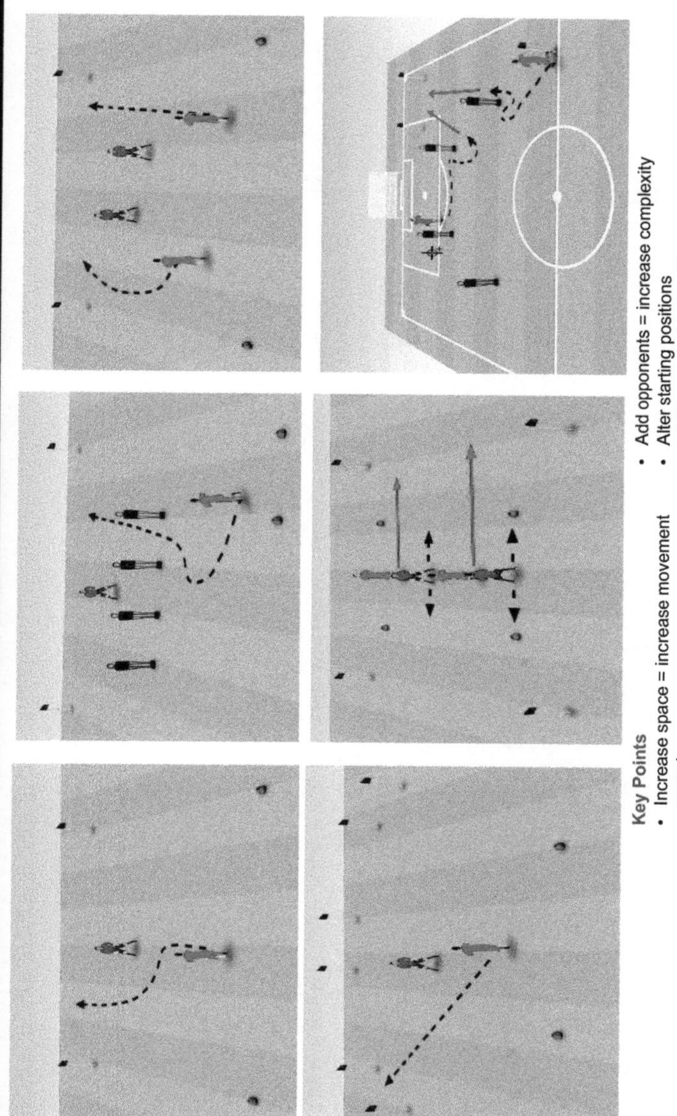

FIGURE 10.3 *(Continued)*

E. Agility development (Phase 3 and movement diversification)

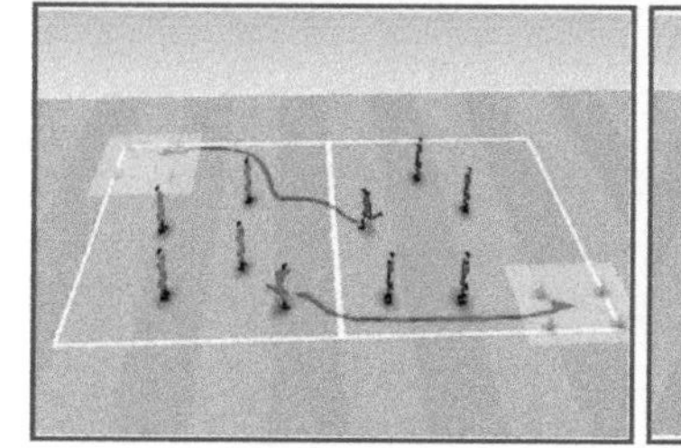

Jailbreak Defence

General objectives: The aim is for players to reach the opposite 'jail' without being grabbed by a member of the other team. If a player reaches the jail and it's empty, their team wins the game.
Own half is a 'safe zone'
Player in jail can be 'freed' by a team mate – teammates hold on to each other until in safe zone

Organisation: 20 x 20 m area; 5 x 5 m jail. Bibs in shorts for tagging

Progressions: Add flag to each zone

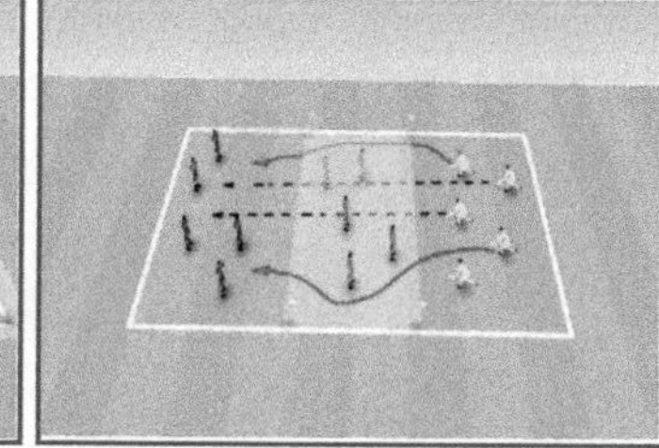

Feed the Monkeys

General objectives: 3-5 teams. Try to get bananas (balls) from one side to the other of the monkey enclosure without the monkeys 'eating' them. Once ball is 'eaten', it is removed - this counts as a point for the monkey team. If ball gets to the other side it is a point for both teams on the outside (both transporter and receiver). Rotate round - keep a tally of points for each team.

Organisation: 10 - 20 m wide monkey cage; Players tuck bibs into shorts

Progressions: Change how bananas travel through cage: add throws (underarm, roll, overarm, bounce). Can add more teams to get across from all 4 sides.

Bulldog

General objectives: The aim of the game is to run from one end of the field of play to the other, without being caught by the bulldogs. When a player is caught, they become a bulldog themselves. The winner is the last player or players 'free'.

Organisation: 20 x 20 m (can adjust depending on numbers); Bibs tucked into shorts

Progressions: Restrict movement (linear, lateral), add obstacles (boxes, trampolines, mannequins)

Capture the Flag

General objectives: When the game begins, players try to cross into opposing teams' territories to grab their flags. When a player is in an opposing team's territory, they can be captured by that team's players. If they tag they must go to jail. Any time a player crosses back to their own team's territory, they are safe and can't be captured. The game ends when one team has successfully grabbed the flag(s) from the other team or teams and returned to their own territory.

Organisation: 20 x 20m area (group number dependent). Flags; add obstacles (i.e., crash mats, boxes, trampolines).

Progressions: Add movement skills in for forfeits or to gain extra flags.

FIGURE 10.3 *(Continued)*

References

Bartlett, R., Wheat, J., & Robins, M. (2007). Is movement variability important for sports biomechanists? *Sports Biomechanics*, *6*(2), 224–243.

Beaulieu, M. L., Ashton-Miller, J. A., & Wojtys, E. M. (2021). Loading mechanisms of the anterior cruciate ligament. *Sports Biomechanics*, 1–29.

Benjaminse, A., Gokeler, A., Dowling, A. V., Faigenbaum, A., Ford, K. R., Hewett, T. E., Onate, J. A., Otten, B., & Myer, G. D. (2015). Optimization of the anterior cruciate ligament injury prevention paradigm: Novel feedback techniques to enhance motor learning and reduce injury risk. *Journal of Orthopaedic & Sports Physical Therapy*, *45*(3), 170–182.

Benz, A., Winkelman, N., Porter, J., & Nimphius, S. (2016). Coaching instructions and cues for enhancing sprint performance. *Strength & Conditioning Journal*, *38*(1), 1–11.

Bober, T., Morecky, A., Fidelus, K., & Witt, A. (1981). Biomechanical aspects of sports techniques. *Biomechanics VII*, 501–509.

Bourgeois, F., McGuigan, M. R., Gill, N. D., & Gamble, G. (2017). Physical characteristics and performance in change of direction tasks: A brief review and training considerations *Journal of Australian Strength and Conditioning*, *25*(5), 104–117.

Chua, L.-K., Wulf, G., & Lewthwaite, R. (2018). Onward and upward: Optimizing motor performance. *Human Movement Science*, *60*, 107–114.

Davids, K., Button, C., & Bennett, S. (2008). *Dynamics of skill acquisition: A constraints-led approach*. Human kinetics.

Dempsey, A. R., Lloyd, D. G., Elliott, B. C., Steele, J. R., & Munro, B. J. (2009). Changing sidestep cutting technique reduces knee valgus loading. *The American Journal of Sports Medicine*, *37*(11), 2194–2200.

DeWeese, B. H., & Nimphius, S. (2016). Program design technique for speed and agility training. In G. G. Haff & N. T. Triplett (Eds.), *Essentials of strength training and conditioning* (pp. 521–558). Human Kinetics.

Donelon, T. A., Dos'Santos, T., Pitchers, G., Brown, M., & Jones, P. A. (2020). Biomechanical determinants of knee joint loads associated with increased anterior cruciate ligament loading during cutting: A systematic review and technical framework. *Sports Medicine-Open*, *6*(1), 1–21.

Dos'Santos, T., Cowling, I., Challoner, M., Barry, T., & Caldbeck, P. (2022). What are the significant turning demands of match play of an English Premier League soccer team? *Journal of Sports Sciences*, *40*, 1750–1759.

Dos'Santos, T., McBurnie, A., Comfort, P., & Jones, P. A. (2019a). The effects of six-weeks change of direction speed and technique modification training on cutting performance and movement quality in male youth soccer players. *Sports*, 7(9), 205.

Dos'Santos, T., McBurnie, A., Thomas, C., Comfort, P., & Jones, P. A. (2019b). Biomechanical comparison of cutting techniques: A review and practical applications. *Strength & Conditioning Journal*, *41*(4), 40–54.

Dos'Santos, T., McBurnie, A., Thomas, C., Comfort, P., & Jones, P. A. (2020). Biomechanical determinants of the modified and traditional 505 change of direction speed test. *The Journal of Strength & Conditioning Research*, *34*(5), 1285–1296.

Dos'Santos, T., McBurnie, A., Thomas, C., Jones, P. A., & Harper, D. J. (2022). Attacking agility actions: Match play contextual applications with coaching and technique guidelines. *Strength & Conditioning Journal*, *44*(5), 102–118.

Dos'Santos, T., Thomas, C., Comfort, P., & Jones, P. A. (2018). The effect of angle and velocity on change of direction biomechanics: An angle-velocity trade-off. *Sports Medicine*, *48*(10), 2235–2253.

Dos'Santos, T., Thomas, C., Comfort, P., & Jones, P. A. (2019c). The effect of training interventions on change of direction biomechanics associated with increased anterior cruciate ligament loading: A scoping review [journal article]. *Sports Medicine*, *49*(12), 1837–1859. https://doi.org/10.1007/s40279-019-01171-0

Dos'Santos, T., Thomas, C., Comfort, P., & Jones, P. A. (2019d). The role of the penultimate foot contact during change of direction: Implications on performance and risk of injury. *Strength & Conditioning Journal*, *41*(1), 87–104.

Dos'Santos, T., Thomas, C., Comfort, P., & Jones, P. A. (2021a). Biomechanical effects of a 6-week change-of-direction technique modification intervention on anterior cruciate ligament injury risk. *The Journal of Strength & Conditioning Research*, *35*(8), 2133–2144.

Dos'Santos, T., Thomas, C., Comfort, P., & Jones, P. A. (2021b). Biomechanical effects of a 6-week change of direction speed and technique modification intervention: Implications for change of direction side step performance. *Journal of Strength and Conditioning Research*, Published Ahead of Print.

Dos'Santos, T., Thomas, C., McBurnie, A., Comfort, P., & Jones, P. A. (2021a). Biomechanical determinants of performance and injury risk during cutting: A performance-injury conflict? *Sports Medicine*, *51*, 1983–1998.

Dos'Santos, T., Thomas, C., McBurnie, A., Comfort, P., & Jones, P. A. (2021b). Change of direction speed and technique modification training improves 180° turning performance, kinetics, and kinematics. *Sports*, *9*(6), 73.

Dos'Santos, T., Thomas, C., McBurnie, A., Donelon, T., Herrington, L., & Jones, P. A. (2021). The Cutting Movement Assessment Score (CMAS) qualitative screening tool: Application to mitigate anterior cruciate ligament injury risk during cutting. *Biomechanics*, *1*(1), 83–101.

Edwards, W. B. (2018). Modeling overuse injuries in sport as a mechanical fatigue phenomenon. *Exercise and Sport Sciences Reviews*, *46*(4), 224–231.

Falch, H. N., Rædergård, H. G., & van den Tillaar, R. (2019). Effect of different physical training forms on change of direction ability: A systematic review and meta-analysis. *Sports Medicine-Open*, *5*(1), 53.

Farrow, D., & Robertson, S. (2017). Development of a skill acquisition periodisation framework for high-performance sport. *Sports Medicine*, *47*(6), 1043–1054.

Fox, A. S. (2018). Change-of-direction biomechanics: Is what's best for anterior cruciate ligament injury prevention also best for performance? *Sports Medicine*, *48*(8), 1799–1807.

Freitas, T. T., Alcaraz, P. E., Calleja-González, J., Arruda, A. F., Guerriero, A., Mercer, V. P., Pereira, L. A., Carpes, F. P., McGuigan, M. R., & Loturco, I. (2021). Influence of physical and technical aspects on change of direction performance of rugby players: An exploratory study. *International Journal of Environmental Research and Public Health*, *18*(24), 13390.

Gabbett, T. J. (2016). The training – injury prevention paradox: Should athletes be training smarter and harder? *British Journal of Sports Medicine*, *50*(5), 273–280.

Gibson, J. (1979). *The ecological approach to visual perception*. Houghton Mifflin.

Hamill, J., Palmer, C., & Van Emmerik, R. E. A. (2012). Coordinative variability and overuse injury. *Sports Medicine, Arthroscopy, Rehabilitation, Therapy & Technology*, *4*(1), 45.

Hamill, J., van Emmerik, R. E. A., Heiderscheit, B. C., & Li, L. (1999). A dynamical systems approach to lower extremity running injuries. *Clinical Biomechanics*, *14*(5), 297–308.

Hendricks, S., Till, K., Oliver, J. L., Johnston, R. D., Attwood, M. J., Brown, J. C., Drake, D., MacLeod, S., Mellalieu, S. D., & Jones, B. (2019). Rating of perceived challenge as a measure of internal load for technical skill performance. *British Journal of Sports Medicine*, *53*(10), 611–613.

Herrington, L. C., Munro, A. G., & Jones, P. A. (2018). Assessment of factors associated with injury risk. In P. Comfort, J. J. McMahon, & P. A. Jones (Eds.), *Performance assessment in strength and conditioning* (pp. 53–95). Routledge.

Hughes, G., & Dai, B. (2021). The influence of decision making and divided attention on lower limb biomechanics associated with anterior cruciate ligament injury: A narrative review. *Sports Biomechanics*, 1–16.

Jeffreys, I. (2010). *Gamespeed: Movement training for superior sports performance*. Monterey, CA: Coaches Choice.

Jones, P. A., Barber, O. R., & Smith, L. C. (2015). Changing pivoting technique reduces knee valgus moments. Free communication. *Journal of Sports Sciences (BASES Annual Conference)*, *33*(Supplement 1), S62.

Jones, P. A., McBurnie, A., & Dos'Santos, T. (2021). Using qualitative technique analysis to evaluate and develop technique of agility actions with your athletes. *Professional Strength and Conditioning*, (63), 25–33.

Jones, P. A., & Nimphius, S. (2018). Change of direction and agility. In Comfort, P., P. A. Jones, & J. J. McMahon (Eds.), *Performance assessment in strength and conditioning* (pp. 140–165). Routledge.

Kalkhoven, J. T., Watsford, M. L., Coutts, A. J., Edwards, W. B., & Impellizzeri, F. M. (2021). Training load and injury: Causal pathways and future directions. *Sports Medicine*, *51*(6), 1137–1150.

Lee, M. J. C., Lloyd, D. G., Lay, B. S., Bourke, P. D., & Alderson, J. A. (2013). Effects of different visual stimuli on postures and knee moments during sidestepping. *Medicine & Science in Sports & Exercise*, *45*(9), 1740–1748.

Lee, M. J. C., Lloyd, D. G., Lay, B. S., Bourke, P. D., & Alderson, J. A. (2017). Different visual stimuli affect body reorientation strategies during sidestepping. *Scandinavian Journal of Medicine & Science in Sports*, *27*(5), 492–500.

Lees, A. (2002). Technique analysis in sports: A critical review. *Journal of Sports Sciences*, *20*(10), 813–828.

Malone, S., Roe, M., Doran, D. A., Gabbett, T. J., & Collins, K. (2017). High chronic training loads and exposure to bouts of maximal velocity running reduce injury risk in elite Gaelic football. *Journal of Science and Medicine in Sport*, *20*(3), 250–254.

Martínez-Hernández, D., Quinn, M., & Jones, P. (2022). Linear advancing actions followed by deceleration and turn are the most common movements preceding goals in male professional soccer. *Science & Medicine in Football*, 1–9. https://doi.org/10.1080/24733938.2022.2030064

McBurnie, A., & Dos'Santos, T. (2022). Multi-directional speed in youth soccer players: Theoretical underpinnings. *Strength & Conditioning Journal*, *44*(1), 15–33.

McBurnie, A., Dos'Santos, T., & Jones, P. A. (2021). Biomechanical Associates of performance and knee joint loads during an 70–90° cutting maneuver in sub-elite soccer players. *Journal of Strength and Conditioning Research*, *35*(11), 3190–3198.

McBurnie, A., Harper, D. J., Jones, P. A., & Dos'Santos, T. (2021). Deceleration Training in team sports: Another potential 'vaccine' for sports-related injury? *Sports Medicine*, 1–12.

McBurnie, A., Parr, J., & Dos'Santos, T. (2022). Multi-directional speed in youth soccer players: Programming considerations and practical applications. *Strength & Conditioning Journal*, *44*(2), 10–32.

McCosker, C., Renshaw, I., Greenwood, D., Davids, K., & Gosden, E. (2019). How performance analysis of elite long jumping can inform representative training design through identification of key constraints on competitive behaviours. *European Journal of Sport Science*, *19*(7), 913–921.

Myszka, S. (2018). Movement skill acquisition for american football – using 'repetition without repetition' to enhance movement skill. *NSCA Coach*, *54*.

Nimphius, S. (2014). Increasing agility. In D. Joyce & D. Lewindon (Eds.), *High-performance training for sports* (pp. 185–198). Human Kinetics.

Nimphius, S. (2017). Training change of direction and agility. In A. Turner & P. Comfort (Eds.), *Advanced Strength and Conditioning* (pp. 291–308). Routledge.

Orangi, B. M., Yaali, R., Bahram, A., Aghdasi, M. T., van der Kamp, J., Vanrenterghem, J., & Jones, P. A. (2021). Motor learning methods that induce high practice variability reduce kinematic and kinetic risk factors of non-contact ACL injury. *Human Movement Science*, *78*, 102805.

Otte, F. W., Davids, K., Millar, S.-K., & Klatt, S. (2020). When and how to provide feedback and instructions to athletes? – How sport psychology and pedagogy insights can improve coaching interventions to enhance self-regulation in training. *Frontiers in Psychology*, *11*, 1444.

Otte, F. W., Millar, S.-K., & Klatt, S. (2019). Skill training periodization in "specialist" sports coaching – an introduction of the "PoST" framework for skill development. *Frontiers in Sports and Active Living*, 61.

Padua, D. A., DiStefano, L. J., Hewett, T. E., Garrett, W. E., Marshall, S. W., Golden, G. M., Shultz, S. J., & Sigward, S. M. (2018). National athletic trainers' association position statement: Prevention of anterior cruciate ligament injury. *Journal of Athletic Training*, *53*, 5–19.

Paul, D. J., Gabbett, T. J., & Nassis, G. P. (2016). Agility in team sports: Testing, training and factors affecting performance. *Sports Medicine*, *46*(3), 421–442.

Porter, J., Nolan, R., Ostrowski, E., & Wulf, G. (2010). Directing attention externally enhances agility performance: A qualitative and quantitative analysis of the efficacy of using verbal instructions to focus attention. *Frontiers in Psychology*, *1*, 216.

Preatoni, E., Hamill, J., Harrison, A. J., Hayes, K., Van Emmerik, R. E. A., Wilson, C., & Rodano, R. (2013). Movement variability and skills monitoring in sports. *Sports Biomechanics*, *12*(2), 69–92.

Rayner, R., Young, W., & Talpey, S. (2022). The agility demands of Australian football: A notational analysis. *International Journal of Performance Analysis in Sport*, 1–17.

Seifert, L., & Davids, K. (2017). Ecological dynamics: A theoretical framework for understanding sport performance, physical education and physical activity. (Ed.),^(Eds.). *First Complex Systems Digital Campus World E-Conference 2015*.

Spiteri, T., McIntyre, F., Specos, C., & Myszka, S. (2018). Cognitive training for agility: The integration between perception and action. *Strength & Conditioning Journal, 40*(1), 39–46.

Taberner, M., Allen, T., & Cohen, D. D. (2019). *Progressing rehabilitation after injury: Consider the 'control-chaos continuum'*. BMJ Publishing Group Ltd and British Association of Sport and Exercise Medicine.

Winkelman, N. C. (2018). Attentional focus and cueing for speed development. *Strength & Conditioning Journal, 40*(1), 13–25.

Young, W., Dos'Santos, T., Harper, D., Jefferys, I., & Talpey, S. (2022). Agility in invasion sports: Position stand of the IUSCA. *International Journal of Strength and Conditioning, 2*(1).

Young, W., & Farrow, D. (2006). A review of agility: Practical applications for strength and conditioning. *Strength and Conditioning Journal, 28*(5), 24–29.

Young, W., & Farrow, D. (2013). The importance of a sport-specific stimulus for training agility. *Strength & Conditioning Journal, 35*(2), 39–43.

Zahidi, N. N. M., & Ismail, S. I. (2018). Notational analysis of evasive agility skills executed by attacking ball carriers among elite rugby players of the 2015 Rugby World Cup. *Movement, Health & Exercise*, 7(1), 99–113.

11

COACHING FOR MULTIDIRECTIONAL SPEED

Motor Learning Principles for Developing Sprint and Change-of-Direction Techniques for Performance and Injury Risk Mitigation

Anne Benjaminse

Motor Learning

Benjamin Franklin once stated, 'Tell me and I forget. Teach me and I remember. Involve me and I learn.' This is especially true for motor learning and has consequences for the way we design practice. Learning motor skills is a problem-solving process. The more athletes are involved in analysing and reflecting on their own actions, the better the learning outcome. Feedback to an athlete, therefore, should serve to help an athlete reflect on what has to be learned or changed. Therefore, the coaching role should be rather a facilitator than an instructor.

To optimally master a motor task, an athlete must be experienced with all possible combinations of that task and environmental conditions under which it can be performed. Since these conditions will never be exactly the same, practice ideally leads to not only developing an overall most optimal way of performing the task for an individual athlete but also developing flexible movement strategies/solutions to deal with the continuous and rapid changes in the environment (Beek, 2000; Bolt et al., 2021). The focus of injury prevention programmes should be on preserving the athlete-environment dynamics (Bolt et al., 2021) while performing relevant and meaningful tasks. This specificity principle states that the dynamics of the athlete-environment relationship should be preserved as best as possible, in order for transfer of the training to the actual sport performance to occur (Bolt et al., 2021; Renshaw et al., 2019). If this is the premise, a coach should stimulate the self-organisation process and athletes' adaptive abilities (Otte et al., 2020). When learning to learn to move, it is the athlete who needs to use information to solve a performance problem and not the coach providing verbal information to solve the problem for an athlete (Otte et al., 2020). In this chapter, applied examples of motor skill learning strategies will be provided to successfully guide the athlete finding their own solutions (Benjaminse and Otten, 2011).

Before doing so, we first need to acknowledge that the perceptual-cognitive capacities of an athlete toward task and environmental factors play an important role in multidirectional sports (Vestberg et al., 2017). Not only should the 'doing' part of a skill (i.e. action) be practised, but the 'reading' and 'planning' part that precede the action (i.e. perception) should also focused on. Athletes of multidirectional sports must perceive essential information from the

DOI: 10.4324/9781003267881-13

rapidly changing playing environment and must then interpret this information correctly to select the most appropriate response based on their goals, the rules of the sport, and the interactions among their teammates, opposing athletes, and the ball (Vestberg et al., 2017). This coupling of relevant perceptual information and accurate motor responses requires athletes to effectively search for and detect external stimuli, direct their attention to the most relevant information related to the movement goal, and plan and execute movements to successfully anticipate or anticipate the dynamic task environment around them (Broadbent et al., 2015; Endsley, 1995).

Second, traditionally, ACL injury prevention has focused on specific biomechanical outcomes of movement such as reducing the knee abduction moment and increasing knee flexion motion during the weight acceptance phase of the 'plant step' of cutting (Alentorn-Geli et al., 2009). Training athletes to avoid high-risk movement patterns is a key component of injury prevention programmes (Arundale et al. 2018). In most cases this involves providing athletes with explicit verbal instructions to alter the way they move. For example, athletes are often given instructions intended to reduce impact forces and lower-body stiffness during landing or weight acceptance – for example, 'While cutting, keep your knees over your toes' or 'While cutting, bend your knees'. It can, however, be questioned if learning one such specific movement form with reduced movement variability is the most efficient way to reduce injuries (Benjaminse and Otten, 2011; Benjaminse et al., 2015). This is because utilising greater movement variability during an agile movement allows for a better distribution of loads across joints and structures in different situations. Human movement is inherently variable, and this plays a vital role in the adaptability and coordination of the movement system (Bartlett et al., 2007) and may reflect the motor systems' automatic process of exploring different kinematic solutions to achieve the desired outcome. This type of 'functional variability', where variability in the movement outcome is minimised while variability in the movement effectors is maximised, is a hallmark of a robust motor control system. The process of exploring different motor control strategies may be critical for ACL injury prevention (Orangi et al., 2021; Benjaminse and Otten, 2011); the athlete will explore and then select the solution that fits best in their body given the situational circumstances (Benjaminse and Otten, 2011).

To serve the two mentioned principles, implicit motor learning and motivation, stimulated by (1) self-controlled learning (i.e. enhancing feelings of autonomy) and (2) enhanced expectancies (i.e. enhancing feelings of competence and self-efficacy) (Wulf and Lewthwaite, 2016), should be considered. This optimising performance through intrinsic motivation and attention for learning (OPTIMAL) theory enhances performance and learning by strengthening the coupling of goals to actions (Wulf and Lewthwaite, 2016).

Implicit Learning Methods

For change-of-direction techniques, the goal is that athletes acquire the ability to sustain optimal motor control while engaging in complex athletic environments whilst minimising their risk to sustain an injury (Gokeler et al., 2018). For this purpose, implicit learning can be induced. Implicit learning methods are methods such as errorless learning, dual tasking, manipulating the environment, external focus of attention (EF), and analogies. For this chapter, the latter two will be discussed. Implicit learning methods aim to minimise declarative (explicit) knowledge about movement execution during learning. Without explicitly telling an athlete what to do, implicit learning stimulates an athlete to search for individual movement solutions (Benjaminse and Otten, 2011). It is for this reason that it can be more effective in more complex tasks. Competitive sports can be physically and psychologically demanding (Kinrade et al., 2015). Implicit motor learning has been shown to be more sustainable in situations with physical (Masters et al., 2008a; Poolton et al., 2007) or mental pressure (Beilock et al., 2001; Hardy et al., 1996; Masters et al., 2008b), which is very relevant to the sports context.

One may think 'the athlete needs to master fundamental skills before they can start exploring' or 'I have to tell them how to do it' (how else does my athlete know what to do?). These thoughts are very understandable. You may not have the time to allow the athlete to explore and find their own optimal solution, or you may think a slow learning process in the beginning leads to poor performance later – both of which can lead you to giving explicit instructions before an exercise. However, it is not recommended to mix different approaches (Winkelman, 2020). If the athlete is presented with explicit solutions at the beginning of the learning process, it will be difficult for them to move away from them later (Winkelman, 2020). In fact, you are not helping the athlete with this. This is not to say that the athlete is not allowed to know the purpose of the exercise. Thus, it is important to differentiate between telling the athlete the goal of the exercise and the instructions and feedback being provided during practice. In case of improving agility, this would mean that you can explicitly tell the athlete the general goal of an exercise. For example, 'the goal of this exercise is to improve your knee bending while changing direction, as this promotes a softer landing, which is better for your knee'. Then, as your athlete is preparing to execute the exercise, it is critical to shift their attentional focus that corresponds closest to the task goal. This means, the coach can choose either an internal focus (IF) of attention (e.g. 'flex your knee when cutting', as most frequently done) or an external focus (EF) of attention (e.g. 'focus on cutting with as little noise as possible' or 'pretend you are going to sit on a chair when cutting') (Singh et al., 2021). For clarity, attentional focus relates closely to what you tell your athlete prior to the execution of the exercise. An EF (i.e. explicit learning) would be induced to focus the attention on body parts and movements. Conversely, for an IF (i.e. implicit learning), the attention is directed to the outcome or the goal of the movement. Hence, adopting an EF of attention simply means the athlete is focusing on the intended movement effect, while preparing for the execution (but has nothing to do with the processing of intrinsic feedback or bodily awareness (Wulf, 2016b). Thus, bodily awareness is not necessarily inherent to an IF (Milley and Quellette, 2021). Learning is not possible without bodily awareness (Wulf, 2016b).

Therefore, learning through implicit learning does not mean that the athlete is unaware of their body movements. It simply means that the athlete focuses on the intended effect of the move when preparing for or while executing the movement. Explicit learning leads to the construction of explicit knowledge and implicit learning to the construction of implicit knowledge. Although explicit learning is closely related to explicit instruction, explicit learning can also take place without explicit instruction: it is possible for a person to acquire explicit knowledge without it being provided from outside. Undoubtedly, a person will often adjust and shift their attention back and forth between the different aspects of the skill, depending on where the 'problem' lies (Wulf, 2016b). For example, an analytically oriented athlete can analyse their own movement performance and consciously draw up implementation rules, which they can also name if requested. Conversely, a more impulsive, associative athlete may benefit little from the explicit instructions of his coach or trainer and master a movement by 'being absorbed in the moment', without using and processing the explicit knowledge offered (Beek, 2000). However, although teachers, therapists, and trainers often tend to organise learning processes explicitly, expertise in many skills is based to a large extent on implicit knowledge. This does not mean that one must never use body related instructions that elicit an IF. Of course, you can use it. It will just not result in most optimal motor learning (Ille et al., 2013; Winkelman et al., 2017).

The benefits of using implicit motor learning are as follows:

- What has been learned holds better under psychological and physical pressure.
- There is room (working memory) left to pay attention to game-related elements (i.e. the ball, teammate, opponent).
- There is greater durability (retention) of what has been learned.

Implicit learning can be done in various ways, including letting the athlete's attention be 'outside the body'. You can stimulate this EF by giving goal-directed instructions or feedback or by using analogies, metaphors, and images.

In summary, it is important to differentiate between telling the goal of the exercise (i.e. description – general instruction) and the specific instruction provided just before the execution of the task. For example, in case of optimisation of cutting performance: 'the goal of this exercise is to improve acceleration'. Then, as the athlete is preparing to execute the exercise, it is critical to shift their attentional focus that corresponds closest to the task goal: for example, 'focus on pushing off the ground as forcefully as possible'.

External Focus of Attention

An important question in the context of motor learning is where the athlete can best focus their attention in order to achieve an optimal motor learning result. IF occurs when the attention is focused on the body and the execution of the movements (for example, in warm-up jumping over hurdles: 'Pull your feet and knees as high as possible'). With an EF, on the other hand, the attention is focused on the environment and the effect of the movements (for example, in warm-up jumping over hurdles: 'Focus on getting over the hurdle' or 'Push off as hard as possible off the ground') (Porter et al., 2010; Makaruk and Porter, 2014). This slight difference in wording directs attention outside the body (e.g. on a target, the hurdle, or the ground, respectively) and is more effective for teaching and controlling motor skills. It frees up the brain (i.e. the athlete does not have to consciously think about difficult movements) and thus also the body, making the athlete move less forced and more autonomous [i.e. subconsciously]). It is recommended to use instructions and feedback with an EF.

The main aim of our movement skill training is to retain and execute agility movements more optimally and subconsciously in sport-specific environments. If movements are not planned with the intended effect in mind (EF), but in terms of specific body movements (IF), this outcome will always be less optimal in the long term. Of course, people make progress when they exercise, even when they consciously try to control their body movements. But they will ultimately not make optimal progress; the learning (i.e. the effect in the longer term) will not be optimal. Why is this such an efficient way of learning? According to the 'constrained action hypothesis', an EF promotes the automatic character of the movement control: unconscious, reflexive, and therefore rapid control processes can take place without hindrance so that the desired result of the movement is realised almost automatically. This is crucial for optimal movement on the sport field. The athlete can then focus their attention on the environment (i.e. the ball, opponents, teammates). Conversely, an IF disrupts the automatic control of the movements. As a result, the movements become slower, less fluid, and less effective (Benjaminse et al., 2017, Benjaminse et al., 2018). Interestingly and crucially, when movements are learned with an EF, they are more resistant to psychological or physical pressure. This is very relevant to sports performance. There is less chance of 'freezing' (less flexible or stiff movements or tension) of a movement since the athlete does not explicitly think about their movement but can continue to execute it in an automatic, fluid way. More automatic movement (i.e. without having to consciously think about how you perform a movement) is related to better reaction times and motor adaptability (Wulf and Dufek, 2009).

For example, applying an external focus instruction when practising agility movements could be instructing the athlete with 'when turning, push yourself as forcefully as possible from the ground' (Porter et al., 2010) to enhance movement form in the sagittal plane, respectively. See Table 11.1 for more examples.

Analogy

Learning analogy is another example of how to efficiently stimulate implicit learning. With this, the trainer provides a simple metaphor or simile that describes the movement he or she wants to elicit. Literally telling an athlete what to do is not always efficient. This is especially true when teaching an athlete, especially young athletes or novices, a move/skill for the first time. Don't you recognise that you often say something like 'pretend . . .', 'it feels like . . .', or 'have you seen

TABLE 11.1 External Focus of Attention/Analogy Instructions as an Alternative to the Internal Focus Instructions

Internal Focus of Attention	*External Focus of Attention (EF)/Analogy (AN)*
To improve knee flexion when changing direction (sagittal plane):	
'Bend your knees.'	'Push yourself off the *ground* as hard as you can.' (EF)
	'Keep your shorts level with the *floor*.' (EF)
	'I want to see your cleats in the *grass*.' (EF)
	'Land as *softly* as possible.' (EF)
	'Decrease the sound of your landing while cutting from 8 to *4*.' (EF)
	'Accelerate as if you are a rocket or coil spring.' (AN)
	'Pretend you are making the cut on eggs, don't crack them!' (AN)
	'Pretend you are going to sit on a chair.' (AN)
	'Make as little noise as possible when making the cut.' (AN)
	'Pretend you have to move underneath a low bridge. Don't hit your head!' (AN)
	'Pretend as if a rattlesnake is close to your foot. Don't let it bike you!' (AN)
Internal Focus of Attention	*External Focus of Attention (EF)/Analogy (AN)*
To improve knee-over-toe alignment when changing direction (frontal plane):	
'Keep your knee over your toes.'	• 'Point the logo of your shirt towards the *new direction/finish*.' (EF)
	• 'Point the tip of your shoes towards the *new direction/finish*.' (EF)
	• 'Imagine your knees are headlights; as you turn, let the light point towards the new running direction.' (AN)
	• 'Pretend you have a laser coming out of your belly button, point it to new running direction.' (AN)

how . . .' in an effort to help your athlete understand what you want to achieve? This is why a coach uses words like 'stiff like a board', 'bounce off like a rocket', or 'spring in like a jumping stick' because it is immediately clear what they mean, as terms are used that the athlete already knows (e.g. plank, rocket, jumping stick) (Winkelman, 2020).

Why is this such an efficient way of learning? You will see that the brain uses analogies in endless situations where 'meaning' is needed. How else do you know your door handle is moving down, using doorknobs to turn, pressing buttons, walking up stairs, and sitting on chairs (Winkelman, 2020)? Sure, there was a moment in the beginning where you first came into contact with these items, and you had to make a decision what to do. By luck or by choice or by someone who taught you, you would have learned how to use these objects in everyday life and you probably won't pull a button or push a door handle anymore. Instead, in your brain there is a long history of using sounds and buttons and by analogy your brain says 'this is something like . . .' and your brain then acts as if it actually is. As you can see, an analogy is a kind of 'mental molecule' that helps us give meaning to something, allowing us to make associations (Winkelman, 2020). Using analogies is certainly not easy. A large vocabulary is needed and a good understanding of the movement and how to 'translate' these 'words' into images or a 'story' for the athlete to use.

When you say 'pretend to be walking on eggshells', the visual and motor parts of your brain kick into action, as if this story, this fiction, is indeed true (Winkelman, 2020). Hearing this sentence, we pretend to see this scene (imagine in your head) and perform the action as described (i.e. embodied simulation), using our perception and motor skills (Winkelman, 2020). This is because hearing a verb is processed in the same brain regions as the brain regions responsible for actually performing that verb. Words can literally 'project' movement onto the brain so that analogies can help an athlete learn an unfamiliar movement pattern with a term that is well known to them.

Basically, there is no perfect analogy. The words you use are highly dependent on culture, age, and experience, and it is important that they are known to the athlete. Instructions and feedback are used by a coach to let the athlete discover their own possibilities for improving that movement (Winkelman, 2020). It is advisable to not want to improve too much at the same time but to focus on the most important aspects of the movement at that moment – for example, emphasising one or two analogies or cues on a technical characteristic that you are attempting to modify. A coach's job is not just to tell *what* needs to be improved but also *how*.

For example, applying an analogy instruction when optimising agility movements could be asking the athlete to 'pretend your knees are headlights and point them towards the new direction' (Winkelman, 2020) to enhance movement quality in the frontal plane. For more examples, see Table 11.1.

Autonomy

Learning is a problem-solving process, and the athlete's involvement during practice to search for their own movement solutions enhances learning. Having some choice appeals to one of the basic psychological needs of human beings and enhances intrinsic motivation (Sanli et al., 2013). It can also stimulate beliefs in one's capabilities (e.g. competence) and enhance feelings of self-efficacy; for example, choosing the variety of the exercises the athlete thinks they can do best or that challenged them most. Conditions that provide an opportunity for choice may be motivating because they indicate control over upcoming events and helps increase adherence and developing the coach-athlete relationship. Therefore, it is advised that coaches try to stimulate the athletes' enjoyment, needs satisfaction, or sense of challenge or curiosity during the activity (Sanli et al., 2013). For a larger group, it is possible to set up a practice condition with three variations or three difficulties of a certain exercise and have each athlete choose which variation or difficulty level of an exercise to practise. Within, for example, 15 minutes, the athletes can select the set up they want to practise, and they can also be free to choose another variation of difficulty. It they feel being ready for another variation when they get satisfied or bored with a previous variation or ready for the next level when successfully executed the previous level a couple of times, they can pick another set up. This switch between set ups also stimulates random practice (see the following).

It is in the nature of teaching, training, and coaching to determine a training situation itself. However, this does not appeal to an individual's psychological needs for any autonomy (Sanli et al., 2013). This also does not encourage internalising behaviour and identifying with it; after all, 'the coach has given the assignment and determines what we are going to do'. When training, you can apply autonomy by offering the athlete simple choices. By giving athletes a certain amount of choice and control during training, feelings of autonomy and competence (for example, an athlete chooses the option that challenges them the most: 'yes, I can do this!'), some basic psychological needs are met (Ryan and Deci, 2000). This, in turn, will enhance the athlete's intrinsic motivation and engagement. This leads to more fun and relatedness because the athlete has chosen the situation that they liked most and, therefore, more ownership on the part of the athletes. In training, autonomy can be supported by providing the athletes with simple but crucial choices. This could be, for example, (1) difficulty of the task, (2) the material to practise with, (3) when feedback is received, and (4) what type of feedback should be received (e.g. verbal or visual or a combination, yourself or expert model). The expertise of the coach is necessary at all times. As an expert, always pay attention to safety and difficulty. That is, make sure an athlete chooses an exercise that is challenging (i.e. learning effect), but not too difficult (i.e. safety). In addition, consider how many choices you will offer during a practice session. Limiting choices is of benefit of your athlete (especially the younger ones) and also logistics in facilitating this.

Language is an important tool to provide athletes feelings of choice. The use of non-controlling language means the avoidance of words such as 'should', 'must', and 'have to', to convey a sense of choice or flexibility (Su and Reeve, 2011) – for example, 'you have to' and 'you cannot' versus 'feel free to' and 'when you are ready'. Granting athletes autonomy equips them with confidence in their ability, diminishes needs for control of negative emotional responses, and creates more positive affect, which may help consolidate motor memories (Hooyman et al., 2014).

Another way to provide feelings of autonomy is by asking questions: 'How can you make this exercise more challenging for yourself?' or 'Let me know when you're ready to move to the next level of this exercise.'

Enhanced Expectancies

Human motivation is dependent on the perception of one's actions having effects on the environment (Eitam et al., 2013). Positive expectations for the near future (i.e. feelings of 'yes, I can do this'), as well as perceptions of autonomy, are intrinsic to motivation (Wulf and Lewthwaite, 2016). Circumstances that enhance athlete's expectations and confidence for future performance success enhance movement automaticity and improve motor learning (Rosenqvist and Skans, 2015). A positive expectation, or confidence, of a future execution of a task can create more success, improvement, and learning. Thus, confidence has been recognised as a predictor of performance.

How can we increase an athlete's confidence? It is advised to shape practice in such a way that performance expectancies are enhanced. First, this can be done by making sure the athlete receives positive feedback and positive reinforcement, as this significantly affects an athlete's motivational state. Meaning providing feedback after good instead of bad trials results in more effective learning, in confirmation of competence and enhancing intrinsic motivation (Saemi et al., 2012). This enhances subsequent learning when processing feedback (Grand et al., 2015). How often don't we give corrective feedback? A common thought is 'how else will the athlete know how to correctly perform a movement?' However, as there is not one perfect movement form, it is advised to have the athletes explore, and then select the movement solution that fits best in their own body to reach the task goal (Benjaminse and Otten, 2011), of course with guidance from the coach and within a safe bandwidth. When athletes are performing a task beyond the optimal bandwidth and potentially increase injury risk, this should be corrected by giving the appropriate feedback. For example, a video instruction of a model correctly performing a movement or a video with the athletes' own best performance works very well to stimulate this search (Benjaminse et al., 2017), and watching plus mimicking the video is an effective learning strategy (Shea et al., 2000; Shea and Wulf, 2005). It appeals to greater intrinsic motivation and satisfaction with performance (Clark and Ste-Marie, 2007). Athletes have well-developed bodily awareness and often prefer to get feedback after relatively good trials, if you let them choose (Benjaminse et al., 2018). It is advised to respect this preference to create an optimal learning environment. A positive feeling about the task at hand improves goal-action coupling and creates a focus on the task goal and reduces a self-focus. Receiving positive feedback helps in giving the athlete a feeling of self-efficacy.

Second, it is the responsibility of coaches to create a learning environment with optimal task difficulty (Guadagnoli and Lee, 2004). It may sound common sense; however, there are tools coaches can use to address this – for example, as addressed in the 'Autonomy' and 'Enhanced expectancies' sections. It is crucial to be aware of processes that lie underneath athletes' concerns when performing tasks. When the difficulty of a task is 'just good' and an athlete experiences success, it builds trust and creates less nervousness about the task. Also, if an athlete performs well or has the feeling to perform well, in a certain situation with slightly more pressure (e.g. 'you have ten seconds to complete five trials'), it can result not only in a higher perceived situational ability but also in enhanced performance in an easier condition (i.e. with no time pressure) (McKay et al., 2012). Feelings of self-ability can also be created by positive comparative feedback, such as 'you are doing better compared to the average athlete' (Lewthwaite and Wulf, 2010).

Training Design

Training that induces high practice variability to guide an athlete's search for their optimal movement solution are promising and warranted (Benjaminse and Verhagen, 2021). Preventative training should support the adoption of non-linear motor learning to stimulate greater self-organisation and adaptability in a meaningful context (DiPaolo et al., 2022).

Random Practice

Random practice (i.e. practising multiple skills in random order with high contextual interference) while adding various constraints should be considered for improving motor learning

(Gokeler et al., 2019; Magill and Hall, 1990). The absence of the consecutive repetition of a given skill during a random execution sequence leads to poorer direct performance than does experiencing a sequence in blocks (Shea and Morgan, 1979). However, the poor direct performance levels of those who practice in a random order mask the greater psychophysiological demands of subcortical structures that this type of condition requires. This increased participation during the practice by brain regions involved in motor skill planning and execution (Wymbs and Grafton, 2009), which is reflected by a higher activation level and cortical excitability, is a critical factor in learning consolidation (Lage et al., 2015). The opposite effect is observed in retention testing, during which random practice leads to decreased activation levels in the indicated regions (Lage et al., 2015), leading to greater automaticity of movement. The variable practice involves performing variations of the task or completely different tasks throughout a training session (Lage et al., 2015). This means, for example, mixing unanticipated deceleration and cutting in different directions, jumping and single-leg landing on the left and right leg, with and without the ball, with and without a defender, from different angles, at different speeds, and so on.

Differential Learning

Lastly, differential learning can be considered to enhance motor learning (Tassignon et al., 2021). Differential learning means that the movement patterns themselves are intentionally varied during practice of a movement skill (rather than only practising the supposedly 'correct' movement form – limiting movement solutions for variable tasks). They are stimulated to engage in a self-organised learning process (Henz and Schöllhorn, 2016, Schöllhorn et al., 2009). This can be done by adding a task or environmental constraint that 'force' the athlete to execute the same task differently. The purpose is to develop control over the body's many degrees of freedom and have adaptable movement strategies available, depending on what the condition is asking for.

For example, applying differential learning when optimising agility movements could be implemented by having the athlete perform multiple variations of a COD task by engaging in environmental variations – for example, passing a football or tennis ball while cutting; cutting while juggling with a tennis ball; having teammates throw or pass balls at the player; having the opponent defend while doing an agility parkour; performing some single-leg hops, a turn, or a jump before cutting; performing cuts on sand or asphalt or within a limited space; and so on. The coach should be creative and make it fun for the players (Benjaminse and Verhagen, 2021).

Perceptual-cognitive Training

The capacities of a multidirectional sport athlete to perceive, anticipate, and respond to environmental factors are related to sports performance (Vestberg et al., 2017) but also play a crucial role in injury prevention. In order to be successful and prevent injury, athletes need to select appropriate goal-directed actions and execute them at appropriate times (Reimer et al., 2006). In other words, the impact of the quickly changing environment, and the players' ability to perceive, interpret, and process the relevant contextual information quickly to execute an appropriate motor response need to be considered when conducting injury prevention exercises (Benjaminse and Verhagen, 2021). For example, in pressing, players injure themselves during non-contact deceleration or cutting, often coupled with a distraction to a ball or opponent immediately prior to injury (Della Villa et al., 2020; Krosshaug et al., 2007).

Neurocognition relates to the cognitive processes and abilities that are closely linked to cortical and subcortical networks of the brain (Diamond, 2013). Neurocognitive functions are responsible for controlling complex, goal-directed behaviour and cover multiple domains. The lower-level cognitive functions include reaction time, processing speed, and visual attention. The higher-level cognitive functions are often referred to as executive functions and are involved in the control and regulation of lower-level cognitive processes. Executive functions enable goal-directed, future-oriented behaviour; it includes skills such as inhibitory control, cognitive flexibility, and working memory (i.e. holding information in mind and manipulating this information in memory) (Diamond, 2013).

A deficit or delay in reaction time or processing speed could contribute to a decreased ability to correct errors in complex coordination, which could result in knee positions with an increased ACL injury risk (Swanik, 2015). Also, knee joint mechanics change unfavourably in response to unanticipated cues (McLean et al., 2010) or while performing dual tasks, such as attending to a ball (Almonroeder et al., 2018; Almonroeder et al., 2019; Norte et al., 2020). Another example of a neurocognitive function, which would be of relevance in this situation, is inhibitory control. The defensive athlete should not be tempted to react to a body feint of an attacker, because after such a move, the defender would have to recover and make up for lost balance or stability. Properly perceiving the feints and actual intended actions of an attacker could aid in positioning the defender favourably to afford successful interception. In pressing, players injure themselves during non-contact deceleration or cutting, often coupled with visually attending to a ball or opponent immediately prior to injury (i.e. distracted) (Della Villa et al., 2020; Krosshaug et al., 2007). There appears also a relation with level of performance in that higher-level football players exhibit more optimal biomechanics in a cognitively demanding task, visually attending to a ball and to one or two defenders, than lower-level players (Lee et al., 2013). In summary, cognitive load may interfere with motor performance (Moreira et al., 2021; Büchel et al., 2022) and kinematics (Brown et al., 2014).

These neurocognitive factors should be targeted with perceptual-cognitive training. Perceptual-cognitive training aims to improve on-field performance by enhancing the athlete's ability to use context-relevant visual information, which facilitates skills like decision-making and anticipation (Hadlow et al., 2018). To facilitate transfer, the perceptual-cognitive training should include a relevant motor component (i.e. cutting and turning). The task constraints during perceptual-cognitive training should relate to the demands of the sport (e.g. include a reactive response component). The perceptual-cognitive training should preserve the dynamics of the athlete-environment relation (i.e. perform the training on field with distractors).

Practical Example

ACL injuries occurring during training or game situations emerge from a complex interaction of internal and external factors (Bolt et al., 2021). One of the primary playing situations in which non-contact ACL injuries occur is defensive pressuring of an attacking athlete (Della Villa et al., 2020; Lucarno et al., 2021), where knee valgus loading is observed frequently. As stated before, training athletes to avoid high-risk movement patterns is a key component of injury prevention programs (Arundale et al. 2018). However, this abducted lower-extremity position is necessary to create a lateral foot plant (Havens and Sigward, 2015; Sigward et al., 2015) and subsequent lateral propulsion for executing sharper CODs (Havens and Sigward, 2014). These sharp CODs and defensive actions are unavoidable in sport and typically performed to evade or pursue opponents or a ball, particularly in unanticipated environments (Dos'Santos et al., 2018). Thus, it is imperative to train athletes to perform these actions with optimal mechanics (Dos'Santos et al., 2018). However, not only biomechanics but also neurocognition should be considered. Expert performance in sport is a combination of both motor (i.e. physical) and perceptual-cognitive skills which address the ability of an athlete to locate, identify, and process information in the surrounding environment (Broadbent et al., 2015). Putting this in a context of injury mechanisms, this indicates that performance deficits may be linked to (1) the physical capacity of the athlete and/or (2) the perceptual-cognitive control of decision-making within a given sport situation (Endsley, 1995). For example, deficits in reaction time and processing speeds indicate a potential cognitive predisposition to ACL injury (Swanik, 2015). Another necessary skill is inhibitory control to not be tempted to fall for a body feint of an attacker.

Using the example of injuries occurring as a result of pressing or defensive actions, we would like to practise a situation in which the athlete typically approaches the opponent with an intention to tackle. In pressing, athletes mostly injure themselves during non-contact deceleration, with distraction immediately before initial contact being frequently observed (Figure 11.1) (Lucarno et al., 2021). To have athletes practice functional movement solutions (i.e. open skills), it is important to practise optimal execution of this situation in a complex context, at different angles and speeds (DiPaolo et al., 2022). Then, the continuous dynamic interactions, perceiving meaningful information in a certain context and translating this into appropriate action, allow for optimal athletic performance (Teques et al., 2017).

Goals for practising directional changes:

Physical goal: defend with optimal mechanics (i.e. sufficient trunk control, knee flexion, and knee abduction within personal boundaries).

Perceptual-cognitive goal: identify kinematic cues from the opponent on time and make appropriate decisions: step forward and defend, inhibit action for a second, and change direction.

Prevention goal: execute these tasks while reducing knee joint loading and subsequent risk of injury. While performing the training sessions with exercises mentioned in the following list, cutting movement can be assessed with the cutting movement assessment score (Dos'Santos et al., 2019). Based on the error scores, cues can be given as indicated in Table 11.1.

Example drills to practise side-step cutting with the previously mentioned goals:

- Cutting with ball (football, handball, basketball, tennis ball, rugby ball) and passing to one or two potential targets.
- Cutting at high speed, with deep knee flexion, with weight vest, dumbbells.
- Agility with, for example, lights to practise working memory (touch order of lights) or inhibitory control (do not touch light/cone when it is a certain colour).
- Agility with, for example, teammates to practise working memory (touch order of lights/cones) or inhibitory control (do not touch light/cone when it is a certain colour).
- Peers mirroring each other in cutting task by, for example, touching cones in front of each other (sideways), with one leader and one follower mimicking the leader, who is indicating which cone to be touched; with or without fake movements included.
- Peers mirroring each other in running back and forth touching cones in a row (acceleration, deceleration), with one leader and one follower mimicking the leader, who is indicating

FIGURE 11.1 (A and B) Defender: reading opponent's body language and anticipating. Attacker: makes a deceiving action. (C and D) Defender: rapid change of movement from right to left, reacting to attacker's deceiving action. (D) Defender ruptures his right ACL. (Reproduced with permission Gokeler et al. (2021). Anterior cruciate ligament injury mechanisms through a neurocognition lens: Implications for injury screening. BMJ Open Sport & Exercise Medicine 7(2):e001091. https://doi.org/10.1136/bmjsem-2021-001091

which cone to be touched; also, with, for example, dribbling a ball with feet/hands, with or without fake movements included.

- Peers mirroring each other in touching cones. Two set-ups with cones in a square/circle/random, with one leader and one follower mimicking the leader, who is indicating which cone to be touched; with or without fake movements included.
- Parkour at high speed with teammates/opponents with multiple uncertain elements included – for example, tag game: try to reach other side of the field without being tagged. This can also be played as rugby with ball in hand, with dribbling ball.
- Rondo game.

- Parkour at high speed/in fatigued condition where single-leg landing, sprint, changes of direction, push-ups, or sit-ups are included. The coach can indicate what to do at which point in parkour so that it is uncertain, making it challenging and fun for athlete.
- A mix of unanticipated deceleration and cutting in different directions, with and without the ball, with and without a defender, from different angles, at different speeds.

Where a defender employs inhibitory control so as to not be tempted to fall for a body feint of an attacker, methods to train this situation could be employing a visual go/no-go task utilising LED lights before a five-metre forward sprint. After the sprint, the defender could be instructed to perform multiple diagonal cuts and turns, but whether the defender goes left or right first depends on the colour of another LED light. After the cutting and turning, the defender could be placed in a square box, where they are tasked with reaching the edge of the square box as fast as possible, opposite to the direction of an arrow on a new other LED light. To mimic backward defending, the drill could be performed in reverse. This example includes a relevant motor component, the task constraints match the demands of the sport, and it preserves the athlete-environment relation. For more details regarding developing perceptual-cognitive abilities and change-of-direction technique, see Chapters 13 and 10, respectively.

Conclusion

When successfully guiding athletes to find their own optimal movement solution, a coach's job is not only to tell *what* needs to be improved but also *how*. The attentional and motivational aspects of motor learning are crucial for optimal outcome. Also, training design should be organised in such a way to optimally stimulate learning – for example, with differential learning and random practice.

References

Alentorn-Geli, E., Myer, G.D., Silvers, H.J., Samitier, G., Romero, D., Lázaro-Haro, C., Cugat, R. (2009). Prevention of non-contact anterior cruciate ligament injuries in soccer players. Part 2: A review of prevention programs aimed to modify risk factors and to reduce injury rates. *Knee Surgery, Sports Traumatology, Arthroscopy 17*(8), 859–879. doi: 10.1007/s00167-009-0823-z.

Almonroeder, T.G., Kernozek, T., Cobb, Slavens, B., Wang, J., Huddleston, W. (2018). Cognitive demands influence lower extremity mechanics during a drop vertical jump task in female athletes. *The Journal of Orthopaedic and Sports Physical Therapy, 48*(5), 381–387. https://doi.org/10.2519/jospt.2018.7739

Almonroeder, T.G., Kernozek, T., Cobb, S., Slavens, B., Wang, J., Huddleston, W. (2019). Divided attention during cutting influences lower extremity mechanics in female athletes. *Sports Biomechanics, 18*(3), 264–276. doi: 10.1080/14763141.2017.1391327.

Arundale, A.J.H., Bizzini, M., Giordano, A., Hewett, T.E., Logerstedt, D.S., Mandelbaum, B., Scalzitti, D.A., Silvers-Granelli, H., Snyder-Mackler, L. (2018). Exercise-based knee and anterior cruciate ligament injury prevention. *The Journal of Orthopaedic and Sports Physical Therapy, 48*(9), A1–A42. https://doi.org/10.2519/jospt.2018.0303.

Bartlett, R., Wheat, J., Robins, M. (2017). Is movement variability important for sports biomechanists? *Sports Biomanics, 6*(2), 224–243. doi: 10.1080/14763140701322994.

Beek, P.J. (2003). Toward a theory of implicit learning in the perceptual-motor domain. *International Journal of Sport Psychology, 31*, 547–554.

Beilock, S.L., Carr, T.H. (2001). On the fragility of skilled performance: what governs choking under pressure? *Journal of Experimental Psychology: General*, *130*, 701–725.

Benjaminse, A., Otten, B., Gokeler, A., Diercks, R.L., Lemmink, K.A.P.M. (2017). Motor learning strategies in basketball players and its implications for ACL injury prevention: A randomized controlled trial. *Knee Surgery, Sports Traumatology, Arthroscopy*, *25*, 2365–2376. doi: 10.1007/s00167-015-3727-0.

Benjaminse, A., Gokeler, A., Dowling, A. V., Faigenbaum, A., Ford, K. R., Hewett, T. E., Onate, J. A., Otten, B., Myer, G. D. (2015). Optimization of the anterior cruciate ligament injury prevention paradigm: Novel feedback techniques to enhance motor learning and reduce injury risk. *The Journal of Orthopaedic and Sports Physical Therapy*, *45*(3), 170–182. https://doi.org/10.2519/jospt.2015.4986

Benjaminse, A., Otten, E. (2011). ACL injury prevention, more effective with a different way of motor learning? *Knee Surgery, Sports Traumatology, Arthroscopy*, *19*(4), 622–627. doi: 10.1007/s00167-010-1313-z.

Benjaminse, A., Verhagen, E. (2021). Implementing ACL injury prevention in daily sports practice-it's not just the program: Let's build together, involve the context, and improve the content. *Sports Medicine*, *51*, 2461–2467. doi: 10.1007/s40279-021-01560-4.

Benjaminse, A., Welling, W., Otten, B., Gokeler, A. (2018). Transfer of improved movement technique after receiving verbal external focus and video instruction. *Knee Surgery, Sports Traumatology, Arthroscopy*, *26*, 955–962. doi:10.1007/s00167-017-4671-y.

Bolt, R., Heuvelmans, P., Benjaminse, A., Robinson, M.A., Gokeler, A. (2021). An ecological dynamics approach to ACL injury risk research: A current opinion. *Sports Biomechanics*, *10*, 1–14. doi: 10.1080/14763141.2021.1960419.

Broadbent, D.P., Causer, J., Williams, A.M., Ford, P.R. (2015). Perceptual-cognitive skill training and its transfer to expert performance in the field: Future research directions. *European Journal of Sport Science*, *15*, 322–331.

Brown, S.R., Brughelli, M., Hume, P.A. (2014). Knee mechanics during planned and unplanned sidestepping: A systematic review and meta-analysis. *Sports Medicine*, *44*, 1573–1588. doi:10.1007/s40279-014-0225-3

Büchel, D., Gokeler, A., Heuvelmans, P., Baumeister, J. (2022). Increased cognitive demands affect agility performance in female athletes – implications for testing and training of agility in team ball sports. *Perceptual and Motor Skills*, *129*(4), 1074–1088. https://doi.org/10.1177/00315125221108698

Clark, S.E., Ste-Marie, D.M. (2007). The impact of self-as-a-model interventions on children's self-regulation of learning and swimming performance. *Journal of Sports Sciences*, *25*, 577–586. doi: 10.1080/02640410600947090.

Della Villa, F., Buckthorpe, M., Grassi, A., Nabiuzzi, A., Tosarelli, F., Zaffagnini, S., Della Villa, S. (2020). Systematic video analysis of ACL injuries in professional male football (soccer): Injury mechanisms, situational patterns and biomechanics study on 134 consecutive cases. *British Journal of Sports Medicine*, *54*, 1423–1432.

Diamond, A. (2013). Executive functions. *Annual Review of Psychology*, *64*, 135–168. https://doi.org/10.1146/annurev-psych-113011-143750

DiPaolo, S., Nijmeijer, E., Bragonzoni, L., Dingshoff, E., Gokeler, A., Benjaminse, A. (2022). Comparing lab and field agility kinematics in young talented female football players: Implications for ACL injury prevention. *European Journal of Sport Science*, 1–10. https://doi.org/10.1080/17461391.2022.2064771

Dos'Santos T., McBurnie A., Donelon T., Thomas C., Comfort P., Jones P.A. (2019). A qualitative screening tool to identify athletes with 'high-risk' movement mechanics during cutting: The cutting movement assessment score (CMAS). *Physical Therapy in Sport*, *38*, 152–161.

Dos'Santos, T., Thomas, C., Comfort, P., Jones, P.A. (2018). The effect of angle and velocity on change of direction biomechanics: An angle-velocity trade-off. *Sports Medicine*, *48*, 2235–2253. doi: 10.1007/s40279-018-0968-3.

Dos'Santos, T., Thomas, C., McBurnie, A., Comfort, P., & Jones, P.A. (2021). Biomechanical determinants of performance and injury risk during cutting: A performance-injury conflict? *Sports Medicine*, *51*(9), 1983–1998. doi: 10.1007/s40279-021-01448-3.

Endsley, M.R. (1995). Towards a theory of situation awareness in dynamic systems. *Human Factors*, *37*, 32–64.

Eitam, B., Kennedy, P.M., Tory, H.E. (2013). Motivation from control. *Experimental Brain Research, 229*, 475–484. doi: 10.1007/s00221-012-3370-7.

Gokeler, A., Benjaminse, A., Della Villa, F., Tosarelli, F., Verhagen, E., Baumeister, J. (2021). Anterior cruciate ligament injury mechanisms through a neurocognition lens: implications for injury screening. *BMJ Open Sport & Exercise Medicine*, 7(2), e001091. https://doi.org/10.1136/bmjsem-2021-001091.

Gokeler, A., Benjaminse, A., Seil, R., Kerkhoffs, G., Verhagen, E.A.L.M. (2018). Using principles of motor learning to enhance ACL injury prevention programs. *Sports Orthopaedics and Traumatology, 34*(1), 23–30.

Gokeler, A., Neuhaus, D., Benjaminse, A., Grooms, D.R., Baumeister, J. (2019). Principles of motor learning to support neuroplasticity after ACL injury: Implications for optimizing performance and reducing risk of second ACL injury. *Sports Medicine, 49*(6), 853–865.

Grand K.F., Bruzi A.T., Dyke F.B., Godwin M.M., Leiker A.M., Thompson A.G., Buchanan T.L., Miller M.W. (2015). Why self-controlled feedback enhances motor learning: Answers from electroencephalography and indices of motivation. *Human Movement Science, 43*, 23–32.

Guadagnoli, M.A., Lee, T.D. (2004). Challenge point: A framework for conceptualizing the effects of various practice conditions in motor learning. *Journal of Motor Behavior, 36*(2), 212–224. doi: 10.3200/JMBR.36.2.212-224.

Hadlow S.M., Panchuk D., Mann D.L., Portus M.R. (2018). Abernethy B. Modified perceptual training in sport: A new classification framework. *Journal of Science & Medicine in Sport, 21*(9), 950–958. doi: 10.1016/j.jsams.2018.01.011.

Hardy L., Mullen R., Jones G. (1996). Knowledge and conscious control of motor actions under stress. *British Journal of Psychology, 87*, 621–636.

Havens K.L., Sigward S.M. (2014). Whole body mechanics differ among running and cutting maneuvers in skilled athletes. *Gait & Posture, 42*(3), 240–245.

Havens K.L., Sigward S.M. (2015). Joint and segmental mechanics differ between cutting maneuvers in skilled athletes. *Gait & Posture, 41*(1), 33–38.

Henz, D., Schöllhorn, W.I. (2016). Differential training facilitates early consolidation in motor learning. *Frontiers in Behavioral Neuroscience, 21*, 199. https://doi.org/10.3389/fnbeh.2016.00199.

Hooyman, A., Wulf, G., Lewthwaite, R. (2014). Impacts of autonomy-supportive versus controlling instructional language on motor learning. *Human Movement Science, 36*, 190–198. https://doi.org/10.1016/j.humov.2014.04.005

Ille, A., Selin, I., Do, M.C., Thon, B. (2013). Attentional focus effects on sprint start performance as a function of skill level. *Journal of Sports Sciences, 31*(15), 1705–1712. https://doi.org/10.1080/02640414.2013.797097

Kinrade, N.P., Jackson, R.C., Ashford, K.J. (2015). Reinvestment, task complexity and decision making under pressure in basketball. *Psychology of Sport and Exercise, 20*, 11–19.

Krosshaug, T., Nakamae, A., Boden, B.P., Engebretsen, L., Smith, G., Slauterbeck, J.R., Hewett, T.E., Bahr, R. (2007). Mechanisms of anterior cruciate ligament injury in basketball: video analysis of 39 cases. *The American Journal of Sports Medicine, 35*(3), 359–367.

Lage, G.M., Ugrinowitsch, H., Apolinário-Souza, T., Vieira, M.M., Albuquerque, M.R., Benda, R.N. (2015). Repetition and variation in motor practice: A review of neural correlates. *Neuroscience and Biobehavioral Reviews, 57*, 132–141. https://doi.org/10.1016/j.neubiorev.2015.08.012.

Lee, M.J., Lloyd, D.G., Lay, B.S., Bourke, P.D., Alderson, J.A. (2013). Effects of different visual stimuli on postures and knee moments during sidestepping. *Medicine and Science in Sports and Exercise, 45*(9), 1740–1748. doi: 10.1249/MSS.0b013e318290c28a.

Lewthwaite, R., Wulf, G. (2010). Social-comparative feedback affects motor skill learning. *Quarterly Journal of Experimental Psychology (Hove), 63*(4), 738–749. https://doi.org/10.1080/17470210903111839

Lucarno, S., Zago, M., Buckthorpe, M., Grassi, A., Tosarelli, F., Smith, R., Della Villa, F. (2021). Systematic video analysis of anterior cruciate ligament injuries in professional female soccer players. *The American Journal of Sports Medicine, 49*(7), 1794–1802. https://doi.org/10.1177/03635465211008169

Magill, R.A., Hall, K.G. (1990). A review of the contextual interference effect in motor skill acquisition. *Human Movement Science, 9*, 241–289.

Makaruk, H., Porter, J. (2014). Focus of attention for strength and conditioning training. *Strength and Conditioning Journal, 36*, 16–22. doi: 10.1519/SSC.0000000000000008

Masters, R.S.W. (1992). Knowledge, "knerves" and know-how: The role of explicit versus implicit knowledge in the break-down of a complex motor skill under pressure. *British Journal of Psychology, 83*, 343–358.

Masters, R.S., Poolton, J.M., Maxwell, J.P. (2008a). Stable implicit motor processes despite aerobic locomotor fatigue. *Consciousness and Cognition, 17*(1), 335–338. https://doi.org/10.1016/j.concog.2007.03.009

Masters, R.S., Poolton, J.M., Maxwell, J.P., Raab, M. (2008b). Implicit motor learning and complex decision making in time-constrained environments. *Journal of Motor Behavior, 40*(1), 71–79. https://doi.org/10.3200/JMBR.40.1.71-80

McKay, B., Lewthwaite, R., Wulf, G. (2012). Enhanced expectancies improve performance under pressure. *Frontiers in Psychology, 3*, 8. https://doi.org/10.3389/fpsyg.2012.00008

McLean, S.G., Borotikar, B., Lucey, S.M. (2010). Lower limb muscle pre-motor time measures during a choice reaction task associate with knee abduction loads during dynamic single leg landings. *Clinical Biomechanics (Bristol, Avon), 25*(6), 563–569. doi: 10.1016/j.clinbiomech.2010.02.013.

Milley, K.R., Ouellette, G.P. (2021). putting attention on the spot in coaching: shifting to an external focus of attention with imagery techniques to improve basketball free-throw shooting performance. *Frontiers in Psychology, 12*, 645676. https://doi.org/10.3389/fpsyg.2021.64567

Moreira, P.E.D., Dieguez, G.T.d.O., Bredt, S.d.G.T., Praça, G.M. (2021). The acute and chronic effects of dual-task on the motor and cognitive performances in athletes: A systematic review. *International Journal of Environmental Research and Public Health, 18*(4), 1732. https://doi.org/10.3390/ijerph18041732

Norte, G.E., Frendt, T.R., Murray, A.M., Armstrong, C.W., McLoughlin, T.J., Donovan, L.T. (2020). Influence of anticipation and motor-motor task performance on cutting biomechanics in healthy men. *Journal of Athletic Training, 55*(8), 834–842. https://doi.org/10.4085/1062-6050-569-18

Orangi, B.M., Yaali, R., Abbas Bahram, A., Kamp, J., Aghdasi, M.T. (2021).The effects of linear, nonlinear, and differential motor learning methods on the emergence of creative action in individual soccer players. *Psychology of Sport & Exercise*, 56. https://doi.org/10.1016/j.psychsport.2021.102009

Otte, F. W., Davids, K., Millar, S. K., Klatt, S. (2020). When and how to provide feedback and instructions to athletes? how sport psychology and pedagogy insights can improve coaching interventions to enhance self-regulation in training. *Frontiers in Psychology, 11*, 1444. https://doi.org/10.3389/fpsyg.2020.01444

Poolton, J.M., Masters, R.S., Maxwell, J.P. (2007). Passing thoughts on the evolutionary stability of implicit motor behaviour: Performance retention under physiological fatigue. *Consciousness and Cognition, 16*(2), 456–468. https://doi.org/10.1016/j.concog.2006.06.00

Porter, J.M., Nolan, R.P., Ostrowski, E.J., Wulf, G. (2010). Directing attention externally enhances agility performance: a qualitative and quantitative analysis of the efficacy of using verbal instructions to focus attention. *Frontiers in Psychology, 1*, 216. https://doi.org/10.3389/fpsyg.2010.00216

Reimer, T., Park, E.S., Hinsz, V.B. (2006). Shared and coordinated cognition in competitive and dynamic task environments: An information-processing perspective for team sports. *International Journal of Sport & Exercise Psychology, 4*(4), 376–400. https://doi.org/10.1080/1612197X.2006.9671804

Renshaw, I., Davids, K., Araújo, D., Lucas, A., Roberts, W. M., Newcombe, D. J., Franks, B. (2019). Evaluating weaknesses of "perceptual-cognitive training" and "brain training" methods in sport: An ecological dynamics critique. *Frontiers in Psychology, 9*, 2468. https://doi.org/10.3389/fpsyg.2018.02468

Rosenqvist, O., Skans, O.N. (2015). Confidence enhanced performance? – The causal effects of success on future performance in professional golf tournaments. *Journal of Economic Behavior & Organization, 117*, 281–295.

Ryan, R.M., Deci, E.L. (2000). Self-determination theory and the facilitation of intrinsic motivation, social development, and well-being. *The American Psychologist, 55*(1), 68–78. https://doi.org/10.1037//0003-066x.55.1.68

Saemi, E., Porter, J.M., Ghotbi-Varzaneh, A., Zarghami, M., Maleki, F. (2012). Knowledge of results after relatively good trials enhances self-efficacy and motor learning. *Psychology of Sport & Exercise, 13*, 378–382.

Sanli, E.A., Patterson, J.T., Bray, S.R., Lee, T.D. (2013). Understanding self-controlled motor learning protocols through the self-determination theory. *Frontiers in Psychology, 3*, 611. https://doi.org/10.3389/fpsyg.2012.00611

Schöllhorn, W.I., Mayer-Kress, G., Newell, K.M., Michelbrink, M. (2009). Time scales of adaptive behavior and motor learning in the presence of stochastic perturbations. *Human Movement Science, 28*(3), 319–333.

Shea, J. B., & Morgan, R. L. (1979). Contextual interference effects on the acquisition, retention, and transfer of a motor skill. *Journal of Experimental Psychology: Human Learning and Memory, 5*(2), 179–187. doi: 10.1037/0278–7393.5.2.179.

Shea, C.H., Wright, D.L., Wulf, G., Whitacre, C. (2000). Physical and observational practice afford unique learning opportunities. *Journal of Motor Behavior, 32*(1), 27–36. https://doi.org/10.1080/00222890009601357

Shea, C. H., Wulf, G. (2005). Schema theory: A critical appraisal and reevaluation. *Journal of Motor Behavior, 37*(2), 85–101. https://doi.org/10.3200/JMBR.37.2.85-102

Sigward, S.M., Cesar, G.M., Havens, K.L. (2015). Predictors of frontal plane knee moments during side-step cutting to 45 and 110 degrees in men and women: Implications for anterior cruciate ligament injury. *Clinical Journal of Sport Medicine, 25*(6), 529–534. https://doi.org/10.1097/JSM.0000000000000001

Singh, H., Gokeler, A., Benjaminse, A. (2021). Effective attentional focus strategies after anterior cruciate ligament reconstruction: A commentary. *International Journal of Sports Physical Therapy, 16*(6), 1575–1585. https://doi.org/10.26603/001c.29848

Swanik, C.B. (2015). Brains and sprains: The brain's role in noncontact anterior cruciate ligament injuries. *Journal of Athletic Training, 50*, 1100–1102.

Su, Y.-L., Reeve, J. (2011). A meta-analysis of the effectiveness of intervention programs designed to support autonomy. *Educational Psychology Review, 23*(1), 159–188.

Tassignon, B., Verschueren, J., Baeyens, J.P., Benjaminse, A., Gokeler, A., Serrien, B., Clijsen, R. (2021). An exploratory meta-analytic review on the empirical evidence of differential learning as an enhanced motor learning method. *Frontiers in Psychology*, 7(12), 533033. doi: 10.3389/fpsyg.2021.533033.

Teques, P., Araújo, D., Seifert, L., Del Campo, V. L., Davids, K. (2017). The resonant system: Linking brain-body-environment in sport performance*. *Progress in Brain Research, 234*, 33–52. doi: 10.1016/bs.pbr.2017.06.001.

Vestberg, T., Reinebo, G., Maurex, L., Ingvar, M., Petrovic P. (2017). Core executive functions are associated with success in young elite soccer athletes. *PLoS One, 12*(2), e0170845.

Winkelman N. (2020). *The language of coaching – the art & science of teaching movement*. 1st edn. Champaign, IL: Human Kinetics Publishers.

Winkelman, N. C., Clark, K. P., Ryan, L. J. (2017). Experience level influences the effect of attentional focus on sprint performance. *Human Movement Science, 52*, 84–95.

Wulf, G. (2016). Why did Tiger Woods shoot 82? A commentary on Toner and Moran (2015). *Psychology of Sport & Exercise, 22*, 337–338. https://doi.org/10.1016/j.psychsport.2015.05.006

Wulf, G., Dufek, J.S. (2009). Increased jump height with an external focus due to enhanced lower extremity joint kinetics. *Journal of Motor Behavior, 41*(5), 401–409. https://doi.org/10.1080/00222890903228421

Wulf, G., Lewthwaite, R. (2016). Optimizing performance through intrinsic motivation and attention for learning: The OPTIMAL theory of motor learning. *Psychonomic Bulletin & Review, 23*(5), 1382–1414. https://doi.org/10.3758/s13423-015-0999

Wymbs, N.F., Grafton, S.T. (2009). Neural substrates of practice structure that support future off-line learning. *Journal of Neurophysiology, 102*(4), 2462–2476. https://doi.org/10.1152/jn.00315.2009

12

METABOLIC CONDITIONING FOR MULTIDIRECTIONAL SPEED

Liam Anderson and Barry Drust

What is Multidirectional Speed?

Multidirectional speed (MDS) can be defined as 'the competency and capacity to accelerate, decelerate, change direction, and maintain speed in multiple directions and movements, within the context of sport-specific scenarios' (McBurnie et al., 2021). In sport match play, CODs can be performed in two ways: MDS of a singular occurrence (i.e. one run in a cricket match) or repeated bouts (i.e. performing an intense rally over various areas of the court in a tennis match). In addition, CODs can occur within training and competition over a range of different approach velocities, turn angles, and exit velocities, all of which can influence the mechanical and metabolic demands, adding to the complexity of these movements.

The Importance of Multidirectional Speed

The ability to perform a rapid COD, whilst running is an important physical component for multidirectional court- and field-based sports (Barber et al., 2016; Besier et al., 2001; Sheppard and Young, 2006; Young et al., 2015; Dos'Santos et al., 2022). The greater the speed that the movement(s) are performed at can elicit an advantage over opponents by manoeuvring past them, making a tackle, reaching the ball before them (or earlier to allow more time to make a shot), or completing a run to score a point. This is important as the ability to perform high-intensity actions, such as unpredictable COD manoeuvres while in motion, have been shown to differentiate players from different playing standards (Haugen et al., 2013; Reilly et al., 2000). In sports such as professional soccer, this is perhaps one of the reasons why higher-quality players possess greater MDS and can score or prevent goals to a greater extent. This is highlighted by high-intensity COD actions preceding ~35% of goals scored in the English Premier League (Martínez-Hernández et al., 2022). Although there were no direct assessments of MDS taken within these observations, higher levels of MDS will likely allow players to manoeuvre quickly past an opposing player to score or find space to perform a clearer shot at goal.

In addition to singular actions to gain an advantage over opponents, court- and field-based sports require the ability to sustain the ability to perform repeated bouts of high-intensity or

DOI: 10.4324/9781003267881-14

multiple MDS actions within a short epoch throughout performances and competition (Iaia and Bangsbo, 2010). Within court- and field-based sports, actions can occur frequently and repeatedly. This will alter the physical requirements as actions are performed over different durations and likely varied intensities. For example, professional tennis consists of alternating short (4–10 seconds) bouts of high-intensity activity and short (10–20 seconds) recovery bouts interrupted by several resting periods of longer duration (60–90 seconds) (Fernandez et al., 2006; Kovacs, 2007). Within this high-intensity activity, a tennis player runs an average of 3 m per shot, a total of 8 to 15 m in the pursuit of one point, with the 4 CODs on average number per point (Deutsch et al., 1988; Fernandez-Fernandez et al., 2007; Fernandez-Fernandez et al., 2009; Murias et al., 2007; Parsons and Jones, 1998). In addition, 'worst-case scenarios' in tennis can extend to 20–30 shots and therefore have 20–30 CODs, with 5% of points in the Australian Open involving more than 7 CODs (Giles et al., 2021). Indeed, the speed at which the tennis player performs these COD can lead to a direct advantage over their opponent, affording them more preparation to coordinate and execute their shot and be more aggressive with play. In addition, the maximum COD demands within 15- and 5-minute periods in a cohort of elite academy soccer players were 62 and 25 bouts, respectively (Morgan et al., 2022). This highlights the importance of singular isolated COD actions and repeated bouts of COD, which can be extreme in certain conditions and therefore are required to be conditioned for. However, before specific training programmes can be designed, it is important to understand the mechanical and metabolic aspect of MDS so that they are aligned with the demands of each sport.

Mechanical Factors Underpinning Multidirectional Speed

Prior to designing physical preparation programmes to develop MDS, understanding the mechanical underpinnings are imperative to effectively develop specific MDS training for athletes. Mechanical loading refers to the forces that both hard (i.e. skeletal) and soft tissues (muscles, tendons, ligaments, etc.) of body are exposed to during different movements (Verheul et al., 2020). From a mechanical perspective, a COD can be broken down into an initial acceleration, followed by a deceleration, a planting of the foot and a reacceleration in a different direction (Sheppard and Young, 2006). Although in theory this breakdown seems simple, each phase of a COD can differ for variables, such as the deceleration intensity and duration, the angle of the new direction and the reacceleration intensity, all of which impact the mechanical loading on the athlete. We will now provide a brief summary of the different mechanical aspects of a COD. For more detailed information on different aspects of the COD, please see Chapters 4 and 5 on COD and deceleration, respectively.

During a COD, the deceleration steps in preparation for the turn require a braking impulse to reduce momentum (Dos'Santos et al., 2017; Dos'Santos et al., 2018; Jones et al., 2016; Dos'Santos et al., 2020). Indeed, this is subject to entry velocity, angle of COD, scenario, and an athlete's physical capacity with multidirectional movements, further complicating movement profiles. This braking impulse that is typical for many COD places an emphasis on muscle lengthening through the braking action with this type of action commonly classified as eccentric muscle actions (Herzog, 2018; Castillo-Rodriguez et al., 2012). After the deceleration into the COD, the foot becomes planted and force is attenuated, requiring isometric strength (McBurnie and Dos'Santos, 2021). Following the foot plant, the reacceleration in a different direction (propulsion) phase of a COD is an important component for producing high levels of MDS (McBurnie and Dos'Santos, 2021). Accelerations require concentric strength and power of the lower-limb triple extensors to produce high vertical, medio-lateral, and horizontal (dependent on angle) and thus resultant forces oriented in the optimal direction (Bret et al., 2002; Lockie et al., 2012; Nikolaidis et al., 2016; Kawamori et al., 2013; Weyand et al., 2000). Within the acceleration phase, it is typical that those athletes that can produce the higher force concentrically will exit the COD at a greater speed, improving MDS.

These mechanical aspects of the different phases within a COD are important to understand before effective training programmes can be administered. Knowledge of the movements and muscle action types during different phases of a COD can help design training programmes aiming to improve whole movements or specific aspects. However, to design and prescribe training programmes aimed at improving athletes' metabolic function, we must further understand the metabolic aspects of COD and MDS.

Metabolic Factors Underpinning Multidirectional Speed

Metabolic factors that underpin MDS refers to the physiological process to provide energy sources and neural activation to produce muscular contraction within a COD. In an acute instance, rapid CODs are of a high-intensity nature. Performing COD in high-intensity exercise significantly increases the energy cost and places an increased energy demand on the anaerobic energy system than straight-line running alone (Stevens et al., 2015; Akenhead et al., 2015; Zamparo et al., 2014; Hader et al., 2014; Buglione and di Prampero, 2013; Hatamoto et al., 2013; Buchheit et al., 2011; Dellal et al., 2010; Tang et al., 2018). Given the high-intensity nature of rapid COD, they require ATP resynthesis through the breakdown of creatine phosphate (CP) and the degradation of muscle glycogen via glycolysis to lactic acid (McCartney et al., 1986; Spriet et al., 1989; Withers et al., 1991). Within practical settings, athletes can perform rapid COD in a singular (i.e. one run in cricket) and repeated (i.e. long rally where the athlete is moving from one side of the court to the other repeatedly in tennis) bouts. However, when repeated bouts of high-intensity exercise are performed, aerobic metabolism begins to play an increased role in energy delivery (Bogdanis et al., 1996). Given the typical durations and intensities of both singular and repeated bouts of COD, they likely have significant contributions of all energy systems, working along an intensity-duration based continuum (see Figures 12.1 and 12.2).

It can be practically difficult obtaining direct measurements of the anaerobic energy system contributions. Physiological measurements during or after performing different activities provides an indication of energy contribution for athletes. During high-intensity anaerobic activity, lactate is metabolised within active muscles (Brooks, 1987). Lactate that is released from active muscles to the blood is taken up by different tissues, such as the heart, liver, kidneys, and inactive muscles (Brooks, 1987). Therefore, when blood lactate is assessed, it represents its balance of production, release, and removal, being an appropriate indirect indicator of anaerobic energy production. Examining the blood lactate response to exercise that included 180° COD reported values, ~10 $mmol^{-1}$, which were 13% greater than distance matched straight-line sprinting (Buchheit et al., 2011). Similar results were found in an intensity matched design between COD running and straight-line running (further matched for accelerations and decelerations), where the five-minute post-exercise lactate response was 8.5 $mmol^{-1}$ vs 1.7 $mmol^{-1}$ for the COD and straight-line running, respectively (Maasar et al., 2021). These data clearly outline the impact of including COD in exercise prescription has on anaerobic metabolism.

In addition to blood lactate values, the assessment of heart rate provides an indication of energy contribution to exercise. Examining the influence of performing a 180° COD during

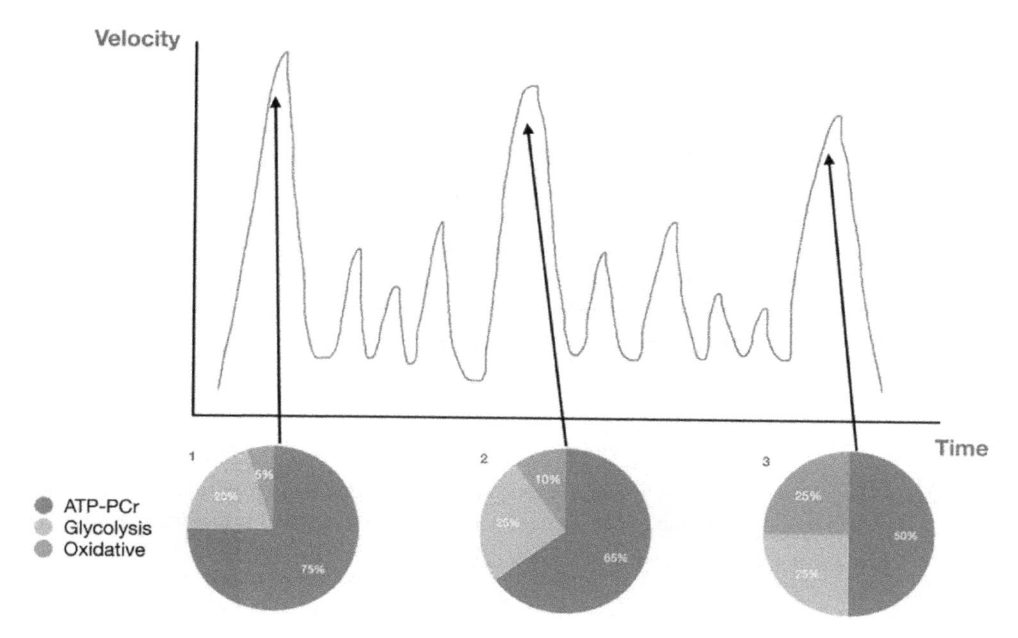

FIGURE 12.1 A hypothetical velocity trace and potential energy system contribution to three high-intensity efforts. High-intensity effort 1 is performed at the start of the exercise bout, with efforts 2 and 3 performed interspersed within a bed of low-intensity activity. Each effort decreases in velocity due to energy system contribution.

high-intensity interval training at different percentages of vVO_2max indicates that the percentage heart rate reserve is ~7.1% greater than straight-line running. Given that performing COD within exercise influences the physiological response, Tang et al. (2018) observed a 54.5% increase in heart rate exertion (a weighted equation depending on time spent in different heart rate zones) when the number of COD increased from 1–3 to 7 in a distance matched study design. Taken together, the blood lactate and heart rate responses to COD exercise indicate a significant contribution by the anaerobic and aerobic energy systems. Targeted training of these energy systems through metabolic conditioning will lead to increased efficiency and an improvement in MDS.

What Is Metabolic Conditioning?

Metabolic conditioning refers to training that targets an energy system and should be specific to the physiological and energy demands experienced during competition (Gamble, 2007). The human body has three different energy systems: phosphagen, glycolytic, and oxidative (see Figure 12.1). They often overlap and work together to produce muscular contractions of different intensities and volumes with one energy system typically dominating at a given time. The ATP-PC pathway provides most of the energy used in high-intensity activities (those that last less than 10 seconds). The glycolytic pathway dominates moderately intense activities (those that last up to several minutes) and the oxidative pathway provides energy for lower intensity activities (those that last more than several minutes). Within court- and field-based sports, where the exercise profile is intermittent, different energy systems can have more pronounced roles within energy delivery for different actions. For

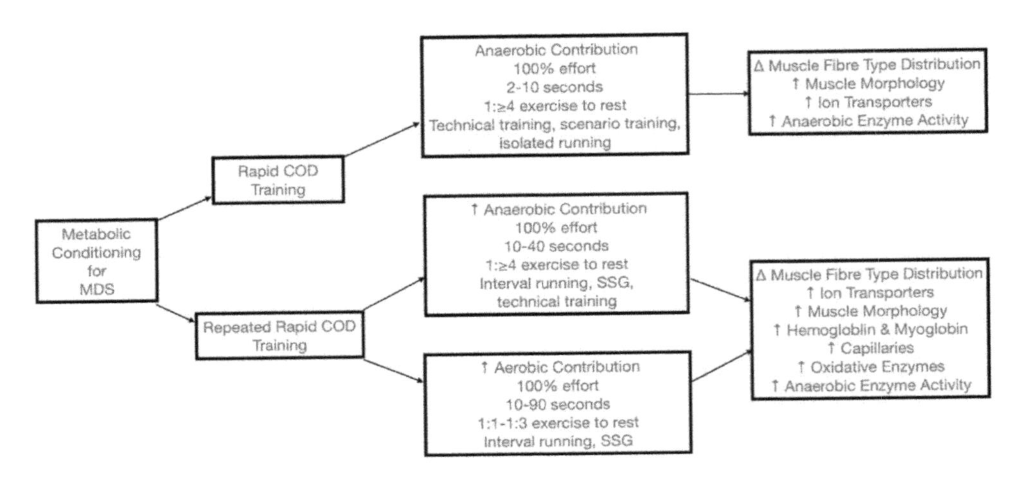

FIGURE 12.2 An overview of energy system training guidelines and physiological adaptations that will occur when metabolic conditioning for multidirectional speed is undertaken.

Key: MDS = Multi-directional speed and COD = Change of Direction

example, when repeated bouts of high-intensity exercise are performed, aerobic (oxidative) metabolism has a greater role in energy delivery (see Figure 12.1) (Bogdanis et al., 1996). The ATP-PC and glycolytic pathway typically operate without oxygen and are known collectively as the anaerobic energy system, whereas the oxidative system operates with oxygen and is known as the aerobic energy system. Targeted training of an energy system can increase the storage and delivery of energy for activities within it. Essentially, this creates more efficient energy production, allowing athletes to perform at higher intensities, improving MDS with a reduced physiological cost.

The anaerobic energy system typically prevails throughout COD over short periods (i.e. <10 seconds) and repeatedly for longer durations (i.e. 60 seconds). Therefore, to improve MDS, metabolic conditioning should look to maximise anaerobic adaptations but also understand the aerobic energy system can also contribute when COD bouts are performed repeatedly with reduced exercise-to-rest ratios and periods of low-to-moderate-intensity activity between. Specifically, in singular COD bouts, the ATP-PC energy system and in repeated bouts the glycolytic energy system are the major contributors of energy source. From a training perspective, metabolic conditioning must yield appropriate motor unit activity, substrate flux, and force-speed production patterns such that the anaerobic pathways are recruited in active muscles (Plisk, 1991). Such training is typically accomplished through sets of repetitions that are often referred to as intervals or sprints and performed intermittently at variable exercise: rest ratios, durations, and intensities. This type of training is often termed high-intensity interval (HIIT) training. From a metabolic conditioning perspective, training is performed at a maximum intensity for durations of 2–90 seconds per repetition with varying work to rest (see Figure 12.2). Working at these maximum intensities for these durations can lead to significant metabolic adaptations that improve MDS.

Whilst many court- and field-based sports can be complex and require multiple training goals, metabolic conditioning can form a vital part of energy system development to improve MDS. As a physical component is being trained, it is important to adhere to the principles of training, understand different metabolic conditioning strategies and how manipulating them can lead to different adaptations. The following sections of this chapter will discuss some practical considerations for training including specific principles of training and strategies used to target different aspects related to MDS.

Practical Considerations for Training

To optimise physiological adaptation to metabolic conditioning, training should be founded on the appreciation of principles of training. Within many court- and field-based sports, there are usually multiple components of fitness required to be developed in addition to technical and tactical components. Due to the multifactorial nature of many sports and the relationship between training load, athletic performance, and injury risk (Verstappen et al., 2021), metabolic conditioning of MDS should be strategically inputted (i.e. periodised) into the training programme. Indeed, training at high intensities induces significant muscle damage and are associated with different injury types (Ekstrand et al., 2011; Malone et al., 2018). Careful considerations should therefore be taken by making players familiar with this type of training through gradual increases in the intensity, volume, and frequency, as well as appropriate management of the overall training load when administering and a thorough warm-up prior to training.

Specificity is widely identified as a fundamental factor in shaping the adaptive response (Morrissey et al., 1995). It is related to the physiological nature of the training stimulus and how it resembles competition. From a MDS perspective, this provides the rationale for understanding the mechanical and metabolic demands of COD before implementing any conditioning. Therefore, training from a metabolic perspective involves anaerobic training that consists of some, or all elements of a COD (i.e. acceleration, deceleration, planting, reacceleration). Within sports requiring MDS, this can be performed using both generic running conditioning and/or sport-specific conditioning (i.e. running without the racquet performing COD in tennis versus performing COD as part of a specific sequence of a rally inclusive of ball strikes). In addition, it is important to understand the multidirectional movement demands of the sport prior to implementing programmes aimed at developing MDS so that they are specific to the demands of competition. For example, cricket batsmen typically perform 180° COD that occur 17.68 m in distance away from each other in a singular movement, whereas badminton players typically have ~90° COD moving laterally back into the centre of the court (~3 m) and usually repeatedly as part of extended rallies. Moreover, within most field sports, differences can exist for positions and a team's tactical strategy, all of which can increase the specificity of the training stimulus to competition (Stolen et al., 2005). Understanding an athlete's individual movement demands will allow training programmes to be designed specifically to meet their requirements. Analysing performance prior to programme design is an important step to facilitate this.

Effective training programmes require a structured approach to continue to elicit adaptations. Given that court- and field-based sports have multiple physical training goals to be achieved within short time periods, alongside frequent and intense competition, it can be important to target overload at specific points in the macrocycle where it is deemed appropriate. Progressive overload is typically obtained through subtle changes in the volume (i.e. the total quantity of the activity performed), intensity (i.e. the qualitative component of the exercise), and frequency (the number of sessions in a period of time-balance between exercise and recovery) of training (Bompa, 1994). Given that MDS training is frequently performed at maximal intensity, manipulation of the volume and frequency will likely provide progressions to the programme to improve MDS. In addition, MDS overload can be created from both mechanical and metabolic load, with increases in mechanical load likely causing a subsequent increase in metabolic response. For example, introducing sharper (increased angle of) CODs elicits greater mechanical and metabolic load. Therefore, manipulating the angle of COD and entry velocity can provide an 'additional layer' to programming and exercise prescription. As the exercise stimulus is progressed, there will be an improvement in an athlete's MDS. Progressive overload of training should be individualised as each athlete will adapt differently to the training stimuli. This outlines the importance of regularly testing and monitoring athletes throughout training programmes to understand adaptations and physiological status.

It must be noted that often MDS training should be considered as part of the overall athletic training programme, which encompasses multiple components that are responsible for holistic performance. It is therefore suggested that the planning and prescription of training to develop MDS should be implemented into an overall periodised plan. For example, during the in-season of professional soccer, it seems logical to perform MDS training in the middle of the microcycle (i.e. Match Day-4 or Match Day-3), where there is enough recovery from/to the competitive matches. Additionally, there are specific periods of the macrocycle where training aspects can be overloaded (i.e. pre-season) to optimise adaptations. Of course, monitoring the physiological adaptations and potential maladaptation from training is important for the overall performance and health of the athletes.

As athletes terminate or reduce participation in training and competition, a loss of physiological and performance adaptations can occur (detraining). After only one or two weeks of training cessation detraining reduces metabolic function, with many training adaptations fully lost within several months. Within the training programme, reversibility occurs typically during the off-season or through periods of injury where traditional training cannot occur. To minimise the detrimental effects of this, athletes should maintain some moderate level of training to slow the decline in metabolic and physiological function.

Training Strategies

Training of MDS can be split into rapid COD (speed) and repeated rapid COD training (speed endurance) training (see Figure 12.2). It can be performed in running drills that are specific to the sport or in conditioned games or practices that overload the specific demands of the sport. Key metabolic adaptations to anaerobic training include an increase in activity of anaerobic enzymes (Ross and Leveritt, 2001), improved K^+ handling (Bangsbo et al., 2009), lactate-H^+ transport capacity (Gunnarsson et al., 2013), H^+ regulation (Skovgaard et al., 2014), and muscle capillarisation (Jensen et al., 2004). Many of these adaptations improve the rate of anaerobic energy turnover during exercise and reduce the inhibitory effects of H^+ within the muscle cell. These factors may improve the ability to produce power rapidly for longer periods and improve recovery after a high-intensity exercise bout, allowing athletes a greater ability to perform high-intensity actions for longer durations and repeat them, with less fatigue, over the duration of the match. In addition, when large motor units are recruited within training, it can lead to further neural adaptations that are associated with COD.

Rapid COD Training

Improving MDS through rapid COD training aims to improve the ability to produce a high amount of force in a relatively short time in the intended direction of travel (DeWeese and Nimphius, 2016). It requires athletes to perform at their maximum effort for short periods of time (2–10 seconds) but allows for sufficient rest between repetitions. Sufficient rest is important between repetitions so that players can fully recover, and rapid and high-magnitude forces can be attenuated and produced in the following repetition (Reilly and Bangsbo, 1998). Therefore, recovery between repetitions should be high (i.e. 1:6 exercise-to-rest ratio), repetitions should be low (<10) and should be performed early in training sessions to maintain maximum output with low levels of fatigue. It is vitally important that this type of training is performed after an adequate warm-up to adequately prepare athletes for the level of intensity. This type of training primarily stresses the ATP-PC energy system.

Rapid COD training should be integrated in a way which is specific to the sport to maximise transfer into competition and should occur in addition to (or carefully placed into the training design) other training load that athletes are exposed to. For example, a hockey defender is looking to improve the MDS on recovery runs when an opposition player breaks the line, the player can perform maximal intensity COD at angles >90° with a reduced acceleration distance (see Figure 12.3). To add further specificity to the drill the player can react to the stimulus of the ball being played through and try to intercept it before it reaches the desired location. This also helps training efficiency by reducing overall training time by linking the training into the requirements of the sessions, limiting unnecessary, low-quality COD exposures.

Rapid COD training can be broken down further (i.e. acceleration training, deceleration training; see Figure 12.4) and be performed as a whole movement. This allows an isolated approach to specific mechanical aspects of the COD. In this instance, the isolation is related to specific

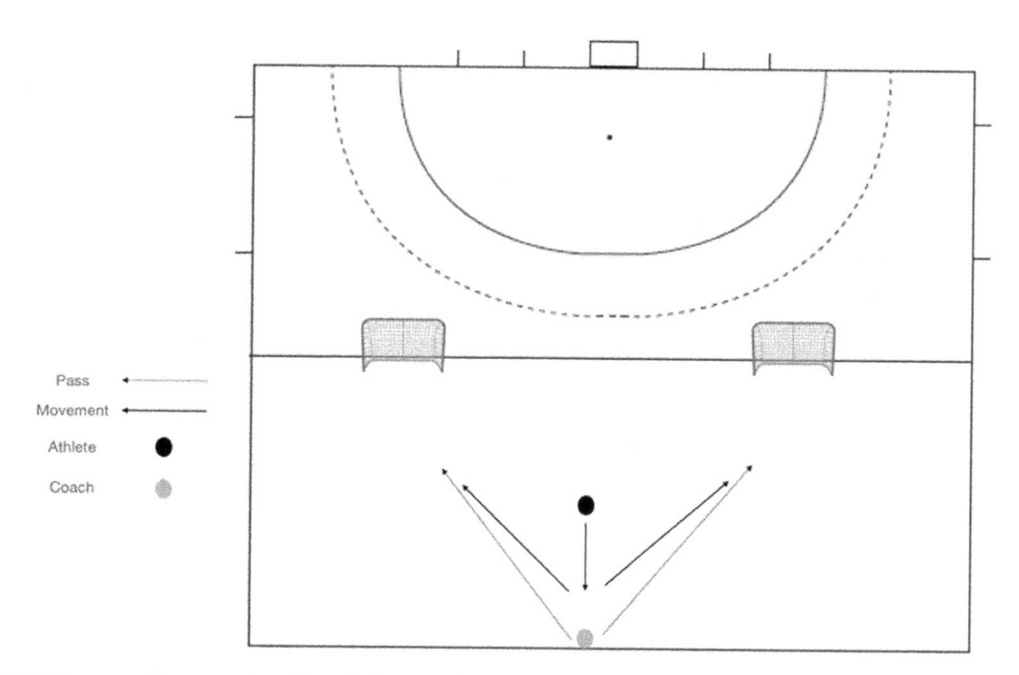

FIGURE 12.3 An example of rapid change-of-direction drill for defending hockey players. Working player accelerates into the coach and decelerates rapidly. Within the deceleration, they assess their body angle for which way they will play the through pass. Working player performs a rapid change of direction 90–130° in the direction of pass in attempt to intercept it before it reaches the goal.

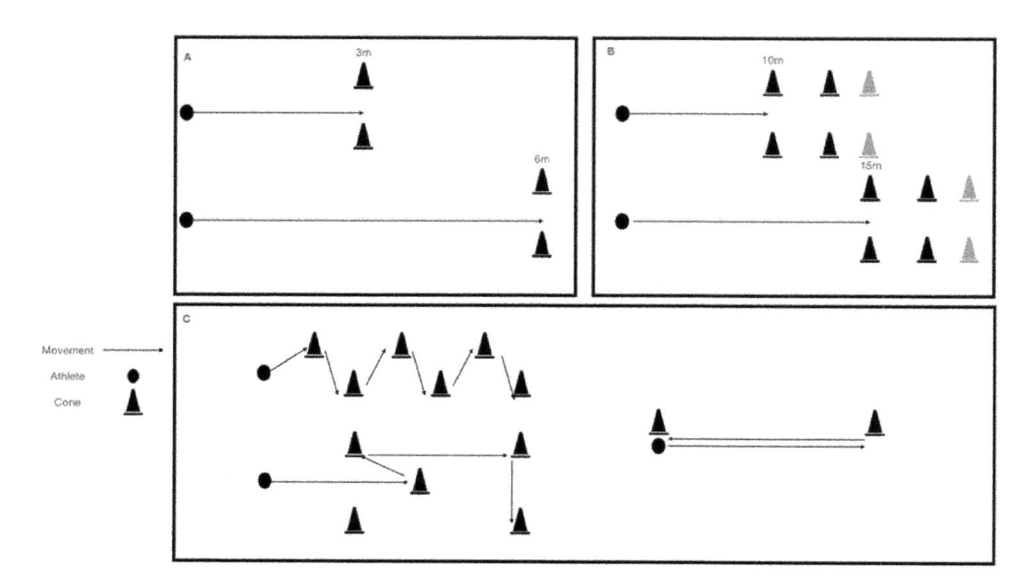

FIGURE 12.4 An example of rapid change-of-direction drills broken down into (A) acceleration phase, (B) deceleration phase, and (C) whole movement. (A) Athlete performs an acceleration through the cones in varying distances of either 3 m or 6 m. (B) Athlete performs an acceleration followed by an intensive deceleration within the designated area (to progress the training, cones can be moved from the far right grey into the black ones to decrease the deceleration distance). (C) Multiple changes of direction in a zigzag fashion, a 130° change of direction followed by a 90° change of direction and a 180° change-of-direction drill.

muscular actions in different actions of the COD but ultimately leading to overall greater MDS. For example, the athlete's ability to accelerate quicker in a straight-line sprint improves the ability to accelerate quicker after the COD plant (Bourgeois et al., 2017). From a deceleration perspective, the physiological adaptations following regular deceleration exposure is unclear. However, in support of the potential for regular deceleration training to elicit positive physiological adaptations comes from high-velocity sprint training where there was an improvement in performance times as well as positive architectural shifts in hamstring muscles (e.g. increased fascicle length) (Mendiguchia et al., 2020). Due to the high eccentric braking demands of a deceleration, likely similar adaptations occur and can be trained within specific sprint context. Therefore, performing both high-intensity accelerations and decelerations in the form of rapid COD training can improve MDS.

Although isolating different aspects of a COD likely leads to improved MDS in rapid COD training, it is likely that performing whole movements (i.e. acceleration, deceleration, or reacceleration in a different direction) is necessary as part of the overall programme. As part of a speed and agility programme, MDS increased over a six-week period in collegiate athletes (Lockie et al., 2014). This programme is perhaps more ecologically valid as it is including other aspects than COD exercises (plyometrics, ladder drills, etc.). To the authors' knowledge, the effect of a rapid COD programme on MDS is not yet known. Given that court- and field-based athletes typically perform many high-intensity COD throughout competition, training this aspect should account for these aspects of performance. However, to prepare players for some 'worst-case scenarios' (intense rallies, repeated pressing, repeated defending or attacking, etc.), where repeated COD occur, repeated rapid COD training is required. An example of a rapid COD training drill specific to hockey defending can be found in Figure 12.3.

Repeated Rapid COD Training

The demands of sports are becoming more intense, requiring athletes to perform at high-intensities for longer and repeatedly to meet competition demands (Barnes et al., 2014; Lago- Peñas et al., 2022). Repeated rapid COD training is a form of speed endurance training that originates from soccer and aims to increase physical performance during high-intensity periods of competition (Iaia et al., 2009; Mohr and Iaia, 2014). Rapid repeated COD training can occur over many different durations (10–90 s) with different exercise-to-rest ratios (1:1 to 1:5) and multiple bouts of COD. Due to the acute nature of a COD, it is likely that rapid COD training improves the high-intensity efforts and that the rapid repeated COD training improves the ability to perform repeated high-intensity COD efforts for more sustained periods of time. This type of training primarily stresses the glycolytic energy system, although as the exercise-to-rest ratio is reduced, elements of aerobic metabolism become more evident.

Rapid repeated COD training is a form of HIIT and can be performed as a sport-specific drill (i.e. small-sided game), running with specific movement demands to the sport (i.e. position specific circuit) or running with minimal specificity to the movement demands of the sport (i.e. repeated 180° turns for soccer players). Although all drills offer differences in terms of the total movement demands, they should all be performed at a maximum intensity. In comparison to linear running, the running velocity will be significantly lower due to the higher physiological load associated with COD movements (Buchheit et al., 2010; Maasar et al., 2021). However, manipulating the exercise-to-rest periods during these drills can elicit different physiological responses to the COD stimulus. Reducing the rest will lead to a higher cardiovascular response, whereas increasing the rest will lead to greater force output and increased blood lactate responses due to the higher intensities the exercise can be performed at (Iaia and Bangsbo, 2010; Ade et al., 2014; Castagna et al., 2017). This indicates that there is some aerobic energy system contribution within exercise where exercise-to-rest ratio is low (i.e. 1:3 to 1:1) and highlights the importance of monitoring the training stimulus to examine if it is providing the desired physiological response.

There are many studies that have identified improvements in high-intensity performance using this type of training (Mohr and Krustrup, 2016; Iaia and Bangsbo, 2010; Iaia et al., 2015; Vitale et al., 2018). Vitale et al. performed two sessions per week over four weeks of all out sprinting for 20s with an exercise-to-rest ratio of either 1:2 or 1:6. Whilst the reduced exercise-to-rest ratio improved the ability to tolerate fatigue during shuttle running performance, the higher exercise-to-rest ratio improved the ability to perform in the first sprint. This is also evident in repeated sprints that occurred in multiple directions over three weeks where junior soccer players performed 20 sprints for a period of 15 seconds and rested for 30 (Born et al., 2016). Here, the sprints performed were repeated multidirectionally across a variety of different angles. This improved performance in MDS, but more specifically in tests that require a visual stimulus that may be more linked to overall performance with agility. An example of a repeated rapid COD drill to improve MDS in tennis players can be seen in Figure 12.5.

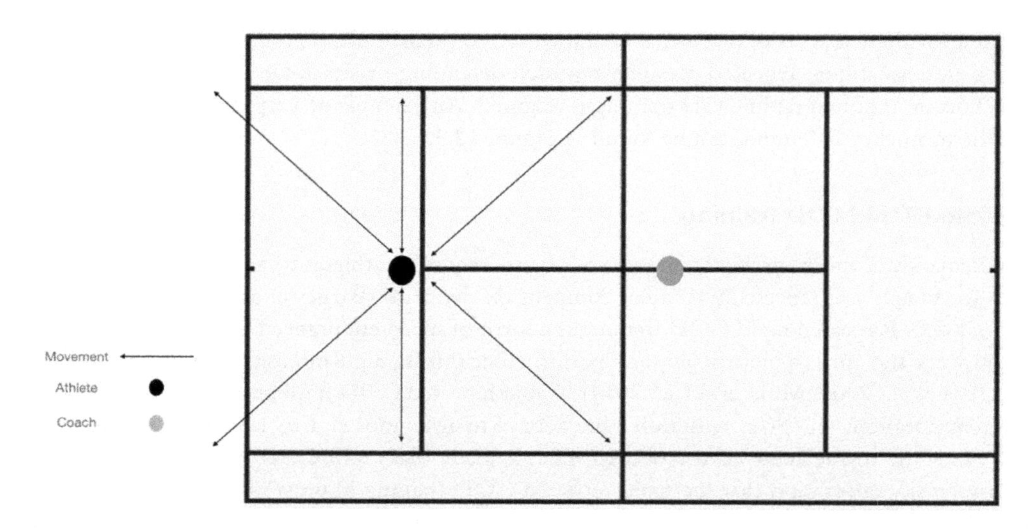

FIGURE 12.5 An example of repeated rapid change-of-direction drill for tennis athletes. The athlete stands on the 'T' in the middle of the court, and the coach serves soft volleys to one of the eight points on the tennis court. Once the player reaches the ball, they return it to the opposite side of the court and return to the start position at the 'T'.

Training Methods

Court and field sports are multifactorial and require many different physiological adaptations for successful performance. In many sports, practices can be developed that account for different aspects of a game to help achieve a specific technical/tactical objective while changing the physiological, physical, and psychological demands (Bujalance-Moreno et al., 2019; Clemente et al., 2021; Davids et al., 2013). Training utilising small-sided games has shown a greater increase in COD performance in basketballers compared with repeated shuffle sprint training (i.e. two sets of 14–17 10 + 10 m shuttle sprints and 9 m jump shots, interspersed with 20 seconds of active recovery) (Dello Iacono et al., 2016). This type of training provides a stimulus for the muscle groups that are actively engaged in during competition. In addition, they can be performed extensively across the season with a specific focus of each drill design with the manipulation of different variables enabling a form of periodisation (Morgans et al., 2014). Small-sided games (or conditioned practises) can therefore offer exponential benefits for the development of holistic athlete performance (i.e. training technical, tactical, physiological, and psychological factors) and can be key in developing MDS from a metabolic conditioning perspective.

Depending on their format, small-sided games and training drills can produce a wide range of physiological responses. From a MDS perspective, manipulating drills using factors such as running distances, reducing player numbers, and altering pitch sizes, durations, and exercise-to-rest ratios can increase the heart rate and blood lactate concentrations of athletes (Hill-Haas et al., 2011; Sarmento et al., 2018; Bujalance-Moreno et al., 2019; Tang et al., 2018; Ade et al., 2021). In addition, these manipulations result in greater accelerations and decelerations and influence the athletes to perform more multidirectional movements. Although this seems an effective training strategy, the variability and complex nature of court- and field-based sports may not allow all players to reach desired intensities required for optimal adaptation. Consequently, running-based drills (i.e. inclusive of drills with and without technical actions) can be performed to ensure that athletes reach the designed intensities in a more isolated manner.

MDS can be trained in numerous ways. From a metabolic perspective, it is important to understand the demands and how they stress each of the energy systems before implementing training strategies. Due to the complex nature of these sports, this can be done in isolated drills that look to develop a specific aspect (i.e. acceleration or sprinting), whole movements (i.e. 180° turn), or sport-specific conditioned games. The manipulation of the duration of exercise block and the exercise-to-rest ratios can be used to obtain the desired adaptive response. It is the role of the practitioner to determine the training plan, content, and structure to deliver the best metabolic adaptations to improve MDS. It must be stressed that monitoring and assessing athletes who are undertaking training programmes to understand potential physiological adaptations or maladaptations. For further information on monitoring MDS and physiological responses, please see Chapter 15.

Future Directions and Conclusions

The demands of court- and field-based sports are continuing to increase with a greater reliance on the anaerobic energy system during competition. These developments are likely due to numerous factors that are associated with improved training methods, greater adaptations, and improved talent identification. Athletes with a higher developed MDS have a distinct advantage over competition and increased research to maximise adaptations is warranted. Advances in technology will allow a greater understanding of the multidirectional demands of court- and field-based sports, paving the way for more metabolic-specific training methods. Such monitoring techniques will likely lead to a greater understanding of the importance of COD and MDS within different sports and allow practitioners to develop more comprehensive movement profiles of their athletes and sport. A greater understanding of movement profiles can lead to more comprehensive research questions around the manipulation of different variables within metabolic conditioning for MDS and provide a greater understanding of how manipulating different stimulus can elicit an adaptation. It is advised that research takes a deeper physiological approach through investigations into molecular and structural responses to different COD stimulus.

The nature of court- and field-based sports make them highly complex with multiple physiological components to be trained. Understanding the mechanical and metabolic demands of different actions are important for implementing training strategies that are aimed at metabolic conditioning. Due to the high-intensity nature of metabolic conditioning, it should look to adhere to the principles of training whilst carefully manipulating drills as part of the overall periodised plan when implementing MDS training. Practitioners should look to develop metabolic function in a way that is specific to their chosen sport through different COD training methods. This can be done in numerous methods with varying results. Monitoring strategies can be utilised to ensure athletes are training specific energy systems in the correct mechanical movements, in the optimal form and dose.

References

Ade, J. D., Drust, B., Morgan, O. J. & Bradley, P. S. (2021). Physiological characteristics and acute fatigue associated with position-specific speed endurance soccer drills: Production vs maintenance training. *Science & Medicine in Football, 5*, 6–17. https://doi.org/10.1080/24733938.2020.1789202

Ade, J. D., Harley, J. A. & Bradley, P. S. (2014). Physiological response, time-motion characteristics, and reproducibility of various speed-endurance drills in elite youth soccer players: Small-sided games versus generic running. *International Journal of Sports Physiology & Performance, 9*, 471–479.

Akenhead, R., French, D., Thompson, K. G. & Hayes, P. R. (2015). The physiological consequences of acceleration during shuttle running. *International Journal of Sports Medicine, 36*, 302–307.

Bangsbo, J., Gunnarsson, T. P., Wendell, J., Nybo, L. & Thomassen, M. (2009). Reduced volume and increased training intensity elevate muscle Na+-K+ pump alpha2-subunit expression as well as short- and long-term work capacity in humans. *Journal of Applied Physiology (1985), 107*, 1771–1780.

Barber, O. R., Thomas, C., Jones, P. A., McMahon, J. J. & Comfort, P. (2016). Reliability of the 505 change-of-direction test in netball players. *International Journal of Sports Physiology & Performance, 11*, 377–380.

Barnes, C., Archer, D. T., Hogg, B., Bush, M. & Bradley, P. S. (2014). The evolution of physical and technical performance parameters in the English Premier League. *International Journal of Sports Medicine, 35*, 1095–1100.

Besier, T. F., Lloyd, D. G., Ackland, T. R. & Cochrane, J. L. (2001). Anticipatory effects on knee joint loading during running and cutting maneuvers. *Medicine & Science in Sports & Exercise, 33*, 1176–1181.

Bogdanis, G. C., Nevill, M. E., Boobis, L. H. & Lakomy, H. K. (1996). Contribution of phosphocreatine and aerobic metabolism to energy supply during repeated sprint exercise. *Journal of Applied Physiology (1985), 80*, 876–884.

Bompa, T. O. (1994). *Theory and methodology of training: A key to athletic training*, Champaign, IL: Human Kinetics.

Born, D. P., Zinner, C., Duking, P. & Sperlich, B. (2016). Multi-directional sprint training improves change-of-direction speed and reactive agility in young highly trained soccer players. *Journal of Sports Science & Medicine, 15*, 314–319.

Bourgeois, F. A., McGuigan, M. R., Gill, N. D. & Gamble, P. (2017). Physical characteristics and performance in change of direction tasks: A brief review and training considerations. *Journal of Australian Strength and Conditioning, 25*, 104–117.

Bret, C., Rahmani, A., Dufour, A. B., Messonnier, L. & Lacour, J. R. (2002). Leg strength and stiffness as ability factors in 100 m sprint running. *Journal of Sports Medicine & Physical Fitness, 42*, 274–281.

Brooks, G. A. (1987). Amino acid and protein metabolism during exercise and recovery. *Medicine and Science in Sports and Exercise, 19*, 150–156.

Buchheit, M., Bishop, D., Haydar, B., Nakamura, F. Y. & Ahmaidi, S. (2010). Physiological responses to shuttle repeated-sprint running. *International Journal of Sports Medicine, 31*, 402–409.

Buchheit, M., Haydar, B., Hader, K., Ufland, P. & Ahmaidi, S. (2011). Assessing running economy during field running with changes of direction: Application to 20 m shuttle runs. *Intternational Journal of Sports Physiology & Performance, 6*, 380–395.

Buglione, A. & Di Prampero, P. E. (2013). The energy cost of shuttle running. *European Journal of Applied Physiology, 113*, 1535–1543.

Bujalance-Moreno, P., Latorre-Roman, P. A. & Garcia-Pinillos, F. (2019). A systematic review on small-sided games in football players: Acute and chronic adaptations. *Journal of Sports Sciences, 37*, 921–949.

Castagna, C., Francini, L., Povoas, S. C. A. & D'Ottavio, S. (2017). Long-sprint abilities in soccer: Ball versus running drills. *International Journal of Sports Physiology & Performance, 12*, 1256–1263.

Castillo-Rodriguez, A., Fernandez-Garcia, J. C., Chinchilla-Minguet, J. L. & Carnero, E. A. (2012). Relationship between muscular strength and sprints with changes of direction. *Journal of Strength and Conditioning Research, 26*, 725–732.

Clemente, F. M., Ramirez-Campillo, R., Sarmento, H., Praca, G. M., Afonso, J., Silva, A. F., Rosemann, T. & Knechtle, B. (2021). Effects of small-sided game interventions on the technical execution and tactical behaviors of young and youth team sports players: A systematic review and meta-analysis. *Frontiers in Psychology, 12*, 667041.

Davids, K., Araujo, D., Correia, V. & Vilar, L. (2013). How small-sided and conditioned games enhance acquisition of movement and decision-making skills. *Exercise & Sport Science Reviews, 41*, 154–161.

Dellal, A., Keller, D., Carling, C., Chaouachi, A., Wong Del, P. & Chamari, K. (2010). Physiologic effects of directional changes in intermittent exercise in soccer players. *Journal of Strength and Conditioning Research, 24*, 3219–3226.

Dello Iacono, A., Martone, D. & Padulo, J. (2016). Acute effects of drop-jump protocols on explosive performances of elite handball players. *Journal of Strength and Conditioning Research, 30*, 3122–3133.

Deutsch, E., Deutsch, S. L. & Douglas, P. S. (1988). Exercise training for competitive tennis. *Clin Sports Med*, 7, 417–427.

DeWeese, B. & Nimphius, S. (2016). Speed and agility program design and technique. *In:* Triplett, N. T. & Haff, G. G. (eds.) *Essentials of strength and conditioning*. Champaign, IL: Human Kinetics.

Dos'Santos, T., McBurnie, A. J., Thomas, C., Comfort, P. & Jones, P. A. (2020). Biomechanical determinants of the modified and traditional 505 change of direction speed test. *Journal of Strength and Conditioning Research, 34*, 1285–1296.

Dos'Santos, T., McBurnie, A. J., Thomas, C., Jones, P. A. & Harper, D. (2022). Attacking agility actions: Match play contextual applications with coaching and technique guidelines. *Strength and Conditioning Journal, 44*, 102–118. DOI: 10.1519/SSC.0000000000000697

Dos'Santos, T., Thomas, C., Comfort, P. & Jones, P. A. (2018). The effect of angle and velocity on change of direction biomechanics: An angle-velocity trade-off. *Sports Medicine, 48*, 2235–2253.

Dos'Santos, T., Thomas, C., Jones, P. A. & Comfort, P. (2017). Mechanical determinants of faster change of direction speed performance in male athletes. *Journal of Strength and Conditioning Research, 31*, 696–705.

Ekstrand, J., Hagglund, M. & Walden, M. (2011). Epidemiology of muscle injuries in professional football (soccer). *American Journal of Sports Medicine, 39*, 1226–1232.

Fernandez, J., Mendez-Villanueva, A. & Pluim, B. M. (2006). Intensity of tennis match play. *British Journal of Sports Medicine, 40*, 387–391; discussion 391.

Fernandez-Fernandez, J., Mendez-Villanueva, A., Fernandez-Garcia, B. & Terrados, N. (2007). Match activity and physiological responses during a junior female singles tennis tournament. *British Journal of Sports Medicine, 41*, 711–716.

Fernandez-Fernandez, J., Sanz-Rivas, D., Sanchez-Munoz, C., Pluim, B. M., Tiemessen, I. & Mendez-Villanueva, A. (2009). A comparison of the activity profile and physiological demands between advanced and recreational veteran tennis players. *Journal of Strength and Conditioning Research, 23*, 604–610.

Gamble, P. (2007). Challenges and game-related solutions to metabolic conditioning for team sports. *Strength and Conditioning Journal, 29*, 60–65.

Giles, B., Peeling, P. & Machar, R. (2021). Quantifying change of direction movement demands in professional tennis matchplay: An analysis from the Australian Open Grand Slam. *Journal of Strength and Conditioning Research*. DOI: 10.1519/JSC.0000000000003937

Gunnarsson, T. P., Christensen, P. M., Thomassen, M., Nielsen, L. R. & Bangsbo, J. (2013). Effect of intensified training on muscle ion kinetics, fatigue development, and repeated short-term performance in endurance-trained cyclists. *American Journal of Physiology. Regulatory, Integrative and Comparative Physiology, 305*(7), R811–R821. https://doi.org/10.1152/ajpregu.00467.2012

Hader, K., Mendez-Villanueva, A., Ahmaidi, S., Williams, B. K. & Buchheit, M. (2014). Changes of direction during high-intensity intermittent runs: neuromuscular and metabolic responses. *BMC Sports Science, Medicine & Rehabilitation, 6*(1), 2. https://doi.org/10.1186/2052-1847-6-2

Hatamoto, Y., Yamada, Y., Fujii, T., Higaki, Y., Kiyonaga, A. & Tanaka, H. (2013). A novel method for calculating the energy cost of turning during running. *Open Access Journal of Sports Medicine, 4*, 117–122.

Haugen, T. A., Tonnessen, E. & Seiler, S. (2013). Anaerobic performance testing of professional soccer players 1995–2010. *Int J Sports Physiol Perform, 8*, 148–156.

Herzog, W. (2018). Why are muscles strong, and why do they require little energy in eccentric action? *Journal of Sport & Health Science*, 7, 255–264.

Hill-Haas, S. V., Dawson, B., Impellizzeri, F. M. & Coutts, A. J. (2011). Physiology of small-sided games training in football: A systematic review. *Sports Medicine, 41*, 199–220.

Iaia, F. M. & Bangsbo, J. (2010). Speed endurance training is a powerful stimulus for physiological adaptations and performance improvements of athletes. *Scandinavian Journal of Medicine & Science in Sports*, 20 Suppl 2, 11–23.

Iaia, F. M., Fiorenza, M., Perri, E., Alberti, G., Millet, G. P. & Bangsbo, J. (2015). The effect of two speed endurance training regimes on performance of soccer players. *PLoS One, 10*, e0138096.

Iaia, F. M., Hellsten, Y., Nielsen, J. J., Fernstrom, M., Sahlin, K. & Bangsbo, J. (2009). Four weeks of speed endurance training reduces energy expenditure during exercise and maintains muscle oxidative capacity despite a reduction in training volume. *Journal of Applied Physiology (1985), 106*, 73–80.

Jensen, L., Bangsbo, J. & Hellsten, Y. (2004). Effect of high intensity training on capillarization and presence of angiogenic factors in human skeletal muscle. *Journal of Physiology, 557*, 571–582.

Jones, P. A., Herrington, L. & Graham-Smith, P. (2016). Braking characteristics during cutting and pivoting in female soccer players. *Journal of Electromyography & Kinesiology, 30*, 46–54.

Kawamori, N., Nosaka, K. & Newton, R. U. (2013). Relationships between ground reaction impulse and sprint acceleration performance in team sport athletes. *Journal of Strength & Conditioning Research, 27*, 568–573.

Kovacs, M. S. (2007). Tennis physiology: Training the competitive athlete. *Sports Medicine, 37*, 189–198.

Lago-Peñas, C., Lorenzo-Martinez, M., López-Del Campo, R., Resta, R. & Rey, E. (2022). Evolution of physical and technical parameters in the Spanish *LaLiga* 2012–2019. *Science & Medicine in Football*, 1–6. https://doi.org/10.1080/24733938.2022.2049980

Lockie, R. G., Murphy, A. J., Schultz, A. B., Knight, T. J. & Janse De Jonge, X. A. (2012). The effects of different speed training protocols on sprint acceleration kinematics and muscle strength and power in field sport athletes. *Journal of Strength & Conditioning Research, 26*, 1539–1550.

Lockie, R. G., Schultz, A. B., Callaghan, S. J. & Jeffriess, M. D. (2014). The effects of traditional and enforced stopping speed and agility training on multidirectional speed and athletic function. *Journal of Strength & Conditioning Research, 28*, 1538–1551.

Maasar, M. F., Turner, D. C., Gorski, P. P., Seaborne, R. A., Strauss, J. A., Shepherd, S. O., Cocks, M., Pillon, N. J., Zierath, J. R., Hulton, A. T., Drust, B. & Sharples, A. P. (2021). The comparative methylome and transcriptome after change of direction compared to straight line running exercise in human skeletal muscle. *Frontiers in Physiology, 12*, 619447.

Malone, S., Owen, A., Mendes, B., Hughes, B., Collins, K. & Gabbett, T. J. (2018). High-speed running and sprinting as an injury risk factor in soccer: Can well-developed physical qualities reduce the risk? *Journal of Science & Medicine in Sport, 21*, 257–262.

Martínez-Hernández, D., Quinn, M. & Jones, P. (2022). Linear advancing actions followed by deceleration and turn are the most common movements preceding goals in male professional soccer. *Science & Medicine in Football*, 1–9. https://doi.org/10.1080/24733938.2022.2030064

McBurnie, A. J. & Dos'Santos, T. (2021). Multidirectional speed in youth soccer players: Theoretical underpinnings. *Strength and Conditioning Journal, 44*, 15–33.

McBurnie, A. J., Parr, J., Kelly, D. M. & Dos'Santos, T. (2021). Multidirectional speed in youth soccer players: Programming considerations and practical applications. *Strength and Conditioning Journal, 44*, 10–32.

McCartney, N., Spriet, L. L., Heigenhauser, G. J., Kowalchuk, J. M., Sutton, J. R. & Jones, N. L. (1986). Muscle power and metabolism in maximal intermittent exercise. *Journal of Applied Physiology (1985), 60*, 1164–1169.

Mendiguchia, J., Conceicao, F., Edouard, P., Fonseca, M., A R., Lopes, H., Morin, J. B. & Jimenez-Reyes, P. (2020). Sprint versus isolated eccentric training: Comparative effects on hamstring architecture and performance in soccer players. *PLoS One, 15*, e0228283.

Mohr, M. & Iaia, F. M. (2014). Physiological basis of fatigue resistance training in competitive football. *Sports Science Exchange*, 27, 1–9.

Mohr, M. & Krustrup, P. (2016). Comparison between two types of anaerobic speed endurance training in competitive soccer players. *Journal of Human Kinetics, 51*, 183–192.

Morgan, O. J., Drust, B., Ade, J. D. & Robinson, M. A. (2022). Change of direction frequency off the ball: New perspectives in elite youth soccer. *Science and Medicine in Football, 6*, 473–482.

Morgans, R., Orme, P., Anderson, L. & Drust, B. (2014). Principles and practices of training for soccer. *Journal of Sport and Health Science, 3*, 251–257.

Morrissey, M. C., Harman, E. A. & Johnson, M. J. (1995). Resistance training modes: Specificity and effectiveness. *Med Sci Sports Exerc, 27*, 648–660.

Murias, J. M., Lanatta, D., Arcuri, C. R. & Laino, F. A. (2007). Metabolic and functional responses playing tennis on different surfaces. *Journal of Strength and Conditioning Research, 21*, 112–117.

Nikolaidis, P. T., Knechtle, B., Clemente, F. M. & Torres-Luque, G. (2016). Reference values for the sprint performance in male football players aged from 9–35 years. *Biomedical Human Kinetics, 8*, 39–44.

Parsons, L. S. & Jones, M. T. (1998). Development of speed, agility, and quickness for tennis athletes. *Strength and Conditioning Journal, 20*, 14–19.

Plisk, S. S. (1991). Anaerobic metabolic conditioning. *Journal of Strength and Conditioning Research, 5*, 22–34.

Reilly, T. & Bangsbo, J. (1998). *Anaerobic and aerobic training*. Chichester: Wiley.

Reilly, T., Williams, A. M., Nevill, A. & Franks, A. (2000). A multidisciplinary approach to talent identification in soccer. *Journal of Sports Sciences, 18*, 695–702.

Ross, A. & Leveritt, M. (2001). Long-term metabolic and skeletal muscle adaptations to short-sprint training: Implications for sprint training and tapering. *Sports Medicine, 31*, 1063–1082.

Sarmento, H., Clemente, F. M., Harper, L. D., Da Costa, I. T., Owen, A. & Figueiredo, A. J. (2018). Small sided games in soccer – a systematic review. *International Journal of Performance Analysis in Sport, 18*, 693–749.

Sheppard, J. M. & Young, W. B. (2006). Agility literature review: Classifications, training and testing. *Journal of Sports Sciences, 24*, 919–932.

Skovgaard, C., Christensen, P. M., Larsen, S., Andersen, T. R., Thomassen, M. & Bangsbo, J. (2014). Concurrent speed endurance and resistance training improves performance, running economy, and muscle NHE1 in moderately trained runners. *Journal of Applied Physiology (1985), 117*, 1097–1109.

Spriet, L. L., Lindinger, M. I., McKelvie, R. S., Heigenhauser, G. J. & Jones, N. L. (1989). Muscle glycogenolysis and H+ concentration during maximal intermittent cycling. *Journal of Applied Physiology (1985), 66*, 8–13.

Stevens, A. W., Olver, T. T. & Lemon, P. W. (2015). Incorporating sprint training with endurance training improves anaerobic capacity and 2,000-m Erg performance in trained oarsmen. *Journal of Strength & Conditioning Research, 29*, 22–28.

Stolen, T., Chamari, K., Castagna, C. & Wisloff, U. (2005). Physiology of soccer: An update. *Sports Medicine, 35*, 501–536.

Tang, R., Murtagh, C., Warrington, G., Cable, T., Morgan, O., O'Boyle, A., Burgess, D., Morgans, R. & Drust, B. (2018). Directional change mediates the physiological response to high-intensity shuttle running in professional soccer players. *Sports (Basel)*, 6.

Verheul, J., Nedergaard, N. J., Vanrenterghem, J. & Robinson, M. A. (2020). Measuring biomechanical loads in team sports – from lab to field. *Science and Medicine in Football, 4*, 246–252.

Verstappen, S., Van Rijn, R. M., Cost, R. & Stubbe, J. H. (2021). The association between training load and injury risk in elite youth soccer players: A systematic review and best evidence synthesis. *Sports Medicine Open, 7*, 6.

Vitale, J. A., Povia, V., Vitale, N. D., Bassani, T., Lombardi, G., Giacomelli, L., Banfi, G. & La Torre, A. (2018). The effect of two different speed endurance training protocols on a multiple shuttle run performance in young elite male soccer players. *Research in Sports Medicine, 26*, 436–449.

Weyand, P. G., Sternlight, D. B., Bellizzi, M. J. & Wright, S. (2000). Faster top running speeds are achieved with greater ground forces not more rapid leg movements. *Journal of Applied Physiology (1985), 89*, 1991–1999.

Withers, R. T., Sherman, W. M., Clark, D. G., Esselbach, P. C., Nolan, S. R., Mackay, M. H. & Brinkman, M. (1991). Muscle metabolism during 30, 60 and 90 s of maximal cycling on an air-braked ergometer. *European Journal of Applied Physiology & Occupational Physiology, 63*, 354–362.

Young, W. B., Dawson, B. & Henry, G. J. (2015). Agility and change-of-direction speed are independent skills: Implications for training for agility in invasion sports. *International Journal of Sports Science & Coaching, 10*, 159–169.

Zamparo, P., Zadro, I., Lazzer, S., Beato, M. & Sepulcri, L. (2014). Energetics of shuttle runs: The effects of distance and change of direction. *International Journal of Sports Physiology & Performance, 9*, 1033–1039.

13

DEVELOPING PERCEPTUAL-COGNITIVE FACTORS IN RELATION TO AGILITY PERFORMANCE ENHANCEMENT

Tania Spiteri

Introduction

Agility manoeuvres are a multidimensional skill (Sheppard & Young 2006; Young & Farrow 2006) requiring athletes to control the individual components and manipulate degrees of freedom of the movement in order to meet the demands of a given situation (Spiteri et al. 2014). Examination of performance times during agility protocols (Jeffreys 2011; Serpell et al. 2011) suggests that when combining perception and action during a task, not only does the task itself become sport-specific, but elite athletes have the ability to produce a faster performance (Farrow & Abernethy 2002; Spiteri et al. 2018). Previous research investigating expert-novice differences during agility tasks have primarily attributed these differences to an improved ability to identify task relevant cues and differentiate between different sources of information to produce an accurate and rapid motor response (Vaeynes et al. 2007; Spiteri et al. 2015b). From this body of research, athletes have been classified into one of two groups – fast thinkers with slow movement and slow thinkers with fast movement (Gabbett et al. 2008) – in an attempt to categorise and identify the main weakness in performance. Despite this, current training practices have predominantly focused on the development of physical qualities, technique (Wheeler & Sayers 2010; Green et al. 2011) and strength (Jullien et al. 2008; Keiner et al. 2014), to overcome limitations in perceptual-cognitive qualities. However, this only addresses half of the equation to optimise an athlete's agility performance. It is well established that an athlete's ability to identify task-relevant cues to produce an accurate and rapid motor response (Wulf et al. 2010a; Roca et al. 2011) is a prerequisite for a faster agility performance (Spiteri et al. 2015a; Spiteri et al. 2015b).

This cyclical relationship between perception and action, termed perception-action coupling (Davids et al. 2013; Spiteri et al. 2018), indicates the importance for an athlete to rapidly recognise relevant stimuli and formulate an adaptive movement response to various task and environmental constraints (Passos et al. 2008; Spiteri et al. 2018). The emergence of movement output through the lens of ecological dynamics, views the athlete as a complex and adaptive system where performer-environment interactions enable multiple movement solutions to emerge for the same or similar task (Araujo et al. 2009; Davids et al. 2013). Specifically, interactions within the sporting environment require the athlete to (1) effectively search for information about the situation,

DOI: 10.4324/9781003267881-15

(2) direct their attention to the most relevant information, and (3) coordinate and execute movements to successfully react or anticipate the ever-changing sporting environment. For example, a basketballer may reduce their approach speed for an upcoming agility moment based upon their current physical capacities (e.g. strength) and specific task/environmental constraints (e.g. the number of defenders, angle of directional change, and/or path they intend to travel) to achieve their desired movement outcome in competition. As agility occurs in a dynamic fast-paced environment, there are various task and environmental constraints that can influence an athlete's agility performance (Figure 13.1). Athletes who have an improved ability to search for and execute alternative task solutions (i.e. perception-action coupling), in response to changing constraints, have a greater capacity to cope with inherent variability as typically encountered in the sporting environment, leading to improved performance outcomes and reduced injury risk as a result of greater movement variability and adaptability.

What are the Perceptual-cognitive Constraints Influencing Agility Performance?

Perceptual constraints refer to an athlete's ability to control their gaze and identify task relevant cues within the surrounding environment, whereas cognitive constraints are dependent upon an athlete's ability to utilise their perceptual skill to identify familiar patterns of play and opponent's movements (Davids et al. 2005). Cognitive constraints are therefore influenced by an athlete's prior knowledge of the situation or playing experience and level of concentration.

When considering the dynamic control of a task like agility, there is a clear integration between higher perceptual-cognitive function and the athlete's technical and physical qualities

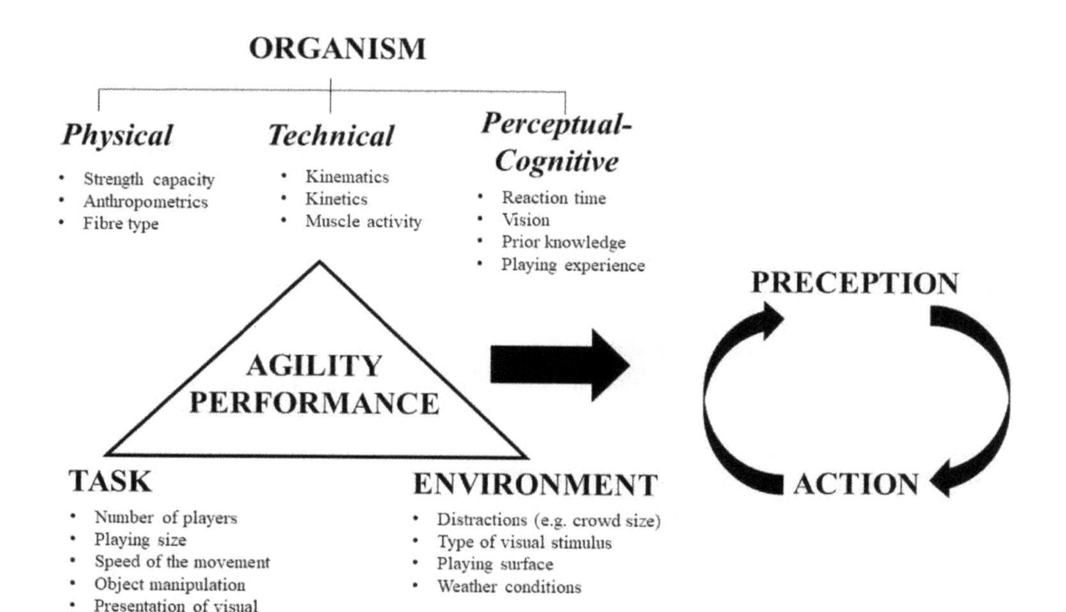

FIGURE 13.1 Specific organism, task, and environmental constraints influencing agility performance, with reference to perception-action coupling. Adapted from Spiteri et al. (2018).

to modulate motor behaviour in response to the surrounding environment. Research has demonstrated that elite or more experienced players appear to be more efficient at utilising their cognitive ability to anticipate opponent's movements quicker than less experience players (Gabbett et al. 2008; Lockie et al. 2014), allowing them to make accurate and efficient sport-specific decisions. Producing a faster initial response to the stimulus enables athletes to prepare and adjust their movement in response through pre-activation of the muscles (McBride et al. 2008; Spiteri et al. 2015b), increasing rate of force development and muscular stiffness, resulting in a faster agility performance (Spiteri et al. 2015b).

While it has been well established that athletes with a more efficient perceptual-cognitive ability produce a faster agility performance (Vaeynes et al. 2007; Veale et al. 2010), the visual cues and search strategies used to achieve a faster agility performance were previously unknown. Recently, researchers examining differences in visual search strategy during a 45° Y-agility movement, requiring athletes to change direction in response to a defender's movements, discovered athletes that produced a faster movement time, utilised a search strategy involving significantly shorter total fixation duration and displayed a greater number, duration, and percent fixation around proximal body segments (e.g. upper leg, lower trunk, and upper trunk) (Spiteri et al., *in review*). In contrast, athletes who produced a slower movement time displayed a greater number of fixations and spent significantly more time fixating on distal body segments (e.g. lower leg and foot) and unspecified viewing areas. These findings emphasise the importance of making effective use of advanced information to rapidly identify relevant proximal kinematic cues from an opponent earlier in stimulus presentation to make rapid and accurate sport-specific decisions (Nunez et al. 2009; Roca et al. 2011). Developing a search strategy that is more efficient at identifying visual cues from proximal body segments allows athletes to find movement solutions in response to task and environmental constraints sooner, providing a tactical advantage to successfully evade or pursue opponents in competition.

Knowing what cues to look for from the task or environment is significantly dependent upon prior experience within that situation. Prior situational knowledge of an opponent's strengths and weaknesses, court or field position, and event probability information (Wulf et al. 2010b; Roca et al. 2011) can assist athletes when searching for relevant cues. Possessing an increased awareness to the surrounding environment has been found to increase the visual representation of sport-specific cues, leading to an increase in motor activation of the muscles involved in skill execution (Yarrow et al. 2009). This increase in motor-evoked potentials enables athletes to prepare the body sooner (i.e. postural adjustments and neuromuscular pre-activation) for the upcoming response (Yarrow et al. 2009; Spiteri et al. 2015b), resulting in a shorter response time. This explains why elite athletes possess the ability to not only identify relevant stimuli sooner but also respond faster to sport-specific stimuli than novice athletes.

While it is impossible to prepare athletes in training for every game-specific situation they may encounter in competition, it is important to create a representative training environment where athletes can develop their perceptual-cognitive ability and explore movement solutions under changing task and environment constraints. Creating a training environment that is designed to reflect the requirements of competition increases the likelihood that a positive learning transfer will occur (Tremblay 2010). Through the ecological dynamics approach, which emphasises the performer-environment system, it is important to select information sources that are representative of the task and competitive environment (Araujo et al. 2009; Davids et al. 2013). For example, playing on different tennis courts (clay, grass, and hard surfaces) and changing direction around the court in response to an opponent's movements and shot selections would allow tennis players to adapt their movement in response to different surface conditions and opponents' movements. This will allow athletes to develop and maintain the coupling between perception and action that is required to successfully control and coordinate their movement responses.

The Effect of Task Constraints on Agility Performance

Task constraints vary across numerous sports due to the aim and rules of the activity. Simply put, they influence the control of movement and the effectiveness of movement outcomes. These constraints include the number of players, speed of the movement, object manipulation, and presentation of the stimulus.

Typically, in sporting environments, movement execution needs to be coordinated and controlled whilst simultaneously occurring rapidly to enable the execution of successive sport-specific actions. While this is directly influenced by an athlete's organismic constraints, the inability to transfer agility performance from training to game environments is in part due to a lack of replicating game speed (Davids et al. 2005). Studies have indicated that when athletes approach the visual stimulus at a faster velocity, the stimulus is presented closer to the point of movement execution, or there is a reduced time to respond to successive stimuli, a slower decision-making time is observed (McLean et al. 2004; Spiteri et al. 2015a). Failing to replicate the required movement speed and time constraints limits the successful transfer to game environments, as athletes may not be able to adequately adjust movement output at the required game speed. Additionally, many sports often require directional changes to occur while simultaneously manipulating equipment (e.g. a lacrosse player holding a stick). Elite athletes have been found to produce a faster performance by successfully adjusting their movement output to account for task constraints (Veale et al. 2010; Spiteri & Hart 2014). This requirement to perform a dual task (e.g. dribbling a basketball or soccer ball) while simultaneous executing an agility movement has been found to increase the cognitive demand placed on athletes, subsequently increasing the mechanical loads, and reducing neuromuscular and postural control strategies of the athlete (Hughes & Dai 2021). This not only requires the athlete to overcome these additional constraints to execute a fast agility movement but also places them at a great risk of injury (Hughes & Dai, 2021) due to the reduced ability to anticipate ground contact and implement appropriate neuromuscular control strategies as a result of impaired decision-making ability and competing attentional demand.

During competition, athletes are required to perform multiple directional changes often to evade or pursue opponents in close proximity. Depending upon the presentation of the stimulus in the visual field, an athlete's perceptual-cognitive ability and speed-of-movement output can be impacted. Research examining offensive (i.e. moving in the opposite direction of the stimulus) and defensive (i.e. moving in the same direction as the stimulus) agility movements discovered distinct differences in both decision-making time and speed-of-movement output between these two categories (Spiteri et al. 2012; Spiteri et al. 2014). Further, when examining decision-making time in response to two closely spaced visual stimuli, faster athletes produced a quicker response time to the first stimulus, allowing them to produce an overall faster agility performance, despite no differences being observed in response time to the second stimulus between groups (Spiteri et al. 2015b). The non-significant difference in response to the second stimuli suggests that when responding to two closely spaced stimuli differences observed between groups appear to be attributed to an athlete's ability to identify and interpret relevant cues from the first stimulus, placing them at a performance advantage for subsequent movement output. It appears that differences in opponents and number of targets can result in an increased cognitive load (Wulf et al. 2010b;

Roca et al. 2011), altering an athlete's perception in the amount of time and space available to change direction (McLean et al. 2004; McRobert et al. 2011). This may compromise biomechanical and neuromuscular postural adjustment strategies, resulting in a slower agility movement (McLean et al. 2004; Spiteri et al. 2015b). Therefore, in training environments, it is important to vary the presentation of the stimulus within the visual field, allowing athletes to couple their movement output to a variety of information sources.

The Effect of Environmental Constraints on Agility Performance

Environmental constraints refer to the environment in which the sport is played – specifically, how the type of stimulus, external distractions, and playing surface influence movement output. Several studies have assessed cognitive function in agility tests by the inclusion of an external sensory stimulus. Stimulus specificity is crucial, as anticipatory and perceptual expertise appears to be dependent upon the type of stimulus used (Sheppard & Young 2006; Veale et al. 2010). Reacting to a stimulus requires processing based on retrieval of information from stored memory; therefore, the greater similarity between the stimulus used within training and the actual sporting environment will allow athletes to generate a faster and context-specific movement response (Vaeynes et al. 2007; Nunez et al. 2009). For example, making an athlete change movement direction in response to another person, as opposed to a generic light stimulus, will allow them to identify and recall relevant kinematic cues from their opponent. This will allow athletes to produce a movement solution reflective of the sporting environment, as there is an inherent link between the stimulus and movement response (Roca et al. 2013; Tremblay 2010). Research has shown that when responding to a more specific stimulus (e.g. video of competition or another person), elite athletes produce a faster reactive time and subsequently faster agility performance compared to novice athletes (Jeffreys 2011). Therefore, it is important to ensure that the type of task and environmental constraints (i.e. stimuli) introduced within the training environment have a degree of similarly between the athlete's sport and their typical sporting environment.

External distractions including the number of players and atmosphere of the crowd can also impact an athlete's ability to identify relevant cues during a game. Compared to tennis, basketball and football have a larger number of athletes on the field and greater crowd engagement, all of which can increase an athlete's arousal and anxiety (Janelle 2002; Wulf et al. 2010b). According to the inverted-U principle, an athlete will miss relevant stimuli if they experience a low or high state of arousal (Janelle 2002). This will negatively affect an athlete's ability to identify relevant stimuli, resulting in a slower decision-making time and agility performance. Therefore, manipulating environmental constraints that mirror game situations, such as crowd noise and number of attackers and defenders, is critical to improve movement output and the ability to identify task relevant cues.

Current Limitations in Perceptual-cognitive Training for Agility Performance

Current training practices to improve an athlete's perceptual-cognitive ability have typically occurred under controlled conditions, with confounding factors such as task and environmental constraints being held constant (Holmberg 2009; Jeffreys 2011). These traditional coaching models often emphasise repetition of 'ideal' movement patterns within a controlled and predictable training environment. Rather than pushing an athlete toward an 'ideal' movement pattern, it is important to consider the various task and environment constraints can influence perceptual-cognitive ability and subsequent movement output. Instead, these current models do not afford the athlete the opportunity to engage in continuous coupling of perception and action through a variety of representative practice conditions (Woods et al. 2020). This lack of perception-action coupling in current training environments is why limited transfer and movement breakdown occurs during competition, as athletes lack the ability to adapt and reorganise their movement strategy to constraints encountered in competition. Thus, to maximise the transfer from training to competition, training environments should sample information from competition to create a representative practice environment through the use of sport-specific stimuli (Robertson et al. 2018; Woods et al. 2020). From an agility perspective, selecting and manipulating various tasks and environment constraints creates activities that are high in action similarity so that emergent performance solutions are reflective of a solution that would occur in competition. This will support the athlete in developing their perceptual-cognitive ability, and adapting their behaviours along with movement output, in response to similar information sources (e.g. ball, teammates, opponents) encountered within competition.

Representative Learning Design for Agility Performance

Agility performance is contextually situated, meaning it is shaped under varying constraints and is the product of a specific movement solution to problems encountered within the sporting environment. This context, or rather lack of context, is why athletes struggle to execute agility movements in competition. As context shapes content, or movement output in this instance, it is important to think about the number of moving bodies of the field or court, gaps in the emergent play, and weather conditions, as this will shape the speed, degree of directional change, and the specific agility movement an athlete performs based upon the information they perceive from their environment (Woods et al. 2020; Pinder et al. 2011). Therefore, it is paramount that training environments encourage exposure of competition specific context that offer athletes opportunities to learn how to adapt movement to emergent problems (Araujo et al. 2009; Davids et al. 2013). Representative learning design emphasises the use of constraints found in competition when shaping the training environment, encouraging athletes to use contextual information to self-regulate their behaviours and movement output (Passos et al. 2008). When applied to agility, representative learning design would observe athletes performing under constraints experienced during competition, leading to greater transfer of performance from training to competition.

Constraints-led Approach to Developing Perceptual-Cognitive Ability

To maximise the development of perceptual-cognitive ability, the creation of a representative practice environment that includes the manipulation of sport-specific task and environmental constraint will help athletes develop functional perception-action coupling, improving performance outcomes (Table 13.1). Dependent upon the level of athlete, drills can be created that vary the cognitive load and contain context-specific information, reflective of the sporting environment. Similar to traditional physical preparation programmes for athletes, applying training principles – progressive overload, specificity, and variation – can assist to progress training based upon the level and/or experience of the athlete. This will allow the development of appropriate drills by gradually introducing and progressing task complexity and environmental constraints to improve decision-making ability.

TABLE 13.1 Development of Perceptual-Cognitive Ability for Agility Performance Utilising Constraints led Approach (Adapted from Spiteri et al., 2018)

Performer	Novice ——————————————————————→ Expert		
Cognitive Load	Low ——————————————————————→ High		
Environment Constraints	• Controlled • Low representation to task environment • Large playing space • Non-specific stimulus (light, cone, hand signal)	• Semi-controlled • Restricted playing space • Sport-specific stimulus (another athlete)	• Uncontrolled • High representation to task environment • Sport-specific stimulus (another person)
Task Constraints	• Consistent movement speed • No object manipulation • Focus on movement execution	• Vary movement speed • Passive defence (stimulus) • Introduce object manipulation	• Vary movement speed and distance • Active defence (stimulus); movement in relation to another person • Object manipulation
Practice Conditions	Blocked practice	Random practice	Differential practice
Feedback	Extrinsic ——————————————————————→ Intrinsic		

When considering training overload, in this case cognitive demand, it is important to vary the strength (i.e. intensity of the cognitive load), duration (i.e. length of drill or training session), and frequency (i.e. number of repetitions of the drill or training session), enabling the athlete to sufficiently adapt. Studies have shown that as cognitive load or demand increases, performance outcomes can decrease as a result (McRobert et al. 2011; Roca et al. 2013). Understanding the experience level of an athlete will allow the cognitive load of the training environment to be manipulated accordingly to progressively expose the athlete to an environment that is representative of both the perceptual-cognitive and physical demands of competition to yield positive adaptations in performance. For example, with novice-level athletes, the cognitive load of the drill should be relatively low. While drills may include a perceptual-cognitive element in the form of a non-specific stimulus (e.g. light, voice commands, hand signals), a 'controlled reactive' environment is established appropriate to the level of the athlete. This creates a training environment with a low cognitive load, emphasising movement execution, while developing an athlete's ability to recognise and react to a stimulus. This provides athletes with a goal-directed search strategy, requiring basic information processing to identify the stimulus and react accordingly. For example, allocating a different directional change to a coloured cone and verbally cueing which colour cone to move to requires the athlete to visually identify the correct cone and execute the appropriate movement response (Figure 13.2). Additional modifications to the practice environment can be achieved by introducing temporal and spatial variability. Temporal variability refers to the timing variance of a signal, whereas spatial variability refers to the various directions from which the stimulus can originate (Čoh et al. 2004). For example, increasing and decreasing the length of time between cueing the stimulus and changing the location of the coloured cones after several repetitions changes the temporal and spatial locating of the stimulus, ensuring athletes do not anticipate or become complacent during the drill.

FIGURE 13.2 'Controlled reactive' environment, changing direction to cued colour cones, focusing on goal-directed search strategy and movement execution.

Traditional decision-making training models emphasise the continuous repetition or rehearsal of 'ideal' movement patterns in a closed, predictable environment, constraining an athlete's learning behaviours. To achieve a representative practice environment, it is important to create variation in training intensity, exercise or drill selection, and speed of movement, by manipulating task and environmental constraints and practice conditions. This will provide opportunities for athletes to engage in perception-action coupling and in exploration and reorganisation of movement degrees of freedom, improving decision-making ability. This in theory fundamentally promotes Bernstein's (1967) notion or 'repetition without repetition' (p. 134). Exposing athletes to this type of movement variability can be achieved by implementing random practice conditions. Random practice refers to a practice sequence where individual skills or drills are executed in a random order during the session, which over time can result in improved skill retention (Wulf et al. 2010b). For example, performing a 180° directional change followed by a lateral shuffle requires athletes to modify their biomechanics to execute the movement efficiently. Varying the order of movement repetition at this level can be predominantly directed by introducing a sport-specific 'passive' stimulus (e.g. another player not actively engaging in defensive actions) or object manipulation (e.g. dribbling a basketball) (Figure 13.3) allows athletes to engage and explore the degrees of freedom of each directional change in response to changing constraints to develop a

FIGURE 13.3 Changing direction in response to a passive 'defender' allows for exploration of movement output under higher cognitive loads.

coordinated and adaptive movement output under a higher cognitive load (Mann et al. 2007; Wulf et al. 2010b). Additionally, manipulating the training space will alter the speed and distance available to execute directional changes, reflecting the constraints of the competitive sporting environment. This will further alter the physical and technical requirements of each directional change requiring athletes to further adjust and manipulate their movement output. Essentially, while these types of changes to the typical agility training drill may make the session itself appear 'messier', the result will be an athlete who displays more masterful movement solutions under a wider diversity of motor problems that are reflective of the athlete's sport.

To maximise the transfer of agility performance from training to sport, athletes need to be exposed to specific mechanical (e.g. movement patterns) and perceptual-cognitive (e.g. sport-specific stimuli) factors to increase the probability of transfer. While the level of specificity will increase with the level of the athlete, creating a high representative training environment, through differential practice methods (e.g. block, serial, and random), allows athletes to be explorative in nature to develop both their perceptual-cognitive skill and movement output, improving their

FIGURE 13.4 Changing direction in response to an active stimulus, requiring object manipulation, within a reduced playing space, further increases the cognitive requirements of the drill.

decision-making ability. For example, athletes are required to identify relevant kinematic cues from an opponent to determine subsequent movement direction in competition. Using a sport-specific 'active' stimulus (e.g. another player actively engaging in defensive actions) during a one-on-one drill will allow athletes to actively search to identify relevant kinematic cues from a defensive opponent (environmental constraint) and perform diverse directional changes within a confined space (environmental constraint) to bypass their opponent (Figure 13.4). Implementing a time restriction required to reach the finish line, adding specific rules to the training drill, increasing the number of defensive opponents, or performing directional changes with equipment used in the sport adds additional task and environmental constraints increasing the specificity and cognitive demand of the drill. Further, this can also improve athletes' knowledge of the situation, allowing them to recall sport-specific actions, when experiencing similar encounters during competition.

In summary, the development of a representative learning environment through manipulation of task and environmental constraints to achieve progressive overload, variability, and specificity of agility drills will facilitate the development of an athlete's perceptual-cognitive ability. This can be achieved by (not limited to) the following:

- Changing the playing space (e.g. making it larger or smaller, constraining the space available to execute directional changes, resulting in changes to movement speed and degree of directional change)
- Modifying the type and number of external stimuli (e.g. a passive defender progressing to an active external stimulus in a 1 vs 1, 2 vs 1, or 3 vs 3 scenario, changing an athlete's visual search strategy and perception of stimulus, which will subsequently change movement output)

- Changing court or field positioning (e.g. starting in a different position will vary the temporal and spatial presentation of the stimulus)
- Changing the rules (e.g. changing the distance of a drill, or adding a time restriction, will vary the task constraint and cognitive load placed upon the athlete)
- Varying equipment used (e.g. performing directional changes with or without equipment used in the sport will change an athlete's perception during the drill)
- Changing the training time and location (e.g. training in the morning compared to the afternoon will change the environmental constraints placed upon the athlete)
- Performing agility-specific drills at different times within the training session (e.g. exposing athletes to agility drills at the beginning versus the end of practice will introduce other confounding performance factors like fatigue, which can influence an athlete's perceptual-cognitive ability and movement output)

The Role of Feedback to Develop Perceptual-cognitive Ability

While the aim of a constraints-led approach to training is to provide athletes with an opportunity to engage in self-directed perception-action coupling, it may be necessary to cue and provide feedback to help guide athlete's attention to further develop their perceptual-cognitive ability. Feedback is obtained throughout agility movements via two primary sources: intrinsic and extrinsic sensory information. Intrinsic feedback describes sensory information sourced internally and externally from the body (i.e. proprioception, vision, audition, and smell), while extrinsic feedback refers to information provided to the athlete via an outside source (e.g. coach) (Janelle 2002; Porter et al. 2010).

When a learner is at the initial stage of movement development for agility performance, it is best to provide external feedback regarding their performance and direct their attention to areas of improvement (Porter et al. 2010). Utilising external cues during agility, such as 'accelerate away from the opponent as quick as possible' or 'push off the ground as hard as possible', has been shown to improve agility performance by creating an external focus of attention allowing motor behaviour to occur automatically (Porter et al. 2010). As the athlete learns to adjust and adapt their movement, intrinsic feedback becomes the predominant information source (Winstein et al. 1990). While extrinsic feedback typically reduces as the learning process continues, it is still important to provide movement and perceptual cues to guide athlete's attention throughout the movement. Adopting an external focus of attention to guide athlete's attention to relevant perceptual-cognitive cues can assist with narrowing an athlete's attentional focus and visual search area. Research has indicated athletes who focus on proximal kinematic cues (e.g. trunk and hips) produce a faster decision-making time compared to those who focus on distal kinematic cues (arms and legs) (Aglioti et al. 2008). For example, directing athletes' attention to a specific cue during the drill (e.g. hips) can be achieved by placing a coloured belt to the region of the opponents' body or utilising cueing words, such as 'hips', before or during the drill, instructs athletes where to fixate throughout the drill, narrowing their attentional focus.

Conclusion

Agility is a fast-paced dynamic skill with many factors that influence performance outcomes. To develop agility performance or, more specifically, decision-making ability, there is a need to create a representative training and learning environment that replicates the demands of competition. Specifically, applying an ecological dynamics approach to agility performance, athletes are viewed as a complex and adaptive system where performer-environment interactions enable multiple movement solutions to emerge for the same or similar task. Redesigning the training environment through manipulation of task and environmental constraints, creating context-specific drills that provide affordances for the athletes to engage in perception-action coupling, strengthens the representation between the stimulus and appropriate movement response resulting in a faster decision and movement execution for a given situation. Utilising these strategies allows coaches the opportunity to create unique training environments that maximise the transfer of agility performances from training to competition.

References

Aglioti, S. M., Cesari, P., Romani, M. and Urgesi, C. (2008). Action anticipation and motor resonance in elite basketball players, *Nature Neuroscience, 11*(9), 1109–1116.

Araujo, D., Davis, K., Chow, J. Y., Passos, P. and Raab, M. (2009). The development of decision making skill in sport: An ecological dynamics perspective in Rabb, M., Araujo, D. and Ripoll, H., eds., *Perspectives on Cognition and Action in Sport*, Suffolk, United States of America: Nova Science Publishers, Inc., 157–169.

Bernstein, N. A. (1967). *The Co-ordination and Regulation of Movements*, Oxford, United Kingdom: Pergamon Press.

Čoh, M., Jovanović-Golubović, D. and Bratić, M. (2004). Motor learning in sport, *Facta Universitatis-series: Physical Education and Sport, 2*(1), 45–59.

Davids, K., Araujo, D., Vilar, L., Renshaw, I. and Pinder, R. (2013). An ecological dynamics approach to skill acquisition: Implications for development of talent in sport, *Talent Development and Excellence, 5*, 21–34.

Davids, K., Renshaw, I. and Glazier, P. (2005). Movement models from sports reveal fundamental insights into coordination processes, *Exercise & Sport Science Reviews, 33*(1), 36–42.

Farrow, D. and Abernethy, B. (2002). Can anticipatory skills be learned through implicit video based perceptual training?, *Journal of Sports Science, 20*(6), 471–485.

Gabbett, T. J., Kelly, J. N. and Sheppard, J. M. (2008). Speed, change of direction speed, and reactive agility of rugby league players, *Journal of Strength Conditioning Research, 22*(1), 174–181.

Green, B. S., Blake, C. and Caulfield, B. M. (2011). A comparison of cutting technique performance in rugby union players, *Journal of Strength Conditioning Research, 25*(10), 2668–2680.

Holmberg, P. M. (2009). Agility training for experienced athletes: A dynamical systems approach, *Strength & Conditioning Journal, 31*(5), 73–78.

Hughes, G. and Dai, B. (2021). The influence of decision making and divided attention on lower limb biomechanics associated with anterior cruciate ligament injury: A narrative review, *Sports Biomechanics, 6*, 1–16.

Janelle, C. M. (2002). Anxiety, arousal and visual attention: A mechanistic account of performance variability, *Journal of Sports Sciences, 20*(3), 237–251.

Jeffreys, I. (2011). A task-based approach to developing context-specific agility, *Strength & Conditioning Journal, 33*(4), 52–59.

Jullien, H., Bisch, C., Largouet, N., Manouvrier, C., Carling, C. J. and Amiard, V. (2008). Does a short period of lower limb strength training improve performance in field-based tests of running and agility in young professional soccer players, *Journal of Strength Conditioning Research, 22*(2), 404–411.

Keiner, M., Sander, A., Wirth, K. and Schmidtbleicher, D. (2014). Long term strength training effects on change-of-direction sprint performance, *Journal of Strength Conditioning Research, 28*(1), 223–221.

Lockie, R. G., Jeffriess, M. D., McGann, T. S., Callaghan, S. J. and Schultz, A. B. (2014). Planned and reactive agility performance in semi professional and amateur basketball players, *International Journal of Sports Physiology & Performance, 9*(5), 766–771.

Mann, D. T. Y., Williams, A. M., Ward, P. and Janelle, C. M. (2007). Perceptual-cognitive expertise in sport: A meta-analysis, *Journal of Sport & Exercise Psychology*, *29*, 457–478.

McBride, J. M., McCaulley, G. O. and Cormie, P. (2008). Influence of pre-activity and eccentric muscle activity on concentric performance during vertical jumping, *Journal of Strength Conditioning Research*, *22*(3), 750–757.

McLean, S. G., Lipfert, S. W. and van den Bogert, A. J. (2004). Effect of gender and defensive opponent on the biomechanics of sidestep cutting, *Medicine & Science in Sports & Exercise*, *36*(6), 1008–1016.

McRobert, A. P., Ward, P., Eccles, D. W. and Williams, A. M. (2011). The effect of manipulating context-specific information on perceptual-cognitive process during a simulated anticipation task, *British Journal of Psychology*, *102*(3), 519–534.

Nunez, F. J., Ona, A., Raya, A. and Bilbao, A. (2009). Differences between expert and novice soccer players when using movement precues to shoot a penalty kick, *Perceptual Motor Skills*, *108*(1), 139–148.

Passos, P., Araujo, D., Davids, K. and Shuttleworth, R. (2008). Manipulating constraints to train decision making in rugby union, *International Journal of Sport Science & Coaching*, *3*, 125–140.

Pinder, R. A., Davids, K., Renshaw, I. and Araujo, D. (2011). Representative learning design and functionality of research and practice in sport, *Journal of Sport Exercise Psychology*, *33*(1), 146–155.

Porter, J. M., Nolan, R. P., Ostrowski, E. J. and Wulf, G. (2010). Directing attention externally enhances agility performance: A qualitative and quantitative analysis of the efficacy of using verbal instructions to focus attention, *Frontiers in Psychology*, *1*, 216.

Robertson, S., Spencer, B., Back, N. and Farrow, D. (2018). A rule induction framework for the determination of representative learning design in skilled performance, *Journal of Sports Sciences*, *37*(11), 1280–1285.

Roca, A., Ford, P. R., McRobert, A. P. and Williams, A. M. (2011). Identifying the processes underpinning anticipation and decision-making in a dynamic time-constrained task, *Cognitive Processing*, *12*(3), 301–310.

Roca, A., Ford, P. R., McRobert, A. P. and Williams, A. M. (2013). Perceptual-cognitive skills and their interaction as a function of task constrains in soccer, *Journal of Sport Exercise Psychology*, *35*(2), 144–155.

Serpell, B. G., Young, W. B. and Ford, M. (2011). Are the perceptual and decision-making components of agility trainable? A preliminary investigation, *Journal of Strength & Conditioning Research*, *25*(5), 1240–1248.

Sheppard, J. M. and Young, W. B. (2006). Agility literature review: Classifications, training and testing, *Journal of Sports Sciences*, *24*(9), 919–932.

Spiteri, T., Cochrane, J. L. and Nimphius, S. (2012). Human stimulus reliability during a reactive offensive and defensive agility protocol, *Journal of Australian Strength & Conditioning*, *20*(4), 20–27.

Spiteri, T., Fransen, J., McIntyre, F. and Hart, N. H. (In Review). What do faster athletes see? Differences in visual gaze and search strategies between faster and slower agility performances, *Journal of Sports Sciences*.

Spiteri, T. and Hart, N. H. (2014). Ball inclusion into the AFL agility test can improve change of direction performance, *Journal of Australian Strength & Conditioning* (Supplement 1), 55–62.

Spiteri, T., Hart, N. H. and Nimphius, S. (2014). Offensive and defensive agility: A sex comparison of lower body kinematics and ground reaction forces, *Journal of Applied Biomechanics*, *30*(4), 514–520.

Spiteri, T., McIntyre, F., Specos, C. and Myszka, S. (2018). Cognitive training for agility: The integration between perception and action, *Strength & Conditioning Journal*, *40*(1), 39–46.

Spiteri, T., Newton, R. U., Binetti, M., Hart, N. H., Sheppard, J. M. and Nimphius, S. (2015a). Mechanical determinants of faster change of direction and agility performance in female basketball athletes, *Journal of Strength & Conditioning Research*, *29*(8), 2205–2214.

Spiteri, T., Newton, R. U. and Nimphius, S. (2015b). Neuromuscular strategies contributing to faster multidirectional agility performance, *Journal of Electromyography & Kinesiology*, *25*(4), 629–636.

Tremblay, L. (2010). Visual information in the acquisition of goal-directed action in Elliott, D and Khan, M., eds., *Vision and Goal-directed Movement Neurobehavioral Perspectives*, Champaign: Human Kinetics, 281–291.

Vaeynes, R., Lenoir, M., Williams, A. M. and Philippaerts, R. M. (2007). Mechanisms underpinning successful decision making in skilled youth soccer players: An analysis of visual search behaviours, *Journal of Motor Behavior*, *39*(5), 395–408.

Veale, J. P., Pearce, A. J. and Carlson, J. S. (2010). Reliability and validity of a reactive agility test for Australian football, *International Journal of Sports Physiology & Performance*, *5*(2), 239–248.

Wheeler, K. W. and Sayers, M. G. (2010). Modification of agility running technique in reaction to a defender in rugby union, *Journal of Sports Science & Medicine*, *9*, 445–451.

Winstein, C. J. and Schmidt, R. A. (1990). Reduced frequency of knowledge of results enhances motor skill learning, *Journal of Experimental Psychology*, *16*(4), 677–691.

Woods, C. T., Rothwell, M., Rudd, J., Robertson, S. and Davids, K. (2020). Representative co-design: Utilising a source of experiential knowledge for athlete development and performance preparation, *Psychology of Sport & Exercise*, 52. doi.org/10.1016/j.psychsport.2020.101804.

Wulf, G., Chiviacowsky, S., Schiller, E. and Ávila, L. T. G. (2010a). Frequent external focus feedback enhances motor learning, *Frontiers in Psychology*, *1*, 190.

Wulf, G., Shea, C. and Lewthwaite, R. (2010b). Motor skill learning and performance: A review of influential factors, *Medical Education*, *44*(1), 75–84.

Yarrow, K., Brown, P. and Krakauer, J. W. (2009). Inside the brain of an elite athlete: The neural processes that support high achievement in sports, *Nature Reviews Neuroscience*, *10*, 585–596.

Young, W. B. and Farrow, D. (2006). A review of agility: Practical applications for strength and conditioning, *Strength & Conditioning Journal*, *28*(5), 24–29.

PART 3

Programming for Multidirectional Speed

14

PROGRAMMING FOR MULTIDIRECTIONAL SPEED IN SPORT

Paul A. Jones and Thomas Dos'Santos; Featuring Sports-Specific Case Studies by Molly Binetti, Cameron Josse, and Chris McLeod

Introduction

The enhancement of multidirectional speed (MDS) should be viewed as multifactorial, whereby practitioners need to consider the physical (mechanical and metabolic), technical, and perceptual-cognitive components in the programme design. Thus far, we have outlined strategies to enhance the physical (Chapters 8 and 12), technical (Chapters 9, 10, and 11), and perceptual-cognitive (Chapters 11 and 13) elements. However, the challenge to practitioners is to integrate these individual components into a cohesive programme to ensure development of MDS and mitigate musculoskeletal injury.

An important first step in designing programmes is to perform a *needs analysis* of the sport and athlete(s) by consideration of the physiological, and biomechanical/movement demands, along with identifying the common non-contact musculoskeletal injuries associated with the sport and their mechanisms/modifiable risk factors (Jones & Comfort, 2020). Specifically, for MDS, this evaluation should consider the agility demands of the sport. For instance, the following questions might apply:

1. What MDS actions (sprints, CODs, etc.) are commonly performed in the sport and how important are they in relation to match deciding events?
2. How do these MDS actions vary (linear vs curvilinear sprints, cutting techniques, etc.)?
3. What are the typical MDS action distances/durations and how are the previously mentioned actions combined?
4. What stimuli do athletes react to before performing these actions?
5. Contextually, why do these MDS actions occur from a tactical/sport-specific context?
6. In 'worst-case scenarios', how frequent are the specific MDS action(s) performed and what are typical peak period demands (e.g. 1 or 3 min period)?
7. If applicable, is there any position specific or tactical role considerations/differences?

Once these actions and their key features have been identified, an evaluation of the biomechanical characteristics and underpinning physical qualities/capacities of these actions is needed

DOI: 10.4324/9781003267881-17

(Chapters 4 and 10) to help inform exercise selection and drill development. In terms of the injury profile of the sport, important questions might be as follows: What are the common non-contact injuries in the sport and are these injuries related to MDS actions? What are the mechanisms of these injuries (e.g. biomechanical characteristics associated with overloading these susceptible tissues)? What modifiable risk factors may relate to the mechanism of injury (e.g. physical qualities required to handle or offset the high loads placed on these tissues)? Answering these questions allows the practitioner to develop a complete picture of the MDS demands of the sport both in relation to performance and injury potential.

Once these demands are evaluated, then an agreed MDS assessment battery related to the sport (Chapter 6) can be developed to evaluate the athlete against along with an evaluation of relevant muscle strength and physical qualities (Chapter 7) to help inform training prescription. It is also important that the evaluation of the athlete considers the training status and experience of the athlete, conducts a retrospective analysis of previous season(s) and their injury history to better individualise the programme. Interestingly, Rawlley-Singh and Wolf (2022) has introduced the concept of aligning strength and conditioning support to the head coach's performance model, principles, and philosophy. Thus, where appropriate practitioners should have an appreciation of the intended tactical (attacking and defensive structures, organisation, style of play, etc.), technical, and action requirements and principles, the coach is looking to adopt for the squad or athlete to better support their practice. In addition, seeking the expertise and feedback from the multidisciplinary team (physiotherapist, skill/technical coach, athlete, motor skill/control practitioner, etc.) and the athletes themselves is also advised for a holistic overview and a varied insight of the MDS demands of the sport and individual's physical and injury risk profile.

Progressive overload of the physical training (strength, metabolic conditioning, etc.) is vital for effective *programming* whether the aim is to improve sports performance or rehabilitate an athlete. This is typically achieved using a periodised approach ('planned distribution or variation in training methods and means on a cyclic or periodic basis' [Plisk & Stone, 2003, p. 19]). Periodisation allows an athlete to exploit complementary training effects at optimal times (e.g. major competition), manage fatigue, and prevent stagnation or overtraining (Plisk & Stone, 2003). Given the high mechanical loads experienced during MDS actions involved in training and competition (e.g. sprinting, changing direction, and deceleration), it is essential that such exposure to these actions is periodised (i.e. planned, sequenced, and phased appropriately) (McBurnie et al., 2022) to provide an appropriate progression in intensity and volume to ensure adaptation to the training rather than injury. This would prevent 'spikes' in volume of these actions in training and competition which is known to lead to soft tissue injury (e.g. overloading the tissue before it is ready) (Duhig et al., 2016; Ruddy et al., 2018; McBurnie et al., 2022). Thus, the monitoring of the MDS actions is also a critical component in the process to particularly avoid these 'spikes' (see Chapter 15). Furthermore, as outlined in Chapter 10, the development of game-related movement skill (agility development framework) should also follow a periodised approach (Otte et al., 2019; Taberner's et al., 2019; Farrow & Robertson, 2017) whereby athletes should work through phases dedicated to technique acquisition, technique retention and integrity, and movement solutions to ensure appropriate development of adaptable movement strategies to use during match play.

An abundance of periodisation models exists within the strength and conditioning field, such as traditional (often mistakenly termed 'linear'), undulating, and conjugate (Plisk & Stone, 2003). Much of the existing literature supports the notion that block periodisation may provide superior results compared to other models (DeWeese et al., 2015a, 2015b; Issurin, 2008, 2010).

Block periodisation is based on the idea that a concentrated load may be used to train one specific characteristic during each training phase while maintaining the previously developed characteristic(s) rather than develop multiple physiological characteristics or motor abilities simultaneously, which may be counterproductive. Such an approach works well for sports where 'peaking' for a single competition in the season is the focus. However, difficulties lie in sports where there are long competitive seasons that require the maintenance of several physical qualities throughout the competitive season. Many field- and court-based sports may have long sports seasons (e.g. six to ten months) and relatively shorter pre-seasons, which presents major challenges to the practitioner (e.g. short time to develop required physical qualities in the pre-season, a long time to preserve such physical qualities during the season, delivery of training around high density of competitions in-season). A typical solution might involve using a blocked periodisation approach during the pre-season prior to the competitive season to develop key physical qualities before shifting to a summated microcycles approach (Baker, 1998, 2001) during the in-season to preserve the physical qualities developed. Munroe and Haff (2018) have discussed an 'emphasis modelling' approach whereby certain qualities are trained concurrently but emphasised at greater densities depending on whether the focus is on development rather than maintenance of certain qualities. Notwithstanding, approaches are likely to vary between sports due to the duration of the season, the density of matches during periods of the season, and specific competition calendars which may involve multiple tournaments and other playing commitments (e.g. international selection).

It is beyond the scope of this chapter to cover every field- and court-based sport regarding programming MDS training. However, applying the information outlined in previous chapters is demonstrated in a series of case studies in the remainder of this chapter. The sport examples included here are basketball (team/court sport), American football (team/field sport) and tennis (individual/court/racket sport) to demonstrate implementation of how to use the information outlined in the previous chapters across the diverse range of multidirectional sports. It is important not to view these examples as definitive for that sport but evaluate how the key principles are applied in each practitioner's working environment that considers the logistical issues in their programme planning. Each case study provides the thought process by which each practitioner in the respective sport programmes their athletes' MDS development programme.

Developing Game Speed for Basketball

Molly Binetti

Basketball, with similarities to other team field or court sports, can be categorised as acyclic, reactive, and random. Movements occur in response to a stimulus and require context to understand movement strategies, making it difficult for them to be pre-programmed or repeatable. These movements can be categorised into jumping and landing, linear (acceleration and deceleration), and multidirectional. Examples include sprints, closeouts, jump stops, lunge stops, angled lateral stops, lateral slides, and shuffle stops. Athletes are required to have a variety of movement strategies to be executed in an ever-changing environment at various forces, angles, and speeds, and over various time epochs (Smith et al., 2020). In basketball, athletes do not have the time or space to reach maximal speeds; thus, the constant need to react to another player or situation (i.e. location of ball) requires athletes to often accelerate, decelerate, and reaccelerate in another direction as quickly as possible. However, it is the ability to change direction combined with the perceptual-cognitive ability to react to a stimulus, such as a defender or bounce of the ball that separates true agility performance from change-of-direction speed (Nimphius, 2021).

Key determinants of effective agility performance can be divided into three major components (Nimphius, 2021) (see Figure 1.1). The first of these components is having adequate physical capacities, such as strength, power, rate of force development, and reactive strength. Each type of strength quality is used during a change of direction as the athlete brakes (eccentric), transitions (isometric), and then reaccelerates (i.e. propulsion) in a new direction (concentric). An athlete's ability to decelerate, change direction, and reaccelerate will be limited by how much force they can rapidly exert into the ground within a given time frame (i.e. net impulse = change in momentum). Movements such as jumping and cutting rely on the ability to attenuate forces effectively to redirect those forces in an optimal direction. The importance of reactive strength (i.e. rapid transition from eccentric to concentric muscle action) for the basketball athlete is to acquire the ability to transfer strength qualities into explosive actions so that they can move quickly and precisely while under stress. The ability to move quickly around the basketball court is highly related to the athlete's ability to transmit force into the ground (Smith et al., 2020), with stronger athletes previously observed to display higher ground reaction forces during dynamic tasks (Spiteri et al., 2013). Due to the high volume and intensity of jumps, landings, accelerations, and decelerations, it is imperative for basketball athletes to have sufficient lower-body muscular strength and for tendons to have the capacity to tolerate stress. Beginning athletes or those without a fundamental strength base should focus their training towards reaching relative lower-body strength values of 1.5–2.0 × body weight, while remaining in beginner-level acceleration, deceleration, and change-of-direction drills (Nimphius, 2021). This approach will help develop an athlete in an appropriate manner without exposing them to exercises they are physically or mentally unprepared for. This will be discussed in more detail when examining programme design.

The second component of effective agility performance is the technical demands (Figure 1.1), such as foot placement, position of the trunk and pelvis, low centre of mass, and proper angles to apply force into the ground in an optimal direction to facilitate effective acceleration and change in direction.

The third and final component of successful agility performance is perceptual-cognitive speed (Figure 1.1). Training to enhance agility must be task and scenario specific. An athlete's decision-making or perceptual-cognitive ability is a key determinant in faster movement skills on the court.

Implications for Programme Design

When designing the training programme, it is important to be clear on the desired outcomes. At the University of South Carolina, the philosophy is to create a learning-rich environment that includes a high degree of variability, chaos, play, and emphasises differential learning to develop highly adaptable and self-organising athletes. It is the job of the performance coach to provide representative learning with specific training stimuli that will induce the greatest transfer to the sporting movements. Marriage of the weight room and court should be top priority. In this setting, athletes are participating in team practices 10 out of 12 months of the calendar year. Practices are designed in a way that exposes them to integrated drills and gameplay every session, which is an important consideration when programming in the weight room. Due to the high exposure to these actions during training within the microcycle, the approach taken here is to focus on specific weight room exercises and physical capacities rather than additional change-of-direction and agility sessions, which is effectively catered for in game-specific practices.

The first step of this approach is testing and evaluation to determine an athlete's physical capacities as described earlier, with the specific tests provided in Table 14.1. A well-constructed testing battery, in conjunction with observing athletes' movement in their natural habitat on the court and constant communication with the sport coaches, can provide information on all components that underpin agility performance (Nimphius, 2021).

Vertical jump testing can assess individual qualities and profile each athlete into one of four categories which provides insight into how they move (Hawkin Dynamics, 2021):

1. High force and fast
2. High force and slow
3. Low force and fast
4. Low force and slow

Understanding these qualities while also collecting information about their technical, tactical, and perceptual abilities on the court provides a detailed roadmap of how to approach training for each individual. This broad range of assessments allows for deeper understanding of an athlete's force, power, speed, and time characteristics bilaterally and unilaterally, which gives insight into which qualities are lacking and if there are any asymmetries present. For example, if an athlete performs well on a bilateral jumping task but shows significant asymmetry on a unilateral jump, training should be directed towards unilateral force and power production. Additionally, if an athlete performs well on a single-leg countermovement jump but has a long ground contact time during a unilateral repeated jump, the training target should be geared toward reactive strength and elasticity.

Off-season

The off-season in Division 1 women's college basketball lasts anywhere between 8 and 12 weeks, depending on how deep of a postseason run a team makes. The purpose of the off-season

TABLE 14.1 Proposed Testing Battery for Basketball

Testing Battery	*Method(s)*	*Metric(s)*
Lower-body strength	Trap bar deadlift, squat variation, split squat variation	Force, relative force (% BW)[i]
Drop jump (18" box)	Just Jump mat, force plate	Jump height, GCT[ii] (RSI)[iii]
Countermovement jump (bilateral)	Just Jump mat, force plate	ECC RFD,[iv] impulse, jump height
Countermovement jump (unilateral, land on two feet)	Just Jump mat, force plate	ECC RFD, impulse, jump height, % asymmetry
Repeat 4 jump (bilateral)	Just Jump mat, force plate	Avg. jump height, GCT (RSI)
Repeat 4 jump (unilateral)	Just Jump mat	Avg. jump height, GCT (RSI), % asymmetry
10-yard acceleration (on-court)	Stopwatch, timing gates	Acceleration speed (sec.)
¾ court sprint (on-court)	Stopwatch, timing gates	Acceleration speed (sec.)

Key: BW: body weight; GCT: ground contact time; RSI: reactive strength index

i Percent body weight

ii Ground contact time

iii Reactive strength index

iv Eccentric rate of force development

programme is to maximise strength and power and prepare the athlete to handle the intensity of future competition. The target strength qualities during this phase are eccentric and isometric strength, which will allow the athlete to tolerate greater loads and the high magnitudes of force necessary to decelerate and cut on the court. This is achieved by using heavy loads, fast eccentric and isometric actions, and manipulating tempos during these phases of movements. Single-leg exercises are heavily targeted during this phase. Specific to improving one's change of direction and speed, this is a key time to expose the athlete to higher volumes and lower intensities of jumping and plyometric exercises to develop tissue tolerance and expose the lower body to specific tensions. These are performed bilaterally and unilaterally and in multiple planes. As the off-season progresses, volume decreases, and intensity of jumping and plyometric exercises increases. This approach looks different based on the individual and their training age or physical capacity. Many COD drills and drills specific to agility development can be incorporated into daily dynamic warm-ups in the weight room and the beginning of practice. These drills can be designated into two categories of high-velocity and high-braking requirements or low-velocity and manoeuvrability.

Pre-season

Pre-season is the 6-week period leading up to the start of official practice where both volume and intensity on the court begins to ramp up. The objective during this phase of training is to focus on rate of force development and reactive strength to peak them for the start of competition. The exposure to high-intensity changes of direction, accelerations, and decelerations increases drastically so the volume of exposures in the weight room will decrease.

TABLE 14.2 Sample Exercise Selection for Change-of-Direction and Agility Enhancement

Eccentric Strength (Braking)	*Isometric Strength (Transition)*	*Concentric Strength (Propulsion)*	*Power/Rate of Force Development (RFD)*	*Reactive Strength (Elasticity)*
Drop landings (loaded/unloaded)	Yielding isometrics (squat/split squat)	Resisted acceleration (bands/chains/sled)	Olympic lifts and derivatives	Pogo progressions
Catch phase of Olympic lifts	Extreme isometrics	Back squat	Loaded jump variations	Jump rope
Low-velocity deceleration drills	Overcoming isometrics	Front squat	Sled accelerations	Skips
High-velocity deceleration drills	Oscillatory isometrics	Split squat variations	Assisted accelerations	Repeat CMJ or SL CMJ (loaded/unloaded)
Loaded rhythm drops		Deadlift variations	Box jump variations	Low box jumps (short coupling)
Accentuated eccentric training		Lateral squat/lunge	Maximal effort sprints and bounds	Extensive bounds (multidirectional)
			Loaded power skips	Repeat hurdle jumps/hops
				Depth jumps

Key: CMJ: countermovement jump; SL: single leg; RFD: rate of force development

In-season

Physical performance ebbs and flows over the course of a season, making it necessary to construct individual in-season microcycles to allow athletes to continue development and reach optimal performance levels. Early on, the athlete is getting accustomed to higher basketball-specific workloads and intensities, making it necessary to focus on higher intensities and lower volumes in the weight room. Programming during this phase is dependent on the role of the athlete, how many minutes they are playing, and how many reps they are getting in practice (i.e. overall exercise volume). Those in limited roles will continue to train in a more developmental fashion. In general, the objective is to train 'reverse specificity' and target qualities the athlete is not being exposed to on the court, maximise recovery, and address any health concerns to optimise performance.

Summary

The development of change-of-direction skill and agility is a multifaceted approach that requires collaboration with the sport coach and marriage of the weight room and specific skill work. A testing battery should be chosen to identify an athlete's current physical qualities and the results used to make informed training decisions. Training COD and agility can be an integrated part of every weight room session, whether as part of the warm-up or selected exercises within the session. It is imperative to measure progress via re-testing and most importantly via on-court movement performance.

American Football

Cameron Josse

Overview of Speed, Change of Direction, and Agility Demands of American Football

Agility and change of direction (COD) are arguably the most significant determinants of game speed in American football. American football is an intermittent game where the dynamics and movement solutions are based heavily on perceptual cues. While the agility demands are complex in terms of the constraints on player performance, the manifestation of movement solutions tend to present with high consistency. For example, if a player needs to redirect themselves laterally, they will use a form of cut step pattern. If that player needs to move laterally while reading

TABLE 14.3 Exercise Variables to Manipulate During Agility Training

Distance
Direction
Body position
Evade opponent/object
Contact
Perturbation
Time pressure
Auditory or visual cue
Rhythm and coordination
Load

environmental cues, they will likely perform a shuffle motion or crossover run. Thus, consistent movement solutions tend to present themselves in similar scenarios.

To help bring a systematic approach to this concept, coach and educator Ian Jeffreys developed what he refers to as the 'movement syllabus' for team sports. Essentially, every movement in the movement syllabus is understood as a 'target movement' to fit a 'target function'. These functions are also divided into three broad movement categories: initiation, transition, and actualisation, as explained in Table 14.4 (Jeffreys, 2017, pp. 80–81).

This movement syllabus presents a roadmap for an array of multidirectional movements that can be trained and developed with football players, particularly from a closed drill standpoint. For example, rather than always performing sprints from a forward-facing start position, athletes may start by facing to the side or facing to the rear so that they have to initiate the sprint effort with a hip turn or drop step, respectively. Closed COD drills may be designed to feature all three movement categories of initiation, transition, and actualisation with a strong emphasis on finishing fast during the actualisation phase.

Likewise, open-reactive drills may be designed to feature various movements through constraint manipulation, putting pressure on the player to discover movement options when affordances for action are limited. It is important that open/reactive activities be included in the off-season training periods and incorporate sport-specific stimuli wherever possible in order to achieve a representative learning effect. For example, one of the most important player-to-player interactions is between a ball carrier and a tackler in the open field. Thus, a basic open field tag situation may be designed where the chaser must run through a chute of cones before being able to pursue the runner, illustrated in Figure 14.1. In this way, there is an emphasis on the pursuit speed with the possibility of a retreating COD action for the chaser, placing a premium on aggressive deceleration, hip turning, drop stepping, and curved running. The movements of the

TABLE 14.4 Ian Jeffreys' Movement Syllabus (Adapted from Jeffreys, 2017, pp. 80–81)

Movement Syllabus Category	*Explanation*	*Example Target Movements*
Transition movements	Moving while maintaining a posture from which the athlete can read and react effectively to key stimuli and carry out effective subsequent movement – includes various angles of deceleration	Lateral shuffle Backpedal Crossover running Forefoot braking Rearfoot braking Lateral brake step
Initiation movements	Starting movements or initiating movement in a new direction, frequently taking an athlete out of his transition movements	Starting to the front (linear acceleration) Starting to the side (hip turn pattern) Starting to the rear (drop step pattern) Turning at high speed (speed cut pattern) Aggressive lateral COD (power cut pattern)
Actualisation movements	Movement where the aim is to achieve a given sport task, often following an initiation movement and involve either acceleration (possibly up to top speed) or the direct application of a sport skill	Linear acceleration High-speed running Curved running pattern

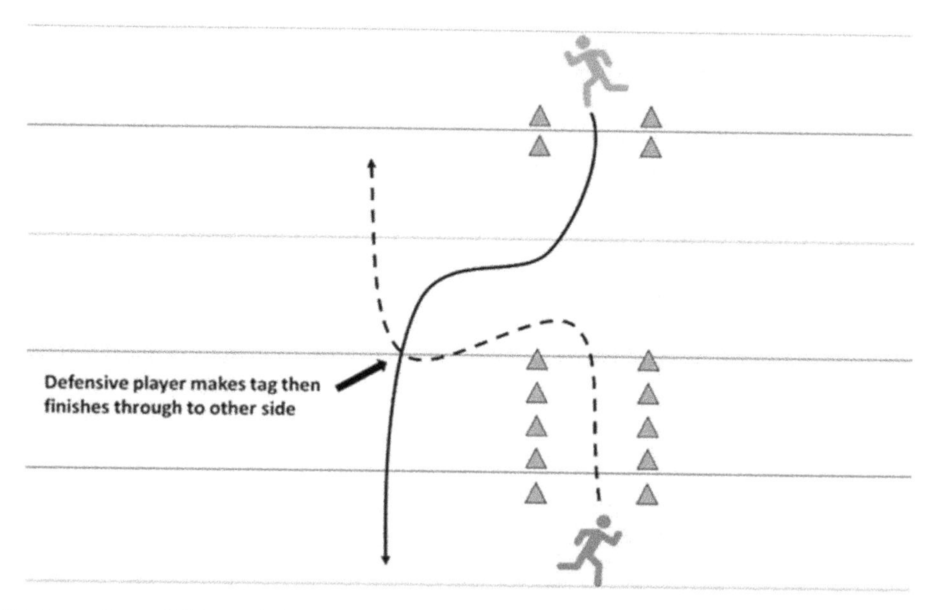

FIGURE 14.1 Open field tag drill with chaser constraint and runner advantage.

runner then emphasise curved running and various cut stepping with acceleration – all of which are fundamental sport-specific actions in American football.

Different player positions in American football will require differing characteristics of exposure to deceleration and COD. For example, the occurrence of high-intensity deceleration efforts (i.e. <-3 m s^{-2}) has been reported as significantly higher for wide receivers (WR), linebackers (LB) and defensive backs (DB) in comparison to other positions, with the down linemen experiencing the lowest frequency (Wellman et al., 2016, pp. 13–15). However, offensive and defensive linemen may perform multiple directional changes in a smaller field space with offensive linemen typically spending a great deal of game-based movement in the transition category, such as shuffling laterally and diagonally. There is a tactical basis for the frequency of these movements, and by staying in these transitionary movements, linemen are able to continuously scan their field of vision to perceive and inhibit the penetration of pursuing defenders to create space for the backfield players with the ball. So the game dynamics can help dictate which areas of the movement syllabus may be worth spending training time on.

Programme Design for Agility and COD in American Football

When incorporating exercises and drills to develop COD ability, players' bodies must be trained in order to adapt in a way that they may safely withstand the bandwidth of intensity they will experience in practices and games. So although 'brain-first' activities like open/reactive drills are paramount in programme design, one cannot neglect the importance of performing enough 'body-first' deceleration and COD activities to enhance motor output and tissue quality through specific movement patterns. Given this, closed activities have an important place in the training process, particularly during early preparation phases. However, these exercises will be more general in nature and primarily used to intensify the exposure to deceleration/COD rather than largely impact sport skill development. In the pre-competition and competition phases, the emphasis shifts heavily in favour of open/reactive activities, as well as specialised skill development. Armed with Jeffreys' movement syllabus as a guide, it becomes possible to get creative and design drills that feature various movement combinations while manipulating the intensity and volume of work to resemble that from sport practice. A sample off-season progression template is provided in Table 14.5, where closed versus open/reactive activities are emphasised and de-emphasised as the program moves closer to the final stage before pre-season training camp.

During the first half of the preparatory period, less volume and frequency of field-based activity may be appropriate to allow for positive adaptation of strength and power qualities. So the microcycle design presented in Table 14.6 could be appropriate, where five total days of training are performed, three of which are devoted to weight-room-based training and two devoted to

TABLE 14.5 Sample Off-season and Pre-season Progression of Agility and COD Training in American Football

Stage and Emphasis	*Training Notes*	*Volume Distribution*	
		Pre-planned Drills	*Reactive Drills*
Stage 1: Primary aim: Introduction to COD mechanics Secondary aim: Minimal volume of low-complexity reactive drills	1. Basic, low-intensity closed drills to introduce various positions and movement planes 2. Activate perceptual-cognitive processing with low-complexity open drills in small spaces	80%	20%
Stage 2: Primary aim: Progress COD intensity and volume Secondary aim: Add more open drills for basic agility development	1. Progress closed drills with combinations of movements, greater entry speeds, and added competition. 2. Increase complexity of open drills and increase the size of the drill spaces.	60%	40%
Stage 3: Primary aim: Maximise COD intensity Secondary aim: Increase intensity and volume of open drills to progress agility development	1. Closed drills reach their maximum intensity in terms of movement combinations, entry speeds, and competition. 2. Complexity of open drills starts to match agility demands of football in isolated situations. Various field sizes and shapes are incorporated.	40%	60%
Stage 4: Primary aim: Maximise intensity and volume of agility development with primarily open drills Secondary aim: Maintain COD capacity with reduced volume of closed drills	1. Open drills reach their maximum intensity in terms of complexity and matching reactive demands of football situations. Various field sizes and shapes are still incorporated. 2. Closed drills are maintained in preparation for the open drills and for maintenance of COD capacity.	20%	80%

Key: COD: change of direction

TABLE 14.6 Sample Microcycle Programming Template for Agility and COD Training in American Football, Phase 1 (Five to Eight Weeks Out from Start of Pre-season Training Camp)

Day 1 – Weight Room Training	*Day 2 – Field Training*	*Day 3 – Weight Room Training*	*Day 4 – Field Training*	*Day 5 – Weight Room Training*	*Day 6 and 7 – Rest and Recovery*
Multidirectional jumps/ plyometrics	Linear Sprinting General agility and COD training Technical/tactical skill training (player-led)	Multidirectional jumps/ plyometrics	Linear sprinting General agility and COD training Technical/tactical skill training (player-led)	Multidirectional jumps/ plyometrics	Individual recovery protocols

Key: COD: change of direction

TABLE 14.7 Sample Strength and Jump/Plyometric Combinations for Multi-Planar Power Development, Phase 1 (Five to Eight Weeks Out from Start of Pre-season Training Camp)

Day 1 – Complex Pairing	*Day 3 – Complex Pairing*	*Day 5 – Contrast Circuit*
1A. Hex bar deadlift – 4 × 3, 80–85% 1 RM 1B. Single-leg hurdle hop to single-leg box jump (45–60 cm) – 4 × 2 each leg 2A. Barbell Romanian deadlift – 4 × 4, 80–85% 1 RM 2B. Box depth drops (45–60 cm) holding dumbbells (12–16 kg) – 3 × 3	1A. Barbell reverse lunge – 4 × 3 each leg, 80–85% 1 RM 1B. Consecutive Heiden jumps – 4 × 3 each way	1A. Barbell squat – 4 × 3, mean bar velocity 0.6–0.8 m/s 1B. Consecutive hurdle jumps – 4 hurdles 1C. Hex bar countermovement jump – 4 × 3 1D. Lateral hurdle hop (15 cm) to single-leg box jump (45–60 cm) – 4 × 2 each leg

field training. However, the work done in the weight room may feature aspects of deceleration/ COD by performing multi-planar jumps/plyometrics, as well as variations of depth drops. In this way, the eccentric and isometric strength characteristics associated with changing direction may be developed using part practice methods. Some examples of strength/power complexes and contrast circuits featuring multi-planar explosive exercises are presented in Table 14.7.

The field training days may be designed as ‘team runs’ where the entire team trains together for the session, upwards of 120 players in the collegiate setting. Due to this logistical challenge, the workout may consist of a battery of exercise stations around which the players are divided and rotated. During the formalised field workout, the movements and exercises may be more general in nature, after which the player’s may come together and perform specialised technical/tactical skill training. Typically, this block of the training session is player-led where the team captains take ownership of their respective position groups and units. An example layout of these field-based training sessions is provided in Table 14.8.

As the preparatory period progresses into the second half, the exposure to field-based training can be amplified to where two more days of agility and/or COD work are added to the days that also feature weight-room training. This is illustrated in Table 14.9. The smaller groups of players

TABLE 14.8 Sample Field Training Sessions for Agility and COD Development for American Football Wide Receivers and Defensive Backs

Field Session 1	*Field Session 2*
Perform the following sequence two times: **1. 60-yard linear tempo runs – 4 total reps** a. 2 repetitions <8 seconds b. 1 repetition <9 seconds c. 1 repetition <10 seconds **Rest 45–60 seconds between each effort.** **2. 30-yard shuttle run – 4 total reps** *Performed as 5 yards out, plant and cut back 5 yards, return back 10 yards out, and plant and cut back 10 yards to finish. Switch plant foot every repetition. Effort should be perceived as 100% in a controlled manner every repetition.* **Align players for a 1:4 to 1:5 work-to-rest ratio.** **3. Sprint, react, and cut 135°, redirect 45°, and finish – 4 total repetitions** *Player sprints towards a cone set 10 yards away, keeping eyes on the coach. The coach may run left or right, after which the player must cut towards the coach at an angle of ~135° towards another cone. The player gets past the cone, plants, and redirects back 5 yards full speed to finish the drill.* **Align players for a 1:4 to 1:5 work-to-rest ratio.** **4. Sprint, react, and cut 90°, redirect 90°, and finish – 4 total repetitions** *Player sprints towards a cone set 10 yards away keeping eyes on the coach. The coach may run left or right, after which the player must cut towards the coach at an angle of ~90° towards another cone. The player gets past the cone, plants, and redirects back 5 yards full speed to finish the drill.* **Align players for a 1:4 to 1:5 work-to-rest ratio.** *Go back to linear tempo runs for one more rotation before moving to technical/tactical skill training. **Technical/Tactical Skill Training (Player-Led)** Players perform various forms of small-sided game-like activities with reduced numbers, such as 1 vs 1, 2 vs 2, or 7 vs 7. All activities are based on specific tactical aims and players are provided a 'script' of the session progression. Total time of skill training is typically about 30 minutes.	**Acceleration, COD, and Agility Stations** *Rotate through each station one time **1. Competitive four-cone drill variations – 5–6 total reps** *Four cones are arranged in a square shape, and the coach designs various activities in which the player must manoeuvre around the cones, such as an 'N' or 'L' pattern. Multiple set-ups are aligned so that multiple players must race and compete to complete the configuration the fastest.* **Align players for a 1:4 to 1:5 work-to-rest ratio.** **2. Reactive 20-yard shuttle – 4–6 total reps** *Players begin facing each other with feet beside each other in an athletic position. One player is the runner, and the other is the chaser. The runner initiates the drill, turning his hips and running either left or right 5 yards, plant and cut back 10 yards, and plant and cut back 5 yards to finish the drill (20 yards total covered). The chaser reacts to the first movement of the runner and then attempts to beat them through the drill configuration. Each player gets 2–3 reps in each role.* **Align players for a 1:4 to 1:5 work-to-rest ratio.** **3. Multi-angle cuts – 6 total reps** *Players sprint 10 yards at full speed, then make a cut step and redirect at angles of 45, 90, and 135° for a 5-yard burst to finish. One cut in each direction (left/right) is performed for each angle for a total of 6 repetitions. Effort should be perceived as 100% in a controlled manner in every repetition.* **Align players for a 1:4 to 1:5 work-to-rest ratio.** **4. Open field tag – 6 total reps** *A playing space is set at 10 yards wide and 15 yards deep. One player is the runner, and the other is the chaser. The runner initiates the drill by running forward into the playing area and attempts to evade the chaser in order to get to the other side of the space. The chaser must pursue and tag the near hip of the runner before finishing through to the opposite end of the space. Each player gets 2–3 reps in each role.* **Align players for a 1:4 to 1:5 work-to-rest ratio.** **5. Linear accelerations – 6 total reps** *Effort should be perceived as 100% in a controlled manner every repetition. Perform 2–3 different sprint start variations for 2–3 reps each, for example:* a. Two-point starts – 2 × 10–15 yards b. Half-kneeling starts – 2 × 10–15 yards c. Push-up starts – 2 × 10–15 yards **Align players for a 1:4 to 1:5 work-to-rest ratio.** *After completing each station, move on to technical/tactical skill training. **Technical/Tactical Skill Training (Player-Led)**

Key: COD: change of direction

TABLE 14.9 Sample Microcycle Programming Template for Agility and COD Training in American Football, Phase 2 (One to Four Weeks Out from Start of Pre-season Training Camp)

Day 1 – Weight Room and Field Training	*Day 2 – Field Training*	*Day 3 – Weight Room and Field Training*	*Day 4 – Field Training*	*Day 5 – Weight Room Training*	*Day 6 and 7 – Rest and Recovery*
Multidirectional jumps/ plyometrics Linear sprinting Position-specific agility and COD training	Linear sprinting General agility and COD training Technical/tactical skill training (player-led)	Multidirectional jumps/ plyometrics Position-specific COD training	Linear sprinting General agility and COD training Technical/tactical skill training (player-led)	Multidirectional jumps/ plyometrics	Individual recovery protocols

associated with having multiple weight-room training groups throughout the day can allow for the performance staff to bring players to the field and divide them up so that position-specific work may be implemented. The team runs are maintained on day 2 and day 4, along with the player-led technical/tactical skill training. The final training day may not feature any work done on the field, but the multi-planar power emphasis is maintained so that players become adapted to consistent exposure of multidirectional movement most days of the week, as will be characteristic of the pre-season and competitive periods of sport.

Along the way, it is vital to monitor the accumulation of acceleration, high-speed running, and deceleration loading, which may be achieved through reports attained from global positioning systems (GPS), as well as monitoring the number of ground contacts when performing jumping and plyometric activities in the weight room. Tracking common bandwidths of intensity and volume associated with different forms of sports practice and gameplay can help provide a progression destination for the performance programme. In this way, players may be progressed appropriately to where they gradually accumulate the capacity to withstand sport-specific decelerative loading. For example, previous research has shown that positions like WR and DB may accumulate up to 20 maximal deceleration efforts in a game, defined as any effort <-3.5 m s^{-2} (Wellman et al., 2016, pp. 13–15). However, the specific number of efforts, as well as the magnitude of their intensity, can largely vary and will be based on specific team tactics as well as the design of sports practice. As far as the performance training is concerned, it is the responsibility of the performance staff to ensure that players have been adequately exposed to a progressive overload of acceleration, high-speed running, and deceleration and COD throughout the preparatory period to reduce risk of injury as well as enhance agility performance when high volumes of sports practice and the competitive periods ensue (McBurnie et al., 2022, pp. 8–9).

Tennis

Chris McLeod

Introduction

It is well known that the development of change-of-direction (COD) performance is highly complex due to the sport-specific demands, the diverse range of influencers, and the individual nature of each athlete. Whilst the exercises employed are obviously crucial in influencing physical and technical adaptations these are often athlete- and context-specific in their application. For this reason, the focus on this case study will be on the thinking process behind COD and MDS programme design in elite tennis. The hope is that this approach highlights key principles and frameworks that may be applicable across sports and individuals.

The Sport of Tennis

Before the specific case study is shared it should be situated within the context of the general demands of the sport. Constraints governing tennis bring about some specific demands that dictate the nature of COD and gives a starting point for influencing individual performance:

- The rules and scoring system of tennis gives rise to short bouts of activity (average rally length of 5–10 seconds) interspersed with extended periods of physical rest (10–20 seconds). Tennis is one of the few sports with no designated 'total time' with matches range from <60 minutes to >5 hours in length. (Fernandez, 2006).
- The court size on each side of the net is 11.88 m × 8.23 m which gives rise to frequent change of directions (4.5–6 per point, or approx. 1 every 2 seconds) (Kovalchik & Reid, 2017). Often after each shot the players are aiming to get back to the centre of the baseline to give themselves more options (and limit the opponents). The players desire to return to this position highlights the importance of COD ability.
- Whilst tennis movement is varied and individual, the fundamentals that underpin any shot/movement are consistent and emerge through a combination of technical/tactical context, player velocity, and physical profile. These constants occur as a combination of run, crossover, shuffle, COD, hop, leap, and rotate.

These three areas/sport-specific constraints mean that whilst there are individual and contextual differences in exact execution, there are patterns of play and consistent movements that can be analysed and targeted.

Case Study

The case study that follows is based on an elite 20-year-old male tennis player. The decision-making framework that will be used in this case study is based on developing/designing a coherent and logical training intervention based on a clear performance/coaching question and varied markers of success. A 'good' decision-making process and programme design is characterised by confidence that it can answer the questions in the five Ps framework (Figure 14.2).

The rest of this chapter will use the framework above to work through the design of the specific training programme using the five Ps framework.

1. Performance

Is There Clarity on What the Change Is We Are Hoping To See in Performance?

Before we could even consider the training programme, we needed to be clear what specific changes the coach/player required and how this linked to their performance. The specific

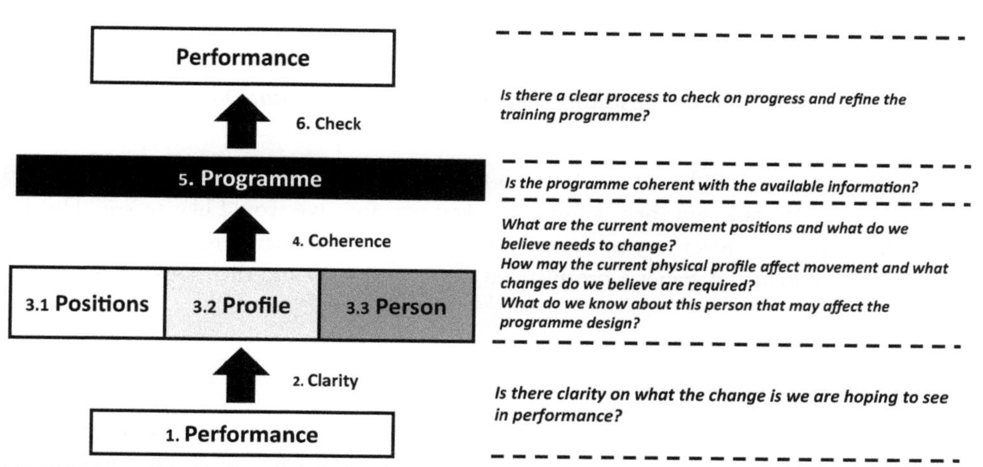

FIGURE 14.2 Five Ps framework for decision-making.

performance issue highlighted by both the player and coach began as a high-level statement during a training session and was described as 'an issue with the players movement to his backhand side'. The following is an abbreviated version of the conversation:

Coach – *Can you see, the player has an issue moving to his backhand?*
Question – **Why** is that an issue?
Coach – *You can see that he takes an extra step after the shot and so cannot change direction and get back onto the court to play the next shot.*
Question – **When** does this usually happen and **when** does it not?
Coach – *It happens a lot but usually when he is being stretched . . . it also seems to get worse as the match goes on, potentially when he is tired. When it does not happen, he seems to just do a better job of putting the brakes on early.*
Question – **Where** do you see it?
Coach – *Often when he pushed wide and so is carrying speed, usually after a crossover or running step.*
Question – **What** specifically do you want to see and **what** difference would it make?
Coach – *I want to see them more balanced, be able to stop quicker, play the shot, and get back into court to stay in the rally.*

2. Clarity

Summary Performance Statement

How might we improve the players movement when stretched to his backhand so that he can stay in the rally to increase the chances of success?

Once there is clarity on the performance issue the next stage is to understand the athletes current state using movement positions, physical profile, and understanding the person.

3.1 Positions

What Are the Current Movement Positions (i.e. Technique), and What Do We Believe Needs To Change?

The first task in beginning to plan a programme is to define the athlete's current key movement positions in the relevant task and then defining the key positions we would like to see. This is done through looking at movement in context (i.e. sport-specific during tennis) or a similar movement out of context (i.e. generic pre-planned movement task) and then looking for similarities and differences.

In-Context Movement – When Stretched to Backhand

Figure 14.3 gives a representation of this players current consistent movement strategy when stretched and moving to his backhand. In partnership with the coach, key changes were suggested/hypothesised linked to the performance question.

Out of Context – 5–0–5 Assessment

This feeling of getting stuck on his left leg and infective penultimate foot contact braking was also observed in the out of context 5–0–5 task. When changing direction off his left side a few key positions were observed:

1. Decreased performance (total time) vs right.
2. Increased lower-limb triple flexion and lateral trunk flexion when changing direction off his left foot.

	Position 1	Position 2	Position 3	Position 4	Position 5
	Pre-shot 1	Pre-shot 2	Shot	Post-shot 1	Post-shot 2
Positions hypothesis	'Poor' preceding penultimate step on right may mean too much speed is carried in pre-shot. Seen through lack of full foot contact on right	To deal with increased velocity left foot externally rotates more than ideal to align to direction of travel	Just post-shot player takes an additional lateral step with left foot (potentially due momentum exceeding capacity)	Left foot external rotation and increase velocity creates 'poor' loading of left leg	Poor and late projection back into court seen by position of 1st step and body angles
Positions 'ideal'	Right penultimate step increase CoM lowering and full foot contact to maximize deceleration	Left foot close to 90° to direction of intended travel	No additional step required at / post-shot	Effective triple flexion and extension of left side	1st step towards direction of intended travel with increased 'projection' onto court

FIGURE 14.3 In context positions overview.

3. High step frequency when decelerating with his right leg. For example, when decelerating on his left, he is able to plant the leg in front and immediately change direction off his right whilst, when decelerating on his right, he takes multiple small steps before changing direction on his left leg (i.e. potential avoidance strategy or inability to effectively load the right limb when decelerating).

The next area to consider is what his physical profile may tell us about his preferences for movement and positions.

3.2 Profile

How May the Current Physical Profile Affect Movement, and What Changes Do We Believe Are Required?

The profile element concerns the physical profile of the athlete. Whilst a more thorough profile was conducted, Figure 14.4 shows the most relevant assessment results (note: the higher the column, the 'better' the score).

The standout results were as follows:

1. A significant difference in 5–0–5 performance between limbs (quicker turning off right leg)
2. A significant deficit (i.e. inter-limb asymmetry) across all single-leg assessments on the athlete's right leg, which is more pronounced when there is less time for force production

Finally, before we try to find coherence and highlight key training intentions, we considered key information about the person that may inform the programme/plan.

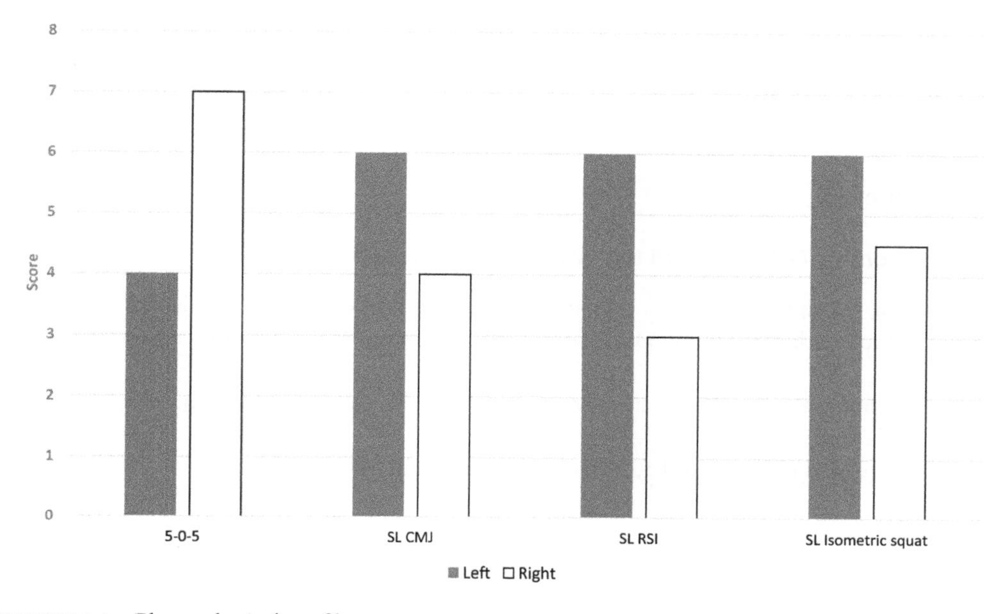

FIGURE 14.4 Player physical profile.

3.3 Person

What Do We Know About this Person that May Affect Programme Design?

1. Previous right ankle injury.
2. Due to the player's ranking, there is high programme uncertainty from week to week due to travel demands and the ranking/tournament entry system within the sport. With the player aiming to play up to 80 matches per year across 20–25 tournaments across the world (each with varied and often unknown training facilities), there are significant challenges in medium-/long-term planning and constraints to consistent exposure to a training programme to provide an adequate training stimulus.

4. Coherence

In exploring this, and looking to define the key factors, the key decision-making questions are as follows:

- **What is similar across all the areas that you believe is important?**

  There is a consistent pattern of the athlete displaying poor rate of force development and impulsive characteristics on his right side (lower body).

- **What is different that you believe is important?**

  The right-side difference described earlier is exaggerated/larger with increasing force demands.

- **What is your current hypothesis that links this information to guide your training design?**

Poor rate of force development and impulse production on the athlete's right-side limits his ability to effectively decelerate on this limb and thus tolerate large mechanical loads associated with high-intensity decelerations. This increases potential injury risk but also negatively affects COD performance on the left/backhand side.

5. Programming

Is the Programme Coherent with the Available Information?

With this clarity in place the training programme can now be designed. The design of the programme is done with the intention of being confident that we can answer two questions:

1. Is the environment giving the athlete/team problems to solve linked to the desired performance outcome?
2. Are the intended physiological adaptations coherent with the desire?

To address these questions, the programme is split into three key areas with associated intentions and key principles seen in the Table 14.10.

As discussed in the person section earlier, one of the major challenges in tennis is the uncertainty in weekly planning (i.e. periodisation) from week to week due to travel demands and the ranking/tournament entry system. To mitigate against the players uncertain schedule whilst still

TABLE 14.10 Programming Principles

Training Areas	*Description*	*Intention/Changes*	*Principles*	*Exercise Prescription*
Potential	Focus on development of single-leg force production/RFD	Maximal force	*Does the exercise selection remove rate limiters to force production in the targeted muscle group?*	Single-leg press Seated calf raise Loaded adductor hold Isometric long lever hamstring holds
Explore	Focus on exploring a variety of single-leg activities of relevant VGRF and contact time	RFD	*Are the VGRF and contact times specific to the outcome task?*	Vertical pogo Horizontal pogo Lateral pogo Zigzag pogo (Use variations of surface and exercises execution; e.g. no arms, light medicine ball in different positions.)
Execute	On-court/in-context situations of that look and feel as close to the match as possible	Specific position and tennis execution	*Does it look or feel and have feedback specific to the real thing (competition skill)?*	Specific 2-to-3-shot rally with intention on cross-court recovery after wide backhand (High intensity, high rest, and high volume to maximise relevant exploration)

RFD – rate of force development
VGRF – vertical ground reaction force

looking to progress, three themed weeks are used dependent on the desired outcome/current context (Table 14.11). These provide a framework for programming and development that could last for up to six months (allowing for variation based on the key principles).

6. Check

Is There a Clear Process To Check on Progress and Refine the Training Programme?

As mentioned earlier, this framework may be used for up to six months and modified/iterated based on feedback and observations. In order to do this well, there must be consistent checks against the agreed performance outcome allowing us to learn about what is working and what needs modify accordingly. To do this well, the outcome measures we need to check against need to be varied in nature. The specific areas selected for this case study can be seen in Figure 14.5.

Conclusion

As was described in the introduction, the intention behind this case study was not to focus specifically on just exercise selection but to share a thinking process that has been used in elite tennis to guide individual, impactful, and coherent programming/planning to enhance a specific aspect of COD and tennis performance. Figure 14.5 provides a summary of the five Ps process involved in the specific case study.

TABLE 14.11 Weekly Framework

Week theme	*Context*	*Examples*	*Intention*	*Week Framework*								
				Potential			*Explore*			*Execute*		
				Frequency	*Volume*	*Intensity*	*Frequency*	*Volume*	*Intensity*	*Frequency*	*Volume*	*Intensity*
Develop	Training volume and intensity can be high	Training week	Significant impact on adaptation	3	High (4–5 sets, 5–8 reps)	High	4 to 5	Low/ Medium	Medium	4 to 5	High	High
Dose	Training volume and intensity can be high in small doses/instances	Low priority tournament week	Keep momentum	2 to 3	Med (2–3 sets, 5–8 reps)	Medium	5 to 5	Low	Medium	2 to 3	Low	High
Don't lose it	Training volume and intensity cannot interfere with on court performance	High priority tournament week	Maintain	1	Medium (2–3 sets, 5–8 reps)	Medium	6 to 5	Low	Medium	N/A	N/A	N/A

1. Performance
How might we improve the player's movement when stretched to his backhand so that he can stay in the rally to increase the chances of success?

3.1 Positions
In context – wide backhand

Out of context 5–0–5
Significant time and positions difference left vs right. Potentially explained by deceleration execution.

Hypothesis – The player has ineffective deceleration when using his right leg as the major load-bearing step. The means that when changing direction to his right, the outside (left) leg is forced to deal with higher VGRF as too much speed is carried in.

3.2 Profile
The physical profile supports the positions hypothesis due to lower capability of his right leg across all tasks. The difference is greater when there is higher VGRF and when RFD is important for the task.

3.3 Person
(1) Previous right-side ankle injury. (2) Uncertain schedule and training week.

4. Coherence
Hypothesis – Poor rate of force development on the athlete's right-side limits his ability to effectively decelerate on this limb. This increases injury risk but also negatively affects change-of-direction performance on the left/backhand side.

5. Programme		
Potential	Explore	Execute
Develop	Dose	Don't lose

6. Check		
Significant change in SL isometric squat	Significant change in SL RSI	Meaningful improvement and symmetry in 5–0–5
Change in in-context positions More effective deceleration and projection in first step post-COD		Meaningful change in % points won in rallies when pushed wide to backhand

FIGURE 14.5 Decision-making framework/process.

Acknowledgements

The author would like to acknowledge that much of the thinking behind this framework/process was developed alongside the previous and current LTA strength and conditioning team of Ian Aylward, Conor McGoldrick, Charlie Faulkner, Steve Bowen, and Ollie Fawls.

References

Baker, D. (1998). Applying the in-season periodsation of strength and power training to football. *Strength & Conditioning Journal, 20*, 18–27.

Baker, D. (2001). The effects of an in-season of concurrent training on the maintenance of maximal strength and power in professional and college-aged rugby league players. *Journal of Strength & Conditioning Research, 15*, 172–177.

DeWeese, B. H., Hornsby, G., Stone, M., & Stone, M. H. (2015a). The training process: Planning for strength–power training in track and field. Part 1: Theoretical aspects. *Journal of Sport & Health Science, 4*, 308–317.

DeWeese, B. H., Hornsby, G., Stone, M., & Stone, M. H. (2015b). The training process: Planning for strength–power training in track and field. Part 2: Practical and applied aspects. *Journal of Sport & Health Science, 4*, 318–324.

Duhig, S., Shield, A. J., Opar, D., Gabbett, T. J., Ferguson, C., & Williams, M. (2016). Effect of high-speed running on hamstring strain injury risk. *British Journal of Sports Medicine, 50*, 1536–1540. doi:10.1136/bjsports-2015-095679

Farrow, D., & Robertson, S. (2017). Development of a skill acquisition periodisation framework for high-performance sport. *Sports Medicine, 47*, 1043–1054.

Fernandez, J. (2006). Intensity of tennis match play * Commentary. *British Journal of Sports Medicine, 40*, 387–391.

Hawkin Dynamics. (2021). *Using a Quadrant Report* [online]. Available from: www.hawkindynamics.com/blog/quadrant-report [accessed 9 May 2022].

Issurin, V. B. (2008). Block periodization versus traditional training theory: A review. *Journal of Sports Medicine &Physical Fitness, 48*, 65–75.

Issurin, V. B. (2010). New horizons for the methodology and physiology of training periodization. *Sports Medicine, 40*, 189–206.

Jeffreys, I. (2017). *Gamespeed: Movement training for superior sports performance*. 2nd edn. Monterey, CA: Coaches Choice.

Jones, P. A., & Comfort, P. (2020). Principles of strength & conditioning: Scientific aspects and principles of rehabilitation. In: *A comprehensive guide to sports physiology and injury management* (Eds. S. B. Porter & J. Wilson). London: Elsevier.

Kovalchik, S. A., & Reid, M. (2017). Comparing matchplay characteristics and physical demands of junior and professional tennis athletes in the era of big data. *Journal of Sports Science & Medicine, 16*, 489–497.

McBurnie, A. J., Harper, D. J., Jones, P. A., & Dos'Santos, T. (2022). Deceleration training in team sports: Another potential 'vaccine' for sports-related injury? *Sports Medicine, 52*, 1–12.

Munroe, L., & Haff, G. G. (2018). Sprint cycling. In: *Routledge handbook of strength and conditioning* (pp. 506–525). Abingdon, OX: Routledge.

Nimphius, S. (2021). Increasing agility. In: *High-performance training for sports* (Eds. D. Joyce & D. Lewindon) (pp. 185–197). Champaign, IL: Human Kinetics.

Otte, F. W., Millar, S. K., & Klatt, S. (2019). Skill training periodization in 'specialist' sports coaching – an introduction of the 'PoST' framework for skill development. *Frontiers in Sports and Active Living, 1*, 61. https://doi.org/10.3389/fspor.2019.00061

Plisk, S. S., & Stone, M. H. (2003). Periodization strategies. *Strength & Conditioning Journal, 25*, 19–37.

Rawlley-Singh, I., & Wolf, A. (2023). A philosophical approach to aligning strength and conditioning support to a coaches' performance model: A case study from a national rowing performance programme. *International Journal of Sports Science & Coaching, 18*(1), 278–291. https://doi.org/10.1177/17479541221105454

Ruddy, J. D., Pollard, C. W., Timmins, R. G., Williams, M. D., Shield, A. J., & Opar, D. A. (2018). Running exposure is associated with the risk of hamstring strain injury in elite Australian footballers. *British Journal of Sports Medicine, 52*, 919–928. https://doi.org/10.1136/bjsports-2016-096777

Smith, S., Sikka, R., & Bosch, T. (2020). Analysis of the sport and sport positions. In: *Strength training for basketball* (Eds. J. Gillett, B. Burgos & National Strength and Conditioning Association) (pp. 913–926). Champaign, IL: Human Kinetics.

Spiteri, T., Cochrane, J. L., Hart, N. H., Haff, G. G., & Nimphius, S. (2013). Effect of strength on plant foot kinetics and kinematics during a change of direction task. *European Journal of Sport Science, 13*, 646–652.

Taberner, M., Allen, T., & Cohen, D. D. (2019). Progressing rehabilitation after injury: Consider the 'control-chaos continuum'. *British Journal of Sports Medicine, 53*(18), 1132–1136. https://doi.org/10.1136/bjsports-2018-100157

Wellman, A. D., Coad, S. C., Goulet, G. C., & McLellan, C. P. (2016). Quantification of competitive game demands of NCAA division I college football players using global positioning systems. *Journal of Strength & Conditioning Research, 30*, 11–19.

15

MONITORING MULTIDIRECTIONAL SPEED TRAINING

Mark Quinn and Steve Atkins

Introduction

Athlete monitoring has become a popular area of research and key aspect of applied practice in contemporary sports science. It involves the use of technology and practices to observe, analyse, and evaluate the preparation and/or performance of athletes (McGuigan, 2017). Recently, athlete monitoring has gained importance as research has continued to show the link between inappropriate load management, illness, and injury (Schwellnus *et al.*, 2016; Soligard *et al.*, 2016). But monitoring athletes is anything but a new phenomenon. Distances, speeds, and time have been measured since competitive sport began and early pioneers used innovative technologies to measure sprint performance. AV Hill (Hill, 1927) measured acceleration by sprinters carrying magnets to induce a current on coils of wire wrapped around a galvanometer. Kistler (Kistler, 1934) used spring scale pressure sensors to measure force during sprint starts, and Dickinson (Dickinson, 1934) used an automatic chronoscope attached to a start gun to measure speed over short distances. Since these early developments, there has been much evolution of technologies and practices to monitor multidirectional speed. However, there have also been many challenges including methodological and practical concerns (Haugen and Buchheit, 2016). It is worth stating from the outset that there is no silver bullet and best practice requires careful consideration of the purpose of monitoring allied to methodology and implementation. This chapter therefore examines appropriate strategies to monitor aspects of speed, acceleration, deceleration, and change-of-direction training in field-based sports through critically reviewing literature leading to practical suggestions of how to effectively monitor multidirectional speed training with athletes.

Measuring Training Load

Classifying the work undertaken by athletes in training and competitive settings can inform coaches, scientists, and clinicians, notably in conditioning and rehabilitation settings. Whilst recent articles have debated the nuances of the term 'load', including its mechanical meaning (Staunton *et al.*, 2022), this chapter refers to training load as a multidimensional construct

DOI: 10.4324/9781003267881-18

(Impellizzeri *et al.*, 2022). Within this construct, there are two key sub-dimensions which are discussed, labelled external and internal load.

Monitoring training load is deemed essential in determining whether athletes are adapting to training plans, understanding individual responses, identifying fatigue, profiling recovery, and mitigating the risk of overreaching, injury, and illness (Bourdon *et al.*, 2017). To begin it is important to establish the purpose of monitoring, practitioners should have a firm understanding of their own reason for monitoring allied to their training programme. In doing so, load monitoring allows for informed decision-making to be undertaken regarding training and competition. The traditional classification of training load reflects internal and external components. Internal components have been defined as relative biological and psychological stressors imposed on the athlete in training and performance settings (Bourdon *et al.*, 2017). Common measurements of internal load include heart rate monitoring, blood lactate, $\dot{V}O_2$, TRIMP scores, and sessional rating of perceived exertion (sRPE). External load reflects the work undertaken by the athlete, expressed by measurements of speed, acceleration, distance covered, 'bespoke' combined player load measures, and overall power output. The external load can be assessed, most commonly using microsensor technologies such as global positioning system (GPS) devices, inertial measurement units, photocell timing gates, or video-based performance analysis.

Whilst there are many different measures of internal and external load, some are more pertinent to monitor multidirectional speed than others. The most common techniques used to determine training load include objective and subjective approaches that reflect both the physical and psychological outcomes associated with training and performance. Embedding the correct measure of external and internal loading will certainly be influenced by cultural and logistical constraints, notably if an already complex test battery is being administrated. Therefore, several key aspects in test selection should be considered:

1. Ability of the method to reflect the demands of the activity
2. Accuracy of the outcome 'signal' relating to specificity of task
3. Reducing 'noise' associated with generating data
4. Complexity and feasibility of the test equipment, notably if being used in field-based settings
5. Utility and 'meaningfulness' of outcomes

As most multidirectional speed training and testing occurs in field-based settings, simple methods would offer the most appropriate solution to monitoring training load associated with multidirectional activity. From a practical perspective, the best load-monitoring methods are the ones that can be easily deployed within settings involving multiple performers and allow for capturing both linear and change-of-direction activity.

External Load

Training Characteristics and Visual Observation

First and foremost, from an external load point of view, it is essential to quantify the general training characteristics (i.e. what did the athletes do within the session?). Whilst various portable intelligent systems are on the market that can assist and quantify training aspects, a simple approach can suffice by regular recording of the frequency, duration, and type of multidirectional speed activity. A common approach would be to record this via database or athlete-monitoring software to give context to other sprint-loading characteristics determined from the methods described further here.

Sprint monitoring can take place across different categories, including periodic testing, integration within the weekly microcycle, specific sprint training, return to play, or other practitioner-determined sessions. With a high number of practitioners reporting sprint training within gym sessions, in addition to field-based sessions, it is important to account for all touch points (Nicholson *et al.*, 2022). There are many external load characteristics of speed and multidirectional running that can be quantified with previous investigations' recording characteristics within the areas of distance travelled, sprinting, high-intensity running, acceleration/deceleration, lateral movement, cutting, and jumping (Taylor *et al.*, 2017). These characteristics can have a plethora of data points objectively collected, with recent investigations outlining 18 different metrics that practitioners collect within high-speed running alone (Bennett *et al.*, 2022). Despite this detail of monitoring, visual observation by simply asking coaches to subjectively see how players are moving and if players are running faster remains an important strategy, being the third most used monitoring method after timing systems and GPS (Nicholson *et al.*, 2022). In these instances, observational descriptors may revolve around biomechanical principles covering kinematics (e.g. posture of the head, shoulders, and trunk), kinetics (e.g. braking impulse), stride lengths and frequencies, flight times, and other movement mechanics. Experiential knowledge and type of practitioner role have been shown to influence the visual search behaviours of coaches when observing sprint performance (Waters *et al.*, 2020). Ultimately, this subjective approach can be liable to disagreement between practitioners. Whilst very useful for quick real-time assessment, a failure to quantify this information can limit future comparison, and therefore, an integrated approach as part of a wider toolkit of strategies is suggested.

Speed Timing Systems and Sensors

Manual timing by use of a stopwatch is one of the most obvious and simple solutions to monitoring speed. Used throughout athletic competitions up until the 1970s, these were replaced by fully automatic timing systems due to concern over large absolute errors that can be attributed to the reaction time needed by the timekeeper (Haugen and Buchheit, 2016). Automated systems consist of pressure-sensitive start bocks and high-resolution photo finish cameras to deliver extremely precise timing. Of course, these 'gold standard' fully automatic systems used in modern-day international athletics are too impractical for monitoring in field-based sports. Therefore, more practical technologies such as timing gates are predominantly used. Other solutions, such as radar or laser guns (e.g. LAVEG), have very high precision during linear sprints, excellent for periodic testing, or when assessing individual athletes, such as monitoring the return to play of an injured performer. Furthermore, light detection and ranging (LiDAR) technologies are emerging as a portable non-invasive solution to continuously track velocity, acceleration, and turning demands but require validation for multiple players (Bampouras and Thomas, 2022; Dos'Santos *et al.*, 2022). Mobile and tablet applications using high-speed video recordings offer a low-cost portable option, although some applications can lack comprehensive validation. For some activities that require less precision, the humble stopwatch can still suffice (generally for distances above 20 m), with a correction factor of −0.20 s commonly applied (Fry and Kraemer, 1991). The most frequently used system for monitoring external load, which can be used with relative ease for both linear and multidirectional activity, is the photocell timing gate (Nicholson *et al.*, 2022). See Chapter 6 for further details regarding the use of these technologies.

GPS and Accelerometery

The introduction of wearable GPS and GNSS devices and inertial sensors (accelerometers, magnetometers, and gyroscopes) has allowed practitioners to objectively quantify many aspects of human movement concomitantly with multiple performers. Via signal transmission from multiple satellites and through inertial sensor derived metrics (Larsson, 2003), these devices offer utility in measuring aspects of speed in gameplay, small-sided games, and general field-based training. Common metrics to monitor speed events revolve around frequencies, distances, and time covered within speed thresholds (e.g. number of sprints), events related to changes in velocity (e.g. total accelerations and decelerations), inertial-sensor-derived metrics (e.g. stride variables and imbalances), and variables that include a hybrid of these categories (e.g. metabolic power) (Torres-Ronda *et al.*, 2022). There are currently a range of commercial systems available which differ in sensors, sample frequencies, device size, body position, and manufacturer-derived algorithms for determining metrics. Each of these should be considered dependent on the movements and outcomes that are needed to be tracked; for example, a gyroscope is needed to detect rotation and turning ability (Stuart *et al.*, 2021). When GPS data is combined with video or other performance indicators, contextual information is provided, which is important to move away from a reductionist approach that investigates multidirectional speed in isolation of rules of play, positions, opposition standards, and tactics (Ju *et al.*, 2023).

Many factors can influence the data that is obtained from these devices and consideration should be given to the running distance, velocity, movement pattern, as well as the device sample frequency, number of satellites acquired, and dilution of precision (Malone *et al.*, 2017). With regard to the latter two, practitioners and manufacturers are encouraged to use data quality control criteria to exclude poor quality data that may not be representative of player output (Shergill, Twist and Highton, 2021). To some extent, these issues, amongst others, contribute to mixed results with validity and reliability. Researchers have shown devices to have low error of measurement for distance and movement at low intensity with longer duration; however, they have shown poorer accuracy in determining high-intensity running, velocity, change of direction, and short linear running particularly with 1 Hz and 5 Hz devices (Scott, Scott and Kelly, 2016). That said, 10 Hz devices are now widely available and provide encouraging results with good to moderate validity shown for instantaneous velocities during constant velocity running, including running with accelerations. Furthermore, acceptable reliability has been demonstrated across studies measuring average accelerations and decelerations (Harper, Carling and Kiely, 2019). Recent investigations also highlight the potential for measuring force-velocity profiles in team sport, with GPS shown to be a valid, reliable, and time-effective measure when compared to radar (Clavel *et al.*, 2022). This information can be obtained during unstructured training and gameplay, offering a truly *in situ* approach without the need for running specific tests (Morin *et al.*, 2021).

The practitioner should be aware of issues at play with respect to definitions, manufacturer differences, and minimum effort durations to determine thresholds of speed. Researchers and practitioners should acknowledge the minimum time needed to identify a sprint effort and understand the influence of manufacturer smoothing and data processing filters, which are infrequently reported (Delves *et al.*, 2021). As outputs can differ between manufacturers, practitioners are advised to avoid using multiple systems simultaneously (Thornton *et al.*, 2019). With regard to analysis, the value of using absolute and relative expressions, via both individualised speed zones alongside sport-specific categorisation, offers benefit for the development of speed and progression of research to understand movement patterns as well as player comparison (although caution is warranted with metrics with large variation).

Local positioning systems (LPS) offer an alternative solution for indoor sports or activities that take place at the same location. The main difference being that the signal propagates from a localised transmitter rather than a satellite. Recent studies attest to the accuracy in comparison with GPS and video (Pino-Ortega *et al.*, 2022). Similar issues exist with reliance on manufacturer filtering techniques, and the high cost, installation time, and facility considerations have limited their use in comparison with other measures (Rico-Gonzalez *et al.*, 2020a).

With regard to accelerometery, an inertial measurement unit (IMU) can be used simultaneously or independently of GPS, offering versatile solutions to quantify movement. A limitation of GPS is that it can only be used outdoors whereas IMUs can be used indoors as well. IMUs can measure multidirectional movements and are often crafted as a bespoke real-world practical solution. For instance, there have been many configurations to utilise IMUs for wheelchair-based sports (Van der Slikke *et al.*, 2022) and foot-mounted devices are used within Association football (Emmonds *et al.*, 2022). Although not yet validated, foot-mounted devices for football (PlayerMaker™) have the capacity to examine limb differences, load strategies between limbs, alongside spatiotemporal characteristics to provide further insight into movement strategies and potential mechanical loads experienced during sport. Whilst results in comparison with GPS are favourable (Waldron *et al.*, 2021), compliance may be more of an issue due to the wearable location.

In summary, lower GPS sample rates, activities with higher velocities, and frequent changes of direction offer lower validity and reliability (Haugen and Buchheit, 2016). Similar results have been found for indoor local position systems (Rico-González *et al.*, 2020b). Fundamentally, the potential deficiencies are perhaps offset due to the ease of integration and benefit of use within regular sports practice, unstructured training, and games. These devices offer a compelling solution for quantifying external load within field-based sports activity. Whilst robust, they are used with contact and high-intensity sports, and so frequent calibration is suggested allied to in-house validation assessments to account for inaccuracies.

Video and Notational Analysis

With the development of GPS, time motion analysis research moved away from the use of video observational methods due to their time-consuming nature, which was unrealistic for frequent use within training or gameplay. However, one limitation of GPS is the lack of detail regarding technique, change of direction, and the contextualisation of sport-specific activity (e.g. why the sprint occurred) while also being limited to outdoor environments and requiring the athletes to put on a wearable device. In contemporary monitoring practice, this is where computerised notational analysis is suitable, and thus, manufacturers of GPS now incorporate systems where GPS derived sprint data can be assessed alongside tagged video of the performance to aid with contextualisation of high-intensity activities. Furthermore, with the ease of access to high-speed video cameras through smartphones (up to 240 frames per second), it allows for simple recording of movement within training drills that can be subjectively or objectively analysed during or after training. Such recordings are essential to cataloguing adaptations in sprint technique. Simply put, the ability to slow video allows practitioners more time to analyse sprint technique whereas real-time assessments need modification of visual search strategies to maximise the information taken in (Waters *et al.*, 2020).

To leverage this further, a thorough video analysis of movement can be completed post-event in computerised notational software (e.g. Hudl Sportscode, Nacsport). This requires the use of detailed classification systems, such as the Bloomfield Movement Classification System, which was previously developed to capture turns, swerves, changes in direction (degrees), and transitions of running types in football (Bloomfield, Polman and O'Donoghue, 2004). More recent investigations have adapted this system to categorise different team sports, decision-making components, and multidirectional running performance in relation to sport-specific actions, such as goal scoring (Talty *et al.*, 2022; Martínez-Hernández, Quinn and Jones, 2022). Importantly, with any video analysis, consideration should be given to the number of camera angles used and positioned around the playing environment, parallax and perspective errors, clear definitions of performance indicators, and agreement through intra- and inter-analyst reliability assessments. Following such procedures, a robustly developed notation system can be influential in monitoring the subtle movements of in-game activity and ensuring these can be developed within training.

Optical Tracking

Advances in technology have also allowed for the use of semi and fully automated optical tracking camera systems. Such systems, consisting of camera arrays embedded in elevated positions in stadia, record two-dimensional positional data at high sample rates (up to 25 Hz) in order to derive data on movement of the performers. Some validation exists to show that linear and curved running at different speeds and distances (Prozone) show excellent correlation with timing gate measurement (Di Salvo *et al.*, 2006). Furthermore, the utility of optical tracking systems is emphasised by their ability to track other technical and tactical performance indices (Ju *et al.*, 2023), and there has been increased integration in elite sport to assist with referee and umpire decisions, which makes these systems more readily available (Naik, Hashmi and Bokde, 2022). More recent validation supports the use of current optical tracking systems (TRACAB) for use in elite football (Linke, Link and Lames, 2020). However, caution is still warranted as these techniques remain tested in very few sports, and there are fewer investigations into validity and reliability compared to GPS. The efficacy to accurately capture change of direction is within its infancy, as improvements in software and computer vision come to the fore, future testing remains essential. They are tools that are firmly at the elite end of performance due to the high cost and associated infrastructure requirements (Cunneen, Smith and Borges, 2020). Yet studies confirming the level of agreement of sprint-running load outputs between optical tracking systems, and to GPS, are starting to allow practitioners to have more confidence when combining different datasets for analysis of multidirectional speed (Taberner *et al.*, 2022; Ellens *et al.*, 2022).

Internal Load

The most deployed internal load methods, applicable to complex field-based test environments, are heart rate monitoring (physiological) and the rating of perceived exertion (psychological). These tests are often chosen due to simplicity of measurement, inherent validity and reliability, and utility of outcomes in informing practitioners and athletes as to the demands of their activity.

Heart Rate Monitoring

Heart rate monitors are one of the most well used microtechnologies available and provide a directly quantifiable unit of measurement, indirectly reflecting the physiological response to physical activity. A variety of wearable devices are now available, ranging from telemetry-based transmitters/receivers (Polar H10) to wrist worn single units (Garmin, Apple Watch, WHOOP, Oura). Recently, even smartphone technologies, notably a simple camera and a flash, have been successfully deployed within bespoke apps to measure complex, and important, aspects of cardiovascular function, such as heart rate variability (HRV4training.com).

The 'gold standard' measurement of heart rate is undertaken using electrocardiography (ECG). ECG testing measures the electrical potential of the skin, recorded via surface electrodes. Using robust measurement and inference analysis, direct measurement of heart rate can be achieved, together with identification of the underpinning electrical waveforms. Whilst portable ECG can be recorded (e.g. Holter monitors), cost and utility in dynamic settings are considered key limitations.

Since the early 1990s, wearable chest strap telemetry has become the *de facto* choice for laboratory and field-based testing of heart rate. Commercially available telemetry systems, such as the Polar H10, have been shown to have excellent validity and reliability, even when measuring beat to beat intervals as when assessing heart rate variability (Gilgen-Ammann, Schweizer and Wyss, 2019). Chest-based telemetry systems are appealing in generating both accurate signals, allied to having great utility in field-based settings. They are, by observation, the *de facto* choice for many professional and non-professional sports teams. Interestingly, contemporary GPS player tracking systems, commonly used by such teams, also offer connectivity with devices, such as the Polar H10. Fitted vests, to house the GPS unit, will often have space to embed a chest strap such as the Polar H10. To date, the authors are unaware of any attempt to validate reading when using this combined measurement approach, though the appeal of recording heart rate simultaneously to GPS is clear.

Recently, there has been much interest in wearable technology, notably wrist-based optical heart rate monitors. These are traditionally embedded into smartwatches and provide a simple approach to collecting heart rate data. These systems operate by detecting fluctuations in blood perfusion to the skin, dominantly at the wrist, occurring during the cardiac cycle. This is referred to as photoplethysmography (PPG). Brands, such as Garmin, Polar, Suunto, and Apple, propose their wrist-worn systems to be accurate in measuring multiple parameters relating to heart rate based on PPG. However, despite many claims for devices being valid and reliable, there remains limited confirmation as to the accuracy of many devices, with the validation quality of wearables often being unknown due to non-transparent standards for testing and reporting (Bunn *et al.*, 2018). This situation is improving, with some reported validation in laboratory-based settings, though this varies by the manufacturer and device type (Fuller *et al.*, 2020). With the pace of upgrades and redesign of wearables, contemporary validation and reliability studies are essential. It is appropriate to be more cautious of using wrist-based wearables, to measure heart rate, than more traditional telemetry systems.

Other forms of heart rate monitoring, such as wearable sensors embedded into clothing, electrode-based ambulatory systems, and smartphone-embedded technologies, are limited by a lack of quality studies into their validity and reliability. Whilst some good evidence is emerging regarding the use of smartphones to detect HRV (Altini and Plews, 2021), these devices have no application in dynamic settings, such as when undertaking multidirectional training.

With a dearth of quality literature available to defend the use of wearable and smartphone technologies in multidirectional settings, and with portability and accuracy being to the fore, the preferred choice for field-based heart rate monitoring would be the chest-based telemetry system. These systems do appear to have the required validity and reliability to be deployed in dynamic settings, such as those associated with multidirectional testing, and represent very good value for money options when assessing the physiological 'internal load' response to training and performance. Whilst many systems do now include the ability to measure a variety of heart rate parameters, ranging from average across a defined period to time spent within set zones, the utility of deploying these systems in sports-specific settings can be considered a key limitation. Chest straps do offer the least intrusive and most adaptable solution for testing/training in high-intensity multidirectional speed settings.

Session Rating of Perceived Exertion

Sessional rating of perceived exertion (sRPE) combines an objective measure of internal training load (time) together with a subjective element (RPE). This creates a training load index, expressed in arbitrary units (Inoue *et al.*, 2022). The sRPE has been accepted as a strong marker of internal load (Foster *et al.*, 2021) and provides a simple, meaningful, profiling tool for training and performance. Simplicity is considered a key element of athlete monitoring (Foster, Rodriguez-Marroyo and De Koning, 2017). As a monitoring and prescription tool, sRPE pleasingly shows good agreement between coach-led prescription and athlete-based subjective rating (Redkva *et al.*, 2017). This suggests the utility of this inexpensive, easy-to-administer tool. However, caution should be exercised when accepting the tool as wholly effective. Inoue et al. (Inoue *et al.*, 2022) reported that whilst there is an agreement between coaches and athletes regarding RPE and sRPE, both overall and between moderate and hard efforts, there were disagreements at the lower intensity of effort.

Using the sRPE is simple. Firstly, the choice of RPE scale for the subjective element needs to be considered. This is best served with the deployment of the Borg's 10-point category ratio (CR-10) (Borg, 1998). When combined with a simple multiplication by time of training (minutes), the sRPE can be determined, normally between 10 and 30 minutes post-training (Turner *et al.*, 2015). A useful 'anchor question' to stimulate the completion of an sRPE rating is simply 'How was your workout?' (Turner *et al.*, 2015). A further, useful application of sRPE is to assess training monotony (Foster *et al.*, 1995) or the lack of variability in training load. sRPE also has good utility as a tool to determine the amplitude of training, allowing subjective determination of both higher and lower training loads. This tool can be used to ensure enough variability in training prescription exists, thereby informing compliance.

Practical Considerations

Alongside internal and external load methods, a growing body of literature exists within sports science that implementation influences desired outcomes (Quinn, 2020; Saw *et al.*, 2016). Put simply, it is the way the monitoring is put into practice, in addition to the correctly chosen tools, that impacts the effectiveness. Indeed, monitoring multidirectional activity is usually just one component amongst wider training and performance monitoring toolkit that should be developed alongside key personnel, including the athlete. It can be constrained by logistical and contextual factors, such as timescales to deliver outcomes, practitioner expertise, experience, and resources (Nicholson *et al.*, 2022). Sprint monitoring can also be influenced by a variety of factors, such as conditions (e.g. wind), clothing (e.g. shoe stiffness), and procedures (e.g. start position) (Haugen and Buchheit, 2016). Therefore, considerations for developing the monitoring practices outlined in this chapter should involve the following:

1. Identifying the purpose of monitoring allied to stakeholder engagement.
2. Planning the data-handling process, including how information will be collected, analysed, and used to influence decisions.
3. Considering and accounting for factors that may act as barriers to monitoring or influence data.
4. Regular evaluation of the effectiveness of the athlete-monitoring methods.

Conclusion

By collecting simple training load measurements, coaches and athletes can generate a powerful series of tools to assess the contribution and magnitude of differing forms of training that occur within prescribed micro- and macrocycles. This mapping of training load to activity will allow coaches to determine the effectiveness and appropriateness of specific training, in both performance and rehabilitation settings. To underpin recommendations on the content discussed in this chapter, Table 15.1 and Figure 15.1 provide a summary and evaluation of the monitoring methods reflecting the most common uses in field-based sports. This includes the typical variables and their most suitable use per training environment in structured or unstructured training, linear, or multidirectional activity. The flow chart (Figure 15.1) also gives due consideration to the minimum monitoring options (i.e. lower budget and resources) or maximum options (i.e. higher budgets and resources) experienced by practitioners. Training characteristics should always be recorded, whilst other monitoring options can be used interchangeably and be tailored to the specific monitoring task.

The internal and external load assessments discussed here can be used to provide a full profile of the volume and quality of work undertaken, yet they do not need to be used in an integrated manner per se. Each individual tool can provide valuable outcomes, yet a truly integrated approach between the objective (heart rate, GPS) and subjective (sRPE, video analysis) can allow the fullest interpretation of imposed load to be undertaken. Given that the metabolic cost of multidirectional work appears elevated when compared to traditional linear work, such tools will be invaluable in the monitoring process.

Whilst this review focuses on monitoring in relation to speed and multidirectional running, it is worth noting that a holistic approach should be taken to review the complete training load, recovery, and external non-sport stressors, which can pose threat to adaptations. Measures not discussed here, such as wellness questionnaires and force plates, amongst others, provide additional information to understand wider training prescription and load and the response to it. Importantly, the essential requirement is that monitoring methods are valid and reliable and facilitate efficient integration to collect relevant data to inform decisions. Ultimately, this chapter outlines some of those tools and the ways to monitor multidirectional activity. Nonetheless, how practitioners go about the monitoring process needs to be tailored to their own environment and to the individual athletes they are working with.

Abbreviations: PTG, photocell timing gates; LPS, local positioning system devices; GPS, global positioning system devices; Optical, optical tracking technologies; Notation, video and notational analysis software; sRPE, session rating of perceived exertion; Mobile, smartphone and tablet applications; Observation, visual observation strategies.

TABLE 15.1 Evaluation of Monitoring Methods Used for Linear and Multidirectional Speed Activity

Evaluation reflects most common uses in field-based sports.

Monitoring Method	*Monitoring Variables*	*Structured Field-Based Training*		*Unstructured Training/ Gameplay*						
		Linear	*Multidirectional*	*Multidirectional*	*Location Data*	*Cost*	*Data Processing*	*Valid*	*Reliable*	*Ease of Use*
Recording training characteristics	Frequency, type, and duration of training	Y	Y	Y	N	L	L	H	H	H
Visual observation	Coach-determined kinetic and kinematic variables, stride lengths	Y	Y	Y	Y	L	L	M	M	H
Stopwatch	Time	Y	Y	N	N	L	L	H	M-H	H
Photocell timing gates	Time, velocity, acceleration, deceleration	Y	Y	N	N	M	M	H	H	L-M
Radar/laser guns	Time, velocity, acceleration, deceleration	Y	N	N	N	M	M	M-H	M-H	L-M
Mobile/tablet applications	Time, velocity, acceleration, deceleration	Y	Y	N	N	L-M	M	M	M	L-M
GPS and LPS	Velocity, distance, acceleration, deceleration, time in speed zones, inertial-sensor-derived metrics	Y	Y	Y	Y	M	M-H	M-H	M	M
Video and notational analysis	Change of direction (e.g. angles, arced runs), tagged performance indicators (e.g. goals), velocity, acceleration, deceleration frequencies	Y	Y	Y	Y	M-H	H	M	M	L
Optical tracking	Velocity, acceleration, deceleration, sport-specific performance indicators	N	N	Y	Y	H	M-H	M-H	M	L
Heart rate	Heart rate, time in zones, HR variability, recovery indices	Y	Y	Y	N	L-M	M	H	M-H	H
sRPE	Single variable in arbitrary units	Y	Y	Y	N	L	M	M-H	M-H	H

Abbreviations: Y, yes; N, no; L, low; M, medium; H, high; GPS, global positioning system; LPS, local positioning system; sRPE, session rating of perceived exertion

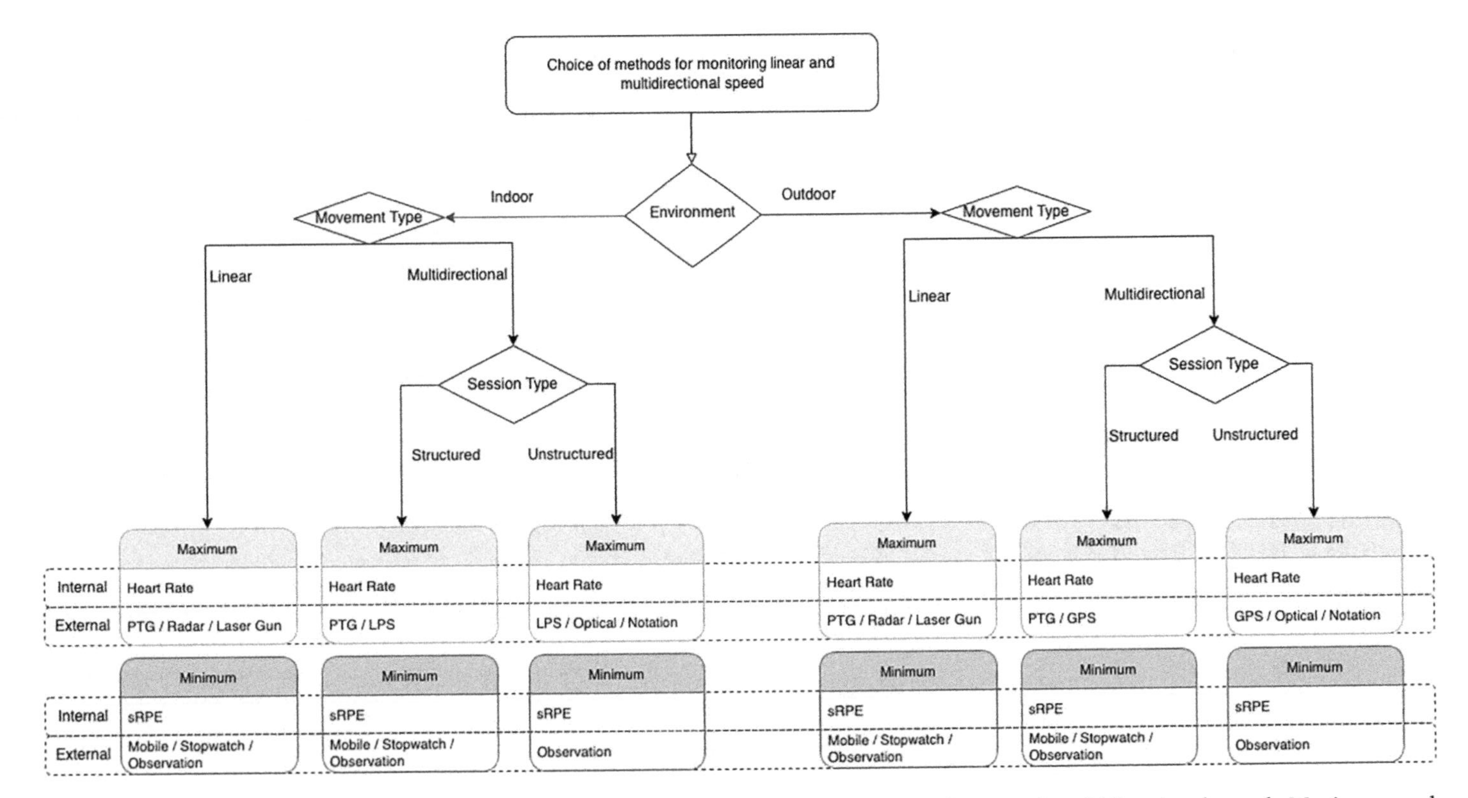

FIGURE 15.1 Considerations and recommendations for choice of methods for monitoring linear and multidirectional speed. Maximum and minimum options, based on resource and budget, can be used interchangeably.

References

Altini, M. and Plews, D. (2021). What is behind changes in resting heart rate and heart rate variability? A large-scale analysis of longitudinal measurements acquired in free-living, *Sensors*, *21*(23), 7932.

Bampouras, T. M. and Thomas, N. M. (2022). Validation of a LiDAR-based player tracking system during football-specific tasks, *Sports Engineering*, *25*(1), 8.

Bennett, T., Marshall, P., Barrett, S., Malone, J. J. and Towlson, C. (2022). Quantifying high-speed running in rugby league: An insight into practitioner applications and perceptions, *International Journal of Sports Science & Coaching*, 174795412211128.

Bloomfield, J., Polman, R. and O'Donoghue, P. (2004). The "Bloomfield movement classification": Motion analysis of individual players in dynamic movement sports, *International Journal of Performance Analysis in Sport*, *4*(2), 20–31.

Borg, G. (1998). *Borg's perceived exertion and pain scales*. Champaign, IL: Human Kinetics.

Bourdon, P. C., Cardinale, M., Murray, A., Gastin, P., Kellmann, M., Varley, M. C., Gabbett, T. J., Coutts, A. J., Burgess, D. J., Gregson, W. and Cable, T. N. (2017). Monitoring athlete training loads: Consensus statement, *International Journal of Sports Physiology and* Performance, *12*(Suppl 2), S2161–S2170.

Bunn, J. A., Navalta, J. W., Fountaine, C. J. and Reece, J. D. (2018). Current state of commercial wearable technology in physical activity monitoring 2015–2017, *International journal of Exercise Science*, *11*(7), 503–515.

Clavel, P., Leduc, C., Morin, J. B., Owen, C., Samozino, P., Peeters, A., Buchheit, M. and Lacome, M. (2022). Concurrent validity and reliability of sprinting force-velocity profile assessed with GPS devices in elite athletes, *International Journal of Sports Physiology and Performance*, *17*(10), 1527–1531. https://doi.org/10.1123/ijspp.2021-0339

Cunneen, N., Smith, H. and Borges, M. (2020). The evolution and practical application of time-motion analysis in rugby league, *Journal of Australian Strength and Conditioning*, *28*(4), 82–93.

Delves, R. I. M., Aughey, R. J., Ball, K. and Duthie, G. M. (2021). The quantification of acceleration events in elite team sport: A systematic review, *Sports Medicine – Open*, *7*(1), 45.

Di Salvo, V., Collins, A., McNeill, B. and Cardinale, M. (2006). Validation of Prozone®: A new video-based performance analysis system, *International Journal of Performance Analysis in Sport*, *6*(1), 108–119.

Dickinson, A. D. (1934). The effect of foot spacing on the starting time and speed in sprinting and the relation of physical measurements to foot spacing, *Research Quarterly. American Physical Education Association*, *5*(Suppl 1), 12–19.

Dos'Santos, T., Cowling, I., Challoner, M., Barry, T. and Caldbeck, P. (2022). What are the significant turning demands of match play of an English Premier League soccer team? *Journal of Sports Sciences*, *40*(15), 1750–1759. https://doi.org/10.1080/02640414.2022.2109355

Ellens, S., Hodges, D., McCullagh, S., Malone, J. J. and Varley, M. C. (2022). Interchangeability of player movement variables from different athlete tracking systems in professional soccer, *Science and Medicine in Football*, *6*(1), 1–6. DOI: 10.1080/24733938.2021.1879393

Emmonds, S., Dalton Barron, N., Myhill, N., Barrett, S., King, R. and Weaving, D. (2022). Locomotor and technical characteristics of female soccer players training: exploration of differences between competition standards, *Science & Medicine in Football*, 1–9. https://doi.org/10.1080/24733938.2022.2089723.

Foster, C., Boullosa, D., McGuigan, M., Fusco, A., Cortis, C., Arney, B. E., Orton, B., Dodge, C., Jaime, S. and Radtke, K. (2021). 25 years of session rating of perceived exertion: Historical perspective and development, *International Journal of Sports Physiology and Performance*, *16*(5), 612–621.

Foster, C., Hector, L. L., Welsh, R., Schrager, M., Green, M. A. and Snyder, A. C. (1995). Effects of specific versus cross-training on running performance, *European Journal of Applied Physiology and Occupational Physiology*, *70*(4), 367–372.

Foster, C., Rodriguez-Marroyo, J. A. and De Koning, J. J. (2017). Monitoring training loads: The past, the present, and the future, *International Journal of Sports Physiology and Performance*, *12*(s2), S2–2-S2–8.

Fry, A. C. and Kraemer, W. J. (1991). Physical performance characteristics of American collegiate football players, *The Journal of Strength & Conditioning Research*, *5*(3), 126–138.

Fuller, D., Colwell, E., Low, J., Orychock, K., Tobin, M. A., Simango, B., Buote, R., Van Heerden, D., Luan, H. and Cullen, K. (2020). Reliability and validity of commercially available wearable devices for measuring steps, energy expenditure, and heart rate: Systematic review, *JMIR mHealth and uHealth*, *8*(9), e18694.

Gilgen-Ammann, R., Schweizer, T. and Wyss, T. (2019). RR interval signal quality of a heart rate monitor and an ECG Holter at rest and during exercise, *European Journal of Applied Physiology*, *119*(7), 1525–1532.

Harper, D. J., Carling, C. and Kiely, J. (2019). High-intensity acceleration and deceleration demands in elite team sports competitive match play: A systematic review and meta-analysis of observational studies, *Sports Medicine*, *49*(12), 1923–1947.

Haugen, T. and Buchheit, M. (2016). Sprint running performance monitoring: Methodological and practical considerations, *Sports Medicine*, *46*(5), 641–656.

Martínez-Hernández, D., Quinn, M. and Jones, P. (2022). Linear advancing actions followed by deceleration and turn are the most common movements preceding goals in male professional soccer, *Science & Medicine in Football*, 1–9. https://doi.org/10.1080/24733938.2022.2030064.

Hill, A. V. (1927). *Muscular movement in man: The factors governing speed and recovery from fatigue*. McGraw-Hill.

Impellizzeri, F. M., Jeffries, A. C., Weisman, A., Coutts, A. J., McCall, A., McLaren, S. J. and Kalkhoven, J. (2022). The 'training load' construct: Why it is appropriate and scientific, *Journal of Science and Medicine in Sport*, *25*(5), 445–448.

Inoue, A., dos Santos Bunn, P., do Carmo, E. C., Lattari, E. and da Silva, E. B. (2022). Internal training load perceived by athletes and planned by coaches: A systematic review and meta-analysis, *Sports Medicine-Open*, *8*(1), 1–32.

Ju, W., Doran, D., Hawkins, R., Evans, M., Laws, A. and Bradley, P. S. (2023). Contextualised high-intensity running profiles of elite football players with reference to general and specialised tactical roles, *Biology of Sport*, *40*(1), 291–301.

Kistler, J. W. (1934). A study of the distribution of the force exerted upon the blocks in starting the sprint from various starting positions, *Research Quarterly. American Physical Education Association*, *5*(Suppl 1), 27–32.

Larsson, P. (2003). Global positioning system and sport-specific testing, *Sports Medicine*, *33*(15), 1093–1101.

Linke, D., Link, D. and Lames, M. (2020). Football-specific validity of TRACAB's optical video tracking systems, *PloS One*, *15*(3), e0230179.

Malone, J. J., Lovell, R., Varley, M. C. and Coutts, A. J. (2017). Unpacking the black box: Applications and considerations for using GPS devices in sport, *International Journal of Sports Physiology and Performance*, *12*(s2), S2–18-S2–26.

McGuigan, M. (2017). *Monitoring training and performance in athletes*. Champaign, IL: Human Kinetics.

Morin, J.-B., Le Mat, Y., Osgnach, C., Barnabò, A., Pilati, A., Samozino, P. and di Prampero, P. E. (2021). Individual acceleration-speed profile in-situ: A proof of concept in professional football players, *Journal of Biomechanics*, *123*, 110524.

Naik, B. T., Hashmi, M. F. and Bokde, N. D. (2022). A comprehensive review of computer vision in sports: Open issues, future trends and research directions, *Applied Sciences*, *12*(9), 4429.

Nicholson, B., Dinsdale, A., Jones, B., Heyward, O. and Till, K. (2022). Sprint development practices in elite football code athletes, *International Journal of Sports Science & Coaching*, *17*(1), 95–113.

Pino-Ortega, J., Oliva-Lozano, J. M., Gantois, P., Nakamura, F. Y. and Rico-González, M. (2022). Comparison of the validity and reliability of local positioning systems against other tracking technologies in team sport: A systematic review, *Proceedings of the Institution of Mechanical Engineers, Part P: Journal of Sports Engineering and Technology*, *236*(2), 73–82.

Quinn, M. E. (2020). *Athlete monitoring in rugby league: A focus on the conceptualisation, implementation and utilisation of a wellness questionnaire* (Doctoral dissertation, University of Central Lancashire).

Redkva, P. E., Gregorio da Silva, S., Paes, M. R. and Dos-Santos, J. W. (2017). The relationship between coach and player training load perceptions in professional soccer, *Perceptual and Motor Skills*, *124*(1), 264–276.

Rico-González, M., Los Arcos, A., Clemente, F. M., Rojas-Valverde, D. and Pino-Ortega, J. (2020b). Accuracy and reliability of local positioning systems for measuring sport movement patterns in stadium-scale: A systematic review, *Applied Sciences*, *10*(17), 5994.

Rico-González, M., Los Arcos, A., Nakamura, F. Y., Moura, F. A. and Pino-Ortega, J. (2020a). The use of technology and sampling frequency to measure variables of tactical positioning in team sports: A systematic review, *Research in Sports Medicine, 28*(2), 279–292.

Saw, A. E., Kellmann, M., Main, L. C. and Gastin, P. B. (2016). Athlete self-report measures in research and practice: Considerations for the discerning reader and fastidious practitioner, *International Journal of Sports Physiology and Performance, 12*(Suppl 2), S2127–S2135.

Schwellnus, M., Soligard, T., Alonso, J. M., Bahr, R., Clarsen, B., Dijkstra, H. P., Gabbett, T. J., Gleeson, M., Hägglund, M., Hutchinson, M. R., Janse Van Rensburg, C., Meeusen, R., Orchard, J. W., Pluim, B. M., Raftery, M., Budgett, R. and Engebretsen, L. (2016). How much is too much? (Part 2) International Olympic Committee consensus statement on load in sport and risk of illness, *British Journal of Sports Medicine, 50*(17), 1043–1052. https://doi.org/10.1136/bjsports-2016-096572

Scott, M., Scott, T. J. and Kelly, V. G. (2016). The validity and reliability of global positioning systems in team sport: A brief review, *The Journal of Strength & Conditioning Research, 30*(5), 1470.

Shergill, A. S., Twist, C. and Highton, J. (2021). Importance of GNSS data quality assessment with novel control criteria in professional soccer match-play, *International Journal of Performance Analysis in Sport, 21*(5), 820–830.

Soligard, T., Schwellnus, M., Alonso, J.-M., Bahr, R., Clarsen, B., Dijkstra, P. H., Gabbett, T., Gleeson, M., Hägglund, M., Hutchinson, M. R., Rensburg, C. v., Khan, K. M., Meeusen, R., Orchard, J. W., Pluim, B. M., Raftery, M., Budgett, R. and Engebretsen, L. (2016). How much is too much? (Part 1) International Olympic Committee consensus statement on load in sport and risk of injury, *British Journal of Sports Medicine, 50*(17), 1030–1041.

Staunton, C. A., Abt, G., Weaving, D. and Wundersitz, D. W. T. (2022). Misuse of the term "load" in sport and exercise science, *Journal of Science and Medicine in Sport, 25*(5), 439–444. https://doi.org/10.1016/j.jsams.2021.08.013.

Stuart, S., Powell, D., Marshall, S. J., Clark, C. C. T., Martini, D. N., Johnston, W. and Godfrey, A. (2021). Sports medicine: bespoke player management. In *Digital health*, 231–251. Academic Press.

Taberner, M., Allen, T., O'Keefe, J., Richter, C., Cohen, D., Harper, D. and Buchheit, M. (2022). Interchangeability of optical tracking technologies: potential overestimation of the sprint running load demands in the English Premier League, *Science & Medicine in Football*, 1–10. https://doi.org/10.1080/24733938.2022.2107699.

Talty, P. F., McGuigan, K., Quinn, M. and Jones, P. A. (2022). Agility demands of Gaelic football match-play: A time-motion analysis, *International Journal of Performance Analysis in Sport, 22*(2), 195–208.

Taylor, J. B., Wright, A. A., Dischiavi, S. L., Townsend, M. A. and Marmon, A. R. (2017). Activity demands during multi-directional team sports: A systematic review, *Sports Medicine, 47*(12), 2533–2551.

Thornton, H. R., Nelson, A. R., Delaney, J. A., Serpiello, F. R. and Duthie, G. M. (2019). Interunit reliability and effect of data-processing methods of global positioning systems, *International Journal of Sports Physiology and Performance, 14*(4), 432–438.

Torres-Ronda, L., Beanland, E., Whitehead, S., Sweeting, A. and Clubb, J. (2022). Tracking systems in team sports: A narrative review of applications of the data and sport specific analysis, *Sports Medicine – Open, 8*(1), 15.

Turner, A. N., Bishop, C., Marshall, G. and Read, P. (2015). How to monitor training load and mode using sRPE, *Professional Strength & Conditioning, 39*, 15–20.

Van der Slikke, R. M. A., Sindall, P., Goosey-Tolfrey, V. L. and Mason, B. S. (2022). Load and performance monitoring in wheelchair court sports: A narrative review of the use of technology and practical recommendations, *European Journal of Sport Science*, 1–12. https://doi.org/10.1080/17461391.2021.2025267.

Waldron, M., Harding, J., Barrett, S. and Gray, A. (2021). A new foot-mounted inertial measurement system in soccer: Reliability and comparison to global positioning systems for velocity measurements during team sport actions, *Journal of Human Kinetics*, 77(1), 37–50.

Waters, A., Panchuk, D., Phillips, E. and Dawson, A. (2020). Experiential knowledge affects the visual search behaviors of sprint coaches and sport biomechanists, *Frontiers in Sports and Active Living, 2*, 95.

16

REHABILITATION AND RETURN TO PLAY FROM DECELERATION AND CHANGE-OF-DIRECTION SPECIFIC INJURIES

Lee Herrington and Paul A. Jones

Introduction

For injured athletes/players to return to match play, not only do they need to be able to tolerate the loads experienced during sports actions that often have caused the injury in the first place (sprinting, landing, changing direction, etc.), but they also must have the confidence and ability to be able to execute the manoeuvres correctly without any performance decrement. When performing sports actions such as rapid deceleration and changing direction, failure to return to pre-injury levels of performance could occur due to three main reasons: compensations to avoid stressing the injured tissue (failure of the injured tissue to tolerate the loads encountered), failure to fully develop the underpinning physical qualities required to undertake the task optimally leading to compensations, and poor technical execution of the task which might be related to kinesiophobia (the fear of the movement/task) or poor movement skill development. As the aim of injury rehabilitation is to return the athlete to pre-injury levels of sports performance whilst minimising the risk of further injury, it is critical that these three potential areas of failure are addressed in any rehabilitation programme and the considerations involved in significantly impacting on them will form the cornerstones of the rehabilitation interventions discussed.

'Why did this injury occur?' is a question frequently asked. The answer to this is at the same time both simple and incredibly complex. The simple answer is injury represents a failure of the tissue to tolerate the mechanical loads applied to it. This is of course the absolute truth of why an injury occurs but why the tissue was unable to cope at that moment is where the complexity lies, and Figure 16.1 illustrates some of the multitude of factors which could influence the tissue's ability to cope with the applied loads.

External Loads During Change of Direction

As presented in Figure 16.1, the 'why' of injury causation is very complex; the 'what' is still mechanical loads exceeding tissue tolerance. It would therefore appear obvious that understanding the external load parameters during deceleration and change-of-direction (COD) tasks would provide a clear indication of what the tissues must cope with and so the levels of load tolerance

DOI: 10.4324/9781003267881-19

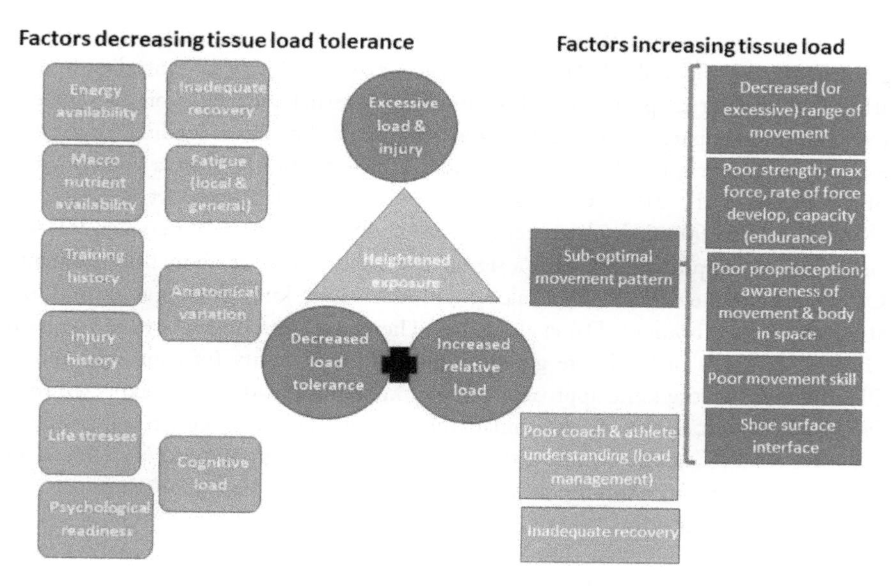

FIGURE 16.1 Factors impacting tissue load.

TABLE 16.1 Average Peak External Moments (Aggregate Based on Literature) During Typical Cutting Angles (Final Foot Contact)

Joint	*Cutting Angle*	*Average Peak External Moment (Nm·kg⁻¹)*	
		Abduction	*Flexion*
Hip	45°	1.28	2.8
	90°	3.2	1.1
	180°	3.0	2.4
Knee	45°	0.67	2.53
	90°	0.96	3.1
	180°	0.91	1.86

Note: the magnitude of external joint moments is influenced by biomechanical modelling and data processing (i.e. smoothing) procedures.

the tissues need to have to minimise tissue stress and reduce injury risk. Table 16.1 presents an aggregated synthesis of current literature sources (Almuzara, 2022) of averaged peak moments (Nm/kg) for three typical COD tasks.

Certain external factors appear to have an impact on why load might vary between specific tissues (joints) during any given COD task – for example, angle of the COD, approach speed, and if the task is anticipated or unanticipated (Dos'Santos et al., 2018). Here is a brief discussion of the implications of some of these factors.

Increasing COD angle from 45° to 90° significantly increases peak internal knee extensor and hip adductor moments, along with knee sagittal plane power absorption, whilst internal hip extensor and ankle plantar flexion moments are decreased significantly (Havens & Sigward, 2015). Sigward et al. (2015) reported knee abduction moments were 2.4 × greater during 110°

vs 45° COD with a disproportionately greater increase in loading in females with the increased cutting angle. Dos'Santos et al. (2021c) found with approach velocity uncontrolled in male team sport athletes that external peak knee abduction and internal rotation moments were greatest during 90° cutting compared to 45° cutting and 180° turns. The lower loading for the 180° turn may be owing to the period of double support as an athlete transitions from a penultimate to final foot contact (Jones et al., 2016). Other studies (Jones et al., 2014; Jones et al., 2016; Schreurs et al., 2017) have also found similar external knee abduction moments between 90° and 180° directional changes. Approach speed has a significant impact on knee abduction moment during 45° COD (Vanrenterghem et al., 2012) along with decreasing knee flexion angle and increasing internal knee extensor moment (Dai et al., 2016). Therefore, it is important to recognise that the biomechanical demands of COD are greatly influenced by velocity (of approach) and angle of the COD. In short, for the same approach, velocity knee joint loads can be expected to increase up to 90°; beyond that, the loads are similar. Increases in approach velocity obviously increase loading during final foot contact, but it does become increasingly difficult to achieve a greater directional change without adopting an appropriate braking strategy (Dos'Santos et al., 2018), which will be discussed shortly.

The nature of the task whether anticipated or unanticipated could also impact on loads. Cortes et al. (2011) and Sigward et al. (2015) undertaking 45° and 90° CODs, respectively, found unanticipated COD to cause significantly greater increases in external knee abduction moments and decreased knee flexion angles along with Sigward et al. (2015) also finding increased hip abduction angles.

Alongside these external factors, how the actual movement is performed can also influence the level of load on tissues/joints. Key elements in the COD movement strategy, which could influence local joints/tissues loads are the relative position of the trunk, the degree of hip abduction (and so lateral foot placement/step width which occurs) and the knee flexion angle.

Trunk position during the COD task is a critical driver to altering loads across the lower limb because of its effect on GRF vector orientation. A contralateral lean (or rotation) of the trunk in the opposite direction to the cut results in a greater laterally directed GRF (Jones et al., 2015). This results in a greater perpendicular distance between the GRF and the knee, increasing knee abduction moment due to a greater moment arm of the GRF in the frontal plane. When trained to reduce this movement strategy, significant reduction in knee abduction moment occurs (Dempsey et al., 2009). Increased trunk flexion during either the final foot contact or penultimate steps is likely to increase internal hip extensor moment and decrease internal knee extensor moment (Warrener et al., 2021), which, though potentially positive for the knee, could increase load for instance in the hamstring muscles.

Excessive levels of hip abduction or lateral foot placement distance (step width) all of which are often used interchangeably, creates increased knee abduction moment through greater laterally oriented GRF resulting in a greater lever arm from the application of force relative to knee joint centre, thus increasing knee abduction moment. Increased hip internal rotation angle can also create increased knee abduction moments through placing the knee in a more medial position to the GRF vector so increasing the perpendicular distance of the moment arm. The presence of increased internal hip rotation during COD is more common in female athletes (Sigward & Powers, 2007).

Greater knee abduction angles will also create greater knee abduction moments, through increasing the medial orientation of the GRF, which results in a greater lever arm from the application of force relative to the knee joint centre. Decreased knee flexion angles will increase the potential for anterior tibial translation (Kvist et al., 2001), and because of the relative increase in flexion impulse could also increase relative loads at the knee (and ankle) (Edwards, 2018).

External Loads During Deceleration

To change direction effectively, at angles greater than 45°, the athlete must first decelerate (Jones et al., 2016). The data presented in Table 16.1 is for the final foot contact of a COD task; prior to this, both limbs are exposed to considerable loads in order to decelerate the athlete to that point. COD tasks demand significant deceleration prior to turning (cuts of 135°–180°), with similar GRFs and trunk acceleration profiles than have been reported during the preparatory deceleration steps (i.e. antepenultimate and penultimate foot contact) of stop tasks (Dos'Santos et al., 2021b). During the final steps of maximal decelerations, the GRFs can be 2.7 times higher than the corresponding steps when accelerating; they also occur over shorter time periods, leading to far greater forces needing to be attenuated during deceleration than acceleration in shorter periods (increased impulse) (Verheul et al., 2021). When decelerating rapidly with the centre of mass (CM) behind the base of support (foot) (Table 16.3), the knee extensors are responsible for generating high eccentric force to counter the external knee flexion moments (Dos'Santos et al., 2018), with the rectus femoris appearing to be the key quadriceps muscle (Mateus et al., 2020). When the trunk adopts a more forward lean, then the gluteus maximus and hamstrings contribute to controlling external hip flexion moment (Mateus et al., 2020). The soleus has also been identified as an important muscle contributing to the attenuation of forces during deceleration (Mateus et al., 2020).

A systematic review on the effect of limb dominance on COD biomechanics (Dos'Santos et al., 2019) found that male and female team sport athletes can show subtle to substantial asymmetries in kinematic and kinetic characteristics related to ACL (anterior cruciate ligament) injury risk, but there was no clear pattern as to which limb (dominant or non-dominant) was affected. More recently in support of these observations, Pollard et al. (2020) reported healthy individuals (male and female) exhibit little side-to-side differences in the majority of lower limb biomechanical parameters when performing deceleration or COD manoeuvres. The lack of differences observed between directional changes with each limb in healthy athletes could be a result of disparity regarding defining limb preference or dominance (often preferred kicking limb) and the implications for potential coordination or strength differences between limbs. Interestingly, Thomas et al. (2020) found that athletes with high single-leg hop asymmetry (≥ group mean + 1 standard deviation [SD] vs low [≤ group mean asymmetry] vs moderate [≤ group mean + 1 SD asymmetry]) used a braking strategy (final to penultimate horizontal GRF ratio) that favoured final foot contact when turning with the 'stronger' limb during a traditional 505 task (180° COD), whereas when turning with the 'weaker' limb, a penultimate foot-contact-braking strategy was favoured (presumably, the 'stronger' limb makes better use of the penultimate foot contact when turning with the 'weaker' limb). Therefore, the presence of unilateral muscle weakness (following injury for instance) could create asymmetry or an avoidance strategy when performing deceleration or COD tasks and so compensatory strategies, which could increase relative joint loads. For example, a reduced ability of one limb to contribute to the generation and distribution of braking forces could create, one limb having to disproportionately contribute more to braking. This would, therefore, expose this limb to greater mechanical loads, neuromuscular fatigue, and potential injury risk whilst also reducing deceleration and COD performance. Similarly, a failure of one limb (knee) to generate adequate braking force during the penultimate foot contact would increase load on the final foot contact, with decreased performance time (and increased horizontal approach velocity) being associated with increased knee abduction and flexion moments and hip flexion moment during final foot contact (McBurnie et al., 2021).

In multidirectional team sport athletes nine months post ACL surgery (n = 156), greater biomechanical asymmetries (between operated and unoperated limbs) during final foot contact of planned and unplanned 90° COD tasks compared to healthy controls (n = 62) were evident. However, these differences were often small and were not revealed in any asymmetry in performance times (King et al., 2019). Nevertheless, in support of the theory mentioned earlier, King et al. (2018) found that male multidirectional team sport athletes nine months post ACL reconstruction (n = 156) revealed no significant differences in planned and unplanned 90° COD task completion times and lower final foot contact times between operated and unoperated limbs. However, lower horizontal velocities at touchdown of final foot contact were found when turning with the operated limb compared to the unoperated limb and was followed by lower; knee flexion, knee extension moment, knee valgus moment, ankle external rotation moment, knee internal rotation angle, and external rotation moment (moments reported as internal moments) at different stages of final foot contact. These observations suggest that while global performance may not be affected, compensations in task execution may occur (e.g. reduced approach velocity, between limb differences in braking strategy) leading to lower knee loading during final foot contact (kinesiophobia). Moreover, Daniels et al. (2021a) examined male multidirectional team sport athletes (n = 144) eight to ten months post ACL reconstruction, performing a pre-planned COD task. Again, approach velocity (horizontal velocity at touchdown of final foot contact) was lower whilst performing the task with the operated limb, and this was followed by lower peak resultant GRF and multi-planar knee joint moments during final foot contact. Moreover, the CM heading angle was more oriented toward the new intended direction of travel at touchdown when cutting from the operated limb and less deflection of the CM took place during final foot contact leading to a lower CM heading angle at take-off. Thus, compensatory whole-body anticipatory changes to lower task demands during final foot contact are evident to reduce knee joint loading. However, such allowances may not be available when tasks become anticipated during match play, which highlights the need to address biomechanical compensations during rehabilitation.

Injuries Related to Deceleration and Change-of-direction Tasks

In most team sports (e.g. Australian football, hockey, rugby league, rugby union, rugby sevens, and soccer), high-intensity (<-2.5 m·s^{-2}) decelerations (often as a precursor to COD) are performed frequently (more frequently than accelerations) during competitive match play (Harper et al., 2019). These actions are performed as an isolated agility action, or preceding COD manoeuvres, and importantly have been proposed to have a significant role in the aetiology of a variety of musculoskeletal injuries, principally ACL injuries, groin (hip adductor) muscle injuries, hamstring muscle injuries, and tendinopathy (possibly rupture) of Achilles and patella tendons. What follows is a discussion of the relationship between these tasks and the loads they generate and the creation of certain specific injuries.

ACL injuries have been linked to deceleration and COD tasks in soccer, handball, basketball and netball (Della Villa et al., 2020; Koga et al., 2010; Mullallay et al., 2021; Takahashi et al., 2019). Likely mechanisms which increase ACL load and create injury could involve increased knee abduction moments (and angles), increased anterior tibial translation generated through high levels of knee extensor force in shallow (20–30°) knee flexion range, and/or a combination of the two. Increased knee abduction moments can be developed if insufficient horizontal braking has occurred during the penultimate foot contact (Jones et al., 2016), the final foot contact involves increased hip abduction/lateral foot placement and is relatively extended (<30° flexion), and/or the trunk is leaning or rotated away from the direction of cut (Donelon et al., 2020).

Hip adductor (groin) muscle injuries frequently occur in sports such as soccer. During the final foot contact of cutting, as the hip extends and externally rotates (towards push off), there is an increase in lengthening velocity of the adductor longus muscle with increasing muscle activity (20–40% of maximum isometric voluntary contraction) (Dupre et al., 2021), placing increased eccentric load on the muscle in a vulnerable lengthened position. Decreased strength in the hip adductor muscles has been prospectively linked to increased groin muscle injury (Moreno-Perez et al., 2019), these weaker individuals may have developed injuries because of an inability to cope with the increased loads on the muscle during cutting. Following a successful exercise rehabilitation culminating in pain-free return to sport, these athletes presented with significantly increased transverse plane rotation of the pelvis toward the intended direction of travel, indicating greater control of the potentially injurious movement (Daniels et al., 2021b); therefore, along with strength, appropriate movement strategies and control appear to be required.

Hamstring muscle injuries are usually associated with high-speed running and specifically the high loads associated with transition from late swing to stance phase. But they can also occur during sharp turns or cutting in ball sports (Biz et al., 2021). Thus, there are possible mechanisms linking deceleration (and/or cutting) movement mechanics and hamstring injury. As the major muscular contributor to deceleration are the quadriceps (Maniar et al., 2019), a reduction in their eccentric strength, for instance, has been shown, following ACL injury and surgery (Kline et al., 2015), to create a need to generate force in other muscle groups, thus increasing load in those muscle groups and so injury risk. When the trunk adopts a more forward lean, then the gluteus maximus and hamstrings contribute to controlling external hip flexion moment (Mateus et al., 2020), this obviously increases load on these structures. Indeed, Kerin et al. (2022) suggest that excessive trunk flexion with an extended knee posture results in increased stretch load on the hamstrings and could explain the observation of deceleration actions involved in hamstring strain injury incidences in rugby union players. Therefore, poor technical ability, failure to decelerate adequately in penultimate steps and maintain an upright trunk with CM behind point of foot contact, could increase load on the hamstrings.

As mentioned, during deceleration tasks, high eccentric forces are generated, with the quadriceps being the main contributors to negative work to bring about CM deceleration, but they are also significantly aided by the soleus (Maniar et al., 2019; Mateus et al., 2020). If these high forces are not appropriately managed (i.e. acute spikes or cumulative high volumes without sufficient recovery), this might heighten the risk of injury to both the patella and Achilles' tendons because of their critical role in energy storage during eccentric actions, the repetitive high loads exceeding tissue capability creating microtrauma, which, if continued, leads to the tendon degeneration found in tendinopathy in line with the mechanical fatigue mechanism as proposed by Edwards (2018).

A Model for 'Safer' Performance

Table 16.2 provides a model of technique for safer side-step cutting (60–110°) and considers the implications for performance (e.g. performance-injury conflict) – *for more information behind the premise of this model, see Chapter 4*. Essentially, successful outcomes of directional changes, such as the side-step cut, are high exit velocity and/or moderate to large deflections/directional changes of the CM to evade an opponent. The former may be influenced by the approach velocity (Jones et al., 2022); both the velocity of approach and angle-of-direction change dictate the intensity of the directional change (e.g. GRFs) and subsequent knee joint loads experienced. To enable this without evoking repetitive high loads on the knee joint, then prior braking during the penultimate foot contact (PFC) (Jones et al., 2016) or earlier (Dos'Santos et al., 2021b) is required. Greater PFC braking helps lower the GRFs experienced and avoid a 'heel contact' at touchdown (David et al., 2017; Donnelly et al., 2017), which subsequently lowers knee joint loads experienced during final foot contact. Decelerative actions like this require increases in touchdown distance (foot to CM distance), rearward trunk lean, shorter steps with large reductions in flight time, and greater knee and hip flexion (Table 16.3) to increase posterior braking impulse. Subsequently, the postures adopted at touchdown of the final foot contact influence the multi-planar loads experienced at the knee. Postures associated with peak knee abduction moments include lateral trunk flexion (Dempsey et al., 2007; Jones et al., 2015), measures of lateral leg plant distance (Kristianslund et al., 2014; Jones et al., 2015; Havens & Sigward, 2015), initial knee abduction (McLean et al., 2004; Kristianslund et al., 2014; Jones et al., 2015) and flexion (Robinson et al., 2015; Weir et al., 2019), hip internal rotation (Sigward & Powers 2007; Havens & Sigward, 2015), and internal foot progression angle (Sigward & Powers, 2007), all of which lead to a more medial knee position relative to the GRF vector in the frontal plane. Except for lateral leg plant distance, all the others can be addressed to lower knee joint loads experienced and do not affect performance (e.g. task completion time, exit velocity); that said, lateral trunk flexion may have performance implications to help deceive an opponent. Narrowing lateral leg plant distance may help reduce knee joint loads but may also compromise the production of medially directed impulse for the required directional change and to increase exit velocity (Jones et al., 2015). Furthermore, encouraging more lower limb flexion during final foot contact will help reduce GRFs and subsequent knee joint loads but would prolong ground contact time and may lead to slower performance (Dos'Santos et al., 2021a). Therefore, the performance-injury conflict associated with these later variables have implications for physical and technical preparation (e.g. develop muscular support structures, 'active' touchdown postures) for athletes/players for rehabilitation and return to play (Table 16.2).

Rehabilitating Deceleration and Change-of-direction Tasks

The aim of injury rehabilitation is to return the athlete to pre-injury levels of performance whilst minimising the risk of further injury. When performing sports actions, such as rapid deceleration and changing direction failure to return to pre-injury levels of performance could occur due to three main reasons: (1) compensations to avoid stressing the injured tissue (because of failure of the injured tissue to cope with the loads encountered), (2) failure to fully develop the underpinning physical qualities required to undertake the task optimally leading to compensations, or (3) poor technical execution of the task, which might be related to kinesiophobia (the fear of the movement/task) or poor movement skill development. These three potential areas of failure need to be addressed in any rehabilitation programme, and the key elements of their development will be considered in the next section. The first of these is to develop the appropriate prerequisite physical qualities; these can be further split in tissue qualities (i.e. tissue load tolerance) and physical attributes required to deliver specific elements within the task itself. The second element is to

TABLE 16.2 A Model for Safer Side-Step Cutting

MKF = max knee flexion

1. *Penultimate foot-contact-braking strategy* involving foot placement in front of the CM, ideally leaning back and encouraging knee and hip flexion during the penultimate step, which all effectively lead to applying horizontal braking force for longer. Penultimate foot contact braking strategy helps manage approaches with greater velocity (e.g. increase controllable approach velocity whilst visual scanning at a velocity they can moderate) and/or directional requirements, as well as reducing knee joint loads through reduced ground reaction forces (GRFs) during final foot contact.
2. *A wide lateral leg plant* increases frontal and transverse plane knee joint loads due to increasing the moment arm distance of the GRF vector laterally outside the knee joint. However, such a strategy helps generate medial-lateral impulse to facilitate the direction change. Thus, developing muscular support structures is essential for return to play. Furthermore, greater attention to avoiding other hazardous lower limb postures (5) is of prime importance, along with encouraging 'active landings' to redirect the force vector during side-step cutting.
3. *Medially directed trunk* toward the intended direction of travel shifts the GRF vector more medially relative to the knee joint, reducing knee abduction moments (KAMs), and leads to faster performance. However, lateral trunk flexion may assist with deception goals of the manoeuvre.
4. *Triple lower-limb co-flexion* may help lower final foot contact GRFs but may lead to prolonging ground contact time and subsequently slower performance. Encourage 'active touchdown' involving an initial flexed posture with muscular support before rapid transition to forceful triple extension.
5. *Avoid initial knee abduction (valgus) and hip internal rotation* as both are associated with greater frontal plane knee joint moments and do not impact performance. Encourage 'strong' frontal plane alignment.
6. *Neutral foot position* should be encouraged when changing direction as excessively internally or externally rotated positions increase KAMs and tibial rotation.

TABLE 16.3 A Technical Model for Pre-planned Deceleration

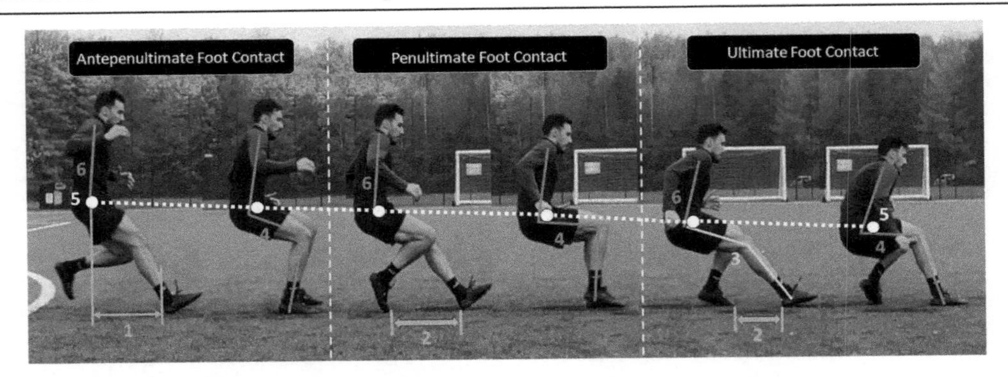

The photosequence depicts the ante-, pen- and ultimate foot contacts during deceleration to a stop. Please note the number of steps involved depends on the velocity of approach with greater velocities requiring greater distances and subsequently number of steps. Typical stopping distances range from 2.9 to 7.9 m from 54.2 ± 3.9 to 89.1 ± 2.5% (4.4 to 7.2 $m \cdot s^{-1}$) of maximum velocity (Graham-Smith et al., 2018). The technique characteristics illustrated here would apply to additional deceleration steps. Furthermore, the time available during match play to decelerate and thus, the number of steps involved depends on the athletes ability to perceive the environment and execute the required deceleration action (perception-action coupling), hence the need to develop a range of braking/deceleration strategies in closed and open situations.

1. *Increased touchdown (TD) distance:* At TD of each foot contact, the foot is placed in front of the CM to increase horizontal braking impulse (force and duration).
2. *Reduced step length:* Step kinematics alter through shorter step lengths and greater step frequency. Notice at TD of the penultimate and ultimate foot contact, the rear foot is still in contact with the ground indicating *no flight phase*, leading to longer braking times (no propulsion phase) of ground contact and thus greater braking impulse (horizontal braking force × braking time)
3. *Initial knee flexion and lower limb alignment:* Flexed (>30°) knee and good lower limb alignment (no knee valgus) in the frontal plane at TD to lower multi-planar knee joint loading. Avoid knee valgus during ground contact.
4. *Sitting position:* Greater knee and hip flexion during each foot contact illustrated by the sitting position. This sitting position ensures the hips and trunk is positioned well behind the foot during ground contact, and the greater knee and hip flexion involves applying braking force for longer, leading to greater reduction in momentum. Greater support leg flexion also enables the subsequent foot contact to be a head of the CM.
5. *Lowering of CM to improve stability:* The marked flexion of the ankle, knee, and hip and the absence of a flight phase leads to a lowering of the CM. Coupled with the periods of double support illustrated in the penultimate and ultimate foot contacts allows a more stable position (lower CM/increase base of support). Lowering the CM (reduces lever arm of CM relative to foot) helps prevent forward rotation about the front foot in the ultimate contact.
6. *Trunk position:* Ideally, the trunk should 'lean back' or at the very least be upright at TD in each foot contact to help shift the CM further behind the foot at TD to increase the braking impulse. Notice this is more pronounced in the antepenultimate foot contact; thus, it is important for early deceleration. Furthermore, an upright or 'leaning back' trunk position avoids large increases in hamstring muscle-tendon lengths.

build optimal movement strategies to minimise compensatory strategies. Finally, the third is to be able to deliver the skilled movement appropriately in the random chaotic environment of sport.

Prerequisite Physical Qualities

Tissue tolerance: At the tissue level an injury occurs when the forces applied to the tissue exceed the load tolerance of the tissue, so one important element of any rehabilitation programme is the graduated exposure of the injured tissue to load to build that tissue tolerance of load back to (or greater than) pre-injury levels. The process of graduated exposure to load involves several elements, the first of which is establishing a stable baseline – that is, what level of load can the tissue tolerate at present; this provides a starting point for reloading. The second element is understanding what loads stress the tissue and which do not; this then provides the parameters for the direction(s) and nature of load and frequency which will drive progression – that is, establishing a low to high tissue load progression paradigm. The third element is then to expose the tissue to progressively greater loads whilst monitoring the tissue for reaction to those loads. It should be noted here that this is about reloading the injured tissue from a stable load baseline, not deloading the tissue as this creates atrophy and a tissue which is less able to cope, so the tissue is always loaded to a maximum level it can tolerate. The obvious consideration when developing reloading progressions are range of movement, intensity of load, velocity of load, repetitions, frequency, and recovery. Having a clear understanding of tissue anatomy and biology aids this process considerably. An example of a tissue loading progression for an injured muscle is shown in Figure 16.2.

Physical attributes to perform: To undertake performance tasks such as rapid decelerations and CODs, certain underpinning physical attributes are required to carry out the tasks in an optimal manner and control the forces involved. These physical attributes or qualities will involve the ability to generate appropriate levels of muscle force (concentrically, isometrically,

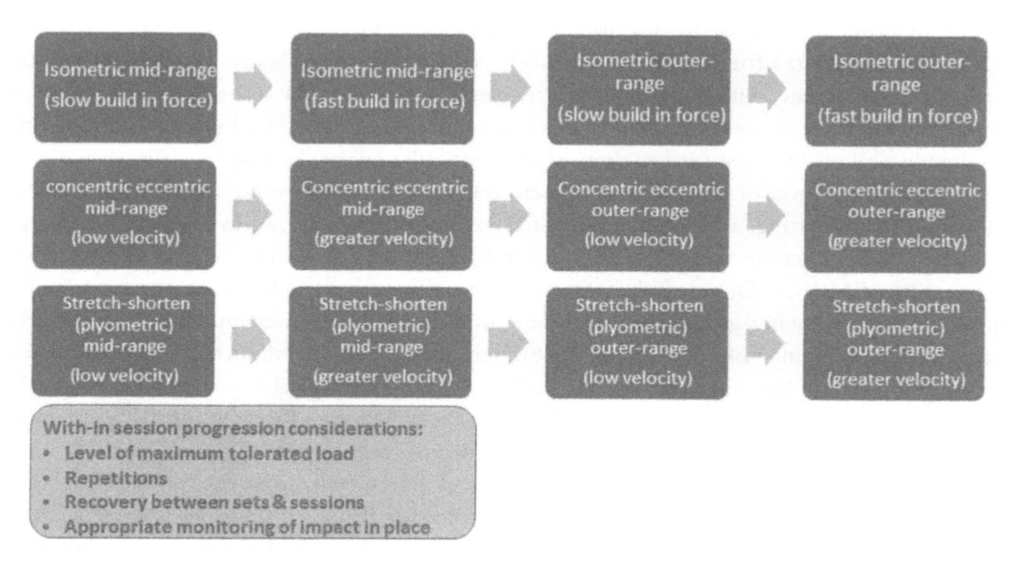

FIGURE 16.2 Loading progression at tissue level for muscle injury.

and eccentrically at the appropriate contraction velocities) and take joints and other soft tissues through appropriate ranges of movement and specifically for certain phases that have controlled elongation of tissue under load. The physical attributes required are specific to the task being undertaken, such as during deceleration and COD, which will now be discussed separately.

Physical attributes for deceleration: During the first to second steps, decelerating the system exposure to ground reaction forces are 2.7 times greater than the corresponding steps accelerating (Verheul et al., 2021), and they occur over a shorter time (Harper et al., 2022), demonstrating the need to cope with and generate both rapid and high peak force with eccentric muscle actions. Therefore, an obvious physical quality required to decelerate effectively is the ability to generate high eccentric forces at relatively high velocities. During these intense horizontal decelerations, when the CM is positioned posterior to the base of support, the knee extensors are mostly responsible for counteracting the large external knee flexor moments; it then becomes imperative that the quadriceps can generate high eccentric forces, as eccentric strength has been significantly linked to cutting and pivoting task performance (Jones et al., 2017; Jones et al., 2022). Alongside the quadriceps, both the soleus muscle and gluteus maximus/hamstrings have been shown to have a contributing but not primary role to controlling these horizontal braking forces (Mateus et al., 2020; Maniar et al., 2022).

What is strong enough for the quadriceps, soleus, and gluteus maximus/hamstring to cope with these loads has yet to be defined in the literature. This means a practitioner needs to use some form of heuristic (rule of thumb) to establish a level of strength, which at least mitigates risk of either excessive stress to the muscles (and their tendons) during the task or failure to undertake the task optimally leading to compensations and potential injury. As presented in Table 16.1, typical peak hip and knee extensor moments are more than 2.5 Nm/kg; it would be reasonable to 'set a bar' at these levels – that is, needing to be able to at least generate 2.5–3.0 Nm/kg eccentric peak moment during an isolated eccentric hip or knee extension task. Limited data exists on ankle plantar flexion peak force or moments, but Jones et al. (2016) reported penultimate foot peak external dorsi-flexion moment as 0.6 Nm/kg and final foot contact as 1.6 Nm/kg during a 90° cut, so again, a reasonable bar for plantar flexion moment might be 2.0 Nm/kg.

Physical attributes for COD: To effectively change direction, plainly one element will be to effectively decelerate, with the exception of angles less than 45°. The second element will then be to rotate the body in the direction of the cut, away from the planted foot prior to pushing off. It is the physical qualities required to do the latter that will now be discussed.

An appropriate level of hip adductor muscle eccentric strength would appear to be critical as during FFC of cutting, as the hip extends and externally rotates (towards push-off), it creates an increase in lengthening velocity of the adductor longus muscle with increasing muscle activity (20–40% of MIVC) (Dupre et al., 2021). Alongside that, those individuals who successfully return to sport following groin injury had decreased (normalised) their hip abduction stiffness during a lateral hopping task (Gore et al., 2018), indicating a potential improvement in resistance to elongation of the hip adductor muscles during the task. As typical hip adduction eccentric peak values are around 3.0 Nm/kg for asymptomatic footballers (van Klij et al., 2021), this would appear to be a reasonable base level of strength required for cutting tasks.

As the cutting task involves rotating the trunk (and pelvis) away from the 'plant' foot – that is, the hip abducting and externally rotating away from the trunk – if this does not occur, then hip internal rotation could occur, which could increase loading at the knee previously discussed (Donelon et al., 2020). To maintain the hip position, the hip abductor and external rotator muscles will need to generate considerable isometric force to counter the turning moment; Table 6.1

indicates this to be typically around 3–3.2 Nm/kg, depending on the task. Typical isometric hip abduction muscle strength in footballers has been reported at 3–3.2 Nm/kg (van Klij et al., 2021); this would appear to be again a reasonable base level of strength required for the cutting task.

Developing Optimal Movement Strategies

A model for safer deceleration and cutting has been presented earlier in this chapter (Tables 16.2 and 16.3), which aims to optimise performance whilst minimising compensatory movements, which could generate excessive stress loading and injury. These models provide the template for developing the athlete's performance during rehabilitation. This next section will cover the principles of developing movement skill and a contextual example. The overarching process is shown in Figure 16.3.

Following on from Chapter 11, there are some key elements with regard to the way practice is conducted, which can help maximise the rate of learning of a movement skill, these are summarised in Figure 16.4. Practice can be block in nature, with the same task being practised repetitively without variation (as opposed to random with constant variations). Block practice is advantageous when the task has high nominal difficulty. So when, for example, the athlete has been initially introduced to the task, and the athlete becomes familiar with the task, the nominal difficulty will decrease, and then they are more likely to benefit from some degree of randomisation to the task elements. Block practice tends to lend itself to perfect practice that is working to a specific 'ideal' goal, whereas random practice allows the athlete the opportunity to work the problem and find solutions which fit, so they develop differential learning. The focus of the athlete's attention has been shown to impact on learning, with initially an internal focus of attention on the action itself being useful, progressing to a more external focus on the goal of the task itself as skill is developed. The explanation of the task can either be explicit – that is, step by step – or more implicit – where analogies, metaphors, or visual feedback is used to show the big picture. Implicit explanation may potentially help whilst still undertaking block closed-skill practice, but explicit explanation generally shows better results through all conditions. The way the practice is structured can either be rigid, mostly devised by

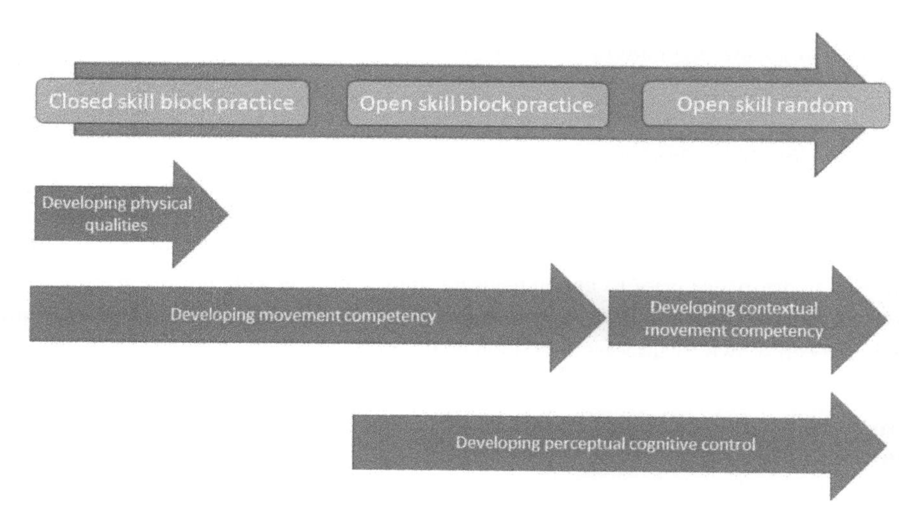

FIGURE 16.3 Progression paradigm for developing movement skill.

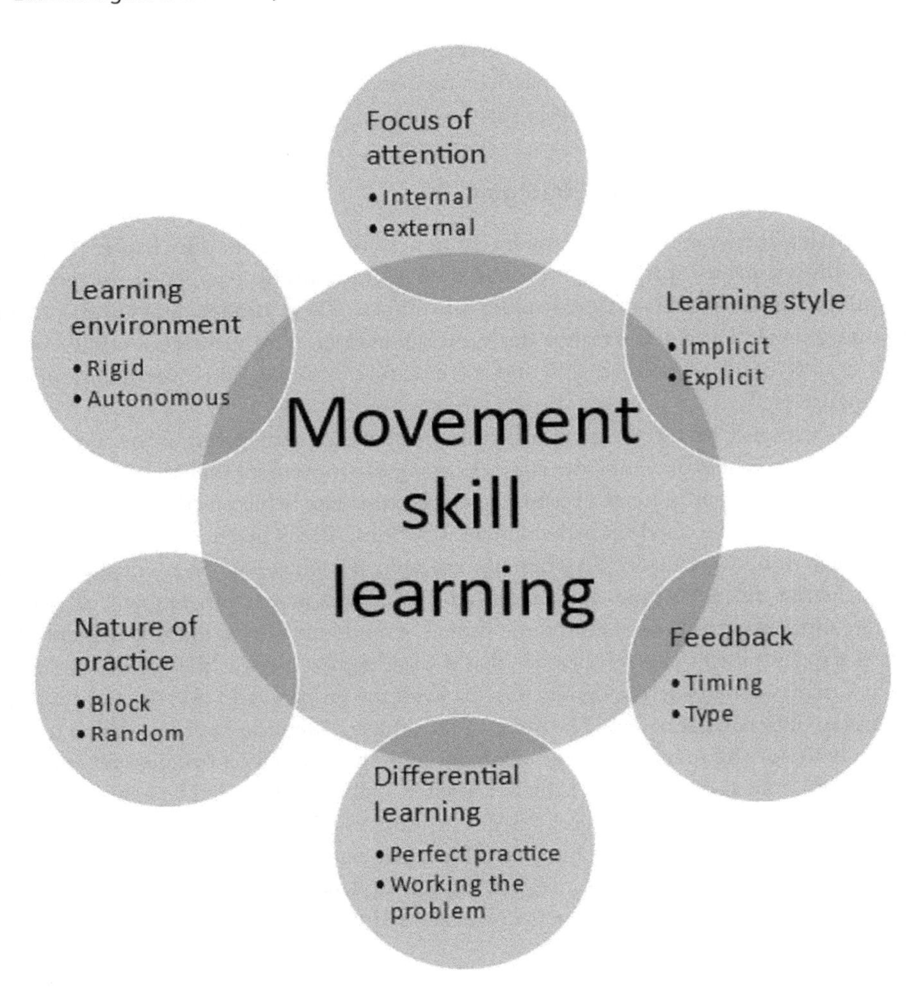

FIGURE 16.4 Key elements in motor skill learning.

therapist/coach, or more autonomous, where the athlete has a role in design. Generally, greater degrees of autonomy help learning. Finally, the timing and nature of feedback plays a role; if the athlete is already cognitively overloaded by the task, then any feedback during the task is likely to contribute further to the overload. Allowing the athlete to describe their thoughts and feelings about the task performance prior to giving feedback allows more specific positive feedback around successful elements to be given; not overemphasising the negative elements the athlete has already identified has been shown to aid learning (Singh et al., 2021).

Delivering Optimal Movement Strategies in the Random Chaotic Environment of Sport

What has been discussed in the previous section involves delivering a specific movement pattern in a very constrained or closed manner; obviously, this does not resemble the chaotic, often random nature of sports competition. What an athlete needs to be able to do is deliver those optimal movement patterns in the open random environment of competition. To do this, the movement skill needs to be progressively challenged. This next section will present a progression paradigm to develop movement skill in more chaotic random environments.

Increased cortical and attentional requirements following injury have been identified, which may be used for example to maintain joint stability but may predispose for re-injury during complex motor tasks or situations with increased attentional requirements (Almonroeder et al., 2018). Simply, if too much attention is being focused on undertaking the task, insufficient brain power is available to respond to the technical and tactical demands of the sport due to a failure of the movement task being automatic; if the brain switches to thinking about the sport, the risk is that as the movement skill is not automatic, it could break down, leading to increased injury risk. The athlete's performance of the task must be trained to be optimised despite having to undertake duel or even multiple tasks at the same time.

Typical activities which could bring random elements to a task would include reaction to stimuli; this could be a verbal command, another athlete, or a ball, for example. The distance to be covered can be varied along with the angle of cut, which are both ways to conservatively manage intensity when rehabilitating injured players. A secondary follow-on task could be included, such as spotting and moving towards a player or even a cone of a specific colour (see Chapter 13 for more details).

Worked example for a cutting task: The task to be undertaken is a 90° cut; what is shown in Figure 16.5 would be an example of the progressions, which could be used from undertaking the task in a closed block manner to undertaking the task in a random, chaotic environment. In the final stages, the ability to deliver performance under fatigue (both cognitive and physiological) must be considered and appropriate stimulus must be added as a progression within each individual element.

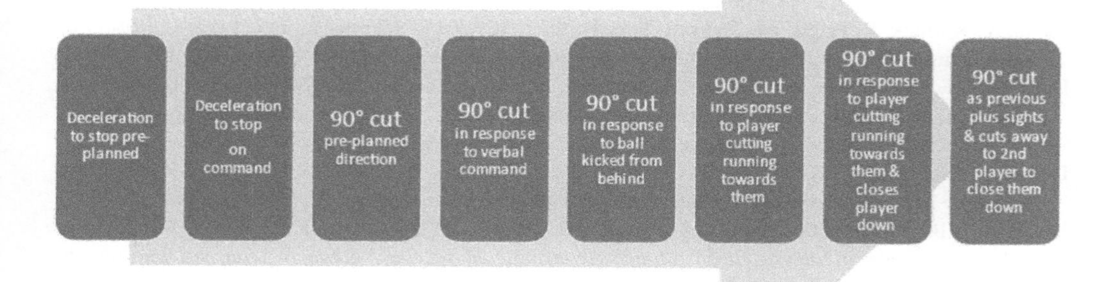

FIGURE 16.5 Progressions for cutting task from closed skill to open random.

Summary

Injury is created when tissue is overloaded beyond its ability to cope. This situation can be avoided by managing load appropriately (exposure) and building tolerance to that load (resilience). Reducing the risk of over exposure is mitigated if various factors which can predispose the individual to elevated levels of tissue stress are reduced or managed (Figure 16.1). One of the most obvious ways to reduce tissue stress is to optimise technique so load distribution is maximised and oriented towards tissues most able to cope (Tables 16.2 and 16.3). When returning from injury, the primary aims of rehabilitation are to return the athlete to pre-injury levels of performance whilst minimising the risk of further injury. This involves preparing the tissues for the tasks – that is, having the prerequisite physical qualities to cope with the task loading demands and then being able to deliver the task in an optimised manner not only in a closed constrained environment but in the chaotic random world of sport.

References

Almonroeder, T., Kernozek, T., Cobb, S., Slavens, B., Wang, J., & Huddleston, W. (2018). Cognitive demands influence lower extremity mechanics during drop vertical jump task in female athletes. *Journal of Orthopaedic and Sports Physical Therapy, 48*, 38–387

Almuzara, L.L. (2022). Neuromuscular response and knee frontal plane projection angle analysis in active people: Implications for anterior cruciate ligament injury prevention. PhD Thesis. Basic Sciences Department, Universitat Internacional de Catalunya Spain

Biz, C., Nicoletti, P., Baldin, G., Gragazzi, N., Crimi, A., & Ruggieri, P. (2021). Hamstring strain injury in professional and semi-professional football teams: A systematic review and meta-analysis. *International Journal of Environmental Research in Public Health, 18*, 100–120

Cortes, N., Onate, J., & Van Lunen, B. (2011). Pivot task increases knee frontal plane loading compared with sidestep and drop-jump. *Journal of Sports Sciences, 29*, 83–92

Dai, B., Garrett, W.E., Gross, M.T., Padua, D.A., Queen, R.M., & Yu, B. (2016). The effect of performance demands on lower extremity biomechanics during landing and cutting tasks. *Journal of Sport and Health Science, 43*, 1680–1685

Daniels, K.A., Drake, E., King, E., & Strike, S. (2021a). Whole-body change-of-direction task execution asymmetries after anterior cruciate ligament reconstruction. *Journal of Applied Biomechanics, 1*, 1–6

Daniels, K.A., King, E., Richter, C., Falvey, E., Franklyn-Miller, A. (2021b). Changes in the kinetics and kinematics of a reactive cut maneuver after successful athletic groin pain rehabilitation. *Scandinavian Journal of Medicine and Science in Sports, 31*, 839–847

David, S., Komnik, I., Peters, M., Funken, J., & Potthast, W. (2017). Identification and risk estimation of movement strategies during cutting maneuvers. *Journal of Science and Medicine in Sport, 20*, 1075–1080

Della Villa, F., Buckthorpe, M., Grassi, A., Nabiuzzi, A., Zaffagnini, S., Della Villa, S. (2020). Systematic video analysis of ACL injuries in professional football (soccer), injury mechanisms, situational patterns and biomechanics study on 134 consecutive case. *British Journal of Sports Medicine, 54*, 1423–1432

Dempsey, A.R., Lloyd, D.G., Elliott, B.C., Steele, J.R., & Munro, B.J. (2009). Changing sidestep cutting technique reduces knee valgus loading. *American Journal of Sports Medicine, 37*, 2194–2200

Dempsey, A.R., Lloyd, D.G., Elliott, B.C., Steele, J.R., Munro, B.J., & Russo, K.A. (2007). The effect of technique change on knee loads during sidestep cutting. *Medicine and Science in Sports and Exercise, 39*, 1765–1773

Donelon, T., Dos'Santos, T., Pitchers, G., Brown, M., & Jones, P. (2020). Biomechanical determinants of knee joint loads associated with increased anterior cruciate loading during cutting: A systematic review and technical framework. *Sports Medicine (open), 6*, 53–60

Donnelly, C.J., Chinnasee, C., Weir, G., Sasimontonkul, S., & Alderson, J. (2017). Joint dynamics of rear- and fore-foot unplanned sidestepping. *Journal of Science and Medicine in Sport, 20*, 32–37

Dos'Santos, T., Bishop, C., Thomas, C., Comfort, P., & Jones, P.A. (2019). The effect of limb dominance on change of direction biomechanics: A systematic review of its importance for injury risk. *Physical Therapy in Sport, 37*, 179–189

Dos'Santos, T., McBurnie, A., Thomas, C., Comfort, C., & Jones, P.A. (2021a). Biomechanical determinants of performance and injury risk during cutting: A performance-injury conflict? *Sports medicine (Auckland, N.Z.), 51*, 1983–1998. doi.org/10.1007/s40279-021-01448-3

Dos'Santos, T., Thomas, C., Comfort, P., & Jones, P. (2018). The effect of angle and velocity on change of direction biomechanics: An angle velocity trade off. *Sports Medicine, 48*, 2235–2253

Dos'Santos, T., Thomas, C., & Jones, P.A. (2021b). How early should you brake during a 180° turn? A kinetic comparison of the antepenultimate, penultimate, and final foot contacts during a 505 change of direction speed test. *Journal of Sports Sciences, 39*, 395–405

Dos'Santos, T., Thomas, C., & Jones, P.A. (2021c). The effect of angle on change of direction biomechanics: Comparison and inter-task relationships. *Journal of Sports Sciences, 39*, 2618–2631. https://doi.org/10.1080/02640414.2021.1948258

Dupre, T., Tryba, J., & Potthast, W. (2021). Muscle activity of cutting manoeuvres and soccer inside passing suggests an increased groin injury risk during these movements. *Sports Science Reports, 11*, 7223. https://doi.org/10.1038/s41598-021-86666-5

Edwards, W.B. (2018). Modelling overuse injuries in sport as a mechanical fatigue phenomenon. *Exercise and Sports Science Reviews, 46*, 224–231

Gore, S., Franklyn-Miller, A., Richter, C., Falvey, E., King, E., & Moran, K. (2018). Is stiffness related to athletic groin pain? *Scandinavian Journal of Medicine & Science in Sports, 28*, 1681–1690

Graham-Smith, P., Rumpf, M., & Jones, P.A. (2018). Assessment of deceleration ability and relationships to approach speed and eccentric strength. Presented at the *International Society of Biomechanics in Sports Conference*, Auckland, New Zealand, September 2018

Harper, D.J., Carling, C., & Kiely, J. (2019). High-intensity acceleration and deceleration demands in elite team sports competitive match play: A systematic review and meta-analysis of observational studies. *Sports Medicine, 49*, 1923–1947

Harper, D. J., McBurnie, A. J., Santos, T. D., Eriksrud, O., Evans, M., Cohen, D. D., Rhodes, D., Carling, C., & Kiely, J. (2022). Biomechanical and neuromuscular performance Requirements of horizontal deceleration: A review with implications for random intermittent multi-directional sports. *Sports Medicine (Auckland, N.Z.), 52*, 2321–2354. https://doi.org/10.1007/s40279-022-01693-0

Havens, K., & Sigward, S. (2015). Joint and segmental mechanics differ between cutting maneuvres in skilled athletes. *Gait and Posture, 41*, 33–38

Jones, P.A., Dos'Santos, T., McMahon, J.J., & Graham-Smith, P. (2017). The role of eccentric strength in 180° turns in female soccer players. *Sports, 17*, 42–50

Jones, P.A., Dos'Santos, T., McMahon, J.J., & Graham-Smith, P. (2022). Contribution of eccentric strength to cutting performance in female soccer players. *Journal of Strength and Conditioning Research, 36*, 525–533

Jones, P.A., Herrington, L.C., & Graham-Smith, P. (2015). Technique determinants of knee joint loads during cutting in female soccer players. *Human Movement Science, 42*, 203–211

Jones, P.A., Herrington, L.C., & Graham-Smith, P. (2016). Braking characteristics during cutting and pivoting in female soccer players. *Journal of Electromyography & Kinesiology, 30*, 46–54

Jones, P.A., Herrington, L.C., Munro, A.G., & Graham-Smith, P. (2014). Is there a relationship between landing and changing direction in terms of 'dynamic valgus'? *American Journal of Sports Medicine, 42*, 2095–2102

Kerin, F., Farrell, G., Tierney, P., Persson, U.M., De Vito, G., & Delahunt, E. (2022). It's not all about sprinting: Mechanisms of acute hamstring strain injuries in professional male rugby union – a systematic visual video analysis. *British Journal of Sports Medicine, 56*, 608–615

King, E., Richter, C., Franklyn-Miller, A., Daniels, K., Wadey, R., Jackson, M., & Strike, S. (2018). Biomechanical but not timed performance asymmetries persist between limbs 9 months after ACL reconstruction during planned and unplanned change of direction. *Journal of Biomechanics, 81*, 93–103

King, E., Richter, C., Franklyn-Miller, A., Wadey, R., Moran, R., & Strike, S. (2019). Back to normal symmetry? Biomechanical variables remain more asymmetrical than normal during jump and change-of-direction testing 9 months after anterior cruciate ligament reconstruction. *American Journal of Sports Medicine, 47*, 1175–1185

Kline, P., Johnson, D., Lloyd-Ireland, M., & Noehren, B. (2015). Clinical predictors of knee mechanics at return to sport after ACL reconstruction. *Medicine & Science in Sports & Exercise, 48*, 790–795

Koga, H., Nakamae, A, Shima, Y., Iwasa, J., Myklebust, G., Engebretsen, L., Bahr, R., & Krosshaug, T. (2010). Mechanisms for non-contact ACL injuries: Knee joint kinematics for 10 injury situations from female handball and basketball. *American Journal of Sports Medicine, 38*, 2218–2225

Kristianslund, E., Faul, O., Bahr, R., Myklebust, G., & Krosshaug, T. (2014). Sidestep cutting technique and knee abduction loading: Implications for ACL prevention exercises. *British Journal of Sports Medicine, 48*, 779–783

Kvist, J., Karlberg, C., Gerdle, B., & Gillquist, J. (2001). Anterior translation during different isokinetic quadriceps torque in anterior cruciate deficient and nonimpaired individuals. *Journal of Orthopaedic and Sports Physical Therapy, 1*, 4–15

Maniar, N., Cole, M.H., Bryant, A.L., & Opar, D.A. (2022). Muscle force contributions to anterior cruciate ligament loading. *Sports Medicine, 52*, 1737–1750 https://doi.org/10.1007/s40279-022-01674-3

Maniar, N., Schache, A., Cole, M., & Opar, D. (2019). Lower limb function during side-step cutting. *Journal of Biomechanics, 82*, 186–192

Mateus, R.B., Ferrer-Roca, V., João, F., & Veloso, A.P. (2020). Muscle contributions to maximal single-leg forward braking and backward acceleration in elite athletes. *Journal of Biomechanics, 112*, 11–47

McBurnie, A.J., Dos'Santos, T., & Jones, P.A. (2021). Biomechanical associates of performance and knee joint loads during a 70–90° cutting maneuver in sub-elite soccer players. *Journal of Strength & Conditioning Research, 35*, 3190–3198

Mclean, S.G., Lipfert, S.W., & Van Den Bogert, A.J. (2004). Effect of gender and defensive opponent on the biomechanics of sidestep cutting. *Medicine & Science in Sports & Exercise, 36*, 1008–1016

Moreno-Perez, V., Travassos, B., Calado, A., Gonzalo-Skok, O., Del Coso, J., & Mendez-Villanueva, A. (2019). Adductor squeeze test and groin injuries in elite football players: A prospective study. *Physical Therapy in Sport, 37*, 54–59

Mullallay, E., Atack, A., Glaister, M., & Clark, N. (2021). Situations and mechanisms of non-contact knee injury in adult netball: A systematic review, *Physical Therapy in Sport, 47*, 193–200

Pollard, C.D., Norcross, M.F., Johnson, S.T., Stone, A.E., Chang, E., & Hoffman, M.A. (2020). A biomechanical comparison of dominant and non-dominant limbs during a side-step cutting task. *Sports Biomechanics, 19*, 271–279. https://doi.org/10.1080/14763141.2018.146123

Robinson, M.A., Donnelly, C.J., Vanrenterghem, J., & Pataky, T.C. (2015). Sagittal plane kinematics predict non-sagittal joint moments in unplanned sidestepping. *XXV Congress of the International Society of Biomechanics*, Glasgow, UK.

Schreurs, M.J., Benjaminse, A., & Lemmink, K.A.P.M. (2017). Sharper angle, higher risk? The effect of cutting angle on knee mechanics in invasion sport athletes. *Journal of Biomechanics, 63*, 144–150. doi:10.1016/j.jbiomech.2017.08.019

Sigward, S., Cesar, G., & Havens, K. (2015). Predictors of frontal plane knee moments during side-step cutting to 45 and 110 degrees in men and women: Implications for ACL injury. *Clinical Journal of Sports Medicine, 25*, 529–534

Sigward, S.M., & Powers, C.M. (2007). Loading characteristics of females exhibiting excessive valgus moments during cutting. *Clinical Biomechanics, 22*, 827–833

Singh, H., Gokeler, A., & Benjaminse, A. (2021). Effective attentional focus strategies after ACL reconstruction: A commentary. *International Journal of Sports Physical Therapy, 16*, 1575–1585

Takahashi, S., Nagano, Y., Kido, Y., & Okuwaki, T. (2019). A retrospective study of mechanisms of ACL injuries in high school basketball, handball, judo, soccer and volleyball, *Medicine, 98*, e16030

Thomas, C., Dos'Santos, T., Comfort, P., & Jones, P.A. (2020). The effect of asymmetry on biomechanical characteristics during 180° change of direction. *Journal of Strength and Conditioning Research, 34*, 1297–1306

van Klij, P., Langhout, R., Van Beijsterveldt, A., Stubbe, J., Weir, A., Agricola, R., Fokker, Y., Mosler, A., Waarsing, J., Verhaar, J., & Tak, I. (2021). Do hip and groin muscle strength and symptoms change throughout a football season in professional male football? A prospective cohort study with repeated measures. *Journal of Science and Medicine in Sport, 24*, 1123–1129

Vanrenterghem, J., Venables, E., Pataky, T., & Robinson, M. A. (2012). The effect of running speed on knee mechanical loading in females during side cutting. *Journal of Biomechanics, 45*, 2444–2449. https://doi.org/10.1016/j.jbiomech.2012.06.029

Verheul, J., Nedergaard, N.J., Pogson, M., Lisboa, P., Gregson, W., & Vanrenterghem, J. (2021). Biomechanical loading during running: Can a two mass-spring-damper model be used to evaluate ground reaction forces for high-intensity tasks? *Sport Biomechanics, 20*, 571–582

Warrener, A., Tamai, R., & Lieberman, D. (2021). The effect of trunk flexion angle on lower limb mechanics during running, *Human Movement Science, 78*, 102817. https://doi.org/10.1016/j.humov.2021.102817

Weir, G., Alderson, J., Smailes, N., Elliott, B., & Donnelly, C. (2019). A reliable video-based ACL injury screening tool for female team sport athletes. *International Journal of Sports Medicine, 40*, 191–199

17

LONG-TERM ATHLETE DEVELOPMENT FOR MULTIDIRECTIONAL SPEED

Robert W. Meyers, John M. Radnor, and Micheál Cahill

Introduction

The importance of multidirectional speed is well established across many sporting performances within adult populations and has been discussed at length in previous chapters (see Chapters 1 and 2); however, it is vital to not assume that this literature, and the understanding of its importance, will transfer directly to youth populations. Put simply, children and youth athletes are not 'miniature adults' and require unique consideration in the planning and delivery of their training programmes to account for the multifaceted factors of advancing age, growth, and maturation (Lloyd, Cronin, et al., 2016). Throughout this chapter, the evidence associated with multidirectional speed for children and youth athlete is explored. Firstly, there is a focus on the development of multidirectional speed across age, growth, and maturation before delving into the biomechanical and physiological underpinnings of these changes. The chapter concludes by discussing the trainability of multidirectional speed as part of a holistic long-term athletic development programme and contextualises these alongside applied examples of training that might be considered appropriate for youth athletes.

The Importance of Multidirectional Speed for Youth Athletes

Sprint speed characteristics are well documented across many youth sports including soccer (Buchheit et al., 2012; Emmonds et al., 2016; Radnor, Staines, et al., 2021), tennis (Galé-Ansodi et al., 2016), basketball (Pino-Ortega et al., 2022; Reina et al., 2019) and rugby union (Till, Cobley, et al., 2016; Till, Jones, et al., 2016), with evidence suggesting that higher-level performers exhibit both increase sprint volumes and overall faster sprint performances (McLellan & Lovell, 2013). Less attention in the literature has been devoted to exploring characteristics associated with deceleration (Vigh-Larsen et al., 2018) despite evidence of marked decreases in deceleration with match play fatigue (Arruda et al., 2015), greater frequency of deceleration compared to acceleration (Harper et al., 2019), and the acknowledgement of the importance of deceleration and change of direction during critical aspects of sport performance, such as goal scoring (Martínez-Hernández et al., 2022). Furthermore, the literature exploring change of direction

DOI: 10.4324/9781003267881-20

within youth sport is also limited, despite its well-established importance for multidirectional sport performance (McBurnie, Harper, et al., 2022; Paul & Nassis, 2015). Some descriptive studies in youth soccer (Morgan et al., 2021) have highlighted the frequency of multidirectional events; however, the diverse nature of change of direction within sporting performance and no universal agreement on classification of change-of-direction events (Talty et al., 2022) have limited the volume of work in this area.

Development of Multidirectional Speed With Age, Growth, and Maturation

Throughout childhood and adolescence, all systems within the body (e.g. nervous, muscular, skeletal) will develop independently and in a non-linear manner (Malina et al., 2004). *Biological maturation* is the process of progressing toward a mature state, and varies in magnitude (extent of change), timing (onset of change) and tempo (rate of change) between different systems in the body (Beunen & Malina, 2005) and between individuals (Lloyd et al., 2014). Whilst the majority of studies in youth athletes have expressed their results in relation to chronological age, more recent work has focused on the role of maturation (Lloyd et al., 2014). Typically, studies have utilised the timing of peak height velocity (PHV), the maximal rate of growth during the adolescent growth spurt (Malina et al., 2004), as an indicator of maturity, with groupings within studies often classified as pre- (at least one year prior to PHV), circa- (between one year before and one year after PHV) and post-PHV (at least one year after PHV) (Lloyd et al., 2014). Importantly, inter-individual differences in size, maturity status, function, and behaviour among youth of the same chronological age may result in those earlier maturing youth athletes being more dominant and favoured for sport selection (Malina et al., 2019), emphasising the importance of understanding and accounting for maturation when working in youth sport.

Sprint speed develops in a non-linear fashion throughout childhood and adolescence, with both pre-adolescent and adolescent spurt in performance identified in the literature (Meyers et al., 2015; Nagahara et al., 2018; Viru et al., 1999). During childhood, sprint speed is similar for boys and girls, but sex differences become apparent around the initiation of PHV, with girls making comparatively limited gains in speed throughout adolescence compared to boys and achieving a higher proportion of their adult performance earlier than their male counterparts (Papaiakovou et al., 2009). In boys, peak changes in sprint performance have been suggested to be around the period of PHV (Philippaerts et al., 2006); however, more recent literature has suggested significant increase both circa- and post-PHV (Meyers et al., 2015), with those having experienced PHV improving sprint speed up to twice as much as their pre-PHV counterparts when followed longitudinally (Meyers et al., 2016). This pubertal spurt in sprint performance has been suggested to translate into ~0.6 s/year improvements over a 40 m sprint distance (Yagüe & De La Fuente, 1998). Furthermore, it has been suggested that some children may experience a temporary period of 'adolescent awkwardness' in the approach to PHV where rapid increases in limb growth may affect neuromuscular control and coordination. During this time, sprint performance may temporarily decline (Philippaerts et al., 2006) before further improvements in sprint performance may be observed; however, it is not clear how many youth athletes experience this phenomenon.

Although the volume of evidence is more limited, a similar pattern has also been found with multidirectional speed tasks, whereby the development of change-of-direction ability is similar amongst boys and girls in the pre-pubescent period (Eisenmann & Malina, 2003) and peak rate of development of change-of-direction speed occurred around PHV (Philippaerts et al., 2006); however, post-pubertal males and females perform multidirectional tasks significantly faster than their pubertal and pre-pubertal counterparts (Lesinski et al., 2020). It is also noted that around the period of PHV, differences in change-of-direction performances emerge between boys and girls (Vänttinen et al., 2011), with diminished increases in multidirectional performance for girls. Collectively, these studies suggest a maturational effect for multidirectional sprint performance that all practitioners working with youth athletes should be aware of and consider in tandem with the developmental changes in motor control and biomechanical capabilities of youth athletes.

Biomechanical Factors in Multidirectional Speed Performance During Youth

Before exploring the biomechanical aspects of multidirectional speed performance in youth, it is important to acknowledge the role of multidirectional speed and its sub-components as fundamental movement skills (FMSs) (Oliver et al., 2013) and athletic motor skill competencies (AMSCs) (Radnor, Moeskops, et al., 2020). FMSs and AMSCs are considered the building blocks of more specialised movements (Radnor, Moeskops, et al., 2020) and have impact upon physical, social, and psychological development of children and adolescents (Lubans et al., 2010). Furthermore, FMSs and AMSCs are acknowledged as fundamental to long-term athletic development (Lloyd & Oliver, 2012). Based on the evidence that less than 7% of a sample of children achieved mastery in running tasks by nine years of age (Duncan et al., 2022), and only 5% of pre-pubescent children in New Zealand demonstrated mature movement patterns across a range of locomotor FMSs (Cowley et al., 2010), the need to ensure FMSs and AMSCs are developed amongst children and adolescence is clear. Furthermore, with adult gait being largely developed by the age of seven (Malina et al., 2004) and evidence to suggest a barrier to prevent the acquisition of more complex skills if the FMSs are not developed (Gallahue & Donnelly, 2003), it is clear that the early engagement with the development of FMSs are likely to be key foundation for latter success in the application of more complex and dynamic multidirectional speed tasks (Lloyd et al., 2013).

The kinematic and kinetic underpinnings of multidirectional speed performance in adults have been covered in other chapters of this book (please see Chapter 3 for linear and curvilinear speed, Chapter 4 for change of direction, and Chapter 5 for deceleration); however, it is important to acknowledge the application of these to youth athletes and consider the principles which underpin performance at pre-, circa- and post-pubertal stages of maturation. Examining the kinematic and spatiotemporal aspects of sprint performance, it is noted that step length increases throughout childhood and adolescence (Meyers et al., 2015, 2017), with some suggestion that growth in leg length may explain some of these changes (Schepens et al., 1998); however, the total explained variance of anthropometric variables in relation to sprint speed is reported as small (Meyers et al., 2017). When examined over a 21-month period, significant increases in step length were found for both those who remained pre-PHV and those who experienced PHV (~8%); however, no significant associations between changes in step length were found with any anthropometric changes (Meyers et al., 2016). It has been reported that step frequency remains stable with advancing age and advancing maturation (Meyers et al., 2019; Schepens et al., 1998), and in keeping with adult literature, flight time remains stable in this period and unrelated to sprint performance (Meyers et al., 2015). When examining the influence of step length and step frequency, it is interesting to note that boys who are pre-PHV may be more reliant upon step frequency (~58% explained variance of maximal sprint speed) to elicit faster sprint performance compared to those who are post-PHV who may be more step length reliant (~54% explained variance) (Meyers et al., 2017), with the changes in the structure and function of the neuromuscular hormonal systems experienced with advancing maturation proposed to underpin these differences.

From a change-of-direction perspective, there is a paucity of literature that examines the determinants of performance in youth athletes. This lack of examination within the literature is largely attributed to the diversity of the multidirectional movement and associated complexities and variation of approaches to testing and assessment (Lloyd et al., 2013); however, the same challenges are true of studies in adult literature where more evidence exists. As such, it is difficult to provide an evidenced-based understanding of the development of multidirectional speed in youth; however, it is also pertinent to note that the neuromuscular and hormonal changes observed throughout childhood and adolescence may help to explain the naturally observed changes in multidirectional speed. Combined with an understanding of the definition around agility and its sub-components of change of direction (Sheppard & Young, 2006), it is perhaps reasonable to suggest that the aforementioned changes in sprint performance, and the development in leg muscle qualities discussed later in this chapter, provide a foundation for the enhancement in change-of-direction performance. Furthermore, with the highest level of skills development evident in the pre- and circa-PHV windows (~8–14 years of age) (Viru et al., 1999), this provides a fertile opportunity for the development and enhancement of technical skills that could support enhanced multidirectional speed at this time. It is also interesting to note that COD performance may not change from U15 to U18 (Trecroci et al., 2020), perhaps suggesting the importance of the physiological and biomechanical factors associated with COD may diminish with advancing age (Thieschäfer & Büsch, 2022). However, the methods to evaluate COD ability throughout youth have mainly used timing gates and using the time to complete a test does not provide a true measure of COD performance. Additionally, considering the increases in both sprint speed and body mass throughout maturation, as youth mature they will experience natural increases in their speed and momentum (Howard et al., 2016). Intuitively, increased momentum may make deceleration and, therefore, COD tasks more difficult for post-PHV athletes, where a greater braking impulse is required to decelerate the body and subsequently redirect their COM, to perform the appropriate manoeuvre. Cumulatively, this section highlights there is a significant lack of research into COD performance throughout youth and is an area that requires more focus to understand the natural development of multidirectional speed.

The forces associated with sprint performance in youth athletes has received some attention within recent studies. Cross-sectional data have suggested that relative vertical stiffness, relative maximal force, and relative leg stiffness are important determinants of sprint speed, accounting for 96% and 97% of the total explained variance in pre- and post-PHV in male youth (Meyers et al., 2019). Furthermore, when examined longitudinally over 21 months, the same variables accounted for 79% of the total explained variance for those pre-PHV and 83% for those who had experienced PHV (Meyers et al., 2016). Studies of male youth on a non-motorised treadmill have also highlighted importance of horizontal force and horizontal power in sprint performance for those pre- and post-PHV, with the relative importance of vertical force increasing for those circa-PHV on account of the rapid gains in body mass experienced at this time (Rumpf et al., 2013). Furthermore, eccentric (absorption) and concentric (production) strength are reported to be strong predictors of sprint speed in male youth (Rumpf et al., 2013). These characteristics have been shown to develop with advancing maturation (Meyers et al., 2019; Rumpf et al., 2013) and, in turn, reinforce the enhanced stretch-shortening cycle function that are evident with advancing age and maturation (Rumpf et al., 2013). Collectively, these data highlight the importance of force and impulse production and power on youth sprint performance yet also highlight some important considerations related to not only the magnitude but also the orientation of these forces.

The concept of force-velocity-power profiling of sprint performance has gained recognition within the literature (see Morin and Samozino [2016] for a review of concepts), with the acknowledgement that in adult populations, horizontal power, and the ability to orient high amounts of force in the horizontal direction are important determinants of sprint performance (Morin et al., 2011). Following this methodology, it has been suggested that increases in speed in boys may result from increases in horizontal power, and when separated into maturational status, those post-PHV demonstrated a greater ability to generate force at higher velocity and also orient high magnitudes of force horizontally (Edwards et al., 2021). Furthermore, a detailed force-plate analysis of sprint kinetics in pre-PHV boys and girls indicated that enhanced sprint performance between groups may be attributed largely to higher antero-posterior forces and shorter ground contacts, likely due to enhanced stretch-shortening cycle function (Colyer et al., 2020). Collectively, these studies further highlight the importance of the magnitude and orientation of force for faster sprint performance but also the need for rapid expression of these forces during brief periods of ground contact.

Once more, the data related to aspects of multidirectional speed performance in youth athletes is limited, with no studies directly exploring the kinetic parameters of performance in youth, nor how these characteristics change with age or maturation. Clearly, there are some aspects of performance, such as the enhancements in eccentric strength and power (Rumpf et al., 2015), that may support the development of deceleration abilities and improvements in the ability of youth athletes to orient forces (Colyer et al., 2020) that may support the reorientation of forces during change-of-direction manoeuvres (McBurnie, Harper, et al., 2022); however, direct evidence to support this is lacking at this time should be an area that is explored in future research.

Physiological Underpinnings of Multidirectional Speed

All human movement occurs as a result of an action potential being transmitted from the central nervous system to the muscles. This action potential stimulates internal force production that is subsequently transferred along the tendon resulting in the movement of bone. Thus, the role of maturation in alterations to the nervous system, as well as the muscle and tendon, and how this influences force production and, consequently, multidirectional speed is important to understand.

During childhood, both girls and boys will experience rapid developments in their central nervous systems (CNS), and it is during this stage of development that the greatest potential for skill acquisition exists due to the heightened neural plasticity commensurate with this age group (Casey et al., 2005). Improvements in speed during childhood are mainly driven by development of the neural system (Malina et al., 2004). Children will experience natural improvements in their ability to recruit or utilise the high threshold type II motor units, improving their force producing capabilities (Dotan et al., 2012). Muscle activation during the 100 ms preceding ground contact is termed pre-activation, and as children mature, they produce greater levels of pre-activation (Lloyd et al., 2012). While this has yet to be explored directly in sprinting, increased CNS development during childhood may explain the greater reliance on step frequency during the pre-pubertal period, where research has suggested that maximal sprint performance in pre-pubertal boys is underpinned more by step frequency rather than step length (Meyers et al., 2017) and may in turn support the notion of a technical focus in multidirectional speed tasks (Lloyd et al., 2013) at the pre-pubertal stage.

As children experience maturation and reach PHV, there is approximately a tenfold increase in testosterone production in boys (Viru et al., 1999). The increases in circulating androgens result in large structural and architectural changes during this time, and these may have an influence on multidirectional speed performance. As females do not experience the increase in testosterone, it is during this period that sex differences in speed (Ramos et al., 1998) and agility performance (Vänttinen et al., 2011) become apparent.

Skeletal muscle architecture refers to the arrangement of muscle fibres and typically comprises architectural variables such as muscle thickness, pennation angle, and fascicle length (Franchi et al., 2018). Muscle architecture has been described as a primary determinant of muscle function, and the architectural arrangement of fibres within the muscle is important because it has implications for the fascicle's *force-velocity* and *force-length* characteristics (Azizi et al., 2008; Lieber & Ward, 2011).

Recent research investigating the influence of maturation on muscle architecture variables has identified that muscle thickness, pennation angle, and fascicle length of the gastrocnemius medialis (GM) and vastus lateralis (VL) all increase with maturation, except for GM fascicle length (Radnor, Oliver, et al., 2020). More specifically, the muscle thickness of GM and VL seem to increase throughout maturation, while the pennation angle of the GM is stable until after the adolescent growth spurt, yet GM fascicle length does not change throughout maturation (Radnor, Oliver, et al., 2020). VL pennation angle and fascicle length have a steady change throughout maturation, where research has identified differences between pre- and post-PHV, but neither group differed from circa-PHV (Radnor, Oliver, et al., 2020). Furthermore, the development of the tendon throughout childhood and adolescence is associated with adaptations to the internal properties in addition to changes in length and cross-sectional area (Waugh et al., 2012). Alterations to these properties lead to increases in tendon stiffness as children experience maturation and approach adulthood, influencing rapid force production by affecting the time lag (i.e. electromechanical delay) between muscle activation and muscle force production (Waugh et al., 2013), and may in part explain the observed changes in stiffness and the influence this has upon sprint performances.

Considering that muscle size is a major predictor of force output in both adults and children (Jones et al., 2008; Tonson et al., 2008), increases in muscle thickness are a significant factor contributing to the improved capacity to produce force as children experience biological maturation and can lead to greater sprint performances (Radnor et al., 2022). Research has identified that muscle thickness of the VL can predict 26.3% of the variance in maximal sprint speed in boys between the ages of 11 and 17 years (Radnor et al., 2022). Previous research has identified that relative peak force is an important determinant of sprint speed in young boys, and the increase in muscle thickness would improve the force producing capabilities of boys as they experience maturation. Considering that post-PHV boys are more reliant on stride length (Meyers et al., 2017), and stride length is underpinned by force production (Weyand et al., 2000), the development of speed during adolescence may be driven by both structural and neural factors that increase force production.

While muscle thickness plays a role in the improvement in multidirectional speed throughout maturation, other muscle and tendon factors may also be important. Maximal sprint speed has been shown to be underpinned by fascicle length of the VL in pre-pubertal and post-pubertal boys (Radnor et al., 2022). In adults, fascicle length has been found to be a positive predictor of rate of force development (RFD), albeit during a countermovement jump (Philippaerts et al., 2006). Similarly, tendon stiffness has a positive correlation with RFD during maximal effort tasks

(Waugh et al., 2013). Considering that ground contact times during sprinting range between 0.137 and 0.147 s for boys (Meyers et al., 2017), there is a need for rapid force production for successful sprint performance. Longer fascicles and stiffer tendons may have a positive influence on RFD, which may ultimately enhance sprinting performance by enhancing the rate of force production in short windows of time available.

There has been little research investigating the underpinning mechanisms of improvements in change-of-direction speed in youth, but essentially, an athlete's physical capacity (i.e. neuromuscular control, rapid force production, strength, and muscle activation) is considered highly important during COD tasks (McBurnie, Harper, et al., 2022). Therefore, the force-producing capacities that develop throughout maturation as a result of the structure (Radnor et al., 2022), size (O'Brien et al., 2010), activation patterns (Dotan et al., 2012), and function (Waugh et al., 2012) of the neuromuscular system are likely driving the COD performance improvements reported as youth mature. High levels of eccentric, isometric, and concentric strength, produced during short ground contact times, are required for the braking, plant, and propulsive phases, respectively (Harper et al., 2022; Spiteri et al., 2014). Lower-limb-muscle thickness and pennation angle have been shown to be correlated with braking and propulsive impulse during maximal rebound jumps in boys (Radnor, Oliver, et al., 2021); however, this has not been studied in COD tasks but may explain the role of muscle architecture in the development of COD ability in youth.

The underpinning adaptations to the neural and structural systems associated with growth and maturation may influence the trainability of speed during childhood. Recent research has shown that children and adolescents may respond differently to specific types of resistance training in terms of speed development (Lloyd, Radnor, et al., 2016; Radnor et al., 2017; Rumpf et al., 2012). Lloyd and colleagues (2016) showed that in response to a short-term resistance training intervention, plyometric training elicited the greatest gains in markers of sprint performance in children who were pre-PHV, whereas combined strength and plyometric training was the most effective in eliciting change in speed for boys who were post-PHV. On an individual response basis, Radnor et al. (2017) concluded that, irrespective of maturation, combined strength and plyometric training may serve as the most potent training stimulus for individuals to make short-term improvements in jump and sprint performance. Considering that pre-pubertal children experience a natural increase in neural coordination and central nervous system maturation during childhood, the high neural demand during plyometric and sprint training may provide an augmented training response, termed 'synergistic adaptation' (Lloyd, Radnor, et al., 2016). Similarly, as post-pubertal children experience increases in testosterone and natural morphological changes that facilitate force generation, the combination of plyometric and strength training may result in a more potent maturity-related training stimulus (Lloyd, Radnor, et al., 2016).

Applied Training Approaches

The development of multidirectional speed throughout childhood is a key factor contributing to competitive success in youth populations (Gissis et al., 2006). As identified earlier in this chapter, the development of multidirectional speed is underpinned by many complex physiological and biomechanical interactions. Therefore, no single variable can be identified to be responsible for the natural improvement in multidirectional speed throughout maturation or the enhanced training effect at different periods of childhood and adolescence (Lloyd et al., 2013). Coaches and practitioners need to ensure a holistic approach is taken when emphasising speed development within any long-term athletic development program for their athletes. It is important to understand how different training modalities and approaches interact with maturity and the competency of the athlete to ensure the stimulus matches the desired training response (Cahill et al., 2020).

Multidirectional speed training can be categorised into both specific and non-specific modes of training (Lesinski et al., 2016; Moran et al., 2017). Specific modalities of training typically (e.g. coordinative overload) occur in a horizontal plane of motion and emulate the actions that occur when linear or multidirectional speed is expressed during competition. Sprint- and COD-specific approaches generally emphasise the technical competence of the action (e.g. sprint mechanics) or adapted forms of sprinting (e.g. resisted or assisted). Non-specific training modalities (i.e. traditional overload) relate more to traditional movements, such as plyometrics and resistance training performed primarily in a vertical plane of motion. Such training methods have been shown to transfer to gains in speed due to improvements in relative vertical force and stiffness (Behringer et al., 2010; Lesinski et al., 2016; Meyers et al., 2019).

Given the complexity and highly variable timing of physiological changes that occur during adolescence, it is not uncommon for youth athletes to be categorised by biological age utilising a maturity offset, which has been viewed as a more accurate way to account for adaptations within biological maturation than chronological age alone (Till & Jones, 2015). As mentioned earlier, the adaption to training can be heavily influenced by the stage of maturation in which the athlete is currently experiencing (Lloyd et al., 2016). Therefore, it seems prudent that planned training should be influenced by the biological age of young athletes to ensure the greatest adaptation, and the purpose for the remainder of this chapter is to identify best practices of training prescription for multidirectional speed development across pre-, circa-, and post-PHV stages of maturation. It is important to note, coaches and practitioners should be cognisant of the implications training age and competency have on their individual athletes when assessing, interpreting, and prescribing training within a long-term athlete development framework. Exercise prescription should not solely be prescribed by stages of biological maturation, as technical proficiency and training age are the most important factors, but should be considered to determine the effectiveness of certain training stimulus and the rate of adaptation.

Pre-peak Height Velocity

As identified earlier in the chapter, natural gains in speed have been shown to be nonlinear in young athletes with no difference in sprint ability identified between immature boys or girls during the initial spurt in sprint performance (Malina et al., 2004). The first spurt in sprint performance occurs during pre-PHV and is largely attributed to the rapid development of the CNS and heightened neural plasticity of the brain during childhood (Viru et al., 1999). Although this neural adaptation has a positive impact on multidirectional speed performance, coaches and practitioners should not solely concentrate on sprint-/COD-specific training modalities to enhance the long-term development of the athlete. This period should place specific emphasis on non-sprint-specific modes of training that develop the building blocks of multidirectional speed training to allow for greater rates of adaptation later in adolescence. Indeed, it has been suggested that the importance of physical factors associated with COD are more prevalent in the pre-pubertal phase (Thieschäfer & Büsch, 2022), highlighting the importance of this phase in the building of robust physical foundations.

Planned training sessions should be age-appropriate, engaging, and low-structured to encourage an exploratory nature of movement in all planes of motion (Lloyd & Oliver, 2012).

Development of AMSCs should transcend throughout each aspect of the training session to ensure a holistic approach to long-term athlete development (Radnor, Moeskops, et al., 2020). These can include less-structured methods, such as animal shapes, playground games, and obstacle courses, as well as more structured approaches. The warm-up is a great time to include a number of the unstructured methods and should consist of whole-body preparatory movements that allow the athlete to express themselves in a multitude of ways facilitating a vast array of AMSCs. Traditional non-specific forms of training, such as plyometrics and resistance training, have shown positive adaptations to sprint speed in pre-PHV athletes (Behringer et al., 2011; Lloyd, Radnor, et al., 2016; Rumpf et al., 2012). Plyometric training has been shown to yield greater improvements in improving speed for less immature athletes as compared to more mature adolescents (Behm et al., 2017; Lloyd, Radnor, et al., 2016). These forms of non-specific speed training can be most effective when incorporated regularly within a periodised plan to promote the transfer of gains in speed performance and improve overall athletic ability (i.e. stiffness, RFD production). As mentioned earlier, these methods can be incorporated in a less structured, more enjoyable way for pre-PHV children, with playground games, such as 'What's the time Mr Wolf?' being adapted to incorporate plyometric exercises.

Specific forms of multidirectional speed training can be incorporated during pre-PHV but should not be implemented in a strict high-structured nature, with the emphasis on specific load and intensity. Rumpf and colleagues (2015) reported differing acute and longitudinal responses to resisted sled towing between pre- and post-PHV athletes. Pre-PHV athletes showed no significant improvement in speed following a six-week sled-towing training intervention compared to post-PHV athletes (Rumpf et al., 2015). Coaches are encouraged to allow young athletes to express speed at high velocities through maximal free sprinting and open game-based play. In addition to free sprinting, coaches can introduce athletes to varied sprint-specific stimulus' such as resisted (e.g. parachutes, sleds, harness) and assisted sprint modalities (e.g. over-speed tow ropes, bungee cords, motorised devices). Such forms of constraint-based training can be used to reinforce and encourage certain aspects of proper sprint technique in addition to providing a new stimulus and resistance. For example, a coach can prescribe a push sled to apply a horizontal resistive load while emphasising technical aspects, such as maintaining a proper forward lean during acceleration or a waist harness to ensure full hip extension at higher velocities. Specific to change of direction, coaches can utilise both closed and open forms of training to reinforce technical competence and reactionary skills, respectively, in a fun and engaging manner. The prescription of training should have a focus not on volume or intensity but rather on varied stimuli, technical reinforcement, proper technique, and movement quality.

Circa-/Post-peak Height Velocity

The second spurt in speed performance typically occurs at the onset of sexual maturation (Viru et al., 1999). Divergent development rates in sprint performance have been observed between boys and girls during this period due to the differences in hormone level increases (Papaiakovou et al., 2009). Boys develop an improved multidirectional speed performance more rapidly due to increased testosterone levels, whereas girls may experience more disadvantageous adaptations due to increased oestrogen levels, causing increases in fat mass accumulation and reduced relative strength (Papaiakovou et al., 2009; Vänttinen et al., 2011). This period of maturation may increase natural gains in speed for boys due to the ability to apply greater relative propulsive forces, thus impulse and change in momentum; however, coaches and practitioners should also be aware that the period around PHV has been associated with a significantly higher risk of injury in youth athletes compared with pre- and post-PHV players (Johnson et al., 2020; Read et al., 2018; van der Sluis et al., 2014). Recent research has identified that growth-related injuries follow a distal to proximal pattern, with Sever's disease more prevalent in the less mature players, with Osgood-Schlatter disease common in the pre- and circa-PHV group, and injuries to the hip and spine (e.g. spondylolysis) more frequently at the post-PHV stage (Monasterio et al., 2021). It is important that coaches understand the implications of this, as there is a large mechanical load during COD tasks that may need to be managed or altered for any athletes suffering from these growth-related injuries.

Training sessions planned during this critical period should have an increased level of structure in comparison to pre-PHV athletes to ensure volume and intensity is more closely monitored from week to week and also individualised based upon the needs of specific athletes who may experience reduced coordination or more pronounced adolescent awkwardness (Davies & Rose, 2000). In these situations, the regression and reinforcement of AMSCs may help youth athletes to regain physical confidence and competence and mitigate risks associated with managing rapid growth in stature and mass. The frequency of training sessions may also need to be reduced to allow for ample recovery time and account for concurrent natural growth of the body and competitive sport schedule during the early years of adolescence (Pfirrmann et al., 2016).

As youth athletes progress through adolescence into post-PHV, natural gains in speed tend to diminish due to physical maturation, and increases in speed are more dependent on specific training modalities and the stimulus employed (Meyers et al., 2015). Both non-specific and specific forms of training should increase in structure across a periodised plan with a specific focus being placed on targeting volumes and intensities. Training stimulus' at higher intensities (80–89% of 1 RM) for youth athletes have been shown to be most effective in transference of non-specific training to gains in speed (Lesinski et al., 2016). Irrespective of the stage of maturation combined training modalities of speed, plyometrics, and resistance training have also been shown to yield greater transference to gains in speed (Radnor et al., 2017), and thus, a mixed multicomponent training programme is advocated for the development of multidirectional speed in youth athletes.

Models of Multidirectional Speed

It is clear from the evidenced presented through this chapter that whilst the development and trainability of multidirectional speed in youth athletes is a complex, multifaceted challenge, it is also apparent that there are many forms of training that might support the development of multidirectional speed performance. In line with this philosophy and evidence, Lloyd and colleagues (2013) proposed a model for the development of agility training in youth athletes (Figure 17.1). In this model, they reference the need for three key components of training across all stages of maturation. These components included FMSs/AMSCs as a foundation of the physiological and biomechanical determinants of performance, as well as the pre-planned COD tasks and exposure to open, reactive agility environments. It is important to note that whilst all stages of maturation are suggested to be exposed to all components of the model, the relative proportions of time devoted to each characteristic adapts based upon the development needs aligned to the maturational group. It is again worth reinforcing the higher percentage of time spent at the FMS/AMSC tasks for those pre-pubertal, ensuring that the physical foundations and movement competencies are achieved at a time where both neural developments peak, and which the association between physical characteristics and multidirectional speed performance remains strong (Thieschäfer &

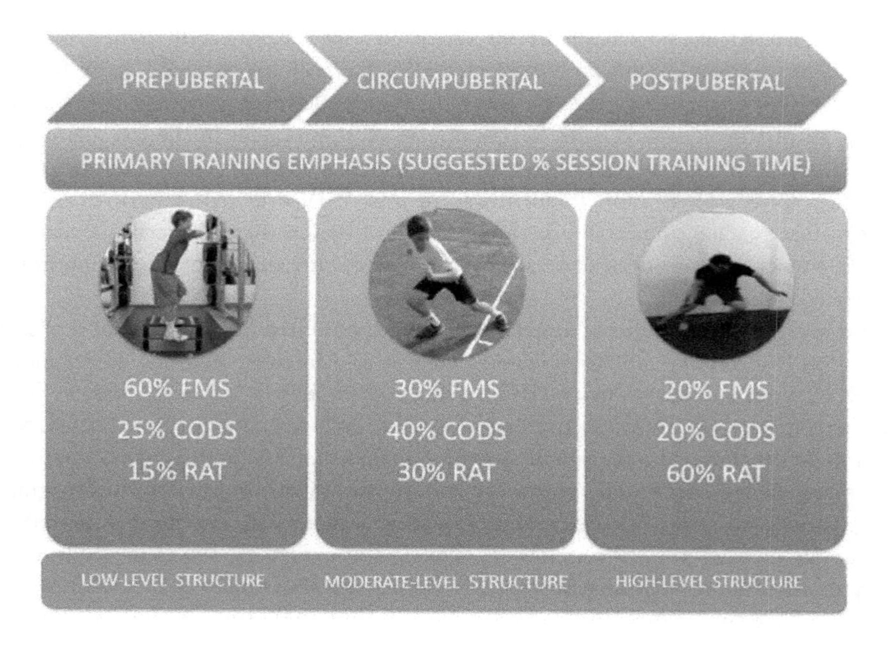

FIGURE 17.1 Primary training focus for pre-, circa-, and post-pubertal children (from Lloyd et al., 2013 with permission).

Büsch, 2022). Furthermore, whilst the circa- and post-pubertal stages move toward less focus on the FMSs/AMSCs, it is important that these characteristics are not removed entirely to ensure continual reinforcement and assist in the management growth related motor control challenges. The utilisation of increased open, reactive training methods, also ensure that the importance of visual/perceptive factors is acknowledged. Research acknowledges the increasing importance of perceptual and cognitive factors with advancing age (Thieschäfer & Büsch, 2022) and also acknowledge that pre-planned change-of-direction task and those open, reactive agility task may be viewed as independent activities in adult populations (Young et al., 2015). To that end, McBurnie, Parr, et al. (2022) have produced a framework (Figure 17.2) which serves as a useful tool for practitioners to consider the development of multidirectional speed, integrating an understanding of training age, training load, growth and maturation, and the need to develop progressive training strategies aligned to these key principles. The following section provides some illustrative examples of how these models may be integrated into training sessions for children who are pre- and post-PHV.

Sample Training Programme

Both the warm-up and main phase of training for multidirectional speed in young athletes should follow a progressive training outline, allowing the coach to increase the structured nature of the training as they progress through adolescence. The authors propose coaches follow the RAMP principle (raise, activate, mobilise, and potentiate) for warm-ups (Jeffreys, 2019) and a whole-part-whole approach to the main phase of multidirectional speed development. This can be segmented into 'express, coach, and compete' in which the athlete is encouraged to *express* maximal

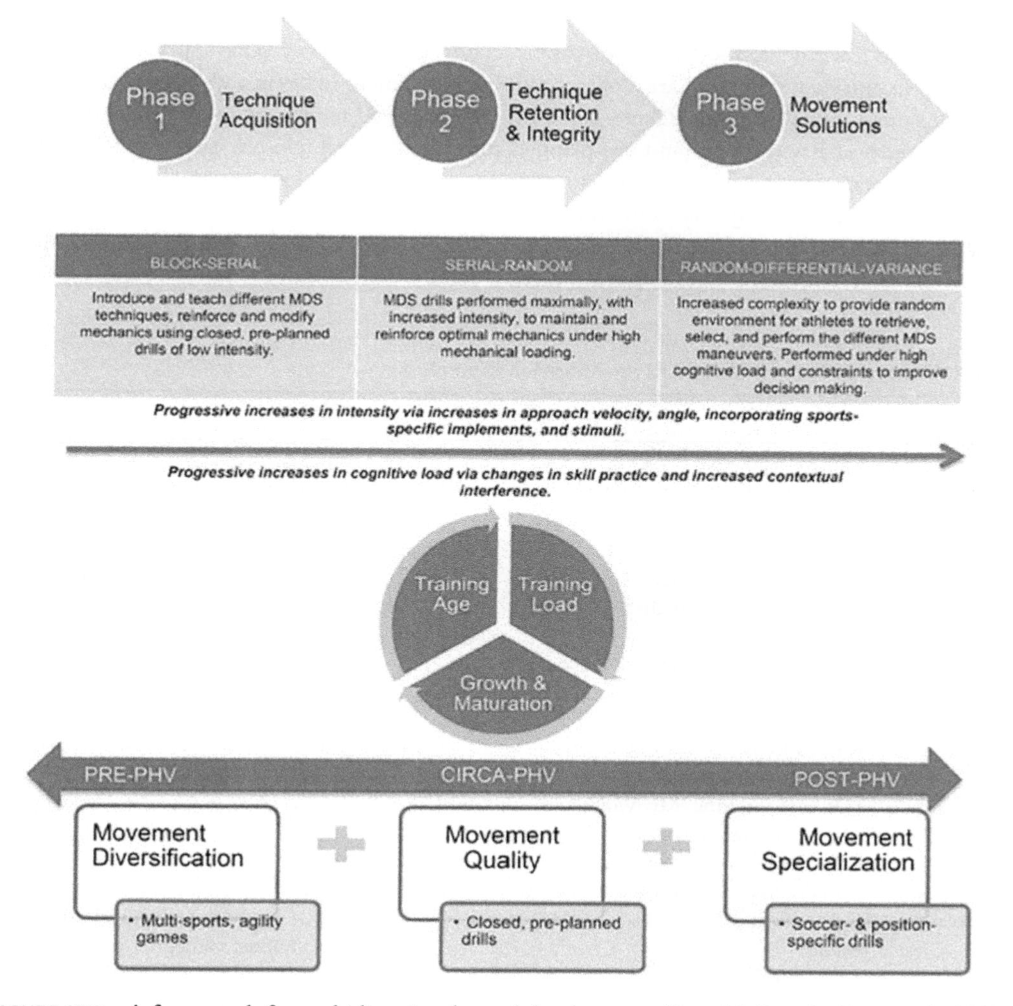

FIGURE 17.2 A framework for multidirectional speed development (from McBurnie, Parr, et al., 2022 with permission).

effort of the movement, allowing the athlete to be exposed to maximal effort, while giving the coach an opportunity to observe and then *coach* a specific aspect to reinforce age-appropriate technical competency activities. Lastly, the athlete can again express maximal effort in a competitive (*compete*) and engaging environment after coach feedback has been provided.

Pre-peak Height Velocity Training Programme

Early adolescent athletes should have a low to moderate overall structure with continued variety throughout each phase of training. RAMP movements should be incorporated into open- and closed-chain fun activities in a challenging nature that involve cognitive decision-making (Radnor, Moeskops, et al., 2020). Activities in the main phase of training utilising the 'express, teach, and compete' progression will ensure young athletes are exposed to both maximal effort repetitions and also a segmented section emphasising technical competency. This approach will allow the coach to emphasise different areas of technique improvement utilising a wide array of modalities to ensure a varied stimulus. Game-based fun activities and technique focus points that vary between reaction-based (open) and pre-planned-movement-based (closed) can be used to allow athletes compete against each other (i.e. races and team relays) in a low-structured fun environment. At this stage, the majority of the session will be focused on AMSC/FMS development and a focus on COD technique. Reactive agility games will be used, but this will form only a small part of the plan. An example session is outlined in Table 17.1.

TABLE 17.1 Pre-PHV Multidirectional Speed Session Example

	Exercise	*Note*
R A M P	Animal shapes • Bear crawl • Crab walks • Flamingo walks Partner stability games • SL balance with high-5 • Mirror drills Low-level plyometrics • Hop + stick • Lateral jumps • Pogo hops Game-based potentiation • What's the time, Mr. Wolf? with conditions (i.e. bilateral vs unilateral stance stop) • Functional movement obstacle course integrating multidirectional movement	Exercises during the RAMP warm-up should focus on teaching the AMSCs/FMSs that underpin multidirectional speed, as well as prepare them for the session.
Express	Game-based in small space for MD speed • Tag • Stuck in the mud • Rock-paper-scissor-sprint!	The use of games will allow children to express their natural gait and COD pattern. Coaches can screen the movement during these drills.
Teach	Drills focused on specific patterns/errors AMSC development *Structured* • Squat, single-leg, and hinge pattern • Lateral shuffle • Cutting movements • Acceleration mechanics – sled push *Unstructured* • Simon says o Focus on AMSCs, stability, and COD technique	As with the warm-up, a significant portion of the main session should focus on AMSC/FMS development, as well as introducing key concept for CODs.
Compete	Acceleration and COD races • 10 m races – different start positions (e.g. lying facedown, facing the other way) • Include different change-of-direction patterns (e.g. 90° cut)	Including competition to this aspect will allow children to achieve appropriate speeds, but using constraints will assist the children with being in the correct patterns.

TABLE 17.2 Post-PHV Multidirectional Speed Session Example

	Exercise	*Note*
R **A** **M** **P**	Activation and mobilisation of key muscles and joints • Glute bridge • Hamstring switches • Mini-band walks • Squat to stand • Lunge complex • Spiderman Partner stability games • SL balance with dowel tug-of-war • Mirror drills Low-level plyometrics • Lateral jump + stick • Pogo hops • Partner perturbations Technique-focused potentiation • 2 m lateral shuffle into linear sprint • Max acceleration into 180° turn	Exercises during the RAMP warm-up should focus on preparing the athlete for the session with key activation and mobilisation exercises. Stability games can be included to prepare the athlete for CODs and the manipulation of centre of mass and base of support. Plyometrics and technical drills can be used to potentiate the athlete for the session.
Express	Game-based in small space for MD speed • Table football Sprints o Three defenders spaced 5 m apart (one in front of the other) and can only move laterally. Attackers need to accelerate and manipulate themselves through all three defenders without getting tagged. • Bulldog!	The use of games will allow youth to react to appropriate stimulus while presenting their natural COD patterns. Coaches can screen the movement during these drills.
Teach	Drills focused on specific patterns/errors Acceleration • Sled push • Resisted sprints • Bounds Initiation • Various starting positions and speeds, learning to move from submaximal into maximal (e.g. crossover step, 180° turn) CODs • Specific drills focused on athletes needs/requirements of the sport o Forward cut o Backward cut o 180° turn	During this element of the session, coaches can work on specific drills for individual errors that athletes may demonstrate. This will depend on athletes' ability, sport, gender, and so on.
Compete	Acceleration and COD races • Acceleration races – different start positions (e.g. lying facedown, facing the other way) • Reactive agility games – capture the flag, one-on-one defend, bulldog	Including competition to this aspect will allow youth to achieve appropriate speeds, but using constraints will assist them with being in the correct patterns.

Post-peak Height Velocity Training Programme

Adolescent athletes should have an increased structure to the training outline which can further segment the RAMP principles into more specific preparatory activities. The main phase of training should still follow the 'express, teach, and compete' progression but allow for a more structured nature, further breaking the skills down into linear and multidirectional skill-based activities in both open and closed formats. Coaches can provide more specific cues to enhance technical competency in different aspects of MD speed (i.e. linear acceleration, crossover, or push to move multidirectional speed). Timing gates can be used in the compete segment of training to encourage intrinsic motivation and to monitor progress over time. An example session is outlined in Table 17.2.

Summary

The development of multidirectional speed throughout childhood and adolescence is impacted by the interaction of age, growth, and maturation, presenting practitioners working in youth strength and conditioning with a complex multifaceted challenge to develop this with youth athletes. It is important for practitioners to understand the natural development of characteristics that underpin multidirectional speed and the evidence base associated with the training methods that might be deployed at different stage of maturation. Whilst the evidence suggests that main forms of training can be effective for the development of multidirectional speed in youth, the model discussed within this chapter provides a framework for practitioners to utilise a range of training approaches whilst adapting the proportions of time/effort devoted to each aspect of training based upon the development needs of the different stage of maturation.

References

Arruda, A. F. S., Carling, C., Zanetti, V., Aoki, M. S., Coutts, A. J., & Moreira, A. (2015). Effects of a Very Congested Match Schedule on Body-Load Impacts, Accelerations, and Running Measures in Youth Soccer Players. *International Journal of Sports Physiology and Performance*, *10*(2), 248–252. https://doi.org/10.1123/ijspp.2014-0148

Azizi, E., Brainerd, E. L., & Roberts, T. J. (2008). Variable Gearing in Pennate Muscles. *Proceedings of the National Academy of Sciences*, *105*(5), 1745–1750. https://doi.org/10.1073/pnas.0709212105

Behm, D. G., Young, J. D., Whitten, J. H. D., Reid, J. C., Quigley, P. J., Low, J., Li, Y., Lima, C. D., Hodgson, D. D., Chaouachi, A., Prieske, O., & Granacher, U. (2017). Effectiveness of Traditional Strength vs. Power Training on Muscle Strength, Power and Speed with Youth: A Systematic Review and Meta-Analysis. *Frontiers in Physiology*, *8*, 423. https://doi.org/10.3389/fphys.2017.00423

Behringer, M., Matthews, M., & Mester, J. (2011). Effects of Strength Training on Motor Performance Skills in Children and Adolescents: A Meta-Analysis. *Paediatric Exercises Science*, *23*, 186–206.

Behringer, M., vom Heede, A., Yue, Z., & Mester, J. (2010). Effects of Resistance Training in Children and Adolescents: A Meta-analysis. *Pediatrics*, *126*(5), e1199–e1210. https://doi.org/10.1542/peds.2010-0445

Beunen, G. P., & Malina, R. M. (2005). Growth and Biologic Maturation: Relevance to Athletic Performance. In O. Bar-Or & H. Hebestreit (Eds.), *The Child and Adolescent Athlete* (pp. 3–17). Blackwell Publishing.

Buchheit, M., Simpson, B. M., Peltola, E., & Mendez-Villanueva, A. (2012). Assessing Maximal Sprinting Speed in Highly Trained Young Soccer Players. *International Journal of Sports Physiology and Performance*, 7(1), 76–78. https://doi.org/10.1123/ijspp.7.1.76

Cahill, M. J., Cronin, J. B., Oliver, J. L., Clark, K. P., Lloyd, R. S., & Cross, M. R. (2020). Resisted Sled Training for Young Athletes: When to Push and Pull. *Strength & Conditioning Journal*, *42*(6), 91–99. https://doi.org/10.1519/SSC.0000000000000555

Casey, B., Tottenham, N., Liston, C., & Durston, S. (2005). Imaging the Developing Brain: What Have We Learned about Cognitive Development? *Trends in Cognitive Sciences*, *9*(3), 104–110. https://doi.org/10.1016/j.tics.2005.01.011

Colyer, S. L., Nagahara, R., Takai, Y., & Salo, A. I. T. (2020). The Effect of Biological Maturity Status on Ground Reaction Force Production during Sprinting. *Scandinavian Journal of Medicine & Science in Sports*, *30*(8), 1387–1397. https://doi.org/10.1111/sms.13680

Cowley, V., Hamlin, M. J., Grimley, M., Hargreaves, J. M., & Price, C. (2010). Children's Fundamental Movement Skills: Are Our Children Ready to Play? *British Journal of Sports Medicine*, *44*(Suppl_1), i11–i12. https://doi.org/10.1136/bjsm.2010.078725.34

Davies, P., & Rose, J. (2000). Motor Skills of Typically Developing Adolescents. *Physical & Occupational Therapy In Pediatrics*, *20*(1), 19–42. https://doi.org/10.1300/J006v20n01_03

Dotan, R., Mitchell, C., Cohen, R., Klentrou, P., Gabriel, D., & Falk, B. (2012). Child – Adult Differences in Muscle Activation – A Review. *Pediatric Exercise Science*, *24*(1), 2–21. https://doi.org/10.1123/pes.24.1.2

Duncan, M. J., Foweather, L., Bardid, F., Barnett, A. L., Rudd, J., O'Brien, W., Foulkes, J. D., Roscoe, C., Issartel, J., Stratton, G., & Clark, C. C. T. (2022). Motor Competence among Children in the United Kingdom and Ireland: An Expert Statement on Behalf of the International Motor Development Research Consortium. *Journal of Motor Learning and Development*, *10*(1), 7–26. https://doi.org/10.1123/jmld.2021-0047

Edwards, T., Weakley, J., Banyard, H. G., Cripps, A., Piggott, B., Haff, G. G., & Joyce, C. (2021). Influence of Age and Maturation Status on Sprint Acceleration Characteristics in Junior Australian Football. *Journal of Sports Sciences*, *39*(14), 1585–1593. https://doi.org/10.1080/02640414.2021.1886699

Eisenmann, J., & Malina, R. (2003). Age- and Sex-associated Variation in Neuromuscular Capacities of Adolescent Distance Runners. *Journal of Sports Sciences*, *21*(7), 551–557. https://doi.org/10.1080/0264041031000101845

Emmonds, S., Till, K., Jones, B., Mellis, M., & Pears, M. (2016). Anthropometric, Speed and Endurance Characteristics of English Academy Soccer Players: Do They Influence Obtaining a Professional Contract at 18 Years of Age? *International Journal of Sports Science & Coaching*, *11*(2), 212–218. https://doi.org/10.1177/1747954116637154

Franchi, M. V., Raiteri, B. J., Longo, S., Sinha, S., Narici, M. V., & Csapo, R. (2018). Muscle Architecture Assessment: Strengths, Shortcomings and New Frontiers of in Vivo Imaging Techniques. *Ultrasound in Medicine & Biology*, *44*(12), 2492–2504. https://doi.org/10.1016/j.ultrasmedbio.2018.07.010

Galé-Ansodi, C., Castellano, J., & Usabiaga, O. (2016). Effects of Different Surfaces in Time-motion Characteristics in Youth Elite Tennis Players. *International Journal of Performance Analysis in Sport*, *16*(3), 860–870. https://doi.org/10.1080/24748668.2016.11868934

Gallahue, D., & Donnelly, F. (2003). *Development of Physical Education for All Children* (4th ed.). Human Kinetics.

Gissis, I., Papadopoulos, C., Kalapotharakos, V. I., Sotiropoulos, A., Komsis, G., & Manolopoulos, E. (2006). Strength and Speed Characteristics of Elite, Subelite, and Recreational Young Soccer Players. *Research in Sports Medicine*, *14*(3), 205–214. https://doi.org/10.1080/15438620600854769

Harper, D. J., Carling, C., & Kiely, J. (2019). High-Intensity Acceleration and Deceleration Demands in Elite Team Sports Competitive Match Play: A Systematic Review and Meta-Analysis of Observational Studies. *Sports Medicine*, *49*(12), 1923–1947. https://doi.org/10.1007/s40279-019-01170-1

Harper, D. J., McBurnie, A. J., Dos'Santos, T., Eriksrud, O., Evans, M., Cohen, D. D., Rhodes, D., Carling, C., & Kiely, J. (2022). Biomechanical and Neuromuscular Performance Requirements of Horizontal Deceleration: A Review with Implications for Random Intermittent Multi-Directional Sports. *Sports Medicine*. https://doi.org/10.1007/s40279-022-01693-0

Howard, S. M. A., Cumming, S. P., Atkinson, M., & Malina, R. M. (2016). Biological Maturity-associated Variance in Peak Power Output and Momentum in Academy Rugby Union Players. *European Journal of Sport Science*, *16*(8), 972–980. https://doi.org/10.1080/17461391.2016.1205144

Jeffreys, I. (2019). The Warm-up: A Behavioral Solution to the Challenge of Initiating a Long-Term Athlete Development Program. *Strength & Conditioning Journal*, *41*(2), 52–56. https://doi.org/10.1519/SSC.0000000000000466

Johnson, D. M., Williams, S., Bradley, B., Sayer, S., Murray Fisher, J., & Cumming, S. P. (2020). Growing Pains: Maturity Associated Variation in Inury Risk in Academy Football. *European Journal of Sport Science, 20*(4), 544–552. https://doi.org/10.1080/17461391.2019.1633416

Jones, E. J., Bishop, P. A., Woods, A. K., & Green, J. M. (2008). Cross-Sectional Area and Muscular Strength: A Brief Review. *Sports Medicine, 38*(12), 987–994. https://doi.org/10.2165/00007256-200838120-00003

Lesinski, M., Herz, M., Schmelcher, A., & Granacher, U. (2020). Effects of Resistance Training on Physical Fitness in Healthy Children and Adolescents: An Umbrella Review. *Sports Medicine, 50*(11), 1901–1928. https://doi.org/10.1007/s40279-020-01327-3

Lesinski, M., Prieske, O., & Granacher, U. (2016). Effects and Dose–response Relationships of Resistance Training on Physical Performance in Youth Athletes: A Systematic Review and Meta-analysis. *British Journal of Sports Medicine, 50*(13), 781–795. https://doi.org/10.1136/bjsports-2015-095497

Lieber, R. L., & Ward, S. R. (2011). Skeletal Muscle Design to Meet Functional Demands. *Philosophical Transactions of the Royal Society B: Biological Sciences, 366*(1570), 1466–1476. https://doi.org/10.1098/rstb.2010.0316

Lloyd, R. S., Cronin, J. B., Faigenbaum, A. D., Haff, G. G., Howard, R., Kraemer, W. J., Micheli, L. J., Myer, G. D., & Oliver, J. L. (2016). National Strength and Conditioning Association Position Statement on Long-Term Athletic Development. *Journal of Strength and Conditioning Research, 30*(6), 1491–1509. https://doi.org/10.1519/JSC.0000000000001387

Lloyd, R. S., & Oliver, J. L. (2012). The Youth Physical Development Model: A New Approach to Long-Term Athletic Development. *Strength and Conditioning Journal*, 12.

Lloyd, R. S., Oliver, J. L., Faigenbaum, A. D., Myer, G. D., & De Ste Croix, M. B. A. (2014). Chronological Age vs. Biological Maturation: Implications for Exercise Programming in Youth. *Journal of Strength and Conditioning Research, 28*(5), 1454–1464. https://doi.org/10.1519/JSC.0000000000000391

Lloyd, R. S., Oliver, J. L., Hughes, M. G., & Williams, C. A. (2012). Age-related Differences in the Neural Regulation of Stretch–shortening Cycle Activities in Male Youths during Maximal and Sub-maximal Hopping. *Journal of Electromyography and Kinesiology, 22*(1), 37–43. https://doi.org/10.1016/j.jelekin.2011.09.008

Lloyd, R. S., Radnor, J. M., De Ste Croix, M. B. A., Cronin, J. B., & Oliver, J. L. (2016). Changes in Sprint and Jump Performances After Traditional, Plyometric, and Combined Resistance Training in Male Youth Pre- and Post-Peak Height Velocity. *Journal of Strength and Conditioning Research, 30*(5), 1239–1247. https://doi.org/10.1519/JSC.0000000000001216

Lloyd, R. S., Read, P., Oliver, J. L., Meyers, R. W., Nimphius, S., & Jeffreys, I. (2013). Considerations for the Development of Agility during Childhood and Adolescence. *Strength & Conditioning Journal, 35*(3), 2–11. https://doi.org/10.1519/SSC.0b013e31827ab08c

Lubans, D. R., Morgan, P. J., Cliff, D. P., Barnett, L. M., & Okely, A. D. (2010). Fundamental Movement Skills in Children and Adolescents: Review of Associated Health Benefits. *Sports Medicine, 40*(12), 1019–1035. https://doi.org/10.2165/11536850-000000000-00000

Malina, R. M., Bouchard, C., & Bar-Or, O. (2004). *Growth, Maturation, and Physical Activity* (2nd ed.). Human Kinetics.

Malina, R. M., Cumming, S. P., Rogol, A. D., Coelho-e-Silva, M. J., Figueiredo, A. J., Konarski, J. M., & Kozieł, S. M. (2019). Bio-Banding in Youth Sports: Background, Concept, and Application. *Sports Medicine, 49*(11), 1671–1685. https://doi.org/10.1007/s40279-019-01166-x

Martínez-Hernández, D., Quinn, M., & Jones, P. (2022). Linear Advancing Actions Followed by Deceleration and Turn Are the Most Common Movements Preceding Goals in Male Professional Soccer. *Science and Medicine in Football*, 1–9. https://doi.org/10.1080/24733938.2022.2030064

McBurnie, A. J., Harper, D. J., Jones, P. A., & Dos'Santos, T. (2022). Deceleration Training in Team Sports: Another Potential 'Vaccine' for Sports-Related Injury? *Sports Medicine, 52*(1), 1–12. https://doi.org/10.1007/s40279-021-01583-x

McBurnie, A. J., Parr, J., Kelly, D. M., & Dos'Santos, T. (2022). Multidirectional Speed in Youth Soccer Players: Programming Considerations and Practical Applications. *Strength & Conditioning Journal, 44*(2), 10–32. https://doi.org/10.1519/SSC.0000000000000657

McLellan, C. P., & Lovell, D. I. (2013). Performance Analysis of Professional, Semiprofessional, and Junior Elite Rugby League Match-Play Using Global Positioning Systems. *Journal of Strength and Conditioning Research*, *27*(12), 3266–3274. https://doi.org/10.1519/JSC.0b013e31828f1d74

Meyers, R. W., Moeskops, S., Oliver, J. L., Hughes, M. G., Cronin, J. B., & Lloyd, R. S. (2019). Lower-Limb Stiffness and Maximal Sprint Speed in 11–16-Year-Old Boys. *Journal of Strength and Conditioning Research*, *33*(7), 1987–1995. https://doi.org/10.1519/JSC.0000000000002383

Meyers, R. W., Oliver, J. L., Hughes, M. G., Cronin, J. B., & Lloyd, R. S. (2015). Maximal Sprint Speed in Boys of Increasing Maturity. *Pediatric Exercise Science*, *27*(1), 85–94. https://doi.org/10.1123/pes.2013-0096

Meyers, R. W., Oliver, J. L., Hughes, M. G., Lloyd, R. S., & Cronin, J. B. (2016). The Influence of Maturation on Sprint Performance in Boys over a 21-Month Period. *Medicine & Science in Sports & Exercise*, *48*(12), 2555–2562. https://doi.org/10.1249/MSS.0000000000001049

Meyers, R. W., Oliver, J. L., Hughes, M. G., Lloyd, R. S., & Cronin, J. B. (2017). Influence of Age, Maturity, and Body Size on the Spatiotemporal Determinants of Maximal Sprint Speed in Boys. *Journal of Strength and Conditioning Research*, *31*(4), 1009–1016. https://doi.org/10.1519/JSC.0000000000001310

Monasterio, X., Gil, S. M., Bidaurrazaga-Letona, I., Lekue, J. A., Santisteban, J., Diaz-Beitia, G., Martin-Garetxana, I., Bikandi, E., & Larruskain, J. (2021). Injuries According to the Percentage of Adult Height in an Elite Soccer Academy. *Journal of Science and Medicine in Sport*, *24*(3), 218–223. https://doi.org/10.1016/j.jsams.2020.08.004

Moran, J. J., Sandercock, G. R. H., Ramírez-Campillo, R., Meylan, C. M. P., Collison, J. A., & Parry, D. A. (2017). Age-Related Variation in Male Youth Athletes' Countermovement Jump After Plyometric Training: A Meta-Analysis of Controlled Trials. *Journal of Strength and Conditioning Research*, *31*(2), 552–565. https://doi.org/10.1519/JSC.0000000000001444

Morgan, O. J., Drust, B., Ade, J. D., & Robinson, M. A. (2021). Change of Direction Frequency Off the Ball: New Perspectives in Elite Youth Soccer. *Science and Medicine in Football*, 1–10. https://doi.org/10.1080/24733938.2021.1986635

Morin, J.-B., Edouard, P., & Samozino, P. (2011). Technical Ability of Force Application as a Determinant Factor of Sprint Performance. *Medicine & Science in Sports & Exercise*, *43*(9), 1680–1688. https://doi.org/10.1249/MSS.0b013e318216ea37

Morin, J.-B., & Samozino, P. (2016). Interpreting Power-Force-Velocity Profiles for Individualized and Specific Training. *International Journal of Sports Physiology and Performance*, *11*(2), 267–272. https://doi.org/10.1123/ijspp.2015-0638

Nagahara, R., Takai, Y., Haramura, M., Mizutani, M., Matsuo, A., Kanehisa, H., & Fukunaga, T. (2018). Age-Related Differences in Spatiotemporal Variables and Ground Reaction Forces during Sprinting in Boys. *Pediatric Exercise Science*, *30*(3), 335–344. https://doi.org/10.1123/pes.2017-0058

O'Brien, T. D., Reeves, N. D., Baltzopoulos, V., Jones, D. A., & Maganaris, C. N. (2010). Muscle-tendon Structure and Dimensions in Adults and Children. *Journal of Anatomy*, *216*(5), 631–642. https://doi.org/10.1111/j.1469-7580.2010.01218.x

Oliver, J. L., Lloyd, R. S., & Rumpf, M. C. (2013). Developing Speed Throughout Childhood and Adolescence: The Role of Growth, Maturation and Training. *Strength and Conditioning Journal*, 7.

Papaiakovou, G., Giannakos, A., Michailidis, C., Patikas, D., Bassa, E., Kalopisis, V., Anthrakidis, N., & Kotzamanidis, C. (2009). The Effect of Chronological Age and Gender on the Development of Sprint Performance During Childhood and Puberty. *Journal of Strength and Conditioning Research*, *23*(9), 2568–2573. https://doi.org/10.1519/JSC.0b013e3181c0d8ec

Paul, D. J., & Nassis, G. P. (2015). Physical Fitness Testing in Youth Soccer: Issues and Considerations Regarding Reliability, Validity, and Sensitivity. *Pediatric Exercise Science*, *27*(3), 301–313. https://doi.org/10.1123/pes.2014-0085

Pfirrmann, D., Herbst, M., Ingelfinger, P., Simon, P., & Tug, S. (2016). Analysis of Injury Incidences in Male Professional Adult and Elite Youth Soccer Players: A Systematic Review. *Journal of Athletic Training*, *51*(5), 410–424. https://doi.org/10.4085/1062-6050-51.6.03

Philippaerts, R. M., Vaeyens, R., Janssens, M., Van Renterghem, B., Matthys, D., Craen, R., Bourgois, J., Vrijens, J., Beunen, G., & Malina, R. M. (2006). The Relationship between Peak Height Velocity and Physical Performance in Youth Soccer Players. *Journal of Sports Sciences*, *24*(3), 221–230. https://doi.org/10.1080/02640410500189371

Pino-Ortega, J., Gómez-Carmona, C. D., Nakamura, F. Y., & Rojas-Valverde, D. (2022). Setting Kinematic Parameters That Explain Youth Basketball Behavior: Influence of Relative Age Effect According to Playing Position. *Journal of Strength and Conditioning Research*, *36*(3), 820–826. https://doi.org/10.1519/JSC.0000000000003543

Radnor, J. M., Lloyd, R. S., & Oliver, J. L. (2017). Individual Response to Different Forms of Resistance Training in School-Aged Boys. *Journal of Strength and Conditioning Research*, *31*(3), 787–797. https://doi.org/10.1519/JSC.0000000000001527

Radnor, J. M., Moeskops, S., Morris, S. J., Mathews, T. A., Kumar, N. T. A., Pullen, B. J., Meyers, R. W., Pedley, J. S., Gould, Z. I., Oliver, J. L., & Lloyd, R. S. (2020). Developing Athletic Motor Skill Competencies in Youth. *Strength & Conditioning Journal*, *42*(6), 54–70. https://doi.org/10.1519/SSC.0000000000000602

Radnor, J. M., Oliver, J. L., Waugh, C. M., Myer, G. D., & Lloyd, R. S. (2020). The Influence of Maturity Status on Muscle Architecture in School-Aged Boys. *Pediatric Exercise Science*, *32*(2), 89–96. https://doi.org/10.1123/pes.2019-0201

Radnor, J. M., Oliver, J. L., Waugh, C. M., Myer, G. D., & Lloyd, R. S. (2021). Influence of Muscle Architecture on Maximal Rebounding in Young Boys. *Journal of Strength and Conditioning Research*, *35*(12), 3378–3385. https://doi.org/10.1519/JSC.0000000000004152

Radnor, J. M., Oliver, J. L., Waugh, C. M., Myer, G. D., & Lloyd, R. S. (2022). Muscle Architecture and Maturation Influence Sprint and Jump Ability in Young Boys: A Multistudy Approach. *Journal of Strength and Conditioning Research*, *36*(10), 2741–2751. https://doi.org/10.1519/JSC.0000000000003941

Radnor, J. M., Staines, J., Bevan, J., Cumming, S. P., Kelly, A. L., Lloyd, R. S., & Oliver, J. L. (2021). Maturity Has a Greater Association Than Relative Age with Physical Performance in English Male Academy Soccer Players. *Sports*, *9*(12), 171. https://doi.org/10.3390/sports9120171

Ramos, E., Frontera, W., Llopart, A., & Feliciano, D. (1998). Muscle Strength and Hormonal Levels in Adolescents: Gender Related Differences. *International Journal of Sports Medicine*, *19*(08), 526–531. https://doi.org/10.1055/s-2007-971955

Read, P. J., Oliver, J. L., De Ste Croix, M. B. A., Myer, G. D., & Lloyd, R. S. (2018). An Audit of Injuries in Six English Professional Soccer Academies. *Journal of Sports Sciences*, *36*(13), 1542–1548. https://doi.org/10.1080/02640414.2017.1402535

Reina, M., García-Rubio, J., Pino-Ortega, J., & Ibáñez, S. J. (2019). The Acceleration and Deceleration Profiles of U-18 Women's Basketball Players during Competitive Matches. *Sports*, 7(7), 165. https://doi.org/10.3390/sports7070165

Rumpf, M. C., Cronin, J. B., Mohamad, I. N., Mohamad, S., Oliver, J. L., & Hughes, M. G. (2015). The Effect of Resisted Sprint Training on Maximum Sprint Kinetics and Kinematics in Youth. *European Journal of Sport Science*, *15*(5), 374–381. https://doi.org/10.1080/17461391.2014.955125

Rumpf, M. C., Cronin, J. B., Oliver, J. L., & Hughes, M. G. (2013). Vertical and Leg Stiffness and Stretch-shortening Cycle Changes across Maturation during Maximal Sprint Running. *Human Movement Science*, *32*(4), 668–676. https://doi.org/10.1016/j.humov.2013.01.006

Rumpf, M. C., Cronin, J. B., Pinder, S. D., Oliver, J., & Hughes, M. (2012). Effect of Different Training Methods on Running Sprint Times in Male Youth. *Pediatric Exercise Science*, *24*(2), 170–186. https://doi.org/10.1123/pes.24.2.170

Schepens, B., Willems, P. A., & Cavagna, G. A. (1998). The Mechanics of Running in Children. *The Journal of Physiology*, *509*(3), 927–940. https://doi.org/10.1111/j.1469-7793.1998.927bm.x

Sheppard, J. M., & Young, W. B. (2006). Agility Literature Review: Classifications, Training and Testing. *Journal of Sports Sciences*, *24*(9), 919–932. https://doi.org/10.1080/02640410500457109

Spiteri, T., Nimphius, S., Hart, N. H., Specos, C., Sheppard, J. M., & Newton, R. U. (2014). Contribution of Strength Characteristics to Change of Direction and Agility Performance in Female Basketball Athletes. *Journal of Strength and Conditioning Research*, *28*(9), 2415–2423. https://doi.org/10.1519/JSC.0000000000000547

Talty, P. F., McGuigan, K., Quinn, M., & Jones, P. A. (2022). Agility Demands of Gaelic Football Match-play: A Time-motion Analysis. *International Journal of Performance Analysis in Sport, 22*(2), 195–208. https://doi.org/10.1080/24748668.2022.2033519

Thieschäfer, L., & Büsch, D. (2022). Development and Trainability of Agility in Youth: A Systematic Scoping Review. *Frontiers in Sports and Active Living, 4*, 952779. https://doi.org/10.3389/fspor.2022.952779

Till, K., Cobley, S., Morley, D., O'hara, J., Chapman, C., & Cooke, C. (2016). The Influence of Age, Playing Position, Anthropometry and Fitness on Career Attainment Outcomes in Rugby League. *Journal of Sports Sciences, 34*(13), 1240–1245. https://doi.org/10.1080/02640414.2015.1105380

Till, K., & Jones, B. (2015). Monitoring Anthropometry and Fitness Using Maturity Groups within Youth Rugby League. *Journal of Strength and Conditioning Research, 29*(3), 730–736. https://doi.org/10.1519/JSC.0000000000000672

Till, K., Jones, B., & Geeson-Brown, T. (2016). Do Physical Qualities Influence the Attainment of Professional Status within Elite 16–19 Year Old Rugby League Players? *Journal of Science and Medicine in Sport, 19*(7), 585–589. https://doi.org/10.1016/j.jsams.2015.07.001

Tonson, A., Ratel, S., Fur, Y. L., Cozzone, P., & Bendahan, D. (2008). Effect of Maturation on the Relationship between Muscle Size and Force Production. *Medicine & Science in Sports & Exercise, 40*(5), 918–925. https://doi.org/10.1249/MSS.0b013e3181641bed

Trecroci, A., Rossi, A., Dos'Santos, T., Formenti, D., Cavaggioni, L., Longo, S., Iaia, F. M., & Alberti, G. (2020). Change of Direction Asymmetry across Different Age Categories in Youth Soccer. *PeerJ, 8*, e9486. https://doi.org/10.7717/peerj.9486

van der Sluis, A., Elferink-Gemser, M., Coelho-e-Silva, M., Nijboer, J., Brink, M., & Visscher, C. (2014). Sport Injuries Aligned to Peak Height Velocity in Talented Pubertal Soccer Players. *International Journal of Sports Medicine, 35*(04), 351–355. https://doi.org/10.1055/s-0033-1349874

Vänttinen, T., Blomqvist, M., Nyman, K., & Häkkinen, K. (2011). Changes in Body Composition, Hormonal Status, and Physical Fitness in 11-, 13-, and 15-Year-Old Finnish Regional Youth Soccer Players during a Two-Year Follow-Up. *Journal of Strength and Conditioning Research, 25*(12), 3342–3351. https://doi.org/10.1519/JSC.0b013e318236d0c2

Vigh-Larsen, J. F., Dalgas, U., & Andersen, T. B. (2018). Position-Specific Acceleration and Deceleration Profiles in Elite Youth and Senior Soccer Players. *Journal of Strength and Conditioning Research, 32*(4), 1114–1122. https://doi.org/10.1519/JSC.0000000000001918

Viru, A., Loko, J., Harro, M., Volver, A., Laaneots, L., & Viru, M. (1999). Critical Periods in the Development of Performance Capacity during Childhood and Adolescence. *European Journal of Physical Education, 4*(1), 75–119. https://doi.org/10.1080/1740898990040106

Waugh, C. M., Blazevich, A. J., Fath, F., & Korff, T. (2012). Age-related Changes in Mechanical Properties of the Achilles Tendon: Determinants of Tendon Stiffness. *Journal of Anatomy, 220*(2), 144–155. https://doi.org/10.1111/j.1469-7580.2011.01461.x

Waugh, C. M., Korff, T., Fath, F., & Blazevich, A. J. (2013). Rapid Force Production in Children and Adults: Mechanical and Neural Contributions. *Medicine & Science in Sports & Exercise, 45*(4), 762–771. https://doi.org/10.1249/MSS.0b013e31827a67ba

Weyand, P. G., Sternlight, D. B., Bellizzi, M. J., & Wright, S. (2000). Faster Top Running Speeds Are Achieved with Greater Ground Forces Not More Rapid Leg Movements. *Journal of Applied Physiology, 89*(5), 1991–1999. https://doi.org/10.1152/jappl.2000.89.5.1991

Yagüe, P. H., & De La Fuente, J. M. (1998). Changes in Height and Motor Performance Relative to Peak Height Velocity: A Mixed-longitudinal Study of Spanish Boys and Girls. *American Journal of Human Biology, 10*(5), 647–660. https://doi.org/10.1002/(SICI)1520-6300(1998)10:5<647::AID-AJHB11>3.0.CO;2-8

Young, W. B., Dawson, B., & Henry, G. J. (2015). Agility and Change-of-Direction Speed are Independent Skills: Implications for Training for Agility in Invasion Sports. *International Journal of Sports Science & Coaching, 10*(1), 159–169. https://doi.org/10.1260/1747-9541.10.1.159

INDEX

Note: Page references in **bold** indicate tables. Page references in *italics* indicate figures and boxed text on the corresponding page.

Milton Keynes UK
Ingram Content Group UK Ltd.
UKHW020406180624
444208UK00019B/448